Sociology

Seward Park Play Grounds, Sedgwick and Hill Sts., Chicago.

STATE AND MADISON STREET, CHICAGO, ILL.

CABLE BRIDGE, GARFIELD PARK, CHICAGO.

184 - Cook County Hospital, Chicago

Sociology

Rodney Stark

University of Washington

Third Edition

Wadsworth Publishing Company
Belmont, California
A Division of Wadsworth, Inc.

Sociology Editor: Serina Beauparlant

Sponsoring Editor: Sheryl Fullerton

Signing Representative: Karen Buttles

Editorial Assistant: Marla Nowick

Production Editor: Sandra Craig

Designer: MaryEllen Podgorski

Print Buyer: Karen Hunt

Art Editor: Marta Kongsle

Copy Editor: Pat Tompkins

Photo Researcher: Stephen Forsling

Compositor: Graphic Typesetting Service, Los Angeles

Cover: Photograph of Chicago by GEOPIC™, Earth Satellite Corporation. The antique postcards were gathered at antique shows and flea markets. Curt Teich postcards appear by the courtesy of The Curt Teich Postcard Collection, The Lake County Museum, Wauconda, Illinois.

Illustration credits appear on pages 665–666.

Printed in the United States of America   56

2 3 4 5 6 7 8 9 10—93 92 91 90 89

Library of Congress Cataloging-in-Publication Data

Stark, Rodney.
    Sociology.

    Bibliography: p.
    Includes indexes.
    1. Sociology.   I. Title.
HM51.S89625   1989   301   88-27954
ISBN 0-534-09600-X

About the Author

Rodney Stark grew up in Jamestown, North Dakota, and received his Ph.D. from the University of California, Berkeley, where he held appointments as a research sociologist at the Survey Research Center and at the Center for the Study of Law and Society. Since 1971 he has been Professor of Sociology and of Comparative Religion at the University of Washington. He is the author of twelve books and many scholarly articles on subjects as diverse as prejudice, crime, suicide, and British politics. However, the greater portion of his work has been on religion and especially on religious movements. He is a past president of the Association for the Sociology of Religion. In 1986 the Society for the Scientific Study of Religion conferred its Distinguished Book Award for his *The Future of Religion: Secularization, Revival, and Cult Formation,* coauthored by William Sims Bainbridge. His most recent book, also with Bainbridge, is *A Theory of Religion,* published in 1987.

About the Cover

There are several reasons why the city of Chicago, shown here in a photograph from outer space, is an appropriate cover for this book. Since Albion Small founded the first American sociology department at the University of Chicago in 1892, more sociological research has been based on Chicago than on any other city in the world. Moreover, a photograph of the entire city helps us recognize that some of the earliest and most significant "Chicago sociology" attempted to understand cities as whole units, to discover and explain the underlying processes of urban ecology. The postcards serve to remind us that sociologists don't always view life from afar—many studies are based on close observations of small groups. Here, too, Chicago sociologists led the way with classic studies of an amazing array of Chicago residents—from juvenile gangs and big-time con artists to stockyard workers, symphony musicians, taxi dancers, prostitutes, realtors, nursemaids, dentists, and public drunks.

Brief Contents

Detailed Contents

NEW POSTOFFICE BUILDING, CHICAGO.

Chapter 11

Intergroup Conflict: Racial and Ethnic Inequality 290

Chapter 12

Gender and Inequality   384

Hull House Settlement, Chicago.

Preface

Several years ago I got my first chance to revise a book that I already had published. Because I had been quite pleased with the first edition of this textbook, I was amazed at how much needed changing for the second edition. So, having had the opportunity to make the book more accurate and more effective, I was very proud of the second edition when it appeared. Now I wonder why, because in writing the third edition I changed even more than I did the second time around. And, once again, the reasons for the changes are the same: my colleagues and our students.

As I noted in the second edition, I am overwhelmed by the generosity of my colleagues across North America, who have volunteered the most extraordinary suggestions. Instead of the scatter of complaints I had expected, I have received scores of extremely cordial letters, many of which enclosed carefully worked out and fully documented suggestions for additions or modifications. I am deeply indebted to each of you who helped make this text more authoritative and a more effective intellectual adventure for our students. In particular, I must acknowledge the vital contributions made by Randall Collins, John Murray Cuddihy, Raymond F. Currie, Phillips Cutwright, Donald Eyler, Gerhard Falk, Roger Finke, Elton Jackson, Virginia M. Juffer, Joan Krenzin, Graeme Lang, Reece McGee, Jerry Michel, Ephraim Mizruchi, Brian Powell, Ira L. Reiss, Alan J. Shields, and Jackson Toby. Many others lent me much guidance through Wadsworth, and they are listed at the end of the preface.

However, if I was surprised by the supportive and valuable mail I received from sociologists, I remain absolutely astonished at the number of students who write me. It seems clear from their comments that the reason hundreds of them have written is because the "over-the-shoulder" style lets students recognize that sociology is a *human activity,* and that by writing to me they can participate. Not only have I greatly enjoyed these letters but several brought new material to my attention—one letter even caused me to write an entirely new chapter for this edition.

I think this level of student response justifies my initial decision to break some norms of college textbook writing. Most textbooks take pains to sound as if they had no authors but were composed during endless committee meetings. Moreover, human beings are equally indistinct within most texts; the books present a field as consisting mainly of printed matter—of papers and books, of principles and findings. This misleads students about the real nature of scholarly disciplines, which consist not of paper but of people. Moreover, a Nobel laureate once told me that if, after the first ten minutes of the first day of introductory physics, his students didn't know that people go into science primarily because it's fun, he would consider himself a failure as a teacher.

So this is a book with a voice, in which a sociologist addresses students directly and describes the activities of a bunch of living, breathing, human beings who are busy being sociologists for the fun of it. Moreover, it attempts to show students that the single most important scientific act is not to propose answers but to ask questions—*to wonder*. As I let students look over the shoulders of sociologists, be they Emile Durkheim or Kingsley Davis, I want students to first see them wondering—asking *why* something is as it is. Then I want students to see how they searched for and formulated an answer. For, as an advertising copywriter might put it, I want students to realize that *sociology* can be a verb as well as a noun.

Changes in the third edition

The single most frequent request made by students as well as colleagues was for a chapter on gender. In the first two editions of the text, I chose to place the discussion of gender issues within the appropriate substantive chapters, such as socialization and family. Sex-role socialization was dealt with as a special topic appended to the chapter on socialization. Issues of gender relations within families were discussed in the family chapter, while analysis of female labor force participation, occupational inequality, and discrimination were in the chapter on the interplay of occupation and education. Female status attainment was examined in the chapter on stratification and conflict, while studies of voter responses to female political candidates brightened the chapter on politics. Similarly, theories and research devoted to the immense gender differentials in crime and delinquency were included in the chapter on deviance. I thought it best to place specific gender issues in their most appropriate context.

Having done this, I couldn't discover how to write an additional chapter on gender. Then a student wrote to suggest that I read a book: *Too Many Women?* by Marcia Guttentag and Paul F. Secord (1983). It is a magnificent piece of sociology. And suddenly I had the basis for a chapter on gender inequalities that could measure up to the rest of the book—that is, a chapter that doesn't merely describe but that *explains*.

All of the material on gender in the first two editions remains where it was, except that the material on sex-role socialization has been expanded and placed within the socialization

chapter. I have used the Guttentag and Secord book as the basis for an entirely new chapter that lets students see sociology at its best and most exciting. In Chapter 12, Gender and Inequality, students watch real sociologists ask a big question: How can we *explain* the immense *variation* in gender inequality observed across time and space? I attempt to let students share the excitement of a moment of authentic insight, as Marcia Guttentag first glimpsed the implications of imbalanced sex ratios. Then I lead students along the road from insight to worked-out theory. Finally, I try to help students experience the immense utility of a powerful theory as it successfully confronts data from many times and places, illuminating puzzle after puzzle.

Coming midway in the text, this chapter serves as a powerful pivot point. First, it provides a comprehensive review of basic materials on theories and research. Second, it lays a solid substantive basis for subsequent chapters on such topics as the family, social change, and population. Finally, I wrote this chapter because I found the material in it irresistible. Perhaps it is only because Chapter 12 is brand new, but it is my current favorite.

A second major change in the book places Chapters 2 through 4 in a much tighter and more explicit structure. These chapters are now preceded by an eight-step model of the sociological process (see pp. 30–34). The model clarifies the fundamentals of the scientific method and serves as a "road map" to help students orient themselves as they encounter basic elements of sociological theories and the primary methods used in sociological research. Because specific discussions are connected to specific steps in the sociological process, the material is much easier to grasp.

The two other major additions in the Third Edition respond to requests for more material on the impact of stratification on the individual and for more discussion of older people. Thus, Special Topic 2 assesses Aspects of Income Inequalities in America. This is not an essay on poverty but rather it focuses on contrasts among income groups. I have separated American adults into five groups based on their annual family income and then used the General Social Survey of 1986 to examine differences in class consciousness, life-styles, politics, attitudes, family structures, and morale. Special Topic 4 is devoted to The Older Family and is also based on the General Social Survey, merging the 1986 and 1987 data sets in order to have a large number of respondents over 65. By comparing older and younger Americans, students will discover many rather surprising things—that persons over 65 are the "happiest" group, for example.

A comparative emphasis

A major new feature of the second edition was the systematic use of Canadian studies and data to provide United States–Canada comparisons. Since then I have had time to become more familiar with many other comparative materials. Hence, data based on the nations of Europe and of Latin America, on the provinces of China, and on the fifty most populous nations are now utilized in many of the chapters. But perhaps the most significant addition of comparative material involves the extensive use of data based on the 186 societies of the Standard Cross-Cultural Sample, as selected by George Peter Murdock. The data are based on coding more than a century of anthropological fieldwork and are, in many ways, the best data for testing macro sociological theories. Tables based on these data appear in many chapters and are especially valuable for showing the variety of family structures and of gender relations and for displaying the links between the development of agriculture and the emergence of social classes.

Point of view and approach

Sociologists considering a textbook often ask what "kind" or "brand" of sociology it reflects. What are the author's theoretical and methodological commitments? I find some difficulty framing a satisfactory answer to such questions, because I don't think I have a brand. First of all, my fundamental commitment is to sociology as a social science. Hence, I want to know how societies work and why, not to document a perspective. Moreover, in constructing soci-

ological theories I am a dedicated, even reckless, eclectic. Competing theoretical sociologies persist, in part, not only because they tend to talk past one another but also because each can explain some aspect of social life better than the others can. Therefore, in my own theoretical writing I tend to take anything that seems to work from whatever school can provide it. The textbook does much the same, but with care to point out which elements are being drawn from which theoretical tradition.

I also have not written a book that favors either *micro* or *macro* sociology. Both levels of analysis are essential to any adequate sociology. Where appropriate, the chapters are structured to work from the micro to the macro level of analysis. And the book itself works from the most micro topics to the most macro.

Methodologically the text is equally eclectic. In my own research I have pursued virtually every known technique—participant observation, survey research, historical and comparative analysis, demography, human ecology, even experiments. My belief, made clear in the book, is that theories and hypotheses determine what methods are appropriate (within practical and moral limits). That is why there is not one chapter devoted to methods and one devoted to theory. Instead, Chapter 3 first introduces basic elements of micro theories and then demonstrates how such theories are tested through experiments and participant observation. Chapter 4 introduces social structure within the context of survey research methods. The chapter then assesses basic elements of major macro schools of sociological theory and concludes with an extended example of testing macro theories through comparative research using societies as the units of analysis. Throughout the book, the interplay of theory and research is not asserted but *demonstrated*. No sooner do readers meet a theory than they see it being tested.

Countless publishers have stressed to me that introductory sociology textbooks, unlike texts in other fields, must *not* have an integrated structure. Because sociologists, I am told, have idiosyncratic, fixed notions about the order of chapters, books must easily permit students to read them in any order. That would be a poor way to use this book. The fact is that later chapters build on earlier ones. To do otherwise would have forced me to eliminate some of sociology's major achievements or else to write a redundant book that repeats itself each time basic material is elaborated or built upon. Clearly, some jumping around is possible—the institutions chapters work well enough in any order (and could even be omitted without harming subsequent chapters)—but the basic ordering of the major parts of the book is organic. Thus, for example, the chapter on socialization expands upon material already presented in the biology chapter. And the discussion of theories of intergroup relations included in Chapter 11 is basic to the examination of models of urban segregation taken up in Chapter 19. In my judgment textbooks can only be highly flexible at the risk of being superficial (imagine a chemistry book with chapters that could be read in any order).

Study aids

To assist readers, each chapter ends with a **complete review glossary** that includes concepts and principles. For example, the glossary for the population chapter includes not only concepts such as "birth cohort" or "crude birth rate" but also a succinct restatement of "Malthusian theory" and of "demographic transition theory." The glossary is ordered in the same way as the chapters, so it serves to summarize and review the chapter.

Boxed inserts of side material have become a standard feature of leading sociology texts. I decided against them. First of all, if the material is worth including, it belongs in the body of the chapter. Placed in a box, the material breaks the narrative flow of the chapter and often gets skipped.

In six instances, however, I have included brief essays—minichapters identified as **Special Topics.** I did this because I wanted to amplify and apply materials from several chapters to give them extra emphasis.

Anyone who reads all of the books and articles recommended for **further reading** at the end of each chapter will know a lot of sociology. To choose them I asked myself what I had read that was of broad interest and had helped me to write the chapter. Obviously I did not think anyone would rush out and read them all. But students attracted by a particular topic may find useful follow-up reading provided in these suggestions. I also have found these works useful in composing lectures.

ShowCase™ presentational software

Demonstrating Sociology, the instructor's resource book distributed with the first edition, was a major departure from the materials offered with other sociology textbooks. It was a first attempt to provide sociologists with a set of classroom demonstrations of the sort that accompany textbooks in the natural sciences. Any chemist, for example, even one teaching in a rundown high school, can go to the front of the classroom and *do* chemistry. I want to make it possible for any sociologist to go to the front of the classroom and *do* sociology.

For the first two editions, the ShowCase demonstrations were limited to ecological data sets. Included with the second edition were ShowCases for the fifty states, the Canadian provinces, and the city of Seattle. For this edition it was possible to add a Survey ShowCase, including selected variables for all 1,470 cases from the 1986 General Social Survey.

The data sets supplied with the second edition remain exactly the same as before so that any demonstrations you have been using can still be used without changing any of the variable numbers. New demonstrations are based on the new Survey data set or on other ShowCase applications available from Cognitive Development, Inc., Suite 141, 12345 Lake City Way, NE, Seattle, WA 98125.

For schools with adequate computer facilities so that students can have individual access, I have prepared *Student ShowCase: A Computer-Based Introduction to Sociology*, available from Wadsworth Publishing Company. The student exercises parallel the textbook and fit snugly with the front-of-the-classroom demonstrations. This student package includes a workbook and a diskette containing both an ecological and a survey ShowCase. The exercises often allow students to test a hypothesis at both the ecological and the individual level.

Other supplements

As for the previous editions, Carol Mosher of Jefferson County Community College in Louisville, Kentucky, has prepared a Study Guide for students. It begins with practical suggestions on studying a text, effective test taking, and essay tests. Each chapter of the Study Guide begins with an overview of the text chapter and narrative summary of major topics, followed by lists of key concepts (with accompanying text page numbers), key research studies discussed, key figures (and their contributions), and key theories. These sections help students identify and focus on what they need to study and remember. They can then follow up their review with multiple-choice, fill-in-the-blank, and sample essay questions that dovetail with, but do not duplicate, the test items included in the Test Bank.

For the first edition, I wrote the Test Bank items because I wanted to provide better quality than typically is achieved by freelance test writers. For the second edition I found I needed help to come up with an adequate number of new questions to satisfy the needs of those who teach many sections. Fortunately, David Treybig of Baldwin-Wallace College, a gifted teacher who cares as much about quality as I do, agreed to help me out, and he did so for this edition as well.

Acknowledgments

Projects such as this depend on many people. My debts to Lynne Roberts and to the staff of Cognitive Development, Inc., can only be expressed, not repaid. Pat Tompkins relentlessly checked everything, meanwhile respecting my prose style, and William Katz was the arbiter of all matters of taste. As usual, Sandra Craig handled the production schedule without letting anyone see her sweat, and perhaps she doesn't. Marta Kongsle helped me run down many new pictures and supervised the graphs and maps. MaryEllen Podgorski gave the book a fine new look.

I am especially indebted to all of my colleagues who devoted time and effort to assessing portions of the manuscript.

First Edition Reviewers

Mary Frances Antolini, Duquesne University

Paul Baker, Illinois State University

David M. Bass, University of Akron

H. Paul Chalfant, Texas Tech University

Gary A. Cretser, California Polytechnic University at Pomona

Stephen J. Cutler, University of Vermont

Kay Denton, University of Utah

Thomas Egan, University of Louisville

Avery M. Guest, University of Washington

Geoffrey Guest, State University of New York College at Plattsburgh

Faye Johnson, Middle Tennessee State University

Frederick R. Lynch, University of California at Los Angeles

Shirley McCorkell, Saddleback Community College

Jerry L. L. Miller, University of Arizona

Carol Mosher, Jefferson County Community College

Barbara Ober, Shippensburg State University

Vicki Rose, Southern Methodist University

James F. Scott, Harvard University

David A. Snow, University of Texas at Austin

Steven Stack, Pennsylvania State University

Kendrick S. Thompson, Northern Michigan University

Susan B. Tiano, University of New Mexico

Second Edition Reviewers

Ben Aguirre, Texas A&M University

Brian Aldrich, Winona State University

William Sims Bainbridge, Harvard University

Mary Beth Collins, Central Piedmont Community College

Larry Crisler, Milliken University

Howard Daudistel, University of Texas, El Paso

William Findlay, University of Iowa

Gary Jensen, University of Arizona

Bruce Kuhre, Ohio University at Athens

Mary Ann Lamanna, University of Nebraska

Dan McMurray, Middle Tennessee State University

Fred Maher, St. Michaels College

Martin Marger, Northern Kentucky University

Robert Miller, University of Central Florida

Kay Mueller, Baylor University

Roger Nett, University of Houston, University Park

Fred Pampel, University of Iowa

Joel Tate, Germanna Community College

Robert Silverman, University of Alberta

Charles Tolbart, Baylor University

David Treybig, Baldwin-Wallace College

Third Edition Reviewers

Patricia Albaugh, Southwestern Oklahoma State University

Robert Alexander, Paterson Counseling Center

John D. Baldwin, University of California, Santa Barbara

Peter Bearman, University of North Carolina

John R. Brouillette, Colorado State University

Brent Bruton, Iowa State University

Joseph J. Byrne, Ocean County College

Greg Carter, Bryant College

Mary Ruth Clowdsley, Tidewater Community College

Maury Wayne Curry, Belmont College

Susan Brown Eve, North Texas State University

Roger Finke, Loyola University of Chicago

Sharon Georgianna, Seattle Pacific University

Erich Goode, State University of New York at Stony Brook

Robert Herrick, Westmar College

Paul Higgins, University of South Carolina

Robert Hirzel, University of Maryland

Brenda Hoke, Michigan Technological University

Robert L. Keller, University of Southern Colorado

Mary Beth Kelly, Genesee Community College

James Kluegel, University of Illinois, Urbana

Michael Kupersanin, Duquesne University

Clark Lacy, Laramie County Community College

Henry Landsberger, University of North Carolina

Martin Levin, Emory University

Janet Huber Lowry, Austin College

William F. McDonald, Georgetown University

Sam Marullo, Georgetown University

Charles Maxson, Grand Canyon College

Lawrence Mencotti, Edinboro University

Jerry L. L. Miller, University of Arizona

David O'Brien, University of Missouri, Columbia

B. Mitchell Peck, Texas A&M University

Peter Venturelli, Valparaiso University

Ira M. Wasserman, Eastern Michigan University

Frank Whittington, Georgia State University

Timothy P. Wickham-Crowley, Georgetown University

John Wildeman, Hofstra University

Robert Wilson, University of North Carolina

Paul Zelus, Idaho State University

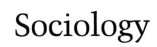

Sociology

Groups and Relationships: A Sociological Sampler

SOCIOLOGY WAS INVENTED early in the nineteenth century because a few scholars in Europe and England began to create and study a new kind of map. It all started when governments began to collect statistics on the causes of death. Suddenly, for the first time, the annual number of suicides became known. These data were used to construct maps like those shown in Figures 1-1 and 1-2, which made it possible to compare one place with another and one year with the next. Almost at once, three amazing patterns were revealed.

First, the rates were extremely *stable* from year to year. For example, Table 1-1 shows that the annual number of suicides per 100,000 people in England and in Sweden changed little from 1830 through 1870. The suicide rates in London and Paris displayed similar stability. Also note the remarkable similarity of the two maps of French suicide rates shown in Figure 1-1.

Second, the rates often *varied greatly* from one place to another. The suicide rate for Paris was more than four times as high as the rate for London. The rate for the Department of Seine in 1856–60 was more than twenty-five times as high as the rate for the Department of Corsica. And, as Figure 1-2 shows, suicide rates for the nations of Western Europe in 1870 varied from a low of 1.5 suicides per 100,000 people in Ireland to a high of 25.8 suicides per 100,000 in Denmark.

Third, all during the century the suicide rates everywhere were *rising*—inching ever upward—also evident in the data shown in Table 1-1.

These three patterns caused nineteenth-century scholars to reassess the causes of human behavior. What could be a more individualistic action, more clearly motivated by personal, idiosyncratic motives, than the act of suicide? But if that were so, why didn't the rates fluctuate wildly from year to year? If individual motives alone were involved, how was it that year after year the same numbers of people in England or Sweden took their own lives? And why were the rates so different from one city or country to another? And why were the rates rising?

Soon many other kinds of rates were being gathered and examined—among them homicide, theft, rape, illegitimacy, military desertion, and charitable donations. These figures displayed the same three patterns—stability, variation, and increase—shown by the suicide rates and therefore raised the same questions. And these questions gave rise to a new science. At first it was called the study of "moral statistics" because of its focus on actions with obvious moral implications (Cullen, 1975; Beirne, 1987).

The founders of moral statistics were a Belgian astronomer named Adolphe Quételet (kĕt-ă-lāy′) and a French lawyer named André Michel Guerry (pronounced "gary"). Quételet came to Paris in 1823, where, among other things, he studied French statistical collection procedures. Returning to Brussels, Quételet published a study of the causes of death in that city, then concentrated on mathematics and astronomy. But his interests kept returning to moral statistics, culminating in his famous and influential book, *Sur l'homme et le développement de ses facultés* (1835). In it Quételet first used the notion of the "average person," a now-famil-

1827–1830: Suicides per 100,000

0.8 to 1.9

2.0 to 3.0

3.1 to 4.7

4.8 to 7.0

7.1 to 34.7

1856–1860: Suicides per 100,000

1.4 to 4.4

4.5 to 6.6

6.7 to 9.1

9.2 to 12.2

12.3 to 35.7

Figure 1-1 ■ **Suicides per 100,000 population in the departments of France.** The darker the department, the higher its suicide rate. The map on the left is a copy of the one first published by André Michel Guerry in his book *An Essay on the Moral Statistics of France*, 1833. Notice the remarkable similarity of the two maps despite the fact that the one on the right is for 1856–60 and thus displays the geography of French suicide about thirty years later than does Guerry's map. In both eras high suicide rates were concentrated in the departments around Paris. (The Department of Seine, which is made up of Paris, had by far the highest rates.) A second area with high suicide rates can be seen in the departments clustered about the port city of Marseilles (see the lower right corner). And in both eras the Department of Corsica (the island to the right) had an extremely low rate. Sociology was invented by scholars who wanted to know why suicide rates, among others, were so stable over time, yet differed so from place to place. Source of data for the 1856–60 map: Le Bras and Todd (1981).

Table 1-1 ■ **Number of suicides per 100,000 population.**

	England	Sweden
1830–40	6.3	6.8
1845–55	6.2	6.9
1856–60	6.5	6.4
1861–65	6.6	7.6
1866–70	6.7	8.5
	Paris	**London**
1827–30	34.7	—
1861–70	35.7	8.1
1872–76	42.6	8.6

Source: Adapted from Henry Morselli, *Suicide: An Essay on Comparative Moral Statistics* (New York: Appleton, 1882).

1870: Suicides per 100,000

Ireland	1.5	Italy	9.0
Spain	1.7	Germany	14.8
Finland	2.9	France	15.0
Netherlands	3.6	Switzerland	19.6
		Denmark	25.8

Belgium	6.0
United Kingdom	6.6
Austria	7.2
Norway	7.6
Sweden	8.5

Figure 1-2 ■ **Suicides per 100,000 in Europe, 1870.** The darker the nation, the higher its rate— no data were available for the uncolored nations. Here we can see the amazing international contrasts in suicide rates. The data for this map were adapted from Henry Morselli's *Suicide* (1882). However, data for seven small states were combined to create a rate for "Germany," which was then still in the process of uniting. This map is of special historical interest because it is based on the same data Emile Durkheim used at the turn of the century to write a classic sociological study, which he also called *Suicide.*

■ Adolphe Quételet.

iar statistical being. And Quételet was among the first to suggest that the stability of suicide and crime rates forces us to look at these phenomena not primarily in individual, psychological terms but rather as the result of *social causes* outside the individual.

Beginning in 1825, the French gathered the *Compte général de l'administration de la justice criminelle en France*, a statistical account of criminal justice activities such as arrests and convictions. The *Compte* was prepared quarterly from reports submitted by the prosecutors in each of the country's departments—the primary geographical units into which France is divided. Because of his position as a Royal Advocate, Guerry had ready access to the *Compte*, and he grew fascinated with it. Why were crime and suicide rates so stable? Why did they vary so much? In 1833 the French Royal Academy of Science published his conclusions in a small book, *Essai sur la Statistique Morale de la France.* In it Guerry was the first to note that crimes of violence and property crimes seem to be unrelated, that places with high levels of one show no tendency to have high levels of the other (see Chapter 7). He also noted the clear need for social, rather than psychological, explanations of suicide and crime. Although Guerry and Quételet ended up as enemies who quarreled over who had been first to note the stability of crime and suicide rates (Beirne, 1987), they attracted a sizable following. Soon moral statisticians were at work all over Europe.

One of the leading moral statisticians in the generation following Quételet and Guerry was an Italian physician, Henry Morselli. Table 1-1 and Figure 1-2 were adapted from Morselli's major work, *Suicide: An Essay on Comparative Moral Statistics* (1882).

Morselli addressed the issues of *variation* and of *increase*. Why did some nations have suicide rates so much higher than others? And why were the rates rising over time? His answer: because of the shift from societies based on small town and rural life to modern, industrialized societies with their huge, impersonal, and disorderly cities. Or, as Morselli (1882) put it, suicide reflects "that universal and complex influence to which we give the name of *civilization*." He argued that some nations had higher rates because they were more modernized ("civilized") and that the rates were rising because modernization was increasing throughout Europe.

In 1897 a Frenchman named Emile Durkheim, who called himself a sociologist rather than a moral statistician, published a book based on Morselli's data and also titled *Suicide*. Durkheim's book further developed the thesis that modern societies were deficient in the kinds of secure and warm *interpersonal relationships* typical of traditional rural life. As a result, many people lacked the social resources to carry them through times of trouble and despair. Thus, Durkheim wrote, the suicide "victim's acts which at first seem to express only his personal temperament are really" caused by "a social condition." That is, high suicide rates reflect *weaknesses in the web of relationships among members of a society*, not weaknesses of character or personality in the individual.

The progressive uncovering of *social causes of individual behavior*—in response to the questions raised by moral statistics—produced the field called sociology. It is the field I would like to introduce you to in this book. You may be sure that although studies of suicide remain of interest to sociologists (Maris, 1969; Pope, 1976; Breault, 1986; Stack, 1987a), the field

abounds with less gloomy topics. But throughout, the topic of sociology is *interpersonal relationships*.

The best way you could learn sociology would also be through relationships, through becoming friends with some good sociologists and helping them do sociology. As a substitute, I have designed this book to introduce you to sociology by allowing you to watch over the shoulders of sociologists as they work. From that vantage point you will soon see that it is as important to know why people asked certain questions about the world and how they searched for answers as it is to learn about their published conclusions. Put another way, no scholarly field is primarily a collection of books and journals in libraries. Any field consists of people, and it exists only because these people think, do research, and write down their conclusions. So in this book I want you to meet the people who do sociology and to learn sociology from them. Along the way, I hope to give you some sense of how much fun I have doing sociology. If by the end of the course you think you might enjoy doing sociology too, consider yourself invited.

Chapter Preview

As an introduction to sociology, this book first must define the field and suggest the difference between sociology on one hand and psychology, economics, anthropology, and the other social sciences on the other. We need not linger over these matters, because the whole book is meant to reveal what sociology is. Since *relationships* are so central to sociology, the human *group* is the primary sociological subject. Hence in this opening chapter we will sample how sociologists distinguish various kinds of groups and some of the principles discovered about how groups function. Next we will see some highlights of sociological research procedures, concentrating on the special difficulties of studying human beings. We also will examine some philosophical questions having to do with whether

■ Sociology is the study of social relations, and its primary subject matter is the group, not the individual. Had sociologists encountered these cowboys (who were on their way to a fair in Bonham, Texas, at the turn of the century), they wouldn't have been eager to know how each felt about being a cowboy or who hated horses. Instead, sociologists would want to know who liked or disliked whom within the group, how young men were recruited and trained for range work, and who was entitled to give orders to whom within the group.

Moreover, sociologists would have been particularly interested in the fact that these cowboys are *black*. A major task of sociology as a science is to separate fact from illusion, to dispel misconceptions about social life. And that is why this is the perfect photograph to begin an introductory sociology textbook.

This picture is fact, not fiction. It helps dispel the widespread illusion that the 40,000 cowboys roaming the western ranges of North America in the late nineteenth century were almost uniformly white. The men who played cowboys in the countless movie westerns were nearly all white Anglo-Saxons, but at least a third of the real cowboys were not. Many cowboys spoke only Spanish. Many others, especially following the American Civil War, were black. In fact, many of the famous personalities of the Old West, including Deadwood Dick and Nat Love, were black.

a *scientific* sociology is possible—or even desirable. Throughout the chapter I will try to keep my promise to let you see sociologists at work. Taken as a whole, this chapter sets the stage for the rest of the book and offers samples of what sociology is like and why and how people pursue it.

What Is Sociology?

What we call **sociology** is one of several related fields known as the **social sciences**. They share the same subject matter: human behavior. They are called *social sciences* because the human is not a solitary beast. Our daily lives intertwine with the lives of others—what we do, even much of what we hope, is influenced by those around us. To study ourselves, we must study our social relations. In fact, as we shall see in Chapter 6, the process by which newborn infants are transformed into competent adults is called *socialization*. Learning to speak, learning to control our impulses, or even learning to play games is learning how to be social.

Despite their common subject matter, there are a number of different social sciences. Psychologists, economists, anthropologists, criminologists, political scientists, and even many historians, as well as sociologists, are social scientists. Divisions among these fields are often hazy. Indeed, sometimes it is impossible to tell which field a social scientist's work belongs in. The field may be determined merely by the university department in which the person is trained or employed. Nevertheless, the following rules of thumb may help you to distinguish sociologists from other social scientists.

Sociologists differ from psychologists because we are not concerned so exclusively with the individual, with what goes on inside people's heads. We are more interested in what goes on *between* people. Sociologists differ from economists by being less exclusively interested in commercial exchanges—we are equally interested in the exchange of intangibles such as love and affection. We differ from anthropologists primarily because the latter specialize in the study of preliterate or primitive human groups,

while we are primarily interested in modern industrial societies. And while most criminologists are trained in and employed in sociology departments, they specialize in illegal behavior, while sociologists are interested in the whole range of human behavior. Similarly, political scientists focus on political organization and activity, while sociologists survey all social organizations. Finally, sociologists share with historians an interest in the past but are equally interested in the present and the future.

As these contrasts make evident, sociology is a broader discipline than the other social sciences. In a sense, the specialty of sociologists is generalization: to find the connections that unite the various social sciences into a comprehensive, integrated science of society. When I had to decide which social science to pursue, I chose sociology precisely because of its greater scope and grand aspirations. Moreover, to be a sociologist is to be free to do psychology, economics, anthropology, political science, criminology, or history as the need arises.

Yet sociologists do have a distinctive subject matter—a turf of their own. Sociologists study the patterns and processes of human social relations. Some of us concentrate on small groups and the patterns and processes of face-to-face interaction between humans. This part of sociology is known as **micro sociology**—*micro* means "small," as in *microscope*. Micro sociologists look at life close up. Others concentrate on larger groups, even on whole societies. From this viewpoint the individual is simply one small dot among many dots that help form a larger picture, much like the dots on a TV screen. This larger-scope sociology is known as **macro sociology** (*macro* means "large"). Macro sociologists attempt to explain the fundamental patterns and processes of large-scale social relations.

As we shall see in Chapters 3 and 4, macro and micro sociology are closely connected, for societies shape the individual and the small group and, in turn, are shaped by them. Suppose sociologists set out to study military battles. Micro sociologists would concentrate on small groups of soldiers, while macro sociologists would concentrate on larger groups, including whole armies. But to understand a battle, you would need to know both micro and macro levels of events: how the great masses of troops were assembled and directed and how the soldiers reacted and fought. Brave troops have been defeated because of a poor plan of battle, and brilliant plans have failed when the troops ran away.

But whether you pursue sociology at the micro or the macro level, the primary focus is not on individuals and individual behavior but on *social behavior*. Since sociologists specialize in studying what goes on between people, the primary subject of sociology is the group. Thus, the true difference between micro and macro sociology is in the size of the groups studied.

■

Groups: The Sociological Subject

A **group** consists of two or more persons who maintain a stable pattern of relations over a significant period of time. Some groups, such as a married couple, are tiny. Other groups, such as the workers in a factory, are large. However, not just any gathering of people qualifies as a group in the sociological sense.

In everyday speech we often refer to ten people standing on the corner waiting for the walk light as a "group." But sociologists would call them an **aggregate** of individuals: *They have come together only briefly and accidentally. They are not acquainted with and may not even notice one another.* For sociologists, people constitute a group only when they are *united by social relations.* If the ten people waiting for the walk light were all members of the same family or baseball team, then they would be a group in the sociological sense of the term.

Dyads and triads

The smallest sociological group is the **dyad**: two individuals who engage in social relations. As we shall see in Chapter 3, an analysis of the basic properties of two-person relationships gives sociology the tools for building a theory of human interaction—for explaining how we influence one another and thereby construct and enforce rules governing social life. Much of our behavior is governed by our need to exchange with others, whether we exchange apples or affection. Such exchanges are possible only if we can anticipate how the other person will respond and vice versa.

However, if the dyad is the fundamental building block of sociology, it is not its primary object of interest. Human social relations consist mainly not of isolated pairs but of multiple relations involving every individual with a number of others. And as soon as we shift our focus from dyads to social relations involving three or more individuals, some very interesting and complex patterns emerge. As a preview, let's consider **triads**: social relations among three persons.

Let's imagine a triad of three women: Ann, Betty, and Cindy. This triad, like all others, includes not one but three relationships. In other words, relationships exist between Ann and Betty, between Betty and Cindy, and between Ann and Cindy. Sociologists have discovered many rules about the behavior of triads. Let's consider two of them.

■ **Transitivity** Triads demonstrate the **transitivity** rule governing human relations. The rule is simple: *Relations among members of a group will tend to be balanced or consistent.* This idea is captured by everyday sayings such as "Any friend of yours is a friend of mine," "Your enemies are my enemies," and "If you like her, you're no friend of mine." Relationships in a triad are transitive when there is no strain on relations between any pair caused by contrary relationships with the third person (Heider, 1946; Newcomb, 1953; Davis and Leinhardt, 1972). To illustrate this, let's look at what happens to people in a transitive triad when it becomes intransitive. Imagine three close friends: Andy, Bubba, and Cal. One day Andy and Bubba get raging mad at each other and never speak again. But both are still buddies of Cal. This is an *intransitive* triad. Now whenever Andy goes bowling with Cal, Bubba is resentful—"How come my buddy bowls with my worst enemy?" Or whenever Bubba and Cal go fishing, Andy grumbles about friends who let you down.

■ A crowd like this one, gathered at an airport gate, is not a group but an aggregate. Groups are united by social relations, while most of these people are strangers to one another. Notice, however, that *within* this aggregate are a number of small groups, many of them families.

Intransitive triads are unstable and usually break up. Sooner or later Cal is going to have to stop seeing either Andy or Bubba, or both. Trying to be friends with two people who hate each other causes too much tension.

■ **Coalition formation**   Suppose Cal decides to go along with one of his buddies and gang up on the other. Maybe he joins Andy as an enemy of Bubba. Now we can say that Andy and Cal have formed a **coalition**. They have combined to oppose someone else.

Now let's introduce *power* into this triadic relationship. Sociologists define power as the ability to get one's way over the opposition of others (see Chapter 9). Many things can cause some people to be more powerful than others, but for now let's limit our attention to physical strength. If all three guys are of equal physical strength, we cannot predict whether Cal will choose to line up with Andy or Bubba if there is going to be a fight. Either choice is equally likely.

Suppose, however, that Bubba is huge and could easily beat up either Andy or Cal, while Andy and Cal are equally matched. Suppose too that Bubba couldn't beat up both Andy and Cal at the same time. Now we can predict that Andy and Cal will gang up on Bubba—that they will form a coalition (Caplow, 1968). Why? Because if Cal chose to join Bubba he would still be at Bubba's mercy after Andy was beaten. The same goes if Andy joins Bubba against Cal. But if Andy and Cal gang up on Bubba they are safe—safe from Bubba and safe from one another, because they are too evenly matched to want to risk a showdown. Figure 1-3 illustrates the principle of coalition formation.

Transitivity and coalition formation are but two of a multitude of principles governing social relations in small groups. I have discussed them here to offer a sample of what micro sociologists study. However, principles such as these are not limited to the behavior of triads. The intimate connections between micro and macro sociology can be seen if we realize that such rules apply equally well to large groups. To illustrate, let's see how intransitivity and coalition formation shape the internal structure of larger groups.

Networks

All groups consist of social relations among members, whether the group contains three or three thousand members. The patterns of relations among members of a group are often called **social networks**. Ideally, even a large group is transitive, with all members liking one another. However, the ideal is rarely realized. Some members do not like others, and thus relations inside a group can become intransitive. And just as intransitivity can lead either to the breakup of a triad or to coalition formation, so can it cause people in large groups to readjust their relations. Intransitivity leads to the formation of internal clusters within the network of the group—clusters composed of persons who like one another and have few friends outside their own cluster. These clusters are often called internal factions or **cliques**. When a pattern of cliques has developed, transitivity is restored: People no longer attempt to remain friends with people who are also friendly with their enemies.

To study the structure of group networks, sociologists often use **sociograms** to chart relationships within a group (see Figure 1-4). For example, a sociologist may ask members of a fourth-grade class, a sorority, or a business office to list the individuals whom they like or admire most in the group (or whom they dislike most). The lines of friendship can then be drawn on a chart. Usually several individuals stand out as "sociometric stars" because they are often chosen as the most liked. If these stars also like one another, then an integrated network exists. People who admire one star will also tend to like another star as well as group members who like other stars.

For example, suppose Sandra and Mary are the two most popular members of a sorority and also like each other. Then those who like Sandra will also tend to like Mary and the other members who regard Mary as the star. Many bonds of friendship exist between members, and

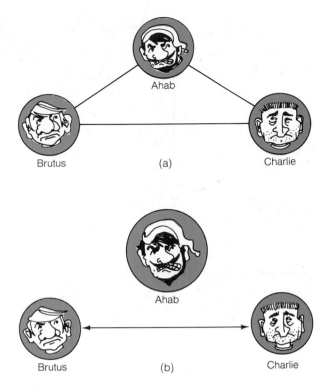

Figure 1-3 ■ **Coalition formation in triads.** In his major work on coalitions in triads, Theodore Caplow (1968) examined relations among three hypothetical smugglers, Ahab, Brutus, and Charlie, who meet on a lonely island to divide their goods. Because they are wicked fellows, they are as willing to cheat one another as to cheat the tax collector. Each is open to a deal to gang up on the third smuggler and steal his goods. In the first condition, each smuggler is of equal fighting ability, as indicated by the size of the circles in diagram (a). When this is the case, we cannot predict which pair may form a coalition against the third. Let's suppose that Ahab is a real brute, able to beat up either Brutus or Charlie but not quite able to beat up both at the same time (b). Now we can predict that neither Brutus nor Charlie will agree to combine forces with Ahab: If one of them did, as soon as he helped Ahab beat up the third member, he would then be at the mercy of Ahab, who could always take all of the goods. Therefore, we can predict that Brutus and Charlie will always combine to rob Ahab. In this way they can split Ahab's goods and need not fear being robbed by one another, since they are too evenly matched. Ahab's superiority ensures that he will always end up the victim.

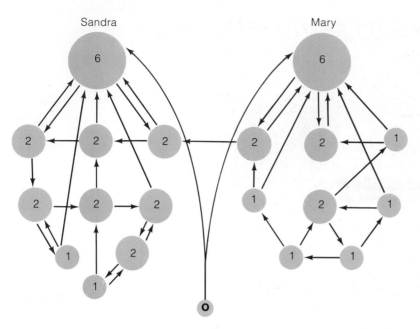

Figure 1-4 ■ **A sociogram of a small group.** Each member of this sorority was asked to name her two best friends. By the use of arrows, the sociogram shows who chose whom. This group has two very isolated cliques, each headed by a "star." The numbers show how many times each person was chosen as a best friend. The two stars were chosen six times, while most others were chosen only twice. Only one person reported a best friend in the other clique. One poor isolated soul was chosen by no one and selected the two stars as her best friends, but wasn't part of either clique.

no clear lines of separation exist within the group.

Intransitivity arises, however, when two stars become enemies—when, in our example, Mary and Sandra suddenly decide they can't stand each other. For then they impose strains between their respective followers just like the strains created in the triad when Andy and Bubba got mad at each other. And just as the intransitive triad led to a coalition, so does intransitivity in larger networks produce a choosing up of sides. Such networks display clearly separated patterns of social relations—distinct cliques or factions. When more than two such internal factions exist, coalition formation is likely: Several factions will cooperate against other factions. Here, too, the coalition rule outlined on page 10 applies. But whether or not coalitions form, internal factions always threaten to produce internal conflict, and in some cases they can break up the group.

Primary and secondary groups

Not all groups are of equal importance to their members. For example, we will more willingly withdraw from a group made up of persons working in our office than from one made up of family or intimate friends. The notions of primary and secondary groups capture this distinction.

Primary groups are characterized by great intimacy among the members. People in these groups do not merely know one another and interact frequently, but they know one another well and have strong emotional ties. As a result, people gain much of their self-esteem and sense of identity from primary groups—as we shall consider in depth in Chapter 3. For example, when retired athletes report how much they miss belonging to a team, they are telling of the pains of leaving a primary group.

The family is the most common primary

■ The family is the most common primary group, characterized by intimate, lifelong attachments. In fact, conflicts among family members cause so much anguish because it is so difficult to "quit" belonging—even many divorced couples must remain in close contact because they remain parents.

group, but many other groups can also become so. Indeed, Charles H. Cooley, who coined the term *primary group*, said a group is primary if its members refer to themselves as "we." Primary groups involve "the sort of sympathy and mutual identification for which 'we' is the natural expression" (Cooley, 1909).

Secondary groups consist of less intimate social networks within which people pursue various collective goals but without a powerful sense of belonging. Business organizations, political parties, even model railroad clubs are typically secondary groups. People find it relatively easy to switch from one secondary group to another and refer to themselves and group members as "we" only casually. However, as we shall see in Chapter 20, primary groups often form *within* secondary groups—a process that can produce internal strains. For example, a group of close friends within a business may promote one another to the disadvantage of other employees and perhaps cause the company to operate less efficiently.

Groups, then, are the primary subject matter of sociology. The aim of sociologists is to con-struct a science of groups, of human social relations. However, not everyone believes that a science of social relations is possible.

■ ▬▬▬▬▬▬▬

Can Sociology Be Scientific?

Can there really be social *sciences*? Anyone who asks that question is usually comparing the achievements of the physical and natural sciences (such as physics and chemistry) with those of the social sciences. From this perspective, the social sciences may appear less scientific, for they do not possess theories as general or as powerful as those of the physical and natural sciences—and the theories of the social sciences cannot be expressed in precise mathematical form. But this is to mistake scientific achievement for the scientific method.

Science is not a set of discoveries but a *method* of discovery. A field is not scientific because of *what* it has achieved but because of *how* the field is conducted. The **scientific method** consists of several related steps. It begins when we observe something about the world that arouses our curiosity—as when Guerry and Quételet noticed the stability and variation of suicide and crime rates. Scientists always begin by asking "Why?" Their next step is to propose an answer to their question—to try to *explain* why. These explanations take the form of **theories,** very general statements about how some portion of the world fits together and functions. Of course, lots of people ask why and suggest answers without ever being scientists. Recently someone told reporters that earthquakes are caused by invisible beings from another planet, but that they will never let us find out. Why isn't that a theory? Because there is no way to show that it isn't true. Maybe aliens are causing earthquakes and maybe they aren't. We can't find out.

What distinguishes scientific explanations is that they must generate *predictions* that can be *checked.* That is, for an explanation to qualify as a scientific theory, *it must be possible to describe observations that would prove it to be false.* When Morselli explained the rising suicide rate in Europe as the result of modernization, he could have been proven wrong by evidence that suicide rates are higher in rural areas and villages than in big cities or that the more urban and industrialized a nation, the lower its suicide rate. When we seek evidence against which to compare the predictions from a scientific theory, we are performing the next vital step in the scientific method—we are doing research. **Research** is systematic observation. The primary purpose of research is to test theories. Good researchers do their best to find evidence that disproves theories. The final step in the scientific method closes the circle—the results of research are used to shape our theories. When predictions from a theory turn out to be incorrect, scientists go back to work on their explanation, trying to reformulate it or replace it with a better one (Wallace, 1971).

Further on in this chapter we will watch several social scientists work their way through this process of formulating and then testing a theory. And in Chapters 3 and 4 we will explore the scientific method in depth. We will see that sociologists can fulfill the rules of science as fully as physicists or biologists can. If physicists

■ Compared with families, people are much less deeply attached to a secondary group like this bell-ringers' musical society. People are quitting or joining all the time. However, people often will forge primary ties with another member or two—members have even married. Thus, secondary groups are not without close interpersonal bonds, but the average relationship in secondary groups is less close than is the average in primary groups.

have achieved more potent results, one reason is that they have pursued their research in a truly scientific way far longer than social scientists have. A second reason, in my judgment, is that the social sciences confront a more difficult subject matter than do the natural and physical sciences. The difference can be summed up in a phrase: *Bacteria don't blush.*

■

Studying Self-Aware Subjects

Suppose a chemistry teacher regularly demonstrated that when two harmless chemicals are mixed together, they explode. Then one day, just as the demonstration was about to begin, one of the chemicals said to the other, "I'm really getting sick of this. Today, let's not explode. Let's do something different. How about helping me make a huge stink instead?" If this could ever happen, chemistry would be a very different field. However, such things routinely happen in the social sciences. Unlike chemicals, people are able to choose among various possible actions. Moreover, they are self-aware. They often know when someone is looking at them, and unlike bacteria under a biologist's microscope, people often do blush when they are looked at. Social scientists must overcome the problem of disturbing what they look at—of being misled because people sometimes act differently when they know they are being observed. While this makes the social sciences difficult, it also makes them fun. People are more interesting than bacteria or isotopes—at least to me. And part of the pleasure of doing sociology is finding ways to keep people from outsmarting your research procedures. A few examples may help demonstrate this point.

Unobtrusive measures

Sociologists don't always need to observe what people do *at the time they are doing it* in order to obtain a good record of what they did. Much of human behavior leaves clear traces. When sociologists examine such traces, they need not worry that self-conscious subjects altered their normal behavior.

For example, one sociologist who wanted to know what radio station people really listened to while driving arranged to have auto mechanics note the dial position of radios in the cars that they serviced (Webb et al., 1966).

Recently, my colleague William Sims Bainbridge and I were interested in geographical patterns in occult and metaphysical beliefs and practices (Bainbridge and Stark, 1980; Stark and Bainbridge, 1985). We might simply have used a national opinion poll to ask people about such beliefs, and in fact we did use Gallup Poll results. But we also knew that we could find many traces of such interest that did not depend upon people being truthful.

One such trace was in the *Yellow Pages* under the listing for "Astrologers" (see Figure 1-5). By looking in the *Yellow Pages* of every major city in the United States, we could easily count how many people offered astrological services to the public. By dividing the number of listings for each city by its population, we identified cities with higher and lower rates of professional astrologers—good evidence of the level of belief in astrology existing in each city (see Figure 1-6).

When astrologers took out listings in the *Yellow Pages*, they were not worried that Bainbridge and I were looking. Nor were we looking when people selected an astrologer by consulting the *Yellow Pages* and thereby ensured that the listings be continued.

Such measures of activity are called **unobtrusive measures.** They gain information without disturbing the objects of the research.

When we decided to repeat our study of religious novelty in Canada, we again consulted the *Yellow Pages*. However, instead of counting astrologers, in Canada we counted listings for unusual religious groups: Scientology, Hare Krishna, the Unification Church (see Chapter 3), and the like. Again we divided the total for each city by the population and eventually transformed the data into rates for each province of Canada. The results are mapped in Figure 1-7.

Of course, sociologists do not rely only on traces of unobserved behavior. Most of the time when we examine what people believe and do, they know we are looking. In fact, we often ask them to tell us what we want to know. We are able to trust such data because a great deal of effort has gone into checking to see if they are accurate and into finding ways to increase their accuracy.

Validation

To ensure that they are getting accurate information, sociologists frequently conduct **validation research.** One way to assess validity is to test data against some independent standard of accuracy.

For example, we can often obtain data known

Astrologers

ADVANCED ASTROLOGICAL SERVICES
Counseling–Specializing In Horary &
Comparison Charts–By Appointment Only
  15346 Stone N ------------------------ **364-3198**
American Institute Of Astrology ----------**362-2606**
Astrological Counseling 16735 10th NE ----**362-6517**
ASTROLOGY CENTER OF THE
NORTHWEST
Bookstore–Computer Calculated Horoscopes–
Classes–Herbs
  522 NE 165th------------------- **363-5313**
ASTROLOGY ET AL
  BOOKS—CLASSES—HERBS
    Professional Counseling
  4728 University Wy NE ----------- **524-6365**

5TH ELEMENT THE
    Astrology & Tarot
  Consultations By Appt.—Books
    Open 10-5 Mon thru Fri
  7527 Lake City Wy NE --------- **522-4535**

Green Jeff 4728 University Wy NE --------**524-6365**
HUGHES DOROTHY B 2322 6th------ **622-7866**
INTERNATIONAL COLLEGE OF
ASTROLOGY
  Horoscopes By Appointment Or Mail
  Astrology Home Courses–Books
    4248 A Southeast Auburn --------- **833-2361**
Jinni ------------------------------ **524-3114**
Meehan Rosalie M
  Rosalie M Meehan–Room 819
    1932 1st----------------------- **622-4770**
Moy Barbara Assoc 1331 3d ------------- **625-0575**
MYRON & CORN
  Bruce I Myron
  Johanna E - Savannah Corn
  By Appointment–Bank Cards Accepted
    Smith Tower ----------------- **622-2554**
Nalbandian Margaret
  4728 University Wy NE --- ----------- **524-6365**
REFLECTING POND
    Books For Creative Living
    Astrological Services By
      David Vikaso Pond
  6211 Roosevelt Wy NE ------------- **527-4333**

ROBERTSON MARC & ASSOCIATES
  -------------------------- **324-3480**
Search Astrology And The Arts ------------ **523-1970**
Wickenburg Joanne -------------------- **523-1970**

Figure 1-5 ■ **Computing an unobtrusive measure.** Suppose you wanted to know how the popularity of astrology differed among cities and regions of the United States. Conducting opinion polls in various parts of the country, asking people if they believed in astrology, would be very expensive. The polls' results would also be subject to error if many people were unwilling to admit to strangers that they accept astrology. However, you could obtain an unobtrusive measure of belief in astrology by consulting the *Yellow Pages* in the nation's cities. There you can discover the number of astrologers in a given city or area who have a business listing. Here is the "Astrologers" section of the Seattle, Washington, *Yellow Pages* from several years ago.

As you can see, there are eighteen separate listings for astrologers in Seattle. By itself, that total isn't very helpful. To compare the figure with those of other cities, population must be taken into account. By dividing the total number of astrologers by the population of the city in which they practice, you can obtain a *rate*. Notice, however, that one of these listings is not actually in Seattle. The International College of Astrology is in Auburn, so we must eliminate it. (Phone exchanges—the first three numbers—indicate those listings in the city being studied, because prefixes have specific geographical boundaries.) You will also notice that several listings have the same phone number. For the sake of accuracy, calls were made to these listings to make sure that they represented several astrologers in a "group practice," not one astrologer using two listings.

By these means we can see that during this year, Seattle had seventeen persons or firms whose astrological practice was sufficiently active to warrant a business listing. Divided by the population of the city, this produces a rate of professional astrologers of thirty-five per one million residents, making Seattle one of the top U.S. cities in terms of astrological interest.

to be accurate, but it can be expensive and difficult to do so. We could determine the exact ages of a sample of American adults by checking official documents (driver's licenses, birth records, and the like), but it is much cheaper simply to ask them their age. To make sure that this information is accurate, we can periodically test the information so obtained by checking it against official records. If what people tell us is close enough to the information obtained

when we check up, we feel confident in the information that is not checked. In this case, studies found that people gave more accurate answers when they were asked their year of birth rather than their age. So that's how we usually ask the question now.

In Chapter 7 we shall examine the results of many studies of delinquency. Most of these studies are based on *self-reports*. That is, samples of teenagers were interviewed or asked to

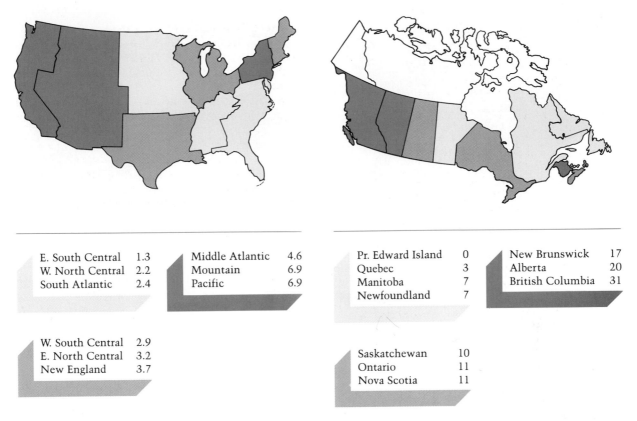

E. South Central 1.3	Middle Atlantic 4.6
W. North Central 2.2	Mountain 6.9
South Atlantic 2.4	Pacific 6.9

W. South Central 2.9
E. North Central 3.2
New England 3.7

Pr. Edward Island 0	New Brunswick 17
Quebec 3	Alberta 20
Manitoba 7	British Columbia 31
Newfoundland 7	

Saskatchewan 10
Ontario 11
Nova Scotia 11

Figure 1-6 ■ **Regional rates of astrologers listed in the *Yellow Pages*.** The numbers indicate professional astrologers per million population in metropolitan areas. Notice the strong regional pattern—the rates are much higher in the West than in the rest of the United States. In Chapter 14 we will see that this same pattern applies to many measures of religious and mystical novelty, both now and at the turn of the century.

Figure 1-7 ■ **Rates of unusual religious groups listed in the *Yellow Pages*.** Here we see the number of unusual religious groups per million population for Canadian metropolitan areas mapped for the provinces. Notice the same regional pattern as with astrologers in the United States—the Far West is highest. In Chapter 14 we will find out why and discover that similar causes are at work on both sides of the border.

fill out questionnaires, and some of the questions pertained to various illegal acts: "Have you ever stolen things from a store?" "How often have you done this?" "When was the most recent time you did this?"

The conclusions drawn from such studies obviously depend upon the validity of people's answers. Because a lot of people may lie, the accuracy of self-reports on delinquency has repeatedly been subjected to stringent validity checks. For example, in Travis Hirschi's delinquency study (1969), he asked boys in Richmond, California, whether they had ever been

picked up by the police. Later he checked out every boy through the police identification bureaus in the area. He found that only a tiny number of the boys actually having a juvenile record had denied being picked up. Other sociologists have interviewed teenagers about their delinquency and then reinterviewed them with a lie detector. They also found the initial interview data to be highly accurate (Clark and Tifft, 1966).

More recently, the validity of a number of different self-report measures of delinquency was tested. In this huge test, answers from these

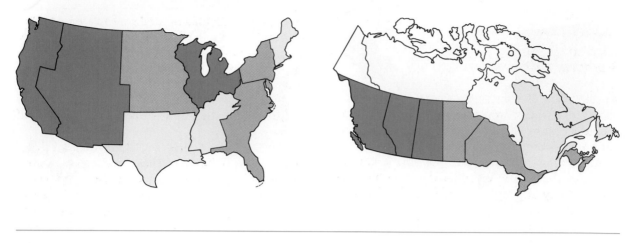

E. South Central	218
W. South Central	295
New England	297

E. North Central	393
Mountain	555
Pacific	565

| Newfoundland | 14 |
| Quebec | 16 |

Pr. Edward Island	25
New Brunswick	26
Ontario	48
Manitoba	54
Nova Scotia	61

South Atlantic	307
Middle Atlantic	308
W. North Central	351

Alberta	75
Saskatchewan	75
British Columbia	94

Figure 1-8 ■ *Fate* **magazine subscription rates: validating the** *Yellow Pages* **data.** Here *Fate* magazine subscribers per million population are shown for both Canada and the United States. This is another independent and unobtrusive measure of interest in novel and mystical beliefs, for *Fate* is North America's leading periodical devoted to occult and mystical phenomena. Notice how closely these regional patterns resemble those for astrologers in the United States and for unusual religions in Canada. And once again rates for the far western parts of both nations greatly exceed those for the rest. When a variety of measures obtained independently gives the same results, our confidence in the validity of each increases.

measures were checked against official police and court records, against answers given while hooked to a lie detector, and even against reports from each person's friends. Again, the self-report data were found to be valid (Hindelang, Hirschi, and Weis, 1981).

A second way to assess the validity of sociological data is to compare results when different measures are used. For example, in our research on occultism, Bainbridge and I found very high agreement between the *Yellow Pages* data, *Fate* magazine subscribers (see Figure 1-8), and many similar measures (including the results of public opinion polls). Any questions raised about the validity of any one of our measures lose their force when various measures collected in different ways all tell the same story.

So far this chapter has focused on what sociology is and how it is done. Now it is time to see someone *do* some sociology. The following examples were selected for several reasons. First, they illustrate the connections between micro and macro sociology. Second, they show how difficult problems of research can be overcome by originality and reflection. Third, they deal with issues concerning the quality of interpersonal relations, of networks, in modern societies—issues that will be central throughout this book. Finally, they may let you see why I think sociology is both interesting and fun.

It's a Small World: Studying Networks

At the start of the chapter we saw that early moral statisticians and sociologists in the nineteenth century feared that the rapid modernization of Europe was disrupting the web of interpersonal relationships that unite human societies. The world was changing rapidly; soon the majority of people would be living in cities rather than in rural communities. Moreover, modernization produced geographical mobility. Although in the past few people had ever traveled more than twenty miles from where they were born, suddenly large numbers began to move hither and yon. Durkheim and many others predicted that modernization would extract a great price in suffering and disorder—high rates of suicide, alcoholism, mental illness, and crime (see Chapters 7 and 19).

As modernization continued unabated into the twentieth century, social scientists continued their gloomy predictions. They expressed special concern about life in large cities where, it was thought, individuals became lost in a sea of strangers; modern cities were said to be too big, too crowded, and too unsettled to let normal human relations form and be maintained (Wirth, 1938). Since sociologists have always regarded interpersonal attachments as the basic structure of social life, they understandably became alarmed at the prospect of nearly everyone living in a city. And, by the 1940s, the belief that people in cities lack relationships was formulated into mass society theories (Beniger, 1987).

Mass society theories

These **mass society theories** were used to *explain* a great many social problems such as crime, suicide, divorce, and alcoholism. They also were used to explain the success of totalitarian political movements of the 1930s and 1940s—especially the appeal of the Nazi and Communist parties. Conditions of modern life created mass societies—ones in which masses of people lacked attachments to one another and were, in effect, isolated social atoms. Such people, it was argued, could easily be influenced by propaganda, and they would throw themselves into new mass organizations in an effort to find some sense of belonging.

But no sooner had social scientists largely accepted mass society theories than the underlying premise of these theories came under serious criticism. Many social scientists began to wonder why the image of city people as lonely, isolated social atoms didn't fit with their own experiences of city living. That is, many sociologists living in major cities still visited their relatives frequently, had lots of friends—even knew their neighbors. Maybe most city people did.

Soon research evidence of many kinds began to support the personal experience of sociologists. For example, the first studies of political behavior based on public opinion polls revealed that people did not fit the image of isolated individuals vulnerable to propaganda appeals through the mass media. Instead, in reporting how they decided which way to vote, people placed little importance on the media—most said they made up their minds through discussions with family and friends (Lazarsfeld, Berelson, and Gaudet, 1948; Berelson, Lazarsfeld, and McPhee, 1954). But these were precisely the kinds of ties that urban Americans were supposed to lack. As research continued, it became obvious that a vast majority of the people living in the largest cities had many stable and intimate ties to family and friends (Fischer, 1976). In this sense, at least, mass society theories were based on a faulty perception; the rise of cities had not overwhelmed human relations. In fact, Table 1-2 shows that place of residence has no impact on social relations. People in big cities are as likely as those living in suburbs, small towns, or rural areas to frequently visit with relatives, neighbors, and siblings.

At this point, those dedicated to mass society theories revised their views. They admitted that most people were still linked to a group of intimate friends, but they argued that these

■ Sociologists now recognize that even in the largest modern cities most people do not experience daily living as a faceless member of a mass of strangers. As with these men playing checkers in a park in New York City, most people spend most of their time surrounded by family, friends, neighbors, co-workers, and others with whom they maintain long-term patterns of interaction.

groups were isolated: They were but islands of intimacy adrift in an ocean of strangers. That is, whereas rural villages were united by links of intimacy that connected the whole community, in modern cities people were connected only to fragments of the overall community, and each of these fragments was isolated. The members of these groups were overwhelmed by a sense of powerlessness and anonymity. Thus, mass society theories were revised to accommodate contrary research findings (Kornhauser, 1959).

Obviously, mass society theorists were correct in arguing that an individual can know every inhabitant in a village of 500 but not every resident in a city of 500,000. But many sociologists began to wonder whether that really meant that cities were composed of large numbers of small, isolated groups. Perhaps these groups were not closed and isolated but were interlocking, so that most people were connected to *chains of attachments* indirectly linking them to huge numbers of other individuals. The issue then became: Are cities collections of small, closed networks of intimacy, or are they huge chains connecting the community as a whole?

At first, this seemed a very difficult question to assess by research—a sociogram of the nation is impossible. But eventually the means to settle the issue arose from a common experience. Time and again we meet a total stranger only to discover after some conversation that we have a mutual friend. Travelers frequently tell of meeting someone far from home who turns out to be a close friend or relative of one of their close friends. This observation from everyday life prompted Stanley Milgram (1967) to conduct his famous "small world" research.

Table 1-2 ■ Social relations by place of residence: National sample of American adults.

Respondent lives in:	Big City	Suburb	Small Town	Rural Area
Percent who spend a social evening weekly with:				
Relatives	32%	33%	32%	34%
Neighbors	32%	20%	24%	33%
Brother or sister	21%	16%	19%	19%

Source: Prepared by the author from: National Opinion Research Center, General Social Survey, 1983.

Milgram's method

 Milgram knew how often complete strangers discover that they have mutual friends and acquaintances. Therefore, he suggested that American society more closely resembled one big friendship network than a multitude of isolated subgroups. But how could he see whether or not this was true? He couldn't simply obtain a list of the friends of every American and then check all these lists for duplicated names. Not even the most powerful computers could deal with that task, even if it were possible to get an accurate list from every citizen. But, he reasoned, what if he selected individuals at random in various parts of the country and tried to find out if they were in fact linked into a common friendship chain? If so, how far apart on that chain are most people?

From this starting point, Milgram invented an extremely clever and simple research method—and with a total budget of only $680. First, he selected a number of individuals from throughout the United States to serve as receivers. Next, he selected other individuals from throughout the United States to act as senders. Then, he prepared letters addressed to the receivers that he distributed to the senders. However, instead of simply asking the senders to mail the letters to the addressee, he told each sender to mail the letter to someone he or she knew personally ("on a first-name basis") who might know the receiver. Each sender was to tell these personal acquaintances that if they didn't know the receiver, they should send the letter on to someone else whom *they* personally knew who might know the receiver.

Arrangements were made to record each person through whom a letter was passed on its way to each receiver. Since senders and receivers had been selected at random in various parts of the country, there was no reason to suppose that any sender had heard of any receiver before being given the letter. Milgram's study was designed to determine whether most senders did belong to a chain of friendships that led to the receivers; that is, did the letters ever reach their destination? And, if they did, how many links between most senders and receivers existed along this friendship chain?

The results powerfully supported Milgram's belief that it is a small world. Not counting those letters that were not received because intermediaries did not send them on, the vast majority of the letters did reach their designated receiver. Moreover, it took an average of only *five* links on the friendship chain for a letter to get from sender to receiver. How did people go about getting the letters to the receivers? In the same way that strangers uncover mutual friends.

If a sender in California, for example, had a letter addressed to someone in New Hampshire, he or she usually proceeded by asking, "Who do I know in New Hampshire?" If the sender knew someone there, he or she sent the letter on to them, much as a stranger learning that another stranger is from New Hampshire might ask, "Do you know my friend Charlie Adams? He lives in Dover, New Hampshire." Senders who didn't know someone in the city or state in which the receiver lived sent the letter to a friend who they thought might have friends in that area. In this fashion, letters were transmitted from friend to friend and thus left a recorded trail of the connections that tie Americans to one another.

Exploring parallel networks

The United States need not be one extended social network in order to refute the assumptions of mass society theories. For example, Milgram's letters might have had much less probability of getting from a white sender to a black receiver and vice versa without supporting the conclusion that the average American is an isolated social atom or part of a small isolated social network. Instead, most black Americans might be closely linked to a nationwide black social network and most whites to a national white network. Of course, when highly separated parallel networks exist within the same society, there is always the potential for serious conflict between them.

Parallel networks can exist for many reasons. Slavery and racism created parallel racial networks in the United States—a separation that is only now being bridged in significant fashion (see Chapter 11). Distance too can have this effect—we are more likely to have friends close by than on the other side of the globe. Language also can create separated social networks. Let's watch how a Canadian social scientist used an unobtrusive measure to assess the impact of distance and language in creating parallel networks of French- and English-speaking Canadians.

Canadian callers

 Some years ago J. Ross MacKay (1958) wanted to know the extent to which French- and English-speaking Canadians maintained interpersonal relationships across boundaries of language and distance. He might have selected samples of French- and English-speakers and asked them how many friends they had in the other linguistic group. But that would have been expensive and it might not have produced accurate results—people might have exaggerated. Instead, MacKay obtained data from the telephone company on the number and length of phone calls between various Canadian cities. The cities were selected for having a very high proportion of French- or English-speakers. MacKay then calculated the travel distance between each pair of cities.

When MacKay examined the amount of telephone traffic between pairs of cities, he found that both distance and language made considerable difference. There were more calls between two French-speaking cities than between French- and English-speaking cities when all were equally distant. And phone traffic diminished with distance within linguistic groups as well as across them. MacKay reported that "English-speaking cities behave as if they were five to ten times as far away" from a French city compared with the phone traffic between two French cities of similar actual separation. MacKay also examined traffic between both French- and English-speaking Canadian cities and cities in the United States. He found that language barriers within Canada are much less powerful than are national boundaries. Compared with the volume of phone traffic between Canadian cities, American cities the same actual distance away appeared to be fifty times farther off.

In a follow-up study, Simmons (1970) was able to separate business and residential phone traffic. His results confirmed MacKay's but also showed that residential calls were much more influenced by distance than were business calls.

To sum up: Canada tends to have parallel social networks based on language boundaries;

Canadians and Americans tend to constitute separate national networks.

These studies helped to refute the assumptions that modern societies were becoming mass societies in which individuals and small social networks were tossed by the tides of propaganda and the mass media. However, the underlying thesis on which these theories were based remains central to sociological analysis: if or when humans lack adequate interpersonal relationships they are prone to a whole array of problems. Mass society theorists misread the course of social change; they were incorrect to assume that urban life would destroy social relations. But as we see throughout this book (especially in Chapters 7 and 19), many people end up lacking social relations and suffer serious consequences as a result.

My primary purpose in this discussion of Milgram's and MacKay's studies was to offer you an initial glimpse of good sociology, of why and how it was done—to show how scientific procedures are used to test our beliefs and hunches about how the world works.

Bias

As we shall see in Part One, the essence of the scientific method is systematic skepticism: Take nothing for granted. Every step of logic in an argument and every set of facts produced by research are to be tested, checked, and retested. Moreover, the proper approach to research is to try to *disprove* those things that the researcher actually believes to be true.

Scientists must be willing to lay their opinions and beliefs on the line—to subject them to rigorous tests and accept the test results. Must scientists then free themselves from their personal biases, commitments, or hopes in order to function properly? The image of scientists as neutral, unemotional beings, like Mr. Spock in *Star Trek*, is romantic nonsense. All human beings are inescapably biased; we all have deep personal beliefs. The scientific method does not aim to strip scientists of their fundamental

humanity or to make them into computers, but to prevent our personal biases from distorting our work. The scientific method consists of rules that, if followed, lead us to the facts, regardless of what we might hope or believe the facts to be. Some of the most important moments in scientific progress have occurred when research turned up results very different from those expected by the researchers.

It would be naive to suggest that scientists never distort their findings or cheat in an effort to support their own convictions. But the public nature of science weakens this temptation and eventually exposes those who cannot overcome their biases. Scientists must report not only what they found but also how and where they found it. This procedure lets others check the results and even repeat the research to see if they obtain the same results.

Personal bias is possibly a more serious problem for social than for natural and physical scientists. Few of us grow up with deep convictions about what color a shark's liver ought to be or about the proper behavior for atomic particles. But we all grow up with many firm beliefs about what people are like and how they ought to behave. Hence, social scientists have to try harder to lay their beliefs aside and look carefully at how things really are.

But this situation also offers some advantages. Social scientists are intimately familiar with their fundamental subject matter: people. In an important sense, every competent human being is something of a social scientist. If we were not good at predicting one another's behavior, social life would be impossible. We would not dare to be in contact with one another if we did not have relatively accurate notions about what makes people tick. Thus, students in introductory sociology have a head start on students taking their first course in biochemistry.

Then why aren't the social sciences far more advanced than sciences such as chemistry and physics? The answer is that common sense and everyday experience take us only so far in understanding human relations. To go further, science is required. And we have applied scientific procedures to human relations for only a relatively short time, as the following review of the history of sociology will show.

The Origins of Social Science and Sociology

Even primitive tribes have understood a great deal about human behavior and the structures and processes governing social life. Yet the physical and natural sciences began centuries before anyone attempted to pursue the social sciences.

It is impossible to date precisely when the social sciences began. Some trace their origins to philosophy and thus back to the Middle Ages or even ancient Greece. But simply to wonder about how social life operates or to assert doctrines about human nature is not social science. Science involves two essential elements. First, its explanations must take the form of *theories*, a term we shall explore fully in Part One. Second, theories must be the object of *testing by systematic research*.

We have already looked at sociologists attempting to use research to discover if certain statements about social life are correct. In Chapters 3 and 4 we shall examine research procedures in depth and see the connection between theories and research. Here I simply want to point out that philosophers such as the ancient Greek Plato did not really formulate social theories, nor did they, or anyone else at that time, attempt to do social research. For these reasons, I regard the economist Adam Smith as the first real social scientist. In his great book *The Wealth of Nations*, published in 1776, he attempted to state formal theories about economic behavior and to use data to test his theories. For this reason, economists regard Smith as the founder of the science of economics (Heilbroner, 1961).

But it was well into the next century before the other social sciences really began. And, as you saw at the start of the chapter, moral statistics played an important role. At first, moral statisticians worked with any interesting data collected by governments. There was little or no specialization. For example, some have claimed Quételet as the real founder of sociology, others believe he was the first scientific criminologist, and still others think he originated differential psychology. Yet he is even better known as a mathematician who pioneered in statistics and probability theory and as an astronomer. As the century passed, however, scholars became more specialized and even began to collect data on their own rather than concentrating on official statistics. In England, Charles Darwin's cousin Sir Francis Galton began to collect data on human traits, initiating work that led to today's behavioral genetics. In 1879 in Germany, Wilhelm Wundt founded the first psychological research laboratory. In France in 1886 Jean-Gabriel Tarde brought much greater theoretical sophistication to the studies of criminology begun early in the century by Quételet and Guerry in his influential *La criminalité comparée*. In 1880 Karl Marx made one of the first efforts to conduct an opinion survey by distributing 25,000 questionnaires to English workers (almost none of whom responded).

The name *sociology* was first suggested in the 1830s by the French philosopher Auguste Comte. But for many years it remained only a suggestion; Comte urged others to do sociology, but he never got around to doing any himself.

It was not until late in the nineteenth century that we can identify people who called themselves sociologists and whose work contributed to the development of the field. Among these were Herbert Spencer in England, who published the first of his three-volume *Principles of Sociology* in 1876, and Ferdinand Tönnies in Germany, who published *Gemeinschaft und Gesellschaft* in 1887 (see Chapter 19). A decade later Emile Durkheim published *Suicide*.

The earliest sociologists in North America, as in Europe, studied moral statistics. Their work proved so popular that it led to the rapid expansion of census questions. However, sociology as an academic specialty was imported into North America from Germany and first appeared at the University of Chicago and at Atlanta University, then an all-black school.

The first department of sociology in North America was founded at the University of Chicago in 1892 by Albion Small (1854–1926). Small did his graduate study at Leipzig, Germany. Returning to the United States, Small published *An Introduction to the Science of Sociology* in 1890, which led the newly opened University of Chicago to select him to create a department there. He also founded the *American Journal of Sociology* and edited it from 1895 to 1925 (Faris, 1967).

The second initial base for sociology in North America was created by W. E. B. Du Bois (1868–1963), a black man who grew up in Great Barrington, Massachusetts, and who was educated at Fisk, Harvard, and then at the University of Berlin. At Atlanta in 1897, Du Bois created a sociological laboratory and directed the Atlanta University Conferences—a major annual meeting devoted to sociological research and analysis on the circumstances of blacks in America. From 1896 through 1914 Du Bois published a book based on his sociological research *every* year and wrote many articles and gave many speeches as well. As a sociologist, Du Bois was devoted to taking an objective, scientific approach. He believed that if the facts were known about social concerns, reasonable actions would follow. "We simply collect the facts: others may use them as they will," he once wrote. After a few years, however, Du Bois decided to shift his efforts from sociology to direct action. He was a founder of the National Association for the Advancement of Colored People (NAACP) and served as editor of its periodical, *The Crisis*, from 1910 through 1934. Although Du Bois still lived when the Civil Rights Movement began to break the bonds of racism against which he had battled so long and so eloquently, as both sociologist and journalist, he had by then committed his hopes to revolutionary Marxism and gone to live in Ghana, where he is buried (Broderick, 1974; Green and Driver, 1978).

Despite these early beginnings in Chicago and Atlanta, sociology grew slowly in North America. The first sociology department in Canada opened in 1922 at McGill University. Not until 1930 did Harvard have a sociology department, and the University of California at Berkeley and Johns Hopkins did not until the 1950s.

As a field less than 100 years old and pursued

■ W. E. B. Du Bois.

by a small number of people, no wonder sociology cannot yet match the achievements of much older and more widespread sciences such as physics and chemistry. Nevertheless, much has been achieved—as will be evident while you read this book.

I find it very attractive and exciting to take part in a young, small field. There is so much to be done that new things happen all the time. Furthermore, it is very satisfying to be able to meet and know a substantial proportion of those active in the field. In fact, it is only because sociology is a small, intimate field that I could attempt to write an introductory book that views the subject from backstage.

While I do not trace the origins of modern social sciences back to early philosophers, a fundamental philosophical issue long delayed the development of the social sciences. It is an issue that lingers still and that often troubles students. But in reality it is a nonissue based on illogic.

■ Choosing is the essential feature of human existence. Whether we are building with Tinkertoys or composing music, throughout our lives we attempt to make good choices and to learn from our mistakes.

■

Free Will and Social Science

For many centuries a major dispute in theology concerned individual responsibility. According to the doctrine of religious determinism (or fatalism), all human actions are preordained, determined by the gods or God; humans are helpless to alter their fates. But, if this were so, how could humans be asked to observe moral codes? If our actions are not ours to choose, how can we be blamed for our evil deeds? Early Christian theologians dealt with this problem by declaring that each individual possesses **free will**. God did make the world and create humans, they argued, but He did not create robots required to do His bidding. Instead, He gave humans the capacity to choose freely among alternatives, and He can therefore reward those who choose good and condemn those who choose evil.

This was a very powerful religious idea. God was no longer to be regarded as capricious, unjust, and terrible—as He must be if He is responsible for what we do, whether good or evil. Instead, it was possible to conceive of a God of mercy, justice, and absolute virtue—a God who gave humans life and choice and asked only virtue in return.

But what does the doctrine of free will have to do with social science? It mistakenly led to the conclusion that because humans possess free will, it is impossible to construct scientific theories to predict and explain their behavior! Thus, it was assumed that if it were possible to achieve social science, then humans must not possess free will; if their behavior is lawful and predictable, then it is inescapable and preordained. If we can predict who will commit crimes, then criminals can't choose good over evil and therefore bear no personal responsibility for their deeds.

In fact, social scientists have sometimes echoed this view, suggesting, for example, that there are no "bad" people in prison, only "sick" people. But, as we shall see in Chapters 7 and 8, sociological theories of crime do not assume that criminals have no choices. Instead, they concentrate on how different people have a different basis for making choices and different alternatives from which to choose. This is contrary to an image of human robots programmed to steal and kill.

Similarly, the first assumption of virtually all social science theories is the same: Humans possess the ability to reason and therefore to select among different lines of action. Social science proceeds from this starting point by postulating that the choices people make can be predicted and explained by assuming that they will *attempt* to do the most reasonable thing, given their circumstances, information, and preferences. That is, *people will seek to maximize their rewards and minimize their costs.* In Chapter 3 we shall see how this simple assumption about human behavior quickly leads to explanations of why and how codes of morality come to exist and why these, in turn, shape individual calculations about what choices are rewarding. Here, let us concentrate on the fact that it is only because people's choices are predictable that it is possible to claim that people have free will.

If people's behavior is not predictable, it must be random. That is, if knowledge of their past actions and their present situation tells us nothing about what people will do next, then the human mind does not reason, but operates like a slot machine or a pair of dice. For only then can there be no consistent patterns between past and future behavior, no link between circumstance and action. Such people would indeed be unpredictable and would frustrate all attempts at social science. But such people would not be human. And surely they could not be judged for their acts or be said to possess free will, for they would have no capacity to choose and no reasoning power at all.

Let's approach this matter in another way. Suppose I set up a money store and offered to sell genuine $20 bills for 35¢ each. As soon as people made sure that there was no hidden gim-mick, that they really could buy money from me at a huge discount, I'm sure I would have more customers than I could handle. When I predict that people will opt for a good deal, I am not reducing them to predetermined robots lacking the power of choice. I am merely saying that by assuming people can select reasonable choices, it is often easy to predict what they will choose to do.

Free will is the essential assumption of social science. Or as W. E. B. Du Bois (1904) put it, sociology "is the science of free will." We do not assume that humans are puppets but that they are reasoning, feeling organisms who learn from experience, who respond to the world around them, who have the power to love, hope, dream, and plan. The goal of social science is to understand why and how humans have these capacities. Moreover, it is because humans can include the findings of social science in making their choices that social science is worthwhile. Social science is not dehumanizing. Rather, it is in some ways the most humanizing of disciplines—it asks what the nature of humanity is and how human life can be enhanced.

Conclusion

The purpose of this book is to introduce sociology not simply as a subject but also as an activity. In letting you see what sociologists do, I hope to convey more effectively what we know, but I also want to show why and how we go about our trade. In this way I hope to enlist some of you to do sociology.

This chapter has attempted to lay an introductory basis for the chapters to come and to engage your interest and curiosity—to serve as an attractive invitation to the rest of the book. Rather than teaching you a first lesson in sociology, it offers sample previews of what is to come, just as TV previews are meant to encourage you to tune in a new show.

I know very well that not every part of every chapter or even some whole chapters will arouse your interest or stir your imagination. That is no surprise. Although every topic included in this book is of primary interest to some group of sociologists, probably no professional sociologist is especially interested in *all* of these topics. To be candid, I'm less interested in some of them than in others. However, since this book is an introduction to the whole field of sociology, it must cover all active topics in the field. Although you should sample and explore all of these topics, it is not necessary that you find each topic of special interest. Any one of the chapters that follow contains enough important, unsolved problems to provide you with a life's work. Indeed, except for Chapter 2, every chapter covers an area of sociology to which any major department of sociology offers at least one whole course and sometimes several advanced courses.

In a sense, then, this book is a sociological sampler whose aim is to survey what sociologists do. In this way you can discover for yourself what kind of sociology most appeals to you.

Finally, I have asked you, as a reader of this book, to explore sociology with me. Although we probably will never meet, we nevertheless will spend a good deal of time together over the next several months. I have made a serious effort to let our author-reader interaction be more intimate than is usual in college textbooks. I want you to share in the fun I have in being a sociologist and telling you about it. For this reason, from time to time I let you look over my shoulder as I do some sociology. Hence, while many of my studies are reported in other introductory textbooks, my work will receive more space in this one. Because I am presuming to tell you what sociology is and how it is done, it seems fair to let you see for yourself what kind of sociologist I am. But I have also chosen to let you watch me work because it was by doing these studies that I truly became a sociologist. Letting my students see my work is the most effective way I have found to reveal to them what being a sociologist means to me.

Review Glossary

sociology The scientific study of the patterns and processes of human social relations. (p. 8)

social sciences Those scientific fields devoted to the study of human behavior, including sociology, psychology, economics, political science, anthropology, criminology, and some branches of history. (p. 8)

micro sociology The study of small groups and of face-to-face interaction among humans. (p. 8)

macro sociology The study of large groups and even of whole societies. (p. 8)

group Two or more persons who maintain a stable pattern of social relations over a significant period of time. (p. 9)

aggregate A collection of people lacking social relations; for example, pedestrians waiting for a walk light. (p. 9)

dyad The smallest possible group, consisting of only two people. (p. 9)

triads Groups with three members. (p. 9)

transitivity A group property that exists when relationships among members of a group are balanced in such a way that no two people when paired disagree in their feelings toward other group members. That is, the two people in all pairs of friends either both like or both dislike other group members. (p. 9)

coalition What is formed when two or more persons join forces to oppose someone else. (p. 10)

social networks Patterns of relationships among members of a group. (p. 11)

cliques Groups within a group. (p. 11)

sociograms Charts showing the social networks within a group. (p. 11)

primary groups Groups whose members have close and intimate relations with one another. (p. 12)

secondary groups Groups whose members have only limited emotional attachments to one another. (p. 13)

scientific method A process by which theories are

formulated, their predictions are tested against systematic observations, and the theory is rejected or adjusted whenever the predictions fail. (p. 13)

theories The explanations scientists formulate; general statements about how some portion of the world fits together and functions and which yield predictions that can be tested. For an extended discussion, see Chapter 3. (p. 14)

research The process of making systematic observations, used primarily to test predictions from theories. (p. 14)

unobtrusive measures Techniques used to measure behavior without disturbing the behavior of the subjects. (p. 15)

validation research Studies conducted to determine whether particular measures used in research are accurate. (p. 15)

mass society theories Attempts to explain many social problems, such as suicide and divorce, as the result of a breakdown in social relations caused by a shift from rural and village life to life in large cities.

People who lack attachments to others are, in fact, more prone to suicide, alcoholism, divorce, and criminality, but the prediction that most people in big cities would show a lack of attachments has turned out to be false. (p. 19)

free will The philosophical and theological doctrine that humans possess the capacity for choosing among alternatives and, therefore, can be held responsible for the choices they make. (p. 26)

■
_____

Suggested Readings

Beirne, Piers. 1987. "Adolphe Quételet and the Origins of Positive Criminology." *American Journal of Sociology* 92:1140–1169.

Berger, Peter L. 1963. *Invitation to Sociology*. New York: Doubleday.

Homans, George C. 1967. *The Nature of Social Science*. New York: Harcourt Brace Jovanovich.

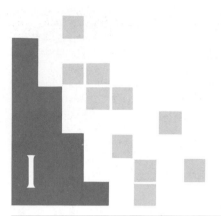

The Sociological Process: An Overview of Concepts, Theories, and Research Methods

I

As with all scientific fields, sociology is a systematic process of discovery. Chapter 1 sketched aspects of this process; there we watched sociologists formulate and test mass society theories. In the three chapters making up this part of the book, we will explore more fully the eight primary steps in the sociological process.

All sciences exist to *explain why*. Imagine several primitive hunters during the Stone Age who wondered why sometimes animals ran away even though they had not seen or heard the hunters approaching, while at other times they could sneak up and almost touch animals before they noticed. Suppose one of the hunters proposed the following answer: When we approach from the same direction that the wind is blowing, our scent is carried ahead of us to warn the herd, but when we approach against the wind, our scent is blown away from the herd and they must rely on sight and sound to detect us. That is a scientific theory. Why? First, because it is *general*—it applies in all instances, not only to last Thursday or to a particular animal. Second, because it makes *predictions that can be checked out*. That is, the hunters can easily discover if their explanation is wrong. All they need to do is try it in a systematic way, sometimes approaching upwind, sometimes downwind, keeping track of the results. According to the theory, if the hunters are always careful not to be seen or make noise, then whenever they come upwind they should succeed in getting close, and whenever they come downwind they should not. If they then found themselves equally successful (or unsuccessful) going with and against

the wind, they would know their theory was false. On the other hand, as repeated tests came out as predicted, the hunters could gain confidence that they had discovered the cause of a vital natural phenomenon.

Here we see the two primary elements of all applications of the scientific process: *theory construction* and *theory testing*. The figure on page 33 identifies these as the two primary aspects of the sociological process. Unlike the primitive hunters, however, modern scientists more clearly understand the fundamentals of the scientific method. Therefore, the sociological process is more clearly outlined and codified. So let's consider each of its eight steps.

The starting point of all sciences, from physiology to sociology, is wonder. Something about the world around us catches our attention and prompts us to wonder what is going on. Why does running cause the heart to beat faster? Why are boys so much more apt than girls are to get into trouble with the police? Here we see Albert Schweitzer (1875–1965), supervised by his cat, at his desk in the hospital he built in Africa on the Ogooué River, where he specialized in the treatment of leprosy. Schweitzer was a great wonderer. He wondered about theology until he was prompted to write *The Quest for the Historical Jesus* (1906). One of the greatest organists in the world, Schweitzer wondered about classical music so much that he wrote *Jean Sebastian Bach: le musicien-poète* (1911). He wondered about philosophy until he was led to write *Philosophy of Civilization* (1923). And through it all he wondered how to cure leprosy. He never found an answer to that question, but in 1952 he was awarded the Nobel Prize for Peace for his efforts on behalf of the "Brotherhood of Nations."

■ **1. Wonder** Science always begins with someone wondering why. Our ancient ancestors wondered why animals could sense them coming. The founders of moral statistics wondered why suicide rates were so stable, yet so variable. In Chapter 2 we will meet sociologists who wondered why Jewish immigrants to North America were successful so much sooner than were some other groups such as the Italians. And in Chapter 3 you will overhear John Lofland and me wondering how people are recruited to new religious movements.

■ **2. Conceptualize** To proceed, all scientists must be precise about *what* they are wondering about. That is, they must *isolate* and *define* their key terms. Put another way, in order to explain the world we must take it apart and classify the various pieces. Hence, chemists separate the material world into the elements shown in periodic tables, while biologists classify all living organisms into groups and subgroups from divisions to species.

Scientific classification is based on concepts. **Concepts** are names used to identify some set or class of things that are said to be alike. Biologists, for example, define all living organisms that are warmblooded and give birth to living offspring (as opposed to laying eggs) as mammals. Used this way, *mammal* is a scientific concept. Sociologists define sets of two or more persons who maintain a stable pattern of social relations over a significant period of time as a *group*. This too is a scientific concept. Just as the concept of mammal ignores all the many differences among cats, dogs, mice, and elephants, treating each as a member of the class of organisms known as mammals, the concept of group ignores gender, race, age, ethnicity, and all other human traits in identifying which sets of persons qualify as groups.

Concepts are **abstractions**; that is, they are ideas, not things. We can see many animals that belong to the class of organisms called mammals, but we cannot see or touch the concept of mammal itself; it exists only in our minds. Nor can we see the concept of group, although we can observe countless sets of people to which it applies. The concept is always more general than any actual set of objects or events to which

it applies. Hence, the concept of a group includes all sets of people having the characteristics of stable and durable social relations—all that ever existed, do exist, will exist, or could exist.

The process of isolating and defining the concepts involved in the phenomenon we are wondering about is the second step in the sociological process, and when sociologists do this they *conceptualize*.

Concepts are the building blocks for theories. The mass society theorists had first to classify certain kinds of human relationships as attachments and some forms of behavior as suicide or as participation in mass movements before they could express their explanations of certain phenomena.

■ **3. Theorize** To take the human social world apart and name the pieces is an essential part of the sociological process, but although concepts identify classes of significant objects or events, they don't explain anything. To call some kind of behavior suicide or to call some set of people a mass movement is to say nothing about *why* suicides or mass movements occur. Theories *supply explanations*. Theories state *why* and *how* several (or more) concepts are related. Because concepts are abstractions and theories are composed of concepts, theories also are abstract: The explanations they provide apply to the range of phenomena included in their concepts.

However, not just any set of statements containing concepts is a theory—or else statements that earthquakes (an abstract concept) are caused by invisible aliens (an abstract concept) would qualify. To qualify as a theory, a set of statements must include or imply some conclusions that can be *empirically verified* by direct physical observation. That is, a theory must *predict* and *prohibit* certain things that can be checked. Theories must risk being proven false. They must be *testable*.

■ **4. Operationalize** The first step to make a theory testable is to be able to identify valid measures of the class of things referred to by each concept in the theory. We already have seen in Chapter 1 how sociologists assess validity— by showing that two measures of the same thing

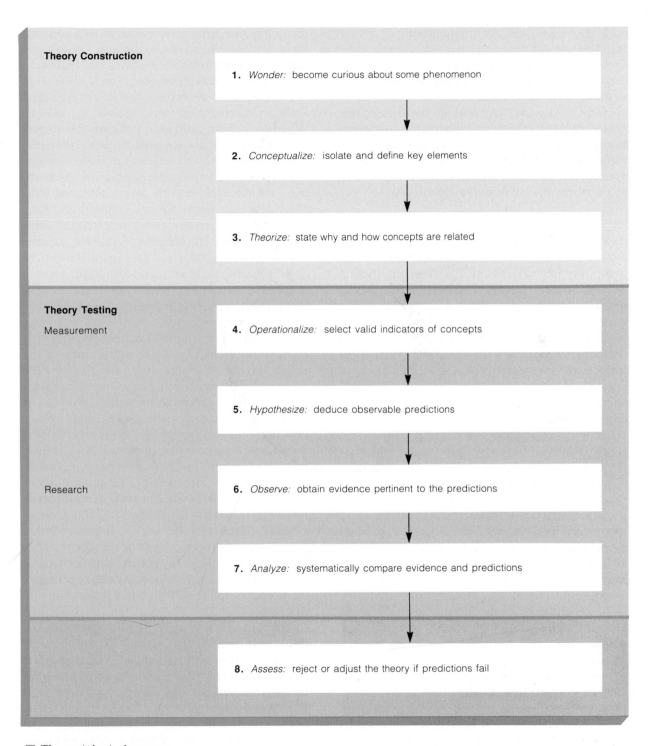

Theory Construction

1. *Wonder:* become curious about some phenomenon

2. *Conceptualize:* isolate and define key elements

3. *Theorize:* state why and how concepts are related

Theory Testing

Measurement

4. *Operationalize:* select valid indicators of concepts

5. *Hypothesize:* deduce observable predictions

Research

6. *Observe:* obtain evidence pertinent to the predictions

7. *Analyze:* systematically compare evidence and predictions

8. *Assess:* reject or adjust the theory if predictions fail

■ The sociological process.

yield the same results, for example. But the question of validity can arise only if the concepts included in a theory *can be measured*. For example, we know how to measure where and when an earthquake has occurred. But there is no way to measure any actions by or even the existence of aliens that are beyond the range of human detection. When sociologists select measures or indicators of a concept, we say they **operationalize** that concept—make it possible to perform observational operations on it.

■ **5. Hypothesize**   The second step to make a theory testable is to formulate predictions about what will be observed in the relationships among indicators of the concepts. That is, the theory tells us what is supposed to happen in general, and a **hypothesis** tells us the implications of that prediction in the specific situation we observe. Here is an example of a hypothesis derived from mass society theory: People living in New York will be less likely to spend social evenings with relatives and friends than people in Mule Creek, Wyoming, will be. This tells us what we are supposed to observe.

■ **6. Observe**   Once we know where and what to look at, and what to expect to see, the next step in the sociological process is systematic observation. Chapters 3 and 4 will exhibit some of the common ways sociologists use to look at the world. Keep in mind that sociologists must always find ways to keep the people they want to observe from outsmarting them or fooling them.

■ **7. Analyze**   Looking is not enough. We must compare what we observe with what the theory, by way of the hypothesis, told us we ought to see. Sometimes these comparisons can be a bit tricky. But the principles involved are simple, as you will see in Chapters 3 and 4.

■ **8. Assess**   The final step in the sociological process is to accept that science requires us to select or alter theories on the basis of evidence—we do not select or alter the evidence to make it fit our theories. When the predicted outcomes keep occurring each time a theory is tested, fine. But when predictions fail, and we are confident that our measurements were cor-

rect, then we must follow one of two courses. First, we can abandon the theory. Second, we can try to reformulate or adjust the theory so that it can yield correct predictions. This is what the mass society theorists did when they shifted from predicting that *individuals* in modern urban societies would lack attachments to predicting that the *groups* within these societies would be isolated. But when that prediction also failed, the theory had to be *abandoned*. In keeping with research results, it was replaced with the following: *If* people are isolated and lack attachments, then they will be prone to pathological forms of behavior—suicide, crime, divorce, alcoholism.

It is vital to recognize that although research can reveal that a particular theory is false, or at least incomplete, *no amount of research ever can prove that a theory is true!* This is because theories are abstractions. Theories apply not only to the past and the present but always to the future as well. For example, the theory connecting attachments and pathological behavior doesn't just apply to North America or to the twentieth century. It applies to all circumstances where human beings lack attachments. It is impossible to test a theory against all possibilities. The future always holds more opportunities for the predicted or prohibited outcomes to be proven false. This is true even for such hallowed theories of physics as the Law of Gravity. Tomorrow, or next year, or next century someone could knock her textbook off her desk and see it fly to the ceiling rather than fall to the floor. Humans will never run out of chances for our theories to fail unless we run out of future.

Fortunately, it is possible to *disprove*, or falsify, our theories. When theories fail we modify or replace them. However, the more times a theory survives efforts to falsify it, and the greater the variety and stringency of the tests we impose upon it, the more confidence we gain that it is valid. So, while we can never say, "That theory is true," there comes a time when we begin to take it for granted. And this lets us grasp a final lesson about the sociological process: Researchers contribute most to scientific progress not by seeking evidence that a theory is true but *by doing their utmost to show that it is false.*

■

Review Glossary

concepts Scientific definitions that identify the members of some class of things as alike, as belonging to the same set or class. (p. 32)

abstractions Ideas or mental constructions rather than material objects. All scientific concepts are abstractions. (p. 32)

operationalize To select valid and observable measures of a concept; such measures are also referred to as indicators of a concept. (p. 32)

hypothesis A specific prediction derived from theories and subject to testing by research. (p. 34)

Concepts for Social and Cultural Theories

2

IN 1907 AN apprehensive American Congress appointed a commission to study whether steps should be taken to slow or halt the flood of immigrants pouring into the nation. That year a record 1,285,349 persons were admitted. Actually, it wasn't *how many* were coming in but *who they were* that really was causing concern. Of all the immigrants arriving in 1907, 81 percent came from southern and eastern nations of Europe—principally from Italy, Greece, Russia, Poland, and what are today Czechoslovakia, Hungary, and Yugoslavia. Of all these people, the two largest groups of immigrants in 1907 were Italians, mainly from southern provinces, and Jews from Russia, Poland, and other parts of eastern Europe.

The commissioners identified the current flow as the "new immigration." They contrasted this with the "old immigration," the pattern that had prevailed from before the American Revolution through the 1870s. The commission noted that in 1882 only 13 percent of immigrants were from southern and eastern Europe, while 87 percent came from Great Britain (including Ireland) and from northwestern Europe—Belgium, France, Germany, Scandinavia, and Switzerland.

The commission was formed primarily because of growing concerns about the impact of the new immigration. In its opening declaration of purpose, the commission suggested that the old immigration brought good citizens "from the most progressive sections of Europe" to America, where "they mingled freely . . . and were quickly assimilated." But the new immigrants were said to be "far less intelligent than the old" and unwilling and unable to assimilate. Many expert witnesses testified that Jews, Italians, Greeks, Poles, Slavs, Hungarians, and other new immigrants would never fit in, never become educated, never contribute to the culture or to the economy.

However, in addition to hearing such testimony, the commissioners did something much more creative: They organized some massive research projects to discover just what was going on. What were the new immigrants *really* like? How were they fitting in? What were their lifestyles?

Published in many massive volumes of statistics, the Immigration Commission Report of 1911 offers a priceless glimpse into the nation at that time. And it includes many surprising findings.

The cleanliness of the new immigrants and their households was found to be "unexpectedly good." And the new immigrants did not form permanent ethnic enclaves in the poor districts of cities, enclaves that would insulate them from all outside efforts to make them into "real Americans." Instead, "as their economic status improves . . . they very generally move to better surroundings." The commission also could find no evidence of greater criminal activity among the new immigrants.

But perhaps their most surprising finding was that some of the new immigrants had already caught up economically. Table 2-1, based on data the commission gathered in 1908, shows that employed Jewish men born in eastern European nations other than Russia had an average weekly income *higher* than that of native-born white

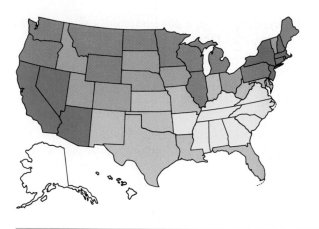

North Carolina	0.3
South Carolina	0.4
Mississippi	0.5
Georgia	0.6
Tennessee	0.7
Alabama	0.8
Arkansas	0.8
Kentucky	1.3
Virginia	1.4

Oklahoma	2.0
Louisiana	2.6
West Virginia	4.2
Indiana	5.2
Missouri	5.5
Florida	5.6
Kansas	6.3
Maryland	7.1
Texas	7.8
New Mexico	8.3

Delaware	8.9
Iowa	9.4
Idaho	9.4
Nebraska	11.6
Ohio	11.8
Vermont	12.6
Colorado	12.7
South Dakota	13.0
Utah	13.2

Wyoming	13.7
Oregon	13.7
Maine	14.0
Pennsylvania	16.0
Montana	17.4
Wisconsin	17.5
Illinois	18.7
Washington	19.6
Michigan	19.9
Minnesota	20.4
North Dakota	20.4

New Hampshire	20.6
Nevada	20.7
California	22.1
New Jersey	23.5
Arizona	24.1
New York	27.2
Connecticut	27.4
Massachusetts	28.3
Rhode Island	29.0

N. W. Territories	1.4
Pr. Edward Island	1.5
Nova Scotia	2.7

New Brunswick	2.8
Quebec	4.2
Ontario	6.2
Manitoba	17.9

British Columbia	19.0
Yukon	23.5
Saskatchewan	26.3
Alberta	29.6

Figure 2-1 ■ **Foreign-born North Americans, 1920–21.** The 1920 census found that 13 percent of Americans were foreign born. A year later, the Canadian census found that 10 percent were foreign born, not including an additional 12 percent who had been born in Britain (because Canada was then a British dominion). In both nations, Jews from Russia and Poland and Italians were among the largest groups of the foreign-born. Notice, too, that Alberta (29.6%) had virtually the same proportion of foreign-born as did Rhode Island (29.0%). However, in Canada at this time immigrants were still being drawn primarily to the rural areas and the frontier, while in the United States most immigrants were settling in the industrial Northeast. In this chapter we examine the transition of Italians and Jews from "foreigners" to "Americans" and "Canadians" in order to understand some key sociological concepts—especially *society* and *culture*. *Note*: At the time, Newfoundland was not part of Canada, and Alaska and Hawaii were not yet states.

Table 2-1 ■ Income of employed males 18 and over in the United States, 1908 (nonfarm only).

	Average weekly income
Native-born:	
White	$13.89
Black	10.66
Foreign-born:	
Canadian (French)	10.62
Canadian (English)	14.15
English	14.13
Irish	13.01
Greek	8.41
Mexican	8.57
Italian (South)	9.61
Jewish (Russia)	12.71
Jewish (Other)	14.37

Source: U.S. Senate Committee on Immigration, *Abstract of Reports of the Immigration Commission,* vol. 1, Washington, D.C.: U.S. Government Printing Office, 1911.

men, while Jews from Russia were just slightly behind native-born whites. In contrast, Italians earned only 69 percent as much as native-born whites, while men born in Mexico and Greece earned only 62 percent as much. In fact, these latter groups earned less than blacks. (The data exclude agricultural workers, whose wages were lower than those of urban workers, and most blacks still worked on farms in this era.) Moreover, this pattern was not limited to the United States. Jews had also achieved very rapid economic success in Canada, and there too they stood out in sharp contrast to the much slower progress of Italians and other new immigrants.

As these facts came to the attention of early sociologists, many of them began to wonder why. Why had the Jews done so well, so rapidly? Or, put in relative terms, why had the Jews achieved success so rapidly compared with the Italians? Both arrived here during the same period and brought little money with them. Both faced considerable hostility from the native-born population. But there were the Jews, new immi-

grants already on a par financially with the old immigrants. How had they done it?

■
_____

Chapter Preview

This is exactly the sort of wondering that is the first step in the sociological process. In this chapter we are going to follow up on this question, looking on as social scientists formulate and test theories aimed at providing an answer. And we are going to give particular attention to efforts to fulfill the second step in the sociological process: to conceptualize.

I have chosen to pursue this particular question because it prompted two broad forms of theory that sociologists often use. Hence, the concepts these two forms of theory require are those most widely used by sociologists. By encountering these key concepts now, you will acquire a sociological vocabulary that will help you in later chapters. Perhaps I could just have written a chapter that defined these concepts and asked you to memorize them. But it's very boring to learn terminology for which you cannot yet see any use—even professors of sociology don't sit around reciting lists of key concepts. Concepts are not meant to be appreciated, but to be used in theories. And the best way to learn them is by using them. So that's how you will encounter concepts in this chapter.

Keep in mind that in time Italians also achieved economic parity with the old immigrant groups in Canada and the United States, so our focus will be not on why only the Jews succeeded but on why they did this so much sooner. As you will see, this question has implications far beyond these particular groups in a certain time and place. For the underlying issue involves the general conditions under which ethnic and cultural minorities achieve economic parity. Moreover, we will be following a question that has attracted the attention of many first-rate sociologists. As you watch them work, you will gain greater insight into what sociologists actually do. And when sociologists wonder about the relative speed of economic progress of Italians and Jews, the next thing they need to do is *conceptualize.* Let's watch.

■ Women taking medical examinations at Ellis Island, the reception station in New York Harbor through which most immigrants passed at the turn of the century. Looking at these women, we see that they are not simply entering a new society but that they are bringing with them a way of life, a culture, that is quite different from that of the two American women examining them.

Society and Culture

Look carefully at the photograph of immigrant women undergoing medical examinations at Ellis Island, for it displays two related and important sociological concepts. These women want to enter the United States, to live in a different nation than the one in which they were born and raised. But more is involved in this shift than simply geography. Compare the immigrant women with the two American women conducting the examinations. The immigrant women not only are *coming from* a different nation but they are also *bringing* many differences with them. These two aspects of

immigrants, coming from a different place and bringing different life-styles with them, are crucial elements in our question about Jews and Italians. So let's isolate and define the two most general sociological concepts: *culture* and *society*.

As the discussion of these two concepts unfolds, you will see that it is somewhat artificial to think of them as two distinct parts of social life. In the real world, society and culture never exist separately—they are, instead, like opposite sides of the same coin. However, as the chapter progresses, you will see that distinguishing between these two concepts helps us explain the phenomenon we are studying. And that, of course, is the whole point of conceptualizing.

The concept of society

Sociologists often use the terms *society* and *nation* interchangeably. But not all nations are societies, and not all societies are nations. A better definition of **society** is a group of people who are united by social relations. Because a society often contains many such groups, the term must also refer to a group that is relatively self-sufficient and independent—a distinct social boundary should set off members of one society from all other persons and groups. Hence, most people will know which society they belong to. In addition, societies tend to occupy a definite physical location—even nomadic societies tend to travel a familiar route within a specific area. Finally, societies tend to have substantial periods of existence; they are not momentary arrangements (Hoult, 1969).

Most nations on earth today meet this definition of society, but some do not. In some nations bitter conflicts rage because two or more societies are enclosed within the same political boundary. The Civil War showed that for a time the United States was not one society. Conflicts between French- and English-speaking areas of Canada have tested whether the nation comprises one or two societies. Conversely, at times, several nations have constituted but one society. In the middle of the past century the area that became Germany consisted of many independent states. The ease with which they merged suggests they may have been one society before they were one nation.

Despite exceptions such as these, sociologists regard most modern nations as societies. However, sociologists also regard most primitive tribal groups as distinct societies. Societies can thus come in many sizes, from millions of members to as few as several dozen. The key is to look for *relatively self-contained and self-sufficient human groups that are united by social relationships*—relationships that make possible coordinated activities such as earning a living and fighting a war.

In 1400, the area that is today North America was occupied by many societies: The social and geographic boundaries between Indian tribes were rather clear cut. Contact between the tribes was limited, and each tribe generally went its own way. Despite their small size, separate tribes were separate societies.

In terms of total population, California is nearly as large as Canada. Both Canada and California are united internally by complex social relations. But California is not a society because it is not very self-sufficient and independent. What happens in California is influenced greatly by what happens elsewhere in the United States—external influences that are much stronger than are outside influences on Canada. Citizens of California are closely connected to citizens of other states by bonds of family, friendship, business, and a sense of common destiny. Moreover, Americans as a whole are bound together by a common *culture* that, to some extent, sets them apart from Canadians. *All societies possess a somewhat distinctive way of life.*

The concept of culture

When people move from one society to another, what happens to them helps us to see the distinction between society and culture. Consider the millions of people who immigrated to the United States and Canada. Some of them adjusted to life in North America easily. Those who came here from England, for example, found a way of life that was very familiar. But others had to make much greater adjustments, such as learning a new language and adopting many new customs.

When we notice the problems that some immigrants have in adjusting to life in a new country, we are recognizing the fact that every society possesses a *culture*. While society is a group of people united by social relationships, their culture is their way of life. What separates Mexico from the United States, for example, is not just a political boundary. Americans and Mexicans speak different languages, eat different foods, wear different kinds of clothes, observe different customs, hold different beliefs, and differ in many other ways. In sum, we can say that Mexico and the United States have different cultures.

If *society* is often synonymous with *nation*, *culture* is often synonymous with *civilization*. **Culture** is the complex pattern of living that humans have developed and pass on from one generation to the next. Culture, then, is a very broad concept. While sociologists use the concept of society to identify people according to their relationships with one another and their independence from others, they use the concept of culture to identify people according to what they believe, what they do, what they know, and how they act: In short, *everything that humans learn is culture.* Culture can also pertain to the various materials and objects that people learn to use. In other words, *technology*, whether it be simple bows and arrows or computers, is as much a mental as a physical phenomenon. It is human knowledge that turns a stick and a string into a bow or that makes it possible to flake stones to serve as arrowheads. Technology does not exist naturally—it is created. A stick is not a club until a human picks it up and hits things with it. To the ant, a statue is only another piece of rock.

As a human creation, culture is strictly a product of human society. Every society is characterized by its culture—its distinctive way of life. Because different societies have different cultures, conflicts between societies arise from cultural differences: What is the true religion? What is the proper form of government? Some conflicts over culture occur within societies, and they may be so severe that they threaten the society's continued existence.

Although society and culture are the two most basic sociological concepts, by themselves they can't explain much of anything. Later in this chapter we will see that many social scientists have tried to explain the rapid economic success of Jews in the United States and Canada on the basis of the culture they brought with them from eastern Europe. But to have such explanations taken seriously, these social scientists had to say more specifically *what aspects* of Jewish culture played this role. So before we start to examine their answers, we need to become familiar with some basic concepts used for social and cultural analysis, for identifying *parts* of societies and cultures.

Concepts for Social Analysis

If the concept *society* refers to certain kinds of groups, then its most basic features have to do with *relationships* among humans. Relationships can be characterized on many different grounds. For example, in Chapter 1 we distinguished primary and secondary groups on the basis of the degree of intimacy of relationship among members. Another way to characterize relations among individuals and groups within societies is on the basis of their relative wealth, power, and social position—on how much inequality exists among members of a group or a society.

Stratification concepts

Sociologists use the concept of **stratification** to identify the unequal distribution of rewards (or things perceived as valuable) among members of a society. In Chapter 9 we will see that these rewards are separated into three major types: property, power, and prestige (or honor). In all known societies, these rewards are unequally distributed—some people have more and some have less. *Stratified* literally means layered; the term *upper crust* reflects the idea that societies are made up of layers. Sociologists identify these layers as **classes:** groups of people who share a similar *position*, or **status,*** in the stratification system. For example, one might think of a particular society as being divided into three classes: the poor, the middle class, and the rich. As we shall see in Chapters 9 and 10, some societies have more than three classes, depending on how

---

*Throughout this text, the terms *status* and *position* are used interchangeably. You will understand why in Chapter 9, where we compare how Marx and Weber conceptualized social class. Although status implies prestige and honor in everyday speech, do not think of those qualities when you read the term in this text. Instead, think only of rank or position within a society, for a person or a group may have *low* as well as high status. Indeed, in this chapter our aim is to see how Jews and Italians escaped from their low status, or low position, in North America.

and to whom rewards are distributed in the society and on the criteria used for analysis.

Sometimes individuals or whole groups change their position in the stratification system. Upward movement is called **upward mobility;** the reverse is called **downward mobility.** When a lawyer's son or daughter becomes a factory worker, we say that he or she has been downwardly mobile. When a factory worker's child becomes a lawyer, we say that he or she has been upwardly mobile.

These concepts of stratification help us to compare the upward mobility of Jewish and Italian immigrants. Upon arrival, both groups were concentrated in the lower class of the stratification system. In time, many Jews and Italians rose to more privileged positions in society. When Jews and Italians were distributed at each class level at about the same proportion as that of established groups, they had achieved equality. In other words, when a Jew or an Italian was as likely as an American or a Canadian of English origin to be rich *or* poor, then being Jewish or Italian no longer determined social position.

Social position can be determined in two general ways. **Achieved status** refers to status, or position, in the stratification system that is derived from individual merit or achievement. When status is derived from inheritance, we call it **ascribed status;** that is, a person's position in society is fixed (ascribed to him or her by others) on the basis of family background or genetic inheritance. So long as women are excluded from lucrative, prestigious, and powerful positions in society, for example, their status is limited by biological inheritance.

The *caste system* in India is an extreme example of a stratification system based on ascribed status. Each level in the Indian stratification system is called a caste. Everyone is born into a caste, and the caste of the parents generally determines the position in society that their offspring will occupy, regardless of individual ability or merit.

When being an Italian or a Jew in Canada or the United States greatly restricted opportunities for improving social position, these groups occupied an ascribed low status. To be a Jew or an Italian was similar to having been born into a lower caste group in India. To the extent that being Jewish or Italian no longer plays any significant role in determining a person's position in society, his or her status is achieved.

Conflict concepts

For a group to be ascribed a low status doesn't just happen; it requires actions by others to limit the opportunities of group members, and these actions, in turn, usually are justified by certain negative beliefs about the group. Put another way, ascribed status is rooted in prejudice and discrimination.

Prejudice refers to negative or hostile attitudes toward a group. People become the objects of hatred, contempt, or suspicion simply because they belong to a particular group and with no regard for their individual qualities: "All Italians are gangsters," "All Jews are cheap," "All Irish are drunks."

Discrimination refers to actions taken against a group to deny members, collectively, rights and privileges enjoyed freely by others. When members of a group are refused consideration for employment, promotion, residence in a neighborhood, and the like, these actions reflect discrimination.

■

Concepts for Cultural Analysis

Each human must learn the culture of his or her society. Among the most significant elements of culture each must learn are *values, norms,* and *roles.* We will begin by exploring these three concepts, and then we will examine concepts involving cultural conflicts within a society.

Values and norms

The **values** of a culture identify its ideals—its ultimate aims and most general standards for assessing good and bad or desirable and undesirable. When we say people need self-respect, dignity, and freedom or that we must all stand up for our country, we are invoking values. Values are not only lofty but also general.

Norms, on the other hand, are quite specific. They are *rules governing behavior.* Norms define what behavior is required, acceptable, or prohibited in particular circumstances. Norms indicate that a person should, ought, or must act (or must not act) in certain ways. We have all been in situations where we were somewhat anxious about how we ought to act. Such anxiety reflects that we are sometimes not sure what the norms are and also that violation of the norms will often lead to disapproval or even punishment. Conversely, conforming to the norms often brings approval and other rewards. In the next chapter we shall begin discussing a theme that runs throughout the book: Why do people conform or fail to conform to the norms?

Values and norms are related. Values justify the norms. For example, we can invoke values of human dignity and self-respect to explain the norm against ridiculing people who are physically handicapped. That is, calling someone a "gimp" not only is violating a norm but is also morally *wrong.* As another example, many societies value the intellectual development of the individual. As we shall see in Chapter 16, this value is the basis for many norms, including the norm that children shall be enrolled in school.

Roles

A **role** is a collection of norms associated with a particular position in a society. That is, these norms describe how we expect someone in a particular position to act or not to act.

Consider a church during Sunday services. To keep things simple, let's assume that there are three roles: minister, organist, and member of the congregation. Each person in each of these roles is expected to act in different ways. The minister is expected to lead the service in the proper sequence and to preach a sermon. The organist is expected to play appropriate selections accurately and at the right times. The members of the congregation are expected to join in hymns, prayers, and rituals at the proper

moments and to sit attentively the rest of the time. A minister who gets prayers mixed up violates a norm attached to his or her role, as does the organist who plays wrong notes or the churchgoer who falls asleep.

Of course, it would be a much more serious violation of role behavior if a member of the congregation ran up and pounded on the organ or if the minister fell asleep during the services. When people blatantly disregard their roles, the integrity of the social situation is called into question. We may begin to ask ourselves, "Is that person really a minister?" "Is that person really a member of this church?" "Is this really a church service or is it a hoax?" (Goffman, 1959).

Social life is structured by roles. In virtually every social situation, we have a relatively clearly defined role to fulfill: student, friend, woman, husband, shopper, pedestrian, cop, nun, bartender, wife. Each of these roles involves a "script" that we are expected to follow.

Some roles are thought to be more demanding than others, and some are thought to be more important than others. Virtually everyone is thought to be competent enough to fulfill the role of friend or spouse, but few are considered able to fulfill roles such as mathematician or sports star. A role that is believed to be more demanding and more important earns greater rewards than do roles that are considered less demanding and less important. However, societies differ in their evaluations of various roles. For example, the role of priest is considered much more important in Italy than in the Soviet Union, while the role of chess player is more highly valued in the Soviet Union than in Italy.

Differences in the rewards attached to various roles in a particular society largely influence what roles persons will seek and what aspects of roles people will try to adopt in their own behavior. For example, if people in the most exalted roles in a society are required to demonstrate intense religious faith, then many other people in that society will attempt to do likewise.

Later chapters (especially Chapter 6) will say much about roles—about how people learn to perform roles, about conflicts among roles, and the like. For now, it is enough to understand that different cultures can evaluate a given role quite differently.

■ First-generation immigrants often stick to the "old ways," to their native culture, but their children inevitably begin to adapt to the culture around them. And back in 1910, that's exactly what these immigrant kids in New York City are busy doing. In an alley between their slum tenements, beneath clotheslines hung with the family wash, it's time to play ball.

Because cultures can vary greatly, what happens when several cultures exist within a single society—as they must in any society undergoing substantial rates of immigration? The result has often been violent conflicts (see Chapter 11). But Canadian and American history also provides examples of more pleasant possibilities.

Assimilation and accommodation

Assimilation refers to the process of exchanging one culture for another. Usually this term is applied to people who adjust to new surroundings by adopting the prevailing culture as their own. Think of assimilation in terms of fitting into or *disappearing into* a new culture. For example, to be fully assimilated into Canadian society an immigrant from the United States would have to drop ways of speaking, acting, and thinking that distinguish the two cultures and would have to substitute Canadian patterns. Or a Mexican would be assimilated into American culture by becoming just like people born and raised in the United States.

Only rarely do individuals manage to become fully assimilated, especially if the cultures differ greatly. Usually it is their children or grandchildren who become assimilated. Moreover, many groups are unwilling *ever* to assimilate fully. For example, when British immigrants began to arrive in Canada they did not begin to speak French or become Roman Catholics, nor did the French switch to English and Anglicanism. Indeed, most immigrant groups in the United States have maintained some central aspects of their original culture, and this tendency is thought to be even more pronounced in Canada (Isajiw, 1977).

The failure of newcomers to assimilate has often caused intense conflicts—but not always and not forever. A second outcome is **accommodation,** which describes the situation where two groups find they are able to ignore some important cultural differences between them and emphasize common interests instead.

In the nineteenth century, Catholic-Protestant cultural conflicts agitated American society. A rapid influx of Irish Catholics, fleeing the terrible famine of 1845–46 in Ireland, caused many Protestants in the United States to fear that their religious culture was threatened. Over the decades the cultural antagonisms between Catholics and Protestants waned until it became possible for them to emphasize their common Christianity rather than historical theological feuds. At that point accommodation had occurred.

Cultural pluralism and subcultures

Accommodation results in the continued existence of several distinctive cultures within a society—or **cultural pluralism**.

Considerable cultural pluralism exists in both the United States and Canada. In each nation immigration has created a cultural mosaic, for most groups have retained some distinctive elements of their native culture—especially religion and food. Moreover, there is constant addition to the overall culture as material from various groups comes to be shared by all. For example, *everybody* eats Italian food, and many Italian and Yiddish words have crept into the vocabulary of English-speaking North Americans (Rosten, 1968). Yet even as the larger culture has embraced elements of ethnic cultures, distinctively Jewish and Italian cultures still flourish (as do many other ethnic cultures). There still are Italian and Jewish neighborhoods, easily recognized as such. Thus, to some extent, Canada and the United States are societies that have not only a distinctive culture but also many cultures.

To deal conceptually with this situation, sociologists have developed the concept of subcultures. A **subculture** is a culture within a culture—in other words, a distinctive set of beliefs, morals, customs, and the like developed or maintained by a group within a larger society. Sometimes the differences between the general culture and a subculture are not very great, as is true today between the general American culture and the subculture of Italian-Americans. Sometimes the differences are great, as between the general Canadian culture and that of the Mennonite communities of Saskatchewan (Driedger, 1982). Often, people are born and

raised in a subculture. But often, too, they *join* subcultures such as those sustained by convents.

Having examined these sociological concepts, now let's put them to use.

Jews and Italians in North America

As already noted, the Immigration Commission was appointed not because of concerns that too many foreigners were entering the country but because of anxieties about them being the "wrong kind" of people. And what made them "wrong" was their culture.

Those making up the new immigration seemed very alien to eyes conditioned by the cultural traditions of western Europe. They spoke strange-sounding languages and ate odd foods. Many went to unusual churches—the Jews even went to church on the "wrong" day. To make matters worse, most of them were desperately poor. Many Americans and Canadians were convinced that these newcomers would always be "foreigners" who would never fit in.

Fears about admitting "inferior racial stocks" rose as the initial stream became a torrent. The 55,000 Italian immigrants to the United States during the decade of the 1870s were followed by more than 300,000 the next decade, more than 650,000 during the 1890s, and then more than two million in the first decade of the twentieth century. The pattern of Jewish immigration to the United States closely paralleled that of the Italians, both in numbers and timing. Meanwhile, Canada also was getting its first substantial immigration from eastern and southern Europe, albeit with smaller totals. Between 1900 and 1914 (when the outbreak of World War I cut off immigration from Europe), about 120,000 Italians entered Canada, many coming north after a brief stop in the United States (Spada, 1969). During this same period about 150,000 Jews also arrived in Canada (Vigod, 1984).

You can see from Figures 2-2 through 2-5 that on both sides of the border Jewish and Italian

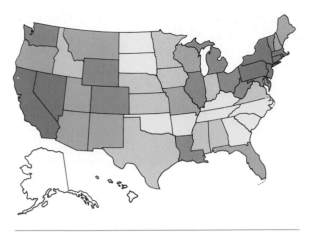

North Carolina	39
South Carolina	46
Georgia	48
North Dakota	52
South Dakota	129
Arkansas	169
Kentucky	172
Tennessee	208
Oklahoma	234

Maryland	1,360
Wyoming	1,369
Washington	1,382
Michigan	1,523
West Virginia	1,831
Ohio	2,075
Vermont	2,188
Louisiana	2,579
Illinois	3,019
Colorado	3,034

N.W. Territories	12
Pr. Edward Island	29
Saskatchewan	91

Quebec	684
Alberta	684
Ontario	1,137
British Columbia	1,637

Virginia	238
Mississippi	242
Alabama	275
Kansas	397
Iowa	403
Indiana	433
Texas	435
Nebraska	518
Idaho	577
Minnesota	620

Delaware	3,730
California	4,895
Pennsylvania	5,394
Nevada	5,823
Massachusetts	6,183
New York	10,827
New Jersey	10,914
Rhode Island	11,699
Connecticut	12,218

New Brunswick	95
Nova Scotia	309
Manitoba	317
Yukon	524

Figure 2-3 ■ **Italians per 100,000 Canadian population, 1921.** The pattern of Italian settlement in Canada somewhat resembles that for the United States, although Canada at this time still had considerable open land. British Columbia had the highest rate, followed by Ontario. The rates for Canada are much lower than rates for the United States despite the fact that the Canadian data refer to anyone claiming Italian descent, while data for the United States are based on place of birth. *Note*: Newfoundland was not part of Canada at this time.

Arizona	698
Maine	727
Wisconsin	843
New Hampshire	885
Missouri	914
New Mexico	964
Oregon	964
Florida	1,064
Montana	1,190
Utah	1,341

Figure 2-2 ■ **Persons born in Italy per 100,000 U.S. population, 1920.** Italian immigrants to the United States settled mainly on the East and West Coasts—a pattern typical of all immigrants at the turn of the century (see Figure 2-1). The reason was simple—these were the areas of greatest economic opportunity at the time. The free land that once drew waves of immigrants to the Middle West had been claimed and settled by the start of the twentieth century. The persistent poverty of the American South held no attraction for immigrants. *Note:* Hawaii and Alaska were not states in 1920.

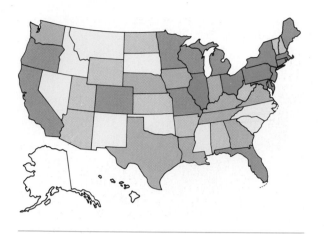

South Dakota	56	Florida	944
Idaho	71	Maine	965
New Mexico	92	Wisconsin	1,130
Montana	123	Oregon	1,355
North Carolina	127	Minnesota	1,601
Mississippi	149	Colorado	1,899
Oklahoma	182	Michigan	1,901
Nevada	192	Delaware	2,155
South Carolina	230	Missouri	2,164
		California	2,569

Arizona	236		
North Dakota	243	Ohio	2,640
Kansas	270	Rhode Island	3,676
Arkansas	272	Pennsylvania	4,246
West Virginia	304	Maryland	4,487
Alabama	364	Illinois	4,736
Wyoming	391	Massachusetts	5,184
Vermont	401	Connecticut	5,945
New Hampshire	466	New Jersey	5,952
Utah	472	New York	16,226

Iowa	520
Kentucky	613
Georgia	632
Louisiana	698
Texas	729
Indiana	758
Tennessee	798
Washington	881
Nebraska	912
Virginia	943

N.W. Territories	12	Saskatchewan	710
Pr. Edward Island	24	Ontario	1,629
Yukon	190	Quebec	2,032
		Manitoba	2,732

New Brunswick	320
British Columbia	323
Nova Scotia	413
Alberta	551

Figure 2-5 ■ **Jews per 100,000 Canadian population, 1921.** Jews in Canada tended to settle not only in the urban East (Quebec and Ontario) but also in several prairie provinces: Jews made up a larger part of the population of Manitoba at this time than of any other province. The first Jews in Manitoba came as traders in the 1870s. Many arrived in the early 1880s as laborers building the Canadian Pacific railroad. Then, when Jews began to flee Russia and Poland in large numbers, Baron Maurice de Hirsch organized and financed a huge resettlement project that founded many Jewish farming communities on the prairies of Manitoba and Saskatchewan. *Note*: Newfoundland was not part of Canada at this time.

Figure 2-4 ■ **Jews per 100,000 U.S. population, 1926.** Unlike the Canadian census, the individual U.S. census form does not ask about religion. However, beginning in 1890 the U.S. government conducted an enumeration of religious membership each decade through 1936 by sending questionnaires to all religious congregations. The data shown here for 1926 indicate that, as with Italians, Jews tended to settle on the East Coast. But, relative to Italians, Jews were more concentrated in Illinois and Ohio and less so in California and Nevada. *Note*: Hawaii and Alaska were not states in 1926.

■ This newspaper cartoon, published at the turn of the century, shows Uncle Sam as a latter-day Moses parting the seas marked *oppression* and *intolerance* to let the children of Israel reach new western homes. The cartoon thus sympathetically acknowledges the outbreak of violence against Jews in Russia that prompted millions to immigrate. But it does not label these immigrants as Jews—readers were expected to *recognize* Jews. Notice the use of harsh anti-Semitic stereotypes: Everyone (including Uncle Sam) has a huge, hooked nose and meaty lips. The women are fat. Despite showing some men with bundles hung from poles over their shoulders, most of the men wear top hats and fine coats—symbols of the "rich" Jewish banker and moneylender.

immigrants tended to settle in the urban East, although a significant number of Jewish immigrants to Canada took up farming in Manitoba and Saskatchewan (Kage, 1981; Sack, 1965; Rosenberg, 1970). And on both sides of the border, Jews and Italians often faced unfriendly receptions (Ages, 1981; Musmanno, 1965).

Prejudice and discrimination

In 1895 Henry Gannett, chief of the U.S. Geological Survey and geographer for the tenth and eleventh censuses, published a popular book that summed up developments in American society since the founding of the republic. Lavishly filled with color maps and illustrations, the book was also regarded as a serious work of social history. In a section presenting statistics on immigration, Gannett noted the concentration of Italians and Jews in the largest cities and remarked:

Hence it appears that the most objectionable elements of the foreign-born population have flocked in the greatest proportion to our large cities, where they are in a position to do the most harm by corruption and violence.

Gannett scattered similar remarks about foreigners throughout the book. Moreover, Gannett's views reflected respectable opinion about Italians, Jews, and other eastern and southern European groups at that time.

Look closely at the cartoon showing Uncle Sam welcoming Jews. It was meant to be *sympathetic* to the persecution Jews were then suffering in Russia. Yet it also depicts Jewish immigrants in terms of harsh anti-Semitic stereotypes. Or consider a book published in Canada in 1909 by the Methodist Church and intended to *improve* attitudes toward immigrants (Woodsworth, 1909). In a chapter devoted to "Hebrew" immigrants, we are told that Jews "may be miserly along some lines" but that they are generous with their own kind. We also are told that "the same keen business instincts are common to both" the Jewish peddler and the Jewish "money-barons who control the world's finances." This is classic **anti-Semitism** (prejudice against Jews) written with the best of intentions by one of the most respected churchmen in Canada at that time.

Italians fared no better (Musmanno, 1965). In 1929 the Italian World War Veterans' Association of Toronto published a book meant to refute public beliefs that Italian-Canadians were criminal, illiterate "undesirables." The book reported, for example, that of all immigrants to Canada between 1901 and 1909, Italians had the lowest rate of deportation (Gualtieri, 1929). Ironically, the book is dedicated to "Giovanni Caboto, the first emigrant in Canada." At the time, every English-speaking schoolchild in Canada was taught that the name of the man who "discovered Canada" was John Cabot, while French speakers learned of him as Jean Cabot (with a silent "t"). He was actually an Italian in the service of the English Crown.

Known as "dagos," "wops," and "guineas," Italians were among those "foreigners" described as "human flotsam" by Madison Grant, chairman of the New York Zoological Society and a trustee of the American Museum of Natural History. He went on to say that "the whole tone of American life, social, moral, and political has been lowered and vulgarized by them." Grant's famous and influential book, *The Passing of the Great Race*, published in 1916, developed elaborate "scientific" and "biological" reasons for halting immigration by people from "the Mediterranean basin and the Balkans."

In 1921 the U.S. Congress heeded Grant's warnings and imposed strict quotas on immigration. Only 154,000 persons a year would be allowed in. Different nationalities were assigned their own quotas. Great Britain received a quota of 65,721 per year. Germany's quota was set at 25,927 and Italy's at a minute 5,802 (Allen, 1985). No Africans could enter, and most Asians were also excluded. These policies remained essentially unchanged until 1967, when the blatant discrimination was finally ended. Canada also adopted very restrictive immigration policies, easing them only in recent years.

Assimilation and accommodation of Jews and Italians

Although prejudice and discrimination greeted Jews and Italians in North America, it was not universal or unrelenting. Among my early sociological research was a study of anti-Semitism in the United States. My colleagues and I found that in the middle and late 1960s, prejudice against Jews had declined greatly and few people still harbored serious feelings against Jews (Glock and Stark, 1966; Stark et al., 1971). Moreover, throughout the United States during the post–World War II period, restrictive real estate covenants preventing Jews from buying homes in certain neighborhoods were overturned by the courts, and many other forms of discrimination subsided as well. For Italians, too, the worst is long past.

In Chapter 11 we will see what sociologists have learned about how prejudice arises and how it dies. Here we will note several things that contributed to changes in attitudes toward Jews and Italians. The first is the substantial degree to which Jews and Italians have become assimilated. Most were born in North America, and so they talk, dress, and act much like others born here. A major aspect of assimilation is *intermarriage*—marrying someone of another ethnic background. Nearly half of the United States citizens who listed their ancestry in the 1980 census as Italian listed a second ancestry as well—which means that their parents or grandparents intermarried. Alba (1977, 1985) estimated that by the third generation, 60 percent of Americans of Italian ancestry married non-Italians. The same pattern seems to hold in Canada. Spada (1969) noted that between 1900 and 1961 439,714 Italians entered Canada. However, despite Italian-Canadians having a high birthrate, only 450,351 Canadians gave their ancestry as Italian in the 1961 census. How could this be? Spada concluded, "The major reason for the disappearance of the Italian population is the high degree of assimilation."

Jewish intermarriage rates are lower than those for Italians, both in Canada and the United States. The primary reason is that Italians are able to marry people of many other ancestries and still marry *within their religion*. For Jews, the boundaries of ethnicity and religion coincide, thus making intermarriage of greater significance. Nevertheless, Jewish intermarriage rates have risen steadily on both sides of the border and are especially high in the western parts of both nations where the Jewish population is relatively smaller (Brym, Gillespie, and Gillis, 1985; Cohn, 1976; Goldstein, 1971).

A second aspect of changed attitudes is accommodation. Despite substantial assimilation, large Jewish and Italian subcultures still exist in the United States and Canada. Jews have not changed their religion, nor have Italians. But these cultural differences no longer generate much conflict. Agreement has been reached within the societies that these differences are not important in comparison with the many common bonds linking all Canadians and all Americans.

Chapter 11 will argue that the underlying basis of such accommodation is economic equality—that prejudice and discrimination against a minority subculture seem to persist until the group has managed to achieve equal status. Put another way, cultural differences are not accommodated until a group has "made it." And this statement brings us back to the sociological question underlying this chapter. By now, both Jews and Italians have achieved economic success in North America. But the Jews were upwardly mobile much sooner than were the Italians. Why?

Theorizing About Ethnic Mobility

Now that we have clarified the needed concepts and identified the question we wish to answer, we can move to the third step in the sociological process. It's time to theorize. We now must say how some set of concepts fits together in a way that offers an answer to our question. We shall examine two such theories. The first was suggested long ago, soon after sociologists first began to wonder about why Jews had been upwardly mobile so much sooner than had Italians. Over many decades this theory was refined and tested, until by the 1970s social scientists had gained great confidence in it. This theory stresses *cultural causes*. It contrasts the values, norms, and roles dominant in Jewish and Italian cultures and concludes that one culture helped while the other hindered the economic progress of the two ethnic groups. The second theory we will examine arose recently to challenge the older theory. It stresses *social causes*, especially aspects of stratification systems, to account for the differences in the economic position of Jewish and Italian immigrants. We shall develop each theory and let them collide with one another, as well as with appropriate research evidence.

The Cultural Theory

Human beings are shaped by their cultures, and most people obey the norms most of the time. If we want to predict how people will behave in any given circumstance, the best way to do that is to know their cultural background. In this way, for example, we can be confident that Italian men will be careful to remove their hats and caps when they enter a church, while Jewish men will be careful to cover their heads when entering a synagogue.

Following this logic, if we want to know why Jews achieved such rapid economic success compared with Italians, chances are that the culture of one group gave them advantages in adjusting to the circumstances they faced in America—both economic and cultural circumstances.

To state the theory briefly: Sociologists proposed that Jewish values of learning, their norms of educational achievement, and the immense respect given to the role of scholar paved the Jewish road to success. Conversely, it was proposed that Italians valued not learning, but family loyalty; their norms led them to drop out of school; and the immense importance placed on the role of father made their original culture slow to change.

Now let's see how this theory squares with appropriate research evidence. In doing so we will not work through specific steps in the sociological process; that is postponed to Chapter 3. Here we simply will watch as researchers attempt to discover whether Jewish and Italian cultures were different in the ways specified by the theory.

Zborowski and Herzog: Jewish Culture

 Over the decades, many prominent sociologists have attributed the rapid upward mobility of Jews to cultural advantages they brought with them from eastern Europe (Slater, 1969; Steinberg, 1974). However, it was two anthropologists who assembled the most detailed and compelling cultural explanation of Jewish success in the United States and Canada.

Mark Zborowski and Elizabeth Herzog painstakingly reconstructed shtetl life in Poland and western Russia, from which the great waves of Jewish immigrants came during the latter nineteenth century and early twentieth. *Shtetl* (rhymes with *kettle*) is the Yiddish word for "village" or "small town." During the centuries of shtetl life, the cultural traditions of ancient Judaism were transformed into the way of life the Jews brought to North America.

Outside eastern Europe, as well, Jews lived almost exclusively in towns and cities. From early medieval times, Jews were prohibited from farming or owning land in most parts of Europe. Thus, most Jews in western Europe were required by law to live in crowded *ghettos**—neighborhoods reserved exclusively for Jews. These ghettos often were walled and the gates were locked at curfew.

Since ancient times the Jewish religion has stressed literacy for men, because each man is expected to read the scriptures and spend time studying their meaning. This tradition stimulated great respect for learning; indeed, learning became a value in Jewish communities. Because they lived in towns and cities, Jews could easily maintain schools and gather in study and discussion groups. Consequently, scholarship became "the dominant force in the Jewish culture" (Zborowski and Herzog, 1962).

These facts about Jewish culture were familiar. What Zborowski and Herzog wanted to do was to re-create the details of shtetl life so that they could see how this "cult of scholarship" worked on a day-to-day basis and understand how the roles and norms of Jewish life reflected and sustained the values about learning and scholarship. Accordingly, they conducted very long interviews with more than a hundred elderly people who had been shtetl residents. (What remained of shtetl life was destroyed during World War II, when shtetl inhabitants were sent to Nazi death camps.) From these recollections by Jewish immigrants and a vast supply of letters, diaries, and life histories, Zborowski and Herzog (1962) produced a rich and compelling account of shtetl life in their book *Life Is with People*.

---

* The term *ghetto* originated in Venice, where the section of the city in which Jews were required to live was, in late medieval times, called the "borghetto." This word derived from the Italian word *borgo*, which meant "borough," which is a major section of a city. *Borghetto* was the diminutive form meaning "little borough." Over time the word was shortened to *ghetto*, and its use spread to all European languages. Today the term is often applied to any neighborhood occupied by an ethnic or racial minority.

■ A teacher in a shtetl school drills Jewish boys in the Hebrew alphabet. Understandably, they are more interested in the photographer than in their books. But most of the time they were required to study long and hard.

They discovered that the *norms* governing schooling, even in the early 1800s, were strict and demanding by modern standards. Children began school between the ages of 3 and 5 years old, and the school day began at 8 A.M. and lasted until 6 P.M. six days a week! Males who showed the greatest academic aptitude were expected to adopt the *role* of scholar and devote their lives to study and learning. In fact, scholars were so highly respected that most parents hoped their sons could become scholars. Wealthy merchants sought to gain scholars as sons-in-law; indeed, the life of a scholar was made possible by his marrying a woman whose family could support him as he devoted himself to full-time study.

When Jews began to immigrate to North America in large numbers, both the United States and Canada were in a period of rapid economic development. This boom attracted millions to come to North America. In both nations, although more so in the United States, the greatest economic opportunities were in the large cities and in the skilled occupations. Consequently, the educational systems were also

expanding rapidly—especially the higher educational systems. Enrollment at colleges and universities grew by almost 1200 percent in the United States between 1870 and 1920. Thus, during the period when most Jewish immigrants arrived, the colleges and universities were making room for and actively seeking much larger enrollments. An amazing number of these new students were the sons and daughters of Jewish immigrants (Steinberg, 1974).

Jews were accustomed to sending their children to school, exalting in their academic achievements, demanding hard study, and making family sacrifices to educate their children. Indeed, an editorial in a Jewish newspaper published in New York in 1902 boasted of the Jewish "love for education, for intellectual effort," and went on to say that "the Jew undergoes privation, spills blood, to educate his child" (quoted in Sanders, 1969).

It was not an idle boast. A 1922 study of high school students (Counts, 1922) found that for every 100 freshmen who were children of native-born, white Americans, there were 44 seniors. Thus, about 56 percent of those who began high

 A Jewish boy delivering bundles of partly sewn men's suit coats in New York about 1910. Like other immigrants, Jewish children often had to help their families earn a living. But compared to most other immigrant groups, they were much less likely to drop out of school to take full-time jobs. Consequently, Jews rapidly entered technical and professional occupations.

school did not finish. Among the children of Italian immigrants, there were only 17 seniors for every 100 freshmen. But among children of immigrant Jews, there were 51 seniors for every 100 freshmen—a slight majority were graduating.

Thus, it is no surprise that by the turn of the century U.S. colleges and universities experienced waves of Jewish enrollment. Indeed, Jews soon formed a majority of the students enrolled in New York University and New York City College and constituted a very sizable minority in other eastern schools, such as Harvard and Columbia. In fact, by the 1920s many of these

schools imposed quotas on the number of Jews admitted. Thus, Columbia reduced its Jewish enrollment from 40 percent to 22 percent two years later. A public furor erupted over formal limits Harvard placed on Jewish enrollment, which exceeded 20 percent by 1920. Consequently, Harvard adopted a policy of regional balance, seeking students from all forty-eight states. In effect, this policy imposed a limit on Jews by limiting enrollments from New York and other eastern states with large Jewish populations.

But despite quotas and simmering anti-Semitism, plenty of room remained in the educational system for Jewish students, and Jews rapidly made their way into high-prestige, high-paying occupations, especially professions requiring advanced degrees: medicine, law, dentistry, and education. As early as 1913 the proportions of doctors, lawyers, and college professors who were Jewish were substantially greater than the proportion of Jews in the general population (Steinberg, 1974).

Thus, Zborowski and Herzog attributed the rapid upward mobility of Jews to the favorable fit between their learning- and schooling-oriented culture and the opportunities existing in the United States and Canada at the time of the greatest Jewish immigration.

Leonard Covello: Italian Culture

Unlike the children of Jewish immigrants, the children of newly arrived Italians did not excel in school and did not seek higher education in order to pursue professional occupations. Italian children tended to quit school at an early age. In the mid-1930s, Leonard Covello, a young teacher and school administrator in an Italian part of New York City, began a lengthy research project to try to understand the educational problems of Italian-American children such as "truancy, absence, cutting classes, lateness, and disciplinary problems." His research lasted until 1944, and he finally published his findings in 1967. His book, *The Social Background of the Italo-American*

School Child, is a superb counterpart to the work of Zborowski and Herzog. For by conducting his research both in Italy and among his fellow Italian-Americans, Covello drew a portrait of the culture Italians brought to North America, a culture that did not fit well with life on this side of the Atlantic.

Covello, like Zborowski and Herzog, focused his attention on education, because Italian-Americans were failing to take advantage of their educational opportunities. Dropping out of school early, they typically were forced to settle for low-paying, unskilled jobs. By the time Covello published his book, this pattern had changed dramatically. Italian-Americans were staying in school and many were going to college. But it had taken many decades longer for this pattern to emerge than it had among Jews. Why?

Covello concluded that Italians had arrived in North America suspicious of schools and accustomed to sending children to work at an early age. These cultural patterns were appropriate to conditions in Italy, particularly the region most Italian immigrants came from— southern Italy.

The government of Italy was controlled by the populous northern regions. Southern Italy was rural, impoverished, and exploited by northerners who regarded the south as an ignorant backwater. Consequently, southern Italy had relatively few schools. Worse yet, these few schools represented the culture of the north— even the language used in them was quite different from the common southern dialects.

Southern Italian parents regarded schooling as a threat to their own values, especially the key value of loyalty to the family, for the schools reflected negative judgments of local life. Moreover, little of what was learned in school was of much importance to life in southern Italy. Whether they went to school or not, the children grew up to be peasants. As one old Italian father told Covello, "What good if a boy is bright and intelligent in school, and then does not know enough to respect his family? Such a boy would be worth nothing."

Furthermore, the absence of children from home while they attended school often threatened the family's well-being. As another father told Covello, "If our children don't go to school,

■ In 1903 when this picture was taken, being a newsboy was not something a boy did only after school. He had to be on his corner all day long or lose his spot to another boy. (The Newsboy Law in New York said boys could work *only* from 6 A.M. to 10 P.M.) Thus it is almost certain that this Italian boy had already dropped out of school to help feed his family. At that time most Italian-American children did quit school early.

no harm results. But if the sheep don't eat, they will die. The school can wait but not our sheep."

The belief that school was not important and possibly harmful was appropriate to life in southern Italy. The things children really needed to learn had to be learned at home anyway, such as how to plant crops and tend sheep. Thus, academic learning was not a value in southern Italian culture. And sending children to school and rigorous study habits were not norms.

Finally, the role of scholar was of little importance. The primary value was family loyalty. The most important norms concerned

■ Italian housewives buying crusty loaves of bread from bakery boys on Mulberry Street in the heart of New York's "Little Italy" in about 1900. Notice that one boy's shoes are worn out—he and his friend may have already dropped out of school. Many of the people shown here probably planned to return to Italy, and perhaps some of them did.

behavior within the family, and the father was the most important social role.

Transplanted to the United States and Canada, these cultural patterns proved inappropriate. Here the Italians did not become farmers. Instead, they found themselves in rapidly growing industrial cities where child labor was of little value and large families were an economic burden rather than an asset. Furthermore, unskilled physical labor paid low wages and offered no opportunity for advancement. Covello concluded that these cultural patterns thwarted the social progress of Italians. So long as these patterns persisted, Italians could not achieve upward mobility.

The patterns of Jewish and Italian cultures differ in the way proposed by the cultural theory so much so that social scientists tended to treat the cultural theory as almost self-evident. Nevertheless, by the 1970s some sociologists were beginning to notice evidence that didn't

fit and to discover predictions that didn't hold. One very troublesome fact was that there was nothing at all unusual about the time the Italians had taken to achieve economic parity. Most other immigrant groups took just as long. So it seemed unlikely that the cultural barriers to achievement identified in Italian culture actually mattered. Groups lacking these values and norms did not rise any faster. From this evidence it followed that the theory really applied only to the Jews, as an explanation of why they were different from other groups.

However, a closer look *within* the Jewish community produced an even more awkward fact. At the pertinent time most Jews did not attend college—most didn't even finish high school. Still, when compared to other recently arrived immigrant groups, poorly educated Jews were far ahead in terms of pay. What do educational advantages have to do with explaining differential rates of economic success between people with the same amount of education? Clearly, nothing.

When a theory and the evidence don't agree, it is time to go back to the drawing board and try to adjust or replace the theory. And that's exactly what Stephen Steinberg did.

■ _____

The Social Theory

In the early 1970s a young graduate student at the University of California, Berkeley, began a study of the religious and ethnic origins of college and university faculty. Noting the substantial overrepresentation of Jews and wondering how this had come about, Stephen Steinberg paused to brush up on the history of Jews in America. He immediately encountered the cultural theory of rapid Jewish upward mobility. But he also noted the growing body of awkward facts and faulty predictions. This led him to formulate a new theory that suggested that the rapid upward mobility of Jews may have been largely an illusion—that it hadn't really happened. How could this be?

Steinberg admitted that the immigrant Jews were poor when they arrived. Table 2-2 shows that only 12 percent of Jewish immigrants from 1904 to 1910 had at least $50 upon their arrival, a figure that is close to that for most other immigrants.

But, Steinberg asked, is money really the issue? What if we meet a ditch digger and an engineer as they arrive in America? What if each has only $50 in his pocket? Are they starting off on equal footing? Steinberg said no. Obviously the engineer brings tremendous potential economic advantages with him compared with the ditch digger, and we would be surprised if the engineer were not making much more money than the ditch digger after a few years. Steinberg argued that the Jews were more like the engineer and Italians were more like the ditch digger in terms of their social class origins.

Specifically, Steinberg attributed the superior economic position of Jewish immigrants in America to their superior economic and social positions in eastern Europe. While people from lower-class origins must acquire new skills to

Table 2-2 ■ **Immigrants having at least $50 upon arrival in the United States, 1904–1910.**

Immigrant Group	Percentage
Jews	12%
Southern Italians	5
Irish	17
Germans	31
English	55
All other immigrants	14

Source: Reports of the Immigration Commission, vol. 3 (1911), reproduced in Stephen Steinberg, *The Academic Melting Pot* (New York: McGraw-Hill, 1974).

rise within a stratification system, he argued, people from more advantaged backgrounds obtain these skills as a matter of course. Upon arriving in new surroundings, people with higher-status backgrounds are likely to be able to *regain* higher-status positions. Let's put this a bit more formally. Among first-generation immigrants, status in their new society will be determined in large measure by their status in their former society. Or, applied to *groups,* their average status in the new society will reflect their average status in the old society.

Steinberg's theory predicts that Jewish status attainment in America and Canada reflected their higher status back in eastern Europe, that Jews arrived in North America with experience, training, and technical skills qualifying them for highly skilled jobs and enabling them to pursue successful business and commercial opportunities.

■ _____

Stephen Steinberg: The Jewish Head Start

 As an initial test of his theory, Steinberg turned to two vital, but neglected, sources of information. The first was an analysis of the economic situation of Jews in Russia and Poland (then under Russian control) based on the Russian census of 1897 (Rubinow, 1970). The second was the massive forty-one-volume report of the Immigration Commission, quoted at the start of this chapter. And so, to work.

First, Steinberg examined the Russian census. At that time Jews were required to live in a restricted region of Poland and western Russia called the Pale of Settlement. Only a few Jews were permitted to live beyond the Pale. As a result, Jews were a concentrated population. As we saw previously, these Jews lived in villages and small towns. Correspondingly, the Russian census found that only 3 percent of Jews were farmers, while 61 percent of non-Jews were (see Table 2-3). In contrast, the Jews were heavily concentrated in higher-status occupations. Nearly a third engaged in commerce, and an even higher percentage were in manufacturing or highly skilled trades. Five percent worked at professions such as law and medicine. Within the Pale, a third of the factories were owned by Jews, who also dominated commerce.

Of course, many of these factories were tiny operations, and much of the commerce was nothing more than selling household items door to door. What is important, however, is not how much money Jews were earning in Russia and Poland, but the training and skills involved. These occupational skills markedly set off the Jews from the non-Jewish, mainly peasant populations in eastern Europe. These skills could have equally distinguished them from most other immigrants to North America, who also were mainly peasants.

We must consider the possibility that only unsuccessful Jews emigrated from eastern Europe. However, since Jews in the late nineteenth century emigrated primarily to flee severe persecution under the Russian czar, that seems unlikely. In any event, Steinberg found detailed records in the Immigration Commission reports that demonstrated the occupational advantages of Jewish immigrants.

Table 2-4 shows that the occupational backgrounds of Jewish immigrants differed from those of other immigrants. Two-thirds of Jewish immigrants worked in skilled crafts in the old country, in contrast with 15 percent of the

Table 2-3 ■ Occupations of Jewish and non-Jewish adults in Russia, 1897.

Occupation	Percentage	
	Jews	Non-Jews
Professions	5%	3%
Commerce	32	3
Manufacturing and skilled trades	38	15
Service	19	16
Transportation	3	2
Agriculture	3	61
Total	100%	100%

Source: Compiled from the Russian census of 1897 and presented in Israel Rubinow, "The Economic Condition of Jews in Russia," *Bulletin of the Bureau of Labor*, no. 72 (Washington, D.C.: U.S. Government Printing Office, 1907).

southern Italians, 13 percent of the Irish, and 6 percent of the Poles. Even immigrants from England were less likely to have skilled occupations than the Jews. In contrast, the Jews had rarely worked as laborers, farmers, or servants, while these were the most common occupations of the Italians, the Irish, and the Poles—indeed of all immigrants as a group.

Canadian authorities did not begin to keep data on the occupations of immigrants until 1931. Kage (1981) points out, however, that since "the sources of Jewish immigration to the two countries were the same, we may assume the American information is valid for Canada."

Jews arrived in North America with highly skilled occupational backgrounds precisely when rapid economic development and industrial growth offered them immense opportunities (Kage, 1981). Consequently, the Jews rapidly reentered their old occupations as printers, jewelers, tailors, watchmakers, cigar makers, tinsmiths, furriers, and the like. Such jobs paid much better wages than the laboring jobs available to most other new immigrants. Although the Jews arrived poor, they came with marketable skills that permitted them to escape pov-

Table 2-4 ■ Occupations of immigrants entering the United States, 1899–1910.

Previous Occupation*	Percentage					
	Jews	Southern Italians	Irish	Poles	English	All Immigrants**
Higher status						
Professions	1%	0%	1%	0%	9%	1%
Commerce	5	1	1	0	5	
Skilled labor	67	15	13	6	49	20
Lower status						
Labor	12	42	31	45	18	36
Farming	2	35	7	31	4	25
Service	11	6	46	17	5	14
Other	2	1	1	1	10	2

Source: Adapted from the *Reports of the Immigration Commission* (1911), as reproduced in Stephen Steinberg, *The Academic Melting Pot* (New York: McGraw-Hill, 1974).

* Excludes immigrants with no previous occupation, including most women and children.

** Also includes other groups not separately listed in the table.

erty rapidly. In contrast, most other groups had to develop such skills after they arrived. Indeed, the majority of them arrived illiterate, while the overwhelming majority of Jewish immigrants could read and write.

Several other immigrant groups have repeated the Jewish pattern of rapid success and for similar reasons. In the late 1950s and early 1960s, a large number of Cuban refugees came to the United States to escape Castro's revolutionary government. Most of them had held middle- and upper-class positions in Cuba before the revolution. Although they came with little more than the clothes on their backs, they rapidly regained their class positions here. More recently, middle-class refugees from Vietnam have shown a similar tendency toward rapid economic advancement.

Steinberg's reassessment of the actual circumstances of Jewish immigrants does not mean that Jewish culture played no role in their success. Rather, he argued that these aspects of Jewish culture reflected the position of the shtetl Jews. Compared with the surrounding non-Jewish populations, the Jews of eastern Europe were middle class. Many studies have shown

that middle-class people everywhere in the world are very concerned about education and push their children to do well in school (Steinberg, 1974). They are especially likely to do so if they have momentarily lost their positions in society (as had Jews, Cubans, and Vietnamese when they fled to America). As we shall see in Chapter 11, education is the cheapest, most rapid, and most reliable path to economic advancement under present conditions.

Steinberg summed up his findings this way:

Jewish immigrants were not simply middle class in their values. . . . There was substance and reality behind these values. Jews did not simply have aspirations for economic mobility—they also had experiences and skills in middle-class occupations. Nor did Jews simply value education and revere learning. They were also literate as a group and had cognitive skills to pass on to their children. Conversely, [other immigrants such as the Italians] did not simply place low value on education and occupational mobility, but were handicapped by factors related to their peasant origins.

■ Jewish-Canadian tailors at work for the Eaton company in Toronto in about 1904. Because so many Jewish immigrants to North America arrived with qualifications for skilled occupations such as this, they rapidly achieved economic success. In contrast, many other immigrant groups had to depend on unskilled laboring jobs to sustain them in Canada and the United States, and hence their climb to economic equality was longer and more difficult.

Keep in mind that Steinberg's theory is not limited to predictions about the relative social class positions of first-generation Jews and Italians in North America. His concept of a first-generation immigrant group applies to *all* such groups, and when he links status in the society of origin with status in the society of residence he is generalizing to *all* societies. Thus many specific *hypotheses* can be deduced from his theory. Recall that a hypothesis is a statement of what we ought to be able to observe according to predictions from the theory.

So why don't we formulate a new hypothesis from Steinberg's theory and check it out? Back when the Immigration Commission was gathering data, a substantial number of Canadians were coming into the United States. The vast majority of these people were French speaking, while the others were English speakers. At the turn of the century the stratification system in Canada was highly skewed on the basis of language. The social status of the average French-Canadian was considerably below that of the average English-Canadian (which was why so many French-Canadians were moving south). Applying Steinberg's theory, we can formulate

■ Jewish immigrants crowd the decks of the *S.S. Westernland* in about 1890, trying to escape the foul air of the jam-packed hold. Notice the many women and children, indicating that these are family groups.

the following hypothesis: Among first-generation Canadian immigrants in the United States, the English speakers will have higher incomes than will the French speakers. Is this true? Turn back to Table 2-1 and see for yourself.

Once again the theory survives an effort to prove it false. Keep in mind, however, that Steinberg's theory does not rule out other factors that also could influence the social status of immigrant groups. Indeed, besides their lower-class origins, Italians and many other immigrant groups faced additional factors that slowed their rate of upward mobility.

Reference groups and Italian traditionalism

At the turn of the century, government studies revealed that, compared with Jews and many other immigrant groups, Italians seemed slow to learn English. For example, in 1911 two-thirds of the Jews who had been in the United States less than five years could speak English. The figure for Italians was only one-fourth. Even Jewish and Italian immigrants who had been in the country ten years or longer showed marked differences in their knowledge of English.

■ This Italian mother, with a bundle balanced on her head, and her children passed through Ellis Island in 1915, on their way to join the father who had come over several years before, planning to return to Italy. But the plans changed, perhaps because of the outbreak of World War I in 1914. They probably still were not certain they would stay in America forever.

Obviously, it is a considerable handicap to be unable to speak the language of the country in which one is trying to earn a living. Furthermore, the children of parents who do not speak the language are hindered in learning to speak it and are thus at a disadvantage in school. In fact, Covello blamed many school problems experienced by Italian-Americans in the 1930s on their poor English skills. The reason the Italians were slow to learn English was a reason for many of their economic problems as well.

Italians were slow not only to learn English but also to adapt to occupational conditions in the United States because most of them did not plan to become Americans. Instead, most Italian immigrants came to America to take advantage of the relatively high wages available to unskilled laborers (compared with wages back in southern Italy) and then returned to Italy with their savings to resume their old ways of life in greater comfort.

It is easy to demonstrate this temporary migration. Immigration Commission statistics reveal that of Italian immigrants between 1899 and 1910, only 21 percent were females (in contrast with 43 percent of Jews). Similarly, only 12 percent of the Italian immigrants were under age 14 (compared with 25 percent of Jews). Therefore, few Italian families were coming to America; instead, it was mostly young, single men. Moreover, most of them did go back. Between 1908 and 1910, for every 100 Italians who entered the United States, 55 others left to go back to Italy. Among Jews, only 8 left for every 100 arrivals during this period. A great many Italians who ended up staying in America had probably not planned to do so. Many of them delayed their returns because of the outbreak of World War I in 1914. By the time the war ended in 1918, economic conditions in Italy were very bad, leading many Italians to stay on and wait for a better time to go back. In the end, large numbers never did return. However, so long as they thought they would go back, they were likely to cling to their Italian culture.

Patterns in Canada were similar. There too the overwhelming proportion of Italian immigrants in this period were young males who had come to earn a nest egg and then return home (Woodsworth, 1909; Spada, 1969).

To describe this situation in a more sociological way, immigrants from Italy continued to regard the folks back home as their **reference group**. This concept refers to the groups that individuals identify with, the groups whose norms and values serve as the basis for self-judgment. In an important sense, our reference groups are the audiences before whom we lead our lives—the people whose approval counts most with us.

A reference group need not actually be present to influence a person's behavior. Even if no member of our reference group can actually see what we are doing, we can still act on the basis of how that group would react. This aspect of reference groups often allows sociologists to make sense of behavior that seems out of place.

Consider a nineteenth-century British gentleman exploring the upper reaches of the Nile. He sets out by himself, accompanied by forty men from an isolated African tribe who are acting as guides and carrying the supplies. There is no other British gentleman, perhaps not even any other white man, within a thousand miles. Yet every night this explorer wears a tuxedo to dinner. His native companions think this is very strange, and if we could see him doing it, we might think it strange, too. But he doesn't care, since we are not the relevant audience. His reference group is other British gentlemen, and a gentleman always dresses for dinner. Once we know this man's reference group, we can explain and even predict much of his behavior. For example, we can be sure that he will always rise from his chair if a woman enters the room and that he will think it vulgar to mention the price paid for a possession.

The reference group for large numbers of Italian-Americans was the inhabitants of rural villages in southern Italy. Once we know that, much of their behavior is understandable. Why reject traditional norms and values of rural Italian life if you are planning to return to it? Brandenberg reported hearing a mother in New York say the following to her son, in forceful Italian, "You *shall* speak Italian, and nothing else, if I must kill you; for what shall your grandmother say when you go back to the old country, if you talk this pigs' English?" (in Woodsworth, 1909).

As time passed, however, the ties to the old country began to fade. Young Italians found it hard to use as a reference group people they had never met, who lived in a place they had only been told about. Their reference groups began to change, and they began to adapt to the culture and conditions around them. In a few years, Italians achieved rapid upward mobility.

The process and results of changing from Italian to North American reference groups is pointedly illustrated by the story of Amadeo Giannini. Born in 1870, the son of an Italian immigrant, he founded a small bank in 1904 in the North Beach district of San Francisco, an Italian neighborhood. Giannini's bank made

■ Following the San Francisco earthquake of 1906, the Bank of Italy occupied these temporary quarters on Montgomery Street. Today, this bank is known as the Bank of America.

loans to the small businessmen of the neighborhood, who found it very difficult to get credit at the city's other banks. Giannini named his institution the Bank of Italy. The bank survived the 1906 earthquake and the fire that destroyed much of the city. Under Giannini's brilliant management, the policy of lending to small businessmen brought the bank considerable success.

By 1928 Giannini had become uncomfortable about his bank's name, which sounded too foreign. Besides, its customers were no longer mainly Italians. So Giannini changed the name from the Bank of Italy to the Bank of America. When he died in 1949, his little neighborhood bank had grown into the largest privately owned bank in the world.

■ A. P. Giannini in about 1906.

Conclusion

Let's look back over this chapter and see how it illustrates the sociological process. We began with a question, with sociologists wondering why Jews had achieved such rapid economic advancement. Over the years sociologists have constructed two major theories to answer this question, so the first thing we needed to do was grasp the concepts these theories require. Having separated society from culture, we examined a series of concepts used in cultural theories, and then we considered concepts often used in social theories. Then we looked at some theorizing.

Cultural theories proposed that the Jewish advantage lay in unique features of their culture—in such things as their love for learning and their strict norms of schooling and study. Initially, when sociologists began to test cultural theories of Jewish mobility, they found the predicted differences between Jewish and Italian culture. And the question of why seemed to be answered. But then, problems began to turn up. For example, less-educated Jews also found rapid economic success. What could account for them, what cultural advantages did they have over Italians and other new immigrants?

So it was back to step three in the sociological process—to more theorizing. This time a social theory was constructed. Italian immigrants came from the bottom of the stratification system in Italy and were qualified only for unskilled labor upon arriving in the United States. But Jews were not from the lower classes in Russia, Poland, and other parts of eastern Europe. They had been not peasants but merchants and craftsmen. This was their real edge over other immigrants. The Jews did not have to gain higher positions in the stratification system; they had merely to *regain* them. Peasants from Italy had to acquire skills that would allow them to rise economically—and typically only their children or their grandchildren achieved higher status. But tailors, diamond cutters, or watchmakers from eastern Europe simply had to find a chance to use their skills.

Thus we discover that we had been wondering about things that either hadn't really happened or at least were rather ordinary. The astounding rate of Jewish economic success was mainly an illusion based on misreading their initial circumstances.

I admit that Stephen Steinberg's explanation of the differential economic success of first-generation Jews and Italians seems a bit of a letdown. But if the aim of science is to explain, it also is to penetrate mysteries. Since mysteries often are far more intriguing than the reality behind them, scientific theories sometimes seem prosaic. Anyone would agree that it is a lot more thrilling to suppose that invisible aliens are sneaking about causing earthquakes than it is to blame them on shifts in the plates forming the earth's surface. But usually the truth is far more useful. And so it is here, too.

So long as our focus was on Jewish culture and its immense capacity for producing economic success, we were missing the lessons of real interest to disadvantaged racial and ethnic groups in North America today. For it is the North American experience of the Italians, not of the Jews, that should command our attention. Unlike the Jews, the Italians really did start at the bottom of the stratification system. How they escaped these circumstances is potentially applicable to others—as we shall see in Chapter 11.

Figure 2-6 ■ **Three waves of U.S. immigration.** Over the past two centuries, there have been three very different "waves" of new Americans, in terms of where they were coming from. In the beginning, nearly all immigrants came from Great Britain, Holland, Germany, and France. By the start of the nineteenth century, many people began to arrive from other nations of northern and western Europe, especially Scandinavia and Ireland. This was the first wave of immigration, or what the Immigration Commission called the "old immigration." The composition of first-wave immigrants can be seen in the column of percentages for 1870. Hardly any immigrants came from Russia-Poland (they were one nation at that time) or from Italy. Few Asians were coming, and virtually all who did were Chinese. Few entered from Mexico, but a substantial number came from Canada.

Now look at 1907—the all-time peak year for immigration (1,285,349). Here the second wave of immigration was in full force. The number of immigrants from England, Germany, and Ireland had plummeted. In their place came people from eastern and southern Europe—26.3 percent from Russia-Poland (most of them Jews) and 22.2 percent from Italy. The Canadian percentage had declined, as had the Chinese.

Immigration dried up during World War I (1914–1918), limited almost exclusively to people from Canada and Mexico. Then, shortly after the war, Congress set tight limits on the number of people to be admitted each year and assigned very discriminatory quotas meant to limit immigration to the pattern of the first wave. In 1967 the immigration law was amended to remove the discrimination against people from Asia, Africa, and Latin America.

Percent of Immigrants From:	1981–1984	1907	1870
Asia	**48.4%**	**3.2%**	**4.1%**
Vietnam	8.8%	none	none
Philippines	7.5%	*	none
China[1]	6.1%	0.1%	4.0%
Korea	5.7%	*	*
India	4.0%	*	*
Japan	0.7%	1.1%	*
North America	**13.9%**	**1.6%**	**10.5%**
Mexico	11.9%	0.1%	0.1%
Canada	2.0%	1.5%	10.4%
Caribbean	**12.6%**	**1.1%**	**0.5%**
Jamaica	3.6%	*	*
Dominican Republic	3.5%	*	*
Cuba	1.7%	*	*
Haiti	1.5%	*	*
Europe	**11.3%**	**93.3%**	**84.9%**
Great Britain	2.4%	6.1%	26.8%
Soviet Union (Russia)	1.6% }	26.3%	0.3%
Poland	1.2% }		
Germany	1.2%	2.9%	18.4%
Italy	0.6%	22.2%	0.6%
Ireland	0.2%	2.6%	14.7%
Central and South America	**10.5%**	**0.3%**	*
Columbia	1.7%	*	*
Guyana	1.5%	*	*
El Salvador	1.4%	*	*
Africa	**2.6%**	**0.1%**	*
Egypt	0.5%	*	*
Other	**0.7%**	**0.1%**	*

*Less than 0.1 percent.
[1]Includes Taiwan.

With the barriers against them lifted, Asians have come to dominate the third wave of immigration. During 1981–84, when well over 2 million immigrants came in, nearly half came from Asia. Thus, while the immediate impact of the first two waves of immigration was felt on the East Coast, today the major impact is on the West Coast. A major difference is that the first and second waves brought hosts of unskilled workers. In contrast, most of the third-wave Asian immigrants are well educated and have the experience and training to do well in business and occupations.

A second characteristic of the third wave of immigration has been a great increase in people coming from Hispanic cultures. Meanwhile, immigration from Africa remains very low, and European immigration is only a shadow of the past.

Review Glossary

society A relatively self-sufficient and self-sustaining group of people who are united by social relationships and who live in a particular territory. (p. 40)

culture The complex pattern of living—made up of customs, values, technology, and other factors—that humans have developed and that they pass from one generation to the next. (p. 41)

stratification The unequal distribution of rewards (or of things perceived as valuable) among members of a society; the class structure. (p. 41)

classes Groups of people who share a similar level in the stratification system. (p. 41)

status Any particular position within a society. (p. 41)

mobility, upward and downward A change of level within the stratification system. (p. 42)

achieved status A position gained on the basis of merit (in other words, by achievement). (p. 42)

ascribed status A position assigned to individuals or groups without regard for merit but because of certain traits beyond their control, such as their race, their sex, or the social standing of their parents. (p. 42)

prejudice Negative or hostile attitudes toward, and beliefs about, a group. (p. 42)

discrimination Actions taken against a group to deny its members rights and privileges available to others. (p. 42)

values Ideals or ultimate aims; general evaluative standards about what is desirable. (p. 42)

norms Rules that define the behavior that is expected, required, or acceptable in particular circumstances. (p. 43)

role A set of expectations governing the behavior of persons holding a particular position in society; a set of norms that defines how persons in a particular position should behave. (p. 43)

assimilation The process by which an individual or a group reacts to a new social environment by adopting the culture prevalent in that environment. (p. 45)

accommodation An agreement between two groups to ignore differences between them. (p. 45)

cultural pluralism When two or more distinctive cultures coexist within the same society as a result of accommodation. (p. 46)

subculture A culture within a culture; a group that maintains or develops its own set of beliefs, morals, values, and norms, which usually are at variance with those of the dominant culture. (p. 46)

anti-Semitism Prejudice and discrimination against Jews. (p. 50)

reference group A group a person uses as a standard for self-evaluation. (p. 63)

Suggested Readings

Alba, Richard. 1985. *Italian-Americans: Into the Twilight of Ethnicity*. Englewood Cliffs, N.J.: Prentice-Hall.

Covello, Leonard. 1967. *The Social Background of the Italo-American School Child*. Leiden, The Netherlands: E.J. Brill. N.B.

Howe, Irving. 1976. *World of Our Fathers*. New York: Harcourt Brace Jovanovich.

Porter, John. 1975. "Ethnic Pluralism in Canadian Perspective." In *Ethnicity: Theory and Experience*, edited by Nathan Glazer and Daniel P. Moynihan. Cambridge, Mass.: Harvard University Press.

Steinberg, Stephen. 1974. *The Academic Melting Pot*. New York: McGraw-Hill.

Zborowski, Mark, and Elizabeth Herzog. 1962. *Life Is with People: The Culture of the Shtetl*. New York: Schocken Books.

Micro Sociology: Testing Interaction Theories

3

SUPPOSE YOU ARE waiting in line at a supermarket check-out stand. If you are like most people, you probably will pass time by reading the headlines splashed across the covers of the many sensational weeklies such as the *National Enquirer*, *The Star*, or *The Globe*. Among the many claims—that Bigfoot has married a Girl Scout leader and moved to Texas or that ancient Egyptians had nuclear power—you happen to notice the following:

Star Blames Her Many Divorces on
Teachers Who Excuse Cute Kids (p. 7)

Turning to page seven you discover that a Hollywood star, known as much for her stormy divorces as for her acting, says that when she was young she often was very cruel to other students but that the teachers always made excuses for "such a cute little thing." The reporter goes on to assert that this is but one of many instances of teacher bias in favor of cute children. However, aside from the star's charges, the story offers not a shred of evidence of a general problem. Nevertheless, you find the idea interesting. Maybe really cute kids do get away with a lot. Suppose you wanted to find out? What could you do?

What about visiting a lot of schools and watching to see if teachers are more lenient with cute kids? Trouble is, no two kids ever do quite the same thing, so you could never compare a

teacher's response to a cute kid and a homely kid guilty of precisely the same infraction. In addition, most kids are neither unusually homely nor extremely cute, and you might have to wait a long time to see even a few incidents involving a child of unusual appearance. Moreover, an observer can only be one place at a time, so it would take a very long time to watch a number of different teachers with their students.

Maybe you could ask a bunch of cute people whether they believe their teachers had given them special treatment? It is fine to ask people to report things they are in a position to know about, such as whether they think it would be wrong for teachers to favor cute kids, but it is useless to ask them things they can't know. In this instance, to ask people if teachers favored them is simply to multiply unfounded testimony. There is no reason to suppose that opinions on a matter such as this would reflect what really takes place.

Maybe you could ask teachers if they do favor cute kids? But would they admit it, even supposing that they were aware of doing it?

So how can you find out? You could do what a young social psychologist at the University of Minnesota actually did. First, Karen Dion (1972) constructed a series of reports purporting to have been turned in by teachers on playground duty. Each detailed a case of serious misbehavior by a 7-year-old, including cruelty to pets and to

Marriages per 1,000 Population

Sweden	4.3	Portugal	7.5
Norway	5.0	Yugoslavia	7.5
Spain	5.0	Bulgaria	7.5
Denmark	5.3	East Germany	7.5
Italy	5.3	Czechoslovakia	7.6
Ireland	5.5	Romania	7.8
Netherlands	5.5	Poland	8.4
France	5.6	Albania	9.0
		U.S.S.R.	10.3

Switzerland	5.7
West Germany	6.0
Belgium	6.0
Finland	6.1
United Kingdom	6.9
Hungary	7.1
Greece	7.2
Austria	7.4

Figure 3-1 ■ **Micro and macro sociological approaches to research on marriage.** This map of variations in the marriage rate across Europe probably would prompt macro sociologists to wonder why there are proportionately so many more marriages in eastern than in western Europe. And soon they would be discussing the impact of urbanization and modernization on the family. As for the photograph, macro sociologists probably would regard it as only a "decoration." In contrast, micro sociologists would tend to ignore the map and be more stimulated by the photo. Thus, they might wonder if church weddings, with their solemn symbols and rituals, create a stronger sense of initial commitment between bride and groom. To find out, they might observe a number of church weddings and a number of informal civil weddings trying to gauge the emotional impact of each. As this comparison reveals, there is a close correspondence between theories and research methods: Different sorts of theories require different sorts of research methods.

other children. Next she secured photographs of a large number of children of the proper age. A panel of judges selected a group of unusually homely and unusually cute children.

Armed with these materials, Dion recruited several hundred young women enrolled in teacher training courses. Each was given a set of reports. Attached to each report was a photograph of the child said to have committed the offense. The student teachers were asked to study each incident and rate the child in terms of the severity of the misdeed. Of course, because Dion had made up all the reports, the photographs weren't those of real offenders. So for each reported incident, half of the student teachers saw the photograph of a cute kid, while the other half were provided a picture of a homely kid. Then Dion compared the results. On all incidents the judgments were considerably less severe when student teachers associated the offense with a cute kid. Now we know.

Notice how well Dion's research procedures overcame the limits of the methods we rejected. Here cute and homely kids "committed" exactly the same offense. There was no shortage of exceptional looking children. Many student teachers could be tested. And there was no need to take their word for what they would do—Dion was able to detect what they actually did.

The final lesson from this example is that there is not just one way to do research. The right method often depends on what one wants to know. Theories not only tell us what we ought to observe but also they often tell us how best to make those observations. Depending upon what kinds of phenomena the theory addresses, different research procedures are appropriate.

In sociology, a primary concern is whether a theory pertains to micro sociology (to the behavior of individuals or small groups) or to macro sociology (the behavior of large social units, even including whole societies). Individual humans and small groups can be studied by direct observation, through personal interviews, or in experiments such as Dion's. But these techniques are of very limited use with large units. We could hardly set out to observe the behavior of all North Americans or invite them all into our laboratory.

Thus we see that the distinction between micro and macro sociology has profound implications for not just *what* sociologists study but also *how* they study it.

Chapter Preview

In this chapter you will meet the key elements of micro theories in sociology. Then the chapter examines the research techniques most appropriate for testing micro theories. This will offer a more detailed view of steps 6 and 7, the research portion of the sociological process—steps concerned with gathering pertinent observations and analyzing them. The first method you will encounter is the experiment. It is the ideal way to do research. Often, however, it is impossible for even micro sociologists to conduct an experiment. Thus we will explore alternatives—nonexperimental methods through which sociologists attempt to approximate the precision of experiments.

Rational Choice Theories in Social Science

All micro theories in the social sciences assert that *choice is the most basic aspect of human behavior* (Phelps, 1975; Hechter, 1983). Life is an endless series of choices, of alternatives from which we must select. Moreover, all micro social science theories share the same view of *how* humans make choices—that we try to do the *rational*, or most reasonable, thing. For this reason all varieties of micro theories in social science recently have been referred to as **rational choice theories** (Hechter, 1983). All micro theorists recognize that factors external to the individual often limit what choices are possible and often shape our perceptions of what choices are the most reasonable. But within these limits, micro theorists work from the assumption that people will attempt to act in the most rational manner.

What does it mean to say humans operate

■ Thomas Hobbes.

on the basis of rational choices? It means they will try to select the option that will benefit them the most—that people will seek to gain rewards and try to avoid costs. Some version of this statement serves as the first step or proposition in all of the many micro theories in the various social sciences. Often it is referred to as the **rational choice**, or **self-interest**, **proposition**.

There is nothing remarkable about the rational choice proposition. Every normal human who has ever lived has been fully aware of the need to choose and has been alert to the principle that good choices pay off while bad ones penalize. Moreover, as Chapter 1 noted, the rational choice proposition permits social science to recognize "free will." Social science is possible because people *do* try to make the best choices available to them. If we know that behavior reflects this principle, then we can hope to predict and explain human actions by examining the choices they confront. In contrast, if people did not follow this rule, if they made their choices randomly, then social science

would be impossible. But then, of course, so would human life itself.

Thomas Hobbes, an English social philosopher, expressed the rational choice, or self-interest, proposition this way in 1656:

I conceive that when a man deliberates whether he shall do a thing or not do it, he does nothing else but consider whether it be better for himself to do it or not to do it.

The rational choice proposition takes slightly different forms in the various social sciences. Micro economists begin their theories with the proposition that humans seek a variety of goods. This premise gives micro economists an active human being whose behavior is rational. From this starting point they can construct laws of supply and demand. Psychologists put it another way: Behavior is shaped by reinforcement. In this way psychologists root the cause of behavior in its anticipated consequences, in the response of the social and physical environment to an individual's behavior. When psychologists say behavior is repeated because it has been reinforced, they are saying that people select their actions on the basis of past experience—we repeat actions that produce the results we desire.

Micro sociological theories also rest on the choice proposition. As Homans (1964) put it, people "are more likely to perform an activity, the more valuable they perceive the reward of that activity to be." This formulation, however, leaves something out. It was adapted directly from psychology during a period when psychologists were inclined to argue that only rewards and not punishments influenced human behavior. Perhaps they took this position because they wanted the world to be a gentler place. Yet people not only seek things they want but also seek to *avoid* things they dislike. Children do not run only to get a ball or to receive candy; they also run to avoid angry dogs, swarms of bees, and sometimes an irate parent. Hence, the formulation I prefer and use in my own theories is: *Humans seek to maximize rewards and to minimize costs.* Bee stings, dog bites, and spankings are costs—things we would prefer to do without. So, too, is the loss of candy.

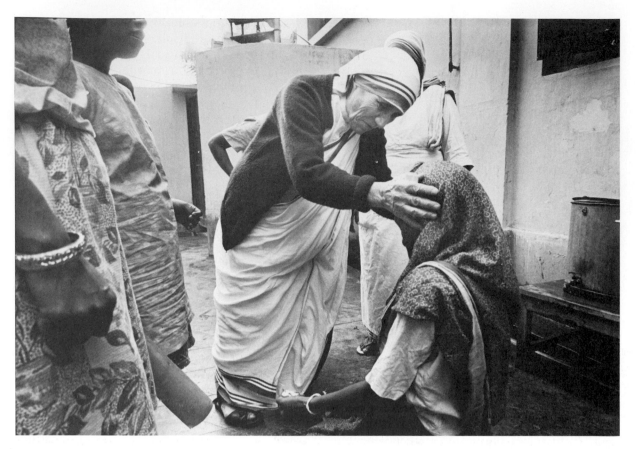

■ Mother Teresa has become the best-known Roman Catholic nun in the world through her devoted work among India's poor. Some would argue that she is an example of an altruist, a person who acts against his or her own desires. But Mother Teresa's greatness lies in what she desires—to reduce the misery of others. That is, Mother Teresa should be admired for how she finds rewards in life, not for living an unrewarding life.

At this point students often express dismay. Do all micro social scientists think people are *always selfish*? What about altruism, unselfish behavior done to benefit others? What about parents who run into burning buildings to try to save a child? How were they acting to maximize rewards and to minimize costs? Or what about soldiers who die for their country or people who give up a comfortable life to aid the sick and the poor?

Social scientists know such people exist. But we also know that their behavior violates the rational choice proposition only if we adopt a very narrow, materialistic definition of rewards.

Human life and culture are immensely rich because of the incredible variety of things people perceive as rewarding. There is no need to suggest that a parent has acted against his or her self-interest by rushing into a burning building. Rather, let us recognize that the ability of humans to regard the survival of a child as more rewarding than their own survival is a credit to the human spirit and to our capacity to love. To call that altruism and place it in opposition to the rational choice premise is to reduce noble behavior to crazy and irrational action. Indeed, the self-interest, or rational choice, proposition of social science is humanistic in the fullest sense. It acknowledges our capacity to find rewards in our dreams, hopes, love, and ideals. This will be clear as we examine what micro sociological theories actually predict about people.

Interaction Theories

Although all micro social theories begin with the same proposition, they soon go their separate ways as more propositions are added. Micro theories become truly *sociological* when they incorporate two key insights.

First, *sociologists greatly expand the concepts of rewards and costs*. For example, while economists tend to restrict these concepts to material commodities, sociologists realize that we do not live by bread alone. There are things we value immensely besides what we can put in our mouths or in our pockets. Chief among these are affection and self-esteem. We want to be loved, liked, respected, and admired.

Second, *sociologists recognize that much of what we want can only be gotten from other people*. Whether we seek candy, love, or learning, we must usually get it from other people. Therefore, to gain rewards, we must induce other people to give us rewards. However, it is costly to give up rewards: When I give you candy, I have less candy; when I provide you with a textbook, it costs me time and energy. To get others to reward us, we must reward them. Perhaps nothing could be more obvious, yet throughout this book we shall trace the profound implications of this simple point.

Because humans seek rewards from one another, they are inevitably forced into *exchange relations*. That is, human beings engage in **social interaction**—they attempt to influence one another. To do this they must exchange rewards. This conclusion is implicit in the rational choice proposition as soon as we shift our focus from the lone individual to the group.

Because, unlike micro economics, micro sociology defines *goods* as the whole range of rewards that people seek and the whole range

of costs that they want to avoid, micro sociology aims to explain the whole range of social behavior by analyzing interaction and the exchanges it entails. Therefore, micro sociology consists primarily of the study of *interaction*, especially face-to-face interaction in small groups. Furthermore, micro sociological theories attempt to *explain the regularities or patterns that arise out of interactions and exchanges*.

For this reason the more formal variety of interaction theories in sociology are referred to as **exchange theories**, and the somewhat less formal, older variety are referred to as **symbolic interaction theories**. Differences between the two are relatively minor matters of emphasis and style. Both are rational choice theories, and both stress the way that our choices involve others.

Micro sociology seeks the causes of human behavior in the relationships between the individual and others. Indeed, sociologists assume that much of each person's individuality arises from one's interplay with the social environment; in the absence of social relations, the human infant would develop into a dumb brute with little self-awareness.

Thus, for micro sociologists, interaction among human beings is the fundamental social process. Interaction is the process by which we influence one another. We are endlessly tangled up in interactions, in influencing and being influenced by people around us. We act and our action affects others. They respond and their responses affect our next action. This, in turn, affects theirs. And so it goes, as we constantly adjust and readjust our activities according to feedback from our exchanges with others.

It is easy to see that human interaction consists primarily of communication. Through language, gestures, and actions we communicate with others and they communicate with us. However, unlike the grunts and hoots of animals, human communication relies heavily on symbols. **Symbols** are things that stand for or indicate another thing. The word *fish* is not a fish—it is intended to convey to a listener the idea of a fish. If humans could not use symbols, then you could know that Lake Washington is full of salmon only if someone led you to the lake and caught some salmon and showed them to you. That is exactly what a mother bear must do to teach her cubs to fish.

The use of symbolic communication can be extremely efficient, but it depends upon the ability of others to interpret or *decode* the symbols used. When we tell people we are happy, they cannot directly perceive how we feel. They must have learned to interpret the meaning of the symbol *happy*.

Symbolic interaction theories have long dominated micro sociology. Their aim is to explain how interaction through the use of symbols makes and keeps people human. Sociologists who pursue these theories are often called *symbolic interactionists*. They focus on the personal, subjective meanings we attach to various symbols. How do participants engaged in interaction perceive their situations and the intentions and meanings of those around them? Is some behavior the result of misunderstandings of the meanings of symbolic communication? Indeed, do symbols mean the same things to different people? Such questions have led symbolic interactionists to conduct detailed studies of people engaged in face-to-face interactions. These researchers have also paid particular attention to children to learn how we develop the capacity to understand one another's use of symbols.

■

Symbolic Interaction: Cooley and Mead

Charles Horton Cooley (1864–1929) and George Herbert Mead (1863–1931) are considered the cofounders of symbolic interactionism. Both wondered how the human infant developed a self, and both concluded that each person's sense of self is *socially created*. In effect, we come to see ourselves as others see us; thus, we learn to view ourselves "from outside." The essence of humanness—our ability to contemplate our own existence, our past, and our future—comes to us from society.

For this reason, sociologists refer to the process by which infants develop into normal humans as **socialization**. When we judge some-

one to be an adequate person, we say that he or she has been adequately socialized—literally has been made social. At the start of our lives, we are not social because we are unable to understand the meaning of the behavior of those around us or to interpret the symbols they use to communicate. Therefore, we are unable to interact effectively. As we will see in Chapter 6, if we are deprived of contact with others from birth, we fail to become socialized.

Cooley (1922) introduced the term **looking glass self** to describe the process by which our sense of self develops. Through symbolic interaction, humans serve as mirrors for one another. Whether we hold a good or poor opinion of ourselves depends on our relationships with other people. The greater our skill in bringing our actions into accord with theirs, the better is their opinion of us; they reflect that opinion back to us, and the more certain we become of our own worth.

Mead (1934) carried Cooley's line of analysis considerably further. He distinguished two aspects of humans that arise out of the socialization process: the *mind* and the *self*. We must acquire certain skills in order to interact: We must learn to use and interpret symbols. Mead used the concept of **mind** to identify our *understanding of symbols*, arguing that the mind arises wholly out of repeated interaction with others. The self also arises through social interaction. As Mead defined that term, the **self** is our learned understanding of the responses of others to our conduct. Through long experience in seeing others react to what we do, we not only get a general notion of who we are but also are able to put ourselves in another's place—to see ourselves and the world as others do. Mead called this "taking the role of the other." From doing this repeatedly, we form a generalized notion of others—of what they want and expect and of how they are likely to react to us. That is, to know what we are like, we also have to know what they are like. Out of this tension between us and others, the self is formed.

Mead pointed out that until children develop a self, until they can take the role of the other, they cannot take an effective part in most games. In baseball, for example, children have to be able to anticipate what others will do in order

■ Charles Horton Cooley.

■ George Herbert Mead.

to play. It is not enough that a shortstop knows to cover second when balls are hit to the right side of the infield; the other players must also know how shortstops play. To play ball, Mead wrote, a youngster must be able to put himself into "the various roles of all the participants in the game, and govern his action accordingly" (1925). The next time you pass a soccer field where very young kids are playing, notice that they tend to be bunched around the ball. Each kid tries to get to the ball, and no one goes into position to receive a pass. It takes time for children to learn to take the role of the other, to reflect that when Tom gets the ball, I will get in position to receive a pass, and then George will break down the far side and I will cross the ball to him, and so on.

We develop a self by interacting with others, but we do not become skilled at interacting until we develop a self. In fact, Mead places the conscience in the self—in our awareness of how others will respond to our actions.

There is much more to symbolic interactionism than ideas about the origins of mind and self. From this simple starting point, we can deduce the existence of regularities, or patterns, in human interactions. Out of the process of interacting and exchanging with one another, we settle into a *pattern of frequent interactions* with certain people. We also *discover and develop rules* governing our interactions.

■

Interaction Patterns: Attachments and Norms

To gain rewards, people must exchange with one another. However, self-interest limits the conditions under which people will exchange rewards. Indeed, the key insight on which Adam Smith based his economic theory is that when an exchange between two persons is voluntary, that is, when neither is being forced to yield rewards to the other, *an exchange will not take place unless both persons believe they will benefit from it.* When we give something to someone else, we expect a return—at the very least we expect them to appreciate our gift, to give us some degree of emotional reward. Perhaps one of the most common complaints expressed about people is ingratitude—"After all I have done for him, is this the way he pays me back?"

■ These children are too young to play games that would require them to take the role of the other. While I watched them they showed the ability to play catch, sort of. The youngest one always tried to catch the ball with his face, and no one went out for a pass—the ones without the ball moved closer instead. Finally, several minutes after the picture was taken, the boy in the rubber boots took the ball and hid behind a tree. The other two did not look for him.

Whenever we engage in an exchange with another person, we risk loss by not receiving an adequate return for what we give. That universal human problem leads to amazingly complex regularities in human interaction. When we exchange with someone and afterward feel cheated, we tend to avoid exchanging with that person in the future. Conversely, when we exchange with someone and are satisfied with our return, we tend to seek exchanges with that person again. Consequently, *over time people tend to establish stable exchange partnerships.*

Attachments

We make most of our face-to-face exchanges with a small number of people. Whether these exchange partners are family, friends, regular customers, or lovers, we recognize them as special to us. We have learned to count on them to provide us rewards in a "fair deal," a deal in which we also come out ahead. But they are important to us in another way as well: We have special

sentiments toward them—these are the people that we like and love.

Human beings do not exchange only goods and services. Indeed, one of our major exchange commodities is sentiment. As Mead and Cooley pointed out, we can feel good about ourselves only if other people give us reason to do so. In a classic study, Miyamoto and Dornbusch (1956) found that college students' self-conceptions were remarkably similar to ratings of them made by their fellow students. Hence, people seek to interact with others who give them emotional rewards by indicating their approval and affection. There is an immense research literature demonstrating this simple point (Byrne, 1971).

Sociologists use the term **attachment** to identify a stable and persistent pattern of interaction between two people. Attachments are of special sociological interest because they are the bonds between an individual and society. That is, *attachments represent something valuable to individuals*—something for which people will expend costs to protect and maintain. But to keep these relationships, we must continue to

■ The saying that "old friends are the best friends" contains much sociological wisdom. The more frequently people interact and the longer the period of their interaction, the more they tend to like one another. For this reason older people shift their attachments less often and with greater reluctance than do younger people.

make it rewarding for others to exchange with us. Common sense tells us that if we begin to cheat our friends, to abuse their affection and trust, we will soon lose them.

Norms

Our attachments to others cause us to conform to certain expectations that they have about how we ought to behave. Although this point is self-evident, it has profound implications. We develop attachments out of our exchanges with others only because we find exchange partners whose behavior is predictable. When we say we can count on Mary and Joe, that we can trust them, we are saying that their behavior follows certain known rules. As we saw in Chapter 2, such rules are called *norms*. *The existence of norms is implicit in the possibility of attachments.* If we can't predict how someone will behave, it becomes too risky to exchange with that person. Moreover, through our attachments, norms gain their force and significance. When we violate norms, we risk our attachments.

In Chapter 7 we shall see that the link between attachments and norms is central to theories of deviant behavior: People lacking attachments are free to violate norms. For now, however, our concern is with the opposite side of that same coin: to see the great costs people are willing to pay to preserve their attachments. When a friend says, "You know, I wouldn't do this for anybody else," that friend is demonstrating a powerful sociological "law." *Human behavior is based on choice, but what we choose to do is greatly influenced by what our friends want us to do.*

In the remainder of this chapter, we shall discover how micro sociologists bridge the gap between abstract interaction theories and the observable world around us. We will watch as sociologists operationalize theories and derive testable hypotheses from them. We will look over their shoulders as they conduct research to test hypotheses, seeing how they gather appropriate observations and analyze them.

Theory Testing: Measurement and Research

Let us begin with a theory: *Within any human group, those having strong attachments to others will tend to conform to the norms, while those having weak attachments to others will tend not to conform to the norms.* This theory consists of a set of abstract concepts: *human group, attachments, conform,* and *norms* being the major ones. The theory also tells us how these concepts are connected. Moreover, the theory applies to all instances of these concepts. That is, the theory applies to all human groups, to all people within all groups, to all attachments and to all norms of all groups—past, present, and future. In this form, the theory is too abstract to test by observations. We can't see "attachments"; we can only observe specific persons, in particular groups, doing certain things.

To test this, or any, theory we must deal in specifics. So first we must select valid instances or indicators of these concepts. As noted in Chapter 2, this is called operationalizing the concept. First, let's select a group. How about a college sorority at Denver University? Next, we need an observable way to measure attachments. Remember the discussion of sociograms in Chapter 1? Let's define *attachment* as being chosen as a close friend by other members of

the sorority—the more choices, the more attached the member; the fewer choices, the less attached. As for conformity to the norms, we could ask each young woman a series of questions about her behavior. Even better, we could arrange to have the housemother keep a log on violations of house rules by each member.

Having settled on measurable, observable instances of each concept, our next task is to form a hypothesis. That is, what does the theory predict about what we will see? In this instance our hypothesis would be: *Sorority members who are more attached to other members will less often break house rules than will members who are less attached.*

Now we know where and at whom to look and what we ought to see. As Chapter 7 will show, sociologists have operationalized this theory and tested hypotheses like this many times. So far the predictions have turned out to be correct.

So let's see how the research process works in greater detail. To begin we must understand the criteria of causation.

Criteria of Causation

Most scientific hypotheses predict causal relationships. That is, they claim that something *causes* something else. The hypotheses we examine in this chapter all predict that attachments to others will cause people to conform. To test these hypotheses, therefore, we need to be able to demonstrate a cause-and-effect relationship between the measures of attachments and of conformity we observe.

To claim that something causes something else, we must show that certain conditions are fulfilled. When any of these is not met, no causal relationships can exist. To demonstrate causation, we must show that a relationship meets three tests, or *criteria*, of causation.

Correlation

To show that something is the cause of something else, we must show that the two tend to occur in unison. That is, as one changes, the other also changes—fluctuations in the proposed cause produce fluctuations in the proposed effect. For example, to demonstrate that lack of attachments to parents causes children to be delinquent, we must show that when the strength of attachments varies, so does delinquency in children. When things vary or change in unison, we say they are *correlated*.

Correlation can be either positive or negative. If one factor rises while the other declines, it is a negative correlation. This would be the case if we observed that auto theft by juveniles declined as attachments to parents rose. If both factors rise or fall together, that is a positive correlation. Either kind of correlation can demonstrate causation—indeed, a hypothesis will predict which kind is expected. As we saw at the start of Chapter 1, when the moral statisticians claimed that modernization caused suicide, they predicted a positive correlation—that as societies became more modern, they would have higher suicide rates. Suppose they had found a negative correlation? Their hypothesis would have been disproved. For a more complete discussion of correlation, see Special Topic 1.

Time order

To establish causation we must also demonstrate **time order**. A cause must occur before its effect. This notion of time order simply recognizes that the idea of cause-and-effect makes no sense backwards. It is absurd to argue, for example, that you fell from a ladder because a friend pushed you if the push came after you had already fallen. Thus, if we observed that boys developed weak attachments to their parents only after they had stolen a car, then we would have to conclude that lack of attachments does not cause delinquency (we might suspect that misbehavior causes bad relations with parents). Or when sociologists argued that lack of attachments causes mental illness, they had to show that people first lost their friends and then became ill. This hypothesis would be refuted if evidence showed that most people became mentally ill first and then lost their friends.

Nonspuriousness

Finally, two factors often appear correlated, one seeming to be the cause of the other, when in fact they are correlated only because each is being caused by some third, unnoticed factor. If that is the case, we are observing **spuriousness**.

For example, we know that the average marijuana smoker will live much longer than the average person who does not smoke marijuana. Therefore, marijuana smoking and life expectancy are correlated. We also can see that smoking or not smoking marijuana occurs before its alleged effect, the time of death. But even though this relationship meets the first two criteria of causation, we would be sadly misled if we believed that marijuana was the fountain of youth and took up smoking it in order to live longer. For we must not overlook the simple fact that the average marijuana smoker is much younger than the average nonsmoker. Smoking marijuana and living longer appear to be correlated only because each is correlated with age. When we examine people the same age, we do not find that marijuana smokers live longer. Correlations like this are spurious. To demonstrate cause and effect, we must establish that the correlation we observe is nonspurious, that it is not being caused by something else.

Many obvious spurious relations appear in the press. In 1985 newspapers reported that a researcher had discovered that elderly men can prolong their lives by marrying younger women. This was based on comparisons of men age 50 to 79 who married younger women and men the same age who did not. The ones who married young women had death rates 13 percent lower than the others. But what *kind* of elderly men would be apt to seek and win a young wife? Probably not those who were in failing health. Good health would seem to be the cause of this spurious relationship.

When sociologists test causal hypotheses, they must attempt to show that each of these three criteria of causation is met. In the next section, we will look over Richard Ofshe's shoulder as he tests a hypothesis and see why the experiment is the ideal method for demonstrating causation. But we will also be able to see why most sociologists do not do experiments. Much of what we most need to study cannot or should not be manipulated in a laboratory. In fact, while thousands of sociological experiments have been conducted, Ofshe's is virtually the only one directly relevant to the proposition that attachments produce conformity. Let's see why, and let's also see how experiments work.

Experimental Research

Once again, let's begin with an interaction theory. We can call this one the theory of loyalty: *Whenever people must choose between rewarding someone to whom they are attached or rewarding someone to whom they are not attached, they will reward the person to whom they are attached.* Put in everyday language, when we must choose between sticking up for our friends or for strangers, we are loyal to our friends.

In the late 1960s, Richard Ofshe, then a graduate student at Stanford, became interested in testing this theory. But to do so, he had first to operationalize it and deduce a hypothesis. He operationalized attachments as the knowledge that people with whom an individual is interacting are acquaintances or strangers. He operationalized rewards as supporting an acquaintance's judgments over those of a stranger, even if you didn't really agree with the acquaintance's judgments. His hypothesis was that people would, in effect, stick up for people they knew.

His next problem: How could he gather appropriate observations that would accurately confirm or deny this hypothesis? The method Ofshe selected was the **experiment**. But to use this method to test this particular hypothesis presented difficulties.

As we examine the inner workings of the experiment, we will see that this method depends upon being able to exert control over the causal factor—to be able to make it vary, rise or fall,

appear or disappear, at will. For example, when Karen Dion wanted to know if appearance influenced perceptions of children's misbehavior, she was able to make appearance vary by simply switching the photographs shown to student teachers. At first glance it is hard to see how one could control the strength of interpersonal attachments to make them vary on demand. You can't just take a bunch of people into a sociology laboratory and assign some to be friends and some to be strangers.

After giving some thought to this problem, Ofshe came up with a clever solution. He constructed a situation where he made some people *believe* that they were participating in an experiment with one of their friends when in fact no one else would be present. In this way he could randomly expose some people to pressure to support their friends.

Although the procedure was tricky, it was not unethical. We shall explore many experiments in this book in which deception was involved. To do experiments, researchers are required to gain approval from committees that review all proposed research involving human subjects. For such a proposal to be approved, the people must not be harmed by having been deceived (or by any other aspect of research), and when deception is involved, the actual nature of the study must be explained to the participants after they have taken part.

In this study, Ofshe recruited students from a nearby community college to be subjects in an experiment. While doing so, he told each student that another study was being planned in which friendship patterns among students would be analyzed. Ofshe then asked each of these students to name his or her four best friends on campus as possible subjects for this other study. About a month later individual volunteers were contacted and scheduled for the experiment. They were told it was vital that they keep the appointment because they would be taking part with two other students, and if anyone failed to show up, the session would have to be canceled.

When a student arrived for the experiment, he or she was told that the object of the study was to measure the physical responses of persons when others disagreed with their opinions.

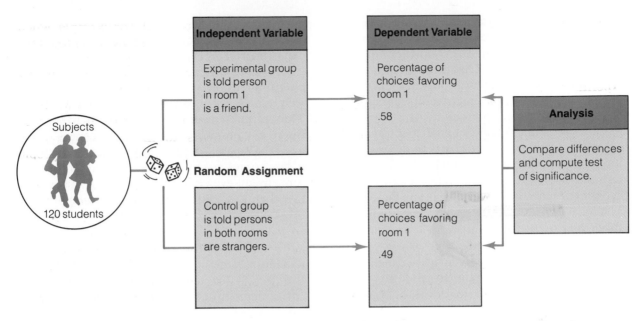

Figure 3-2 ■ **Ofshe's experiment.** The precision of the experimental method rests in the ability of researchers to control what happens, when, and to whom. Here we see that Ofshe could randomly assign a student to either the experimental or the control group. Students in the experimental group all believed that the person in room 1 was a friend of theirs, while the person in room 2 was a stranger. Students in the control group believed that both of the other people were strangers. By comparing the results for the experimental group with those for the control group, Ofshe could assess the extent to which the experimental group oversupported the choices of the person in room 1—a friend. Using a test of significance, he could determine that the differences he found were unlikely to have occurred simply by chance.

Two other students would be hooked up to devices that would record their physical reactions whenever they made a judgment that disagreed with the judgments of the others. These other two students were said to be in other rooms, and all communication was to occur electronically. The actual student subjects were told that their own physical reactions were not part of the study. Instead, they would be shown the judgments of the other two students, and their job was to register with whom they agreed when the other two students disagreed. Their judgment would then be communicated to the other two students.

The judgments involved selecting the more artistically attractive of two visual patterns. After each pair was shown, the "choice" made

by the person in room 1 would appear on the upper half of the projection screen, while the "choice" of the student in room 2 would appear on the lower half. After these instructions were given, half of the subjects were told that the person in room 1 was a friend of theirs while the person in room 2 was a student they did not know. The other half of the subjects were told that both of the other participants were strangers. Figure 3-2 illustrates Ofshe's experimental design.

Of course, there were no other subjects in the experiment. The judgments made by the other two "people" were fixed so that the same patterns occurred each time the experiment was run. What Ofshe wanted to know was the extent to which the judgments of people who thought a friend was in room 1 agreed with those of that person, and to compare this with the figures for the subjects who thought both other "participants" were strangers. Ofshe found a substantial bias by subjects toward the judgment of the person in room 1 when that person was believed to be a friend.

Now let's take Ofshe's experiment apart to see how it solves the problems of demonstrating causation. To proceed, you need to learn two terms used in research: the independent and the dependent variable. A variable is any factor that can have two or more values. For example, in this experiment friendship was a variable that took two values: A friend either was or was not included in the "three-person" experiment. For the moral statisticians, the suicide rate was a variable taking higher or lower values from one nation to another.

The term independent variable indicates a cause. When Morselli claimed modernization caused suicide, modernization was his independent variable. The term dependent variable indicates an effect—something that is being caused. In Morselli's hypothesis, suicide is the dependent variable. We can say that variation in the dependent variable depends upon or is caused by variation in the independent variable. In Ofshe's study friendship was the independent variable and bias in favor of friends was the dependent variable.

Experiments and Causation

Ofshe wanted to demonstrate bias in favor of a friend's judgments. Thus, he needed to put people in situations where nothing differed from subject to subject except their belief about who was in room 1. Recall that the criterion of nonspuriousness requires that all other potential causes be ruled out so we can assume that variations in the independent variable cause the variations in the dependent variable. In experiments we accomplish this by experimental controls. These are measures taken to eliminate all other potential causes. This is why Ofshe made sure that all subjects had an identical

experience, saw the same patterns of responses, got identical instructions, and spoke to the same experimenter in the same room.

However, the experiment itself is not the only potential source of spuriousness. The subjects were not identical, since no two people are alike. Thus, differences among subjects had to be eliminated as a possible source of spuriousness. Some were males and some were females, some were older; some, doubtless, were more timid, and some might even have liked their campus friends less than others did. How could Ofshe prevent these differences from influencing his findings?

Randomization

Ofshe determined *at random* which students would be told they were taking part with a friend and which with strangers. He could have done this as easily as by flipping a coin before each student's appointment and letting heads mean a friend was in room 1 and tails a stranger. Because you can't make people alike, you try to make *groups* alike; that is, by *random assignment*, experiments make it possible *to compute the probability* that groups will contain the same mix of ages, sexes, attitudes, and other traits. Because he used randomization, Ofshe could assume that both his groups were alike.

Time order

Experiments are ideal for establishing that causes occur before their presumed consequences because experimenters can control *when things happen*. Ofshe arranged for students to know whether they were participating with a friend or with strangers before they were asked with whom they agreed.

Correlation

In any kind of research, it is easy to determine whether an independent variable and a dependent variable are correlated. One measures both variables and then sees if they vary together.

Ofshe found that bias in favor of room 1 varied depending on the assumed relationship between the subject and the person in that room.

But a final matter must be dealt with in evaluating the results of an experiment. Ofshe found a correlation in support of his hypothesis, but he still needed to know whether that correlation reflected a causal relationship or whether it could have occurred simply by chance. That is, he had to examine the probability that his results were produced by the failure of his random assignment to make the groups sufficiently alike. Here experimenters use a **test of significance**.

Significance

In determining whether to trust the results of an experiment, two things are taken into account: (1) the *number* of subjects on which the results are based and (2) the *size* of the correlation (that is, the amount of change produced in the dependent variable). (See Special Topic 1.) The logic involved is simple. We know that if we flip a coin many times, we eventually get about the same proportion of heads and tails. As Table 3-1 shows, however, the fewer times we flip a coin, the greater the likelihood that we will get an unequal proportion of heads and tails. The same principle applies when subjects are randomly assigned to experimental groups. The more subjects involved, the greater the probability that potential differences between groups will be minimized. However, for any given number of subjects, the odds that a correlation is produced by random differences among the groups rather than by changes in the independent variable depend on the size of the correlation obtained. The larger the correlation is, the lower the probability that the finding is due to chance.

In this instance, when Ofshe computed the test of significance, he found that the odds were 20 to 1 against chance findings. That meets the usual standards social scientists use.

Ofshe's study was a very strong test of his hypothesis not only because of the precision of experimental research but also because it was

Table 3-1 ■ **The more times you flip a coin, the higher the odds against all heads.**

Number of Flips	Odds Against All Heads
1	2 to 1
2	4 to 1
3	8 to 1
4	16 to 1
5	32 to 1
6	64 to 1
7	128 to 1
8	256 to 1
9	512 to 1
10	1,024 to 1
11	2,048 to 1
12	4,096 to 1

a relatively weak situation. That is, as employed in his experiment, attachments lacked most of the power they usually possess in real life. Subjects did not know which of their friends was in room 1, they had no reason to suppose that the friend knew their identity, and they were not asked to support their friends on a matter of much importance. By the same token, they knew that the strangers were not true outsiders but were fellow students, possibly even acquaintances. Hence, the motive to support their friends against the strangers could not have been very strong. Yet even in this weak situation, Ofshe found strong effects. Therefore, his experiment was a demanding test of the theory of loyalty.

Now suppose Ofshe had wanted to study conformity in a much stronger situation. Perhaps he might have wanted to examine the effects of deeply felt attachments, such as those between lifelong friends or lovers. He might have wanted to impose a much more demanding test on such attachments, such as asking people to accept a new religion because their friends had done so. In this case, Ofshe would have been forced to abandon the experimental method. As already noted, it took originality and some deception to create even this weak attachment situation in a laboratory. But it is impossible to bring people into a lab and randomly assign them as lifelong friends or lovers, just as one could not randomly assign them to be young or old, male or female, or black or white. And no review committee for human subjects would approve plans for an experiment to change people's religions, even if some sociologist were silly enough to propose such an experiment.

Yet sociologists need to study strong attachments, and they also need to study the effects of age, sex, and race on social behavior. And some of us even want to know about the role of attachments in religious conversion. Thus, much of our work cannot be done in the laboratory. For this reason, most sociological research is **nonexperimental research**. A number of research techniques have been developed to try to meet the criteria of causation, even though we cannot manipulate what happens to people. In the remainder of this chapter and in the next, we shall see how this research is done.

■ The Reverend Sun M. Moon.

Field Observation Research

A question of long-standing interest to sociologists as well as the general public is why people join new religious movements. For example, why do people in the United States from conventional religious backgrounds suddenly become Hare Krishnas or members of the Unification Church or go to live in an ashram and study yoga with a guru from India?

When I began graduate school, that was something I wondered about. During several years as a newspaper reporter, I had been assigned to cover stories about a number of exotic new religions, including several based on revelations said to have been brought to earth by friendly aliens on flying saucers. During my first week of classes at the University of California at Berkeley, I met John Lofland, who was also interested in conversion to new religions. Much had been written on this topic over the years, but we found this work unconvincing. For one thing, nearly all of it seemed to have been

researched in libraries, because there was very little to suggest that the authors had ever met any members of the groups they claimed to explain.

There was widespread agreement among these authors, however, that people joined a new religion because of the correspondence between the beliefs of the religion and the problems suffered by those who joined. The research procedure each scholar seemed to have followed was to study the ideology of a group in order to answer the question: What does this faith promise to do for people? Having determined this, they next asked: To whom do such promises most appeal? Thus, for example, if a new religious movement, such as Christian Science, claimed the ability to cure illness, it seemed likely that it would most appeal to those with chronic illnesses or physical handicaps. Having deduced who ought to join a particular religious movement, these scholars seemed content to conclude that, in fact, those were indeed the people who actually did join.

But was that true? Lofland and I were not so sure. Moreover, we suspected that ideological appeals were emphasized as the cause of conversion primarily because that's about all you

■ When John Lofland and I studied them in the early 1960s, there were fewer than 30 American members of the Unification Church, sometimes called the Moonies. They have grown a lot since then; in this photo 2,000 couples are taking part in a mass wedding ceremony held by the church in New York's Madison Square Garden. These people did not become Moonies because they were "brainwashed" or because they were desperate to find a new religion. Most joined the church primarily on the basis of their attachments to members—they accepted the religion that their close friends and relatives had accepted.

can study about religious groups in the library. In the library, you can't watch anyone join a religious movement or even observe members' activities. About all you can find are books and articles written by the group to explain their ideology and works written by others to attack or criticize that ideology. But what really happens, we wondered? The only way to find out was to go into the world and look, applying the methods of **field observation research**.

So we began looking around the San Francisco Bay Area for a group to observe. We wanted one that was new and growing but still small enough so that the two of us could closely ob-

serve most of what went on. After much hunting, we found exactly what we wanted. We discovered a group of about a dozen people who had just come to San Francisco from Eugene, Oregon, where they had been recruited to be the first American members of a new religion that had begun in Korea.

The group was led by a Korean woman, a former college professor, who had been sent to America to seek converts for a religious movement founded by Sun M. Moon. Moon was a Korean electrical engineer who believed that he had a revelation from God that Judgment Day was only a few years away. Although this group was tiny and unimpressive when Lofland and I found it and was still very small when our study was finished, today it has become famous as the Unification Church, whose members are known to outsiders as "Moonies."

As Lofland and I began our field observations of the Moonies, we formulated a theory of conversion: *Conversion to a new religious group occurs when people have or develop stronger attachments to members of this group than they have to nonmembers.* In this theory, which has much in common with the theory of loyalty, attachments play the primary role. From this viewpoint, interaction between members of a group and outsiders is the key to conversion because to gain new converts group members either must bring in their family and friends or find ways to gain new friends. Put another way, Lofland and I were proposing that attachments, not ideology, played the central role in conversion—that people accepted new religious beliefs because their friends held these beliefs.

Here is our specific hypothesis: *Of all the people the Moonies encountered in their efforts to spread their faith, only those with attachments to members that overbalanced their attachments to nonmembers would join.* So we settled down to watch, keeping careful notes about everything we saw. From the very beginning the evidence ran strongly in favor of our hypothesis.

During her first months in Eugene, Miss Kim, the Moonie missionary, failed to make any converts. She attended many churches and gave talks to a number of women's clubs, but no one found her message attractive. But then, having moved to the edge of the city, Miss Kim became friends with a young housewife. Slowly she developed this woman's interest until one day the woman professed her belief in Kim's religious message. This woman then arranged for Kim to begin instructing two other women in the neighborhood. Soon they, too, joined. Then the husband of one of them joined, and he invited several men who worked with him home to hear Kim. They also converted. By the time the group decided to leave Eugene and attempt to build the movement in San Francisco, it had a dozen members, all of whom had been friends long

before Kim met them. Thus, *the initial growth of this movement moved entirely along lines of pre-existing attachments.*

Once in San Francisco, the group continued to draw some members from among their old friends in Eugene, but for some months they failed to convert anyone in San Francisco. They had no friends in that city, and they did not begin to gain new converts until they learned how to form friendships with other newcomers to San Francisco. Lofland and I spent as much time as possible with the group, watching the members convey their message to new people and waiting to see who accepted it. We soon found persuasive evidence that conversion required not only strong attachments to Moonies but also weak attachments to non-Moonies. We saw a number of people who formed strong friendships with Moonies, attended meetings regularly for a considerable time, and even professed belief in Moon's teachings, but they did not become Moonies. In each of these cases, the person had very strong attachments to outsiders who were not enthusiastic about the group. We watched people waver about joining the Moonies as they reacted to contrary influences.

People who joined were free of such pressures. Often they were strangers themselves in the Bay Area, and their attachments were to people far away who were unaware of their evolving conversion. We even observed some people who formed strong attachments to Moonies while expressing complete disbelief in their doctrines. Several of these people moved into the apartment house owned by the group because of their friendships with members. This house also served as the Unification Church headquarters. Their decision to actually convert to the religion came months later, and then only after intimate, daily interaction with group members.

Lofland and I concluded that while elements of the Moonie doctrine did play a role in who joined—atheists never joined no matter how much they may have liked some members—the primary basis of conversion was attachment. Rather than being drawn to the group mainly because of the appeal of its doctrines, people were drawn to the doctrines because of their ties to the group.

Thus, attachments can make people accept "deviant" norms. That is, though many outsiders regard Moonies as weird, even as crazy, people willingly paid that price to align their behavior with that of their close friends. They were much less concerned about what the outside world thought of their actions than what their friends thought (Lofland and Stark, 1965; Lofland, 1966).

You will notice that Lofland and I could not be nearly so precise about meeting the criteria of causation in our study as we could have through an experiment. Of course, there was no way we could randomly assign people to have or not have Moonie friends and then sit back to await conversion. Nevertheless, we could meet causation criteria to some extent. First, by keeping careful records on each person who came into contact with the Moonies, we established a correlation between attachment and conversion. No one ever joined without having close attachments. Second, because we observed the group over a considerable period of time, we were able to demonstrate time order. The friendships occurred before the conversions. Indeed, in many cases the friendships had already existed for years.

To demonstrate nonspuriousness is a much more difficult problem in nonexperimental research. We could do little to ensure that people who had friendships with Moonies weren't different in other significant ways from those without such friendships. We didn't notice such differences, but they might have existed. Hence, there is always an element of risk in accepting nonexperimental research findings. In Chapter 4 we shall examine some statistical procedures that help to decrease the possibility of spuriousness in nonexperimental studies, but these usually do not apply to the observational variety of nonexperimental research.

You may be wondering what Lofland and I told the Moonies we were up to while we did our study. At first we told them nothing. We met one of their missionaries, who invited us to come and learn about their message, and we simply took her up on the offer. After a little while, however, we decided to explain to them what we were doing, since it was beginning to get awkward to sneak off to the bathroom every time we wanted to write down our observations.

Miss Kim was quite willing to let two young sociologists from Berkeley study her group. If nothing else, she thought we might compile a useful historical record. In fact, not long ago a young Moonie enrolled at a major Protestant seminary drew upon our published study and interviewed us in order to write a history of the founding of his church in America.

Replication

Scientific tests of hypotheses rarely rest upon a single piece of research. Instead, the original researcher or other researchers repeat the studies to see if they obtain the same results. Such studies are called **replications**.

It usually is quite easy to replicate an experiment. For example, to replicate Ofshe's study, one would only need to create the same laboratory setup, recruit experimental subjects in the same way, and then repeat the experiment. If the result came out the same way again, we would have even greater confidence that the hypothesis is correct.

It is more difficult but even more important to replicate nonexperimental research. For example, perhaps attachments play a major role in conversion only among the Moonies but not among other groups, such as the Hare Krishnas. The only way to learn if the results that Lofland and I obtained have broad applications would be to examine conversion to many other religious groups. However, to do that might have taken Lofland and me the rest of our lives. Fortunately, sociology is not a solitary calling. Sociologists pay attention to one another's work and are often prompted to follow up on something someone else has proposed or observed.

In the two decades since Lofland and I published our study of conversion, I have learned of more than twenty replications (for example, Gerlach and Hine, 1970; Richardson and Stewart, 1978; Snow and Philips, 1980; Barker, 1984).

These replications have involved a great variety of groups, from Adventists to Zen Buddhists. While there is evidence that attachments may not play so central a role in accepting mystical beliefs when no participation in a religious group is involved (accepting the truth of astrology columns, for example), attachments have consistently been found to play the major role in explaining who converts to a new religious group.

Conclusion

This chapter has introduced the fundamental building blocks of micro sociological theory. We have seen that humans must interact and exchange with one another and that they therefore tend to form attachments and conform to one another's expectations. In this way, norms arise to guide and structure our behavior. Throughout the rest of the book, we shall see how this elementary theoretical scheme serves as the basis for elaborate theories from which a great variety of hypotheses can be derived.

This chapter also more closely looked at portions of the sociological process—especially those steps devoted to research. We saw that the experimental method excels in satisfying the criteria of causation, which is why it is the common research method in fields that do not require human subjects: Not only do bacteria not blush when they are being observed, but they also have no legal rights and elicit no sympathy. However, because sociologists study people, we often cannot use the experimental method. In this chapter we examined an observational field study and saw how it attempted to approximate the precision of experiments. In the next chapter we shall encounter more sophisticated nonexperimental forms of research. We shall also encounter macro sociological theories.

Review Glossary

rational choice theories All micro science theories that proceed from the rational choice, or self-interest, proposition (p. 70)

rational choice, or **self-interest, proposition** The assumption on which social science is based, that human beings attempt to make choices that will maximize their rewards and minimize their costs. (p. 71)

altruism The name applied to behavior that is alleged to be contrary to self-interest and to occur entirely for the benefit of someone else. (p. 72)

social interaction Human efforts to influence one another. (p. 73)

exchange theories A common form of interaction theory, emphasizing ways in which people reward one another. (p. 73)

symbolic interaction theories The traditional form of interaction theories places primary emphasis on the use of symbolic communication by humans as they interact. (p. 73)

symbols Things used to stand for and indicate another thing. For example, the word *fish* is not really a fish, but is used to convey the thought or idea of a fish. (p. 73)

socialization The process through which infants develop into normal humans; literally, to be made social. (p. 74)

looking glass self Cooley's term for the self-conception humans develop on the basis of feedback from others—how we see our image as it is reflected in the eyes of others. (p. 74)

mind As used by Mead, *mind* refers to the human capacity to understand symbols. (p. 74)

self As used by Mead, *self* refers to our learned ability to gauge the responses of others to our conduct. (p. 74)

attachment A stable and persistent pattern of interaction between two people. (p. 76)

correlation What exists when variation in one phenomenon is matched by variations in another phenomenon—for example, when fluctuations or variations in outdoor temperatures coincide with variations in how warmly people dress. For something to be the cause of something else, the two must be correlated. (p. 79)

time order The determination that changes in a cause occur prior to changes in its effects. (p. 79)

spuriousness The appearance of a correlation between two phenomena because each is related to some third phenomenon. For example, the number of firefighters at a fire and the amount of damage done by the fire appear to be correlated because both are related to the size of the fire. For a cause-and-effect relationship to exist, the correlation must be nonspurious. (p. 79)

experiment A research design in which the researcher has control over the independent variable; that is, the researcher can manipulate when and how strongly the independent variable occurs, and has the ability to determine randomly which subjects are exposed to which level of the independent variable. (p. 80)

variable Something that can take more than one value; something that varies. As used in science, the term **independent variable** is used to identify a cause, while the term **dependent variable** refers to the consequence of some cause. (p. 82)

experimental controls Methods to ensure that nothing varies in an experiment except the independent variable, thus ensuring nonspuriousness. (p. 82)

randomization Use of chance to assign people to experimental treatments to equalize groups exposed to different levels of the independent variable. (p. 82)

test of significance A computation of the odds that a correlation occurred simply by chance; social scientists usually require that the odds against a chance finding be 20 to 1 or greater (the .05 level of significance) before they will trust a result. (p. 83)

nonexperimental research All forms of research that are not experiments. (p. 84)

field observation research Studies done by observing what people do in their normal situations (in contrast with observing them in a laboratory). (p. 85)

replications Studies that repeat earlier research and thus serve both to check against chance findings and to extend the range of research findings by showing that the findings apply in another time or place. (p. 87)

■
_____

Suggested Readings

Barker, Eileen. 1984. *The Making of a Moonie— Brainwashing or Choice?* Oxford and New York: Basil Blackwell.

Blau, Peter M. 1964. *Exchange and Power in Social Life.* New York: Wiley.

Hechter, Michael, ed. 1983. *Microfoundations of Macrosociology.* Philadelphia: Temple University Press.

Homans, George. 1974. *Social Behavior: Its Elementary Forms.* New York: Harcourt Brace Jovanovich.

Phelps, Edmund S., ed. 1975. *Altruism, Morality, and Economic Theory.* New York: Russell Sage Foundation.

Popper, Karl R. 1959. *The Logic of Scientific Discovery.* New York: Basic Books.

Macro Sociology: Testing Structural Theories

4

SUPPOSE THAT YOU have volunteered to take part in a discussion group organized by two of your professors. When you arrive, they show you to a booth equipped with a microphone. They explain that to let each participant remain anonymous, the discussion will take place over an intercom system. When it is your turn to talk, a light will come on and your mike will be open. Five other people will take part in the discussion, which will be about problems in adjusting to college. After explaining this, the professors leave.

The discussion begins, and each person takes a turn. Suddenly one of the others, who had already mentioned that he had been a bit scared about going to college because he sometimes has epileptic seizures, begins to stammer and breathe hard into the microphone. He gasps out, "Help." Then there is a crash, like a body falling to the floor. You can't speak to the others because your mike is not on. You don't know where your professors have gone, but they promised not to listen in. What do you do?

What you are most likely to do depends upon *how many other people you believe are part of the discussion group*. In the actual experiment, no one else was really present. All the other voices were simply tape recordings, including that of the young man who had the seizure. When John Darley and Bibb Latanè (1968) did this experiment, some subjects were told that they would be one of two people in the discussion. Others were told there were three, and still others were told there were six (Figure 4-2). When subjects thought that they were part of a two-person group—therefore, they alone knew the young

man was having a seizure—*all* of them quickly left the booth to seek help. But when subjects thought it was a three-person group—and thus one other person was also aware of the emergency—only 80 percent left the booth to seek help, and they also took longer to respond. Subjects in the six-person situation were even slower to seek help, and only 60 percent attempted to do so.

What is going on here? Clearly, these differences in the apparent willingness of people to help someone else are not due to differences of individual character. Because people were randomly assigned to groups of different sizes, the three groups should have contained the same mix of personality types and other individual characteristics. What is going on here is **social structure**. Quite beyond individual characteristics are characteristics of the groups—such as size—in which we exist, and these group features operate as structures that influence our behavior in the same way that physical structures—such as the position of doorways—do. All characteristics of groups are social structures.

In this instance, Darley and Latanè were conducting research on *group size* as a social structure. They had hypothesized that the larger the group believed to be present, the less an individual will feel personal responsibility to act in an emergency. And that is precisely what the results of their experiment showed.

While micro sociology focuses on the individual and his or her immediate social surroundings, macro sociology focuses on social structures. This includes features of groups, organizations, and even whole societies, how

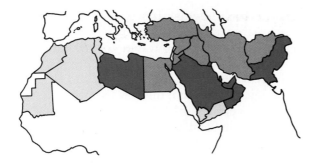

Number of Males per 100 Females

North Yemen	90
South Yemen	97
Mauritania	98
Algeria	99
Morocco	100
Tunisia	101

Syria	103
Egypt	103
Iran	104
Iraq	104
Afghanistan	105
Turkey	106
Jordan	106

Pakistan	108
Libya	111
Oman	112
Saudi Arabia	120
Kuwait	138
Bahrain	146
Qatar	177
United Arab Emirates	216

Figure 4-1 ■ **Gender as a social structure.** A social structure is a characteristic of a group, not of an individual. All individual humans have a specific gender. But as they move from group to group the gender composition of their environment can change dramatically. For example, students often are shocked at how much their day-to-day life changes if they transfer from an all-male or all-female college to one that is coeducational. The sex ratio of groups is a social structure, an aspect of the group or the society. Here we see variations in the number of males per 100 females in the principal nations of Islam. Imagine how different it would be to live in North Yemen, where there are only 90 men for every 100 women, compared to living in one of the United Arab Emirates, where there are 216 men for every 100 women. When individuals move from one of these nations to another, their own gender doesn't change, but the social conditions surrounding gender roles will shift remarkably. Indeed, the whole of Chapter 12 is devoted to the immense impact of sex ratios on gender inequality and cultural definitions of *man* and *woman*. *Source*: ShowCase Presentational Software: Principal Nations of Islam (Seattle: Cognitive Development, Inc., 1987).

social structure is created, how one aspect of structure affects another aspect, and how these larger social collectivities function as whole systems.

Chapter Preview

This chapter begins with another example from micro sociology to familiarize you with one of the most widely used methods of social scientific research—the survey. To do this I will let you look over my shoulder as Travis Hirschi and I *failed to confirm* a hypothesis that everyone assumed would turn out to be true. Then, to let you more fully appreciate the differences between micro and macro sociology, we will see how repeated failures by other researchers to replicate what Hirschi and I had found caused a great deal of confusion and concern. In assessing the contrary evidence, it became clear that the theory needed to be shifted from the micro to the macro level of analysis—from characteristics of individuals to characteristics of groups. Thus, we will confront social structures. And against this background we shall explore elements of societies as systems and how sociologists formulate theories to explain these systems. Finally, we will watch a macro sociologist perform the entire sociological process from wonder to analysis, as Jeffery Paige sought to understand why some small, preliterate societies are torn by bitter conflicts that result in terrifying rates of mayhem and murder, while others are extremely peaceful and nonviolent.

Survey Research

For several years Travis Hirschi and I were both on the staff of the Survey Research Center at the University of California in Berkeley. One afternoon, sitting on the lawn, we started to talk about how religion plays a role in interaction theories of conformity to the norms. Imagine a young boy faced

with an absolutely risk-free chance to steal $50. There is absolutely no way that any other human being would ever find out if he took the money. According to the rational choice proposition, this boy will take the money. Now add religion to the equation. What if this boy strongly believes in the concept of sin? If he takes the money he must face the cost of knowing that he is dishonest, that when no one is looking he is not a moral person. Loss of self-respect is a significant cost to human beings. Moreover, in many religions the concept of sin includes belief that misdeeds will require atonement in the world to come. Thus, to explain when people will and will not steal, we need to recognize that many people will include religious rewards and costs in their calculations.

However, this was not the point Hirschi was trying to make. Instead, he was using this example to illustrate how sociologists also operate on the basis of the rational choice premise. Thus, although every sociological theorist has accepted the claim that religion sustains conformity to the norms, no research had been done on this issue because the point was so obvious that there would be no rewards to justify the effort required to test it. Would a sociology journal even publish a study reporting that religious kids are less likely than other kids to be delinquent, we wondered?

But one thing led to another and all of a sudden he and I decided that we would go back into the center and waste a little time demonstrating the obvious by testing this hypothesis: *Among teenagers in Richmond, California, those who believe in the concepts of sin and hell and who attend church and Sunday school will be less likely than other teenagers to commit delinquent acts.* Appropriate observations were already at hand from a huge survey Hirschi had gathered to write a book called *Causes of Delinquency*. By analyzing some of these data, we could see if they supported the hypothesis.

The sociological method called **survey research** has two basic elements. First, the data are collected by *personal interviews* or by having each individual complete a *questionnaire*. Thus, if you want to know how religious people are, you ask them a series of questions about

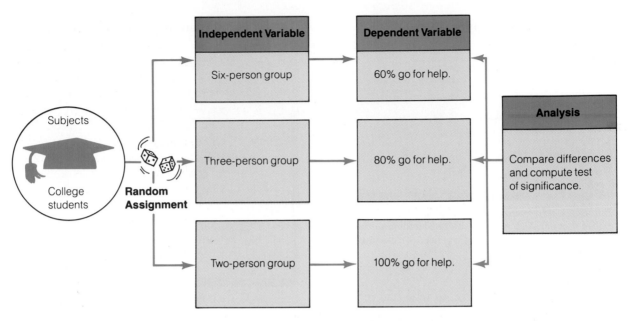

Figure 4-2 ■ **The bystander intervention experiment.** Random assignment of subjects ensures that, although each subject differs from all others, the three groups of subjects will be alike (except for random variation). For this reason perceptions of group size, not something else, must have caused the differences among these three groups on the dependent variable—going for help. As the perceived size of the group declined, the proportion who went for help increased.

what they believe and do. If you want to know about their delinquency, then you ask them questions about violations they may have committed.

Obviously, problems can arise about whether people answer truthfully and whether they are even able to give accurate answers. For example, research has demonstrated that people do not report their TV viewing habits very accurately. To get good information about this subject, it is necessary to have people keep daily logs on what they watch. However, an immense amount of effort has gone into perfecting survey research techniques, and the data so obtained can be quite reliable when people employ proper techniques and safeguards.

The second feature of survey research is the use of *samples*. When we want to know about the religious behavior of the American public, we do not attempt the huge task of asking every single citizen. Instead, we use techniques developed to obtain accurate results by questioning only a selected few, or a sample from the larger population. If the sample is chosen properly, we can assume that the results will reflect on the whole population. Special Topic 1 describes how sampling is done.

Hirschi and I proceeded to investigate the effects of religion on delinquency on the basis of questionnaires filled out by a sample of students enrolled in junior high schools and high schools in Richmond, California, a city of about 100,000 people across the bay from San Francisco.

Our first concern was to see if there was a correlation between religion and delinquency. To do this, we first separated the data according to two categories of students: those who attended church frequently (at least once a month) and those who did not. Then we sorted each of these

Table 4-1 ■ Church attendance and delinquency.

| | Church Attendance | |
	Frequent	Infrequent
Delinquent	22%	38%
Not delinquent	78%	62%
	100%	100%

Source: Adapted from Hirschi and Stark (1969). The results shown here have been modified and simplified for clarity. However, they accurately reflect patterns in the actual data.

Table 4-2 ■ Controls for sex reveal a spurious relationship.

| | Church Attendance | |
	Frequent	Infrequent
Boys		
Delinquent	50%	50%
Not delinquent	50%	50%
	100%	100%
Girls		
Delinquent	10%	10%
Not delinquent	90%	90%
	100%	100%

Source: Adapted from Hirschi and Stark (1969). The results shown here have been modified and simplified for clarity. However, they accurately reflect patterns in the actual data.

groups into delinquents (those who had recently committed two or more delinquent acts) and nondelinquents (those who had recently committed no more than one delinquent act). When we were finished, the results looked like those shown in Table 4-1, which shows the percentages of delinquents and nondelinquents within each religious category. The findings clearly seem to support our hypothesis. Frequent church attenders are much less likely to be delinquent (22 percent) than are infrequent church attenders (38 percent). Thus, our results fulfilled the first criterion of causation (see Chapter 3). But what about the other two?

It is much more difficult to establish *time order* for questionnaire data than for data from experiments. Perhaps people become delinquents and then become infrequent church attenders. However, other research shows that patterns of church attendance among teenagers primarily reflect family religious patterns, which are usually established long before children reach junior high. Indeed, these patterns may have been established well before a child was born. So it is reasonable to assume that this study met the criterion of time order.

But what about the criterion of nonspuriousness? Obviously, delinquent and nondelinquent teenagers are likely to differ in many ways other than church attendance. Could one of these other, uncontrolled factors cause a spurious correlation between church attendance and delinquency? The answer turned out to be yes.

Spuriousness

Although there had been no prior research on the connections between religion and delinquency, much had been devoted to each of these topics. Therefore, it was well known that boys are much more likely than girls to be delinquent. It was equally well known that girls are more likely than boys to be active in church. So we knew we had to examine the possibility that sex differences were the real cause of the correlation in Table 4-1. We used a simple technique to check this out. First, we divided the sample into males and females. Then we examined the relationship between church attendance and delinquency separately for males and females.

The results were like those shown in Table 4-2. There we can see that boys who attend church are no less likely to be delinquent than boys who do not (50 percent of both groups are delinquents). The same holds among females: Ten percent of the girls who attend church frequently are delinquents, as are 10 percent of the girls who do not.

Thus, we must conclude that the correlation found in Table 4-1 is spurious—religion *does*

■ Will these children be less likely to commit juvenile crimes because they attend church? The answer to that question depends upon *where* this picture was taken. If it was taken in a city where the majority of citizens belong to a church, which is the case in most North American cities, then going to church greatly reduces the probability of juvenile delinquency. But if it is in a city like those along the West Coast, where the majority do not belong to a church, then church attendance seems to have no influence on delinquency.

not cause people to refrain from delinquent behavior. We know a relationship is spurious if it disappears when some third variable is controlled. As a check, we tried many other measures of religiousness, including belief in heaven and hell, Sunday school attendance, and even parents' church attendance. None of these was correlated with delinquency either when sex differences were controlled.

Hirschi and I were astonished at these results. After all, we had set out to test something that everyone knew to be true. Recall that we had not even been sure the study was worth the time and trouble. In fact, had the data not already been available to us, we probably would not have bothered with it. However, what we found turned a lot of what everyone had believed about the world upside down . . . for a while.

After our findings were published (Hirschi and Stark, 1969), most sociologists accepted our results, and the paper was frequently cited and often reprinted. Within several years the

"knowledge" that religion fails to guide teenagers along the straight and narrow was enshrined in undergraduate textbooks. But then problems began to turn up as other researchers tried to *replicate* our research.

Conflicting results

Several years after our study was published, two other scholars replicated it with a sample of teenagers from several cities in the Pacific Northwest (Burkett and White, 1974). They too could find no religious effects on delinquency. While no one could explain why religion did not influence delinquency, it still seemed that it did not.

But then two more studies yielded very different results. The first, based on a sample of teenagers in Atlanta (Higgins and Albrecht, 1977), found a very strong negative correlation between church attendance and delinquency—exactly what Hirschi and I had expected to find. The second, based on teenagers living in six wards (congregations) of the Mormon Church (Albrecht, Chadwick, and Alcorn, 1977), found the same thing. That same year a paper on religion and drug use appeared in a Canadian journal (Linden and Currie, 1977). Based on a sample of teenagers in Calgary, it also reported very strong negative correlations—religious kids were much less likely to use illegal drugs. At this point a study that had gone unnoticed came to light (Rhodes and Reiss, 1970). Based on a sample of Nashville students, it also reported a substantial negative correlation between church attendance and delinquency.

Does religion inhibit delinquency or not? The research score stood at four to two—four studies said yes, while two said no. To shrug and say that sometimes religion does inhibit delinquency and sometimes not is not a satisfactory scientific response. When does religion have this effect, when doesn't it, and why? That was the pressing issue.

From Micro to Macro: Adjusting the Theory

As I assessed the published research studies, I saw that they did not hold the key to clearing up the confusion. Each study was well done. The data all seemed reliable and pertinent. Each analysis was careful and complete. It simply was true that sometimes the predicted results appeared and sometimes they didn't. So it was time to take seriously the final step in the sociological process—to reject or adjust the theory. But how?

One day the light dawned. I had been thinking only about individuals, about how the beliefs of the individual were supposed to shape behavior. But I should have been thinking about groups and about how religious culture is sustained through interaction. Put another way, I began to see that religion is not primarily an individual characteristic, a set of beliefs and practices of particular persons, but that it is first and fore-

most a social structure. What counts is not only *whether* a person is religious but also the *proportion* of religious people in their environment.

Teenagers form and sustain their interpretations of norms in day-to-day interaction with their friends. If most of a young person's friends are not actively religious, then religious considerations will rarely enter into the process by which norms are accepted or justified. Even if the religious teenager does bring up religious considerations, these will not strike a responsive chord in most of the others. This is not to suggest that nonreligious teenagers don't believe in the norms or discuss right and wrong but that they will do so without recourse to religious justifications. In such a situation, the effect of the religiousness of some individuals will be smothered by group indifference to religion, and religion will tend to become a very compartmentalized component of the individual's life—something that surfaces only in specific situations such as Sunday school and church. In contrast, when the majority of a teenager's friends are religious, then religion enters freely into everyday interactions and becomes a valid part of the normative system.

From these ideas I reformulated the theory to include an element of social structure: *Religious individuals will be less likely than others to break the norms, but only in communities where the majority of people are actively religious.* The relevant hypothesis is that surveys done in communities and other social settings where most people belong to a church ought to find that teenagers active in religion are less delinquent than others. In contrast, studies done where most people do not belong to a church should find no correlation between religion and delinquency. With this hypothesis in mind, I once more examined the published studies.

As a result of other research, I already knew a great deal about the religious geography of the United States and Canada. The most striking feature is a remarkable "unchurched belt" running along the shores of the Pacific. Beginning at the Mexican border it stretches all the way through Alaska. California, Nevada, Oregon, Washington, British Columbia, the Yukon Territory, Alaska, and Hawaii have church membership rates far lower than those in the rest of

Canada or the United States. In most other states and provinces a substantial majority belongs to a church, but on the West Coast only about a third belong (see Chapter 14).

These geographic patterns strongly supported my macro explanation of the contradictory research. Hirschi and I had found no correlation in our data from California, and Burkett and White had found none in theirs from Washington and Oregon. But studies in Georgia, Utah, Tennessee, and Alberta had found strong correlations. So I began to seek further tests of this geographic effect.

Survey studies are very expensive, and they usually collect far more data than the initial researchers can use. For that reason, computer tapes containing the original data from a survey are usually placed in public archives. I searched such archives for surveys on delinquency that had included data on religion. I found one done in Provo, Utah, which has the highest church membership rate in the United States. If I was right, these data ought to show a strong negative correlation, and they did. Next, I gained access to a survey of high school students in Seattle, which has one of the lowest church membership rates in the nation. Here I expected no correlation to show up, and none did.

Finally, I was able to locate a huge national survey based on samples of 16-year-old boys at eighty-seven U.S. high schools. Rather than simply relying on the geographic location of these schools, I was able to assess the proportion of religious students in each. I then hypothesized that religion would be negatively correlated with delinquency in the schools where the majority of students were religious, but that no correlation would be found in those schools (nearly all of which were on the West Coast) where most students were not. And that's exactly what the data showed (Stark, Kent, and Doyle, 1982).

Thus we meet social structure. In Richmond, Seattle, and many other West Coast cities, apparently it did not matter that some parents raised their children to be religious—at least not when it came to keeping them out of trouble with the law. This was because the surrounding social structure, in this case the lack of an active religious affiliation of the majority,

overwhelmed the effects of religion on the individual. In most of the rest of North America, however, a religious upbringing does decrease delinquency among young people, because individual religiousness is reinforced by the surrounding religious majority. Thus the expected correlation between religiousness and delinquency that got "lost" for a while, when Hirschi and I failed to find it in California, turned out to be alive and well on the other side of the mountains. Once again we see why there must be macro as well as micro sociology: *Social structure is as real as personal traits, and when we fail to consider structural effects, we often can make no sense out of our research.*

Social Structures and Social Systems

Macro sociology is the study of larger social structures, and macro social theories attempt to explain the existence of social structures (how they arise and the causes of different kinds of structures), the relationships among social structures, and the interplay between the individual and social structures. While macro sociology has its own distinctive subject matter, it is not independent of micro sociology any more than micro sociology can ignore macro phenomena—as we have just seen. In fact, all macro theories include, either explicitly or implicitly, micro assumptions. For example, all macro theories assume that human beings operate on the basis of rational choice, or self-interest. For a specific example, when a macro theory generates the prediction that a rapid decline in the average standard of living in a society will produce political conflict, such a statement implies that people pursue rewards and try to avoid costs. When their rewards fall sharply, they get unhappy. Although there are several competing schools of macro sociological theory, they make similar assumptions about micro sociology. Moreover, these schools of thought also make many common assumptions about the fundamental features of social structures. For example, common to all schools of macro sociological theory is the assumption that the social structures in a society are connected, because societies are social systems.

Macro sociologists assume that societies are not chance collections of people, culture, and social structures—they assume instead that societies are systems. The idea of a **system**, whether we are discussing the solar system or a social system, has three important elements (von Bertalanffy, 1967). First, a system consists of a number of separate parts, or *structures*. The solar system, for example, primarily consists of the sun and nine planets. Second, these parts are *interdependent*, or connected, so that changes in one part produce changes in at least one other part. If one planet explodes, all the others will be affected. Third, because parts are interdependent, they tend to fall into some kind of *equilibrium*, or balance or steadiness, in their interrelations. No planet is free to fly off on its own path, for its connections (gravitational attractions) with other planets limit its actions. Let's examine how societies fulfill each of these elements of a system.

Social structures

Societies consist of innumerable structures such as sex ratios and religious composition. Here it is sufficient to note two social structures that are often treated in macro sociological theories: *institutions* and *classes*.

■ **Institutions** Sociologists recognize that social roles, groups, and activities are not randomly arranged within societies, but tend to be clustered. Moreover, each of these clusters makes fairly specific contributions to the overall welfare of a society by satisfying basic needs the society requires to exist. For example, children must be born and prepared to replace adults, or else the group will die out. Arrangements must also exist to produce and distribute goods and services among members of a society; without food, shelter, and clothing, humans cannot live.

Relatively permanent patterns, or clusters, of specialized roles, groups, organizations, customs, and activities devoted to meeting fundamental social needs are called **social insti-**

tutions. From examining many societies, both primitive and modern, sociologists have concluded that at least five basic social institutions exist in all societies: the family, the economy, religion, the political order, and education (see Figure 4-3). Part Four discusses each of these institutions in detail.

Many macro theories use institutions as basic elements of social structure and attempt to relate one institution to another. For example, because the Protestant Reformation and the rise of industrial capitalism both occurred in Europe during the sixteenth century, there has been a long theoretical debate over which might have been the cause of the other (see Chapter 17). That is, did changes in religious institutions cause changes in economic institutions, or vice versa? Indeed, a third school of thought holds that neither caused the other, but that both changed because of changes in the political institutions.

■ **Classes** Every known society has been *stratified*. That is, some members have had more power, property, and prestige than others. *Classes* are another major element of social structure, for, as we saw in Chapter 2, classes are groups of people having a similar position within a society's stratification system. (In Chapter 9, we shall expand this definition of classes and assess disputes about how to conceptualize stratification systems.) To explain how a society operates, macro sociologists often examine relationships among its various classes, arguing that *conflicts* among classes can cause crises in a society and be an important source of change (see Figure 4-4). For example, class conflict can erupt into revolutions.

Institutions and classes are major concepts in most macro sociological theories. Many theories focus on the interplay between these social structures—for example, on how class interests shape the structure of a society's institutions.

Interdependence among structures

Because societies are systems, the various social structures are connected; consequently, a change in one structure produces changes in some other

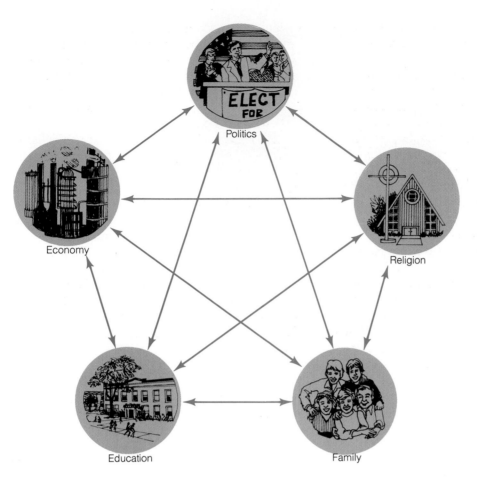

Figure 4-3 ■ **Society as a system of institutions.** To discover why and how one social institution influences another is a major activity among macro sociologists. Will changes in family structure prompt religious or economic changes? Part Four of this book is devoted to the study of institutions.

structures. If you have a number of tiny parts spread out on a workbench—say, small gear wheels, springs, and screws—moving one part has no effect on the remaining parts. But if these parts are assembled into a watch and thus become a system, then the movement of one part affects at least several other parts, and the overall state of the system changes.

Macro sociologists work from the assumption that societies resemble watches more than an array of disassembled watch parts. As noted earlier, they seek to explain why and how various social structures show **interdependence**. They do not, however, assume that every structure is related to every other structure, nor do they assume that the same degree of interdependence among structures exists in all societies. In fact, as we shall see in Chapter 17, sometimes so little connection exists among social structures that a society falls apart.

Equilibrium and change

The interdependence among structures of a social system necessarily limits the possible variation in any given structure. If we continue our mechanical analogy, a given social structure can be pulled only so far before its connections with other structures begin to limit fur-

Figure 4-4 ■ **Society as a system of classes.** Imagine how different are the lives led by people living in these houses and you will begin to understand why so many sociologists think that class conflicts play the primary role in shaping societies. Part Three of this book is devoted to conflict and inequality.

ther pulling. Such mutually limiting connections among social structures mean that the overall system tends toward a state of balance, or **equilibrium**. That is, the free movement of structures is limited by their connections with other structures. However, societies are never wholly static. Even those with the greatest equilibrium fluctuate constantly as their parts shift to remain in general alignment. This occurs, if for no other reason, because societies are *open systems*. Just as they are composed of living organisms who must interact with the physical environment, societies also constantly react to outside forces.

There is nothing magical or mysterious about the notion that systems, including social systems, tend toward equilibrium. If we bend a cogwheel in a watch, the watch will no longer keep time. Likewise, not just any arrangement of the parts of a society will suffice to keep that society going. Societies can fall apart when their fundamental structures fail to be compatible. Equilibrium reflects the tendency for social structures to remain mutually compatible—not

only when they are standing still but also when they are *changing*. In Chapter 17 we shall pursue this in much greater detail and see that periods of rapid social change are often dangerous times for societies because of the risk of structural misalignment and malfunction.

■

Macro Sociological Theories

Keeping in mind how characteristics of systems shape and delimit what goes on within them, let's now examine how macro sociologists attempt to explain how social structures arise, how they fit together, and how they change. Macro sociological theories come in three major forms: functionalist, social evolutionary, and conflict. Although some sociologists regard the disputes among these three theoretical approaches as so basic that one must choose sides, I tend to regard them more as complementary than as conflicting; each helps solve some problems better than the others.

Functionalism

Because societies are open systems—systems that exchange with their environments—it proves useful to explain social structures on the basis of their consequences, or functions for other parts of the system, especially as these parts come under pressure from the environment. Theories taking this form are called **functionalist theories**, and the school of macro sociology that favors them is called **functionalism**.

Functional theories are common throughout science. Sociologists adopted functionalism from biology, so let's start with a simple biological example to clarify the logical structure of functional theories. Why do we have sweat glands? Biologists answer that humans have sweat glands (a physiological structure of that system called the human body) because of their function, namely, to prevent the body temperature from rising too high for our organs to survive. Such a cooling mechanism is needed because the human environment is often warm enough to endanger the organism. When the environment causes a person to overheat, the sweat glands release water stored in the body. The evaporation of this water on the surface of the body causes cooling. By explaining sweat glands in this way, biologists display the basic elements of all functionalist theories.

According to Arthur Stinchcombe (1968), functionalist theories have three components. First, there is the *part of the system* to be explained. In our example, this is the sweat glands. Second, we explain the existence of this part by identifying how it *preserves* some other part of the system from disruption or overload. In our example, sweat glands prevent other organs of the body from being damaged by high temperatures. Third, the theory must identify the *source* of this potential disruption or overload. In our example, this is identified as high temperatures in the environment.

Now let's apply these principles to a socio-logical example. When we examine primitive societies, we frequently find that the family unit is defined differently from the family in modern societies. While most North Americans grow up in a **nuclear family** (one adult couple and their children), primitive societies often have **extended families**, which include several adult couples and their children. For example, in many societies the sons remain at home; when they marry, they bring their wives home rather than set up a new household.

Suppose we want to explain why the extended family is common among primitive societies. According to functionalism, we must see what contribution or "function" the extended family makes to some other part of such societies. Looking closely, we see that in such societies the family serves to support dependents, be they young, handicapped, ill, or elderly. To do this, the family must always include an adequate number of able-bodied adults. That is, there must be enough family members to support dependents.

However, under the conditions of life in many primitive societies, the death rate is so high that it constantly threatens the capacity of the family to support dependents. So many adults die while still young that if other adults were not on hand to assume their responsibilities, many dependents could not be supported. The extended family, by clustering adult couples into a single unit, minimizes the impact of this source of disruption (Figure 4-5). When a man dies, other men in the family remain to feed and shelter his widow and children; when a woman dies, other adult women remain to raise her children and cook for her widower. The extended family substitutes for welfare programs, retirement plans, and insurance policies; these latter programs identify functional alternatives.

Although functional theories attempt to explain social structures by describing their contributions to the system, functionalists do not assume that only one structural form can fulfill a particular function. For example, while all mammals die if they become too warm, many mammals, including dogs, do not have sweat glands. Instead of sweating when they get hot, dogs hang out their tongues and pant. The evaporation of water from their large tongues cools

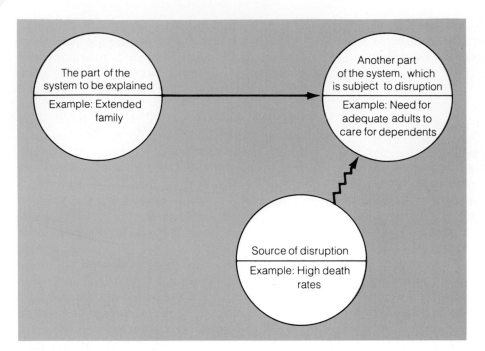

Figure 4-5 ■ **Diagram of a functional theory.** Functional theories explain why a given part of any system exists by showing how it prevents some other system part from being disrupted. In this example the extended family is explained as a social structure designed to provide an adequate number of able-bodied adults within families to support dependent family members. Here the source of disruption is a high death rate in preindustrial societies where extended families are common. High death rates threaten the capacity of smaller families to provide for their dependents.
(Adapted from Stinchcombe, 1968.)

the air as they inhale to keep their body temperature within tolerable limits. This is a **functional alternative** to the sweat gland—another structure by which the same function can be accomplished. By the same token, modern societies have released the family from having sole responsibility for supporting dependents by creating welfare programs. In this way the extended family has been replaced.

Nor do functional theories propose that all social structures have beneficial effects for social systems. Indeed, such theories often identify *dysfunctions*, arrangements among structures that harm or distort the system. Nor do functionalist theories assume that all social systems *ought* to survive. In discussing the survival of societies, we raise the fundamental

subject matter of the second major form of macro sociological theories: social evolution.

Social evolution

Functional theories imply evolution. Thus, they do not directly answer the question of how social structures developed. For example, explaining how sweat glands or extended families make vital contributions to other parts of their systems does not tell us how they got there in the first place. Biologists use the principle of natural selection to explain the origins of sweat glands. They argue that animals with more efficient cooling mechanisms are more likely to survive and reproduce than are animals with less efficient cooling mechanisms. Thus, biologists rely on evolutionary theories to explain the origins of sweat glands while relying on functional theories to explain why sweat glands are an advantage for survival.

Functional theories in sociology imply an evolutionary mechanism to explain the origins of structures just as functional theories in biology do. **Social evolutionary theories** suggest that societies with structures that enable them to adapt to their physical and social environments have a better chance of survival than do societies that fail to develop such structures. Because of this selective process, certain highly adaptive social structures tend to exist in societies. For example, many primitive societies may have failed to solve the problem of sustaining dependents in the face of high death rates by failing to develop the extended family or some comparable structure. Perhaps the lack of such societies simply reflects their failure to survive.

The implicit evolutionary assumptions of functionalism have led a number of contemporary macro sociologists to construct theories about the evolution of human societies. In so doing, however, they have been careful not to simply apply biological theories of human evolution directly to explain social structure. This was a tragic failure in late nineteenth-century theories of social evolution, and the needless and objectionable substitution of biology for sociology caused sociologists to avoid the topic of social evolution for several generations.

Late in the nineteenth century, social evolutionists attributed cultural differences among societies to genetic differences in their populations. Thus, if one society had advanced technology while another relied on stone axes and digging sticks, then the persons in the advanced society were considered to be more highly evolved. Such conclusions provided justification for extreme racist policies. However, as we shall see in Chapter 17, these conclusions are disproven by the actual patterns of cultural development and change throughout history.

A second faulty assumption nineteenth-century social evolutionists made was that social change is inevitable and *progressive*—that societies always change in beneficial ways. This view was so obviously incompatible with the historical record that it caused theories of social evolution to fall into disrepute. As Gerhard Lenski (1976) put it:

Not every society has grown in size and complexity. . . . Some have remained hunters and gatherers or horticulturists [simple gardeners] down to the present day. Some societies have even regressed from levels they achieved at an earlier time.

Evolutionary theories need not assume that all societies always evolve toward more complex cultures. Also, evolutionary theories are not meant to apply to specific cases. Instead, they apply to the population of cases. For example, no biologist believes that any *one* horse evolves. Rather, they believe that because of selection for adaptive traits, the *species* of horses changes over time. By the same token, modern social evolutionists do not apply their theories to one particular society, but to all societies. Nor do modern social evolutionists assume that the direction of change is necessarily good or beneficial. Good and bad are moral, not scientific, judgments. Instead, modern social evolutionists propose that since the dawn of human history, societies have tended to become larger, to accumulate more effective technology, to become more efficient at producing food, to become more complex (in the sense of having more specialized occupations and organizations), to become more urban, and to become more powerful.

The evidence supporting these long-term trends is persuasive. Archeology reveals that the pace of change was extremely slow during the first several million years of human existence. Nevertheless, later human societies tended to be larger, more complex, and more technologically powerful than earlier societies (Lenski, 1976).

History reveals a similar pattern of social evolution. Of course, Rome fell—as have other civilizations. But the long-term trends are not obscured by the many bumps in the road of human history. Indeed, we have recently determined that the belief that Western society was ignorant and backward after the fall of Rome is much exaggerated. Instead, technological progress continued throughout the so-called Dark

Ages, as medieval societies discovered or perfected much important technology unknown to the Romans (White, 1963).

Social evolutionary theories in macro sociology explain these long-range trends by referring to the pressures that the environment places on human societies. These pressures favor the survival of societies that have found the means to become larger, more complex, and more technologically advanced. Environmental pressures can result from nature. For example, if the climate turns cold, societies having shelter, fire, and clothing are more likely to survive.

Environmental pressures can also come from other societies. A society with a large number of warriors equipped with better weapons will be able to seize the resources of fewer, less sophisticated neighbors. The competition for survival results in winners and losers, and hence societies will evolve in the direction of winning characteristics. In later chapters we shall examine some specific theories about the evolution of societies.

Conflict theories

A third school of macro sociological theory focuses on the conflicts that occur within societies and how these in turn shape social structures. Where functionalists ask how a structure serves other structures in a social system and evolutionists seek the survival benefits of a particular structure, **conflict theorists** ask how social structure serves the interests of various competing groups within a society.

Karl Marx (1818–1883) was an early conflict theorist. He argued that social structures were created by the most powerful members of a society, the ruling class. He wrote that "the ruling ideas of any age are the ideas of its ruling class." He further argued that the ruling class constructs social structures that best serve its own interests and, conversely, that the social structure determines who will be the ruling class. Thus Marx traced the origins of social structures to class conflicts.

As we shall see in Chapter 17, Marx was also an early social evolutionist who believed that class conflicts within societies are the cause of social evolution. He argued that communist societies (which he believed would not possess a ruling class) were the inevitable outcome of social evolution, since they would not have internal class conflicts.

Many modern macro sociologists seek to explain social structures by referring to conflicts within societies, but most do not limit their attention to conflicts among different classes. Taking a very broad view of possible conflicts, they follow the lead of a great German sociologist, Max Weber (1864–1920). Weber argued that while class conflicts are an important social influence, there are many other causes of group conflicts. For example, groups often form to pursue common aims on the basis of a great variety of cultural interests or identities (Hechter, 1978). Weber called these groups "status groups."

An ethnic group is a good example of a status group. Persons of different classes may find a common purpose and unity in their shared cultural heritage (such as a common language or shared customs), which in turn may bring this group into conflict with other ethnic groups. The present dispute between French- and English-speaking Canadians is the kind of internal conflict that can shape social structure. The conflict between Canadian ethnic groups has produced substantial changes in many parts of Canadian society.

Conflict theories, then, are concerned with the distribution of power in societies and how various interest groups (including classes) seek and gain power and use their power to shape social structures. From this perspective, any society at any given moment is the result of past compromises and power struggles (Dahrendorf, 1959; Habermas, 1975). These conflicts arise from such things as class, race, region, ethnicity, religion, occupation, age, and gender; and they supply the energy and motivation for constructing and maintaining social structures.

In the remainder of this book, we shall encounter many macro sociological theories of each major school. Often they disagree, but in my judgment each tells us something important that the others don't. The most powerful and comprehensive macro theories often contain elements from all three schools.

Later in this chapter, we shall look over the shoulder of a macro sociologist as he derives an important hypothesis and then tests it through research. We shall see just such a blending of the three schools of macro theory. We shall also see that good macro theories rest upon micro theories.

Comparative Research

Micro sociological research is usually based on individuals. As you will recall from Chapter 3, Ofshe's experiment was based on comparisons of students who took part in his study. Lofland and I studied conversion to the Unification Church by observing which individuals did or did not join. And in this chapter you have seen that Hirschi and I initially studied religion and delinquency by comparing students in Richmond, California. But when I wanted to see if social structure influenced the religion-delinquency relationship, I could no longer compare only individuals: I had to compare cities and high schools.

Individuals don't have social structures. They live *within* social structures, since these are the properties of groups. So macro sociological research always must be based on comparisons among groups, which is why it is known as **comparative research**. Put another way, comparative research always involves aggregate units—the "things" it compares always include more than one person. Sometimes comparative research involves small groups such as college sororities or professional basketball teams. More often, larger aggregates such as cities or counties are involved. And, in recent years, a growing body of research has been based on comparisons among whole societies.

However, even when macro research is based on whole societies, the logic of the comparative research is the same as that for research based on individuals. Correlation is demonstrated by separating societies according to the independent variable and then comparing them with respect to the dependent variable. Time order must be dealt with by showing that changes in the independent variable occurred before the

changes in the dependent variable. Finally, the possibility that something other than the independent variable is causing the correlation must be addressed by controls for spuriousness. Let's watch a good macro sociologist at work.

Jeffery Paige: violent and peaceful primitives

 In early 1988 an anthropologist reported in *Science* the latest results of many years of research among the Yanomamö Indians, who live in the remote tropical rain forests along the border between Brazil and Venezuela. When he first arrived among the Yanomamö, Napoleon Chagnon (1988) of the University of California, Santa Barbara, was impressed by their simple life-style and their carefully tended gardens. But as he continued his field observations, he began to learn of murders and to realize that the Yanomamö were much less peaceful than they appeared to be. Revenge killings are frequent among the Yanomamö, although Chagnon himself never saw one during any of his thirteen field trips over a twenty-three-year period. Most killings occur in raids by a male kin group from one village during which they ambush and kill one or two males from another village. The raids usually are made in retaliation for an earlier killing—chains of revenge that often span many years.

But even though Chagnon knew that such events often took place, he was unprepared for the bloody reality that began to emerge when, in recent years, he reconstructed a complete genealogy for each of twelve Yanomamö villages. Finally, twenty-three years after he began his field observations, Chagnon published these major statistical results:

1. Nearly 70 percent of adults over the age of 40 have had at least one close relative—parent, spouse, sibling, or child—killed by other Yanomamö.
2. More than 30 percent of all male deaths were due to violence.
3. Nearly half of males over 25 have taken part in a killing.

What events initiated a series of revenge killings? Almost always a conflict over women: infidelity, seduction, kidnapping of brides, and the like. For the Yanomamö, as do many societies, have a severe shortage of women—in some villages there are 130 men for every 100 women. This occurs because the Yanomamö and most other premodern societies practice female infanticide. In Chapter 12 we shall explore the whole syndrome of high male sex ratios caused by killing many females at birth. Here our concern is with violence in general.

Chagnon's findings add to a growing awareness among social scientists that extraordinary violence often lurks beneath the peaceful appearance of primitive groups. However, *some* primitive groups are as peaceful and nonviolent as they appear. In fact, social scientists now tend to classify primitive societies into two basic types: *factional* and *communal* (Swanson, 1968, 1969). The basis for this classification rests on patterns of decision making within the group. In *factional* societies such as the Yanomamö, groups or factions within the society pursue their own interests at one another's expense. In consequence, levels of conflict and competition within the society are high and frequently erupt in violence. In *communal* societies such as the Navaho Indians of the American southwest, factional disputes and conflicts are regarded as improper, and elaborate processes of deliberation are used to delay decisions until general agreement can be reached. Having avoided conflicts, these societies also minimize violence within the group.

Social scientists have been aware of these contrasts for a long time. And they have frequently wondered why? Why are some primitive groups communal and peaceful while others are factional and violent?

Then a sociologist had a very clever idea. While in graduate school at the University of Michigan, Jeffery Paige had been carefully introduced to the central premise of conflict theories that social structures are shaped by conflicts among groups within societies. But later, as he pondered the variations in the levels of conflict within primitive societies, he suddenly realized that *social structures can, in turn, shape internal conflicts*. Conflicts within these

societies tend to occur between factions or cliques—subgroups having a high level of attachments with the subgroup and few and weak attachments across subgroups (see Chapter 1). So the critical question is what causes factions to form? Why do some societies seem relatively immune to factionalism, while in others factions flourish? Paige believed the answer must lie in differences in their social structures. Moreover, he thought he knew *which* social structures were involved.

Paige began with two key concepts that identify the two primary bases for factionalism in primitive societies. The first is *kinship*, ties based on family relationships. The second is *residence*, the composition of households. The first two steps in his theory link each of these concepts to the concept of faction: (1) *Factions in primitive societies will form along divisions based on kinship*, and (2) *factions in primitive societies will form along divisions based on residence*.

The reasoning behind these steps in Paige's theory is simple. Family members will interact more often with one another than with outsiders, hence attachments within families will be stronger than attachments between families. Residents of the same household will interact more often with one another than with residents of other households, hence attachments will be stronger within households than between them.

The third step in Paige's theory identifies males as the primary participants in violence: (3) *In primitive societies, violence primarily occurs between male factions*. Finally, he was ready to lay out the truly significant step in his theory: (4) *Primitive societies will tend to lack factions and to have little violence when kinsmen do not share common residence*.

Paige's fourth step reflects variations in rules of residence—the norms about who lives with whom. In some primitive societies, the bride leaves home after marriage, and the couple take up residence with or close to the husband's family. This is called the **patrilocal rule of residence**. In such societies, male kin live in close proximity. A man's male neighbors are primarily his father, uncles, brothers, and sons. This maximizes interaction among males who are already united by ties of kinship. It also minimizes a man's interaction with males who are not his relatives. In such societies, kinship and residence structures coincide and are mutually supportive.

However, some primitive societies observe a **matrilocal rule of residence**, and newlyweds reside with or near the bride's family. Consequently, male kin in matrilocal societies are scattered and lack day-to-day interaction. After marriage, males interact mostly with males who are not their relatives. Therefore, their tendencies to form factions with their kinsmen would bring them into conflict with the men with whom they live, while residential factions would force men to oppose their closest relatives.

Finally, Paige was ready to formulate a hypothesis: *Matrilocal societies will be low in factions and violence, while patrilocal societies will be high on measures of each.*

His next steps were to collect appropriate observations and then to see if they supported or contradicted his hypothesis. Because Paige's theory is about societies, not about individuals, his research was based on the comparative method. What he needed to observe were overall features of primitive societies. So Paige selected a sample of primitive societies, ten with patrilocal residence and ten with matrilocal residence. Then he examined the amount of factionalism and violence within each. Of the ten patrilocal societies, eight were high on both measures. Of the ten matrilocal societies, only one was high on factions and violence. Thus Paige found a very strong correlation between rules of residence and levels of conflict, just as hypothesized. But to argue that the former actually causes the latter, Paige also needed to demonstrate the correct time order: to show that rules of residence occurred first and that current levels of factionalism and violence followed. It would be plausible to argue that violence causes patrilocal rules of residence because families want to keep the men at home to protect them. Unfortunately, Paige could not assess time order because the necessary data were not available.

He drew his sample of societies and the information on each from an extraordinary work called the *Ethnographic Atlas*, created by George P. Murdock (1967b) and his colleagues. The *Atlas* contains comparable information on hundreds of primitive societies. These data have been taken from field studies conducted by generations of anthropologists. Unfortunately, most of these societies existed long before anthropologists studied them. Consequently, it was impossible to determine time order on residence and conflict—both had been established long before the studies.

However, because contemporary research shows that interaction produces attachments and that anything that impedes interaction tends to encourage the formation of factions, most sociologists find the time order proposed by Paige to be persuasive.

Spuriousness could also invalidate Paige's findings. Although he selected two groups of societies on the basis of their matrilocal or patrilocal rules of residence, he could not, of course, randomly assign societies to have one rule or the other. Hence, some other factor might be the real cause of the correlation Paige observed. Could patrilocal rules of residence simply reflect the dominance of males and of male values in these societies and thus account for the higher levels of factionalism and fighting? For lack of adequate measures available in the *Ethnographic Atlas*, Paige could not test this alternative or others.

Clearly, then, Paige's research did not fully meet the criteria of causation. When forced by their theories to rely on nonexperimental research procedures, sociologists often must settle for somewhat iffy results. Nevertheless, this study rests on two powerful additional supports. First, by using differential levels of attachments as the basic micro element in his theory, Paige relied on a theory that has generated thousands of hypotheses that have stood up to very stringent tests—as we saw in Chapter 3. Whatever limits apply to his research methods seem of little importance here. The second source of strong support for his theory is something we have not mentioned before: the *force of logic*. It is virtually self-evident that attachments would be greatly shaped by residence and kinship in the manner Paige proposes, for how could these factors *not* have great impact on patterns of interaction?

Keeping in mind that scientific theories never can be proved and that all scientists must try to disprove their theories, we still can admit that some theories seem so silly it is hardly worth disproving them (eating meat causes people to be political conservatives, for example), while others seem so self-evident that it is hard to imagine them being invalid. Many social scientists would agree that Paige showed great insight in constructing his theory, but would also suggest that once these connections have been pointed out they are obvious. Keep in mind too, that for all the problems Hirschi and I caused when we were thought to have proved an obvious theory to be wrong, that's not really what happened. Religion *does* influence conformity to the norms; it just doesn't do it in as simple a way as had been supposed. In time we may discover that Paige's theory also needs some adjustment, but it seems unlikely that it ever will need to be rejected.

■

Conclusion

In this chapter we studied social structure and saw that there is much more to human behavior than individual psychology. People act to gain rewards and to avoid costs, but social structures often determine what rewards are available and how they can be gained, thereby placing a powerful matrix upon human behavior. Thus, although attachments encourage conformity to norms, social structures can determine to whom we become attached and to whose norms we will conform.

We also examined the fundamental elements of three major schools of macro sociological theory and saw that all three work from

■ This rare photograph taken from above a valley in New Guinea shows a battle among primitive warriors armed with spears. Sometimes such battles occur between societies competing for resources, but often they erupt between factions within a single society. Paige's research showed that the degree of internal conflict in primitive societies was highly correlated with their rules of residence.

the assumption that societies are systems. We looked at the elements of systems and of societies as social systems. Finally, we watched a macro sociologist blend elements of these schools of macro theory with a fundamental premise of micro theory to formulate a hypothesis about why different societies have different amounts of internal factionalism and violence. We watched him test this hypothesis using whole societies as the units of analysis.

Thus we have concluded the preliminaries. We have identified key sociological concepts and elements of sociological theories and examined principles of sociological research. Now it is time to see how well sociologists have applied their theories to many major topics and what they have learned from their research.

Review Glossary

social structure Any characteristic of a group, rather than of an individual. (p. 90)

survey research (also called public opinion polling) A common form of sociological research based on interviews of or questionnaires from a sample of a population. (p. 92)

system Any set of interdependent parts. (p. 98)

social institutions Relatively permanent patterns or clusters of specialized roles, groups, organizations, customs, and activities devoted to meeting fundamental social needs. Five major social institutions are the family, economy, religion, political order, and education. (p. 98)

interdependence A relationship among parts of a system such that if one part changes, at least one other part is affected. (p. 99)

equilibrium A state of balance among interdependent parts of a system. (p. 100)

functionalist theories, functionalism Theories that attempt to explain some part of a system by showing its consequences for some other part of the system. These consequences are called *functions*; for example, the function of the sweat gland is to keep organisms from overheating. (p. 101)

nuclear family A family group containing one adult couple and their children. (p. 101)

extended families Those families containing more than one adult couple. (p. 101)

functional alternative The existence of more than one system structure that satisfies the same system need. (p. 102)

social evolutionary theories Theories that account for the existence of a social structure on the basis of its survival benefits for societies. For example, technologically superior societies will be better able to withstand environmental challenges; hence, societies will evolve toward increased technological capacity. (p. 103)

conflict theories Marxist conflict theories seek to explain all social arrangements as the result of class conflicts, especially the capacity of the "ruling class" to impose its interests on the whole society. Non-Marxist conflict theories examine a much wider range of conflicts within societies (for example, between groups divided by language, race, culture, and even region) and seek to show how competing groups use their power to shape favorable social structures. (p. 104)

comparative research In a sense, all forms of research are comparative, since they involve comparing individuals or groups, but sociologists use this term for all research involving comparisons of aggregate units, from small groups to whole societies. (p. 105)

patrilocal rule of residence A situation in which married couples live with or near the man's family. (p. 106)

matrilocal rule of residence A situation in which married couples live with or near the woman's family. (p. 107)

Suggested Readings

Babbie, Earl R. 1986. *The Practice of Social Research*, 4th ed. Belmont, Calif.: Wadsworth.

Blau, Peter M. 1977. *Inequality and Heterogeneity: A Primitive Theory of Social Structure*. New York: Free Press.

Boulding, Kenneth E. 1970. *A Primer on Social Dynamics*. New York: Free Press.

Harris, Marvin. 1979. *Cultural Materialism: The Struggle for a Science of Culture*. New York: Random House.

Stinchcombe, Arthur L. 1968. *Constructing Social Theories*. New York: Harcourt Brace Jovanovich.

Correlation and Sampling

The first pages of Chapter 1 recounted the birth of the moral statistics movement. In France, André Michel Guerry began to create maps showing crime and suicide rates for each department. Figure 1-1 on page 3 shows the map Guerry created for suicide rates based on the years 1827 to 1830 and compares it with a map of the same rates for 1856 to 1860. By examining the maps we can note how little the geography of suicide had changed during those years. The department in which Paris is located was highest both times and Corsica was lowest.

What that indicates is that the suicide rates in France were *correlated*—that variations across departments in one era closely matched variations in the rates thirty years later.

The moral statisticians used maps to show correlations because the only alternative was to list numbers. As Guerry himself noted, "The shadings of our maps strongly accentuate proportions relative to geographic position that might otherwise have gone unnoticed in long lists of numbers" (Stark and Reinking, forthcoming). Guerry was right. A glance at his map of suicide is enough for anyone familiar with the geography of France to spot the immense impact of urbanism and industry. In contrast, one would need to spend a lot of time reading a list of the eighty-six departments of France in 1830, noting the suicide rate of each, while trying to construct a mental pattern of them.

Figure ST1-1 displays two maps of the city of Chicago, probably the most-studied city in the Western hemisphere. Recall that the first major department of sociology developed at the University of Chicago. And these early sociol-

ogists at the University of Chicago popularized the use of methods like Guerry's in American sociology. Over the years an immense number of books and articles have used Chicago data.

These maps are based on seventy-six Community Areas of the city. The first shows the delinquency rate—the number of juvenile residents of each area referred to court during the year per 1,000 residents age 10 through 17. Basing the rate only on the teenage population takes into account that some areas have relatively more teenagers. The second map shows the percent of employed residents from each area who ride to work on public transportation. This is an excellent measure of the degree to which an area is part of the center city. More people depend upon public transportation the closer they live to the center of the city, for that's where public transportation is more plentiful, where traffic is more congested, and parking more expensive and difficult to find.

Below each map, the same information is presented as a list in which the areas are ranked from low to high. It is much easier to see that delinquency rates tend to show the same pattern as use of public transportation—that both are higher in the city center—by comparing the maps than it is to reach this conclusion from comparing the lists. So for decades this is exactly what the moral statisticians and early sociologists did. When they wanted to demonstrate a correlation between two rates, they provided readers with a map of each and pointed to how similar they were. Or to show a lack of correlation, they would point out that the maps were unlike. As a result, their books and scholarly

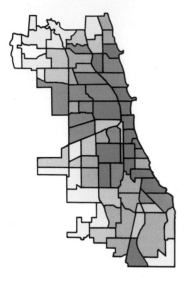

1980: Juveniles Referred to Court per 1,000 Age 10–17

Norwood Park	6.5
Edison Park	7.1
Beverly	7.5
Montclare	8.8
Forest Glen	9.1
Mount Greenwood	9.2
Clearing	9.7
West Lawn	11.0
Jefferson Park	11.1
Archer Heights	11.8
Ashburn	12.7
Dunning	13.3
Hegewisch	14.2
West Ridge	15.0

Pullman	15.4
Belmont Cragin	17.2
Morgan Park	17.4
West Elsdon	17.6
Calumet Heights	18.9
Garfield Ridge	19.1
North Park	19.2
East Side	19.7
Lower West Side	20.3
Portage Park	20.4
Burnside	23.9
Armour Square	27.8
Lincoln Square	28.6
Auburn Gresham	28.8
Brighton Park	29.0

Washington Heights	29.2
South Deering	30.8
Chicago Lawn	32.1
Irving Park	32.5
West Garfield Park	33.1
West Pullman	33.3
Hyde Park	33.5
Roseland	33.8
Hermosa	34.4
Avondale	36.0
Rogers Park	38.2
Edgewater	38.3
Chatham	38.5
Gage Park	40.0
McKinley Park	40.1
Greater Grand Crossing	40.2

Austin	40.8
South Lawndale	41.4
Kenwood	41.9
Albany Park	43.6
Lincoln Park	44.4
South Chicago	44.6
West Town	45.1
Avalon Park	45.9
Humboldt Park	46.1
Englewood	46.2
North Lawndale	46.5
Lakeview	46.5
Bridgeport	46.8
Logan Square	50.9
East Garfield Park	52.0

Near South Side	53.9
West Englewood	54.4
New City	54.9
Fuller Park	56.1
South Shore	60.1
Woodlawn	62.1
North Center	66.5
Near West Side	67.7
Riverdale	69.4
Oakland	71.5
Douglas	79.6
Near North Side	83.7
Uptown	90.5
Loop	102.0
Grand Boulevard	109.3
Washington Park	114.3

Figure ST1-1 ■ **Using maps to study Chicago.** These maps depict the seventy-six "community areas" making up the city of Chicago. The map on the left shows the delinquency rate. The map on the right shows the percent of the employed residents of each area who use public transportation to go to work. No data were available for the O'Hare Community Area, which is located around the famous O'Hare Airport and has only a small population. *Source*: ShowCase Presentational Software: Chicago (Seattle: Cognitive Development, Inc., 1987).

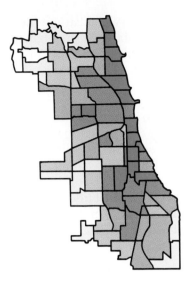

**1980: Percent of Workers Who Commute via
Public Transportation**

Mount	
Greenwood	15.8
Ashburn	15.9
Clearing	17.0
East Side	17.4
Hegewisch	18.9
West Lawn	19.3
Forest Glen	19.5
Edison Park	19.7
Norwood Park	19.8
Dunning	20.2
Montclare	20.7
West Elsdon	21.6
North Park	22.1
Gage Park	22.3

Hermosa	23.3
Calumet Heights	23.5
Chicago Lawn	23.7
Beverly	23.7
Garfield Ridge	24.2
Morgan Park	24.6
Belmont Cragin	24.8
West Ridge	25.2
Armour Square	25.4
Portage Park	25.5
Archer Heights	26.2
Jefferson Park	26.2
South Lawndale	26.4
Irving Park	28.1
New City	28.4
West Pullman	28.7

Washington	
Heights	28.8
Brighton Park	29.0
South Deering	29.2
Hyde Park	29.3
Pullman	29.4
Humboldt Park	29.5
Albany Park	29.8
Riverdale	30.0
North Center	30.1
Avalon Park	30.9
Lower West Side	31.0
South Chicago	31.1
Austin	31.1
Bridgeport	31.3
Lincoln Square	31.8

McKinley Park	32.2
Roseland	32.4
Loop	32.9
Avondale	33.3
Logan Square	33.4
Near West Side	33.9
West Town	34.3
West Garfield	
Park	34.5
Auburn	
Gresham	34.8
North	
Lawndale	35.0
Burnside	36.3
Chatham	38.5
Kenwood	38.6
West	
Englewood	38.7
South Shore	38.7
Greater Grand	
Crossing	39.5

Near North	
Side	40.4
Douglas	40.6
Uptown	41.5
East Garfield	
Park	41.5
Edgewater	43.6
Woodlawn	44.0
Lincoln Park	44.4
Fuller Park	44.6
Englewood	45.2
Rogers Park	45.3
Oakland	49.0
Lakeview	49.4
Near South	
Side	52.6
Washington	
Park	53.3
Grand	
Boulevard	54.7

journals are filled with beautifully printed maps.

However beautiful, maps have shortcomings for revealing correlations. It is easy to look at these maps of Chicago and note the similarity. But, what if, instead of a map based on seventy-six neighborhoods, we needed to compare two Chicago maps based on hundreds of census tracts? That could be very difficult. Again, it is easy enough to compare two maps of the United States based on the fifty states, but it can be very hard to grasp the similarities or differences of two U.S. maps based on all 3,142 counties. Moreover, it is easy to determine that two maps are very similar but more difficult to say whether they are somewhat similar or not very similar. So it was a matter of great importance when, in the 1890s, a British scientist named Karl Pearson discovered a way to compare maps or lists of data. His method is very simple and easy to demonstrate.

To see what he did, we can draw a line across the bottom of a piece of paper. This line represents the Chicago map of the percent using public transportation. So, at one end of the line we will write 15.8, which indicates the area with the lowest rate, Mount Greenwood. At the other end of the line we will write 54.7, the rate for the highest area, Grand Boulevard.

```
15.8                        54.7
```

Next we will draw a vertical line from the left end of the horizontal line up the left side of the paper. This line represents the map of delinquency. To the left of the lowest point on this

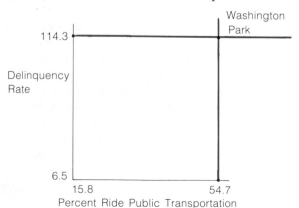

line we will write 6.5 for Norwood Park, which has the lowest delinquency rate. At the highest point on the line we will write 114.3 for Washington Park, the area with the highest delinquency rate.

Now that we have a line with an appropriate scale to represent each map, the next thing we do is refer to the listing of the two maps, find each area and locate its score on each line. Let's start with Washington Park. With a rate of 53.3, it is second highest on public transportation. So mark that point on the horizontal line. Next we must locate Washington Park on the vertical line. Because it has the highest score, put a mark at 114.3. Now that we know where Washington Park is located on each map, we can draw a line up from the horizontal line and another out from the vertical line. Where the lines cross, we can make a dot. That dot shows the combined map location of Washington Park.

If we follow this procedure for every one of the seventy-six areas, then we will have seventy-six dots within the area designated by the horizontal and vertical lines. What we have done is to create a *scatterplot*, and it will look like this:

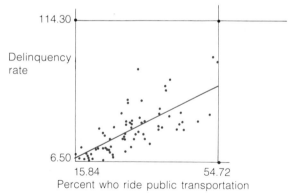

r = 0.74
N = 76

Notice the line running from the lower-left corner of the scatterplot up to the upper-right corner. This is the *regression line*, which is the best-fitting attempt to draw a line that passes through each of the dots. This is done through a simple calculation that we need not pursue here. When two maps are absolutely identical, if every shift in the percent riding public transportation were matched by an equivalent shift in the delinquency rate, then all of the dots representing areas would be smack on the regression line, like a string of pearls.

As you can see most of the dots are close to the regression line, which indicates that the maps are very similar, but not identical. They almost never are. So Pearson added another little twist to his method. He measured the distance from the regression line out to each dot. Then he added all of these distances together. His method rests on the fact that the *smaller* this total is, the more perfect the match between maps. Pearson expressed his results in the form of a *correlation coefficient*. This is a number that can take any value from 0.00 to 1.00. The closer it is to 1.00, the more perfect the match, or correlation, between two measures. The closer it is to 0.00, the less correlation between the two. Correlations can be either positive or negative. If the more bus and train riders an area has, the more delinquents it has (if, as one rises so does the other), then this is a *positive correlation*. But if the more bus and train riders in an area, the fewer delinquents it has (if, as one rises the other declines), then this is a *negative correlation*. When correlations are positive, the regression line slopes from lower left to upper right. When correlations are negative, the regression line slopes from upper left to lower right. And when there is no correlation the regression line is horizontal.

In the lower-left corner of the scatterplot illustration, you will find the correlation coefficient: $r = 0.74$. The letter r stands for Pearson's measure, and in this instance it shows that a very strong, positive correlation exists between delinquency and public transportation use in Chicago. We can interpret this as showing that in Chicago, as in most cities, delinquency is highest in the center city neighborhoods.

Of course, correlation coefficients are useless without data. To get the data for the map of delinquency, someone had to sit down with the juvenile court records and use the home address of *every* kid sent to court during 1980 to add up a total for each of the seventy-six community areas. The data on use of public transportation were collected during the 1980 census. That is, *every* employed person was supposed to report on his or her census form how he or she got to work. Then the totals were calculated not only for these areas of Chicago but also for every significant geographical unit in the nation. Obtaining information on every relevant case, every delinquent or every commuter, is a solid basis for research. Similarly, if we wanted to know how many people watched the last Super Bowl or smoke, we could go out and ask everyone. The trouble is, asking everyone usually is extremely expensive. It cost more than $1 billion to conduct the 1980 census.

If a census were the only reliable way to get such information, very little sociological research would be possible. Fortunately, we don't have to get information on every member of a population to obtain valid results. Instead, we can select relatively few members of a population, find out about them, and assume that the results apply to the entire population. Such a procedure is called *sampling*.

Random Samples

The method of sampling requires that those included in the sample are like those who are not included. The procedure used is identical to the means used in experiments to make sure that groups of subjects are not different. Recall that when Richard Ofshe wanted to be sure that people who thought they were evaluating a friend were not different from those who thought they were evaluating a stranger, he randomly assigned people to the groups. That made it possible to use the laws of probability to compute the odds against chance findings.

Drawing a sample from a population rests on the same principle. The aim is to make certain that people in the sample are just like those left out. To achieve this, decisions about who gets into the sample and who is left out are made randomly.

To select a simple random sample from a population, all that is needed is a complete list

■ This young man is conducting an interview for a national public opinion polling firm. When about 1,500 similar interviews have been completed, they will provide an accurate picture of national opinion. This technique won't work, however, unless each person interviewed is selected by random procedures so that every person in the nation has an equal probability of being selected.

of the population. If we had a list of everyone in the United States, for example, we could put every name in a barrel, stir the names up, and then draw names until we had the total we wanted for our sample. Since every American's name would be in the barrel, everyone would have an equal chance of being selected, and because selection was random, we could calculate the probability that the sample is just like the population as a whole.

The odds that a sample will be like a whole population depend only on the absolute size of the sample and not on the ratio of the sample size to the population size. Hence, a sample based on 1,500 cases is more accurate than one based on only 1,000 and less accurate than one based on 2,000 cases. That is true whether the population being sampled has 20,000 or 200 million members. Thus, a sample including 1,500 persons (a common size) is equally good for

describing the whole U.S. population, the population of Canada, or the population of Fargo, North Dakota.

■
─────────────

Stratified Random Samples

It is impossible to choose a simple random sample of Americans or Canadians, because there is no complete list. Nor is there a complete list for particular cities. The telephone book is the closest thing to a complete list of residents of a city, but it omits people who do not have phones and the many people with unlisted numbers. So we must use another way to sample such populations randomly. This method is called *stratified* random sampling, because the sampling proceeds through a series of levels, or strata.

The U.S. Census Bureau has divided the

country into many small geographic units known as *census tracts*. Cities, for example, are made up of a number of these tracts. To select a sample of the United States, researchers essentially put every census tract into a barrel, mix them up, and then draw some out. In fact, the drawing is rigged so that the probability of each tract being drawn is equal to its portion of the U.S. population, thus ensuring that every American has the same chance to be selected. After a random set of census tracts is selected, sampling is then focused on each. Most tracts are in cities (because that is where most people live). City census tracts are made up of blocks. Again taking into account the total population of various blocks, procedures are used to select at random a sample of blocks.

Once blocks have been selected, interviewers are sent out to discover the identity of *every* person living on each of the sample blocks. From this operation a list emerges: names and addresses of everyone living on all of the sampled blocks. Finally, these names are subjected to random selection and a sample of Americans is obtained (when the names of those selected from rural tracts have been added). Only at this point can the actual research begin. For only when we know who is in the sample do we know who should be interviewed and who sent a questionnaire.

While samples are much cheaper than a census, they are still fairly expensive. Fortunately for sociologists, big commercial polling companies, such as the Gallup Poll, often include questions of great research value in their surveys and are extremely helpful in making their findings available to scholars. When a sociologist has funding to interview a national sample, he or she takes great care to collect data useful for many different research questions and eventually makes the data available to other researchers.

You may notice that some of the tables used in this textbook give the General Social Survey as their source. That survey is conducted every year by the National Opinion Research Center at the University of Chicago. This study is not done for a specific researcher. It is designed to gather useful data on a wide range of topics and to make these quickly and freely available for analysis by any social scientists who ask. It is an amazing resource. As I sit here at my computer writing these lines, whenever I get an interesting idea it only takes a few seconds to shift from my word processing program to the program I use to analyze survey data and to have immediate access to the General Social Survey. All fourteen years of the survey, totaling more than 23,000 interviews, are stored in my hard disk. When rewriting Chapter 1, I suddenly wanted to see if people in big cities had lower levels of interpersonal relations than did people in small towns and rural areas. It took me less than five minutes to find out and to print out Table 1-2. Sociologists can only afford to have data such as these because of samples. Not even the government could afford to go out and interview every person every year. Fortunately, it is sufficient to interview only about 1,500 *if* they have been chosen properly.

Individuals and Groups

II

How we become and remain human is a fundamental sociological question. In the beginning, of course, our biological heritage determines that we are human infants, not kittens. But from then on we must rely on our interactions with others to acquire the complex culture we need to be competent members of our societies—a learning process known as *socialization*.

In this photograph we see an example of group socialization as school children hold a "toothbrush drill." Each child holds a glass of water, each has applied toothpaste to his or her brush, and now—with their brushes at the ready—they await the signal to begin brushing.

Today schools no longer think it necessary to teach students how to brush their teeth (although many dentists think a lot of people grow up without learning proper techniques). But at the turn of the century, when this picture was taken, stores in North America had only just begun to sell toothbrushes and toothpaste, and many people had never used either. Today gum disease, not tooth decay, is the primary reason people lose their teeth, but back then decay was a major problem. Some people had lost all of their teeth by their late teens, and many people had lost them all by the time they were forty.

To help prevent decay, the Tennessee Coal, Iron & Railroad Company instituted drills like this at schools it maintained for children of its employees. Notice that boys and girls stand in separate columns at this company school in Fairfield, Alabama. Note, too, that most of the boys wear neckties. And in those days no occasion was complete without an American flag.

In addition, notice that all of these children are white, although nearly half of the school children in Alabama at this time were black. Segregation in the American South meant that even private schools reserved for company employees were all white or all black. So a few blocks away from the Tennessee Coal, Iron & Railroad Company's school for white children in Fairfield was another school for children of their black employees. And the same day that this picture was taken of toothbrush drill at the white school, a similar picture was taken of the same drill at the black school.

If human beings were not subject to dental problems, children would not need to learn to brush their teeth. This reminds us that biology as well as culture influences our behavior. Thus Chapter 5 explores the complex ways in which biological, cultural, and social forces combine and interact. Chapter 6 then examines the socialization process in detail. Among the many aspects of culture transmitted by socialization are norms—rules specifying how people are expected to act and to not act. Chapters 7 and 8 explain why in all societies and groups some people violate norms and explore how societies attempt to prevent people from doing so.

Biology, Culture, and Society

5

EARLY IN THIS century many social scientists were really biologists in disguise. They argued that most human behavior was caused by inborn, or inherited, features of our biology. Major figures in psychology at the turn of the century, including Sigmund Freud, E. L. Thorndike, and John Dewey, embraced instinctual theories of behavior (Allport, 1968). An **instinct** is a form of behavior that occurs in all normal members of a species *without having been learned*. For example, a spider hatched in isolation from all other spiders will still spin webs identical to webs made by others of the same species. Thus, psychologists who proposed instinct theories of human behavior discounted the impact of the *environment*—of cultural and social influences—on human development. To them what was given to humans by heredity was final.

The major proponent of instinctual theories was the social psychologist William McDougall, who was on the faculty of Harvard before moving to Duke. In a very influential textbook of its time, *An Introduction to Social Psychology*, McDougall (1908) listed a number of human instincts and attempted to show how even elaborate forms of behavior are produced by "compounds" of several instincts. Religiousness, he explained, is caused by a blend of four instincts: curiosity, self-abasement, fear, and the protective, or parental, instinct. Other psychologists suggested other instincts, and in his 1932 book McDougall revised his list and proposed that human behavior could be explained by eighteen different instincts.

Not to be outdone by psychologists, many sociologists of the period proposed biological and

hereditary explanations for cultural differences among societies. For instance, less technologically advanced societies were believed to be made up of people with inferior intellects. Others claimed that the Swedes were stubborn, the Italians were excitable, the Spanish cruel, and the Dutch obsessed with cleanliness because of their heredity. Recall from Chapter 2 that biological arguments were used to justify the exclusion of "genetically inferior" groups such as southern and eastern Europeans, Africans, and Asians from entry to the United States in 1921.

All these biological theories were simple-minded and obviously inadequate. Studies of children subjected to extreme neglect showed that they were not capable of speech, let alone sophisticated thought, and thus proved that most human behavior is not instinctual (see Chapter 6). As for the "backward races," soon some of them were going to Harvard. Moreover, no one could demonstrate that humans exhibit any instinctual behavior, with the possible exceptions of a sucking response in infants and an infant's tendency to imitate facial expressions (see Figure 5-2). Soon social science books ceased to mention instincts, and even some of the major proponents of the instinct approach eventually discarded it. In fact, social science textbooks soon made no mention of human biology at all.

By the 1930s, the social sciences were dominated by purely environmental theories. Heredity was assigned no role. Everything humans do was said to be entirely the result of cultural and social influences (White, 1949). Some researchers grudgingly admitted that

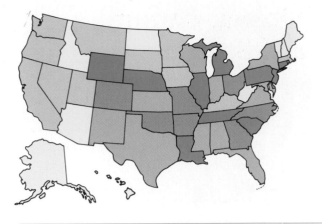

1982: Percent of Black Infants with a Low Birth Weight (Under 5 Pounds 8 Ounces)

Vermont	3.6		Arkansas	12.3
New Hampshire	4.0		Rhode Island	12.3
Idaho	5.5		North Carolina	12.4
North Dakota	7.8		Colorado	12.4
Maine	8.4		Ohio	12.6
Alaska	8.6		Missouri	12.6
Arizona	9.1		Delaware	12.6
Hawaii	9.4		Oklahoma	12.6
West Virginia	10.0		Georgia	12.7
Montana	10.1		Louisiana	12.8
Washington	10.1		New Jersey	12.9
South Dakota	10.3		Nebraska	12.9
Minnesota	10.4		South Carolina	13.0
Oregon	10.6		Pennsylvania	13.2
Iowa	10.9		Tennessee	13.2
Massachusetts	11.0		Connecticut	13.4
California	11.0		Illinois	13.6
Utah	11.2		Michigan	13.8
Kentucky	11.3		Wyoming	15.7
Nevada	11.6			

New Mexico	11.7
Florida	11.9
Alabama	11.9
Indiana	12.0
Mississippi	12.0
New York	12.1
Wisconsin	12.1
Maryland	12.1
Kansas	12.2
Virginia	12.2
Texas	12.2

Figure 5-1 ■ **The geography of birth weights of black infants in the United States.** A black infant in the United States has a much greater risk than a white infant of being born small due to inadequate nutrition—an effect that can be traced back to the grandmother's diet, which often harmed the health of the child's mother. Health researchers have set 5 pounds 8 ounces as the threshold for classifying a baby as small. Low birth weight is associated with many physical and developmental problems and illustrates the intimate connections among biology, culture, and society. Cultural justifications of racism sustained social patterns of discrimination and privation that, in turn, caused biological harm. In their turn, these biological consequences have influenced the social fate of many individuals by reducing their physical and intellectual capacities to compete. Examining the map, you might be somewhat surprised to find that low birth weight for black infants is not a Southern phenomenon. Only three of the top ten states are in the South.

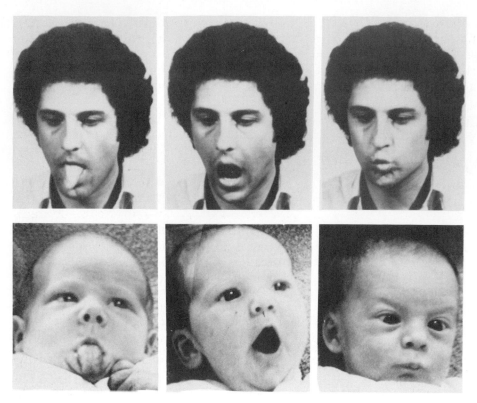

Figure 5-2 ■ **"Same to you, fella!"** Until recently it was believed that human infants did not learn to imitate facial expressions until they were 8 to 10 months old. However, recent research has shown that infants are born with this ability. Andrew N. Meltzoff and M. Keith Moore (1977, 1983) found that newborns, some only 60 minutes old, would imitate facial expressions. These sample photographs from video recordings show 2-week-old infants imitating tongue protrusion, mouth opening, and lip protrusion.

societies and cultural patterns would be different if human biology had produced but one sex, if infants grew up in only several months, or if the average person lived for 10,000 years. But these were regarded as nothing more than silly hypothetical possibilities. The accepted view was that our biology may set some limits, but within these, human nature is essentially plastic and can be shaped into virtually any form.

As we shall see in Chapter 6, anthropologists such as Margaret Mead studied remote tribes for the express purpose of "proving" how plastic human nature really is. We shall also see that at least some of these reports probably contained as much fantasy as fact. Moreover, more careful research began to show that heredity does

sometimes overcome environmental influences. For example, while environmental factors can make people short, they cannot make them taller than their hereditary potential.

Today the absolute environmentalist position is judged to be as extreme as the absolute hereditarian position it was reacting against. Few social scientists accept that humans have instincts, but most believe that human beings are the result of the interplay between their biology and their social and cultural environment. To illustrate this, let us consider symbolic interaction, which was defined in Chapter 3 as the essential human capacity. Clearly, we are not born with this capacity. If no one talks to us, we never learn speech on our own. To learn the meaning of symbols takes much time and immense stimulation from the environment. However, it is equally true that our biology makes symbolic interaction possible. Only because the human brain evolved in size and complexity are we able to learn symbolic interaction skills; persons whose brains are too damaged or deficient cannot learn these skills.

Chapter Preview

In this chapter we shall focus on how biology interacts with culture and society to shape human behavior. First, we shall examine several basic concepts and principles of heredity. Next, we shall explore the developing field of behavioral genetics. Here we shall find out how geneticists demonstrate whether a human trait is hereditary. For example, geneticists have recently found evidence for a hereditary element in mental illness and in intelligence.

The major portion of the chapter will address how social and cultural factors modify the fulfillment of our genetic potentials. For this discussion, we shall examine two examples in detail and watch biologists and sociologists at work on the same question. Our first example will involve the sudden, very recent, and dramatic changes in the age of puberty and the size of human beings. The second will trace the bitter controversy over race and IQ. Our goal is to see the subtle ways in which environment and heredity combine. Finally, we shall examine recent studies that compare humans and other primates to see what similarities and differences exist. Are humans truly unique? Do only humans possess culture and language? Can animal studies provide us with useful insights?

Heredity

We know that cats never give birth to pups and that the offspring of humans will always be human. The reason is that tiny parts of the male's sperm and the female's ovum contain an amazing amount of information that determines the kind of organism that results from the mating. Since offspring grow up to be whatever their parents' cells specify, an individual biological organism inherits its particular makeup; that is, the physical aspects of an organism are inherited.

In the case of humans, a male sperm contains twenty-three **chromosomes**, as does the female ovum. These combine to form twenty-three pairs (Figure 5-3). The specific instructions on each pair of chromosomes combine to determine various traits, such as eye color. These instructions are encoded in complex chemical chains called DNA, which are contained in tiny structures called **genes**. Each chromosome contains many genes, and humans are estimated to have more than 1,000 genes. No two sperm and no two ova, even from the same male or female, are likely to have the same array of genes. That is why the same parents can have one child with red hair and another with brown. However, a person's hair color is determined by the particular genes he or she has received. Geneticists have worked out some precise rules of heredity, and in many cases they can often specify the odds that a given trait will show up in a child.

Two other genetic concepts will be useful in this chapter: **genotype** and **phenotype**. The sum total of the genetic instructions that an organism receives from its parents is called the genotype. However, the physical development of organisms does not always exactly follow the genetic blueprints, or genotypes. Environmental forces sometimes deflect or prevent the fulfillment of the genotype. For this reason, we refer to any specific organism as a phenotype to take into account the interplay between the genotype and the environment in physical development. In other words, the phenotype is what we see when we look at any organism. As we will see later in this chapter, for example, throughout nearly the whole period of human existence the genotype of the average person "planned" for him or her to become much taller than the environment actually permitted. We can view the genotype in part as a genetic potential, while the phenotype is the actual outcome of the interplay between the genotype and the environment. A second reason to distinguish between genotype and phenotype is that

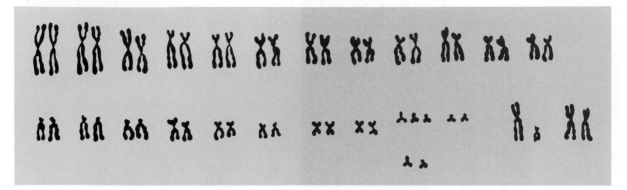

Figure 5-3 ■ **Human chromosomes.** A photomicrograph of the twenty-three pairs of chromosomes in a human cell. The actual hereditary information (the genes) carried by each chromosome pair is contained in DNA molecules.

much of a person's genetic inheritance does not show up in his or her phenotype, but it can show up in the phenotypes of that person's children. For example, brown-eyed parents can have blue-eyed children, thus showing that both parents had a blue-eyed gene in their genotypes.

The importance of heredity to sociologists does not depend on whether some human characteristics are wholly determined by genetics, for without question some are. Blue-eyed parents, for example, can only produce blue-eyed children (although brown-eyed parents can produce blue-eyed children). The important question is what traits are determined to what degree by genetic inheritance. Do any of these traits influence human activities of interest to social science? Sociologists don't care much about eye color, but they do care very much about variations in humans that determine what people can and cannot do and how they do or do not act.

■

Behavioral Genetics

Just because instinctual theories were silly does not mean that heredity plays no role in human behavior. In 1960 the publication of the first textbook in **behavioral genetics** marked the rapid rise of a new scientific field (Fuller and Thompson, 1960). In recent years behavioral geneti-

cists have claimed considerable success in isolating human characteristics and behavior that are influenced to a substantial degree by genetic inheritance (Hay, 1985; Ehrman and Parsons, 1981). Among these are such characteristics as intelligence, major forms of mental illness, alcoholism, and a tendency toward impulsive and aggressive behavior.

To show that any particular trait is inherited, one must first demonstrate that blood relatives are more alike in terms of this trait than are randomly selected, unrelated individuals. For example, David Rosenthal (1970) summarized dozens of studies reporting that schizophrenia, a mental illness, clusters in families; that is, relatives of a schizophrenic are considerably more likely to become schizophrenic than are people without known schizophrenic relatives.

However, this approach has encountered major criticism. Not only do two brothers who develop schizophrenia have a similar genetic inheritance but they also grew up in the same home with the same parents and were exposed to similar social circumstances outside the home. Opponents of behavioral genetics argue that the similar environment in which relatives are raised makes it seem as if heredity plays a part.

For this reason, studies of twins, especially identical twins separated at birth, are central to research in behavioral genetics. We have seen that children of the same parents each have a

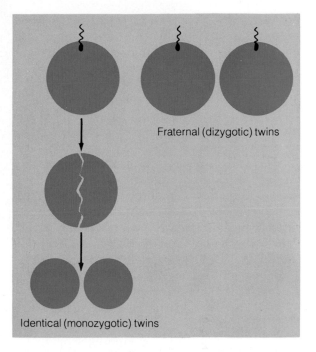

■ Identical twins are genetic duplicates. As a result, *all* differences they display can only be caused by environmental factors. Of course, being the same age and sex, looking the same, and having the same parents, they will tend to have very similar environments, so it is difficult to know whether personality and behavioral similarities between them are genetic or environmental.

Figure 5-4 ■ **Twins.** Identical (or monozygotic) twins occur when a fertilized ovum (or zygote) splits, forming two infants with precisely the same genetic inheritance. Most twins are dizygotic and occur because the mother produced two ova and both were fertilized. Such twins often are not even of the same sex and are no more similar genetically than are brothers and sisters not born at the same time.

unique genotype, although their genotypes are more alike than are those of children with different parents or children with only one parent in common. Most twins are not identical and are the result of their mother producing two ova at the same time, each of which was impregnated by a different sperm. Such twins are no more genetically similar than are children born at different times to the same parents. However, once in a while, after an ovum has been impregnated, it splits in half and develops into two babies (Figure 5-4). When such splits occur, each half has the same genetic content. Identical twins, the results of this phenomenon, thus have identical genotypes.

Any hereditary trait that shows up in one identical twin will show up in the other unless

outside forces intrude. Suppose schizophrenia has a genetic basis. Then if one twin becomes schizophrenic, the other should, too. The same holds true if intelligence is genetic. However, studies that showed amazingly similar mental health or intelligence in identical twins were subject to the same criticism mentioned earlier. Since these twins look exactly alike and are the same age, they will have been treated in almost identical ways. Once again, similarity of environment offers a very plausible counter-explanation.

However, not all identical twins grow up in the same house. Sometimes they are adopted by two different families and grow up without even knowing they have a twin. For some decades now, behavioral geneticists have focused on locating such sets of identical twins. Such twins permit a more stringent test of hereditary and environmental explanations.

For example, if intelligence has no hereditary basis, the IQs of identical twins raised separately should not be more similar than IQs of randomly selected pairs of persons. In fact, a great many studies, done in different countries by many different geneticists, show that the IQs of identical twins raised apart are extremely similar, although not identical. Environmental factors, therefore, can and do influence intelligence. But the IQs of identical twins are too much alike to allow us to reject the notion that genetics also plays a major part in determining intelligence (Erlenmeyer-Kimling and Jarvik, 1963; Omenn, Caspari, and Ehrman, 1972; Lewontin, 1973; Ehrman and Parsons, 1981; Hay, 1985).* Studies of twins raised separately also have supported the role of heredity in many forms of mental illness, including schizophrenia and depressive disorders (Rosenthal, 1970). Researchers recently have discovered that a gene located on chromosome 11 seems to cause depressive disorders among the Old Order Amish of Pennsylvania (Egeland et al., 1987).

Aside from studies of identical twins, behavioral geneticists also rely on studies based on persons who were adopted as infants. They seek to separate heredity from environment by testing whether adoptees more closely follow a behavioral pattern of the adoptive parents who raised them or that of their biological parents. Here the work of Marc Schuckit and his colleagues on alcoholism is an excellent example. He found that adoptees with an alcoholic biological parent had a nearly 50 percent rate of alcoholism regardless of whether or not one of their adoptive parents was an alcoholic. This finding suggests a strong genetic influence. Among adoptees whose biological parents were not alcoholics, the risk of alcoholism was far lower. But here environmental factors were felt, for *the odds of becoming an alcoholic were twice*

as high if an adoptive parent was an alcoholic (Schuckit et al., 1972 a,b, 1979). These results have been replicated in Denmark and Sweden using the same technique of comparing adoptees with their real and adoptive parents. Moreover, recent studies based on twins, including identical twins, have yielded similar support for a genetic component in alcohol abuse (Hay, 1985).

Many social scientists resent behavioral geneticists and cling to the belief that the environment causes all or nearly all variation among humans. But it seems to me unwise to ignore a field conducted in a scientific manner and guided by theories that have amply explained less controversial human traits. Of course, social scientists did not feel threatened when geneticists unraveled the hereditary transmission of diseases such as sickle-cell anemia or diabetes. But when geneticists discuss the heredity of mental illness or intelligence, they tread on ground social scientists were accustomed to having all to themselves. Yet social scientists have as much to tell geneticists as geneticists have to tell us. This will be obvious in the next two sections of this chapter, where we shall see the immense power of the social and cultural environment to modify fulfillment of human potentials. Here the combined resources of sociologists and geneticists help to illuminate many mysteries.

■

The Growth and Puberty Revolutions

Over the past several decades, people have clearly been getting bigger. The change has been especially obvious in sports. In the 1930s, centers selected to the all-American basketball teams sometimes were no taller than 6 feet 2 inches, the size of a good small guard today. The line of the Chicago Bears' famous "Monsters of the Midway" averaged less than 200 pounds in their National Football League championship season of 1933. Good high school football players are bigger than that today.

To some degree athletes are larger because

---

*There are indications that the British geneticist Cyril Burt faked some twin studies late in his career. However, even discarding all of Burt's studies does not weaken the evidence in favor of the role of heredity in intelligence.

■ Here we see the University of Washington's super varsity basketball team of 1929. They went undefeated until losing the Coast Conference championship game to California's Golden Bears. The tallest man in the picture is 6 feet 2 inches. The previous year Washington had been a real powerhouse because they had a center who was 6 feet 6 inches. Today these men would be too short to have much chance of making the Washington team—or even a Seattle high school team.

they are now recruited from a much larger population, both because the U.S. population has grown and because the population enrolled in high school and college has grown even more. Thus, if a person 7 feet tall occurs only once in a million births, there will be more 7-footers when the population is over 200 million than when it is 100 million.

However, not only sports stars have become bigger. The size of the average American has increased substantially. In fact, people in all the advanced industrial nations are bigger than their parents and grandparents. In Japan the rapid increase in average height has required major

changes. A few years ago most of the desks in Japan's elementary schools had to be replaced by larger ones.

In addition, a second change has recently been noticed. Not only are people growing larger than before but they are also growing faster—achieving their full size at a much younger age. Data from various nations reveal that a century ago most people still grew a lot in their late teens and usually did not reach their full adult height until age 25 or even later (Tanner, 1970). Today, most people stop growing by 18 or so, and most achieve nearly their full growth much sooner than that.

■ Napoléon Bonaparte, the Emperor of France, talks with his officers on December 1, 1805, the night before the Battle of Austerlitz. In this painting by Lejeune, Napoléon is one of the taller men in the group. Yet for more than a century he has been referred to by historians as the "little corporal," a man of humble origins, suffering from a "small man complex," who changed the course of European history. Recently, the historian Michael Burns (1985) has explained that Napoléon's height has been misinterpreted because of the rapid shift in human growth. In Napoléon's day, the average man in southern Europe was probably 5 feet 2 or 3 inches. At 5 feet 6 inches, Napoléon was tall for the place and time. He was classified as short by later historians, especially by British and northern European writers, for their better health and diet had, even in Napoléon's time, resulted in greater stature.

Concern with the rapid shift in growth patterns led scientists to notice another change. James M. Tanner, a British physiological psychologist, found that the age at which girls begin to menstruate has also declined in recent decades. Moreover, Tanner and others noted anthropological reports that girls in remote primitive tribes usually do not begin to menstruate until about age 17, or as much as five years later than the average age for girls in Europe and North America. Tanner suddenly suspected that the recent changes in the age at the onset of menstruation might be the very end of a truly rapid and dramatic downward trend. Could it be, he wondered, that not long ago girls everywhere did not enter puberty until their late teens?

These suspicions spurred Tanner and many other scientists to do a great deal of research involving old medical and school records. Across Europe, scientists reconstructed when girls typically began to menstruate during the nineteenth century. When Tanner gathered all this information together and added data for the twentieth century, a very consistent, clear, and amazing picture emerged. Data from Norway, Germany, Sweden, Finland, Denmark, Great Britain, Canada, and the United States all showed the same thing: As recently as 1850, the average girl did not menstruate until about age 17. Since that time, the age of first menstruation has rapidly declined; now the average girl in these nations begins to menstruate several months after her twelfth birthday.

The onset of male sexual maturation is not marked by so signal an event as menstruation. But since boys at present reach puberty at a later age than girls, Tanner thought it reasonable to assume that back when girls did not menstruate until age 17, boys did not begin to shave until 18 or so. This assumption has been confirmed by an unexpected source, music history. Boy choirs have long been popular in Europe, and conductors of such choirs are always concerned with the loss of boy sopranos when their voices change at the onset of puberty. Music historians know that back when Johann Sebastian Bach (1685–1750) and Wolfgang Amadeus Mozart (1756–1791) composed choral music, boy sopranos often could sing until the age of 18 or so. Today, boy sopranos are usually washed up by the age of 13.

New research by Bullough (1981) indicates that Tanner's data portrayed a too-rapid decline in the age of first menstruation in the nineteenth century. That is, the average young woman in western Europe in about 1850 may have begun to menstruate at 15½ or 16, not 17 as Tanner claimed. Moreover, women may have begun menstruating considerably younger in some earlier times—in Rome during the height of the empire, or in the Greek cities during the golden age of Hellenic culture. But these are matters of detail. The larger picture seems clear:

■ One aspect of this portrait of a Chinese-American man posing with his parents would be found in the huge majority of similar families—the son, born and raised in the United States, is much taller than his father. While people in industrial nations generally have been getting larger, the shift has been especially marked for Asian immigrants to Europe and North America.

There has been a dramatic shift in the human phenotype in modern times. We are much bigger than our ancestors, and we grow much faster and mature much sooner than they did. Before we examine the consequences of these changes, let's attempt to see why these changes took place.

Environmental suppressors

No trained biologist could believe that these rapid changes in human physiology were caused by genetic changes. No such change could spread so far so fast. Thus, the answer had to be sought elsewhere. In fact, the answer lies in the potent capacity of environmental factors to modify genetic potential. Indeed, to ask why humans suddenly began to get so large so fast is to raise the wrong question. The right question is: What kept humans so small and delayed their maturation for so long? What we are examining is a rapid change in the phenotype of human beings that reveals the previously unfulfilled potential of the human genotype.

Much research still needs to be done to explain how the environment suppressed our natural growth patterns, but the major factors are easy to determine: inadequate nutrition (especially shortages of vitamins and proteins) and chronic poor health.

As we shall see many times in this book, one of the major impacts of the Industrial Revolution, of modernization, has been healthier and longer lives. Until modern times, most people, even farmers, ate meager diets, deficient in vitamins and proteins. Most people had meat, eggs, or dairy products very rarely, hardly ever had fruit, and ate vegetables only in summer (Braudel, 1981). They lived almost exclusively on bread and on mush and soup made from grain. As a result, their growth was stunted and their maturation delayed. Poor diet also made people more susceptible to illness and contagious diseases, the latter being most common among children. A lack of sanitation and poor personal hygiene (see Chapters 13 and 19) further contributed to poor health. For these reasons, large numbers of children, often as many as half, did not reach adulthood. Nor were those who survived strong and healthy. The average person died by age 35.

Under such privation, we are hardly surprised that human development was stunted and maturation long delayed. Then the Industrial Revolution suddenly began to change these conditions. People began to eat much more food, which was also much more nutritious (see Chapter 18). Sanitation and immunization practices eliminated many common diseases. Infant mortality declined rapidly as the average life expectancy doubled. And suddenly people got much bigger and began to mature much younger. And that change, in turn, has had some profound implications.

Social consequences of early maturation

Thus far we have seen how social and cultural forces affected human biology. We shall now change our point of view: How does our biology modify social and cultural patterns? Strict environmentalists would say that our biology does not greatly affect cultural patterns, that human nature is sufficiently adaptable to allow an immense range of cultural patterns. Clearly, many cultural arrangements *are* possible, since many different ones have been observed. Yet developments in the wake of the growth and puberty revolutions suggest that we are not so easily shaped. For this reason, let's look briefly at how changes in sexual norms and authority relations between adults and teenagers may be related to changes in human maturation.

■ **Changing sexual norms**   Until modern times, most people 17 and under were still biological children in both size and development. Not surprisingly, they usually did not marry until they were in their early twenties. In 1890, for example, the median age at first marriage in the United States and Canada was 22 for women and 25 for men. In 1980 it was nearly the same. While the age of physical and sexual maturity fell rapidly, the age at marriage did not. Thus, the time between maturation and marriage has grown longer and longer. In each generation people have had to wait longer from the time they were sexually capable until the time they married. This put severe strains on the norms restricting sex to marriage. It is not difficult for prepubic teenagers to refrain from sex, but it is a challenge for persons who are sexually mature to refrain from sex for more than ten years.

Clearly, this strain could not be relieved by letting people marry soon after they became sexually mature. No one believes that 13- or 14-year-olds are mature enough to marry, regardless of their physical development. Thus, the traditional means of dealing with sexuality—marriage soon after sexual maturity—became increasingly inappropriate. The result was a great shift in sexual norms. Premarital sexual behavior is now widespread and has gained considerable social acceptance (see Chapter 12).

Besides changes in human biology, reliable methods of contraception, legalized abortion, and effective treatment of common venereal diseases also contributed to a relaxation of sexual norms (just as the threat of AIDS may be causing the old restrictions to be renewed). Furthermore, as we shall see in Chapter 12, a radical shift in the proportion of males to females also took place during this period—and when females outnumber males, norms of virginity and chastity usually fade. Still, the fact remains that until the twentieth century, few teenagers were sufficiently mature for norms against premarital sex to be much of an issue.

■ **Adult authority**   Throughout most of human history, physical and social maturity have coincided. The phrase "You're not big enough to do that yet" referred to both size and maturity. When people were big enough, they were taken to be old enough. For this reason, very small adults have always had trouble being accepted as grown-ups (Truzzi, 1968). Today, however, people are big enough long before adults are willing to regard them as old enough. This has caused problems of authority because adult authority over children has always rested on the fact that adults were bigger and stronger.

Consider student-teacher relations. Until this century, even female high school teachers tended to be taller than all but their largest male students. As a result, when teachers told students to sit down or be quiet, the students were not inclined to refuse. Many authority problems in schools and in families today are exacerbated because teenagers are now of adult size. It seems that new bases of adult authority will have to develop. Kids today grow too big to be spanked long before they are old enough not to need adult supervision and direction.

Since biology can influence cultural and social arrangements in these ways, then perhaps it can do so in other ways as well. As we proceed on our tour of sociology, you will continue to catch glimpses of human flesh and blood in social behavior we examine. Humans are biological organisms as well as social beings. Indeed, in the last part of this chapter we shall see how humans compare with their primate cousins. Before taking up that topic, however, we must examine how the interplay of biology, culture, and society shapes something that determines the whole of human behavior: the ability to think and to learn.

■

The IQ and Race Controversy

Intelligence testing was begun by the French psychologist Alfred Binet (1857–1911) at his laboratory in Paris in 1906. Binet wanted to distinguish between students who lacked the ability to learn and those who were not learning because of a lack of effort. He postulated that people have an innate, or inborn, capacity for learning, and therefore the greater that capacity, the more a given individual should learn over a given time.

Binet set out to measure a person's **mental age** on the basis of how much that person had learned by a given calendar age. For example, variations in the ability of 8-year-olds to perform intellectual tasks will reflect variations in their innate ability to learn. Some 8-year-olds will perform as well as the average child of 9 or even 10. Such children, then, are said to have a mental age of 9 or 10, well above their calendar age. Similarly, some children will perform below their age level and thus have a mental age that is less than their calendar age.

An **IQ**, or intelligence quotient, is a person's mental age divided by the calendar age. The result is then multiplied by 100 to get rid of the decimal point. If a person's mental and calendar ages are the same, that person has an IQ of 100, the average IQ score. If a person's mental age is 25 percent higher than his or her calendar age (for example, a person of 8 performs at the average for 10-year-olds), the IQ is 125. An 8-year-old who performs at the 6-year-old level has an

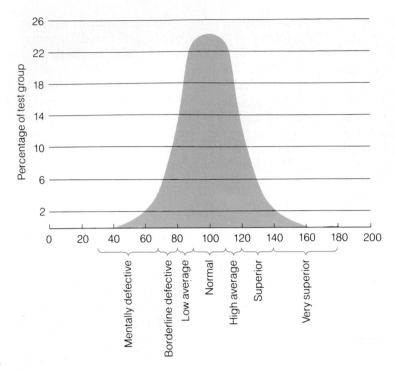

Figure 5-5 ■ **The normal curve.** The normal curve (shown by color shading) illustrates the theoretical distribution of IQ scores that would be obtained from a very large group of people. Note that the average score would be 100 and that 68.26 percent of all individuals would score between 85 and 115 and about 95 percent between 70 and 130.

IQ of 75. Having launched massive testing programs for French schoolchildren, Binet found that his test produced a normal distribution, the bell-shaped curve shown in Figure 5-5. Thus, for everyone who scores 125 (25 points over the average), someone will score 75 (25 points below the average).

Binet's test was soon translated into many other languages. At Stanford University Lewis M. Terman translated it into English, which is why the test is known in this country as the Stanford-Binet Test of Intelligence. Since Binet developed his test more than eighty years ago, a great deal of research has been done to validate his and other IQ tests. Two facts about IQ tests are significant. First, they are very powerful predictors of school performance and occupational success. Second, test scores are highly consistent over the course of a person's

life. Most people score about the same when they take the test several times at different ages (Brown and Herrnstein, 1975).

IQ testing has aroused opposition from some social scientists who claim it measures only environmental influences, not an innate ability. In response, supporters of IQ tests point out that whatever the tests measure, it is something that has immense impact on how well people succeed in school and on the job. Moreover, since this quality seems to be fixed by the time children are old enough for their IQ to be measured, it does not react to environmental influences in later childhood or adulthood. Why would the environment be so potent only in the first five or six years of life, but not later? Surely much happens to people that could influence how much they learn after the age of 6. That scores remain stable suggests that IQ tests measure

■ Young American draftees taking the Army Alpha IQ test just after the United States entered World War I in 1917. The rapid and massive influx of new troops far exceeded the available facilities at military posts, so these soldiers are sitting on the floor to take their tests. Note that a civilian is giving the test. Today the services have their own trained psychologists to supervise the many tests given new recruits.

not only what a person happened to learn by a given age but also his or her underlying ability to learn. But perhaps the most powerful support for IQ tests has come from the studies done on identical twins who were raised separately. If IQ is just the result of social and cultural influences and not heredity, then why do the IQs of identical twins who were reared apart correlate so highly?

Conflicts over the real meaning of IQ scores suddenly intensified when some social scientists claimed that blacks have less innate intelligence than whites.

Arthur Jensen drops a bomb

 IQ testing was widespread in the United States by World War I, and the U.S. Army developed a short test called the Army Alpha, which was given to all men drafted for the war. The army test had been validated against the Stanford-Binet and is still regarded as a satisfactory measure of IQ. As the test results were analyzed, it was noticed that the average score for black soldiers was substantially lower than that for white soldiers.

Through the years, the results of mass IQ testing continued to show a difference in the average scores of blacks and whites. Then in 1969, Arthur Jensen, a professor of educational psychology at the University of California at Berkeley, published an article in the *Harvard Educational Review*. In this article, he claimed that interracial differences in average IQ were the result of genetic differences. Jensen's reasoning was simple. First, persistent IQ differences between blacks and whites have appeared in study after study for decades. Second, obviously whites and blacks are genetically different in some respects, as evidenced by physical traits. Third, heredity is known to play a major role in the IQs of people of the same race. Jensen therefore concluded that genes affecting IQ are somewhat different between blacks and whites, causing the average black to have a lower IQ than the average white.

Understandably, Jensen's article touched off a raging controversy. If his position were true, then blacks were trapped by their heredity, not just their environment—blacks would always score lower on IQ tests, do less well in school, and occupy a lower position on the occupational ladder. Stated more bluntly, Jensen was claiming that blacks are naturally not as smart as whites. It is worth noting that Jensen was not happy about his conclusion. He didn't want it to be true, but he thought the evidence left no other explanation.

Many people rushed to condemn Jensen's findings and indeed to condemn Jensen himself (students at Berkeley demonstrated off and on for several years, demanding that Jensen be fired). Those who had always rejected the validity of IQ tests and the evidence that heredity influences intelligence found in the Jensen case new reason to attack the tests and behavioral geneticists. However, even if Jensen were wrong, haunting questions remained. Why was the average IQ score of blacks lower than that of whites? And would the difference ever disappear?

For nearly a decade, the race and IQ controversy raged on: Jensen maintained his position, and social scientists who disagreed failed to provide convincing answers to the basic questions. Then a prominent black social scientist solved most of the mystery.

Thomas Sowell solves the puzzle

 In the mid-1970s, Thomas Sowell, now at Stanford University, took Jensen's conclusions as a scientific, not a political, challenge. As he wrote in the introduction to his now famous study (Sowell, 1978, p. 203):

Despite the emotionally charged philosophical and political issues involved, this is ultimately an empirical question—independent of anyone's beliefs, hopes, or fears.

Sowell believed that adequate data would show that Jensen was wrong, that black-white IQ differences resulted from social and cultural differences rather than genetic differences.

Sowell started from a proposition that we shall pursue at length in Chapter 11—that in many crucial respects, the situation of most American blacks resembles that of recent immigrants more than that of groups long resident in the United States. Until recent times, most blacks lived in the rural South under laws and customs of segregation. The migration to northern cities, undertaken by millions of blacks since 1940, was thus more like a trip from rural Italy to the United States than from Detroit to Chicago. Sowell argued that the social and cultural backgrounds of most American blacks depressed their IQ scores. In fact, the model he proposed for investigating this issue of race and IQ is the same model developed to explain the growth and puberty revolutions. That is, Sowell argued that culture and society greatly stunt genetic potential. But how could he demonstrate this?

Sowell needed to compare the IQ results for blacks with those for white immigrants from deprived backgrounds during their early days in the United States. Unfortunately, World War I data from the Army's Alpha testing identified only the race of each test taker, not his ethnic background. However, Sowell remembered that earlier in this century schools routinely recorded the ethnic background of each student. (When my mother enrolled me in the first grade, the teacher asked, "And what is Rodney's nationality?" I thought the answer would be "American" but was surprised to learn that it was "Norwegian, Swedish, and German.") By the end of World War II, most schools had stopped asking for this information, in part because there were no longer many first-generation Americans.

Sowell also knew that by the 1920s many schools were administering IQ tests. Did any of these records still exist? Could he get access to them? Yes. Digging in dusty and forgotten file cabinets and combing through storerooms and attics, Sowell eventually discovered records from early in the century providing the ethnicity and IQ scores of more than 70,000 students. Also using some data on ethnicity and IQ that had been published between 1915 and 1925, he was able to assess the average IQ scores of many immigrants soon after they arrived in the United States.

What Sowell found confirmed his initial suspicions and dramatically proved the power of social and cultural forces to modify heredity. Around the turn of the century, the average IQ scores among recent white immigrants were well below those of white groups that had been in the country longer.

Thus, there was nothing unusual about black IQ scores. Indeed, average black IQ scores today are well above those of many white ethnic groups back in the 1920s. For example, in the 1920s Italian schoolchildren had an average IQ score of about 85 (100 is the expected average IQ). The IQs of Slovaks, Greeks, Poles, Spaniards, Portuguese, Syrians, Croatians, Lithuanians, and even French-Canadians also averaged below 100. Thus, sixty years ago these white ethnic groups scored at the same level as blacks were scoring in the 1940s and 1950s. Consequently, most scholars of that time were convinced that these scores also proved genetic inferiority. Indeed, laws limiting immigration, which Congress adopted in the 1920s, were justified as a means to limit the influx of "inferior" groups from eastern Europe and Mediterranean nations.

But these views of genetic inferiority were wrong. Today members of the white ethnic groups just listed score at or above the national average; as we shall see, this improvement could not have been caused by changes in their genetic makeup. Indeed, Sowell found the same pattern of low average IQs early in this century among

■ Thomas Sowell.

Japanese- and Chinese-Americans, but today both groups regularly achieve average scores above 100.

Sowell made an important second discovery: Sixty years ago black students born and raised in the North had a higher average IQ than did these same groups of recent white immigrants. Moreover, throughout the century, the longer their families have lived in the North or the younger blacks were when they moved to the North, the higher their IQs. By the same token, Sowell found that the IQs of whites in poor rural areas of the South were also well below the national average and that their IQs also rose following migration to the North.

It is impossible to attribute these improvements to genetic change. No plausible reason and no known genetic principle can explain why moving from one place to another would alter genetic structure. Even if a selective breeding program had been undertaken to prevent people with low IQs from having children, it would have taken centuries to produce the changes that took place in only a few decades. Instead, Sowell's findings demonstrate that, as in the cases of height and age at puberty, the environment can suppress fulfillment of the genotype, resulting in phenotypes that fall short of their potential.

Poor diets, poor health, and poor schooling, plus a way of life that does not require or reward abstract thinking, all can reduce intellectual capacities regardless of genetic potential. In this way, Sowell's careful scientific research demolished notions of inborn racial superiority.

But Sowell did not destroy the validity of intelligence tests. To the contrary, he argued that such tests reflect how social and cultural deprivations can damage people's abilities. Moreover, Sowell argued that intelligence testing is even more valuable for the disadvantaged than for people from privileged backgrounds. College board examinations (Scholastic Aptitude Tests, or SATs) for the first time opened high-quality colleges to students from poor high schools by enabling their talents to be compared directly with those of others. Sowell (1978, p. 231) wrote:

Unusual intellectual ability among minority schoolchildren is less likely to be recognized [when objective tests are not used]. Dr. Martin D. Jenkins, who pioneered the study of high-I.Q. black children in the 1930s, repeatedly found black youngsters with I.Q.s of 150 and above whose teachers were wholly unaware of their ability.

Sowell himself is a classic example of this point. He was born in the rural South and moved to Harlem in his youth. Today he is a graduate of Harvard with a doctorate from the University of Chicago, in part because intelligence testing conducted by the New York City school system revealed his exceptional intellectual talent.

Humans and Other Animals

Social scientists have always been very ambivalent about classifying humans as animals. None denies the obvious biological similarities. But, when it comes to saying just what *sort* of animals we are, social scientists have tended to see little resemblance between humans and other species. At odds are two long traditions among social scientists: One stresses the immense *intellectual superiority* of humans even over other primates; the other stresses the *moral and ethical inferiority* of humans when compared

with the rest of nature—or even in comparison to our biologically more primitive ancestors.

The first tradition stresses the unique human capacity to *create culture* and to pass it on to younger generations. Some social scientists argue that only humans need years of education and training to be able to fulfill normal adult roles—for only humans can create and acquire knowledge and technology. Indeed, social scientists long took it for granted that only humans have *sufficient intelligence* to acquire a *language* and thus to have the means to share culture.

The second of these traditions suggests that the gift of intelligence is, itself, the curse of Cain—that humans are, in the words of Jean-Jacques Rousseau (1712–1778), *"un animal dépravé"* (a depraved animal). Back when humans lacked true consciousness, they, like other animals, were happy and good, according to Rousseau. But consciousness permits humans to suffer from envy, to remember grievances and seek revenge, to recognize that "crime" can pay. Since Rousseau's day, the idea that humans represent nature gone wrong—that we are a species of depraved apes who have lost their natural virtues—has been influential. Indeed, Konrad Lorenz (1966) argued that murder is uniquely human, that other animals rarely attack members of their own species. Lorenz blamed this on humans having become meat-eaters only late in their evolution, far too late to have developed instinctual inhibition mechanisms that curb intra-species aggression among carnivores. To make matters worse, according to Lorenz, humans have developed a murderous arsenal.

In 1973 Lorenz won the Nobel Prize—partly for his work on human aggressive instincts. Among others who have sustained the image of humans as uniquely carnivorous, killer apes is Robert Ardrey in his three immensely influential best-sellers, *African Genesis* (1961), *The Territorial Imperative* (1966), and *The Social Contract* (1970).

But is this image of humanity correct? Indeed, is it true that human intelligence also is unique, giving us alone the capacity to create culture and master language? To assess these views, let's travel to Africa and watch Jane Goodall, one of the most talented and celebrated field observers of our time, studying a band of chimpanzees in the wild.

Jane Goodall's great adventure

 Few scholars in modern times have come to their careers in a less likely fashion than did Jane Goodall. She grew up in England and at 18 she left school, took a secretarial course, and then spent four years working in London. In 1957 a friend invited her for a visit in Kenya so Goodall left London and returned home to Bournemouth, where she spent the summer working as a waitress to save money for her trip. After spending a month at her friend's farm, Goodall decided to stay on in Africa a while and took "a somewhat dreary office job" in Nairobi (Goodall, 1971). One day, someone who knew of her great interest in animals suggested that she ought to meet Louis Leakey (1903–1972), the most famous anthropologist and paleontologist in the world and curator of the National Museum of Natural History in Nairobi.

Leakey, his wife and sons, and his many students and assistants spent much of each year at their immensely important digs for early hominid fossils in the Olduvai Gorge, across the border in Tanzania (Cole, 1975). When Jane Goodall turned up in his office and explained that she wanted to "get closer to animals," Leakey promptly hired her as a secretary. Soon she accompanied the Leakeys back to Olduvai. She found the digging fascinating. And she was even more fascinated to sit in camp in the evenings as Louis Leakey conducted a free-wheeling seminar for everyone present.

After a few months Leakey decided that the quiet, carefully organized, young Jane Goodall was precisely the right person to go off to study a band of several hundred mountain chimpanzees—a study he had been suggesting for twenty years. Never mind that she lacked a Ph.D. degree—she hadn't even gone to college. Never mind that she had no training in fieldwork or in biology. Never mind that she was only 23. And never mind that she had no money. All that mattered to Leakey was that these chimps be

■ Louis Leakey painstakingly probes for fossils with a dental pick. Here in Olduvai Gorge, located in Tanzania's Serengeti Plain, Leakey and his wife and sons uncovered bones of creatures who lived millions of years ago and who many paleontologists believe were early human ancestors. Because Leakey thought knowledge of the behavior of primates might shed light on the behavior of the hominids he was unearthing in the Olduvai, he promoted field observational studies of primates. After a stint at Olduvai, Jane Goodall agreed to Leakey's suggestion that she study chimpanzees in a nearby game reserve.

studied properly. It would take a long time to do it right, he pointed out. Two years would probably just be a good start. Leakey told Goodall that he was

particularly interested in the behavior of a group of chimpanzees living on the shores of a lake—for the remains of prehistoric man were often found on a lakeshore and it was possible that an understanding of chimpanzee behavior today might shed light on the behavior of our Stone Age ancestors [Goodall, 1971].

■ Jane Goodall accepts a banana from a wild chimpanzee on the Gombe
Reserve. But the chimps were not always this friendly. It took Goodall six frus-
trating months to get them even to let her come within sight. But she kept
trying until finally the two largest males, apparently as curious as she, let her
come quite close. Over the next several years, Goodall established close relationships with the chimps, learning to imitate the hoots and gestures they used to
express themselves, and eventually she got to be one of the bunch.

Goodall could "hardly believe that he spoke seriously" when he asked if she would undertake this work. When she agreed, Leakey dismissed all other objections as minor matters easily dealt with.

Within a short time Leakey sent Goodall back to London to study primates for a year. Next, he talked a small foundation in Des Plaines, Illinois, into putting up $3,000 to buy Goodall a tent, some supplies, and a plane ticket back from London. Then, Leakey secured a government permit to conduct a study on the Gombe Stream Chimpanzee Reserve. However, when officials at the Game Department learned that the actual study was to be done by a young woman, they refused to permit her to live alone in the bush. Goodall solved this problem without Leakey's aid—she simply took her mother along!

So, in 1960, Jane Goodall and her mother headed into the bush to observe the behavior of chimpanzees in the wild. Each day Goodall climbed into the mountains to seek the chimps while her mother passed the day in camp, sometimes providing minor first aid to local fishermen. And every evening Goodall returned disappointed. The chimps wouldn't let her near them. Once in a while she spotted them on a distant slope, but she could never get close enough even for the most superficial observations. This went on for six months. Then, one day, Goodall walked into a clearing and there, less than twenty yards away, were the two largest male chimps calmly grooming. Soon a female and a youngster peeked at Goodall from the tall grass nearby. Goodall sat motionless. After about ten minutes the two big chimps arose, looked at her, and sauntered away. She was ecstatic:

The depression and despair that had so often visited me during the preceding months were as nothing compared with the exultation I felt when the group had finally moved away and I was hastening down the darkening mountainside to my tent on the shores of Lake Tanganyika [Goodall, 1971].

Thus began a decade during which Goodall virtually became a member of this pack of chimpanzees. She came to know each one and learned to recognize and simulate the facial expressions, gestures, and hoots by which they communicated. And once the chimps began to let her come close, Goodall soon made discoveries that brought her international fame.

First of all, Jane Goodall saw chimps make and use tools. As she looked on, several chimps plucked long blades of grass, stripped off the leaves, licked one end to make it sticky, and poked the stem into a termite nest, pulling it out covered with termites. These they licked off as a child would a lollipop. Was this tool use? A **tool** is an object that has been *modified* to suit a particular purpose. A long blade of grass is not a tool. But when it has been stripped so it will slip down the hole in a termite nest, and when it has been made sticky so the termites will adhere to it, and when it is used to pull out termites, then it is a tool. Granted it isn't a very fancy or sophisticated tool. But, then, neither are stone tools like those the Leakeys were discovering in the Olduvai Gorge. In any event, this one observation was sufficient for Louis Leakey to tour the international lecture circle to proclaim that Goodall's work meant we must revise our definition of humans as "the tool-making animal." Chimps could do it too.

Goodall's second sensational discovery directly challenged the image of humans as depraved killer apes. Maybe humans did not take up meat eating until late in their evolution, as Lorenz and others have claimed, but chimpanzees, who clearly are less evolved primates than the hominids at Olduvai, eat meat. Regularly. Goodall frequently saw them catch, kill, and devour bushbucks and bushpigs. She also saw them frequently kill and eat monkeys and young baboons. Indeed, Goodall saw her chimps use sticks as clubbing weapons and throw rocks.

These early discoveries ensured Goodall's fame and ended all problems of financing further research—the National Geographic Society gave her annual grants. But what has ensured her immense scholarly reputation is the cumulative impact of her work. She has devoted years to her study, and this has caused her to modify and clarify many of her early conclusions as she came to know more. If she went out with no experience in observational field research, she soon developed superb work methods. Always evident in her work are the primary rules Goodall followed:

1. Record everything you notice, always, and file it so you can find it again.

2. After you have drawn a conclusion, search for evidence that *you are wrong.*

3. Never, ever think you understand everything that's going on.

Goodall's research was not the only work to undermine the notion that animal behavior is mainly unlearned and instinctive. A lot of animal behavior *is* instinctive, of course. That is, a pattern of behavior is somehow programmed into the biological heritage of a species so that all normal members of the species exhibit this behavior automatically and without any learning. For example, squirrels raised in an isolation cage and fed only a liquid diet will, in their first trial, bury nuts in exactly the same way as do adults that had observed and practiced nut burying from infancy (Eibl-Eibesfeldt, 1970). We can cite such examples almost indefinitely.

However, the list of animal behaviors that are *not* instinctual, and that must be learned, also has been growing long in recent decades. What could be more catlike than bathing? Yet, kittens separated from their mothers at a young age grow up to be cats that do not bathe. Moreover, many animals raised in a zoo are unable to mate. In 1975 the Sacramento Zoo in California finally resorted to showing a movie of two adult gorillas mating to their prized young gorilla pair, who seemed to want to mate but didn't know how. The film successfully provided them with the needed sex education. Clearly, then, for these species these are learned patterns of behavior that parents must pass to offspring just as humans must pass along their culture.

For many scientists, some of the most overpowering evidence of animal culture came from Harry and Margaret Harlow's years of experimentation with rhesus monkeys at the University of Wisconsin. In one major experiment, the Harlows (1965) raised three groups of infant monkeys. Monkeys in the first group were raised in total isolation and fed mechanically. Those in the second group were raised in isolation cages,

each with its mother. Infants in a third group were raised together but isolated from adults. Later all the monkeys were placed in a normal monkey colony, where their behavior was carefully recorded and assessed.

The behavior of monkeys raised in total isolation was extremely abnormal. They avoided all contact, cowered in corners, and never learned to engage in sex. Perhaps surprisingly, the monkeys who had been isolated with their mothers were nearly as abnormal as the first group; they also failed to learn sex or to adjust to social relations. Those raised in isolated groups without mothers showed the least abnormality and adjusted best to life in the colony, but they never became completely normal either.

These results indicate two things. First, monkeys must be exposed to monkey society from an early age, or they will fail to become normal monkeys. Second, many of the effects of isolation seem irreversible. None of the monkeys ever made up the deficits of infant isolation fully. As we shall see in Chapter 6, the effects of severe deprivation on humans bear striking resemblance to the same effects on the Harlows' monkeys.

Some social scientists object to applying the term *culture* to fighting or mating behavior, which many animals do not inherit but must learn. They would treat as culture only technology and claim that humans are the only animals who have it. If by technology we mean machines, then only humans have technology. But then are human groups without machines not in fact human?

In order to keep our ancestors within the human race, we must accept the very simple definition of tools already given, as purposeful alterations of objects. And, if we do, then we must acknowledge the existence of technology among nonhumans such as Jane Goodall's chimpanzees. Although recent human culture is immeasurably more complex and powerful than animal culture, we are not unique as toolmakers or in teaching our young how to behave.

Nonhuman language

One reason why nonhuman animals cannot develop more elaborate cultures is their lack of

■ In another famous experiment shown here the Harlows isolated infant monkeys each with two artificial "mothers." The mother at left is made of wire and has a nipple at which the infant can nurse. The second mother has no nipple but is made of cuddly terry cloth. When the Harlows frightened an infant it fled not to the wire mother (as Freudian theorists predicted) but to the terry cloth mother. This was evidence that the primary tie between infants and their mothers is not based on nursing, but on cuddling.

efficient communication. We recognize that animals do have some capacity for communication. Cries and calls meaning "Danger!" or "I'm looking for a mate!" are widespread among animals and birds. Also, animals often communicate with gestures and body movements. Male baboons challenge others to a fight by displaying their very light colored eyelids, for example. But animals can communicate little information through such means compared with

the immense amount that human language can communicate quickly and accurately. Lacking language, other animals have been stymied in sharing their experience and thus in accumulating and passing on knowledge. Consider how little a human parent, without speech, could teach a child. Teaching by showing is slow, and it seriously limits what can be taught. Without doubt, language is the human trait most responsible for our great superiority over other animals. If we are the kings of beasts, we talked our way into the title.

But why do only humans have language? No one is quite sure. For centuries people assumed that only humans were sufficiently intelligent to develop speech. But, in recent decades many careful observers of the higher apes, such as chimpanzees, have been uneasy with this assumption. Through long observation of ape behavior, they became convinced that apes display considerable intelligence. Their ability to solve problems, for example, is sufficient to suggest that they are smart enough to learn a language. And this has led to a series of efforts to teach chimpanzees to speak.

Several couples took an infant chimp into their home and raised it with their own children, hoping that the chimp would learn speech as the human child did. The Kelloggs (1933) may have been the first to try. Their ape did not learn to speak, but their child learned to scrape paint off the wall with his teeth and to give the characteristic chimp "food bark." Perhaps the most celebrated of these attempts involved a chimp named Viki, reared by two psychologists in the late 1940s. In six years of intense effort, they managed to teach Viki to utter four sounds which some listeners thought crudely approximated English words (Hayes and Hayes, 1951).

Speaking is impossible for chimps because they lack the vocal apparatus needed to produce speech sounds. In the wild they are usually silent and produce vocal sounds only during moments of extreme excitement. To try to teach them to talk was a little like trying to teach a human to swing by the tail. And blaming their failure to talk on a lack of intelligence was a little like blaming the human inability to swing through trees on stupidity instead of an unsuitable physique.

Washoe learns to sign

The breakthrough in determining the language-learning capacity of higher primates came in the late 1960s, when two daring psychologists at the University of Nevada realized that language does not require speech. In the wild, chimps seem to communicate mainly through gestures. Although these gestures do not constitute anything like a language, Beatrice and Allen Gardiner struck upon the idea of exploiting this natural tendency of chimps by attempting to teach a chimp the American sign language (used for communication by the deaf).

In June 1966, the Gardiners obtained a year-old female chimpanzee from Africa, whom they named Washoe. Verbal speech was never used in Washoe's presence; only American sign language was used. The Gardiners also undertook teaching sign language to Washoe. They were soon successful. The chimp began to acquire a vocabulary, much as any human toddler begins to pick up words. In time Washoe began to form the simple word combinations that pass for sentences among young humans (Gardiner and Gardiner, 1969).

As word began to leak out in the scientific community of these efforts, the Gardiners were much ridiculed and their claims quickly dismissed. But the Gardiners kept on working, and Washoe continued to develop a greater vocabulary and to fashion more sentences. Scientists were impressed when the Gardiners invited some deaf people without any previous contact with the project to come and communicate with Washoe. The scientists were sign-deaf, but the deaf people found no difficulty understanding Washoe. And Washoe understood them.

By October 1970, 5-year-old Washoe had a vocabulary of 160 signs (Fleming, 1974). Since chimps mature at much the same rate as humans, this was no minor accomplishment for her age. However, she was also getting big. A full-grown chimp weighs more than 120 pounds and is much stronger than any human male. So the Gardiners decided it was time to find her a different environment. Roger Fouts, who had studied with the Gardiners and worked with Washoe, took her with him when he joined the Institute for Primate Studies at the University of Oklahoma.

In Oklahoma, Washoe joined a number of other chimps and monkeys gathered for research on communication. A number of them were taught sign language, and Fouts and his colleagues were then able to study communication among chimps (in contrast with chimp-human communication). They were especially eager to see what would happen when chimps who had learned sign language had infants. Would they teach their infants to sign?

When Washoe was sexually mature, she was allowed to mate, and the researchers waited for her to give birth. Unfortunately, she miscarried. Two subsequent pregnancies ended in miscarriage and the early death of the infant. So Fouts obtained an infant male chimp named Loulis from the Primate Research Center at Emory University. Loulis was given to Washoe to raise. Within eight days of being adopted by Washoe, Loulis began to imitate her signs. By the age of 17 months, Loulis knew ten signs, including "hug," "drink," "food," "fruit," and "give me." Thus, apes can transmit at least some language to their young.

What do chimps have to say when they learn sign language? Obviously they do not begin to recount the history and traditions of chimpanzees. Lack of language has prevented such a culture from ever developing. If chimps do develop their own history, it can begin only now. Perhaps they will not prove to be sufficiently bright to develop and pass on a complex language or to contemplate their own existence. But before you dismiss the idea of chimps developing an elaborate culture as something that could happen only in *Planet of the Apes*, ponder the following account based on Washoe's first few days in her new Oklahoma home.

When she arrived in Oklahoma, Washoe had never seen any monkeys. Fouts therefore taught her a new sign: "monkey."

She was happy to use it for the squirrel monkeys and for the siamangs, but she concocted a different name for a rhesus macaque who had threatened her. She called him dirty monkey. *When Fouts asked her the sign for the squirrel monkeys again she quickly went*

■ Most social scientists were surprised to discover that apes could learn sign language and carry on conversations. They were even more surprised when these apes grew up and taught their infants to sign.

back to just plain monkey. But when they returned to the macaque, it was dirty *monkey. Before this incident, Washoe had used* dirty *to describe only soiled objects or feces. Since her meeting with the aggressive macaque, she has applied this sign to various teachers when they refuse to grant her wishes* [Fleming, 1974].

Washoe had invented an appropriate invective for what she didn't like. And as with any human 5-year-old, her first "bad word" was the equivalent of "poop." Who then can say how much more Washoe can learn?

Animal societies

To better understand the connections among biology, culture, and society, many social scientists now specialize in studies of social behavior among animals, the primary focus of Jane Goodall's work with chimpanzees. A major purpose of these studies is to seek basic elements of social organization by examining soci-

eties that have not been overlaid with a great deal of culture. That is, all human groups have cultures that are both elaborate and ancient. Even when we locate an isolated tribe with only Stone Age technology, we have not found people just inventing a culture. Such a group has a culture that has existed for centuries. We cannot return to the plains of Africa several million years ago to see human culture and society in its elementary forms. But if we are willing to assume that differences between humans and other primates are only of degree, not kind, then we can observe primates as substitutes for our most ancient ancestors.

A second virtue of animal studies is that we can manipulate the environment to study adaptation. Members of a primitive human tribe cannot be rounded up and moved to a new location to see what happens. But we can move animal societies—indeed, sometimes we have moved them to protect them from advancing human settlement. Recently, social scientists moved a group of macaques from Japan to Oregon. The results were surprising.

These macaques had long been studied in

Japan, but the troop grew too large. Scientists decided to move half of the animals to a new colony in Oregon. Thus, two groups with the same genetic heritage and, in the beginning, identical social and cultural patterns now faced a different climate and a different physical environment.

The group that remained in Japan continued as before, but the Oregon troop soon began to change in remarkable ways. In the Japanese troop, dominance among males is not based on their size or ferocity. Instead, it is determined by the size and ferocity of their mothers! When young male macaques fight, their mothers quickly come to their aid, and the tougher mother beats up the other mother and her son. Thus, young males learn not to mess with some mothers' sons. This dominance carries over into adulthood. Even a quite small male will dominate larger males if his mother won his fights for him when he was young (Eaton, 1976).

In Oregon, however, this pattern rapidly disappeared. This behavior was apparently a cultural, not a biological, trait. In Oregon the macaques live in a smaller area than in Japan, where the adult males tend to congregate far from the females and their young and hence do not intervene in youthful quarrels. But in Oregon, when a fight breaks out, the adult males quickly move in and break it up. Thus, mothers are not permitted to win fights for their sons, and male dominance is not established by the mother's fighting ability. Instead, males establish their own dominance system by fighting when they are mature.

In Oregon the macaques also encountered snow. They responded by inventing snowballs, which they can throw so far that the handlers must be cautious during the brief periods when there is snow on the ground. The macaques also learned to roll huge snowballs and sometimes make them into piles and play on them. But so far they have not built a snowman or even a snowmacaque (Eaton, 1976).

By observing primates, social scientists have gained insights into the creation of simple social structures and the invention of culture. Perhaps the link between humans and other animals can best be summed up as follows: Sometimes they appear to act just like us; sometimes we appear to act just like them.

Conclusion

This chapter has traced the radical turnabouts in how sociologists and other social scientists have dealt with the implications of biology for society and culture. At the start of this century, many social scientists attributed most individual behavior and many cross-cultural differences to biology. Then biology was excluded from all consideration. More recently, scientists have recognized the fascinating interactions among biological, cultural, and social elements. Moreover, the study of animal behavior, once the sovereign province of biology, has now attracted the interest of many social scientists. As a result, in about seventy years we have moved from the view that nearly all human behavior is produced by instincts governed by heredity to the view that much animal behavior is learned rather than instinctive.

The next chapter builds upon the interplay of biology, culture, and society as we ask how the potential humanity of newborn infants is fulfilled. We shall see that the process of socialization does not simply mean growing up or how children are raised. In a significant sense, we never finish growing up. Socialization is a lifelong process.

Review Glossary

instinct Any behavior that occurs in all normal members of a species without having been learned. (p. 120)

chromosomes Complex genetic structures inside the nucleus of a cell, each containing some of the basic genetic units (genes) of the cell. Chromosomes combine in pairs; thus, in humans, twenty-three chromosomes from the father combine with twenty-three from the mother. (p. 123)

genes The basic units of heredity within which specific genetic instructions are encoded in complex chemical chains. (p. 123)

genotype The sum total of genetic instructions contained in an organism's genes. (p. 123)

phenotype The observable organism as it has developed out of the interplay between the genotype and the environment. (p. 123)

behavioral genetics A scientific field that attempts to link behavior, especially human behavior, with genetics. (p. 124)

mental age The amount a person has learned by a given calendar age; for example, an 8-year-old who knows as much as the average 10-year-old has a mental age of 10. (p. 131)

IQ The abbreviation of *intelligence quotient*, which is mental age divided by calendar age, with the result multiplied by 100. The average IQ score is thus 100, for the calendar age of the average person is exactly equal to his or her mental age. (p. 131)

tool An object altered or adapted from natural materials in order to increase the ability of an organism to achieve some goal. (p. 139)

■

Suggested Readings

Eaton, C. Gray. 1976. "The Social Order of Japanese Macaques." *Scientific American*, Oct.

Gardiner, R. Allen, and Beatrice T. Gardiner. 1969. "Teaching Sign Language to a Chimpanzee." *Science* 165:664–672.

Goodall, Jane. 1971. *In the Shadow of Man*. Boston: Houghton Mifflin.

Rosenthal, David. 1970. *Genetic Theory and Abnormal Behavior*. New York: McGraw-Hill.

Sowell, Thomas, ed. 1978. *Essays and Data on American Ethnic Groups*. Washington, D.C.: The Urban Institute.

Tanner, James M. 1970. "Physical Growth." In *Carmichael's Manual of Child Psychology*, 3rd ed., edited by Paul Mussen. New York: Wiley.

Socialization and Social Roles

6

IN JUNE 1983, a Seattle judge gave permanent custody of a 6-year-old boy to the county welfare department. He asked that efforts be made to have the child adopted, despite protests from the child's father and mother. The judge based his decision on the fact that the child could not speak intelligibly, crawled rather than walked, and barked like a dog when people approached him. When found in his home by social workers, who had been alerted by a neighbor, the child was "filthy, smelled of urine, his teeth were rotten, he had sparse and brittle hair and a pale, pasty complexion" (Hopkins, 1983). After placement in a foster home, the boy was soon toilet trained and began to walk and talk.

This little boy's tragic condition was the result of isolation and almost total neglect. From infancy he had spent most of his days and nights alone in a filthy one-room home. His father was in prison, and his mother was rarely home, stopping by now and then only to feed him. Aside from his mother, he rarely saw a human being.

There have been countless cases like this, of children whose parents so neglected them and so isolated them from all human contact that when they were discovered, they acted more like wild animals than human beings. In fact, children like this are often called **feral children** (the word *feral* means "untamed"), and some people have mistakenly assumed that such children had been reared in the wild by an animal (Malson, 1972; McClean, 1978; Shattuck, 1980).

Human children cannot be raised by mother wolves, dogs, or other animals—such stories are fantasies. Unfortunately, demented or cruel human parents can raise their children like animals. Sometimes children thought to be feral are actually victims of mental retardation or severe mental illness, not neglect. But others, like the little boy in Seattle, are born with normal capacities, for they make rapid progress once they are rescued from isolation (Davis, 1940, 1947, 1949).

Feral children demonstrate an important principle: Our biological heritage alone cannot make us into adequate human beings. Only through social relations—constant intimate interaction—can the rich cultural legacy that sets humans apart from other animals be transmitted to new humans. An infant is born without culture. Reared in isolation, a human being will not even learn to talk or walk, let alone to sing or read.

The learning process by which infants are made into normal human beings, possessed of culture and able to participate in social relations, is called **socialization**. This process, which literally means to be "made social," begins at birth and continues until death—we never cease to be shaped by our interactions with others. As we pass through life, what others expect of us and the roles we are expected to fill all change. And we change, too.

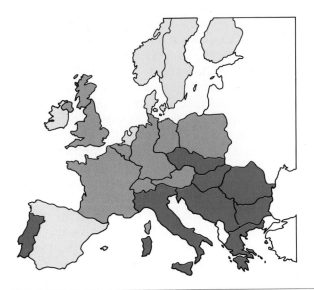

Percent of Women Married Before Age 20

Sweden	0.7
Denmark	0.9
Finland	2.0
Norway	2.1
Netherlands	2.5
Ireland	2.7
Spain	3.1

West Germany	3.4
Switzerland	3.7
United Kingdom	4.5
Austria	4.5
Poland	4.5
France	4.6
East Germany	4.9
Belgium	6.8

Italy	6.9
Portugal	7.3
Czechoslovakia	8.0
Greece	11.2
Hungary	14.3
Romania	16.0
Yugoslavia	16.1
Bulgaria	17.8

Figure 6-1 ■ **Teenage brides.** Because not all children are raised in the same way—even within the same family—we can expect variations from one nation to another to be substantial. A major factor in childhood socialization is the parents' expectations about what the child's adult roles will be. For example, in western Europe very few women marry while still in their teens. In eastern Europe many do. This dichotomy not only reflects differences in how they were raised but also justifies such differences to their parents. Parents in western Europe will be more likely than parents in eastern Europe to see a need for preparing their daughters to be self-supporting. That is, if young women are likely to marry in their teens, parents will be less willing to spend money sending them to school; this unwillingness, in turn, tends to encourage early marriage.

Chapter Preview

In this chapter we shall examine how humans are socialized. First we will see how infants acquire basic skills such as speech and the ability to reason. Next we examine how we discover that we are human—that we have a unique and independent identity separate from the external world. This is, how do humans develop a *self*? We then consider the concept of *personality*. What is its place in social science? How do people develop personalities? This sets the stage for an extended look at the link between culture and personality. How do societies shape people so they fit into particular cultural patterns? Here we will assess the rise and fall of cultural determinism. Midway in the chapter we reach the central sociological contribution to the study of socialization: Even in the same family, not all children are socialized in the same way. Instead, from infancy we are sorted out on the basis of the roles our parents expect us to perform as adults. Moreover, each time we enter a new role we undergo additional socialization as we learn how to perform it adequately. For example, much socialization is involved in performing such roles as parent, spouse, teacher, lawyer, or priest. Because of the crucial link between roles and socialization, the rest of the chapter will explore *differential socialization*—socialization related to roles and to role expectations. Next, we will connect roles and differential socialization with the development of *self-conceptions*—our perceptions of ourselves. Finally, we apply the principles of socialization to a major focus of current sociological interest: *gender*. How are we socialized on the basis of roles rooted in male-female differences: How are infants raised to be boys and girls, men and women?

Biophysical Development

Physicians and psychologists have done much of the research on socialization—aiming to discover the normal processes involved in the bio-logical and physical development of infants and children. Their ultimate aim is to further discover how normal development can be modified by the environment.

Years of testing infants at various ages have made it possible to determine patterns of normal development. For example, with reasonable parental care, children will usually learn to stand up by about the age of 8 months and to walk by about 14 months.

Statistical norms like these help parents and physicians to be alert to signs of slow development, in which case treatment or special training may be sought. But the norms also serve as a basis for assessing whether development is impeded by particular environmental circumstances or even whether enrichment of the environment can accelerate development.

Chapter 5 mentioned the work by Harry and Margaret Harlow (1965) with infant monkeys raised in isolation. As with feral human children, monkeys raised in isolation failed to develop normal monkey skills and displayed symptoms of acute maladjustment when placed in contact with normal monkeys. Similar studies cannot be conducted on human infants, yet cases of child neglect have supplied comparable data. For example, researchers have studied infants raised in orphanages for signs of impaired development.

In a classic study, Skeels and Dye (1939) conducted research in an orphanage on infants whose development at 19 months was judged so retarded that they were considered unfit for adoption. These infants were transferred to an institution for the mentally retarded, where Skeels and Dye arranged for each to be put under the personal care of an older, mildly retarded girl. Four years later the infants showed dramatic improvement. Their estimated IQs had risen by an average of 32 points, while similar infants who had remained in the orphanage had lost an additional 21 points over the same period.

Twenty-seven years later Skeels (1966) did a follow-up study of these same subjects. Most of the orphans who had been mothered by retarded girls had graduated from high school and a third had gone on to college. Nearly all of them were self-supporting and rated as normal. However, most of the people who had been in the control

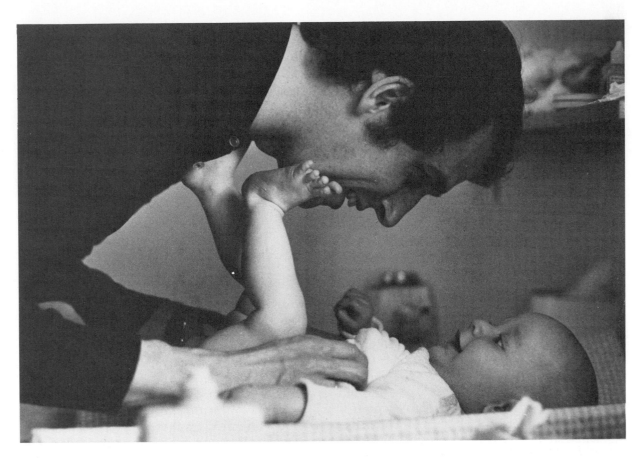

■ While special efforts to speed up infant development have little effect, neglect can cause development to be tragically retarded. Children need a great deal of daily interaction like this in order to fulfill their potential. This is no surprise if we remind ourselves how much each infant must master in a few short years to be normal.

group and remained in the orphanage had not progressed beyond the third grade and either remained in institutions or were not self-supporting.

Clearly, infants who lie unattended and unstimulated in crowded orphanages are deprived in much the same way as the Harlows' monkeys and feral children. As a result, despite a normal biological heritage, they fail to develop normally. Skeels and Dye's research prompted major reforms in the treatment of orphaned infants to prevent this sort of retardation. Today, most such infants are placed in foster homes rather than in institutions and thus receive more

normal levels of attention. Even when infants are raised in institutions, great effort is made to handle and cuddle each one often.

Can normal development be accelerated by special treatment? The answer seems to be only a little bit. One study showed that children who have toys suspended above their cribs, such as different-colored objects that attract interest and invite handling, can reach and grasp objects about six weeks sooner than children who lack such crib toys (White, 1971). However, the infants with crib toys did not begin to look at and explore their hands as soon as those without the toys.

There are two reasons why development

cannot be greatly accelerated for normal infants in normal settings. First, at least in modern times, the average infant seems to receive adequate stimulation and care (for a contrast with preindustrial times, see Chapter 13). Second, development is not only a psychological and social process. Fundamental physical and mental development must occur before infants can acquire certain skills. Coaching before such development takes place is to no avail, as we shall now see.

Cognitive Development

Learning is the key process in socialization. Thus, a primary issue in socialization theory and research is, How do we learn? Indeed, how do we learn to learn? Here we must know how the human brain operates, how it physically develops from birth, and how it builds up its capacities to solve problems and make choices.

Despite an immense amount of research and considerable theoretical progress, the brain still withholds many of its vital secrets. For example, when someone asks you if you know Bruce McElroy, you can say almost instantly whether you do. Computer experts are eager to know how humans can answer such a question so quickly. So far, the only way to answer this question with a computer is to have the computer search all names in its memory to see if "Bruce McElroy" is there. But that's not how our brain does it. We know the speed at which brain impulses travel, and people can answer too soon to have done a computerlike memory search. So the human brain must have more than just a simple file of all acquaintances; instead, a single bit of information such as "knowing Bruce McElroy" must be stored in a great many different files that are interconnected in the most complex ways. But, to say that is really to say little except that it's still a mystery.

If we don't understand exactly how the brain does many things, we do know a great deal about general patterns of what the brain can do—about the processes of learning and intellectual development. Here again, however, the brain has

turned out to be a subtler and more intricate mechanism than was first suspected. We do not simply build up knowledge and learning skills in a constant, gradual way. Instead, normal cognitive development passes through a series of stages, periods of slow progress interrupted by sudden spurts. One man played the major role in discovering fundamental patterns of cognitive development, or reasoning ability, so let's go back in time and look over his shoulder.

Piaget's theory of cognitive stages

 Jean Piaget (1896–1980) was a Swiss professor of psychology who successfully challenged the conventional stimulus-response theory of how children learn. In fact, he demonstrated that strict application of the **stimulus-response (or S-R) learning theory** led to a contradiction: People could not have thought up something like the S-R theory itself if our minds operate as stated by the theory.

The S-R learning theory, which for a long time dominated psychology, proposes a simple model of learning in which humans play only a passive role. The theory says that behavior is merely a response to external stimuli, and we repeat whatever behavior has been reinforced by our environment in the past. According to this view, the brain is little more than a memory bank capable of recalling past reinforcements, but it is not an active participant in the learning process; that is, it does not construct general rules or principles to guide future behavior. For example, S-R psychology dismisses the proposition that grammatical rules are acquired in learning to talk. Instead, it postulates that language is acquired word by word and then sentence by sentence through reinforcement. One of the attractive features of this view was that it freed psychology from relying on introspection and focused research on observable behavior. While psychologists can never be sure what is going on in people's minds, regardless of what people might say is going on, they can observe what people say and do.

Piaget found this extreme form of behaviorism unrealistic. If nothing but S-R learning is

■ The elderly man sitting on the bench, smoking his pipe, and watching the children play is Jean Piaget, the famous Swiss psychologist. Piaget's work on stages of cognitive development redirected the field.

going on, he argued, invention is impossible. How can anyone ever say a new sentence, for example, if we only acquire language by repeating what we are taught? *Any behavior that goes beyond what is present in our environment cannot possibly be a mere copy of the environment.* And Piaget pointed out that we invent all the time. In fact, much of modern mathematics cannot possibly be regarded as a reflection of external reality because it has no counterpart in reality. It is a human mental creation. Thus, Piaget (1970) wrote, "To present an adequate notion of learning one first must explain how the [person] manages to construct and invent, not merely how he repeats and copies."

Early in his career, Piaget became convinced that the human mind develops and functions on the basis of **cognitive structures**, or general rules for reasoning. His initial insight into this matter came from administering Binet's IQ tests to youngsters (see Chapter 5). What struck him were the consistent patterns of wrong answers. That is, time and again kids gave the *same* wrong answer to a given question. Why? Piaget concluded that the children were applying the same, but incorrect, rule to a problem.

This led Piaget to suspect that cognitive development involves coming to comprehend a set of basic principles or rules of reasoning; normal development consists of acquiring these rules by particular ages. Thus, the difference between children who correctly answered a particular IQ test question and those who chose the same incorrect answer was that the first group had acquired the rule needed for giving a correct response, while the *other group was still applying an inadequate or incorrect rule.*

Thus, Piaget set out to discover basic rules of reasoning and the ages at which normal children acquire them. First, he carefully observed his own children as they grew up; then he conducted a long series of experiments with large numbers of children. In the end he proposed that cognitive development passes through four fundamental stages: (1) sensorimotor, (2) preoperational, (3) concrete operational, and (4) formal operational. In a number of experiments, he showed that humans at one stage of cognitive development cannot solve problems requiring understanding at a higher stage and cannot be taught to solve these problems before they reach that stage of development. Let us briefly examine these stages and some of the pertinent experimental evidence.

The **sensorimotor stage** begins at birth and lasts until around the age of 2. During this period, infants discover and develop their senses and their motor skills. A major cognitive discovery during this stage is the *rule of object permanence*—the principle that objects continue to exist even when they are out of sight. Young infants immediately lose all interest in an object as soon as it is blocked from view; they do not search for it. But by about 10 months, children will search for an object when it is suddenly covered with a cloth or otherwise removed from sight: They know the rule of object permanence. However, a child takes a bit longer to begin searching for an object where it was last seen. Instead, young children will search where they last found the object.

The **preoperational stage** begins at about age 2 and ends at about 7. The earliest years of this period are devoted to language learning. However, the other major task during this period is to overcome egocentrism, or, to use a symbolic interaction concept discussed in Chapter 3, to learn to take the role of the other.

During the preoperational stage, children cannot solve problems that require them to put themselves in someone else's place. In a classic experiment, Piaget and Edith Meyer-Taylor constructed a model mountain range out of clay. Children were placed by the model and asked to describe it. Then they were asked to describe how it would look from where another child was standing (from a quite different perspective). Children in the preoperational stage were unable to get the point of the request and con-

tinued to describe the model from where they stood. As George Herbert Mead pointed out, this kind of limitation prevents younger children from participating adequately in team games.

The **concrete operational stage** begins at about 7 and ends at about 12 (many people never progress beyond this stage). In this stage children develop a number of logical principles that permit them to deal with the concrete, or observable, world. One such principle is the rule of *conservation*—that is, a given amount of material does not increase or decrease when its shape is changed. Children still in the preoperational stage do not yet understand this. If you present them with identical clay balls and then flatten one of the balls, they will say that the flattened ball is smaller and contains less clay. Similarly, when such children are presented with two identical rows of checkers and then one row is clustered into a smaller space, they will say the cluster contains fewer checkers than the row.

The **formal operational stage**, the final stage in Piaget's theory of cognitive development, often begins at about age 12. In previous stages children learn mainly by trying things out to see what happens. Eventually, however, some people learn to think abstractly and to impose logical tests on their ideas.

Recall the distinction between theories and hypotheses. Theories are abstract, general statements of a principle, while hypotheses are specific statements about the concrete world. In the concrete operational stage, people deal with the world only at the level of hypotheses, and they test hypotheses by examining concrete evidence. But when they reach the formal operational stage, people can formulate and manipulate theories and logically deduce from these theories that certain things are likely to be true or false. With this comes the ability to think hypothetically—to say "what if?" and then trace the logical implications of this supposition.

People still in the concrete operational stage miss the point of hypothetical assertions and often find them distressing. Suppose someone says, "Let's assume, for the moment, that humans were of only one sex and that every individual could bear infants. Would humans still form family units in order to make child

rearing easier?" People in the formal operational stage are able to pursue such a hypothetical line of reasoning, add to it, and evaluate it.
In so doing they may more fully understand why
the family is a universal human institution (see
Chapter 13). But people in the concrete operational stage will immediately object: "But people don't come in only one sex. Why are you
saying something so stupid? How can I suppose
that a lie like that is true? That's all just idle
nonsense. Let's go study families if we want to
really know what goes on."

Obviously, the formal operational stage never
ends. Some humans can continually refine their
ability to think logically and abstractly. Unfortunately, not everyone can do so. After testing
large numbers of people, researchers have concluded that perhaps half of all adults do not reach
the formal operational stage of cognitive development and thus are limited to literal interpretations of the world around them (Kohlberg and
Gilligan, 1971).

Several factors may prevent people from
achieving the ability for formal operations. Some
people may lack the necessary intelligence.
Others may not have the opportunity or the
need to develop powers of abstract reasoning at
this level. Although all normal humans have
constant practical experience with the concrete
world, many have little occasion for abstract
thought.

Because of Piaget's work, few psychologists
now propose that all learning is purely the result
of S-R mechanisms. Even many who devote most
of their own research to improving the S-R model
acknowledge that cognitive structures influence what is learned and when (Bandura, 1974).

Piaget's theory does not reject the importance of S-R mechanisms for a great deal of what
we learn. Rather it adds to this model. In particular, it adds an active human consciousness
that is capable both of formulating rules of reason to interpret the constant flow of environmental stimuli and of generalizing from a few
instances. For example, by falling from several
objects (such as trees and bicycles), we not only
learn that it hurts to fall from them but we also
learn the general principle that falling can hurt.
That saves a lot of bruises.

Brown and Bellugi: language acquisition

 If learning is the key to socialization, language is the key to
learning. Most of what we know,
we were told. Thus, a major area
of socialization is devoted to discovering how children develop the capacity to
use and understand language. Work on this topic
fills a large section in any good social science
library. By watching Roger Brown and Ursula
Bellugi (1964) conduct one of the landmark
studies in this area, we can see a sample of this
work and also understand how it supports
Piaget's stage theory.

In October 1962, Brown and Bellugi began
intense observation of two children whom they
called Adam and Eve. Adam was studied from
the age of 27 months to 36 months; Eve from
the age of 18 months to 36 months. These two
children were selected from an initial pool of
thirty because they talked a lot and because
Brown and Bellugi could understand what they
said. Brown and Bellugi visited Adam and Eve
in their homes every two weeks, took notes,
and tape-recorded everything said by each child
and by each mother as mother and child went
about their normal routines. The aim of the study
was to see how the acquisition of speech
progresses.

A number of important findings emerged.
First, Brown and Bellugi found that young children's speech is stripped of all but the most vital
words. Even when young children repeat a sentence just spoken to them, they tend to retain
only the nouns and verbs; they omit auxiliary
verbs, articles, prepositions, and conjunctions.
For example, when a mother said, "Fraser will
be unhappy," the child repeated, "Fraser unhappy"; when a mother said, "No, you can't write
on Mr. Cromer's shoe," the child replied, "Write
Cromer shoe." Only very gradually do children
begin to include more words in their sentences.

A second major finding was that not only do
children repeat what parents say but also that
parents frequently echo their children. In so
doing they expand and correct childish sentences. Thus, when Adam said, "There go one,"
his mother echoed, "Yes, there goes one." Brown

and Bellugi suggested that this interaction of repeating a phrase back and forth was a key to the development of speech. This may explain why the little boy in Seattle, mentioned in the introduction to this chapter, could not speak despite having had a fair amount of exposure to television. The TV never talks *with* you.

But perhaps the most important of Brown and Bellugi's results was clear evidence that young children experiment with speech in ways that appear to involve a search for grammatical rules. Often Adam and Eve spoke sentences that they could not possibly have heard from someone else:

"You naughty are."

"Cowboy did fighting me."

"A this truck."

"Put on it."

Brown and Bellugi believed that sentences such as these reflect a trial-and-error effort to discover the rules determining what words are allowed in which positions in sentences. Such a search for grammatical rules strongly confirms Piaget's theory of cognitive structures underlying learning. In fact, kids could hardly be speaking sentences like those above on the basis of S-R learning alone, for the sentences appear to be original. And that, of course, was Piaget's whole point. A mind is not simply a passive memory bank: Someone is in there thinking, not just recalling.

Interaction and cognitive development

Although Piaget criticized S-R learning for neglecting the active role the individual plays in his or her own development, other social scientists soon began to criticize him for neglecting the role of *social interaction* in his own work. That is, Piaget based his work primarily on studies of how children learn by manipulating *things*—inanimate objects. But, as Jerome Bruner (1977) and others pointed out, it is vital that the child deals with *objects that answer back*. In acquiring language, the human is also learning to engage in *symbolic interaction*. Consequently, these critics argued, the tradition of research and theory going back to Cooley and Mead (see Chapter 3) must be added to the work

by Piaget and by Brown and Bellugi. Two principal additions recommended were (1) recognizing the importance of strong bonds of attachment between an infant and his or her parents (or primary care-givers) and (2) recognizing the existence of special patterns of adult-to-infant verbal interaction that are crucial to infant language development. Let's examine each of these.

■ **Attachments and language** A number of child development theorists have stressed attachments as fundamental to language acquisition (Ainsworth et al., 1978; Bretherton et al., 1979). Inge Bretherton and her colleagues stated it this way:

Infants who can feel assured of their mother's availability and responsiveness, especially in situations of stress, can devote themselves more fully and enthusiastically to interacting with the physical environment. . . . They can learn more about the environment and properties of objects by teaching themselves.

But secure attachments also ought to result in more interaction between parent and child and in emotionally more satisfying interaction. Bretherton and her colleagues referred to this as the "attachment-teaching hypothesis."

Over the past several years an immense amount of research has been done to assess the importance of attachments for cognitive development and language acquisition. Social scientists have been amazed by the results. Attachments don't seem to matter. Of course extreme isolation and neglect do greatly impair child development, as in the case of the little boy in Seattle. But, within the *normal range* of adult-infant attachments, variations seem unimportant. As Elizabeth Bates and her colleagues (1982) put it, the degree of attachment a child enjoys "in normal circumstances is enough to acquire language, and more is not necessarily better."

■ **"Motherese"** A second aspect of interaction that has been a major focus of recent studies of language acquisition expands upon the attachment-teaching hypothesis. Brown and Bellugi noted that mothers not only echoed their children but also tended to use a somewhat childish language to communicate with a child. A number of later investigators have noted the same thing and have intensively analyzed it. Research in many different societies reveals the same phenomenon: When parents speak to young children they use a simplified, repetitive form of language that often exaggerates the aspects of a given language that children find most difficult to learn. Because it typically has been mothers whose speech to infants was studied, this modified language has been named *motherese*. Many studies have found that motherese is ideally suited to teaching languages. For example, Williams found that Spanish, English, and Chinese versions of motherese stress those sounds in a language that are hardest to tell apart (in Bates et al., 1982). Chinese is a tone language, using pitch or tone level to distinguish meanings among words that otherwise are alike. Consequently, Chinese motherese emphasizes the tone distinctions Chinese kids find hardest to learn. In the English version of motherese, extra stress is used to distinguish similar sounds—*d* and *b*, for example, will receive exaggerated stress.

These features of motherese have so impressed developmental theorists that there has been considerable speculation on how so powerful a "teaching tool" evolved (Moerk, 1975). In any event, it seems to exist everywhere. And without it, kids would probably find it much more difficult to master linguistic skills—or would they? Once again a great deal of research has been done. And once again the obvious seems not to be true. Kids not exposed to motherese acquire language as rapidly as those who are (Bates et al., 1982). But the *amount* of verbal interaction with adults matters; kids who are talked to more learn to talk sooner and better. However, the style of verbalization does not seem to make any difference. It has been suggested that motherese reflects parental frustration, not a superior teaching method. That is, parents engage in motherese in response to a child's errors in an effort to improve infant speech, but to no avail: The kids learn when they're ready.

Clearly infants require a great deal of interaction to learn how to speak and think. Clearly, too, kids need attachments to adults. But within these general limits, variations in the closeness

of attachments and in the patterns of verbal interaction seem relatively insignificant.

Emotional Development

Humans not only think but they also have feelings about things—feelings called emotions. Even newborn infants display strong emotions: Deny an infant something it wants, and watch the anger boil up. Part of socialization is learning self-control so that we have appropriate emotional reactions to the world around us. But to do so we must first develop what George Herbert Mead called the *self*. Recall from Chapter 3 that Mead identified the self as our learned understanding of the responses of others to our conduct. By seeing how others react, we gain understanding not only of them but also of ourselves. Once a self is formed, it begins to take on particular patterns of preference and response—patterns that can be described as a *personality*.

Let's briefly examine the origins of the self and the formation of personality.

Emergence of the Self

If you asked a baby, "Who are you?" you could not expect an answer. We have to discover who we are. In fact, we first must discover that we exist. Just as infants must discover their hands, they also must discover they are separate from the world around them. And, just as Mead argued, they must learn that from others through interaction.

In a classic sociological study, Reed Bain (1936) charted the vocabulary development of infants. Unlike Brown and Bellugi and other more recent language researchers, Bain didn't want to know *how* kids learned to talk. Instead, he wanted to know *when* they acquired words to indicate *others* and when they acquired words to indicate *self*. He discovered that we acquire other-related words sooner than self-related words. That is, we know "they" are out there before we learn that "we" are in here. And we learn about "us" from "them."

In Mead's analysis the self emerges but gradually, and the essential self-discovery occurs as we gain the ability to "take the role of the other"—to put ourselves in another person's place and gear our behavior to external perspectives. Until we can do that we cannot play team sports or perform any actions requiring coordination with others.

In addition to Bain's research on self-related and other-related words, the emergence of the self has been charted carefully in many studies of cognitive and linguistic development. For example, young children's speech is very egocentric in the sense that it often is uttered with little or no regard for being heard or understood. In fact, at the same time Mead was writing and teaching (in English) about taking the role of the other, Piaget (1926) was teaching and writing (in French) that children speak egocentrically, without regard for the hearer:

The talk is egocentric, partly because the child speaks only about himself, but chiefly because he does not attempt to place himself at the point of view of his hearer.

This point was well documented in a study by Flavell and his colleagues (1968). They asked a group of 8-year-olds and a group of 14-year-olds to explain the rules of a board game successively to two other students their age. One of the students in each pair was blindfolded. The 8-year-olds gave the same instructions to each listener—instructions completely inadequate for the blindfolded listener. The 14-year-olds gave much more elaborate instructions when addressing the blindfolded student than when addressing the one who could see. They could put themselves in the place of the blind. The 8-year-olds could not yet do so. Many other studies confirm this aspect of the emergence of the self (Schmidt and Paris, 1984).

Personality Formation

In Chapter 1 we saw that because humans have the capacity of choice—of free will—their behavior is predictable. In Chapter 3 we saw that most behavior is governed by norms that arise out of interaction. Norms are rules governing behavior and serve the function of making behavior predictable, for only if we can predict one another's behavior with considerable reliability is it possible for us to interact. If I have no idea of how you will react, I will not feel sufficiently safe to risk interaction. When we meet strangers we rely on our general knowledge of the norms and of human nature to anticipate how they will act. But through repeated interactions with others we gain much greater precision in anticipating their actions. Such anticipations are made possible because individuals typically display a *consistent pattern of thoughts, feelings, and actions*. We refer to such a pattern as their **personality**.

In terms of their personalities, all humans are alike in certain ways; in other ways, every human is like *some* other humans; and in some ways each human is unique, like no one else (Kluckhohn and Murray, 1956). By seeing how all three claims can be true, we can examine elements of personality.

All humans are alike because some factors that form our personalities are universal. We all share the biological endowments of humanity. We all are subject to the same general physical environment governed by the same laws of nature. All normal humans acquire language. All of us reason. Each of us seeks to make more rewarding choices from among the options we perceive. All of us must learn the culture of our group and society.

All humans are like only *some* other humans because the contents of culture vary from group to group. Norms do not simply limit behavior, but they frequently are incorporated into the personality as well. That is, usually people not only know the rules but they also *believe in them*. Because norms differ from place to place, so too will the belief systems of typical members of different societies. This also will be true of their emotional reactions and, ultimately, of their behavior. Thus, for example, a normal person in one society will be provoked into a towering rage by something that will be passed off as trivial in another culture.

Finally, no two people ever have identical biographies, and, therefore, no two people ever have precisely the same personality. Each of us has a unique historical pattern of interaction with our social and physical environment, and this pattern provides us with individuality. While we are interesting to one another because of our unique qualities, these are of limited interest to social scientists (except for those engaged in psychotherapy). The business of science is to seek *generalizations*, and that turns our attention from the unique to the common. No social scientist cares that your friend Jack hates cats. But we would be interested in a cat-hating society.

Thus far in this chapter we have attended to the universal aspects of socialization. There is every reason to suppose that children deep in the Amazon jungle acquire language in much the same way as Adam and Eve did in Boston and that parents in Guam use motherese. We expect children everywhere to develop a self and learn to take the role of the other much as Mead and Piaget proposed. However, for the remainder of the chapter we shall explore how particular cultural and social structural patterns and the socialization process interact. That is, how are people socialized to be like *only some other people?*

■ Franz Boas.

Culture and Personality

Chapter 5 discussed the reaction of social scientists in the 1920s and 1930s against extreme biological determinism—theories that attributed most of human behavior to such things as instincts rather than learning. This reaction involved the equally extreme claim that biology was insignificant and that environment alone determined human behavior.

A leader of the environmentalists was Franz Boas (1858–1942), the first appointed professor of anthropology at Columbia University. Boas published and taught the principle of **cultural determinism**. According to this principle, regardless of how a given culture came into being, the culture wholly determined the behavior of all persons who were socialized within it. Moreover, Boas argued that human nature is infinitely plastic, that cultural forces can create

virtually any kind of personality type and any patterns of roles and behaviors. For example, he argued that sex roles had no biological basis but simply reflected cultural forces that blinded us to other possibilities. Moreover, Boas took the view that culture made its deep and permanent effects on people during early childhood. That is, a particular culture determined how people would think and act as a result of specific patterns of child rearing, which shaped the immature personality into the desired mold.

By postulating this powerful link between child rearing and personality, Boas was, in effect, *equating culture and personality*. Or, as his famous student Ruth Benedict (1934) put it, culture is "personality writ large." That is, the individual personalities of the members of a society are tiny replicas of their overall culture, while their culture is the summation of their personalities.

The major problem facing Boas and his supporters was to demonstrate exceptions to all generalizations that had been made about human behavior and personality so that they could claim that existing patterns are only common, not necessary—that an almost infinite array of cultural and social forms is possible.

Cultural determinism reached its peak of influence during the long career of Margaret Mead (1901–1978), Boas's most famous student. In 1931 Mead traveled to New Guinea in search of tribes that would prove Boas was correct in his claims that patterns of socialization in early childhood strictly determine the adult personality—or what he and Mead often called "temperament." More specifically, Mead intended to prove that sex roles can take virtually any form. To do this, she hoped to locate a tribe in which both male and female members develop "feminine" temperaments and another in which both genders have "masculine" temperaments. And she planned to demonstrate that these patterns of gender temperament were the result of early childhood socialization practices.

Once in New Guinea, Mead quickly discovered tribes she believed exhibited precisely these patterns, and she found them "conveniently within a hundred mile area" (Mead, 1935). In her famous book, *Sex and Temperament in Three Primitive Societies* (1935), Mead claimed that among the Arapesh of New Guinea, the ideal personality type for both men and women is gentle, unaggressive, responsive, cooperative, and passive—that is, both male and female Arapesh have "feminine" temperaments. Mead argued that this was the result of extremely gentle child-rearing practices in which both parents played equal roles. For example, Arapesh children were not weaned or toilet trained until they were relatively old. This avoided repression and shaped their personalities into a gentle, feminine disposition.

In contrast, among the cruel Mundugumor, Mead found the temperament of both men and women to be "masculine," that is, unrelentingly aggressive, cruel, suspicious, and violent. The Mundugumor were (and are) cannibals and treated one another almost as savagely as they did enemy tribes. Mead explained this on the basis of their brutal child-rearing practices. Mothers resented nursing their infants and used slaps and shoves to wean them at an early age. Children were cuffed and kicked whenever they displeased their parents. This, according to Mead,

soon turned them into little monsters destined to become adult monsters like their parents.

From these findings, Mead concluded that male and female temperaments have no biological basis whatever. She further concluded that culture is the source of personality, imposing its marks indelibly during infancy.

Mead was often criticized for working too fast and for invariably finding the world to be as she expected it to be. Thus, when asked to write a preface for a new edition of her book, she took the opportunity to scorn unnamed critics who suggested that her findings were "too good to be true," and that she must have just "found what I was looking for" (Mead, 1950). In the decade since her death, a raging battle has erupted between Mead's supporters and critics of her scientific objectivity and methods (Freeman, 1983).

But let's not worry more about the accuracy of Mead's observations in New Guinea. Let's take her at her word. In doing so, we can spot some of the omissions and logical shortcomings of extreme cultural determinism.

The first shortcoming is insensitivity to physical realities. Mead tells us that the gentle Arapesh live in an almost inaccessible part of New Guinea, unsuited to growing crops. The Mundugumor, on the other hand, live on a rare tract of excellent growing land—high, well drained, and clear of the jungle. Let's pretend we know nothing about the Mundugumor except the desirability of their location and the fact that dozens of other tribes would like to live there as well. Might we not suspect the Mundugumor to be the meanest, toughest bunch of warriors on the island? If they weren't, why wouldn't tougher folks have driven them off and taken their land? This reminds us that culture isn't just the accidental result of mental processes. There is always a real world to be reckoned with that imposes its tests of fitness on any culture (Harris, 1979). Indeed, if the Arapesh were at all as gentle as Mead portrayed them, that might explain why they ended up with the worst piece of real estate on the whole island.

But a more compelling problem is the assumption of a direct and everlasting link

■ Among New Guinea tribes such as this one, Margaret Mead claimed to find proof that early child-rearing practices determine the adult personality and that human nature is essentially plastic, making virtually any cultural pattern possible. For sociologists, however, the most striking thing to be seen in this picture is differential socialization. The little boy in the foreground already is becoming a very different kind of person from those the young girls in the background are becoming. This process is not limited to childhood. The adult males in this picture lead daily lives far different from those of their wives, and thus basic male-female personality differences are recreated and constantly reinforced.

between early childhood socialization and adult personality. Consider this question: At what age would a child taken from the Arapesh and given to the Mundugumor still grow up with an Arapesh personality? Would it be too late to change at 2, or 5, or 15? At what age is it impossible to transform an individual? There is no clear answer because *socialization is not something that happens to infants and then stops.* It is a life-long process. A lot happens between the time when children are weaned and the time when they become adults, just as a lot can happen to change people remarkably between the ages of 30 and 40 or 60 and 70.

The whole structure of Mundugumor and Arapesh life, not just early childhood experience, supported their particular styles of behavior. A Mundugumor warrior who began to mellow might end up in a neighbor's cooking pot. Being fully aware of that, he would not need to draw upon his early childhood training to remember to stay tough.

Despite these problems, however, we must recognize that the major shortcoming of the cultural determinists was that they pushed their position too far. No one would deny that cultures can differ greatly and that among these differences are great variations in how people are expected to act. For example, the average Mundugumor, male or female, is obviously very different from the average German. If we acknowledge such differences, we must also acknowledge that they are produced by differences in socialization—that a Mundugumor infant sent off to be raised in Germany would become a German. Of course, early childhood socialization is not irrelevant—it simply is the start of a lifelong pattern by which, for example, Germans become and remain Germans.

The failures of the cultural determinism advocated by Boas and Mead are those of exaggeration and omission. Boas and Mead were correct in arguing that culture is extremely important in shaping humans, but they were excessive in saying that it is the *only* thing that matters. They were correct in arguing that human nature can be shaped into a great variety of expressions, but they were excessive in saying that virtually any cultural and personality pattern is possible. Finally, they were correct in arguing that child-rearing practices constitute a major aspect of the socialization process, but they were excessive in saying that only childhood socialization matters.

Suppose an adult Mundugumor warrior moved to Texas. He probably would never become just like a native Texan, but he would soon be very different from his friends back in New Guinea. Moreover, the ways in which he would change would depend a lot on the kinds of roles he assumed in Texas. Suppose he became a linebacker for the Dallas Cowboys or a cowboy on a ranch. The socialization involved in these two roles would produce rather different outcomes.

We will now leave the South Seas and examine processes of **differential socialization**: how roles determine how people are socialized, and how this process prolongs socialization throughout an individual's lifetime.

■

Differential Socialization

Whatever the shortcomings of Margaret Mead's fieldwork, one thing is certain: In no society she visited were all children being raised in the same way. For example, not all Mundugumor children were expected to be equally fierce, to develop the same basic personality, or to learn the same physical and mental skills. Instead, from infancy, children are sorted out in a variety of ways and socialized in different directions because they are expected to lead different lives. Put another way, they are being groomed to fill quite different social roles.

Recall from Chapter 2 that a social role is a set of shared expectations about the behavior of a person occupying a particular position in a society. A role consists of a set of norms applying to a particular position, and these norms serve as a script to be followed by those people filling that position.

Every society can be conceived of as a collection of related roles. Even simple societies have a number of different positions—son, daughter, father, mother, aunt, uncle, cousin, warrior, hunter, cook, gardener, grandfather, grandmother, chief, and priest, to name but a few. Each of these positions has a unique role associated with it; the role of priest, for example, is quite different from that of hunter, although the same person may alternate between these roles.

Many social roles make major demands on those who fulfill them, and thus people must often undergo long and rigorous training before taking on such roles. Moreover, not just anyone is thought to be eligible for any role—for example, males are not qualified to be daughters. In addition, people often aspire only to some roles and not to others. In short, people are socialized to hold certain positions and fulfill those roles.

All societies have differentially socialized people on the basis of sex: Males and females fulfill quite different sets of roles, and from infancy they are prepared to lead different lives. Although gender is the most universal and dramatic instance of differential socialization, it is but one of innumerable bases determining how people are socialized.

To illustrate this point, let's examine the differential socialization of two brothers born a year apart in England at the turn of the century. From birth, the eldest son was the legal heir to his father's title as Baron of Buncombe and to the family estate: 2,000 acres of land and Buncombe Hall, an eighteen-room Gothic manor house. The younger son would inherit no title and no estate. At most, he could hope for a modest cash inheritance. From the day of their births, these boys faced very different futures, and they knew they would play completely different roles as adults. Almost from the day of their births, they were treated differently by parents and servants.

The elder son was taught to ride and hunt and was instructed in the management of the estate. While still a lad, he rode with his father to call on the tenants who farmed various portions of the estate. On these trips he was constantly instructed in how to act like a proper lord of the manor, and he often encountered sons of tenants who were being prepared to replace their fathers and one day be his tenants.

Meanwhile, the second son was left out of most of these socialization activities. As long as he could remember, he had been aware that he would have to prepare for an occupational career—not just any career, of course, but one fit for the younger son of a baron. Usually, this meant a career in the army or in the church. Since his mother preferred that he go into the church, his father agreed that he should be prepared to become a priest of the Anglican Church. As a result, he was left in the company of his mother more often than of his father, and his tutor made him study hard. The elder brother could get away with little study and with modest school achievements, but the younger brother was drilled hard in Latin, Greek, history, classical literature, and music, although, unlike his brother, he was not made to learn accounting.

At the appropriate age, each boy was sent off to a famous boarding school, but the elder was given more money to spend and was not expected to do better than passing work. The younger was pushed relentlessly in school because he would need to attend the university.

As an adult, the elder brother was self-confident, bold, and extremely well mannered—many regarded him as a born leader. He was a terrific rider and sportsman. The younger brother grew up to be somewhat shy. He often seemed ill at ease in large gatherings and preferred not to ride, hunt, or fish. While the elder brother spent many years as a popular and eligible bachelor and did not marry and settle down until he was past 40, the younger brother married at 25 and soon had a large family. As a father, the priest was mild and undemanding and treated all his sons much the same. In contrast, the baron was soon taking his eldest son on visits to the tenants. His younger son, however, was meant for the army, so both boys did an equal amount of riding and hunting.

This is a classic case of differential socialization based on differing expectations of roles that the children would assume. Notice, too, that each brother was socialized somewhat differently to perform some of the same roles. The role of father carried a different script when it was combined with the role of Anglican priest instead of with the role of baron. Indeed, the role of husband was also scripted somewhat differently.

Differential socialization has long been the object of considerable sociological research. Of particular concern has been the way in which parents' expectations about their children's future influence patterns of socialization. Perhaps no one has pursued this question longer and more effectively than Melvin Kohn.

Melvin Kohn: occupational roles and socialization

 Melvin L. Kohn is chief of the Laboratory of Socio-environmental Studies of the National Institute of Mental Health in Washington, D.C. In 1956 he conducted a study of the values guiding child-rearing practices among American parents. The results revealed some notable class differences.

Working-class parents (manual laborers and blue-collar workers) placed greater stress on such values as obedience, neatness, and cleanliness than did middle-class parents. The latter thought such values as curiosity, happiness, consideration for others, and especially self-control were more important. Both groups gave equally high importance to honesty (Kohn, 1959).

Kohn argued that these findings reflected two underlying value clusters. Working-class parents were more concerned about their children *conforming* to the expectations of others, especially expectations concerning good behavior; middle-class parents were more concerned about their children being capable of *self-expression* and independence. Put another way, working-class parents placed more importance on values involving external judgments (on pleasing others), while middle-class parents stressed values involving internal judgments (on pleasing oneself).

Kohn was careful to point out that these class differences were only tendencies. Parents of all classes regarded all of these values as important in raising children. But the emphasis given to these two clusters of values differed among the two classes.

Kohn then asked whether these differences in how parents socialized their children affected how they actually treated their children. His research led him to identify two primary differences in child-rearing practices. The first pertained to why parents punished their children, the second to who punished them.

Kohn found that working-class families tended to punish children on the basis of what a child did. That is, if a child was prohibited from jumping up and down on the couch or yelling and then did so, the child was punished. In contrast, middle-class parents tended to be more concerned about the motives behind behavior than about rule violations as such. Thus, if a child broke a rule against yelling in the house, the parents would punish on the basis of why the child yelled. Yelling done out of anger or a loss of self-control would tend to be punished. But if it was done out of enthusiasm or happiness, middle-class parents would ignore it. In

effect, working-class parents reinforce conformity to external authority, while middle-class parents reinforce self-control and self-expression.

Middle-class parents feel an obligation to be *supportive* of children to encourage self-expressiveness. Moreover, they feel both parents should be supportive, just as they feel both should share responsibilities for disciplining children. Working-class parents, on the other hand, tend to have a division of responsibility in child rearing. Mothers take primary responsibility for the children and tend to be the supportive parent. Fathers are delegated the responsibility of enforcing the rules. Thus, when a child is caught jumping on the bed in a middle-class family, a family conference is likely to be held. In a working-class family, the child is told, "Well, when your dad gets home, he's not going to be happy about this." Again, Kohn was careful to point out that these are only tendencies; in many middle-class families, husband and wife divide the discipline and support responsibilities, while in many working-class families, parents take equal roles in child rearing.

The next question Kohn faced, of course, was why do these different tendencies exist between working- and middle-class families? Kohn's initial answer was that these tendencies reflect a parent's own experience with how the world works. He especially emphasized work experience. Working-class parents are more successful in jobs when they observe the rules: when they are prompt, do what they are told, and show up for work looking neat and clean. Middle-class parents find they are more successful in jobs when they can work without supervision, take individual initiative, and get along well with co-workers. Parents draw upon this personal experience in deciding how to raise their own children—they raise them to succeed in the adult roles they expect their children to adopt.

This interpretation led Kohn to decide that social class as such was not the significant independent variable. Instead, he realized that the actual work conditions the parents experienced should be the real focus of research. Although class differences are correlated with the nature of working conditions, the correlation is far from perfect. Thus, some working-class people have jobs, such as repairing home appliances, that

■ These two Seattle fishermen do not hold high-status, high-income jobs. But they are their own bosses. Not only does no one supervise their work—usually no one else is even in sight when they are pulling in their nets or their crab traps. In contrast, many high-status professionals work under close supervision and constant observation. Melvin Kohn has found that the degree to which people work under supervision is more important than their income or job status in determining how they raise their children. Degree of supervision even influences the basic personality of many workers.

require a great deal of self-supervision and individual initiative. Conversely, many middle-class people work in highly supervised and controlled office jobs. So Kohn set out to refine his results by examining occupational, and not simply class, effects.

The results were as predicted: Parents' work conditions, not their social class, influenced whether they stressed conformity or self-expression in raising their children (Pearlin and Kohn, 1966; Kohn and Schooler, 1969).

Kohn also demonstrated that experience with adult occupational roles not only influenced child-rearing practices but also reflected basic personality characteristics of the parents. That is, parents whose work experience placed a premium on conformity stressed this in raising

children and had more conformist and less flexible and expressive personalities themselves (Kohn and Schooler, 1969). This raised a new question. Did correspondence between job experience and personality reflect *selection*? Were people with flexible, self-expressive personalities more likely to obtain jobs requiring little supervision and rewarding initiative and innovation? Or was this evidence of **adult socialization**? Were people changed by socialization into adult roles and thus taught to be more flexible or conformist, depending upon the conditions of their occupation?

Such a question could be answered only by a **longitudinal study**, in which observations are made of the same people at several different times. In this way, one can see what people are like before they enter a role and after they have performed it for a while. Since Kohn had already based one of his studies on a national sample of more than 3,000 employed American men, ten years later (in 1974) he arranged to reinterview them. Once again the results were striking.

Both selection and adult socialization account for the correlation between work conditions and personality. People with more flexible, self-directed personalities are more likely to obtain jobs with little supervision and much opportunity for individual initiative. Conversely, less flexible, less self-directed people gravitate toward more structured and more supervised occupations. However, people's personalities also tend to suit their jobs better as time goes by. People in highly structured jobs become less flexible and less self-directed. People in less-structured jobs tend to become more flexible and self-directed (Kohn and Schooler, 1982).

The two primary lessons from Kohn's pioneering research are:

1. Children are socialized differentially on the basis of parental expectations about the roles the children will assume as adults; understandably, parents base these expectations on their own experiences.

2. Socialization is a lifelong process. In Kohn's sample, even men 50 and older showed shifts in basic personality traits in response to their occupational roles.

In the past decade Kohn's work has been replicated in many other nations, including Taiwan, Italy, Japan, Ireland, Germany, and Poland (Kohn and Schooler, 1983). In each society, the nature of the parent's work experience greatly influences his or her values governing child-rearing practices. Moreover, in recent work, Kohn and his associates have found that *variations in housework* influence a woman's psychological flexibility and the value she places on self-directedness (Kohn and Schooler, 1983). That is, the more complex the household tasks a woman performs, the greater her psychological flexibility and the more she values self-direction.

However, a new study done in Canada suggests serious limits to the socialization effects demonstrated by Kohn. On the basis of longitudinal data from Ontario, E. Dianne Looker and Peter C. Pineo (1983) found the same strong correlations between parental working conditions and parental orientation toward self-direction or conformity in child rearing found elsewhere. However, they failed to find any indication that these parental orientations were effectively transmitted to their children. That is, there were no significant correlations between parents' self-direction/conformity values and those of their teenage children. This does not mean that the parental values isolated by Kohn have no impact on what happens to their children but only that such effects, if they exist, do not depend upon children having adopted these values from their parents.

Thus far we have seen that socialization prepares people for roles and that roles, in turn, shape socialization. At this point we need to consider more closely how people go about performing social roles.

Erving Goffman: performing social roles

Elizabethan playwright William Shakespeare (1564–1616) wrote in *As You Like It*:

All the world's a stage,
And all the men and women merely players:
They have their exits and their entrances,
And one man in his time plays many parts.

But it was sociologist Erving Goffman (1922–1982) who most effectively analyzed social interaction from the point of view that life really is a stage and that much of the time we are putting on performances for one another.

Goffman (1961) made an important distinction between role and role performance. *Role* refers to how a person would act if he or she did only what the norms attached to a particular position directed. **Role performance**, in contrast, is "the actual conduct of a particular individual while on duty in [a] position."

Goffman pointed out that while roles do greatly shape our behavior, we rarely act only according to the script. "Perhaps there are times," he wrote, "when an individual does march up and down like a wooden soldier, tightly rolled up in a particular role." But most of the time we are not wholly confined by a role. Instead, we constantly display glimpses of ourselves, or the individual "behind" or "inside" the role. Moreover, we sometimes give an unconvincing, discreditable, incompetent, resentful, or even defiant performance.

Like a drama teacher, Goffman identified the basic techniques for giving adequate role performances (Goffman, 1959, 1961, 1963, 1971).

First of all, Goffman examined the costumes and props we use in role performances. Simply by wearing the appropriate clothing or carrying the right props, we can often make a convincing appearance in a role. As a young newspaper reporter, I once gained access to the medical files of a celebrated mass murderer by putting on a white coat and hanging a stethoscope around my neck. In a huge county hospital, that was sufficient proof that I was a resident physician with the right to wander onto wards and look at charts. (Such a deception would violate the role of sociologist, but not the role of reporter.)

Of course, if I had not also had the right kind of haircut, been of the appropriate age, and been able to exude the impression of bored self-confidence, someone might have asked me who I was. This illustrates Goffman's insight that a major aspect of the way we present ourselves in roles involves **impression management**—the conscious manipulation of scenery, props, costumes, and our behavior to convey a particular role image to others.

■ Just a few weeks ago these young men wore jeans and T-shirts and acted like most other people just out of high school. Now they wear a suit and tie every day and are rapidly trying to learn how to act mature and serious. They are undergoing several weeks of intensive training to prepare them to conduct themselves in the role of Mormon missionary for the next two years. Nearly half of young Mormon men (and a growing number of young women) volunteer to serve as one of the more than 30,000 unpaid missionaries their church has at work around the world. But before they go, they must be socialized into this new and demanding role.

Goffman also pointed out that roles in life, like those in the theater, have both a *stage* and a *backstage*. Waiters in a restaurant, for example, give a stage performance to customers and a more relaxed backstage performance in the kitchen, where only the cooks and other waiters see them. Professors act out their roles somewhat differently when they chat with students in the hall from when they are in front of a class.

In addition, *teamwork* is often involved in an adequate role performance. For example, a husband and wife holding a party will often prompt one another in their roles. Moreover, an effective role performance often requires that others play along. A hostess cannot play her part if the host begins to swear at her, throws his plate on the floor, takes off his clothes, or otherwise falls out of his proper role. Similarly, a parent cannot convincingly scold a child if the other parent is laughing at the misbehavior.

Another kind of teamwork plays a vital, but often little noticed, role in facilitating adequate role performances. Goffman called this **studied nonobservance**. For Goffman, this is a powerful and civilizing norm based on the acceptance of our common humanity. It is summed up by the phrase, "After all, we're only human." Through nonobservance, we come to one another's aid by covering up miscues in role performance. When we are embracing a lover and his or her stomach grumbles, we pretend not to hear it. When someone unconsciously scratches inappropriately, we pretend not to see it. Day in and day out, we are careful not to notice the little slips that mar role performances. In fact, a major aspect of good manners is to not notice bad manners.

Of course, we don't ignore all failures in role performance. While actors on the stage may only risk bad reviews for a poor performance, in real life people sometimes lose their friends, their jobs, their families, and even their liberty because they have violated their roles.

Moreover, people sometimes suffer these consequences even when they have given a superb role performance—because they were acting out a **deviant role**. Some positions in society and their roles are against the law. Thus, while the bank officer who embezzles risks jail for an inadequate role performance, the robber who withdraws funds from the same bank risks jail for performing a deviant role. In Chapters 7 and 8 we shall examine deviant behavior and deviant roles.

Self-Conceptions and Roles

Symbolic interactionists postulate that we see ourselves as others see us, that the self is a social construction. An immense amount of research effort has gone into assessing how we evaluate ourselves (Wylie et al., 1979). Do we hold a favorable or unfavorable self-conception, and what factors influence our judgments? The primary finding of this research is that the roles we play greatly shape self-conceptions.

Sociologists have often asked their students to take the following test: Number a sheet of paper from 1 to 20. Then using twenty different words or phrases, answer the question, Who am I? If you are like most people who have done this, your answers will be dominated by roles (Kuhn and McPartland, 1954). For example:

1. A student
2. A basketball player
3. A senior
4. A man

But it isn't enough to just ask people who they are. We also need to know *how they feel about being the person they believe themselves to be.* So, after each of your answers you could rate yourself on each. First, are you satisfied or dissatisfied with this characteristic? Second, would you like to change this characteristic? Third, in terms of this characteristic, do you feel you are as good as most, better than most, worse than most?

Recently, Anne McCreary Juhasz (1985) used a technique very like this to assess the self-esteem or self-conceptions of 219 seventh- and eighth-grade students in a midwestern city in the United States. Her major finding was that gender has a potent effect on self-conceptions. Boys see themselves more favorably than do girls. Moreover, many studies have found that girls tend to rank male traits higher than they do female traits (Wylie et al., 1979; Richer, 1984).

Of course, gender roles are not the only roles that influence self-conceptions. Occupations, hobbies, education, marital status—all influence how we see ourselves. But none has as much influence as do our gender roles. Therefore, to conclude this chapter let's examine how people are socialized to become "men" and "women."

Sex-Role Socialization

Most human societies have drawn sharp distinctions between male and female roles. And most of them have thought that these differences simply reflected biological facts of life. Obviously, males and females are different anatomically. Equally obviously, these differences have played *some* part in structuring a division of responsibilities. Only women can bear children. Only women can nurse an infant. In premodern times these two facts were quite significant. With high rates of fertility, women often had restricted mobility, and they also tended to suffer from chronic infections caused by childbirth. Prior to modern baby formulas, infants could only be nourished by breast-feeding. That meant a mother had to stay sufficiently near her infant to be able to feed it frequently. In addition to reproductive differences, most women also are smaller than men, which had social significance when much labor depended on muscle power.

But while these biological facts are self-evident, how important are they? Most human societies have thought them to be so important that they justified the subordination of women to the control of men. Yet, the fact that some societies have taken a much different, more egalitarian approach to gender relations makes it clear that most of the differences we can see between the sexes in most societies are cultural, not biological (O'Kelly and Carney, 1986). Hence, Chapter 12 is devoted entirely to exploring and explaining cross-cultural variations in gender inequality.

Of course, no matter what view they take of proper sex roles, to most members of any society it is seldom obvious that such basic features of their culture are optional and arbitrary. As we have seen, that's not how socialization works. Instead, to the extent that a culture defines gender roles as distinctly different, parents will raise girls and boys so that they *will be different*. In addition, these girls and boys will grow up *wanting* to be different, believing that these differences in sex roles are not only normal but also necessary. So if a society believes, as most have, that men are supposed to be aggressive while women are supposed to be gentle, that's how most men and women in that society will be.

With this in mind, let's look at patterns of differential sex-role socialization in North America.

From the earliest days of life, an infant is not simply a child, but a boy or a girl. Boys get blue blankets; girls get pink ones; boys are nicknamed Buck and Butch; girls are called Honey and Sweetie. Not surprisingly, one of the first things a child learns is whether he is a "he" or she is a "she." And from a very early age children show marked gender-specific preferences, such as for sex-typed toys and activities (Huston, 1983).

How does this happen? Do little boys arrive already programmed by their biology to prefer playing with toy guns and dump trucks while little girls have a biological propensity for tea parties? Of course not. These are things they must learn. Hence our interest must focus on *who* is socializing young children and *how*.

Although it is fashionable to blame many of our current child-rearing problems on such impersonal forces as "society," or the "media," the fact is that parents, and especially mothers, still do most of the socializing of youngsters. If we want to know how children in North America so quickly and so firmly adopt traditional conceptions of sex roles, the place to look is in parent-child interactions. And that's exactly what three sociologists at the University of Illinois did. So let's watch them while they observed mothers reading children's books to their offspring.

DeLoache, Cassidy, and Carpenter: Baby Bear is a boy

 One of the most common forms of interaction between parent and child takes the form of reading to the child. With very young children, the reading usually involves picture books with a minimum of text, and the child often sits on the parent's lap and follows along. Often the gender of characters is unknown—we know the gender of Goldilocks and of Papa and Mama Bear, but not that of little Baby Bear. And in many other stories there are no clues as to the gender of any characters.

How do parents deal with gender-neutral characters? Do they assign them a gender? If so, which? And how do they decide?

To find out, Judy S. DeLoache, Deborah J. Cassidy, and C. Jan Carpenter at the University of Illinois recruited mothers with young children to participate in an observational study. Each mother and child was scheduled for a session in a playroom designed to permit all interactions to be taped. The women were told that the researchers were interested in mother-child interaction in two situations, playing with toys and looking at books together. The mother and child were left alone to play with some toys for about ten minutes and then were seated in a large upholstered chair and given three books. In the first phase of the study these were widely known books. The researchers reported that:

The mother was asked to look at, talk about, or read the books with her child however they would normally do at home. The mothers thus had no idea we were interested in their assignment of gender to the characters in the books [DeLoache, Cassidy, and Carpenter, 1987].

Each of the three books included a number of gender-neutral characters. They did not have male or female names, did not wear any gender-specific clothing (such as hair ribbons), and were not engaged in any sex-typed activities. So, how did mothers refer to these characters? As *males*:

In all, the mothers used a total of 104 gender-specific labels, of which 102 (98%) were masculine references. . . . One of the only two feminine labels was one mother's reference to a large duck pictured with two smaller ducks as "Mrs. Duck."

The researchers conducted a second version of their study, this time using books specially prepared to present gender-neutral characters engaged in highly sex-typed activities. Thus, for example, an animal without any gender identity was shown standing in the front of a classroom filled with small animals. The researchers expected that this "teacher" would be identified as female. Another picture showed two bears in the front seat of a car, one of them driving. They expected the driver to be identified as male, the passenger as female.

Once again a group of mothers and children were recruited, and the instructions given them were as before. And so were the results, or nearly so. Sixty-two percent of the characters were identified as male, 22 percent as neither, and only 16 percent as females. Variations in gender-typed behavior had only the weakest effects. For example, the "teacher" was more likely to be identified as female than as male, but not by much.

The importance of these findings is related to prior studies that have revealed that characters depicted in children's books are overwhelmingly shown to be male. Many have claimed that this enforces harmful perceptions of sex roles—that children learn it is a man's world in which women are on the sideline. Consequently, many people have demanded that children's books be revised to present gender-neutral characters. But what DeLoache, Cassidy, and Carpenter's work shows is that such books do not reduce perceptions that characters are males. Mothers rarely identified animal characters as female unless they had female names, wore female clothing, or were obviously female. Otherwise they referred to them as male. Hence, the authors concluded, "The only strategy that is likely to succeed in achieving more egalitarian sex roles in young children's picture books is to portray more overtly female characters in a wider variety of nonstereotyped roles" (DeLoache, Cassidy, and Clark, 1987).

Of course, children are not socialized only by their parents; they also do much to socialize one another. A major mechanism in peer socialization among children is play. So let's watch a fine observational study of the connections between play and sex roles.

Stephen Richer: games and gender

 Several years ago, Stephen Richer, a sociologist at Carleton University in Ottawa, conducted an observational field study of play patterns with three groups. The first consisted of kids age 6 to 14 at a summer camp. The other two were of kids age 3 to 4, who attended day-care centers.

Richer's study was motivated by the lack of previous research on the conditions under which *boys and girls play together*. Much research has shown that boys and girls usually don't play together, that most of their play is done in single-gender groups. Other research shows that both boys and girls evaluate boys' play activities more positively than they do girls' play activities. In addition, boys monopolize physical, competitive, team games.

Richer also knew from his own prior research and from the published findings of other sociologists that most play involving both boys and girls can be described as "courtship play." As Richer describes it:

The most common type is a chasing game, in which the girls chase the boys and kiss them when they are caught. In my own work I have seen two slightly different versions. The game called "kissing girls" . . . [or] "kissing catchers" . . . involves any number of girls chasing any number of boys. If the boy is caught a kiss can be given by one or several of the girls. In a variant of this, several boys might themselves catch one of their number and bring the typically wildly resisting boy to the girls to be kissed. . . . It is striking that the boys rarely do the chasing [Richer, 1984].

As Richer pointed out, such games perpetuate traditional sex-role relations. They suggest that a woman's main interest is to catch a husband and that "the major impetus for cross-sex interaction is some kind of sexual activity."

What Richer wanted to know was *when* and *why* do boys and girls play together in nonsexual ways? This was one reason he chose to include very young kids (3 to 4) in his study: Is sex-segregated play present at a young age, or is it something that develops over time?

In his research with the older children at the summer camp, Richer found only one circumstance under which girls and boys would play together, without manifesting strong gender preferences: when they formed a single team to compete either with the staff or with outsiders from another camp. When it became "us-against-them," internal divisions based on gender dissolved, "albeit temporarily." However, efforts to create mixed-gender teams within the group failed to have such an effect.

But Richer found that younger children *did not display gender preferences in their play*. Instead, boys and girls not only played together but they also showed few preferences for different kinds of play; boys were equally willing to play house and girls were equally willing to play army.

Richer's results suggest that the strong gender preferences of slightly older children are

learned, and, given that the opposition of camp counselors to sex-segregated play had no impact, these preferences may be learned primarily from older children. Whatever the case, the process by which younger children are socialized into gender-segregated play norms is an area in need of further study.

■
―――――

Conclusion

This chapter first studied early childhood socialization, but it soon was revealed that socialization is a lifelong process. Because socialization is the transmission of culture and the shaping of character, it does not cease so long as we continue to interact and have new experiences. Moreover, because so much socialization is aimed at preparing people for, and comes as a result of, playing new roles, socialization continues as we pass through life's successive roles.

Socialization during infancy and early childhood has received the greatest attention from social scientists, because serious failures in this period can have profound, long-lasting effects. A child who never learns to take the role of the other, for example, will never be able to play team sports; he or she may even grow up to be an egomaniac. A child who grows up in a modern society without learning to read is condemned to a life of marginal employment and ignorance.

However, even if early socialization is crucial, not all problems or patterns of adult behavior are rooted in childhood. Socialization failures can occur at any age and be wholly independent of anything that came before. In the next chapter we shall see that people who fall into "bad company" during their teens, or even as adults, may become socialized into new and deviant patterns of behavior. People who have successfully performed a whole series of adult roles suddenly may fail to be adequately socialized into a new one—as grandparent or retired person, for example.

Just as socialization occurs throughout our lives, so does the topic of socialization occur throughout this book. For example, when we examine social institutions such as the family, religion, school, or the economy, we also examine major sources of socialization. In fact, this textbook is part of your present socialization.

■

Review Glossary

feral children The name often applied to children who, because of severe neglect, act as if they were raised in the wild (*feral* means untamed). (p. 146)

socialization The process of being made social, of learning to act in ways appropriate to our roles. (p. 146)

stimulus-response (S-R) learning theory The theory in which behavior (responses) of organisms is said to be the result of external stimuli; that is, organisms only repeat behavior that has been reinforced by the environment. (p. 150)

cognitive structures General rules or principles that govern reasoning. (p. 151)

sensorimotor stage According to Piaget, the period from birth to about age 2 during which the infant develops perceptual abilities and body control and discovers the rule of object permanence—that things still exist even when they are out of sight. (p. 152)

preoperational stage According to Piaget, the period from age 2 until about 7 during which a child learns to take the role of the other. (p. 152)

concrete operational stage According to Piaget, the period from 7 until about 12 during which humans develop a number of cognitive structures, including the rule of conservation. (p. 152)

formal operational stage According to Piaget, the time after about age 12 when some humans develop the capacity for abstract thought, that is, for using theories rather than only empirical observations. (p. 152)

personality Consistent patterns of thoughts, feelings, and actions. (p. 156)

cultural determinism The claim that an almost infinite array of cultural and social patterns is possible and that human nature can be shaped into almost any form by cultural forces. (p. 157)

differential socialization The process by which different members of the same society or even the same family are raised differently because of varying expectations about the roles that each will need to fill as an adult. (p. 160)

adult socialization Processes by which adults are enabled to perform new roles. (p. 163)

longitudinal study Research in which observations are made of the same people at different times. (p. 163)

role performance The actual behavior of people in a particular role, in contrast to how they are supposed to behave. (p. 164)

impression management Conscious manipulation of role performance. (p. 164)

studied nonobservance The way in which people pretend not to notice minor lapses in one another's role performance. (p. 165)

deviant role A set of norms attached to a position which, in turn, violates the norms adhered to by the larger society. For example, a proper performance of the role of burglar will deviate from other people's norms. (p. 166)

Suggested Readings

Elkin, Frederick, and Gerald Handel. 1978. *The Child and Society*, 3rd ed. New York: Random House.

Freeman, Derek. *Margaret Mead and Samoa: The Making and Unmaking of an Anthropological Myth*. 1983. Cambridge: Harvard University Press.

Goffman, Erving. 1959. *The Presentation of Self in Everyday Life*. New York: Doubleday.

Goffman, Erving. 1971. *Relations in Public*. New York: Basic Books.

Kohn, Melvin L., and Carmi Schooler. 1982. "Job Conditions and Personality: A Longitudinal Assessment of Reciprocal Effects." *American Journal of Sociology* 87:1257–1286.

Piaget, Jean, and Barbel Inhelder. 1969. *The Psychology of the Child*. New York: Basic Books.

Deviance and Conformity

7

MOST OF US play by the rules. As we shift from role to role and from situation to situation, we usually conform to the norms that define how we are supposed to act—but not always. Each of us breaks the rules some of the time, and some of us break them a lot of the time. When we violate norms, our behavior is called **deviance**: We deviate from, or fail to conform to, the norms. Deviance ranges from the trivial to the acute— from sleeping in class to committing murder. How others react to a deviant act indicates how serious the violation is. When people ignore or mildly disapprove of an action, the offense is minor. But when the offender is taken to jail, referred to a psychiatrist, or pursued by an angry mob, he or she has broken an important norm.

Some actions are regarded as deviant only in some societies, while other actions seem to be regarded as deviant in all societies. For example, no society condones unrestricted killing of its members or unlimited taking of goods from others against their will. On the other hand, drinking alcohol is seriously deviant in Iran, while refusing to drink in certain circumstances is slightly deviant in France.

Variations in *what* is defined as deviant *where* are of interest to sociologists, but sociologists of deviant behavior concentrate on a more basic and universal phenomenon. Although norms may differ from one society to another, *all societies have norms, and all societies punish those who violate important norms. Yet in all societies some people commit acts of serious deviance anyway. Why?* Sociologists of deviance try to answer this question—why do some people

deviate whatever the norms may be? To do so they seek general theories of deviant behavior.

Serious deviance depends not only on the *importance* of the norm violated but also on the

Figure 7-1 ■ **Property crimes per 100,000 population.** On both sides of the border the news media create the impression that property crime thrives in the urban East. For example, the media have often told us that many people in eastern cities have been driven to install three and even four locks on their outer doors to stave off burglars. Maybe there are more locks and more fearful people in the East, but the thieves seem to prefer to live out West. Aside from Florida, western states dominate the map of property crime in the United States. For example, the property crime rate of Texas is more than 40 percent higher than New York's rate, while Oregon's rate is 138 percent higher than Pennsylvania's. In Canada, the two northern territories have the highest property crime rates while British Columbia, the most western province, has a rate nearly 80 percent higher than the rate for Quebec and nearly 70 percent higher than the rate for Ontario. This is not a recent development. As far back as the data go, the West has been the site of high property crime rates. The same thing shows up in Table 7-1, where we see that Americans living in the West are more than 80 percent more likely than those in the East to admit having been picked up by the police. In this chapter we will consider why crime rates vary so much from one place to another. (Comparisons between Canadian and American rates are misleading because the latter exclude several less-serious kinds of offenses that are included in Canadian rates.)

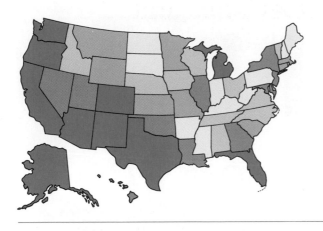

1986: Property Crimes per 100,000

West Virginia	2,152	New Jersey	4,669
North Dakota	2,554	Illinois	4,746
South Dakota	2,591	Maryland	4,769
Pennsylvania	2,743	New York	4,782
Kentucky	2,758	Georgia	4,868
Mississippi	3,071	Utah	5,212
New Hampshire	3,191	Louisiana	5,320
Maine	3,314	Hawaii	5,426
Arkansas	3,530	Nevada	5,571
Indiana	3,547	Oklahoma	5,578

Virginia	3,554	Alaska	5,676
Nebraska	3,593	Michigan	5,688
Alabama	3,730	California	5,842
Vermont	3,828	New Mexico	5,900
Wisconsin	3,839	Washington	6,443
North Carolina	3,856	Colorado	6,508
Iowa	3,916	Oregon	6,531
Ohio	3,938	Arizona	6,663
Idaho	3,984	Texas	6,749
Tennessee	3,995	Florida	7,192

Wyoming	4,064
Missouri	4,076
Minnesota	4,078
Massachusetts	4,167
Montana	4,322
Connecticut	4,403
Delaware	4,405
Kansas	4,454
South Carolina	4,463
Rhode Island	4,567

1986: Property Crimes per 100,000

Newfoundland	2,932
Pr. Edward Island	3,032
New Brunswick	3,616
Nova Scotia	4,431

Quebec	4,874
Ontario	5,188
Alberta	6,311
Saskatchewan	7,042

Manitoba	7,625
British Columbia	8,641
Yukon	9,362
N.W. Territories	9,396

Table 7-1 ■ Percent of American adults who say they have been "picked up" by the police for something other than a traffic violation.

Region	Percent Arrested
East	10.0%
Midwest	11.4
South	9.8
West	18.4

Source: Prepared by the author from National Opinion Research Center, General Social Surveys, 1973 and 1984.

frequency of norm violation. No one would get upset if a student walked backward out of class, or even all the way across campus. But if that student always walked backward, day after day, this behavior would raise serious concern. Moreover, people with past records of observing the norms (such people are often described as being "of good character") will be forgiven even a very grave norm violation. For example, people with no prior police record often receive probation for quite serious crimes, such as burglary or armed robbery (see Chapter 8), while some people with records of repeated violations may be harshly penalized for relatively minor infractions, such as being drunk in public.

People who frequently break important norms are called **deviants**. The behavior of such people is seen as a problem for others. In Chapter 8, we shall examine efforts to prevent deviance and to reform or change deviants. Here we ask, Why does deviance occur?

■ This proud husband and father is a pillar of Muslim society and has fulfilled the ideal of having four wives. In Europe and the Western Hemisphere he would be a criminal polygamist. What behavior will be regarded as deviant differs from society to society and even from one subculture to another within the same society. The important point for sociology is that in all societies and subcultures some people violate the norms. Theories of deviance attempt to explain why they do.

■──────

Chapter Preview

This chapter ignores minor acts of deviance: It says little about why some of your friends might have vulgar eating habits or write on lavatory walls. Rather, it explores the causes of serious acts of deviance.

In modern societies, important norms are usually written into law; therefore, most serious acts of deviance are considered crimes.

Because sociologists of deviance concentrate on serious deviance, they also tend to concentrate on crime, which is why many sociologists also call themselves criminologists.

However, not all sociologists of deviance specialize in crime. Many attempt to understand mental illness, for example; and while the mentally ill are sometimes subject to legal proceedings, mental illness is not a crime. Nor is alcoholism, although public intoxication and drunk driving are illegal. Both criminal and noncriminal deviance are discussed in this chapter, but crime will receive much greater attention.

Deviance is one of the most active areas of sociological study. This activity simply reflects the fact that deviance is a serious and chronic threat: the more burglars in our midst, the more we fear losing our belongings; the more murderers, the more we fear losing our lives. Other forms of deviance are not so threatening, but there are still widespread efforts to aid alcoholics and addicts and to treat the mentally ill. Consequently, sociologists have devoted much effort to formulating and testing theories of deviant behavior.

This chapter shall examine the more significant of these theories. However, simply because there are a number of theories of deviance does not mean that the field is a muddle of competing, contradictory claims. Instead, most of the theories are complementary. That is, many are directed at different aspects of the problem and thus try to answer somewhat different questions.

As a result, there are many partial theories of deviance. As we examine these, you will see that they suggest the outlines of a general theory. No one has yet attempted to construct such a general theory, but someone is bound to do so soon. Of course, not every aspect of every current theory fits with other theories or even with the basic facts of deviant behavior that research has revealed. As the chapter proceeds, we shall consider various theoretical disagreements and see how these square with the known facts.

Because I have chosen to work from the micro to the most macro in the overall design of this book, in this chapter we shall begin with human biology and end with the effect of societies upon deviance.

Biological Theories of Deviance

For centuries humans have wondered why some people are chronic deviants—why some people cannot be trusted to conform to important norms. Virtually every facet of life has been

■ Cesare Lombroso.

blamed by someone as a cause of crime and deviance. But perhaps the oldest claim about deviance is that some people are just "born bad": Some people have an inborn personality flaw that stimulates misbehavior or prevents them from controlling their deviant urges. This view became very influential in the 1870s, when an Italian physician, Cesare Lombroso (1836–1909), began to gather systematic data on prison and jail inmates and to develop a biological theory of criminal behavior.

"Born criminals"

Lombroso believed he had found the key to criminal behavior in human evolution. His years of careful observation and measurement of prison inmates convinced him that the most serious, vicious, and persistent criminals (who he believed made up about one-third of all persons who commit crimes) were "born criminals" (Lombroso-Ferrero, 1911). **Born criminals** were less evolved humans who were biological "throwbacks" to our primitive ancestors, according to Lombroso. The born criminal is "an atavistic being who reproduces in his person the ferocious instincts of primitive humanity and inferior animals."

Lombroso believed that, because of their genetic makeup, born criminals could not restrain their violent and animalistic urges. Because the trouble was biological, he argued, little or nothing could be done to cure born criminals; society could be protected only by locking them up. However, because their criminality was not their fault, born criminals ought to be treated as kindly as possible in dignified, decent prisons.

Lombroso and his students presented a great deal of evidence to support his theory. He claimed that criminals tended to be more ape-like than normal people, having abnormal skulls, huge jaws, flat noses, and long arms. Because Lombroso developed a testable theory, we know today that his theory was incorrect. His error lay in examining only prisoners and assuming that they displayed a higher proportion of physical abnormalities than nonprisoners did. However, when the British physician Charles Goring (1913) measured nonprison populations, he found the same incidence of physical abnormality as Lombroso had found among convicts. Thus, Goring showed that there was no correlation between these physical characteristics and committing crimes. As Chapter 3 made clear, something cannot be the cause of something else if the two are not correlated. Lombroso's theory was therefore disproved.

However, even though criminologists have known for more than seventy years that Lombroso was incorrect, they have not dismissed the possibility that human biology plays a role in crime and deviance. Indeed, in his book that exposed Lombroso's faulty methods, Goring reaffirmed his belief that criminals can be distinguished from noncriminals on the basis of body build and physiology. And throughout this century researchers have continued to try to discover and demonstrate such biological differences (Wilson and Herrnstein, 1985).

Behavioral genetics

In Chapter 5 we examined the new field of behavioral genetics, which has attempted to assess the role of heredity in various forms of human behavior. As we saw, studies of twins have been a primary research method for behavioral geneticists. One study done in Denmark examined 3,586 twin pairs (Christiansen, 1977). The researcher checked each twin through the criminal record files of the Danish police, recording only serious offenses. The results were highly suggestive. For identical (or monozygotic) twins, if one twin had a serious criminal record, the odds were 50 percent that the other twin did too. But for fraternal (dizygotic) twins (using male sets only, to eliminate gender differences within pairs), if one twin was a criminal, the odds were only 21 percent that the other twin also was a criminal. Because each set of twins grew up in the same home, their environment was held constant, and thus these differences suggest that the more genetically similar, the more similar the pattern of deviance or conformity. Adoption studies also have sustained interest in a hereditary component in criminal behavior. In terms of criminal records, adoptees much more closely resemble their biological than their adoptive parents (Mednick et al., 1984).

Keep in mind that even if there is a genetic "predisposition" to break the law, much more is involved in criminal acts. For one thing, such actions, like all human behavior, must be learned. Spiders may be genetically programmed to spin webs, but no human is born with instincts to break into houses or to write bad checks. Moreover, geneticists still have a long way to go to discover just *what* people inherit that can predispose them to deviance. Wilson and Herrnstein (1985) have suggested that much deviant behavior results because some people seem unable to control their impulses or to consider long-term costs versus short-term gains. Perhaps genetic aspects of the nervous system play some role here.

In any event, most sociologists are uncomfortable with the idea that a tendency to commit crimes might be partly rooted in physiology and genetics. On the other hand, they long have been puzzled by the marked gender and age differences in patterns of deviant behavior, traits having obvious physical as well as social aspects. Then Walter Gove suggested a new synthesis of biology and sociology.

Walter Gove: Age, Gender, Biology, and Deviance

 Walter Gove set himself the task of explaining a number of well-known, but little understood, aspects of crime and deviance. The first of these has to do with changes in deviant behavior with age. As Gove (1985) noted, "Virtually all forms of deviance that involve substantial risk and/or physically demanding behavior occur mainly among young persons, and the rates of such deviance decline sharply in the late twenties and early thirties."

First, he pointed out that the arrest rate for violent crimes such as homicide, rape, and assault is highest among persons 18–24; the 13–17 age group is second highest while the 25–30 age group is third. After age 30 the rates fall. The same patterns are reported for drug and alcohol abuse, so much so that the phrase "to mature out" is part of the language used in the drug culture to describe how people quit as they pass 30. These age trends are similar for males and females (Cline, 1980) and hold in a wide variety of societies (Hirschi and Gottfredson, 1983).

Secondly, although both males and females tend to cease deviance in young adulthood, these forms of risky, physically demanding deviance are *overwhelmingly* committed by males.

Table 7-2 shows the proportion of females among persons arrested in a number of nations. Everywhere males predominate. But the proportion of female offenders is much higher for some kinds of crimes than for some others. Table 7-3 shows these contrasts for Canada and the United States. Few of those arrested for robbery, aggravated assault, burglary, or homicide are female. In contrast, females make up a substantial proportion of those arrested for forgery, fraud, embezzlement, larceny-theft, and shoplifting. Overall, in both nations more than twice the proportion of those arrested for property crimes are females as compared with those arrested for crimes of violence.

Gove then reviewed the major social science theories of deviance—those we will examine in

Table 7-2 ■ Percent of females among those arrested.

Nation	Percent Female
Finland	6.7%
Japan	9.7
Canada	9.8
Netherlands	10.3
South Korea	10.5
Israel	11.7
England and Wales	13.6
United States	13.7
Austria	13.8
France	14.3
West Germany	16.7
New Zealand	20.5

Source: Adapted from Simon and Sharma (1979).

Table 7-3 ■ Percent of females among persons arrested for various crimes.

	Percent Female	
Offense	United States	Canada
Robbery	3.6%	7.0%
Burglary	7.5	3.9
Homicide	13.1	11.8
Aggravated assault	13.4	11.0
Larceny-theft	30.3	31.8*
Forgery	33.8	**
Embezzlement	38.0	**
Fraud	39.5	24.1
Shoplifting	**	43.0
All violent crimes	10.7	9.7
All property crimes	23.5	20.0

Sources: U.S. Department of Justice (1985); Canadian Centre for Justice Statistics (1984).
*Theft
**Not reported as a separate category

this chapter—and concluded that they did little to explain why gender differences are so pronounced with some kinds of deviance and why these also are the forms of deviance that fall most rapidly at around age 30. Many of the theories could predict a *gradual* decline with age, as we shall see. But none predicts the sudden and rapid decline that actually takes place.

At this point Gove assessed a growing literature that links aggressive or assertive forms of deviance to physique. Beginning with the work of Sheldon (1940) in the 1930s, through studies by Cortés and Gatti (1972) and Cortés (1982), research has found that an athletic (or mesomorphic) body build is conducive to these forms of behavior. This is not to suggest that being muscular causes people to commit assault or robberies but that it requires some degree of strength and self-confidence to act in these ways: The proverbial 98-pound wimp does not make a successful mugger. Moreover, the life-style of the drunk or the addict is often very physically demanding as well. Consider the testimony of this heroin addict:

[It was] the worst period of my life. I found myself wandering around the streets of New York filthy all the time. I had no place to stay. I slept on rooftops, in hallways, in damp cellars, any available place and always with one eye open. . . . I was really low then, not eating . . . and cold all the time [Tardola, 1970].

Finally, Gove was ready to put these pieces together.

Why do these forms of deviance rapidly decline at around age 30? First of all, because *physical strength* peaks in the early twenties and then declines. Secondly, *physical energy* also peaks in the twenties. Gove postulates two aspects of energy. The first is endurance, or conditioning. We remain strong enough to perform various actions to a later age than we retain the endurance or conditioning to do them for a long time. An aging boxer may still be a dangerous opponent for a few rounds, but may be forced to try for an early knockout, knowing he will tire badly in later rounds. A second aspect of energy, according to Gove, is the ability to *re-*

bound, or recover, from injury and exertion; for example, an older alcoholic will recover more slowly from a drunken spree. Thirdly, Gove argues that *psychological drives*, especially those sustained by the production of hormones such as testosterone and adrenaline, decline suddenly too.

This line of theorizing leads easily to explaining the differential patterns of male and female deviance. Gove suggests that females are so much less likely than males to commit certain acts simply because they are weaker and smaller. He notes the differences shown in Table 7-3 indicate the need to explain not simply why women are less likely than men to commit crimes but also why the difference is so much greater for the high-risk, physically demanding crimes. Moreover, among both males and females, those with more muscular builds are more prone to these forms of deviance, and both genders show a notable drop in these behaviors as they begin to pass their physical prime. Gove concluded with the observation that, at the age when some people are winning Olympic medals, others their age are busy committing assaults, robberies, rapes, and burglaries and that both groups consist of "young adults who withdraw from the field as they age."

Although Gove's new approach may help explain certain aspects of deviance, it leaves many others unaddressed. Most people do not stop committing risky and physical crimes as they pass their prime because *most people never commit these offenses at any age.* What distinguishes those who do from those who don't? Let's turn to other theories of crime and deviance in search of answers.

Personality Theory

 Despite an immense amount of research, efforts to link various forms of deviant behavior to abnormal features of the personality have been disappointing (Sagarin, 1975; Liska, 1981). An assessment of ninety-four studies, which were conducted between 1950 and 1965 and meant to distin-

■ This street scene by the German expressionist George Grosz implies that conformity is but a superficial human mask—that inside us all, just beneath the surface, lurks a violent and dangerous beast ruled by dark passions and deep-seated psychological pathologies. However, efforts to explain deviant behavior by uncovering its psychological basis have not been very successful. Although sudden outbursts of abnormally aggressive behavior do seem to have a psychological basis, most deviance is based on conscious planning and choice.

guish between criminals and noncriminals by using various personality tests, found the overall results to be weak and contradictory (Waldo and Dinitz, 1967).

The most promising line of psychological research has been on extremely aggressive behavior. Hans Toch (1969) found that *men who repeatedly assaulted others* had very weak self-esteem. This trait made them extremely resentful of even slight criticism or discourtesy, especially if it occurred in the presence of others. The violent rages of these men stemmed from the fear of loss of face, combined with the belief that others already held them in low esteem.

In-depth interviews with men frequently convicted of assault led Leonard Berkowitz (1978) to expand on Toch's position. Berkowitz concluded that these men had such fragile self-esteem that they flew into uncontrollable rages even when no one except the offending person was present. An audience might spur them to even wilder reactions, but they could suddenly become violent even without such a spur.

Berkowitz's respondents consisted of sixty-five white males between the ages of 18 and 43; most were in their late twenties. Each was serving time in an English jail for assault, and most had served many previous sentences for violent behavior—one had twenty-seven prior convictions. Another, with fourteen previous convictions for assault, had gotten into an argument with a policeman and knocked him down. Then the man ran into his house, got a machete, and battled eight cops, wounding two of them. Why had he done it? His answer was, in effect, Why not? The cop "just got on me back. . . . That was it, [I] just elbowed him, brought him over me shoulder, and stamped him with me foot."

Arguments were the most common preliminary to violent outbursts by these men. The interviews showed remarkably little sign of rational calculation—of deciding whether or when to hit someone. Of course, men in jail may wish to deny responsibility for the act that got them there. Still, that these same men had repeated such behavior so often despite jail sentences strongly suggests that there is truth to their claims that these things just seem to happen to them. As one man with a long record of assault convictions put it, "At the time I'm not thinking at all, you know. It's afterwards I think this all out, but at the time I don't stop to think. At the time it seems the natural thing to do or the right thing to do" (Berkowitz, 1978).

A second approach to studying aggression through personality analysis suggests not only that the inability to control rage is a frequent cause but also that *too great* control over rage may lead to extreme violence. Thus very passive, mild-mannered people who suppress their anger during a long period of provocation may cause others to provoke them excessively; eventually the quiet people erupt in acts of extreme retribution. Had they been less controlled, they might have prevented the increased mistreatment. Instead, they took it as long as they could and then earned newspaper headlines as the person who "wouldn't hurt a fly" but who suddenly took an axe to a spouse or a neighbor or went to the office one morning with a shotgun (Schultz, 1960; Megargee, 1966).

Later in this chapter we shall see that some forms of deviant behavior do seem to be acts of sudden impulse. We shall also see that sociological theories are not well suited to deal with these forms of deviance, which are probably best understood through psychology.

However, *most of the deviant acts that prompt so much interest in criminology are not acts of impulse.* And at least so far, personality theories have not helped much in explaining acts of deviance involving conscious choices. We shall return to these matters toward the end of the chapter. Now we should see just what sociologists think they know about deviance.

Deviant Attachments

We have already encountered the fundamental proposition on which most sociological theories of deviance are based: Our behavior is shaped through interaction with others, especially those to whom we have formed strong attachments. These attachments to others cause us to live up to their expectations about how we should act. In Chapter 3 we examined research showing the power of attachments to influence our behavior—people will even adopt a new religion to please their friends.

However, although attachments produce conformity to the expectations of others, that does not necessarily mean that we will conform to the norms of our society. What happens if our attachments are to people who themselves break norms? What if our friends are burglars or auto thieves? Questions such as these have led to the formulation of several sociological theories seeking to explain deviance on the basis of attachments to *deviant others.* These theories elaborate on the sentiments of many proverbs about falling in with "bad company."

Differential association— social learning

Edwin H. Sutherland (1883–1950) is remembered as the most influential early American sociologist of deviant behavior. In 1924 he first proposed a theory based on deviant attachments, a theory now known as the **differential association theory**. Sutherland argued that all behavior is the result of socialization through interaction. That is, how we act depends on how those around us desire us to act. How much we deviate from or conform to the norms depends on differences (or differentials) in whom we associate with.

Thus, Sutherland argued, boys become delinquent because too many of their attachments are to others who engage in and approve of delinquent acts. In this view, the causes of deviance lie not in the individual but in the normal processes of social influence. However, Sutherland's differential association theory did not precisely explain how our friends influence our behavior and teach us to conform or deviate. Therefore, in 1966 Robert Burgess and Ronald Akers reformulated Sutherland's theory into a set of specific propositions based on learning theory.

Burgess and Akers argued that Sutherland had correctly identified the source of deviant behavior: attachments to people who supported deviance. Such friends teach us to deviate by rewarding us for deviant behavior and not rewarding (or reinforcing) nondeviant (conformist) behavior. Thus, a boy may receive a great deal of attention and respect from his friends when he steals a bike or breaks a window but be ignored when he is "good."

Consider this more elaborate example. A person may have companions in the local tavern who reinforce heavy drinking and nightly visits by not staying home or abstaining. Through such a pattern of *selective reinforcement*, a person may become a habitual heavy drinker. As time goes by, such a person may become increasingly dependent on regulars at the tavern for social relations and become a problem drinker. Indeed, this may be why so many persons treated for alcohol or drug abuse resume such behavior even after hospitalization has cured their physical addiction. The patients return to the same social settings and the same sets of attachments through which they originally formed their problem behavior and quickly relearn it.

Unquestionably, differential association and learning processes play a significant role in much deviant behavior. Having assembled the findings of many studies done over a forty-year period, Maynard L. Erickson (1971) showed that the great majority of delinquent acts occur in cooperation with others. Vandalism, for example, is rarely done by a lone juvenile. Most juveniles who steal a car or burglarize a house do so in groups. And research consistently finds that delinquents tend to have delinquent friends (Liska, 1981). Yet the theory fails to explain many aspects of deviance and does not jibe with many research findings.

A major problem is research suggesting that delinquent kids end up together because others reject them (Hirschi, 1969; Jensen, 1972; Liska, 1981), not because these friends encouraged each other's delinquency. Diana Gray (1973) found that teenage girls becoming prostitutes did not begin to associate with pimps or other prostitutes until *after* they had already begun to sell sexual favors. Travis Hirschi (1969) found that only some boys with delinquent friends engaged in delinquency—those who did well in school and were attached to their parents were not more likely to engage in delinquency if they had delinquent friends than if they did not.

A second problem is that differential association–social learning theory does not address the question of why delinquent friends exist. That is, if attachments to deviant friends cause deviance, what caused the deviance of the friends? At some point someone must have begun to act in a deviant way without supportive friends. In addition, why do some people but not others have deviant friends? And why are only some people susceptible to the influence of deviant friends, as research shows?

Finally, what explains the many acts of deviance that could not possibly be responses to the expectations of deviant friends? Many acts—indeed, many of the most serious deviant acts—are done on the sly by people who hope no one ever finds out: the man who kills his wife and hides the body, the embezzler, the secret alcoholic. Clearly, these kinds of deviance cannot be attributed to reinforcement by friends.

Here we must recognize something that will be significant at many points in this chapter: *Some forms of deviance are directly rewarding.* Some people enjoy the effects of alcohol or drugs and require no additional reinforcement from others. Some people enjoy peeking through windows to see others naked. As for stealing, people seldom take things they don't want or don't hope to sell. A child caught shoplifting will often explain that "it was such a neat cap gun." Granted, our friends can lead us astray. But people are perfectly capable of getting into mischief on their own (Wilson and Herrnstein, 1985).

The problems of the differential association–social learning approach are but sins of omission. That is, problems do not arise because of what the theory explains but because of what it does not explain. Other theories of deviance attempt to fill these gaps.

Subcultural deviance

One way to supply the deviant others needed by differential association–social learning theory is to recognize the existence of subcultures within a society. In Chapter 2 we discussed how a subculture is a culture within a culture—a group of people who maintain or develop a set of values, norms, and roles that are different from those of the surrounding society. As we saw in Chapter 3, sometimes subcultures arise around a new religion; those who become attached to persons in such a subculture can consequently become members themselves. In a similar fashion, a subculture can arise around drug use; in fact, during the 1960s many people were recruited to be drug users just as others were recruited to be Moonies or Hare Krishnas.

Recognition of subcultures lets us understand that deviance is often a matter of definition. An outside observer noting the behavior of a member of a subculture may regard that person as deviant. But that same person is conforming to the norms of his or her group. For

■ To conform to the norms of one group often is to seriously break the norms of another group. The punk rock fans above have gone to great pains to be "normal" in the eyes of other punks. Their dress and deportment break norms of society in general and especially those of older professionals like the two men on the right. Of course, these men also make a considerable effort to be "normal." Some forms of deviance, such as these having to do with norms of appearance, reflect subculture conflicts. Which of these styles is seen as more acceptable often will be determined by which subculture is the more powerful.

example, Jehovah's Witnesses are members of a religious group who, among other things, accept a norm against saluting flags (they regard it as idolatry). Many Americans observing a Jehovah's Witness refusing to salute the U.S. flag might define the behavior as deviant, but to

other Jehovah's Witnesses it would be an act of conformity.

Particularly in complex modern societies, many subcultures exist, and thus some deviant behavior can be explained as conflicts over norms, or **subcultural deviance**. Public controversies over pornography, marijuana, abortion, and sexual behavior are conflicts over whose norms will be represented in legal codes and public policies and whose will be judged deviant.

Some subcultural views of deviance can be summed up as "different strokes for different folks." Thus, the norms in any society are often determined by who has the power to pass laws and set policies. Because Jehovah's Witnesses are a tiny minority, they are unable to ban flag ceremonies. Because the majority of Americans oppose the use of narcotics, narcotics are illegal.

Subcultural theories also help explain how some forms of deviance that do not begin as conformity to the norms of a subculture can become stabilized as an individual enters into a subculture. We have seen that Diana Gray (1973) found that girls began prostitution on their own. However, in time some of them did begin to associate with pimps and prostitutes and become part of this deviant subculture. Many of the other girls soon gave up prostitution.

Although subcultural theories add to our understanding of deviance, they also fail to provide a full explanation. For one thing, many forms of deviance seem to have no subcultural basis. Aside from the occasional gangland slaying, very few homicides seem to be the result of conforming to the norms of a subculture. In fact, although sociologists long attributed much serious violence to subcultures having norms that favored violence, such as juvenile gangs or working-class men, research has uniformly failed to confirm this view. Even teenage gangs turn out to be much less approving of member violence than had been supposed (Ball-Rokeach, 1973; Kornhauser, 1978). And that raises the major omission of subcultural theory: *deviance within any subcultural group.*

All human groups, regardless of their norms, include some members who fail to conform. Some members of juvenile gangs steal from other members. Some gangsters squeal to the authorities. Some ministers commit adultery. Some scientists fake their results. And many people feel deeply ashamed and guilty after committing some act, which makes no sense if what they were doing was "right" according to their group norms. Subcultural explanations cannot explain deviance of this kind. Again, the solution is not to discard a theory but to add to it.

Structural Strain Theory

We now encounter a closely related group of theories that attempt to explain deviance on the basis of **structural strain**, or frustration caused by a person's position in the social structure, especially the stratification system.

The ideas underlying structural strain theories are very old. Whenever someone says that people commit crimes because of poverty or some other disadvantage, that person is invoking strain theory. Back in 1938, Robert K. Merton formulated a theory of how disadvantage can lead to deviance, and theories based on his work are called **structural strain theories**.

Merton began with the assumption that humans have a natural tendency to observe norms, a tendency instilled in us by regular processes of socialization. Indeed, this tendency is reflected by that part of our personalities often called the conscience. Because of our conscience, breaking the norms causes us to feel some degree of guilt and remorse. Yet people often act against their conscience. Why? Merton thought it was because of the terrible strain upon them.

These strains arise because people are socialized to have certain desires, or goals, and to regard certain means as proper ways to achieve these goals. However, the proper means don't work as well for some people as for others. People who are poorly placed in the stratification system will find themselves unable to achieve their goals or at least unable to achieve them as easily as people better placed in the system, if they only use legitimate means (that is, if they obey their conscience). So long as disadvantaged people stick to the rules and obey the norms, they will experience frustration because they will fail to achieve wealth, happiness, fame, comfort, influence, and all the other things socialization has taught them to value. The resulting strain forces people to use deviant or illegitimate means to achieve goals.

Merton argued that deviance is a built-in consequence of stratification. *Strain theory portrays a deviant as a person torn between guilt and desire, with desire gaining the upper hand* (Hirschi, 1969). In effect, Merton argued that poverty causes the poor to turn to crime, to alcohol, to drugs, and even to killing friends and relatives in order to escape their unfulfilled desires for a better life.

By itself, the structural strain theory of deviance runs into serious problems. First, the theory would seem to predict far more deviance than actually occurs. Of those poorly placed in the stratification system, the great majority do not commit acts of significant deviance. What distinguishes them from those who do?

Second, most of the deviant behavior committed by persons under structural strain cannot alleviate their frustrations. Most crime pays very little—even menial jobs would provide more luxury. That is, illegal behavior offers scant hope for achieving goals that cannot be met by legitimate means.

Third, the theory offers no explanation for deviant acts committed by people in the privileged social positions, such as middle- and upper-class teenage delinquents. Nor does it explain why wealthy people shoplift or why bankers embezzle. Indeed, if people deviate only when driven by intense frustrations caused by societal deprivation, deviant behavior committed by privileged people is inexplicable.

Perhaps the worst problem strain theory faces is that a person's social class is barely, if at all, related to committing crimes. Table 7-4 is based on two national samples of American adults. It

Table 7-4 ■ Family income of Americans at age 16 and being "picked up" by the police.

"Thinking about the time when you were 16 years old, compared with American families in general then, would you say your family income was":			
"Far below average"	"Below average"	"Average"	"Above average"
Percent who have been "picked up" by the police			

	"Far below average"	"Below average"	"Average"	"Above average"
Percent who have been "picked up" by the police	12.6%	12.5%	11.3%	12.9%

Source: Prepared by the author from National Opinion Research Center, General Social Surveys, 1973 and 1984.

shows that 12.6 percent of those who reported that their family income when they were 16 was "far below average" have been picked up by the police for something other than a traffic offense. Of those whose family income was "above average," 12.9 percent have been picked up by the police. This is as close to a perfect *zero correlation* as one could expect. Moreover, scores of studies have failed to show that poor kids are more likely to commit delinquent acts than are kids from privileged homes (Tittle et al., 1978). On the other hand, when we focus on very serious offenses such as arson, robbery, and burglary of commercial firms, then we find people from the very lowest stratum of society are substantially overrepresented (Hindelang, Hirschi, and Weis, 1981). But even if this behavior does represent a response to strain, it applies to only a tiny segment of the population and accounts for only a small proportion of the crime and deviance that occurs.

Whenever the unemployment rate rises, the news media begin to cite that as a "root cause" in their stories about crime or drug abuse. Yet although social scientists frequently have predicted a positive correlation between unemployment and property crime rates, research has failed to detect it (Cantor and Land, 1985).

Within cities, crime and delinquency *are* concentrated in the poorer neighborhoods (Shaw and McKay, 1942; Bursik and Webb, 1982;

Simcha-Fagan and Schwartz, 1986), but numerous reasons for this do not depend on strain theory (Stark, 1987a). Poor neighborhoods tend to *attract* people who *already* engage in crime and deviance because social control is weakest in these parts of town. Control is weak here because of high rates of population turnover (residents constantly moving in and out), poor policing, and lack of community organization. Hence, chronic offenders tend to drift into the most run-down, poverty-stricken areas of cities because they are the safest places for them and because their crimes pay so poorly that they can't afford better surroundings. Indeed, this is where people tend to go following their release from jails and prisons. Ironically, this is also where they commit their crimes. Burglary rates, for example, are highest not in wealthy neighborhoods where homes contain many valuables but in the poorest neighborhoods. Most burglars pick on homes and stores within six blocks of their residence.

Another factor elevating crime rates in the poorest parts of cities is that these neighborhoods also tend to be mixed-use neighborhoods. Where homes, apartments, retail stores, and even light industries are all mixed together, the *opportunities* for crime and delinquency are higher. Kids living in many residential suburbs would have to ask mom or dad for a ride in order to shoplift or break into a liquor store. Many kids in mixed-use neighborhoods can do these things without even crossing a street (Stark, 1987a).

"White-Collar" Crime

Nothing is more embarrassing for strain theory than the frequency with which high-status people commit crimes. Merton's famous essay, "Social Structure and Anomie," essentially ignores the banker who embezzles or the physician who sells prescriptions to addicts, for only in this way could Merton sustain his thesis that crime and deviance are caused by the pains of poverty and want. While a graduate student, I asked a famous strain theorist how he explained upper-class criminals and was astonished when he said that was a job for psychotherapists because such people must be crazy. Eventually, however, social scientists accepted that many middle- and upper-class people commit crimes. And, from this recognition arose a new concept: white-collar crime.

White-collar crime is distinguished from other crime on the basis of the *social status of the offender*. The term *white-collar* indicates that a person wears a suit (with a white shirt or blouse) to work as opposed to blue-collar workers, who wear "work clothes" and do manual labor. Hence, white-collar crimes are those committed by "a person of respectability and high social status in the course of his occupation" (Sutherland, 1983).

For many sociologists, the value of the concept of white-collar crime is to call attention to the fact that crime does not occur only among the lower classes—that when brokers dip into their clients' stock accounts they are doing something as fully criminal as when high school dropouts steal cars and sell their parts. All classes have thieves. However, for other sociologists, white-collar crime serves as a conceptual device to protect strain theory from empirical falsification. That is, they argue that crime has different causes depending on the social class of the criminal. Hence, strain theory should be applied *only* to crimes committed by lower-class people. Crimes committed by middle- and upper-

■ Ivan Boesky was one of the wealthiest and most famous speculators on Wall Street when he was indicted for violating laws against using confidential information to profit in securities trading. Here Boesky leaves court after having paid a fine of $100 million, and on March 23, 1988, he entered a federal prison at Lompoc, California, to serve a three-year term. Some sociologists argue that cases like Boesky's are so different from ordinary cases of theft that they require a special theory, for clearly Boesky was not driven to steal because of poverty. However, other sociologists suggest that no special theories are needed to explain "white-collar" crime; temptations afflict people at all levels of society, and explanations of who succumbs and who resists are the same regardless of the sums involved.

class people do not, therefore, challenge strain theory because the causes of their criminality must be sought elsewhere.

Indeed, there have been many efforts to formulate specific theories to explain white-collar crime (Sutherland, 1983; Coleman, 1987). In the end, however, each of these attempts is forced to argue that quite different motivations impel poor people and rich people to break the law. But is this true? Must we suppose that a gas station attendant stole from the cash register because he wanted more money but accountants have another motive when they embezzle? Is it useful to suggest that different causes lead doctors, on the one hand, and patients, on the other, to defraud Medicaid? Recently, Travis Hirschi and Michael Gottfredson (1987a) argued that it is not. White-collar crime, they argued, causes problems only for some theories. Other theories have no difficulty with the fact that princes as well as paupers can be overcome by greed and temptation. Let's examine such a theory.

Control Theory

To formulate a more comprehensive sociological theory of deviance, the famous French sociologist Emile Durkheim (1858–1917) proposed, in effect, that we dismiss the question "Why do they do it?" and ask instead "Why don't they do it?" Since Durkheim's time, his advice has been heeded by many leading sociological and criminological theorists; this approach to deviance is known as **control theory**.

The initial assumption all control theories make is that life is a vast cafeteria of temptation. By themselves, *deviant acts tend to be attractive, providing rewards to those who engage in them*. To some, theft produces desired goods and alcohol and drugs supply enjoyment. Indeed, control theorists argue that norms arise to prohibit various kinds of behavior because without these norms such behavior would be frequent.

Put another way, when we consider what things people should not be allowed to do, we don't bother to prohibit behavior that people find unpleasant or unappealing. We assume that people won't do these things anyway. So we concern ourselves with things that people find rewarding and therefore might be tempted to do.

Thus, control theorists take deviance for granted and concentrate instead on explaining

This famous painting by Hieronymus Bosch (1450–1516), entitled *Garden of Earthly Delights,* is an allegory on temptation prompted by the painter's deep religious concerns. Bosch's vision of the human condition as an unrelenting opportunity to sin foreshadowed the insights of modern control theory, which asks not why do people deviate but why do they ever conform?

why people conform. Their answer is that people vary greatly in the degree of control their groups have over them. In any group, some people are rewarded more for conformity and punished more for deviance than other people are. Control theorists argue that conformity occurs only when people have more to gain by it than they have to gain by deviance.

In a classic paper, Jackson Toby (1957) described teenagers as differing in terms of their **"stake in conformity."** This phrase referred to *what a person risks losing* by being detected in deviant behavior. Toby suggested that all of us are tempted but that we resist to the extent that we feel we have much to lose by deviant behavior; for instance, a boy with a low stake in conformity has little "incentive to resist the temptation to do what he wants when he wants to do it." Therefore, like strain theorists, control theorists accept that access to desired rewards is unequal among members of any society. Some people succeed, some get left out. But while strain theory argues that inequality pushes the have-nots to deviate, control theory stresses how the have-nots are *free* to deviate. In the words of the song, "Freedom's just another word for nothing left to lose." Some people are free to deviate because they risk very little if their deviant behavior is detected. But for others the costs of detection far exceed the rewards of deviance.

For control theory, the causes of conformity are the **social bonds** between an individual and the group. When these bonds are strong, the individual conforms. When these bonds are weak, the individual deviates. Because the strength of these bonds can fluctuate over time, control theory can explain shifts from deviance to conformity (and vice versa) over a person's lifetime. Because many bonds are not related to social class, control theory can explain both the conformity of the poor and the deviance of the wealthy. But what are these bonds? There are four kinds between the individual and the group: *attachments, investments, involvements,* and *beliefs* (Hirschi, 1969; Stark and Bainbridge, 1987).

Attachments

We are already familiar with the concept of **attachments**—they are stable patterns of interaction between individuals. Moreover, attachments have a psychological component: We tend to like and even love those to whom we are attached. The degree to which an individual is attached to others depends upon the number and closeness of his or her bonds: how much that individual cares about others (and is cared about in return) and, therefore, how much the person cares about what others think of his or her actions. When we are strongly attached to others, we are likely to desire their continuing good opinion of us, and we therefore worry about how our actions will influence their regard for us. Conforming to norms helps to ensure the affection and respect of our friends—it protects our reputations.

When we are alone, we often break norms—we pick our noses, belch, and otherwise act grossly. We usually do not break these norms so freely in company. Moreover, if we knew for certain that our friends would never find out, we might even commit serious norm violations. Those who lack significant attachments are, in effect, *always alone*, and their friends never know about the norms they break. They do not put relationships with others at risk because they have none to risk. For them, the costs of deviance are low.

By focusing on bonds of attachment, control theory is able to deal with a great many research findings about deviant behavior. The more that young people care about others—parents, friends, and teachers—the less likely they are to commit acts of delinquency (Hirschi, 1969; Liska, 1981). Conversely, delinquents are very weakly attached, even to their delinquent friends (Hirschi, 1969; Kornhauser, 1978).

As Gove noted, sociological theories have trouble explaining why deviance declines with age. Delinquency rates rise rapidly from age 12 through about age 16 and then begin to fall rapidly. Gove's theory of physical fitness would not apply here. In addition, deviant behavior is much higher in the late teens and early twenties than it is after age 30. This is the phenomenon Gove addressed. But Gove's theory does not address the fact that all forms of deviance decline with age, not just those forms requiring physical prowess. Gove's theory is pertinent because it may tell us what causes some deviance rates to fall so rapidly with age. But we also must know why "sit down" crimes such as embezzlement also decline with age—albeit not so dramatically.

Control theory fills this gap. With the onset of the teens, deviance rates rise rapidly not only because people become stronger but also because attachments weaken for many. Adolescence is a time when parent-child relations often become stressful, and teenagers often feel alienated from

Table 7-5 ■ Current marital status and arrest among American males and females (not including widowed).

		Married	Single	Divorced and Separated
Percent who have been "picked up" by the police	**Males**	16.9%	26.3 %	36.6%
	Females	4.4%	6.6 %	9.0%

Source: Prepared by the author from National Opinion Research Center, General Social Surveys, 1973 and 1984.

other family members. As this occurs, they have reduced stakes in conformity. Then, in their later teens many young people form strong new attachments—often to persons of the opposite sex. Hence their stakes in conformity rise. Young adults are frequently very deficient in attachments. Often they leave family and childhood friends behind and go out on their own, relatively unattached. With marriage, the birth of children, and steady employment, they form new attachments; thus the tendency to commit even sedentary crimes falls as people get older.

Perhaps the most powerful aspect of control theory is its ability to account for weak or missing correlations between social class and most forms of deviance. Close attachments are not confined to the middle and upper classes. Most poor kids love their parents, too, and most poor adults love their families and friends. Thus, most poor people have a strong stake in conformity. By the same token, some middle- and upper-class kids don't love their parents, and not all privileged people love their families and friends. Thus, their stake in conformity is low.

Durkheim answered the question "Why don't they do it?" on the basis of attachments. As he put it, "We are moral beings to the extent that we are social beings."

The family serves as the primary source of the strong attachments that most effectively make us "social beings." Table 7-5 shows the impact of marital attachments on the percentage of American adults who have been picked up by the police. Among both men and women, those who were currently married were much less likely to have been picked up by the police than were persons who had never married or who were currently divorced or separated. By being detected in deviant behavior, married people have more to lose—their families.

Investments

The idea of **investments** is simple. We are tied to conformity not only through our attachments to others and through the stakes we have built up in life—the costs we have expended in constructing a satisfactory life and the rewards we expect. The more we have expended in getting an education, building a career, and acquiring possessions, the greater the risks of deviance. That is, we could lose our investments if we were detected in deviant behavior. An unemployed derelict may have very little to lose if caught sticking up a liquor store and a considerable amount to gain if he or she gets away with it. But it would be crazy for a successful lawyer to risk so much for so little, and most people rarely make really irrational decisions. When successful lawyers and bankers fail to resist the temptation to steal, they usually steal huge sums that seem to them to make the risks worthwhile. But the underlying processes of choice are the same for rich and poor.

Variations in investments also help account for the tendency of delinquents to reform as they reach adulthood. At age 14, most people have little investment at stake when they deviate. However, after people have begun to build normal adult lives, their investments mount rapidly.

Involvements

The *involvement* aspect of control theory takes into account that time and energy are limited. The more time a person spends on activities that conform to the norms, the less time and energy that person has to devote to deviant activities.

To a considerable extent, **involvements** are a consequence of investments and attachments. People who have families, or play football after school, or are engrossed in hobbies, or are busy with careers have much less time and energy left for violating norms than do people with few attachments and investments. Popular wisdom has it that "idle hands are the devil's workshop." Many studies have reported that the more time young people spend "hanging around" or riding in cars, the more likely they are to commit delinquent acts (Hirschi, 1969). The more time young people spend on schoolwork or even talking with friends, the less likely they are to get into trouble. That is, people neglect to do all sorts of things for lack of time. College couples even delay breaking up until between quarters or until the summer holiday, when they have more time (Hill, Rubin, and Peplau, 1976). People also tend not to do deviant things when they are pressed for time.

Beliefs

Control theory stresses human rationality—whether people tend to deviate or conform depends on their calculations of the costs and benefits of deviance or conformity. But control theorists also recognize that through socialization we form **beliefs** about how the world works and how it *ought* to work. That is, we develop beliefs about how people, including ourselves, should behave. Sociologists often describe this as the **internalization of norms**, instead of using the word *conscience*.

We accept norms not only because our friends expect us to but also because we risk our self-respect if we deviate. The phrase "I'm not that kind of person" indicates that we hold certain beliefs about proper behavior. When a friend suggests a deviant act and assures us that nobody will know, we display internalized norms if we respond, "Yes, but *I* will know."

By themselves, our beliefs may or may not cause us to conform. As we saw in Chapter 4, individual religious beliefs will prevent delinquent behavior only when the person is part of a community in which the majority belong to religious organizations. However, because most Americans live in such a community, a national sample of adults ought to display a negative correlation between church attendance and having been picked up by the police. Table 7-6 shows that this hypothesis is confirmed. People who attend church less than once a year are more than three times as likely as weekly attenders to have been picked up by the police.

Put another way, a religion gains the power to alter behavior when it is supported by attachments to others who accept the authority of the moral beliefs that religion teaches. This fact helps us to recognize that all four elements of control theory are interconnected. Attachments are also investments—much time and energy go into building close relations with others. Attachments and investments both act as involvements: Time spent with friends or at work is time not available for deviance. In addition, our beliefs will also determine with whom we choose to become attached and what investments we decide to make.

As with other explanations of deviant behavior, control theory also cannot stand alone. It seeks to explain conformity to the norms of a social group, but it doesn't identify which group or note that conformity to the norms of one group may be deviance from the norms of another group. In combination with subcultural theory, we have a more complete explanation of deviance. And control theory clearly implies and therefore requires elements of differential association–social learning theory to specify mechanisms by which attachments generate conformity.

To help pull these arguments together, let's

Table 7-6 ■ Church attendance and arrest among American adults.

	Attend Church			
	Weekly	Monthly	Yearly	Less Than Yearly
Percent who have been "picked up" by the police	5.9%	10.5%	12.9%	22.0%

Source: Prepared by the author from National Opinion Research Center, General Social Surveys, 1973 and 1984.

watch while two sociologists combine aspects of control theory and differential association while replicating Travis Hirschi's classic study.

Linden and Fillmore: A Comparative Study of Delinquency

 Travis Hirschi's *Causes of Delinquency* (1969) was based on a sample of American students in the public schools of Richmond, California (see Chapter 4). Hirschi's book reformulated control theory and then subjected many hypotheses to rigorous empirical testing.

Subsequently, Rick Linden and Cathy Fillmore (1981) undertook a parallel study based on a sample of Canadian students in Edmonton, Alberta. One of their aims was to demonstrate that studies of delinquency done in one modern society would generalize to other modern societies—that it would not be necessary to have different theories of delinquency for Canada, the United States, France, and Japan. A second aim was to more adequately combine elements of control and differential association theories of delinquency.

As mentioned earlier, differential association theory fails to explain why some teenagers have delinquent friends and others don't. The theory also has suffered from research evidence that teenagers often begin their delinquent activities *before* they begin substantial association with other delinquents. Moreover, Hirschi had found that having delinquent friends had no impact on some teenagers. Linden and Fillmore sought to repair these shortcomings of differential association theory by combining it with control theory. They proposed that teenagers with low stakes in conformity have little to lose by associating with other delinquents and that such association will further amplify their delinquency as they learn new criminal techniques and are reinforced for new acts of deviance. Figure 7-2 illustrates Linden and Fillmore's model.

Table 7-7 compares the delinquency of Richmond and Edmonton teenagers, based on self-report data. More serious property crime was a bit more common in Richmond than in Edmonton at this time. But overall the data are very similar. Notice that here too we see huge gender differences.

Linden and Fillmore measured stakes in conformity on the basis of attachments to parents and liking school. They found that in both Edmonton and Richmond these were negatively correlated with being delinquent and with having delinquent friends. Finally, in both nations those with delinquent friends were more apt to be delinquent.

But the more important comparison involves applying the reformulated theoretical model to both samples. Linden and Fillmore found that in both nations their model fit the data well. In

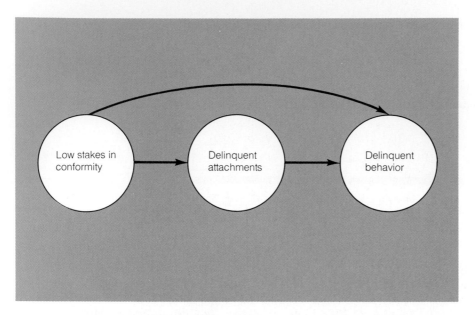

Figure 7-2 ■ **Linden and Fillmore's model combining control and differential association theories.** People with low stakes in conformity not only have little to lose by breaking the law but they also have little to lose by associating with others who break the law. Thus teenagers with weak attachments to parents and poor school records will tend to hang around with other delinquents, and taking up with "bad" friends increases the tendency to commit illegal acts. (Adapted from Linden and Fillmore, 1981.)

both Canada and the United States low stakes in conformity seem to lead to the formation of attachments to delinquent peers, and these attachments greatly increase the level of delinquency. That is, teenagers with little to lose by giving in to temptations are very likely to do so. But they are even more likely to do so if, in addition, they have friends who support them in their decisions to skip school, shoplift, stick up a store, steal a car, vandalize property, or beat somebody up.

Sociology is not a description of what goes on in a particular time or place. That is the job of journalism. Sociology is an attempt to formulate explanations that apply to human social life—here, there, and everywhere. Thus, Linden and Fillmore were not surprised to find that their model applied on either side of the U.S.-Canadian border.

While the theories we have examined thus far are meant to apply in any society or in different regions within any society, they are not

designed to explain *differences* from one society or region to another. To do this, we now must examine a more macro theory of deviance.

■

Anomie and the Integration of Societies

In Chapter 1 we saw that the rapid growth of large cities during the nineteenth century caused many early sociologists to fear a breakdown in human relations—that people would come to live in a world of strangers, lost and alone. Emile Durkheim, one of the founders of modern sociology, feared that as people lost their links to one another through long-standing attachments, society would suffer from **anomie:** a condition of *normlessness*. People would not know what the norms were, and attachments would not motivate them to obey the norms even if they knew them, for humans would lack

Table 7-7 ■ Self-reported delinquency for Richmond and Edmonton youth.

	Richmond, California		Edmonton, Alberta	
	Boys	Girls (percent)	Boys	Girls (percent)
Have stolen something worth $2–50	19.1%	7.7%	14.1%	5.6%
Have stolen something worth over $50	6.6	2.0	2.4	0.2
Have stolen a car	10.8	3.6	5.9	0.7
Have damaged property	25.5	8.6	40.3	16.0
Have beaten someone up	41.7	15.6	40.9	16.0

Source: Adapted from Linden and Fillmore (1981).

the moral direction provided by others. Indeed, Durkheim argued that in modern urban societies the individual is morally in "empty space." Without social ties, "no force restrains them" (Durkheim, 1897), and in such circumstances people literally lose the ability to tell right from wrong. Ephraim Mizruchi (1964) has suggested the term *deregulation* as the best translation of anomie into English. When social relations break down, society loses its ability to regulate behavior.

Durkheim contrasted conditions of city life with those of more traditional rural villages and identified the latter as **"moral communities."** He stressed two components of the moral community. The first of these is **social integration.** Here he referred to the number and intimacy of attachments enjoyed by the average person. In traditional village life, Durkheim argued, the average person was firmly anchored in an extensive network of close attachments. The second aspect of moral communities, according to Durkheim, is **moral integration.** Here he referred to shared beliefs, especially religious beliefs, that provide members of a community with a common moral conception—mutual beliefs about what the norms are and why the norms are correct.

Both social and moral integration are eroded

by life in large cities, according to Durkheim. People lose their attachments, and thus social integration erodes. While a single religion unites traditional communities, many competing religions flourish in cities, and each weakens the others. Thus, Durkheim concluded that cities would destroy the power of societies to control their members and therefore become locations for excessive serious deviance.

Durkheim's theory describes how macro changes in social structures can have devastating effects at the micro level. Indeed, the correspondence between his anomie theory and control theory is obvious: The sheer size and disorganization of big cities reduce the average person's attachments and beliefs. Thus, free to deviate, people will do so.

Durkheim attempted to demonstrate his thesis by showing that suicide rates were much higher in urban areas and in areas where a variety of Protestant faiths existed than in rural areas and places that remained solidly Catholic (Durkheim, 1897).

As we saw in Chapter 1, research does not support the thesis that city life inevitably produces "mass societies" in which people lack attachments and thus fall victims to anomie. Thus, Durkheim's predictions about the future were overly pessimistic. However, that does not

■ Emile Durkheim.

invalidate his theory. Durkheim's assertions about the consequences of weak moral and social integration can be applied to the extent that societies (or different areas of societies or even different areas in a city) vary in their degree of social and moral integration. Durkheim's theory predicts that deviance rates will change as integration varies; for example, crime and suicide rates will be higher wherever moral and social integration are lower.

During the 1930s and 1940s, many researchers attempted to test Durkheim's predictions about the relationship between integration and deviance. Clifford R. Shaw and Henry D. McKay (1929, 1931, 1942) found that delinquency is much higher in urban neighborhoods with a high population turnover than in more stable neighborhoods. In neighborhoods of newcomers, social integration is necessarily lower than in places where people have had time to form attachments with their neighbors. Robert C. Angell (1942, 1947, 1949) found that cities higher in "moral integration" had lower rates of crime and suicide.

Although Durkheim's theory of integration and anomie has been repeatedly described in

textbooks as a major contribution to sociological knowledge, during the 1950s and 1960s researchers seldom tested it. A major reason was the lack of good, readily available measures of social and moral integration of cities or parts of cities and the immense expense apparently required to come up with adequate measures.

Earlier research had many flaws because of these limits. Thus, Angell used rates of contributions to charitable fund-raising drives as a measure of moral integration on the grounds that these rates would reflect the degree of consensus on values and norms in a community. He also used these rates because they were available in reports published by charitable organizations, not because they were particularly appropriate for testing Durkheim's thesis. Other studies tended to be circular. Often a high crime rate was used as an indicator of weak social and moral integration, thus making it impossible to say that weak integration *caused* high crime rates. Moreover, measures of social integration, such as statistics on population turnover, were available for just a few cities—in fact, much of the research was based solely on comparisons of Chicago neighborhoods.

Only recently have problems of obtaining good measures for testing Durkheim's theory been overcome. The results have strongly supported Durkheim's predictions, but they have also consistently revealed strange correlations. These patterns have forced sociologists to reconsider the concept of deviance. So I invite you to watch as this research was conducted and the odd results were reinterpreted.

Social integration and crime

 In 1980, while Robert Crutchfield was still a graduate student in sociology at Vanderbilt, he decided to test Durkheim's thesis about the impact of the social integration of communities on crime.

As we have seen, research on this question had long been frustrated for want of a practical way to measure the social integration of cities. How can we determine the number and intimacy of the attachments of average citizens in various cities? It is much too expensive to select

■ Robert Crutchfield.

Table 7-8 ■ **Correlations between moral and social integration and crime rates.**

	Moral Integration	Social Integration
Total crime rate	−.44	−.63
Burglary	−.46	−.64
Larceny	−.44	−.55
Rape	−.41	−.53
Assault	−.14	−.28
Homicide	−.12	−.26
Robbery	−.16	−.08
Auto theft	−.18	−.08

Sources: Stark, Doyle, and Kent (1980); Crutchfield, Geerken, and Gove (1983).

large samples from a number of cities and ask individuals how many close friends they have, how often they see them, how long they have known them, and so forth.

Crutchfield therefore adopted the method used by Shaw and McKay to estimate variations in attachments among American city dwellers. Recently both the U.S. Census and Statistics Canada began to publish statistics on population turnover for all major North American cities. This is the proportion of a city's population who are recent newcomers or have recently moved to a new neighborhood within a city. Crutchfield agreed with Shaw and McKay that in cities with high rates of population turnover—where many people are always moving in, moving out, or moving around—social integration will necessarily be reduced. Attachments will be disrupted, and large numbers of people will be strangers and transients. He then computed these rates for major cities and examined whether these were correlated with crime rates (Crutchfield, Geerken, and Gove, 1983).

He found very high correlations: Cities with high population turnover (and thus low social integration) had high official crime rates, while those with low population turnover had low crime rates (Table 7-8). He also controlled for many other factors, including racial composi-

tion and poverty, to demonstrate that the relationship was not spurious. (Figure 7-3 shows rates for population turnover.)

However, Crutchfield was not content to examine only the total crime rate. He also examined each of the seven offense rates that compose the total crime rate: burglary, larceny, auto theft, robbery, rape, assault, and homicide. The results were very strange. Burglary, larceny, and rape were strongly negatively correlated with social integration, but homicide, auto theft, and robbery were virtually uncorrelated with social integration. Because the overwhelming proportion of all reported crimes are burglary and larceny, this produced a strong correlation with the total crime rate. However, social integration seems to affect only these two categories of offense plus rape but has no effect on the other kinds of crime. Why? For a time, no one knew.

Moral integration and crime

 While Crutchfield was reopening research on social integration, I was doing the same thing on moral integration. At the time we were unacquainted and did not learn of one another's work for another year. I

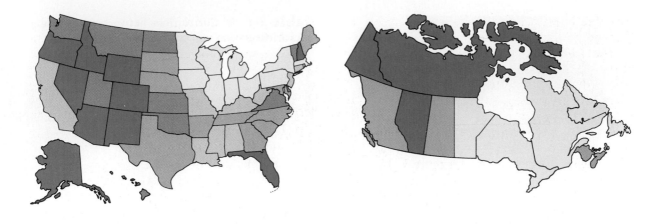

1975–1980: Newcomers per 1,000

New York	35.5	Kansas	116.5
Michigan	47.5	North Dakota	119.7
Pennsylvania	48.4	Delaware	124.3
Ohio	52.8	Oklahoma	126.5
Illinois	56.2	Virginia	130.0
Wisconsin	61.6	Vermont	133.2
Massachusetts	65.5	Montana	137.6
Minnesota	67.5	Utah	139.0
Indiana	70.0	Washington	150.3
Iowa	73.1	Hawaii	155.4

New Jersey	73.2	Oregon	156.7
Louisiana	77.2	New Mexico	158.8
California	79.3	New Hampshire	172.2
West Virginia	79.9	Idaho	180.3
Alabama	82.2	Florida	184.8
Rhode Island	82.3	Colorado	190.8
Kentucky	82.7	Arizona	220.2
Mississippi	84.6	Alaska	244.4
Connecticut	87.2	Wyoming	255.7
Missouri	87.3	Nevada	293.3

North Carolina	91.5
Nebraska	97.2
Maryland	97.6
Tennessee	98.2
Maine	100.2
Texas	100.9
South Dakota	102.0
South Carolina	106.2
Georgia	106.5
Arkansas	114.7

1979–1980: Newcomers per 1,000

Quebec	4.2	Pr. Edward Island	33.6
Ontario	10.7	Alberta	49.4
Newfoundland	20.1	N.W. Territories	84.4
Manitoba	24.8	Yukon	108.7

Nova Scotia	26.2
New Brunswick	26.6
Saskatchewan	28.8
British Columbia	29.9

Figure 7-3 ■ **Newcomers reduce the level of attachments in communities.** Nearly one-third of the residents of Nevada in the 1980 census had moved to the state within the past five years. Other western states also had high rates, while New York, Michigan, and Pennsylvania had the lowest newcomer rates. The Canadian newcomer rates are based on people who moved into a province during a two-year period (1979–80). If the Canadian rates are adjusted to reflect the same length of time as those for the United States, the two nations are quite similar—the Yukon would then have a rate of 271.8, very close to that for Nevada. Newcomers usually arrive with few, if any, attachments in their new community, and where there are many newcomers, they reduce the level of attachments for those who did not move. You can stay put and still become a stranger in your neighborhood if everyone else moves. Because sociologists place so much importance on attachments for restricting crime and deviance, measures like this are of major use in research. By comparing these maps with Figure 7-1, you will see why.

was able to proceed with the first good test of Durkheim's notions about moral communities because I had figured out how to estimate accurate rates of church membership for American cities, counties, and states (see Chapter 14). Like Crutchfield, I chose to focus on major cities and see if variations in church membership correlated with variations in crime rates. I also looked at the total crime rate first and found a very high negative correlation—the higher a city's church membership, the lower its crime rate. Then I also examined the seven crime categories composing the total crime rate and found the same odd pattern (Table 7-8). Church membership reduces burglary, larceny, and rape, but it has little or no effect on homicide, assault, robbery, and auto theft (Stark, Doyle, and Kent, 1980).

I learned about Crutchfield's same strange results in the next year, when I received an early draft of his paper. That fall he became a faculty member in my department, and we became friends and eventually collaborators. During our first conversations about our odd findings, neither of us could be certain they weren't simply an accident or the result of some momentary circumstance. But soon we were able to replicate both studies (Stark et al., 1983) using data for the 1920s. Once again we got the same pattern of results. At that point it was clear that something was wrong either with Durkheim's theory or with the concept of deviance. The latter seemed more likely, since the theory worked very well with some (though not all) forms of deviance.

Reconceptualizing Deviance

 Each sociological theory of deviance discussed in this chapter makes several basic assumptions. First of all, these theories are not directed at momentary nonconformity. Rather, they conceive of deviance as a pattern of nonconformity having significant duration. Subcultural theories, for example, treat deviance as part of a normal way of life—as conformity to the norms of stable subcultures. Moreover, sociological theories of deviance assume that behavior is based on conscious motivation or at least self-awareness. Strain theory characterizes humans as driven to acts of deviance in response to thwarted desires. Control theory regards conformity and deviance as based on calculations of potential gains and losses (even if these calculations are sometimes in error).

The picture of deviant acts that emerges from all of these theories, then, is of deeds by self-aware actors who knowingly violate norms and engage in sustained periods of deviant behavior. But when we closely examine deviant acts, only some fit this description. Burglary fits. The typical burglary is committed by someone who is fully aware of the illegality of his or her actions, who planned the action in advance, who has acquired certain basic skills relevant to entering premises and selecting and selling loot, and who engages in a series of such offenses. Burglars are conscious deviants.

But this image does not fit the usual homicide. Only a minority of murders are premeditated or committed for gain. Typically, homicides occur during a sudden burst of rage, which is followed by deep remorse. In fact, of every four homicides, three involve victims who were relatives, friends, or close associates of the killer (Smith and Parker, 1980). Persons rarely repeat this form of homicide. Hence, murder often does not involve a conscious decision to violate norms or a sustained period of deviance. Instead, murderers tend to resemble the impulsively violent English men studied by Berkowitz (1978), discussed earlier in this chapter.

These reflections led Crutchfield and me to conclude that our strange results were due to the inclusion of crimes that lacked the rational elements postulated by sociological theories. We therefore proposed that deviance be reconceptualized as of two types, with sociological theories applying to only one of these types. These two types reflect the differences between burglars and murderers.

Intentional deviance involves rational calculation and duration. **Impulsive deviance** lacks calculation and duration; it includes sudden, momentary acts of deviance that do not involve reflections about norms. For example, people

■ A French museum guide points to the bare spot on the wall where a famous painting by the Impressionist Claude Monet once hung. The previous morning five armed men burst into the museum and took Monet's *Impression, Soleil Levant* and eight other master-pieces, including four more by Monet and two by Pierre-Auguste Renoir. Carefully planned crimes like these are the kind most effectively explained by sociological theories of deviance. But suppose that when he went off duty, this museum guide stopped in a bar, got into an argument with his brother-in-law, and was stabbed to death. Crimes based on sudden impulses in the heat of passion pose much greater difficulty for sociological explanations.

tend to kill or assault one another during sudden bursts of uncontrolled (possibly uncontrollable) rage. These tend to be impulsive, even dangerous people, but they are not intentional deviants. Their morning-after feelings are typically guilt and remorse, not satisfaction with a job well done. Indeed, impulsive deviants often have a hangover the next morning.

Armed with this distinction between impulsive and intentional deviance, Crutchfield and I set out to make sense of our findings by showing that social and moral integration can limit conscious acts of deviance but not acts that were not considered.

At first glance, our new scheme did not seem to fit very well with our research results. Obviously, burglary and larceny are acts of intentional deviance for the most part, and they respond to social control as predicted by the theory (see Table 7-8). Rape, too, is usually an act of intentional deviance; most rapists are repeaters who plan ways to commit their acts without getting caught. Rape rates are also strongly influenced by social and moral integration. Homicide and assault, which are typically acts of impulse, also fit the prediction that they will tend not to be responsive to integration. But robbery and auto theft, both apparent acts of conscious, intentional deviance, do not respond to community integration.

We could have just discarded our new concepts at this point as a nice try that failed. Instead, we asked what kinds of acts were really being reported as instances of auto theft and robbery. Checking with the FBI, we quickly learned that although some autos are stolen by professional thieves, who strip them and sell the parts, most cars are stolen by teenagers for a little joyriding, after which the car is abandoned and recovered. Juvenile joyriding more closely fits the image of sudden impulsive action than intentional deviance. Thus, we realized that auto theft rates should be only very weakly related to community integration, which agreed with our results.

But that left robbery. Like most people, we believed that most robbers make a career of crime—masked gunmen who stick up store after store until arrested. As it turned out, however, this is not the kind of robber who accounts for most of the statistics. Instead, the robbery rate primarily consists of a mishmash of relatively trivial and impulsive actions. When a wino shoves another wino to the ground and runs off with his bottle, that is a robbery. If one kid twists another kid's arm (or even threatens to do so) and takes his lunch money, that's robbery, too. And people who go into stores or even banks and pull a classic stickup are often drunk or deranged.

Clearly, the official robbery rate includes many intentional robberies, but the bulk of the offenses are best described as impulsive or trivial. Having learned these facts, we gained confidence in our reconceptualization. Moreover, when we computed a robbery rate based on persons serving jail and prison sentences for robbery (and who ought mainly to be intentional deviants), we found a very substantial correlation between the robbery rate and social and moral integration, as the theory would predict.

If our reconceptualization is valid, then it follows that *sociological theories of deviance should apply only to instances of intentional deviance*; failure to find correlations when impulsive deviance is examined leaves these theories intact. People who truthfully say "I didn't know what I was doing" or "Something just came over me and I didn't stop to think" cannot be deterred from deviance by their stakes in conformity. Moreover, here an effective dividing line between sociology and psychology presents itself. Sociologists have correctly criticized psychologists for not attending to social structure and for attributing irrationality to deviants who clearly calculate the potential gains

and losses of their deviance. But sociologists may have been equally naive for failing to recognize the significance of psychological factors in many forms of deviance—those that reflect impulsive, unthinking, momentary acts.

Interestingly enough, Durkheim anticipated this critical distinction before the turn of the century. He thought that acts of despair, such as suicide, reflect weak social and moral integration. Research has confirmed this prediction (Bainbridge and Stark, 1981a; Stack, 1983). Durkheim also argued that "crimes of passion" would be more common in more highly integrated communities, for these occur within networks of close attachment, not between isolated strangers. This prediction still awaits adequate research.

The Labeling Approach to Deviance

So far in this chapter we have assumed that the members of any society or group know its norms. Consequently, when people seriously violate norms, it is reasonable to ask why they did so. Now we must consider a sociological approach to deviance suggesting that this question is often inappropriate. Instead, we should ask why we label people as deviant when they break norms. Sociologists taking this approach claim that most deviance results from some persons having been identified, or labeled, as deviants. Not surprisingly, this approach is called **labeling theory**.

Labeling theorists distinguish between primary and secondary deviance. **Primary deviance** involves whatever behavior a person engaged in that caused others to identify or label him or her as deviant. **Secondary deviance** is behavior that is a reaction to having been labeled a deviant. Most labeling theorists suggest that primary deviance involves relatively transient, insignificant, quirky behavior that most people engage in from time to time. Usually, others ignore such behavior (Lemert, 1951, 1967; Scheff, 1966; Schur, 1971). Sometimes, however, others react strongly and negatively to the primary deviance of some people, who are then publicly labeled as deviant.

Having been stigmatized as deviants, many

people are driven to fulfill our expectations of them. Because they have a bad name, they come to see themselves as bad, and so they do bad things. The labeling approach, therefore, concentrates on identifying and criticizing the process by which norms arise and are enforced and by which some people are labeled for behaving a certain way while others are not. The labeling approach also specifies how a label forces people to adopt a career of secondary deviance.

Allen E. Liska (1981) has identified three major ways in which labels incline people to deviate. First, a deviant label, such as burglar, alcoholic, or prostitute, limits legitimate economic and occupational opportunities. Many employers will not hire ex-convicts, for example, and some reject applicants who have been arrested even if they were acquitted (Schwartz and Skolnick, 1962). At the same time, being labeled deviant may increase illegitimate economic opportunities (serving a jail term may make a person more proficient in crime).

Second, a deviant label limits a person's interpersonal relations. Thus, an ex-convict may find few chances for attachments with conventional people and thus be limited to attachments with others who also have been labeled as deviant.

Third, being labeled a deviant can affect self-conceptions. Sociological theories of interaction have long held that we see ourselves as others see us. If others see us as deviants, we may come to accept their judgments. Then when we act as we are "supposed" to act, we will be acting in deviant ways.

Labeling theories have made some important contributions to understanding deviance. As with subcultural theories, they have sensitized us to the fact that norms are not absolute but are created by humans. Therefore, it is useful to examine how a particular norm was established, by whom, for what reasons, and, perhaps, *against* whom. Many norms are born in conflict, and many laws are passed by close votes. According to labeling theorists, this demonstrates that norms are often arbitrary. Thirty years ago, a doctor who performed abortions risked a prison sentence and expulsion from the medical profession. Today abortions are routine medical procedures. Labeling theorists

therefore suggest that the question to be asked is not why deviants behave as they do but why we decide to prohibit certain actions.

Labeling theories also closely examine the process by which some people are labeled as deviant while others who do the same thing go unlabeled. Labeling theorists argue that the higher a person's status, the less chance that he or she will be labeled for deviant behavior.

Finally, labeling theory calls attention to how the reactions by society to primary deviance can produce continuing patterns of secondary deviance—that by attempting to stop deviant behavior, we may cause it.

However, over the past twenty years, many hypotheses drawn from labeling theory have not been confirmed by research. For example, numerous studies have failed to show that people labeled as delinquents as a result of arrest and conviction subsequently increase their level of illegal activity (Gibbons and Blake, 1976; Klein, 1976; Liska, 1981). In fact, some studies show that juveniles who are labeled and punished for an offense are less likely to commit subsequent offenses than those who escaped being labeled (McEachern, 1968; Thornberry, 1973). We shall consider this further in Chapter 8.

Nor has the view been sustained that primary deviance is usually insignificant and harmless. To the contrary, quirky, transient, and trivial norm violation is almost always ignored (Gove, 1975); people usually get labeled as a deviant after committing a serious act. People are labeled as rapists after they have raped someone, as robbers after they have robbed, as murderers after they have killed. Thus Liska asks, "Are these actions unimportant when committed by primary deviants?" That is, are they to be considered not serious if the person does not already have a deviant label?

This brings us to the major shortcoming of labeling theory. While it may help us to explain why ex-convicts often commit new offenses and go back to prison, it cannot explain the initial act of deviance by which people get labeled as deviants. Thus, to explain why an ex-convict commits new offenses does not explain why he or she became a convict in the first place. Why they *start* to do it lies beyond the scope of labeling theories.

Conclusion

This chapter has reviewed a number of partial theories of deviance. I mentioned at the start that these theories were much more complementary than conflicting and that the next step for sociologists is to fit them into a general theory of deviance. An introductory textbook is hardly the place to undertake such a task. Nevertheless, as an effective summary of the chapter, some of the components of such a general theory can be described.

First, any general theory of deviance must include elements of learning theory. Nearly all human behavior is learned, including deviant behavior.

Next, a general theory must specify the sources from which conformity and deviance are learned. Here we need to apply theories of early childhood socialization as well as theories of differential and adult socialization (see Chapter 6). For example, because males are much more prone than females to commit criminal and delinquent acts, aspects of *sex-role* socialization must be part of a general theory on deviance. Furthermore, elements of differential association theory should prove useful. In learning to deviate or conform, what a person's friends reward will matter.

We know, too, that some people seem to be more easily influenced by their friends than others are. Thus, a general theory of deviance may need to draw upon personality theories dealing with traits such as weak self-esteem. We must also keep in mind the distinction between intentional and impulsive deviance, relying on psychology to help explain the latter.

To account for the existence of deviant groups that can provide differential association, elements of subcultural theory must be included. Although much deviance is not supported by subcultures, certainly some forms are, and some forms of deviance are stabilized by association with deviant subcultures.

All of the above elements help to clarify and extend control theories. Consider attachments—the bonds of affection between people. Clearly, learning provides the mechanism by which attachments form and influence our behavior. Differential association and subcultural theories help explain to whom we become attached. If we are attached to persons who reward conformity, then we tend to conform. If we are attached to persons who reward deviance, then we tend to deviate. And if we are unattached, then we tend to do as we please. Other things being equal, it will probably please us to commit deviant acts, because most of them are inherently self-reinforcing. Here, too, psychological theories can help explain the inability of some people to form and maintain strong attachments (Wilson and Herrnstein, 1985).

The investment aspect of control theory incorporates the basic tenets of structural strain theory. If our investments in life are low, we are in a deprived condition: Life has rewarded us little and promises never to reward us very much. This does not drive us to break the norms as much as it frees us to do so. Moreover, because control theory examines all deviance in terms of relative gains and losses, it can explain the behavior of not only the unemployed burglar but also the wealthy embezzler.

Labeling theory can also contribute important insights to a general theory of deviance. To the extent that past acts of deviance stigmatize a person with a deviant label, his or her attachments to others may be severely limited. Conventional people may tend to avoid ex-convicts, prostitutes, or problem drinkers. This in turn frees the deviants of attachments that might cause them to conform. Moreover, lack of conventional attachments may prompt those who share a deviant label to associate with one another and thereby form a deviant subculture. Indeed, to the extent that deviant labels prevent people from building investments in conventional activities, they will also have greater freedom to deviate.

Finally, theories of social and moral integration place a general theory of deviance within the framework of large-scale social structures. That is, the overall condition of societies as whole systems can affect rates of internal deviance. For example, high rates of population instability hinder attachments, prompting deviance to rise. If there is a great decline in religious commitment, then deviance ought to rise as moral integration weakens.

This sketch of obvious connections among current theories is meant to show you that despite the proliferation of partial theories, social scientists have been making progress in understanding deviance and conformity.

Review Glossary

deviance Behavior that violates norms. (p. 172)

deviants People who are known to frequently break relatively important norms. (p. 174)

born criminals Lombroso's term for people whose deviance he attributed to their more primitive biology. (p. 175)

differential association theory A theory that traces deviant behavior to association with other persons who also engage in this behavior. (p. 181)

subcultural deviance Behavior through which a person deviates from the norms of the surrounding society by conforming to the norms of a subculture. (p. 183)

structural strain Frustration or discontent caused by being in a disadvantaged position in the social structure. (p. 184)

structural strain theories Theories that blame deviance on the stress of structural strain; for example, one such theory claims that people commit crimes because of their poverty. (p. 184)

white-collar crime According to Sutherland (1983), these are crimes committed by "a person of respectability and high social status in the course of his occupation." (p. 186)

control theory A theory that stresses how weak bonds between the individual and society make people free to deviate, while strong bonds make deviance costly. (p. 187)

stake in conformity Those things a person risks losing by being detected committing deviant behavior; what a person protects by conforming to the norms. See *social bonds*. (p. 187)

social bonds Bonds that, as used in control theory, consist of the following:

1. **attachments** Bonds to other people. (p. 188)

2. **investments** The costs expended to construct a satisfactory life and the current and potential flow of rewards expected. (p. 189)

3. **involvements** The amount of time and energy expended in nondeviant activities. (p. 190)

4. **beliefs** Our notions about how we ought to act. (p. 190)

internalization of norms The sociological synonym for *conscience* refers to the tendency of people not simply to learn what the norms are but also to come to believe the norms are right. (p. 190)

anomie A condition of normlessness in a group or even a whole society when people either no longer know what the norms are or have lost their belief in them. (p. 192)

moral communities Groups within which there is very high agreement on the norms and strong bonds of attachment among members. (p. 193)

social integration The degree to which persons in a group have many strong attachments to one another. (p. 193)

moral integration The degree to which members of a group are united by shared beliefs. (p. 193)

intentional deviance Norm violations that stem primarily from rational calculation and that persist for some significant period; for example, most burglaries are such norm violations. (p. 197)

impulsive deviance Norm violations that occur suddenly without calculation and that do not persist for a significant period; for example, most homicides are such norm violations. (p. 197)

labeling theory A theory that explains deviant behavior as a reaction to having been socially identified as a deviant. (p. 199)

primary deviance Actions that cause others to label an individual as deviant. (p. 199)

secondary deviance Actions carried out in response to having been labeled as deviant. (p. 199)

Suggested Readings

Canadian Centre for Justice Statistics. *Crime and Traffic Enforcement Statistics*. Ottawa: Statistics Canada (issued annually).

Criminology. 1987. Special issue on theory. 25:783–989.

Hirschi, Travis, and Michael Gottfredson, eds. 1987. *Positive Criminology*. Beverly Hills: Sage.

Kornhauser, Ruth. 1978. *Social Sources of Delinquency: An Appraisal of Analytic Models*. Chicago: University of Chicago Press.

Liska, Allen E. 1981. *Perspectives on Deviance*. Englewood Cliffs, N.J.: Prentice-Hall.

Silverman, Robert A., and James J. Teevan, Jr. 1980. *Crime in Canadian Society*. 2nd ed. Toronto: Butterworths.

U.S. Department of Justice. *Sourcebook of Criminal Justice Statistics*. Washington, D.C.: U.S. Government Printing Office (issued annually).

Social Control

8

WE HAVE EXAMINED why people deviate. In this chapter we take a different point of view: How do groups attempt to prevent deviance? All collective efforts to ensure conformity to the norms are forms of **social control**.

The most common forms of social control occur during face-to-face interaction. Most of us conform most of the time to avoid offending those around us. Mild norm violations in the presence of others embarrass us and indicate our responsiveness to social control. Even when we are alone, we often limit our deviance for fear that someone might find out. Yet not everyone is equally responsive to social control. We all know people who are regarded as "outcasts," "misfits," or "jerks." Everyday speech includes a huge and colorful set of terms for people who lack the approval of those around them. These terms make it clear that while informal disapproval prevents much deviance, it doesn't prevent it all.

When *informal* methods of control fail and more serious acts of deviance occur, *formal* methods of social control are activated. A number of special roles and organizations exist in societies to enforce conformity to important norms: police, courts, psychiatrists, prisons, mental hospitals, even collection agencies.

These formal agencies of social control tend to operate as backup systems—they react to complaints. The police seldom try to discover that a crime has been committed; they go into action after a crime is reported to them.

Chapter Preview

In this chapter we examine both informal and formal methods of social control. From the very start of this book, we have been discussing informal methods of social control; interaction with others, particularly with those to whom we are attached, is the major channel of informal social control. So, in this chapter, we will simply expand on our understanding by examining some classic experiments that reveal the power of groups to control members' behavior and the response of groups to members who persist in deviance.

The bulk of the chapter is devoted to *formal methods* of social control—activities by organizations created to ensure conformity to the norms. First we assess programs and policies designed to prevent deviance. We shall watch an amazing program designed to prevent young boys from becoming delinquents and see the results of the experiment used to measure its effectiveness. Next we examine whether punishment can deter deviance: Can punishment cause some people to cease being deviant and prevent some others from ever starting to deviate? Finally, we look at the criminal justice system—the police, courts, and prisons. How well does this system operate? Can it serve to reform and resocialize deviants?

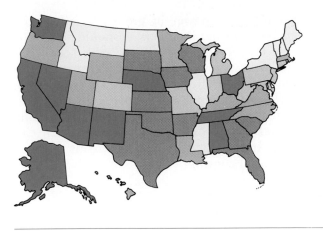

Vermont	0.00	Texas	4.19
New Hampshire	0.00	Kansas	4.22
Montana	0.00	Georgia	4.27
North Dakota	1.06	Arkansas	4.27
Maine	1.47	Florida	4.29
Mississippi	2.29	Wisconsin	4.30
Idaho	2.61	South Dakota	4.36
Illinois	2.73	Iowa	4.38
New York	2.77	Oklahoma	4.44
		South Carolina	4.59

Pennsylvania	2.84		
Colorado	2.89	Ohio	4.68
Rhode Island	2.98	Washington	4.80
Maryland	3.12	Tennessee	4.92
New Jersey	3.13	New Mexico	4.94
Indiana	3.13	Arizona	5.21
West Virginia	3.18	Nevada	5.22
Missouri	3.21	California	5.60
Connecticut	3.49	Alaska	6.00
Michigan	3.54	Nebraska	6.55
		Alabama	7.32

Minnesota	3.58
Oregon	3.67
Louisiana	3.68
Kentucky	3.74
Wyoming	3.76
Hawaii	3.84
North Carolina	3.85
Virginia	3.89
Utah	3.90
Massachusetts	3.96

Pr. Edward Island	3.0	Ontario	6.8
New Brunswick	3.6	Saskatchewan	7.3
Newfoundland	4.0	Yukon	8.7
Nova Scotia	5.0	Manitoba	9.1

British Columbia	5.8
N.W. Territories	5.8
Quebec	5.9
Alberta	6.0

Figure 8-1 ■ **Percent of prison inmates who are female.** Women are much less likely than are men to be involved in crimes, and, therefore, they are much less likely to be arrested or sentenced to prison—a generalization that holds in all societies for which information is available. However, in some places the ratio of female to male offenders is higher than in other places. Thus we see that although the percent of female prison inmates is about the same in the United States and Canada, the percentages vary greatly within each nation. Three states had no female prison inmates in 1980. Overall, female prisoner rates are higher in western states, although Alabama has the highest rate of any state. In Canada, too, the higher rates tend to be in the western provinces, and Saskatchewan, Yukon, and Manitoba have rates higher than any state. Note: There were no data for Delaware.

Informal Control

The culture in which we are socialized greatly shapes our behavior. Had we been born among the Arapesh studied by Margaret Mead, chances are we would be gentle. Had we been born among the Mundugumor, we would probably be cruel headhunters. Through socialization, people learn what is expected of them, that is, to conform to group norms.

When very young, we require considerable coaching to conform, but as we mature we learn to take the role of the other, to see ourselves as others see us. We are able to evaluate our own actions from their point of view. For many of us, long exposure to a consistent set of norms, or **informal social control**, seems to create strong internal standards governing our behavior. That is, the norms become *internalized:* They become part of our own beliefs about how we should act. Sometimes norms are so firmly internalized that the person's conformity no longer seems to depend upon others being present to provide feedback. As mentioned in Chapter 2, nineteenth-century British adventurers and explorers dressed each evening for dinner, despite being in the wilderness amid natives who knew nothing of this norm. The code of manners governing how a gentleman behaved had become part of their self-esteem.

Chapter 2 introduced the concept of reference group, pointing out that people who ignore the norms around them may be conforming to the norms of an absent group whose standards they have adopted. The professor who ignores the good opinion of students and colleagues to devote his or her efforts entirely to research is often conforming to the norms of a reference group made up of specialists scattered over many universities.

Similarly, major portions of Chapter 7 assumed the power of others to influence the individual. Control theory stressed how attachments to others limit an individual's deviance. Differential association attributed deviance to the influence of deviant friends upon an individual. Labeling theory assessed how others can stigmatize the individual for past deviance and thus cause further deviance.

Given the power of groups to affect the behavior of their members, it should be no surprise that for the past few decades social scientists have conducted many experiments to find out how effective groups are in creating conformity and to assess how groups react to deviance by their members. Closely examining several classic examples of this research can reveal much about basic mechanisms of informal social control.

Group pressure

 It is self-evident that people tend to conform to the expectations and reactions of others around them. But what are the limits of **group pressure**? Can group pressure cause us to deny the obvious, even physical evidence?

Over thirty-five years ago, Solomon Asch (1952) performed the most famous experimental test of the power of group pressure to produce conformity. Since then his study has been repeated many times, with many variations confirming his original results. Perhaps the best way to understand what Asch discovered is to pretend that you are a subject in his experiment.

You have agreed to take part in an experiment on visual perception. Upon arriving at the laboratory, you are given the seventh in a line of eight chairs. Other students taking part in the experiment sit in each of the other chairs. At the front of the room the experimenter stands by a covered easel. He explains that he wants you to judge the length of lines in a series of comparisons. He will place two decks of large cards upon the easel. One card will display a single vertical line. The other card will display three vertical lines, each of a different length. He wants each of you to decide which of the three lines on one card is the same length as the single line on the other card. To prepare you for the task, he displays a practice card. You see the correct line easily, for the other lines are noticeably different from the comparison line.

The experiment begins. The first comparison is just as easy as the practice comparison. One of the three lines is obviously the same length as the comparison line, while the other two are very different. Each of the eight persons answers in turn, with you answering seventh. Everyone answers correctly. On the second pair of cards, the right answer is just as easy to spot, and again all eight subjects are correct. You begin to suspect that the experiment is going to be a big bore.

Then comes the third pair (Figure 8-2). The judgment is just as easy as before. But the first person somehow picks a line that is obviously wrong. You smile. Then the second person also picks the same obviously wrong line. What's going on? Then the third, fourth, fifth, and sixth subjects answer the same way. It's your turn. You know without doubt that you are right, yet six people have confidently given the wrong answer. You are no longer bored. Instead, you are a bit confused, but you go ahead and choose the line you are sure is right. Then the last person picks the same wrong line everyone else has chosen.

A new pair is unveiled, and the same thing happens again. All the others pick an obviously wrong line. The experimenter remains matter-of-fact, not commenting on right or wrong answers but just marking down what people pick. Should you stick it out? Should you go along? Maybe something's wrong with the light or with your angle of vision. Your difficulty lasts for eighteen pairs of cards. On twelve of them, all the others picked a line you knew was incorrect.

When the experiment is over, the experimenter turns to you with a smile and begins to explain. You were the only subject in the experiment. The other seven people were stooges paid by Professor Asch to answer exactly the way they did. The aim of the experiment was to see if social pressure could cause you to reject the evidence of your own eyes and conform.

In his first experiment, Asch tested fifty people in this situation. Almost a third of them went along with the group and gave the wrong answer at least half of the time. Another 40 percent yielded to the group some of the time, but less than half of the time. Only 25 percent refused to yield at all. Those who yielded to group pressure were more likely to do so as the experiment progressed. Nearly everyone withstood the group the first several times, but as they con-

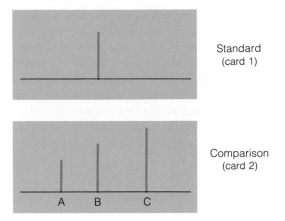

Figure 8-2 ■ **Asch's comparisons.** These two cards are one of the pairs used in the classic experiment by Solomon Asch to measure conformity to group pressure. Subjects were asked to pick which of the three lines on the second card matched the line on the first card. The correct choice is very easy to see. But when everyone else said the line on card 1 matched line A on card 2, many subjects would agree.

tinued to find themselves at odds with the group, most subjects began to weaken. Many shifted in their chairs, trying to get a different line of vision. Some blushed. Finally, 75 percent of them began to go along at least a few times.

The effects of group pressure were also revealed in the behavior of those who steadfastly refused to accept the group's misjudgments. Some of these people became increasingly uneasy and apologetic. One subject began to whisper to his neighbor, "Can't help it, that's the one," and later, "I always disagree—darn it!" Other subjects who refused to yield dealt with the stress of the situation by giving each nonconforming response in a progressively louder voice and by casting challenging looks at the others. In a recent replication of the Asch study, one subject loudly insulted the other seven students whenever they made a wrong choice. One retort was "What funny farm did you turkeys grow up on, huh?"

The Asch experiment demonstrates that a high proportion of people will conform even in a weak group situation. They were required merely to disagree with strangers, not with their friends, and the costs of deviance were limited to about half an hour of disapproval from people they hardly knew. Furthermore, subjects were not faced with a difficult judgment—they could easily perceive the correct response. Little wonder, then, that we are inclined to go along with our friends when the stakes are much higher and we cannot even be certain that we are right.

Cohesiveness

In a variation on his original experiment, Asch (1952) found that the influence of groups on conformity did not depend on the size of the group. Subjects were as likely to yield to the group when only three or four confederates were used. However, yielding was influenced greatly by the degree to which the group stuck together. When just one of the confederates was instructed to give the correct answer, yielding to the others dropped dramatically. Only 5 percent of the subjects conformed as much as half the time. This is perhaps experimental evidence that misery loves company.

Other research has demonstrated that the social integration of a group determines how effective group pressure will be. For example, Festinger, Schachter, and Back (1950) found that housing units occupied by married college students differed in the degree to which the occupants were united by bonds of friendship. The higher the proportion of friendships, the smaller the proportion of occupants who deviated from the unit's norms. Similarly, the more that church congregations are united by bonds of personal friendship, the greater their consensus on religious doctrines (Stark and Glock, 1968). Thus we shall see that Durkheim's theory of integration, discussed at length in Chapter 7, applies not just to large groups but also to small ones.

Group responses to deviance

 Group pressure, even when imposed by highly cohesive groups, does not produce conformity among all members. How do groups respond to a member who fails to conform?

In 1951 Stanley Schachter conducted an experiment that was the opposite of Asch's approach. Instead of setting up a group of confederates who conspired against a single subject to cause conformity, Schachter recruited subjects to form a number of groups, and within each he placed one or two confederates whose job was to deviate.

Each group was read a story about a young man who had had a difficult childhood in a tough neighborhood and who now awaited execution on death row. Then each group discussed the case, with the experimenter acting as moderator. After a period of discussion, each member's position on what should have been done about this young man was assessed. Groups tended to agree closely on a scale of reactions ranging from love to punishment, with a strong bias toward the love end of the scale. The paid deviant, however, took a strong stand for extreme punishment. As discussion continued, clerks watching through one-way mirrors kept close track of who said what to whom. At the end of the experiment, each group member filled out a sheet indicating how much they liked or disliked the other group members.

The data yielded two clear patterns. First, as soon as the paid deviants expressed their views to the rest, they became the center of attention. More remarks were directed toward the deviants than toward any other group member. Second, when the paid deviants stuck to their position, they began to receive less attention. By the end of the experiment, few remarks were directed to them. When the rating sheets were examined, the deviants stood out clearly—others tended to like everyone but the deviants.

These patterns are easily understood. The initial reaction of these groups to deviance was to try to squelch it. Group members ganged up on the deviant and tried to convince him or her to share their point of view. But when it became clear that the deviant member would not conform, they reacted by cutting the deviant out of the group and no longer talking to him or her. To judge from the ratings given the deviant, had this been a real-life occurrence, group members would have avoided the deviant in the future.

Schachter then introduced a variation into some of these discussion groups. Using two confederates, he had both begin taking strong, deviant stands in favor of punishment. But while one kept resisting pressure from the group, the other gradually gave in. This confederate, called the "slider" because he or she slid from deviance to conformity, was not rejected by the group. Although the slider did not receive as high a liking score after the experiment as group members who had conformed from the beginning, his or her scores were noticeably better than those the deviant received.

Schachter's experiment also supports the importance of social integration to conformity. Schachter was able to distinguish groups on the basis of how much members indicated liking one another. In groups where average liking scores were high—indicating greater integration—the deviant was more strongly disliked, while groups whose members liked one another less also disliked the deviant less.

These studies reveal why most of us probably play by the rules most of the time. Even in the brief and artificial setting of a social science laboratory, groups exert considerable pressure to conform and react quite strongly to deviation from group norms. Yet these studies also reveal that group pressure does not guarantee conformity. Groups have long recognized that more drastic and formal measures of social control must often augment informal methods.

Formal Control

When you invite friends to dinner, you can assume that they will use silverware and not eat with their fingers, that they will use their napkins and not wipe their chins on the tablecloth, and that they will not throw plates of food against the wall. You can also assume that when they leave, they won't take your stereo system or your car. Your friends will not act this way because they *are* your friends—they respond to informal pressures to conform. But not everyone does. When people do not, we often call upon formal agencies of social control to act on our behalf.

Formal social control is not applied to just any norm violation. The police won't come just because you happen to have friends who *do* eat with their hands or wipe their chins on the tablecloth. They might come if plates thrown against the wall bother your neighbors. And they definitely will come if people steal your belongings. Formal means of social control are used only for acts of deviance that are also illegal or otherwise defined as providing legal grounds for intervention. Thus, even private collection agencies are limited to pursuing the payment of legal debts, rather than debts from illegal gambling or claims having no standing in common law.

Formal social control is attempted in three principal ways. The first is to *prevent* deviance by removing opportunities for it to occur or by eliminating its causes. The second is to *deter* deviance by the threat of punishment: to make people afraid to deviate or at least to deviate again. The third is to *reform* or *resocialize* people so they cease wanting to deviate. Let us see how each of these methods of social control functions in our society.

Prevention

For people to commit a deviant act, they must have the *opportunity* to do so. Thus, many approaches to formal social control are based on **prevention**, or the attempt to reduce opportunities. Campaigns encouraging people to lock their cars are meant to reduce the opportunity for auto theft, for example. The prohibition of alcoholic beverages in the United States during the 1920s was intended to prevent alcohol abuse, as laws today against the sale of certain drugs are intended to prevent drug abuse.

Many recent prevention programs are guided by a new approach to deviance called *opportunity theory*. Lawrence Cohen and Marcus Felson (1979) recognized that for a crime to occur requires not only people motivated to commit an offense, but also *suitable targets* (property or individual victims), and the *absence of effective guardians*. Opportunity theory traces a substantial part of the rise in household burglaries in recent years to the great increase in female employment. Female employment has greatly increased affluence and hence the proportion of households that contain possessions worth stealing. Moreover, female employment has substantially decreased the proportion of homes where someone is home during the day. Empty homes full of valuables create an opportunity for those motivated to commit burglaries. Other proponents of opportunity theory have demonstrated the increased opportunities for crime caused by changes in the structure of urban neighborhoods. Many new house designs seek to increase privacy and inadvertently greatly decrease the ability of residents to note suspicious persons or circumstances and thus protect one another from becoming victims of crimes (Taylor et al., 1980). David Cantor and Kenneth C. Land (1985) recently have suggested that the reason burglary, larceny-theft, and auto theft decline as unemployment rises is due to an increase in the number of adults who stay home and who can, therefore, protect their own and their neighbors' property.

Anything that draws teenagers and young adults to a neighborhood increases the crime rate, because people this age are the ones most apt to commit crimes. Hence, neighborhoods near public high schools have higher crime rates than do neighborhoods farther away (Roncek and Lobosco, 1983), and crime rates fall as one gets farther away from a fast-food restaurant (Brantingham and Brantingham, 1982).

A frequent and relatively successful response to the insights of opportunity theory are efforts such as block-watch programs designed to increase effective guardianship. The same aims are reflected in the booming sales of home security systems.

During the past few years, criminologists even have proposed substantial changes in the design of cities as a means of reducing crime. Marcus Felson (1987) noted how the physical setting of shopping malls produces a very low crime rate in comparison with retail areas laid out along regular streets. Similarly, by greatly restricting access by strangers and providing secure parking, condominiums provide much better security against crime than do single-family dwellings. This led Felson to suggest that many other "stand-alone" aspects of urban life could be gathered together. For example, an educational facility could consolidate elementary, junior, and senior high schools for a substantial area, combine them with an adult night school, and create one well-lighted, patrolled, traffic-free campus with greatly reduced rates of assault, rape, drug dealing, burglary, and arson compared with a scatter of schools that stand empty for all but a few hours on weekdays.

However, the major effort in preventing crime and deviance has been directed toward removing its causes. Here the emphasis has been placed on childhood *socialization*. A long-standing article of faith, among social scientists and nearly everyone, is that adult deviance results from a long journey down the "wrong road," a journey that begins in youth. The most persistently addressed question has been, What can be done to intervene soon enough? How can we get kids headed on the right road before it's too late?

The Cambridge-Somerville experiment

 In the middle 1930s a New England physician, Richard Clarke Cabot (a member of one of the oldest upper-class families in the East), decided that it was time to launch a major effort to help young boys grow up to go straight. More importantly, he was determined to test the results of this effort rigorously. He thus initiated and funded a ten-year social experiment that even today is regarded as a model attempt at a delinquency prevention program and a model sociological experiment.

In essence, Cabot decided to give poor boys many of the same opportunities as boys from well-to-do homes. First, he tried to provide for their physical well-being. Second, he sought to enrich their experiences and broaden their horizons. Finally, he tried to provide close relationships with adults who could give the boys good advice and serve as models of well-adjusted adults.

In 1937 Cabot launched his project by selecting two economically distressed industrial communities near Boston—Cambridge and Somerville. He hired a staff of counselors and researchers, who selected 650 boys (with an average age of about 11) as subjects for the delinquency prevention program. To know whether his program really did prevent delinquency, Cabot could not place all the boys in the program, for then there would have been no control group for comparing the delinquency rates. So he *randomly* divided the group into two groups of 325.

The *experimental group* consisted of boys who would receive the experimental prevention program. Another name for an experimental group is a *treatment* group—they get the treatment. In a medical experiment, for example, the experimental group would receive a new treatment, perhaps a new drug. In this case the experimental or treatment group was recruited to take part in Cabot's delinquency prevention program. The parents of each boy were contacted and arrangements made for their son to take part. Cabot had no trouble getting all the boys in the experimental group to take part. Little wonder, for during the depths of the Great Depression he offered to furnish these youths with free health care, tutoring, vacations at summer camps, field trips, an elaborate recreational program, and individual counseling.

To determine whether his program worked, however, Cabot needed a *basis of comparison.* This was provided by the other 325 boys who randomly were excluded from the program. They made up what is called the *control group.* By comparing an experimental group with a control group, one can assess the effectiveness of some treatment. Suppose 650 boys with flu were located and 325 were randomly selected to receive a new drug. By comparing their speed of recovery with the 325 who were left untreated, we could see whether the new drug made any difference. In this case, the boys left out of the program provided a basis for comparison to see if the program made a difference: Were boys in the program less likely to become delinquents than were boys left on their own?

In May 1939 the program got under way. Unfortunately, Dr. Cabot died just as his ambitious undertaking began, but in his will he provided the needed funds, and his family supervised the project. Some aspects of the program had to be reduced during World War II—gas rationing cut into field trips, for example. Nevertheless, the project was carried through to its projected end (when the boys all reached 18).

What were the results of this massive project? To find out, the researchers compared the criminal records of boys in the control group with those of the boys in the experimental group. They found that 40 percent of the boys in the control group had been convicted of a crime. They also found that 40 percent of the boys in the program had been convicted of a crime! Moreover, boys in the experimental group had committed as many crimes as those in the control group (Powers and Witmer, 1951). Obviously, the program had had no effect on delinquency. Boys who were left on their own were no more likely to get into trouble than were boys who were part of the elaborate program (Figure 8-3).

Those associated with the study were astounded by these results and in the end refused to accept them. This is understandable. You can spend a number of years trying to help young people stay out of trouble only if you believe your efforts can make a difference. Sure, you can't help them all, but daily you see some kids going straight and you take comfort in that fact. Of course, you lack similar intimate observations of those outside the program, and so you cannot notice that they are doing just as well (or as badly) without your care. Having built up years of personal "experience" with the efforts of your program, you will not readily accept research findings that your perceptions are biased and your effects negligible. Indeed, in their effort to show that the results of the experiment were wrong, the directors of the Cambridge-Somerville study simply discarded the control group altogether.

Instead, they engaged in a minute examination of the case records of each boy in the experimental group. For only these data could

satisfy the clinical worker, who, by the nature of his task, has little interest in averages. What such a person wants to know is whether there were any cases—even if only a few—in which the introduction of the [program] tipped the balance in a boy's favor [Powers and Witmer, 1951].

From this private reading of the files, Powers and Witmer concluded that there was clear evi-

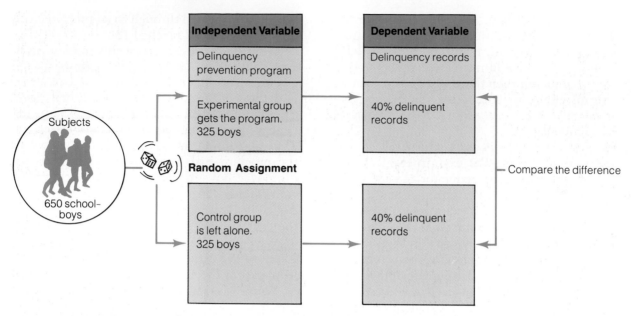

Figure 8-3 ■ **The Cambridge-Somerville experiment.** To see if Cabot's prevention program worked, 650 boys were randomly assigned to be in either the experimental or the control group. If the program had worked, the boys in the experimental group would have been significantly less likely to acquire delinquency records than would the boys in the control group. But, as you can see, the program made no difference. Control and experimental groups were equally likely to have delinquency records—40 percent of each.

dence that fifty-one of the boys in the project had been helped. But if this was true, why did the experimental group not have a smaller proportion who were arrested? Did the program also push some boys into crime who otherwise would have gone straight? That seems unlikely. But that leaves us to ask what was helping the boys in the control group. As Cabot understood, the experimental results were the only reliable basis for judging the worth of the programs. Because random assignment made the two groups equally prone to commit crimes, the program could be termed successful only if the experimental group had fewer crimes. There is no better evaluation method available.

This can be underscored by a poignant example. In an effort to show that the experiment was insensitive to the real results of the prevention program, the directors wrote to former participants and asked if the participants believed they had benefited from taking part. Many said they had, including one young man

who wrote this testimonial about how much his counselor had helped him:

He told me what to do—what's right and wrong—not to fool around with girls [emphasis added]. It gives a boy a good feeling to have an older person outside the family to tell you what's right and wrong—someone to take an interest in you [Powers and Witmer, 1951].

Several years later, this same young man began serving a five-year sentence for a serious sex offense (McCord and McCord, 1959).

Later, social scientists reopened this classic study, hoping that some evidence in favor of the program could still be found. William and Joan McCord had the useful hypothesis that perhaps the research had ended too soon, that possibly the effects of the program would not stabilize until later in life. So they reexamined the police records of the experimental and control groups

■ Immense effort has been and continues to be invested in various therapeutic techniques aimed at correcting patterns of deviant behavior or preventing its recurrence. This group of young people is taking part in an encounter group led by an adult therapist. No research evidence suggests that such therapy succeeds.

for ten years after the original study had ended. But this hypothesis also turned out to be false; no difference could be found (McCord and McCord, 1959).

Thus ended the first experimentally evaluated attempt to prevent delinquency by trying to influence socialization of the young. But it did not end efforts to achieve this goal.

Other prevention programs

In the decades following the Cambridge-Somerville study, scores of delinquency prevention programs have been tried and evaluated. Until recently, the result was an unbroken string of failures (Weis, 1977). During the 1950s and 1960s, immense effort was made to utilize forms of psychotherapy to reform delinquents. None

succeeded (Toby, 1965). Prevention efforts were also taken into the streets by social workers attempting to reform juvenile gangs. These efforts were also judged failures (Miller, 1962). Toward the end of the 1970s, just as sociologists became convinced that nothing would work, the first evidence appeared that something might. A group of psychologists in Oregon began to have at least modest success with their efforts to train the parents of problem kids to more effectively control their children's behavior. We shall examine this project in depth in Chapter 13. But it now appears that many kids simply never outgrow the selfish, aggressive, antisocial behavior that is normal for two- and three-year-olds. In fact, children don't cease such behavior unless their parents punish them for it. Studies of really misbehaved children show that their parents do not consistently punish them.

■ This public beheading took place in China around 1860. For centuries it was believed that public executions served to deter the onlookers from committing similar crimes. But for most of this century, social scientists rejected this view. Only recently has support for deterrence theory reappeared in social science journals.

Although the Oregon group has had some success in training parents to cope with their children, it remains to be seen how applicable the results are. For one thing, many parents (especially those of the worst-behaved kids) are unwilling or unable to improve their parental performance. Secondly, intervention must occur at a very early age to be effective. Finally, such intense levels of training seem needed that it may be economically impossible to make such training widely available.

Why did none of the other programs work? Because they failed to truly change the circumstances of people. Training adults to be better parents may strengthen weak attachments within a family; simply providing a kid with a counselor will seldom have such an effect. A counselor is not an adequate substitute for parents or close friends, and a delinquency program fails to give kids a stake in conformity—

it may even do the reverse. Kids who mess up do not risk being kicked out of a delinquency program.

However, even if we can't set up programs to make kids want to conform, couldn't we make them afraid to be deviant?

Deterrence

As far back as written records go, humans have constructed legal codes that specify not only which acts are prohibited by law but also which punishments are to be given to offenders. The Code of Hammurabi, written about 3,700 years ago, tells us that if a man destroys another man's eye, the offender's eye should be taken out; if a son strikes his father, the son shall have his hand cut off. Early legal codes tried to achieve symmetry—to provide justice by matching the punishment with the offense. This approach is repeated in many places in the Old Testament. In the Book of Deuteronomy we read, "Life shall go for life, eye for eye, tooth for tooth, hand for hand, foot for foot."

However, even in these early philosophies of justice, punishment was not meant merely to serve as revenge for victims or their relatives. Instead, punishment has long been intended as a means of making life and property more secure by reducing the likelihood of a person committing a crime or a second offense.

This aspect of social control is called **deterrence**—the use of punishment to deter people from deviance. As Plato put it 2,300 years ago, "Punishment brings wisdom; it is the healing act of wickedness." This occurs, Plato explained, because the point of punishment is not to "retaliate for a past wrong," but to make sure that "the man who is punished, *and he who sees him punished* [emphasis added], may be deterred from doing wrong again."

As human societies evolved into complex states, governments increasingly sought to deter crime; hence punishments became increasingly severe as crimes continued to occur. **Capital punishment** (execution) became common; in England during the eighteenth century, more than two hundred different crimes carried the death penalty. Additionally, executions typically were conducted in public, often drawing large crowds, in an effort to deter those who witnessed the punishment from committing similar acts.

However, many began to speak out, calling capital punishment cruel and uncivilized. In time the opponents of capital punishment succeeded in restricting the death penalty to fewer and fewer offenses in most of Europe and North America (see Figure 8-4). By the twentieth century, some nations dispensed with it altogether. Canada suspended the use of capital punishment in 1967 for a five-year trial period. In 1973 another trial period was adopted. Then, in 1976, the Canadian Parliament abolished the death sentence (except under provision of the National Defense Act). The last execution in Canada occurred in 1962. In 1972 the U.S. Supreme

Court prohibited capital punishment in the United States on the grounds that it was applied in a discriminatory fashion—that blacks and poor people stood in greater jeopardy. Since then, however, many states have redrafted their capital punishment statutes in a way acceptable to the Court, and in 1977 the first execution since the late 1960s took place in the United States. It was followed by a number of others. By the end of 1986, more than 1,200 persons were in U.S. prisons under sentence of death.

While much of the debate over capital punishment has centered on moral issues, a major element has been the argument that it does not deter crimes for which it has been used (mainly homicide, but also rape). Indeed, by the 1950s the accepted view among social scientists, presented in most introductory textbooks, was that the threat of punishment does not prevent deviant behavior, and the experience of having been punished does not cause people to cease their deviant behavior. Deterrence was dismissed as an obsolete notion, exposed as such by scientific research. In fact, very little research had ever been done. As we shall see, especially with regard to capital punishment, what little research had been done was flawed by poor methods and the great difficulty in obtaining appropriate data.

By the early 1970s, however, a growing number of social scientists began to reconsider the deterrent effects of punishment. For many, it was simply a response to their realization that they attuned their own behavior on the basis of potential punishment. For example, on trips across the country, they drove faster or slower depending on a state's reputation for enforcing speed limits. Are these self-observations merely illusions? Can it really be that if penalties for crimes were repealed, the crime rate would not go up? The case for deterrence was reopened.

Jack Gibbs, a sociologist, led the way by reformulating the theoretical issues concerning deviance. Isaac Ehrlich, an economist, reopened research on the effects of capital punishment on homicide. Both men provoked angry reactions from many of their colleagues. Together, however, they have stimulated an immense amount of theoretical and research effort; deterrence is no longer a discarded concept.

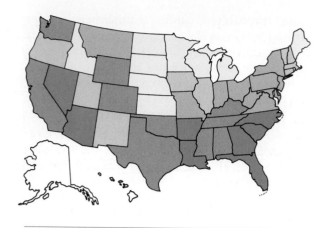

1930–1939: Prisoners Executed per 100,000

Idaho	0.00	Washington	1.32
Kansas	0.00	Oklahoma	1.46
Nebraska	0.00	California	1.56
South Dakota	0.00	Wyoming	1.60
North Dakota	0.00	Tennessee	1.61
Minnesota	0.00	Kentucky	1.83
Wisconsin	0.00	Texas	1.87
Michigan	0.00	Alabama	2.12
Rhode Island	0.00	Mississippi	2.20
Maine	0.00	Colorado	2.23

New Mexico	0.04	Florida	2.32
Oregon	0.18	Louisiana	2.45
New Hampshire	0.20	Arkansas	2.72
Vermont	0.28	Delaware	3.00
Connecticut	0.29	Arizona	3.40
Iowa	0.32	South Carolina	3.53
Utah	0.36	North Carolina	3.67
Massachusetts	0.42	Georgia	4.39
Illinois	0.77	Nevada	7.26

Pennsylvania	0.83
Maryland	0.88
Montana	0.89
Indiana	0.90
Missouri	0.95
New Jersey	0.96
Virginia	1.05
West Virginia	1.05
New York	1.14
Ohio	1.19

1938–1940: Persons Sentenced to Death per 100,000

Pr. Edward Island	0.00	British Columbia	0.73
Alberta	0.13	New Brunswick	0.88
Nova Scotia	0.17	Manitoba	1.22

Quebec	0.33
Saskatchewan	0.45
Ontario	0.45

Figure 8-4 ■ **Use of capital punishment in the 1930s.** Capital punishment has been the focus of strong feelings and heated political debate over most of this century. Here we see variations in the use of capital punishment during the 1930s. In the United States, ten states did not execute anyone during the decade. Others used it but rarely. In Nevada, Arizona, and a number of southern states, executions were relatively frequent. The data for Canada are for only two years, not ten, and reflect the number sentenced to death, not actual executions. Even if we assume that all Canadians receiving the death sentence were executed and multiply the Canadian rates by five to equate them to the U.S. statistics, we find that capital punishment was much less common in Canada than in the United States during this period. In any event, while these statistics were piling up, social scientists were attacking the belief that capital punishment deters people from committing murder. Eventually, both nations ceased using capital punishment. Recently, however, executions have resumed in the United States, and a new debate rages about whether capital punishment "works." Note: Alaska and Hawaii were not states at that time; Newfoundland was not part of Canada; Northwest Territories and Yukon Territory were without local jurisdiction.

Jack Gibbs: a theory of deterrence

 As Jack Gibbs examined the grounds on which deterrence had been dismissed from social science, he recognized that much of the reasoning and the evidence cited missed the mark. The case against deterrence came down to this: Many people are punished for committing crimes, including some who are executed for homicide; nevertheless, the crime rate, including the homicide rate, remains high. Moreover, most people who serve a prison or jail sentence for a crime turn right around and commit new crimes when they are released. Clearly, then, punishment fails to deter.

Gibbs concluded that this argument is irrelevant to the fundamental issue. It claims, in effect, that if *some* people seem not to be deterred, *no one* is. When the issue is posed this way, it is impossible to demonstrate any deterrent effects of punishment unless it is 100 percent effective. This is the same as saying that aspirin has no effect on headaches unless it cures every headache for everyone. To see if punishments influence people to conform, Gibbs pointed out, we cannot look at just those who were not deterred; rather, we must look at everyone. That is, we need to know more than the fact that some people do risk punishment; we need to know whether the fear of punishment influences those who do not commit offenses. This is, of course, a much more difficult research problem.

Although Gibbs was very concerned with improving research on deterrence, he recognized that he first had to formulate an adequate theory. Why and how should punishment produce conformity? Until such an explanation was proposed, we could not say what empirical observations would be predicted or prohibited and therefore what research ought to be undertaken.

Gibbs (1975) set out to formulate a clear theoretical statement of the effects of deterrence. Drawing on social learning and control theories of deviance, he proposed that it is not only the severity of punishment that matters but also the rapidity and certainty of punishment. Gibbs's **deterrence theory** can be summarized as follows: *The more rapid, the more certain, and the more severe the punishment for a crime, the lower the rate at which such crime will occur.*

Thus, Gibbs predicted that severe sentences will not effectively deter crimes if people realize that they have little chance of being caught or that their punishment will be long delayed if they are caught. On the other hand, not even quick and certain punishment will deter crime if the punishment is very mild, for then the costs of detection often will be outweighed by the rewards of the crime. Here Gibbs's theory links with control theory to explain why the same punishment might be much less severe for some than for others. For example, two years in jail is a much greater cost to someone with a happy family and a good job than to an unemployed drifter. Deterrence thus fits into control theory as another of the costs to be considered by the potential deviant. The higher that cost and the swifter and more certain it is to be imposed, the greater the conformity.

Remember that Gibbs's theory of deterrence, like other sociological theories of deviance, does not apply to all deviant acts. Clearly, a person who acts on impulse or in a drunken rage is not likely to be deterred, because he or she is unable to consider the consequences of the crime (Geerken and Gove, 1977).

Even though what Gibbs's theory predicts and prohibits is very clear, proper testing has been difficult. As we shall see later in this chapter, punishment for crimes in the United States today is often far from certain or swift and often not severe. This makes it difficult to test the theory against available statistics. Gibbs was able to show, however, that people are less likely to be convicted for an offense a second time when the police have a high rate of success in solving such cases. For example, the police can solve rape cases far more often than burglaries. Thus, the certainty of arrest is greater for rape. Examining prison statistics, Gibbs found that far fewer people are arrested a second time for rape than are arrested a second time for burglary: Only 16 percent of those in prison for rape were second offenders, compared with 51 percent for burglary.

Once Gibbs's theory was published, many social scientists began to design studies to test it more rigorously. The most important break-through was to recognize that what matters most is not the actual certainty, swiftness, or severity of punishment but the *perceptions* of these aspects of punishment. Suppose the actual odds of being caught for some offense were very high. A person who mistakenly thought that they were very low would act on that perception. Indeed, Gibbs's theory assumes a link between reality and perception, that the true conditions governing punishment will act as a deterrent because people will perceive these conditions. Thus, Gibbs's theory can be tested without encountering problems concerning the present operations of the criminal justice system. Instead, we can simply find out how people perceive the situation and see if that perception influences their rates of deviance and conformity.

In the past few years, many such studies have been done (see Gibbs, 1986). The findings strongly support deterrence theory. People who think that it is hard to get away with crimes, that justice is swift, and that present levels of punishment are severe are much less likely to commit such offenses than are people who think that the opposite conditions are true.

Later in this chapter, we shall see that people who have actual experience with police, courts, and the prison system often perceive lower risks in crime; this perception can be a major factor in sustaining chronic criminal behavior. This has led many deterrence researchers to discuss the importance of naiveté in social control. Indeed, many have suggested that a primary way in which differential association (see Chapter 7) can influence deviance is by exposing a naive individual to a perception of much lower risks (G. Jensen, 1969; Parker and Grasmick, 1979; Minor and Harry, 1982).

Sherman and Berk: deterring wife beating

 Recently two sociologists conducted a careful experiment in Minneapolis to test the deterrent effects of arrest on wife beating. Lawrence W. Sherman and Richard A. Berk (1984) arranged to have police offi-cers *randomly* apply one of three intervention tactics when called to a home because a husband had been beating up his wife: arrest, ordering the man to leave the premises, or offering some form of advice and mediation. The offi-cers referred to a report pad, color-coded to indicate which action they should take in any given case, to ensure random treatment. The procedures were applied *only* to those cases where the police were *authorized but not required* to make an arrest, thus excluding cases where a serious injury already had occurred or where a life-threatening situation existed (such as when weapons were involved). The experiment began in March 1981 and ran until August 1982, during which time 330 cases had been dealt with randomly.

In addition to noting which of the three responses the police used, the researchers closely monitored each case for six months—they even conducted an interview every two weeks with each victim. Their primary concern was to discover whether a new wife-beating incident had occurred.

Sherman and Berk designed this experiment to test two contrary hypotheses. The first, derived from deterrence theory, is that men who are arrested for beating their wives will be more reluctant to commit a new offense than will men who were simply ordered to leave or men given verbal advice. That is, the more severe the punishment a person anticipates, the less willing he will be to run the risk. A second, contrary hypothesis can be deduced from labeling theory—that those arrested and given an official label as a wife-beater will be confirmed in that deviant role and therefore will be more apt to repeat the offense than those not arrested.

What were the results? Strong support for deterrence theory: The husbands who were arrested were much less likely to commit a new offense than were those ordered to leave, and men who were simply advised had by far the highest rate of new offenses.

In 1985 Berk teamed with Phyllis J. Newton to test the deterrent effect of arrest on wife beating using nonexperimental techniques. Berk and Newton analyzed 783 cases of wife-battery in a county in California where arrests had been made in 207 cases, while officers had decided against arrests in the remainder. Once again the analysis showed a very strong deterrent effect; men who were arrested were much less likely to commit a new offense (as measured by subsequent police involvements).

Despite the growing body of research supporting deterrence theory, vigorous opposition continues; some sociologists even claim that it doesn't matter whether punishments deter crime or not, because, they argue, punishment is immoral. Closer examination of these views suggests that the real issue is not deterrence in general but concern that the renewed interest in deterrence will reopen a much more sensitive question—whether capital punishment deters homicide. For many people, the idea of the legal system putting people to death is so repugnant that there can be no valid scientific purpose in researching the deterrent effects of capital punishment. For many others, including most American citizens (see Figure 8-5), some acts of murder are so repugnant that the killer has no right to life.

Here we can see the pressures that inevitably come to bear on social scientists. On the one hand, we are active participants in the world we study, and like all human beings, we must deal with moral issues. On the other hand, we have a responsibility to provide facts pertinent to many moral controversies. In this instance, a most pertinent fact is whether capital punishment deters homicide. If it does not, then there may be no reason to debate the morality of the matter. Of course, we cannot know the facts until adequate research has been done. Often sociologists have difficulty switching back and forth between the role of scientist and that of concerned citizen—to insulate our research procedures from our moral convictions. Keeping this in mind, let's observe the interplay of moral commitments and scientific research in this controversial area.

The capital punishment controversy

People have opposed capital punishment for many reasons. Some have opposed it for religious reasons. In fact, we shall see later in this chapter that the Quakers were the first to insti-

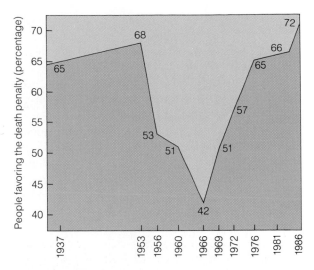

Figure 8-5 ■ Support for capital punishment. The graph shows the percentage of American adults who favored use of the death penalty for murder during the past five decades, as reported by the Gallup Poll.

tute prison sentences as punishment in an effort to eliminate torture and execution. Some have opposed it on grounds of racial discrimination, because blacks were executed more often than whites (53.5 percent of the persons executed in the United States between 1930 and 1967 were black). Other opponents of capital punishment have even argued that executions actually increase homicides because capital punishment brutalizes public perceptions of the value of life (Bowers and Pierce, 1980).

However, a major aspect of the debate over capital punishment has been social scientific research that seemed to show that capital punishment does not deter homicides. If this is so, many have argued, then we should not risk executing an innocent person or risk other possible negative consequences of capital punishment, since nothing is gained. Unfortunately, this conclusion was based on uncritical acceptance of highly deficient research.

The deficiencies in the research were due partly to the limited statistical techniques social scientists used in the 1930s and 1940s, when the research was done. They also were due partly

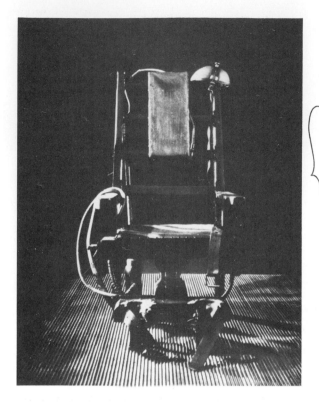

■ This is "Old Sparky," New York State's electric chair. It was the world's first, going into service in 1890. A total of 695 persons were put to death in this chair from 1890 through 1963.

to problems in the data available for analysis. In effect, these early studies simply compared the homicide rates of states that used capital punishment with the rates of states that did not. These comparisons showed no correlation: States without capital punishment did not have higher homicide rates than did states with capital punishment.

Unfortunately, little or no concern was given to the problem of spuriousness, even though states differed in many ways besides the use of capital punishment. For example, New York, which used capital punishment, had a homicide rate as high or higher than in North Dakota, which did not use capital punishment. However, to conclude that capital punishment did not deter homicide was to assume that these two states were identical in other ways. A much better test would have been to see what would

happen to the homicide rate in New York if capital punishment were repealed and what would happen to the homicide rate in North Dakota if capital punishment were reinstated. But, of course, no such data exist.

Nevertheless, most social scientists in the 1950s and 1960s, few of whom had read the pertinent research studies, assumed that capital punishment had no deterrent effect. But then Isaac Ehrlich, an economist, challenged the accepted belief.

In an article in the *American Economic Review* of June 1975, Ehrlich used sophisticated statistical techniques to see if the homicide rate and execution rate for the United States from 1933 through 1969 were correlated. Ehrlich concluded that there is a negative correlation between the two and that the deterrent effects of capital punishment were huge. In fact, he concluded that each execution prevented eight additional homicides. That is, each time someone was executed for committing a murder, eight other people escaped becoming murder victims. Ehrlich concluded that, by putting to death those who have taken a life, we save many additional lives.

Ehrlich's article provoked a storm of protest and moral condemnation. Many attempted to dismiss his findings as the result of improper statistical procedures (McGahey, 1980). Other scholars rose to Ehrlich's defense, including statistical experts who claimed his methods were superior to those used by his critics (Yunker, 1982). Moreover, when the data used by Ehrlich were extended to the 1980s, when the first executions since the Supreme Court decision of 1972 occurred, the results were even stronger (Yunker, 1982).

The homicide rate tended to fluctuate with the execution rate from 1930 through the late 1950s. Then, when executions became very rare and eventually ceased entirely, the homicide rate began a rapid ascent. However, as we saw in Chapter 3, correlation alone is not sufficient proof of causation. And it is difficult to conclude from only these data whether executions really do deter homicide. A major problem is that the data are crude and apply to the United States as a whole. However, many states did not have capital punishment during this period, and states differed greatly in their homicide rates. Perhaps these are meaningless averages that are accidentally correlated.

These difficulties showed the need for research able to detect subtler influences. So, let us watch how David Phillips found better ways to study the deterrent effects of capital punishment.

David Phillips: deterrence through the press

Recall that Plato believed we may be deterred from deviance by seeing someone punished for a crime. Plato was discussing punishments administered in public, where people actually saw a person tortured or executed. In modern times, executions are not held in public, and only a small number of people actually see an execution. Thus any deterrent effects of punishments do not result from actual observation. Rather, we "see" such punishment only to the extent that mass media make us aware of it.

This line of reasoning led David Phillips to formulate a new approach to detect the deterrent effects of capital punishment on the homicide rate (Phillips, 1980). He argued that deterrence does not depend upon how frequently people are executed for murder but on how much publicity the executions receive. Moreover, Phillips argued that previous studies ignored the possibility that the impact of a given execution may not be long lasting. Thus, while previous studies compared homicide rates for periods of a year or longer, it might be crucial to examine the possibility of marked but relatively brief changes. Unfortunately, virtually all statistics on homicide are yearly.

After a long search, however, Phillips discovered that weekly homicide statistics had been published for London from 1858 through 1921. Next, he consulted an encyclopedia of notorious murders to construct a list of the most heavily publicized English executions during this period. Finally, he consulted the London *Times* and counted the column inches of coverage given to each case. For each execution he computed the number of homicides that occurred for several weeks before the execution and for several weeks following the execution. His hypothesis was that the homicide rate would be lower for several weeks after a well-publicized execution than for the weeks just before.

His results supported the hypothesis. A very significant drop in homicides consistently occurred immediately after a well-publicized execution. Indeed, the week after one of these executions averaged more than a third fewer homicides than in a normal week. Moreover, the greater the number of inches the newspaper devoted to the story, the greater the drop in homicides. However, as Phillips had suspected, the impact of executions seemed to be short, lasting only about two weeks. After that the homicide rate rebounded. However, Phillips's findings are somewhat weakened by a tendency for the homicide rate to rise slightly above normal for the third through fifth weeks following a highly publicized execution. This raises the possibility that many murders were not deterred but were simply postponed. Hence the controversy continued (Kobbervig, Inverarity, and Lauderdale, 1982; Zeisel, 1982a). Then a sociologist found a way to replicate Phillips's research using recent data for the United States.

Steven Stack's replication

In 1987 a new study of the impact of publicized executions on homicide rates appeared in the *American Sociological Review*. The author was Steven Stack, a sociologist at Auburn University. Stack had discovered that since 1950 homicides have been reported on a monthly basis in the *Vital Statistics of the United States*. Unlike homicide rates used in most American research, which are based on reports forwarded to the FBI by local police, these data are based on death certificates. Moreover, because these were monthly rather than annual rates, Stack suspected they might be sufficiently sensitive to reflect the deterrent effects of highly publicized executions—if such effects actually occur.

Stack decided to base his study on the thirty-year period 1950–1980, during which more than 700 executions took place. However, these executions rarely attracted much press attention, even locally. Searching *Facts on File* and *New York Times Index*, Stack discovered sixteen executions sufficiently publicized so that most Americans could have been aware of them at the time. He then compared the homicide rates of months in which one of these publicized executions occurred with other months. (For three executions that occurred after the 23rd of the month, the next month was used.)

Stack's results agreed with Phillips's. On average there were thirty fewer homicides in the United States in months during which a highly publicized execution took place. However, Stack found no evidence of an elevated rate during the next month. This contradicts the argument that murders were only delayed, not deterred. Moreover, Stack was able to add several control variables to guard against spuriousness. One of these was the proportion of the population age 16–34, because people in this age group are the most likely to be murdered and to commit murders and their proportion in the population rose during these decades. A second control variable was the unemployment rate—homicide tends to fluctuate with unemployment (for unemployment increases family quarrels). Both of these control variables had strong effects on shifts in the homicide rate during this period, but they did not eliminate the deterrence effect. Finally, Stack looked for deterrence effects of executions that received little or no publicity. None could be found.

At the end of his article, Stack makes it clear that despite the support his findings give to deterrence theory, he personally opposes the use of capital punishment. That caveat helps clarify the point raised earlier that we must be careful not to confuse scientific and moral responsibilities. Many readers have asked me to omit the entire topic of deterrence and especially of capital punishment from this chapter. Unlike Steven Stack, such readers fail to understand that whether capital punishment works and whether it is morally justified *are wholly unrelated questions.* Granted, if it could be demonstrated

that capital punishment did not deter, it might be easier to repeal or prevent reinstatement of the death sentence. But even if executions were known to have a huge deterrent effect, that is irrelevant to the question of whether executions are morally justified. Scientific research is no substitute for moral judgment. Nor has a textbook author the right to be a censor. It is my responsibility to report active areas of theory and research, but it is neither necessary nor appropriate for me to weave essays on moral philosophy into these reports.

Even if we set aside the question of deterrence and capital punishment, many difficult problems still surround the subject of deterrence. Common sense tells us that we often conform from fear of punishment. Yet as we have seen, it is difficult to show that deviant acts that do not happen were deterred. And it is easy to show that some people are not deterred—the prisons are full of them. Thus, we must return to the argument against deterrence that Gibbs dismissed as irrelevant: If punishment deters crime, why are the prisons filled with people, most of whom have served previous sentences? To answer this question, we must examine how the American and Canadian systems of criminal justice operate.

The Wheels of Justice

Let's imagine a young Canadian or American male who is contemplating a career of crime. He will need to take into account three vital facts: It's far from certain that he will be punished for committing a crime; if he is punished, it will likely be long after the crime; and it is quite likely that the punishment will not be very severe, at least not the first few times he is caught. To see why this is the situation, we must look at the police and the courts.

The police

Except for traffic officers, Canadian and American police officers spend little time looking for violations of the law. Instead, the police respond primarily when offenses are reported to them;

Graham Dies for Plane Bomb Murder

THE DENVER POST
FINAL EDITION

The Voice of the Rocky Mountain Empire

Vol. 65, No. 163   Denver, Colorado, Climate Capital of the World   Saturday, Jan. 12, 1957   5 Cents   16 Pages

Slayer Meets Death Quietly

By ZEKE SCHER
Denver Post Staff Writer

CANON CITY, Jan. 12.—John Gilbert Graham, 24, died Friday night in the lethal gas chamber of the Colorado penitentiary.

With no display of emotion, he sat down in the death seat, sniffed at the hydrocyanic fumes, gasped for air, gave a scream and then lapsed into silence —forever. It took 11 minutes—the flying time from Denver to the Weld county scene of the crash of a plane he had sabotaged—before Graham was pronounced dead by prison doctors at 8:08 p. m.

Doctors marveled at the physical stubbornness of the heart of the murderer of his mother, Mrs. Daisie King, and 43 other plane passengers.

Warden Harry C. Tinsley said he found Graham jovial when he appeared at the doomed man's cell at 7:36 p. m. to read the "death warrant."

"How are you doing, Jack?" Tinsley asked.

"Fine," Graham replied with gusto.

JOKES WITH WARDEN

As Tinsley fumbled in his pocket for the cell door key, Graham cracked:

"You wouldn't want to lose that now."

Graham was escorted from his second floor cell in the maximum security building to the third floor death house by Tinsley, Deputy Warden J. William Kinney, the Rev. Justin McKernan and three guards.

At 7:50 p. m. Graham entered the "preparatory" cell, about 25 feet from the steel gas chamber.

"You'll have to put these shorts on," Tinsley told Graham, handing him a pair of prison-made white undershorts. The condemned wear only shorts. Otherwise gas might cling to their clothing.

Graham undressed and put on the shorts. A guard then placed an elastic band holding a stethoscope over Graham's upper chest.

"Jack, you can go . . ." Tinsley said.

Graham did not hesitate. He walked quickly toward the chamber. He nodded to Undersheriff Charles Rudd and Capt. Logan Ketchum of the Denver sheriff's office. The two men had guarded Graham full time in Denver through his lengthy district court murder case.

ENTERS DEATH ROOM

The young father of two stepped into the chamber, turned around and sat down. It was 7:52 p. m. Two prison officers placed a black mask over his eyes.

Stout leather straps were fastened about his arms and shoulders, holding him to the straight-backed, black steel chair. His legs were strapped together. A guard, holding a scoop of cyanide pellets, knelt down to pour them into a funnel underneath the chair.

The stethoscope was connected to a tube leading out of the chamber. The guard stepped out.

Warden Tinsley leaned in, gave Graham a firm pat on the right shoulder and said "God bless you."

"Thanks, warden," Graham replied.

Father Justin, the prison's Roman Catholic chaplain, stepped in, blessed Graham and said: "I hope God will forgive you your sins. Take it like a man."

"O. K." Graham mumbled and gave a nod.

Deputy Warden Kinney was the last to enter and leave the chamber and told Graham "Goodbye and good luck."

"Thanks," Graham replied.

The chamber door closed quietly at 7:56 p. m.

Graham's breathing was unhurried, his coloring normal. His hands hung limply at the end of the arm rests. He sat quietly.

Choose Champs

The reserve champion steer of the junior show was Hereford "Ernie" owned and exhibited by Gary Minish, 16, of Dysert, Ia., and bred by Ernest Means of Sargent, Colo.

Both steers were champions of their respective breeds and went on to take top honors in interbreed competition at the close of the junior show judging shortly before noon Saturday.

The champion Shorthorn steer was "Ally," owned and shown by Larry Eisenach, 14, of Eaton, Colo. "Ally" was bred by Phil Miller of Castle Rock, Colo.

A 10-year-old Rankin, Tex., boy, Corky Thornton, who raises sheep in a pen in his backyard showed the champion fat lamb, a Southdown, in other junior division judging Saturday morning.

Corky is the son of a Rankin railroad worker.

RANKIN GIRL

Carolyn Branch, 14, who lives on a ranch near Rankin, showed the reserve junior champion fat lamb, also a Southdown.

Gerald Anderson, 14, of Leland, Ill., showed his Poland China barrow, "Prairieview King," to win the junior championship of the fat barrow competition.

Gerald appeared headed for a repeat of his performance here a year ago when he showed the junior champion fat barrow, then took it on to win the 1956 National Western open fat barrow contest.

Mary Helen Holtorf, 17, who lives on a farm 37 miles northeast of Akron, Colo., showed her Duroc barrow to win the reserve junior championship.

ELIGIBLE TO COMPETE

Junior division winners were eligible to take their animals into open competition against adult professional livestock producers to vie for the over-all 1957 National Western championships.

Saturday morning shopping throngs saw a colorful six-band, 500-horse western parade. The affair was a salute to Stock Show week and the National Western Stock Show.

Features included music by high school bands from Denver and points as far as Sterling and a variety of mounted units.

Lakewood sent its Westernaire mounted teenagers. Also represented were the Round-up Riders of the Rockies, Arvada Hoof Printers, Arapahoe Sheriff's Posse and members of the Rodeo Cowboys Assn.

More details, photos on page 3

w Parade

The highly publicized execution of mass murderer John Gilbert Graham was one of those included in Steven Stack's study of deterrence. Graham, who was convicted of killing forty-four passengers and crew aboard a United Airlines flight from Denver to Salt Lake City by planting a powerful bomb in his mother's suitcase, died in the Colorado State Prison's gas chamber on January 11, 1957. According to Stack's projections, there should have been 602 homicides in the United States that month had no execution occurred. In fact, there were only 536, a reduction of 66 killings.

only then can they attempt to solve a case. A major reason why the odds of getting caught for a crime are so low is that a large proportion of the crimes that occur is never reported to the police.

Table 8-1 is based on a huge national survey designed to measure the true incidence of major crimes. Every several years, the U.S. Justice Department sends interviewers to 60,000 randomly selected American households to ask detailed questions about crime victimization. For each crime that respondents say has been committed against them during the past year, the question is asked, "Was this incident reported to the police?"

The data in Table 8-1 show that about half of the time the answer was no. Larceny is the least frequently reported crime (25 percent), while auto theft is the most frequently reported (68 percent). The latter reflects the fact that victims may not collect their auto insurance unless the theft is reported; in addition, people realize that there is a very good chance that the police will find their car. Still, a third of auto theft victims did not report the crime. When the police don't even know about a crime, they are obviously unlikely to catch the criminal. Thus, about half the time one can expect to get away with a crime simply because the victim fails to report it.

Of course, even when a crime is reported, the police are often unable to find the criminal. Table 8-2 shows the proportion of various reported offenses that led to an arrest. Most murders are solved because most are sudden acts of passion committed by a friend or relative of the victim; often the murderer is apprehended at the scene of the crime. Reported assaults and rapes result in arrests about half of the time, whereas only a quarter of reported robberies result in arrests. Notice that in each of these latter three offenses, the police are aided by the fact that the victim sees the person who commits the crime. Without this advantage, the police do poorly in solving larcenies, burglaries, and auto thefts.

Clearly, the odds of being caught seem low. Yet Table 8-2 overstates the chances of being caught, because it gives the percentages of *reported* cases that led to an arrest. About twice

Table 8-1 ■ Proportion of crimes reported to the police.

Offense	Percent Reported
Larceny	25%
Assault	42
Burglary	48
Rape	51
Robbery	55
Purse snatching	59
Auto theft	68

Source: U.S. Department of Justice, 1982.

Table 8-2 ■ Reported crimes cleared by arrest.

Offense	Percent Cleared	
	Canada	United States
Homicide	85%	74%
Assault	78	61
Rape	56	54
Robbery	29	26
Larceny	*	20
Theft	10	*
Burglary	22	14
Auto theft	23	15

Sources: Canadian Centre for Justice Statistics, 1984. Federal Bureau of Investigation, 1985.
*Not reported as a separate category.

as many crimes are committed as are reported, so the proportion of cases that are solved by arrest is only about half of what is shown in the table. For example, 3.7 million burglaries were reported to the American police in 1981, 14 percent of which led to an arrest. However, based on the victimization survey for that year, an estimated 7.7 million burglaries actually occurred. If we base the computation on the actual number of burglaries, then slightly less than 7 percent were solved by the police. That means that the odds against getting caught for committing an act of burglary are nearly 20 to 1.

Of course, that does not mean that only one burglar in twenty gets caught. Burglars tend to commit a series of crimes, so eventually the odds catch up with them. Yet they have such a good chance of avoiding arrest that they tend to explain getting caught as simply "bad luck" or a "silly mistake" (Irwin, 1970). Similarly, studies find that juveniles who have had contact with the police by being arrested or stopped and questioned have a lower, not a higher, expectation of being caught for an offense (Piliavin and Briar, 1964; G. Jensen, 1969). Of course, this expectation is further depressed for crimes such as burglary, for which the actual odds of being caught are low anyway. Recall that Gibbs found that of people serving prison sentences for burglary, 51 percent had served a prior sentence for the same offense. Clearly, then, the threat of jail fails to deter burglars in part because they do not see punishment as certain—in fact, they see it as unlikely. Other offenders have similar feelings.

The courts

What about people who are arrested for a crime? It is still not certain that they will be punished, and even if they are, punishment is likely to be long delayed.

In both Canada and the United States many people arrested for a crime are never punished for it. First of all, prosecutors drop many charges because of flaws in the arrest procedures—officers didn't follow the rules with sufficient care or file their paperwork properly. In many other cases the charges are dismissed at preliminary hearings because of problems of evidence; often key witnesses fail to appear. Of cases surviving these barriers, the majority are resolved by a plea bargain. That is, the charges against the person are reduced to less serious ones in exchange for a plea of guilty. For example, a frequent plea bargain known in the United States as "swallowing the gun" involves reducing charges of armed assault to simple assault, an offense carrying a far shorter maximum sentence, if the accused person will plead guilty.

This spares the government the effort and expense of a trial, but it also makes punishment much less severe. In fact, the majority of persons convicted even of quite serious offenses do not go to prison, but receive suspended sentences or are placed on probation. And of those who do go to prison, very few will serve their full sentence: Most will be out on parole long before their time was up. Moreover, time runs on a unique calendar in prison. In American prisons, for example, three days equal four in the outside world. That is, unless one gets in repeated trouble with prison officials, time off for good behavior equals 25 percent of one's sentence (Cole, 1983).

Zeisel (1982b) offered the following summary of the American criminal justice system. Of every 1,000 felonies committed in the United States, 540 are reported to the police. Of these, 65 result in an arrest. Of all those arrested, 36 are prosecuted and convicted—many of those arrested are juveniles, who usually are not taken to court. Of those convicted, 17 are sentenced to serve time in jail or prison. Of these, 3 are sentenced to serve more than one year. In sum, for those who commit crimes in the United States, punishment is very uncertain, not often swift, and rarely severe. Consequently, crime is not highly deterred, and those convicted of crimes are very likely to commit subsequent offenses: A recent survey of all persons being held in state correctional facilities in the United States showed that 64 percent had served a previous sentence (U.S. Department of Justice, 1982).

Reform and Resocialization

Few people today realize that prisons as places where people serve sentences for crimes are quite new. For centuries, prisons and jails were merely places where people were held while awaiting trial or until they received their sentences. Punishment did not involve spending time in prison but took the form of execution, mutilation, branding, or flogging. Authorities regarded it as unthinkably expensive to confine and feed able-bodied offenders for an extended period. Not

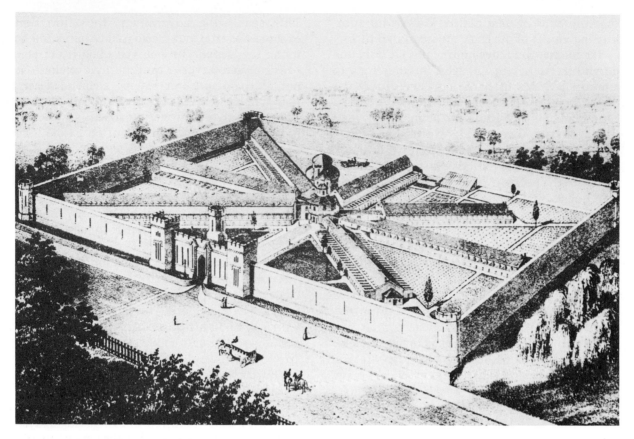

■ This painting by architect John Haviland in 1825 shows his design for the Eastern Penitentiary at Philadelphia, which was constructed on the Auburn model. Within the outer walls the cell blocks were stacked several stories high in wings radiating from the central hub like the spokes of a wheel. Guards in the hub had an unobstructed view of each cell entrance simply by looking down a row. Haviland designed prisons like this throughout the United States and Canada, and they were copied all over the world. The French sent a team of architects and prison officials to study American prisons in 1833 and again in 1837.

until the late eighteenth century was confinement in prison used as an alternative to physical punishment.

The first serious experiments with prisons began in Pennsylvania under the direction of William Penn, whose Quaker beliefs caused him to oppose physical punishment. Penn directed that prisoners spend their sentences at hard labor to pay for their own upkeep and to pay damages to their victims. Penn's prisons became notorious for vice. Men, women, and juveniles were locked together, and the guards profited from the sale of liquor. So, in 1790 the Quakers of

Pennsylvania tried a new approach—the penitentiary.

The new name reflected a whole new philosophy for dealing with criminal offenders. They were to be placed in circumstances much like monasteries, where they would be forced to contemplate their sins and become penitent (hence the name). Each prisoner was placed alone in an 8-by-6-foot cell and lived under a rule of silence. The Quaker example was copied by other states. Soon prisoners were required to work to pay the costs of their support, although the rule of silence prevailed.

Problems continued, however. Convicts learned to get around the rule of silence and continued to cause problems of disorder and frequent escape. Then, in 1816 a new prison was built in Auburn, New York. This prison was novel both architecturally and in operating principles. Cells were built in tiers five floors high, making it possible for a few guards to observe the interiors of cells from strategically placed viewing points. Prisoners were divided into three groups. Dangerous troublemakers were placed in solitary confinement. A second group was allowed out of their cells for work only. The third and by far the largest group worked and ate together during the day and went into seclusion in their cells only at night. Internal discipline was maintained by adopting military procedures. Prisoners were marched from their cells to their places of work or the mess hall.

Modern prisons are typically modeled on the Auburn design. However, a major change occurred during the 1930s and 1940s, when finding work to keep most inmates busy was no longer possible. In state after state, political opposition, especially from labor unions, to the sale of prison-made goods and the use of prisoner labor to construct roads and bridges resulted in the termination of prison work projects. This left wardens with few jobs to occupy inmate time and, of course, it immensely increased the cost of prisons, which were once virtually self-supporting. At the same time, efforts to reform the prisons by making them more humane and turning them into therapeutic institutions also made them much more expensive to staff. At present, it costs more than $40,000 a year to keep a person in prison in the United States.

Encouraged by the social sciences, especially psychology, many prisons have discarded their punishment philosophy in recent years and adopted a therapeutic philosophy of reform and resocialization. Because the Quakers had meant prisons as places where criminals regained their moral judgment through solitary meditation, the therapeutic prison has sought to use psychological therapists and social workers to help inmates gain the necessary insights and to make the needed personality adjustments so they do not return to crime. But just as counselors proved ineffective with juveniles in the Cambridge-Somerville project, so too have they failed to find a method for making adult prison inmates conform to patterns of nondeviant behavior. The **recidivism rate**, the proportion of those released from prison who are sentenced to prison again, is as high among the new, therapeutic prisons as among the older, punitive prisons: about 60 percent.

While the threat of going to prison probably causes many people to obey the law, clearly it does not deter some, even after they have served a prison sentence. Nor do the prisons seem able to achieve the **resocialization** of inmates so they will not want to continue in crime. If we take seriously the theories of deviance discussed in Chapter 7, we should not be surprised that prisons fail to create conformity. If a lack of attachments tends to lead to deviance, then taking people who already have inadequate attachments out of the community will weaken these attachments even more.

Moreover, labeling theory suggests that, upon release from prison, the stigma of being an ex-convict will further limit the ability of offenders to form attachments with conventional people. Indeed, prison may well foster new attachments to other deviants. In this fashion, tiny subcultures of deviants form in prison and survive as members are released.

Furthermore, whatever investments the person had prior to prison (which failed to be a sufficient reason to conform) must diminish while a person is in prison. Most people leave prison with little money, no job, and no promising career. Ex-convicts thus have very little to lose by subsequent deviance. And in prison they may gain a distorted view of how much can be gained by deviance and how low the odds of being caught are. In this way the prison system contributes to career deviance, especially as inmates return again and again.

Many efforts have been made to break this vicious cycle and prevent ex-convicts from committing new crimes. One of the most ambitious of these programs, and one that was subjected to the most careful evaluation by research, involved paying convicts salaries during their first months back in society. By watching carefully as this study was conducted, we can gain

■ Early in this century inmates in American prisons spent little time in their cells during the day. Most were employed full-time in prison industries—many worked on labor gangs building roads and bridges far from the prison. During the 1930s reformers stopped the use of work gangs and brought an end to prison industries in most states. As often happens, the reforms may not have improved prison conditions. Today many prisoners have little or nothing to do with their time and spend long, tedious hours in their cells.

a better understanding of the problems the criminal justice system faces.

Salaries for ex-convicts: the TARP experiment

 Critics of the criminal justice system have stressed the economic plight of persons just released from prison. Lacking jobs, ex-convicts may be forced to commit new crimes to get money to live. Thus, these critics argued that recidivism could be reduced substantially if the government pro-

vided economic support to tide people over during their transition from prison back into society. In 1976 Kenneth J. Lenihan persuaded the U.S. Department of Labor to support an experimental program to test this hypothesis. Lenihan also recruited his colleagues Peter H. Rossi and Richard A. Berk to direct research to study the effects of the program.

The study was designed as an experiment, thus allowing the most accurate evaluation possible. Arrangements were made with authorities in Texas and Georgia to identify all persons serving time in state prisons who were scheduled to be released soon; approximately 2,000 adult men and women were listed. These

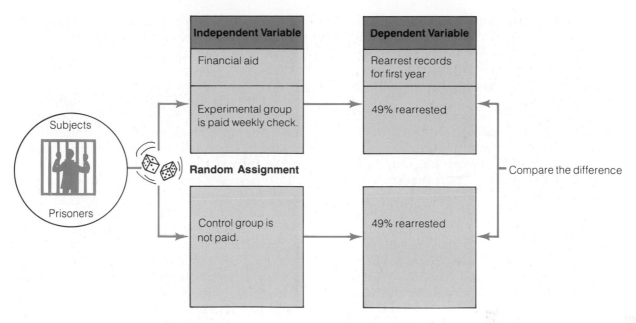

Figure 8-6 ■ **The TARP experiment.** As the Cambridge-Somerville experiment showed that a delinquency prevention program failed, this experiment showed that an effort to help ex-convicts stay out of jail by giving them financial aid while they reestablished their lives had no effects either. Because of random assignment of ex-convicts to experimental and control groups, the possibility of spuriousness is eliminated.

inmates were randomly assigned to two groups. One group was given a weekly paycheck ($70 in Georgia and $63 in Texas). These payments continued for about six months. The other group received no checks and left prison in the usual manner and condition.

The study, referred to as the TARP study (for Transitional Aid Research Project), was carried out with the strictest experimental controls. Because prisoners were randomly assigned to receive or to not receive payments, and because a large number of subjects were involved, the group that was paid should not have been different from the group that was not paid.

The dependent variable was also clearly defined. The goal was to see if payments eased the way back to a conventional life, and people were judged successful in doing so if they managed to avoid arrest for one year after release from prison. Thus, the experimenters kept track of each person in the experimental and control

groups and recorded when anyone was arrested.

What were the results? Among those who had not received TARP checks, 49 percent had been rearrested within a year of their release— a pretty dismal picture. But then the sociologists found that 49 percent of those who had been given financial aid had been rearrested during the first year. The payments had made no difference at all (Figure 8-6). Keep in mind that this was only the proportion who got into trouble within the first year. Others undoubtedly got arrested in later years.

Like delinquency prevention programs, the attempt to prevent recidivism by giving released convicts financial aid totally failed. But just like those who conducted the Cambridge-Somerville delinquency prevention study, the social scientists who conducted the TARP study also refused to accept the clear results of their own research. They, too, have ransacked the files on those in the experimental group and offered arguments that the program really did help some of them (Rossi, Berk, and Lenihan, 1980, 1982; Berk, Lenihan, and Rossi, 1980). Other scholars with no emotional stake in the study, however, regard the results as clear—the program failed (Zeisel, 1982b).

It would be comforting to argue that the failures of the prison system to reform convicts are caused by a lack of effort, investment, and public enlightenment—and people untrained in criminology often make such charges. But the facts are that legions of dedicated men and women have worked hard to provide effective therapies and programs to reform convicts and that immense energy and many resources have gone into the prison system. There has been no shortage of new ideas, and every few years new programs and styles of prisons are introduced. The problem is that nothing has worked. The most modern therapeutic treatment centers have achieved no better results than did the Quaker penitentiaries: The majority of those who leave the prisons commit new offenses.

But if prisons are unable to reform, they do serve to isolate from society for the duration of their stay persons who have been judged dangerous to life and property. The policy of locking up serious offenders is more acceptable in our culture than physical torture or frequent resort to execution. That is, while we attempt to restructure prisons so that inmates are reformed or to discover other means of doing so, it is worthwhile to remember why prisons were invented in the first place—as a more humane form of punishment.

Conclusion

It is easy to draw overly pessimistic conclusions from this chapter and to assume that social control doesn't work. Granted, social control doesn't prevent some people from committing acts of serious deviance—more than 13 million crimes are reported to the police in North America each year, and the actual number of crimes committed is probably about twice that number. Keep in mind, however, that even if each of these crimes were committed by a dif-

ferent person, then only about one person in ten engaged in a criminal act each year. And because we know that some people commit many crimes, only a tiny fraction of North Americans are responsible for the crime rate.

Viewed this way, social control usually seems to work—most of us usually conform to the law. And, to a great extent our conformity is rooted in informal social control. Long before we wonder if the police will catch us or the courts jail us for committing a crime, we restrain such impulses because we know how our families and friends would react. Thus, as noted at the beginning of the chapter, formal methods of social control are activated only when informal methods fail. In an important sense, the police, the courts, and the prisons must assume responsibility for the people whom we—all of us in society—have failed to bind to the moral order. If the justice system typically fails to reform these people, this failure must be evaluated in light of the kinds of people it confronts. To keep even 40 percent of such people from committing new offenses might be judged a substantial achievement.

Clearly, however, formal social control could be more effective. Improving the reporting of crimes should be possible. In fact, recent police efforts to educate the public and to treat victims more sensitively have greatly increased the reports of rape. Better coordination among the police, prosecutors, and the courts could probably prevent the dismissal of so many cases on technical grounds. And many proposals exist for speeding up court procedures and preventing serious offenders from getting off lightly.

But if crime can be reduced somewhat by overhauling the criminal justice system, it would be unrealistic to expect truly dramatic changes. For the fact remains that in every human group known, some people break the norms—not just in small ways but also in very serious ways. Even in tiny, isolated, utopian religious communities, where each person has voluntarily chosen to join the group in its retreat from a "wicked" world, some people commit grave crimes. Surely, then, we shouldn't be surprised that some people commit crimes in a much less socially and morally integrated society such as ours.

As we have seen in the past two chapters, sociologists can explain much about why people deviate and conform. But to know why deviance occurs often does not provide the knowledge for preventing it. Moreover, social scientists do not know how to reform many people who exhibit chronic patterns of serious deviance.

■

Review Glossary

social control All collective efforts to ensure conformity to the norms. (p. 204)

informal social control Direct social pressure from those around us. (p. 206)

group pressure The impact of group expectations and reactions on the behavior of the individual. (p. 206)

formal social control Actions by organizations and groups that exist to uphold the norms. (p. 209)

prevention As a form of social control, all efforts to remove the opportunity for deviance or to deactivate its causes. (p. 209)

deterrence The use of punishment (or the threat of punishment) in order to make people unwilling to risk deviance. (p. 215)

capital punishment The death penalty. (p. 215)

deterrence theory The proposition that the more rapid, the more certain, and the more severe the punishment for a crime, the lower the rate at which that crime will occur. (p. 217)

recidivism rate The proportion of persons convicted for a criminal offense who are later convicted for committing another crime. Sometimes this rate is computed as the proportion of those freed from prison who are sentenced to prison again. (p. 227)

resocialization Efforts to change a person's socialization, that is, to socialize a person over again in hopes of getting him or her to conform to the norms. (p. 227)

■

Suggested Readings

Geerken, Michael R., and Walter R. Gove. 1977. "Deterrence, Overload and Incapacitation: An Empirical Evaluation." *Social Forces* 56:424–447.

Gibbs, Jack. 1975. *Crime, Punishment, and Deterrence.* New York: Elsevier.

Phillips, David P. 1980. "The Deterrent Effect of Capital Punishment: New Evidence of an Old Controversy." *American Journal of Sociology* 86:139–148.

Stack, Steven. 1987. "Publicized Executions and Homicide: 1950–1980." *American Sociological Review* 52:532–540.

Yunker, James A. 1982. "The Relevance of the Identification Problem to Statistical Research on Capital Punishment." *Crime and Delinquency* 28:96–124.

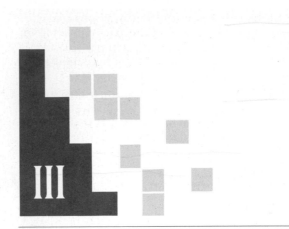

Stratification and Conflict

III

Evalyn Walsh McLean and her son Vinson are pushed along a curving walk on their lush estate in Palm Beach, Florida, in 1913. Evalyn and her husband, Ned McLean, were famous not only for their extraordinary wealth but also for their wild spending and notorious life-style. She was the daughter of Tom Walsh, an Irish immigrant who struck a fabulously rich silver mine in Colorado in 1880. He was the son of a newspaper magnate, owner of the *Washington Post* and the *Cincinnati Enquirer*, among other publications. When Evalyn and Ned got married, their fathers chipped in and gave them $200,000 to spend on a honeymoon in Europe— a sum that would be close to $2 million at today's prices. After several months abroad they had to cable home for money to pay their hotel bill, and then they left hundreds of unpaid bills behind them in Europe. Several years later Ned bought Evalyn the famous Hope diamond.

Soon Evalyn became addicted to morphine, hiding packets in furniture and under rugs all over her many mansions, while her husband became the most celebrated public drunk of the day. Ned liked to walk into saloons and knock the hats off other men with his cane and then stomp the hats flat—his bodyguards patiently took down names and addresses so new hats could be sent. Ned also offended many hostesses, including the wife of President Harding, with his habit of relieving himself in fireplaces.

When little Vinson was born, the press called him the "hundred-million-dollar baby," and his parents lavished expensive gifts on him. In addition to the poodle riding with him in this photo, young Vinson had two pet lion cubs. He also had his own playhouse, which was larger than the house in which the servant pushing the carriage was raising his family. Because Ned McLean had grown up with a black playmate, his parents decided Vinson ought to do the same. However, as his mother remarked, "We could not buy a colored boy, of course, although it was our habit to buy anything we wanted" (Birmingham, 1973). So they leased a five-year-old black child for a ten-year period.

This picture suggests central themes of the four chapters that follow. The first is stratification. In all known societies some people end up with more of life's rewards than other people do. Chapters 9 and 10 will attempt to explain why this happens, why some people get so much more than others.

However, there is more than wealth separating Evalyn and Vinson from the servant who is pushing them. They are white; he is black. In Chapter 11 we will attempt to understand what causes prejudice and discrimination on the basis of racial and ethnic differences.

Finally, Evalyn, despite her immense wealth, was excluded from many activities open to her husband and even to her black servant. When this picture was taken women were not allowed to vote. Nor were women permitted to enter the saloons where her husband did his hat tricks. Chapter 12 tries to explain variations in sex roles.

Concepts and Theories of Stratification

9

STRATIFICATION—THE ORGANIZATION of society whereby some members have more and others have less—has been a constant theme in moral, political, and philosophical writing through the ages. Millions of words have been written to denounce inequalities in wealth and power. Millions have also been written to justify these inequalities. From the point of view of modern sociology, this is an irresolvable conflict based on two stubborn facts. First, stratification has many undesirable consequences. People at the bottom of stratification systems often suffer greatly, both physically and emotionally. Second, some degree of stratification seems to be an unavoidable feature of social structure.

Chapter Preview

This chapter examines the basic concepts and theories sociologists use to describe and explain stratification. It begins by examining various concepts of social class. In Chapter 2, social classes were defined as groups of people who share a similar position, or level, within a stratification system. Now we shall pursue this definition in greater depth and explore differences in how leading sociologists have conceived of classes. We will also analyze the phenomenon of *social mobility:* upward or downward movement by individuals or groups within a stratification system. Armed with these conceptual tools, we shall then explore theories of stratification. Why are societies stratified? To what extent can stratification be minimized? In Chapter 10 we shall apply these principles by examining stratification and mobility in different kinds of societies.

Conceptions of Social Class

People have used many different schemes to identify social classes, or divisions of rank and wealth, within societies. Some schemes have used broad distinctions and others have used narrow ones in deciding which people occupy similar positions in a stratification system. Are classes large and few in number, or are they small and numerous?

Plato saw only two classes in ancient Greek society, the rich and the poor, and he believed them to be locked into eternal conflict. Aristotle divided Greek society into three broad classes: a rapacious upper class, a servile lower class, and a worthy middle class that, having all virtues and all failings in moderation, could be trusted to see after the common good of all. The word *class* comes to us from the Romans, who used the term *classis* to divide the population into a number of groups for the purpose of taxation. At the top were the *assidui* (from which the word *assiduous* comes), who were the richest Romans. On the bottom were the *proletarii*, who possessed nothing but children.

However, not until the mid-nineteenth century was the concept of class given significant meaning for modern social theorists. The person who first did this was Karl Marx (1818–1883).

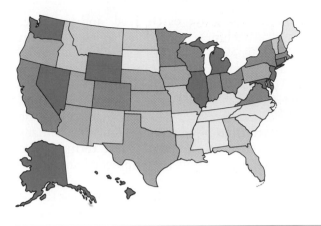

Arkansas	$14,356	New York	20,385
Mississippi	14,922	Virginia	20,423
Maine	16,208	Indiana	20,540
Tennessee	16,245	Delaware	20,658
Kentucky	16,399	Ohio	20,710
South Dakota	16,431	Wisconsin	21,113
Alabama	16,602	Minnesota	21,217
North Carolina	16,805	Massachusetts	21,329
West Virginia	17,042	California	21,479
South Carolina	17,105	Colorado	21,485

New Mexico	17,151	Washington	21,635
Idaho	17,278	Nevada	21,666
Georgia	17,403	Michigan	21,886
Vermont	17,549	Illinois	22,007
Florida	17,558	Wyoming	22,497
Louisiana	17,822	New Jersey	22,830
Oklahoma	17,846	Maryland	22,850
North Dakota	18,239	Connecticut	23,038
Missouri	18,746	Hawaii	23,066
Montana	18,839	Alaska	28,266

Nebraska	19,110
Arizona	19,150
Texas	19,372
Rhode Island	19,441
Kansas	19,575
New Hampshire	19,796
Oregon	19,837
Utah	20,035
Iowa	20,243
Pennsylvania	20,259

Pr. Edward Island	$16,392	British Columbia	23,042
New Brunswick	17,675	N.W. Territories	23,894
Nova Scotia	17,894	Alberta	24,547
Newfoundland	18,584	Yukon	27,718

Manitoba	18,895
Saskatchewan	19,086
Quebec	20,007
Ontario	22,553

Figure 9-1 ■ **Median family income, 1980.**
Stratification refers to variations within any society in the amount of wealth, power, and prestige members possess. Some people always have more, while others have less. Here we see that, in a manner of speaking, there even is stratification among states and provinces. In some places the average family has a much higher income than does the average family in other places. Thus, in the United States the family in the South tends to be much less affluent than are families in the North. In Canada, the maritime provinces have the lowest family incomes, while incomes are highest in the Far North and Far West. Comparisons between Canada and the United States are misleading in these data because the Canadian dollar had a lower exchange rate than the U.S. dollar.

Marx's Concept of Class

Marx aimed to explain social change and produce a theory of history: Why and how do societies change, and what will they be like in the future? He believed that the answer lay in conflicts among social classes. The whole of human history, Marx and Friedrich Engels wrote in *The Communist Manifesto* in 1848, has been "the history of class struggles." These struggles are the engines that pull societies into new forms; the history of human societies is a history of one ruling class being overthrown by a new one.

Marx saw that there is no single answer to the question of how many classes to identify in societies. Instead, the answer depends upon which society and when. Thus, he identified four classes in ancient Rome—patricians, knights, plebeians, and slaves—and a larger number in Europe during the Middle Ages. But Marx expected modern capitalist societies to consist of only two classes.

The bourgeoisie and the proletariat

A capitalist society, according to Marx, is one having a free-market economy based on private ownership of property. Chapter 17 develops a fuller definition of capitalism. In this chapter Marx's definition suffices. By the middle of the nineteenth century, when Marx wrote his major works, all of the nations of western Europe, as well as the United States and Canada, fit his definition of capitalism. Therefore, he predicted that each of them soon would undergo a great simplification of their stratification systems into two fundamental classes. As he wrote in *The Communist Manifesto*, "Society as a whole is more and more splitting up into two great hostile camps, into two great classes directly facing each other: Bourgeoisie and Proletariat."

Marx defined these two classes in terms of their different relationship to the means of production. The **means of production** are everything besides human labor that goes into producing wealth. Chief among these are land (on which crops grow, cattle feed, and buildings stand), machines and tools, and investment capital. One class, the **bourgeoisie,** owns these means of production. The other class, according to Marx, is everyone who does not own such means and therefore must sell his or her labor to the bourgeoisie. Marx called this class the **proletariat,** employing the name the Romans used to identify the poor. These terms essentially refer to owners (or employers) and workers (or employees).

Marx realized that all capitalist societies in his time had many people who did not fit into his two-class scheme, but he believed that these groups would not significantly affect history. One such group was the middle class, including small merchants and self-employed professionals, such as doctors and lawyers. Marx believed that as the capitalist system evolved, the middle class would eventually be crushed and forced into the proletariat. He also dismissed many people who were marginal to the economy—vagrants, migrant workers, beggars, criminals, gypsies, and the like. He classified such persons as **lumpenproletariat** (literally, the "ragamuffin proletariate"). Such people had so little social purpose and self-respect, Marx believed, that they would have no effect on the impending revolutionary struggle. Finally, Marx excluded farmers and peasants from his conception of class because he believed that the drama of historical change would occur in the urban industrial sector of capitalist societies; rural people would play little or no part in shaping social change. He wrote that the "peasants form a vast mass, the members of which live in similar conditions, but without entering into manifold relations with one another. Their mode of production isolates them from one another . . . and the identity of their interests begets no unity, no national union, and no political organization"; therefore, "they do not form a class."

Ironically, the great revolutions Marx predicted never did occur in the urban, industrialized, capitalist nations. However, revolutions claiming to be Marxist have occurred in a number of less developed nations and have found their primary support among peasants. This suggests that, were he alive today, Marx would rethink his concepts to include rural populations.

■ Class conflicts within industrial societies often take the form of strikes. Indeed, the right to have unions and to strike were major concessions employees won in the late nineteenth and early twentieth centuries. This young textile worker was arrested in Lawrence, Massachusetts, in 1912. She and hundreds of other strikers had demonstrated in the streets in violation of a court injunction.

Class consciousness and conflict

In addition to *material* position in society, Marx also included an important *psychological* component in his notion of class. To be considered a real class, people must be similarly placed in society and share comparable prospects, but they must also be aware of their circumstances, their mutual interests, and their common class enemy. Marx called this awareness **class consciousness.** Much of his theory about the coming of the communist revolution concerns how the proletariat will achieve class consciousness, at which point their superior numbers will ensure their success. Marx also worried about the tendency for workers to believe they had common interests with the ruling class and called this **false consciousness.**

By incorporating assumptions about class consciousness into his definition of social class, Marx inserted portions of his *theory* of revolution into his *concept* of class. This made key portions of his theory true by definition and thus untestable. By Marx's definition, if people with a common economic position in society do not recognize their common interests and organize to pursue them, they are not a class. To say that classes will be self-conscious and organized, then, is to predict nothing about the course of history; it simply states a definition. Indeed, Marx denied that classes could exist without class struggle, again by definition. He wrote, "Individuals form a class only in so far as they are engaged in a common struggle with another class." Hence, when Marx said class struggle is inevitable, he had already made that statement necessarily true by his definition of the word *class.*

■ Karl Marx.

■ A young radical, helping to organize demonstrations in support of the Industrial Workers of the World in 1913, wears his slogan on his hat.

Economic dimension of class

The most important feature of Marx's definition of class is that it is determined only by the *economic* dimension. Property ownership is the sole factor for ranking people, and then they are divided into only two groups: those who own the means of production and those who do not.

When he rested his distinction between the bourgeoisie and the proletariat entirely on this single criterion, Marx necessarily implied that *all other differences* in position among people in society are *wholly* the result of property ownership. Thus, if some people are more powerful than others, or if some people are more admired or respected than others, it is entirely due to the underlying economic differences between them. For, Marx claimed, the relationship to the means of production is "the final secret, the hidden basis for the whole construction of society." The rest of a society's culture results from the underlying economic arrangements. Indeed, for Marx culture was a "superstructure of various and peculiarly formed sentiments, illusions, modes of thought, and

conceptions of life" that arises from economic relations.

Marx nowhere gave empirical evidence that economic differences were the sole basis of other social differences such as power and respect (Dahrendorf, 1959). His claim, however, was an empirical one that other social scientists could test. If power or prestige can be shown to *vary independently of property*, then Marx's statement is at least excessive and perhaps false. Indeed, the likelihood that the economic dimension of property does not govern all aspects of stratification made many sociologists who came after Marx very uneasy with his single-factor conception of class. Among them was Max Weber.

■

Weber's Three Dimensions

Max Weber (1864–1920) is one of the great names in the history of sociology. We shall assess his work on religion and social change in Chapter

■ Max Weber.

17 and his work on bureaucracy in Chapter 20. In Weber's lifetime, as in ours, the influence of Marx on social theory was immense. And some of Weber's major works were attempts to modify Marxist positions.

Weber believed that Marx's wholly economic view of stratification could not capture primary features of modern industrial stratification systems. Looking around in Germany, Weber noticed that social position did not always seem to be simply a matter of property ownership. Many Germans who belonged to the nobility lacked wealth yet possessed immense political power; for example, only they could be officers in the army. On the other hand, Weber noted that some German families possessing very great wealth, who owned factories and other great companies, lacked political power and social standing because they were Jewish.

Strictly applying Marx's conception of class would classify these Jewish families as bourgeoisie, while many powerful *Junkers* (aristocrats) would belong to the proletariat. Thus, Weber thought Marx's scheme was too simple. He proposed that stratification is also based on

other, independent factors. He suggested three such factors: *class, status, and power*.

Modern social scientists have found several of Weber's terms somewhat confusing; therefore, they have renamed them to constitute "three P's" of stratification: *property* (what Weber called "class"), *prestige* (what Weber called "status"), and *power* (as Weber defined it).

Property

By *class* Weber meant groups of people with similar "life chances" as determined by their economic position in society—the goods they possess and their opportunities for income. This is what modern social scientists refer to as **property.** Weber stressed class membership based on *objective* economic position. Unlike Marx, he did not reserve the word *class* only for groups that had developed class consciousness and had organized for class conflict. Instead, Weber regarded the banding together by persons with the same economic position as merely possible or potential. Thus, a key question for Weber was when and why class conflicts occur. Making class conflict part of the definition of class would not answer the question.

Furthermore, Weber did not stress ownership of property, but realized that in some circumstances *control* of property might be independent of ownership. If a person can control property to his or her personal benefit, then it matters little whether the person legally owns the property. Thus, Weber was able to recognize the high class position of managers (whether of capitalist corporations or socialized industries) who control firms they do not own. Marx had placed such persons in the proletariat.

Prestige

Weber recognized that economic position can rest on control without ownership because he saw that prestige (or "status" in his terms) and power were not wholly the *consequence* of property relations. Instead, they could be the

■ All of these senior officers of the German General Staff in 1871 could claim membership in the nobility. Yet some of them had no private wealth and had to depend mainly on their army pay. Weber conceptualized stratification as multi-dimensional and therefore could take into account the power and prestige of these commanders while also recognizing their relative lack of property.

source of property relations. To use a trivial example, when famous sports stars or military heroes endorse a commercial product, they are exchanging their **prestige,** or social honor, for economic advantage. Indeed, people often enjoy high prestige in a society while having little or no property. For example, poets and saints may have immense influence in a society while remaining virtually penniless.

Power

The case for power as being independent of wealth is even more obvious. Weber defined **power** as the ability to get one's way despite the resistance of others. People may be very powerful without acquiring much property. For example, a corporation president may wield great power within the corporation and even in the political process of a society without personally owning any substantial part of the corporation. The same is often true of senior civil servants who run such powerful agencies as the CIA, the FBI, the RCMP, or the Federal Reserve while receiving relatively modest salaries. Additionally, power is often traded for economic advancement. Many politicians manage to retire rich even though they received only modest salaries while in office. The whole notion of influence peddling assumes the sale of power, while Marx seemed to believe that power can only be bought.

Status Inconsistency

In Chapter 2, *status* was defined as any position within the stratification system. (This is not what Weber meant by the term, and that is one reason why sociologists often use the term *prestige* for Weber's concept.) This definition says nothing about the *basis* for status in a stratification system. Thus, a particular status or position can be high or low on the basis of the property, prestige, or power (or all three) associated with that position. We can also refer to *status characteristics*—certain individual or group traits that determine status. For example, various ethnic or racial minorities may be confined to a low status in society. Therefore, ethnicity and race are status characteristics: Variations in them influence position in society.

Because the term *status* denotes any particular position in the stratification system, it is a more general concept than class, which is just one measure of status. As Weber pointed out, there is more to stratification than simple economic differences.

If there are at least three basic dimensions of stratification in society, and if these can vary independently of one another, then individuals or groups can hold different ranks (or different status levels) on each of the three dimensions. For example, a person could be rich but have low prestige and little power. This state of affairs is called **status inconsistency.**

Status inconsistency theories predict that people whose status is inconsistent, or higher on one dimension than on another, will be more frustrated and dissatisfied than people with consistent statuses will be. A major proponent of status inconsistency theory, Gerhard Lenski (1954, 1956, 1966), explains the process this way: When people rank higher on one status dimension than on another, they will emphasize their highest claim to rank and deemphasize their

lowest. Thus, in presenting themselves to others, they will expect to be judged according to their highest status. Others, however, will tend to respond to them according to their lowest status, for others will seek to maximize their own position.

Consider the case of university professors. They seek to be treated by others on the basis of their advanced educations. But many people outside of universities ignore this claim and treat professors as having low status on the basis of their lack of power and wealth. Similarly, the Jewish industrialists in Germany in Weber's day sought to be ranked on the basis of wealth, but often were treated with disdain on the basis of their ethnicity. A somewhat parallel example exists in the United States and Canada in the denial of status to "hick" millionaires—people lacking education and social graces who hit it rich and then unsuccessfully attempt to move in fashionable circles. The phrase "the vulgar rich" expresses the status inconsistency of many wealthy people.

Lenski argued that persons who are denied the social rank that they believe they deserve become antagonistic toward the rules governing status in their society. Consequently, persons suffering from status inconsistency will favor political actions aimed against upper-status groups; that is, they will support liberal and radical parties and proposals. This very important theoretical conclusion helped explain why persons of considerable social standing often seemed to turn their backs on their own class interests and support the claims of the less privileged.

To test status inconsistency theory, Gary Marx reasoned that, in the 1960s, all wealthy, famous, or highly educated black Americans suffered from status inconsistency. Therefore, according to the theory, upper-status blacks ought to be *more* militant about changing racial conditions than were blacks with consistent low statuses. So Gary Marx predicted that black bankers and physicians, for example, would be more radical than black janitors and housekeepers. Research based on large national samples confirmed his hypothesis (G. Marx, 1967).

By the same token, as members of an ethnic minority, Jewish bankers and industrialists in

North America and Europe ought to have a record of support for liberal and radical parties, and they do (Cohn, 1958). The theory also explains the strong preference of wealthy and powerful American Catholics for the Democratic Party (Baltzell, 1964). And few groups have demonstrated a greater propensity for left-of-center politics than college and university faculties, not only in North America, but worldwide.

In opting for political responses, people suffering from status inconsistency place the blame on others, on the "system." But not everyone responds in this fashion. Sometimes people blame themselves for their problems. Let's look over Elton Jackson's shoulder to see how he conducted a classic study of this aspect of status inconsistency.

Elton Jackson: status inconsistency and psychological stress

Soon after Lenski had generated renewed sociological interest in status inconsistency, a young sociologist completing his Ph.D. at the University of Michigan decided to explore the psychological consequences of having inconsistent or discrepant statuses. Elton Jackson (1962) argued that "conflicting expectations" are the basic interaction problem people with inconsistent statuses face. Individuals' status determines what others expect of them and what they expect of themselves. But "when a person holds high rank on one status dimension and low rank on another, the expectations (both those held by the individual and by others) mobilized by the rank positions will often be in conflict."

These conflicts can produce two general consequences. The first is *frustration.* Social relationships will be stressful because of frequent conflicts over which status will determine how the inconsistent individual will be treated. The second consequence, according to Jackson, is *uncertainty.* What can the individual expect from others, what can they expect of him or her? These problems can cause a person to lose self-esteem and to suffer from even more profound forms of psychological distress.

To test these hypotheses about status inconsistency, Jackson analyzed data based on a national sample of American adults. He measured status inconsistency on the basis of three status measures. The first was occupation. Each person's occupation was classified as falling into one of three categories: 1 (high)—professional, managerial, and business operators; 2 (medium)—clerical and skilled labor occupations; 3 (low)—semiskilled and unskilled occupations. The second status measure Jackson used was education, also sorted into three groups: 1 (high)—persons with at least some college; 2 (medium)—persons who attended high school; 3 (low)—persons with eight years of school or less. Jackson's third status dimension was "racial-ethnic background." Here his three categories ranked people of English or old American family backgrounds as 1, those of northwest European ancestry as 2, and placed southeastern Europeans, Jews, and nonwhites in group 3.

By combining an individual's rank on each of these three measures, Jackson could categorize them as of consistent or inconsistent status. People whose three scores were all the same (111, 222, 333) were rated as consistents. Moderate inconsistents were all those with two similar ranks and a third that was only one rank-step different (121, 223, or 332, for example). More sharply inconsistent were persons with no two ranks the same (123, 312, 231, and so forth). Those classified as suffering the greatest inconsistency were those with one rank that was two rank-steps above or below the other two (113 or 313, for instance). An example of the latter would be a college-educated person of old American family background who works as a janitor.

Jackson drew upon a rich survey research tradition of mental health studies for his measures of psychological stress. Table 9-1 shows Jackson's key findings and two illustrative questions included in his overall psychological stress index. Persons with consistent statuses were less than half as likely (16 percent) as those with a two-rank discrepancy (36 percent) to score high on psychological stress. This same pattern shows up on the items concerning a nervous breakdown and clammy hands.

Table 9-1 ■ Status inconsistency and psychological stress.

	Consistents	Inconsistents		
		Moderate	High	Extreme
Percent scored high on psychological stress	16%	18%	24%	36%
"Have you ever felt that you were going to have a nervous breakdown?" Percent "Yes"	15%	17%	22%	23%
"Are you troubled by your hands sweating so that you feel damp and clammy?" Percent "Yes"	28%	31%	35%	41%

Source: Adapted from Elton Jackson (1962).

Thus, Jackson's data strongly supported his hypothesis: Status inconsistency can have mental health consequences. But as he pursued the analysis, Jackson discovered something even more significant: Different patterns of inconsistency had different outcomes. When people were of high-status ethnic backgrounds and had low-status jobs, they were highly subject to psychological stress but showed no affinity for liberal politics. However, in the opposite case (people of low-status racial and ethnic background with high-status occupations), there was no evidence of unusual psychological stress but a very marked preference for liberal politics. These findings fit well with others mentioned earlier. The research on blacks, Jews, and Catholics had found political reactions to a condition of wealth and occupational prestige combined with lack of power and prestige—precisely the pattern Jackson found too. Notice that race and ethnicity clearly are *group* traits. When these are accorded low status, the blame does not easily fall upon the individual group member ("Why blame *me* for being a Swede?"). Rather, when people are accorded low status because of belonging to a group that is the target of prejudice by the majority, their normal reaction is to blame their tormentors and seek to change the "system." However, when a person has a

group trait that is accorded high status and nevertheless ends up with a low-status job, the blame is much harder to externalize. Such people tend to blame themselves: "My ancestors came over on the *Mayflower*, and my folks sent me to prep school and then to Dartmouth. Yet here I am mopping floors."

The notion of status inconsistency is possible *only* if we accept Weber's view that there are multiple bases for rank in societies. If we follow Marx and accept only one basis for rank, then, of course, it is impossible to conceive of inconsistency. However, no matter how we conceptualize stratification systems, questions arise about how people gain their positions. And this brings us to the topic of social mobility.

■

Social Mobility

Societies differ greatly in the amount of upward and downward movement that goes on within their stratification systems. In some societies few people rise above or fall below their position at birth. In other societies there is a great deal of mobility. The amount of mobility in societies depends on two things. First, the *rules* governing how people gain or keep their posi-

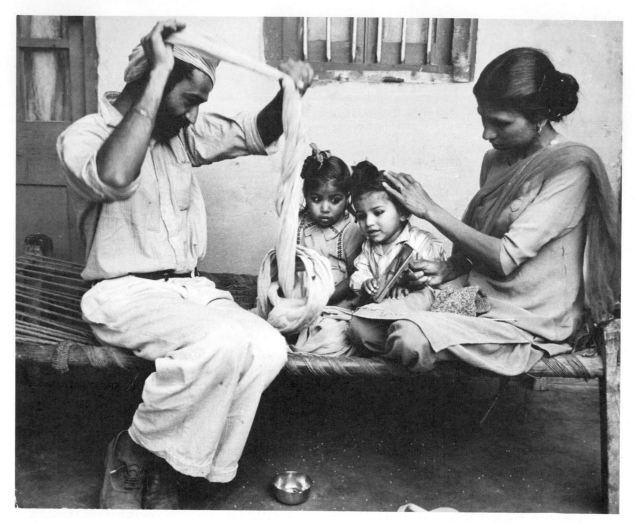

■ Fifty years ago the adult status of these Indian children would almost certainly have been exactly the same as that of their parents. Today, India's caste system is not as strictly observed as it used to be. However, it is still very likely that these children will inherit their parents' caste position.

tions may make mobility difficult or easy. Second, whatever the rules, *structural* changes in society can influence mobility.

Rules of status: ascription and achievement

Chapter 2 introduced the two primary rules by which societies determine status. *Achieved* status is a position gained on the basis of merit, or achievement. *Ascribed* status is a position based on who you are, not what you can do. When a society uses ascriptive status rules, people are placed in status positions because of certain traits beyond their control, such as family background, race, sex, or place of birth.

In all known societies, both achievement and ascription operate, but societies differ in which rule dominates. In medieval Europe, for example, one's status was predominantly based on ascription. Persons born of the nobility were likely to remain in high positions; persons born of peasants were likely to remain in low positions.

When ascription is the overwhelming basis for status, we often speak of *caste* systems. Traditional society in India was composed of dozens of castes. Each person's caste group was defined by the caste he or she was born into, and each group was restricted to certain occupations. All the filthy and demeaning jobs, such as garbage collecting, were reserved for one caste, whose members were permitted to hold no other occupations. Similarly, highly skilled occupations such as goldsmithing were the exclusive right of another caste. However, even in caste systems, some people managed through luck and talent to rise above their origins—great prowess as a soldier, in particular, was often a ticket to higher status. And some high-born persons managed to fall to low positions because of misbehavior or incompetence.

Achievement is the primary basis of status in the United States, Canada, and other advanced industrial nations. The majority of North Americans are socially mobile; they rise above or fall below the positions of their parents. Nevertheless, ascription plays a significant role in these societies, too. Although blacks and women are not wholly excluded from upper-status positions, they are underrepresented in such positions and overrepresented in lower ones. One reason for this is discrimination based on race and sex.

Social mobility is much more frequent when achievement rather than ascription is the primary basis for status. But societies also differ in the amount of social mobility that occurs because of the direction of structural change in their overall status systems.

Structural and exchange mobility

When the proportion of upper-status positions in a society increases, some upward mobility is inevitable. Because more openings exist at the top for the present generation than existed for the previous generation, some children of lower-status parents must be placed in high positions in order to fill them.

A simple example will make this clear (see Figure 9-2). Suppose that in 1960 a society had 100 jobs, 25 of which were high-prestige, high-paying jobs and 75 low-prestige, low-paying jobs. However, the economy changed. As machines replaced humans on the job, there was less need for people to do unskilled work and a greater need for people to do highly skilled work (such as designing and maintaining the machines that replaced unskilled laborers). Thus, in 1990, this society still contained 100 jobs, but 50 were high-status positions.

Suppose that in 1960 each of the 100 people holding the 100 jobs had one child who replaced him or her in the economy. Then by 1990, 25 children of persons who held low positions would have entered high positions, simply because 25 low positions had been eliminated from the status system and 25 high positions had been created. Thus, a third of the offspring of low-status people in 1960 become upwardly mobile simply as a result of changes in the status system. The reverse would have occurred if the proportion of high positions had decreased rather than increased.

Social mobility that results from changes in the distribution of statuses in society is called **structural mobility.** Note that structural mobility occurs *regardless of the rules governing status.* Had our hypothetical society been based on ascriptive status rules, the outcome would have been the same. For example, if the demands of a particular occupation exceeded the capacity of the appropriate caste group, members of other castes would have filled the openings. Therefore, we can learn little about the rules governing status in a society merely by knowing its rate of mobility. We must also know whether that mobility is structural or exchange mobility.

Mobility that is not structural is called **exchange mobility.** The word *exchange* indicates a trade-off. In exchange mobility, some people rise to fill positions made available because other people have fallen in the status system. Let us reconsider a simple illustration in Figure 9-3. Suppose that the proportion of upper-status positions did not increase between 1960 and 1990. Thus, in 1990 there are still 25 upper-status positions and 75 lower positions. The only way that the offspring of persons in lower positions can gain an upper position is if

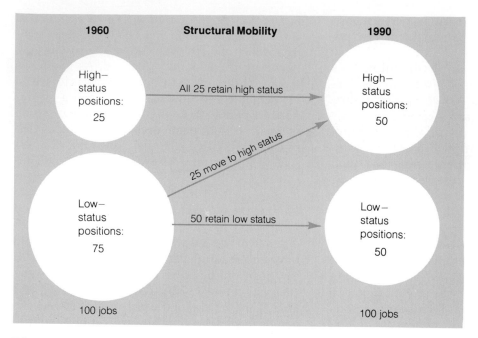

Figure 9-2 ■ **Structural mobility.** Structural mobility occurs because of changes in the ratio of upper-status to lower-status positions. When there is an increase in positions at the top, some people will have to be upwardly mobile in order to fill them. There has been a great deal of structural mobility in industrial nations during the twentieth century.

someone born of upper-status persons moves to a lower status, thus making room at the top.

There is little exchange mobility when the ascriptive status rule operates, but if status is through achievement, there is a fair amount of such movement. Many children of talented and ambitious parents do not inherit the talent or ambition that earned their parents high rank. Conversely, many children of low-status parents are more talented and ambitious than their parents are. Hence, if the status system is truly based on achievement, then we can expect a good deal of reshuffling each generation. In Chapter 10, we shall examine mobility in the United States and other industrial nations.

Thus far we have examined concepts of stratification, but now we must confront the basic theoretical issues: Why are societies stratified and can stratification be eliminated? As noted at the beginning of this chapter, these issues have been debated for centuries. In the remainder of this chapter, we shall see that the debate continues among contemporary sociologists. However, before examining the three principal sociological theories of stratification, it will be useful to relate the contemporary debate to its roots in the nineteenth century.

■

Marx and the Classless Society

Karl Marx lived and wrote during a period of extremely rapid social change, which produced a great deal of social displacement and individual suffering. Across Europe the Industrial Revolution was in full swing. Great factories dotted the countryside, belching forth noxious smoke as well as an unprecedented volume of production. Until that time, most human beings had lived on farms or in tiny villages. But soon most people were to be living in cities, and it seemed that most would end up sweating over machines in factories.

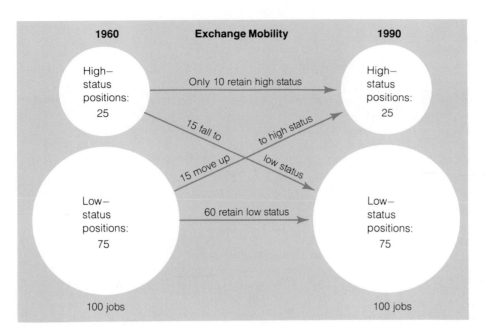

Figure 9-3 ■ **Exchange mobility.** Exchange mobility occurs when openings are created at the top by downward mobility. That is, as some people move downward they exchange positions with others who move up to fill their vacancies.

To many, trading a life in a cow barn for a life in a factory was not real progress. The successful rise of industrial unions was yet to come. Many people, including Marx, found existing conditions intolerable, and out of their anger and frustration came an immense burst of utopian social thought.

A **utopian** constructs plans for an ideal society. Thousands of utopian schemes have been proposed over the past two centuries alone. Indeed, many have been tried. During the nineteenth century, for example, scores of groups in the United States set up their own separate communities, where they attempted to enact a utopian living plan (Nordhoff, 1875; Noyes, 1870). Some of these groups, such as Oneida and Amana, were based on a common set of religious beliefs. Some, such as New Harmony, embraced socialism. The religious commune groups tended to last much longer, but they all broke up in the end. Nevertheless, whether religious or socialist or both, these groups reflected

a deep discontent with the quality of life in nineteenth-century industrial societies (Kanter, 1972).

Within this context of rapid social change, widespread social unrest, and rampant utopian thought, Marx set out to create a scientific theory of history. The aim of his theory was to show how the inevitable forces of history would produce a revolution of the proletariat, which in turn would produce socialism and a communist society. After years of writing, Marx concluded that the coming revolutionary societies would be "classless"; that is, everyone would belong to a single social class.

Marx's conclusions, which were joyfully received by many, sharply contrasted with the predictions of **anarchists,** who were a major force in radical thought and politics at the time. The anarchists had reached a conclusion similar to that held by modern sociology: Stratification is an inescapable feature of human societies. Unlike most modern sociologists, the anarch-

■ During the nineteenth century, the word *industry* mainly meant huge factories and plants, powered by coal-burning steam engines that belched immense clouds of smoke and pollution. Marx believed that life in these "Satanic mills" was so intolerable and degrading that it would soon produce a revolutionary proletariat. Here we see Pittsburgh, Pennsylvania, in 1903. The huge Homestead steel plant (soon to become United States Steel) pours out grime—while inside the huge mill sheds, the fathers and older brothers of these boys suffered from intense heat. Recently, Pittsburgh was rated as one of the most livable cities in North America; a lot has changed since this picture was taken.

ists reacted to this conclusion by proposing to dispense with society. Indeed, they earned their name by proposing to "smash the state" and to live without social organization. However, because anarchists failed to explain convincingly how humans could live apart from society without also living in constant fear, danger, and disorder, most people found their solution worse than the problem. Then, in a few sentences, Marx claimed to prove the anarchists incorrect by showing how both society and equality were possible.

To see how he arrived at this conclusion, we must recall how he defined social class. As stated earlier in this chapter, Marx conceived of only two classes in modern industrial societies, and these classes differed on the basis of the ownership (or nonownership) of the means of production. By Marxist definition, classes exist only because privately owned property exists. This alone separates people into the bourgeoisie and proletariat. Thus, to achieve a classless society, the *private ownership of the means of production* must be abolished. Then, the bourgeoisie ceases to exist and everyone becomes a proletarian.

But how can this be done? If the state seizes ownership of the means of production, then no person will own these means. Moreover, because everybody will belong to the same class, there will be no class conflict.

Following Marx, communist regimes that have come to power have proclaimed their societies to be classless because they have placed ownership of the means of production in the hands of the state. These claims have long caused heated debate among people in noncommunist nations because communist societies have remained very noticeably *stratified*. For example, party members in the Soviet Union have luxuries unavailable to other citizens. How could this be a classless society?

Dahrendorf's critique

The most penetrating analysis of Marx's claims about the creation of classless societies was written by Ralf Dahrendorf (1959), a leading conflict theorist of stratification. Later in this chapter we shall examine elements of his work. Here we shall concentrate on his argument that Marx's claim about classless societies was a "magic trick" that didn't mean what it appeared to mean.

Dahrendorf pointed out that everything Marx said about communist societies being classless was true, *but true only by definition*. Marx defined *class* according to the ownership of the means of production. If the state owns all means of production, then everyone falls into one class *as Marx defines class.*

But, Dahrendorf continued, notice that Marx never said this would produce *unstratified* societies. Indeed, communist societies have one class only in the limited sense expressed by Marx, but Marx did not say that everyone would have equal power or equal prestige. Moreover, it does not even follow that people in communist societies would be equal economically. For, Dahrendorf asked, *who is the state?* Is it really all of the people? Or is the state in fact controlled by political specialists?

Here Dahrendorf turned to Weber. What would happen to Marx's prediction of a classless society if he had based his definition not simply on the ownership of the means of production but also on its *control?* People do not have equal control over the means of production, even if private ownership is outlawed. Human affairs still require organization and direction. Someone still must manage each factory, for example. Because Weber argued that variations in the control of the means of production are often more significant than technical ownership, the socialization of industry clearly does not create classless societies as Weber used the term. Instead, people still differ greatly in their *control* over the means of production. Those who run the government in effect "own" the means of production.

Indeed, Dahrendorf argued, Marx did not escape the anarchist's conclusion at all. He only resorted to a solution by definition that did not alter the brute reality of stratification. As Weber himself noted, Marx was only proposing to replace the capitalist boss with a communist boss, and there is no reason to suppose that this substitution would reduce stratification.

Interestingly enough, Dahrendorf's critique

of Marx had been anticipated in 1896 by a young Italian sociologist, who also anticipated major elements of both modern functionalist and conflict theories of stratification.

Mosca: stratification is inevitable

In his book *The Ruling Class* (1896), Gaetano Mosca (1858–1941) laid out a three-step "proof" that societies must be stratified. His first proposition was that *human societies cannot exist without political organization.* Mosca used the term *political organization* in the broadest sense to mean all forms of coordination and decision making in human activities. This proposition simply recognizes that human society is impossible if everyone runs around helter-skelter. Instead, group life requires mutual undertakings, and the actions of individuals must be directed and coordinated. Put another way, in order to have societies, humans must take collective actions.

Mosca's second proposition resembles the conclusion the anarchists reached: *Whenever there is political organization (or society), there must be inequalities in power.* Here Mosca simply recognized that coordination requires leaders, and leaders, by definition, have greater power than their followers have—to lead, a person must be able to give orders and have them obeyed. Thus, according to Mosca, differences in power are built into the basic social roles by which societies are created and maintained—an insight that anticipated modern functionalist theories.

By themselves these two propositions establish that societies will always be stratified in terms of power. But Mosca carried his reasoning one step further and anticipated modern conflict theories of stratification. He argued that *because human nature is inherently self-seeking, people with greater power will use it to exploit others and therefore to gain material advantages.* Thus, given the existence of power inequalities, material inequalities will always exist too. Mosca concluded that stratification is not something that human societies can avoid, but is an inescapable feature of collective life.

For advancing this view, many of Mosca's contemporaries dismissed him as a cynic and a reactionary. But today, a century later, his ideas have become part of the sociological mainstream. Indeed, as we now examine in detail modern theories of stratification, it will be obvious how fully Mosca anticipated them.

■

The Functionalist Theory of Stratification

The modern functionalist view of stratification is most closely identified with the work of Kingsley Davis and Wilbert E. Moore (1945, 1953). The key to their **functionalist theory of stratification** is in seeing society as a system of roles or positions. *Inequality or stratification exists in societies because it is built into these roles and into the problem of filling them adequately.*

Davis and Moore began by arguing that positions in society differ in the degree to which they are functionally important. That is, poor performance in some roles is more damaging to the society than is poor performance in some other positions. For example, while it is true that a society engaged in a war requires both soldiers and generals, a general is in a position to make more devastating errors than is any given soldier. Remember that for every famous general who won a battle that he should have lost there was a general on the other side who lost a battle he should have won. History tends to be unkind to societies that appoint generals who snatch defeat out of the jaws of victory (Fair, 1971).

Some positions are inherently more important to the system, and Davis and Moore argued that some are also inherently more difficult to fill adequately. These positions require qualities that are naturally rare or that require a considerable preliminary investment in time, training, and effort. For example, some positions in a society require occupants with very high intelligence or great tact or other characteristics that are always in short supply in any population. Others—surgeons, for example—also require many years of training. Extensive training is always potentially in short supply, for new people constantly must begin training to fill future needs.

Thus, all societies face a general problem of motivation—"to instill in the proper individual the desire to fill certain positions, and, once in these positions, the desire to perform the roles attached to them" (Davis and Moore, 1945). How can this be accomplished? Davis and Moore argued that the only way to produce this kind of motivation is to adjust the reward system. Theirs is a supply-and-demand argument. To ensure an adequate supply of the right people, it is necessary to attach higher rewards to the positions that are most important and hardest to fill. Why would anyone want to become a general if the rewards were the same as those of a private?

Furthermore, it isn't enough to find some people who want to be generals—it is important to attract the right kind of people to the position of general. Stratification, therefore, exists because the positions in society differ in their importance to the system and because it is necessary to ensure that competent people fill the most important positions. Indeed, people also vary in their ability to perform important positions. Hence, as Davis and Moore (1945) put it, stratification or social inequality

is an unconsciously evolved device by which societies insure that the most important positions are conscientiously filled by the most qualified persons. . . . Those positions convey the best reward, and hence have the highest rank, which a) have the greatest importance for the society and b) require the greatest training or talent.

Differential rewards, according to Davis and Moore, prevent less essential or less important positions in society from competing with the more important for scarce talents.

Replaceability

Many have attacked Davis and Moore for attempting to justify social inequalities—for arguing that people get pretty much what they deserve in life. Davis and Moore rightfully

respond that they are not trying to justify stratification, merely to explain it. They no more chose to make stratification an inevitable part of society than physicists chose to make gravitation a part of the physical universe. Nevertheless, the Davis and Moore explanation of stratification has been criticized justifiably because it comes dangerously close to being circular (Stinchcombe, 1968). The trouble stems from their inability to define the notion of functional importance adequately.

Davis and Moore based their analysis on the proposition that positions or roles in society differ in functional importance, that is, in their consequences for the continued operation of society. This is vital to their argument that stratification results from the need to motivate the most qualified people to take these positions. Unfortunately, they found it difficult to establish that one position is more important than another except on the basis of how hard it is to fill that position. That is an inadequate standard.

Today it is very hard to fill the position of housekeeper; to ensure an ample supply would require wages to be set at a level most potential employers are unwilling to pay. Clearly, it does not follow that this position is extremely important. But should we then count it as of low functional importance because we are not willing to pay much to fill the position? To rate the importance of a position on the basis of how much people are paid for filling it leads into a trap. Then one must argue that rewards differ because of functional importance, but that is to say that rewards differ because rewards differ, since functional importance has been defined as a difference in rewards. This is a tautology, or circular argument.

Fortunately, positions can be ranked according to functional importance without leading to contradiction or tautology. A position is of high functional importance to a society depending on its **replaceability,** that is, to the degree that *either the position itself or its occupants are hard to replace.* Let us return to the example of housekeepers. The salary people are paid to clean other people's houses is low, even when those willing to take such jobs are in short supply, because the position of housekeeper is very replaceable. That is, their employers are fully able to take over the functions of the house-keeper, and when they are sufficiently motivated to do so (by the financial savings involved), they will tend to do so.

A *position* is highly replaceable when its functions can be performed by people in many other positions. Thus, hospital janitors are highly replaceable because all other hospital workers could perform their job. Orderlies are next most replaceable because doctors and nurses could perform their functions. Doctors are least replaceable because, presumably, not even nurses could fully take on their hospital duties.

People are highly replaceable when little skill is needed to perform their particular roles. Little training or skill is required to mop floors, for example, and thus people who hold such positions are always potentially in competition with all other workers to hold their own positions. On the other hand, very few people have the talent and the years of training needed to be surgeons, and so few people can compete for these positions. Thus, positional replaceability is the dominant basis of functional importance. People in highly replaceable positions also tend to be individually highly replaceable. Given the replaceability notion, the functionalist theory can easily be shown as a supply-and-demand argument about the existence of stratification.

A toy society

People who study the operation of systems often employ models to try out different arrangements to see what happens. Sometimes these models are small replicas of the actual system, but often they are very simplified versions of the system. The latter models omit many components of the original system in order to study a few features of the system more closely. In a sense, such a simplified model is an educational toy, for, as George Homans (1974) has aptly put it, such a toy "should be taken lightly like the serious thing it is. . . . At the very least the toy may show how inadequate our assumptions and formulations are."

To help explain stratification systems, we can

Table 9-2 ■ Abilities of space survivors to provide needs.

Survivor	Ability to Produce			
	Air	Water	Food	Heat
Ay	X	X	X	X
Bee		X	X	X
Cee			X	X
Dee				X

learn much by closely inspecting a very simplified toy society. Imagine a spaceship on a long voyage that is suddenly forced to crash-land on a tiny asteroid. Four people live through the crash. Let's call them Ay, Bee, Cee, and Dee. To survive, they will need four things: food, air, water, and heat. The survivors differ greatly in their technical skills. Ay is able to produce all four critical products, as shown in Table 9-2. Bee can produce everything but air; Cee can produce food and heat; and Dee can produce only heat.

Clearly, Ay is irreplaceable. If Ay dies or stops making air, then everyone will die. Moreover, if Ay stops *sharing* air with the other three, then they will die. Yet Ay can live without any of the others. To an exaggerated degree, Ay is like a doctor in relation to the rest of a hospital staff—he or she can do all the jobs.

Conversely, consider the situation of Dee. Everyone can get along without Dee, while he or she can't live without aid from the others. Clearly, Ay can make the most favorable exchanges with the other survivors. Ay has a monopoly on air and needs nothing from anyone else. He or she may decide not to bother making heat and let Dee provide heat in exchange for air. But Ay will not trade air for heat if it takes more effort to make air for Dee than for Ay to make his or her own heat. Similarly, Ay may bargain with Bee and Cee, perhaps to get water from Bee and food from Cee, in return for air. As a result of this bargaining process, Ay will always end up with more food, water, and heat than the others have. This is because Ay will supply his or her own food, water, and heat and refuse to trade air, whenever the terms of exchange do not favor Ay.

Now let's introduce time into this model. Like all humans, these marooned travelers will eventually die. Let's assume, however, that they have children and therefore our toy society has a future. If the next generation is to survive, then these children must be prepared to take over the vital productive functions. Finding a replacement for Ay is clearly imperative. Without an air maker, all will die. But suppose that air making requires a rare talent or a long period of difficult training. Someone with talent must be motivated to become an air maker or to invest the time and effort needed to learn air making. How can this best be assured? The most efficient way is to make every child desire to be an air maker. Thus, the only person with the potential for air making will not be wasted by becoming a heat maker. The way to do this is to greatly reward air making so that people will aspire to this occupation. Indeed, we have already seen that air making will be highly rewarded so long as it is the least replaceable skill.

This toy society reveals the essential points of the functionalist theory of stratification. We can see how specialization and exchanges between specialists result in stratification. Of course, many aspects of real societies have been omitted from this toy society. Among these are forces that limit the potential exploitation of Cee and Dee by Ay and Bee. These will be discussed in the section on the conflict theory of stratification.

■
The Social Evolution Theory of Stratification

Chapter 4 pointed out that all functionalist theories depend upon an evolutionary premise. Indeed, recall that Davis and Moore referred to stratification as "an unconsciously evolved device." No functionalist theory completely explains any phenomenon unless it is connected to an evolutionary theory. Thus, we need to know how social stratification evolves.

The fundamental premise of all social evolutionary theories is that *humans will retain that culture which they believe is rewarding.* Humans persist in efforts to find ways to gain rewards—to find procedures and implements that will achieve the desired results. Those that don't seem to work will be discarded; those that appear to work best will be preserved. If humans preserve culture, then as time passes culture will accumulate—that is, over time humans will possess a more complex culture (Lenski, 1966, 1976).

As culture becomes more elaborate, something important happens—any given individual can master less of it. Why? The human mind can learn only a limited amount of information. As culture becomes more complex, it soon exceeds the capacity of any individual to master all of it.

According to the **evolutionary theory of stratification,** when no single individual can master all aspects of a culture, specialization must occur. That is, individuals will master parts of their culture and enter into exchanges with others who have mastered other parts. In this way the accumulation of culture inevitably leads to a division of labor and therefore to stratification.

Some aspects of culture are more valued than others. That is, people desire or need certain things more than they do other things. As people and groups within a society specialize, some will be able to command higher prices for their goods and services than others can. Stratification means the existence of such inequalities.

Therefore, the accumulation of culture, because it results in cultural specialization, also results in stratification. The notion of replaceability is pertinent in determining the relative advantage of one specialty over another. Indeed, at this point a social evolutionary theory must draw upon functionalism to assess how specialties will be valued in the stratification system. Furthermore, as we shall now see, a full understanding of stratification must also incorporate the important insights of conflict theory.

The Conflict Theory of Stratification

Modern conflict theory provides a needed corrective to functionalist theory. Like the functionalists, most conflict theorists accept that stratification is unavoidable (Harris, 1979; Ossowski, 1963; Lenski, 1966). But the **conflict theory of stratification** adds several key insights about how stratification systems are subject to distortion. The first of these concerns how persons high in the stratification system will take advantage of their position to exploit others. This makes societies more stratified than can be accounted for by functionalist theory alone. The second of these insights concerns how the political process can be used to influence the stratification system, particularly by limiting replaceability.

Exploitation

Modern conflict theories build upon Mosca's third proposition: Humans pursue their own self-interests (Dahrendorf, 1968). It follows that people in a position to exploit others will tend to do so. Thus, if societies must be stratified, those on top will use their position to increase their rewards. As a result, societies are always more stratified than they need to be (Lenski, 1966).

Let's reexamine our toy society. Ay is functionally irreplaceable, being the only air maker. While Ay alone can provide others with air, he or she can do without the others because Ay can also make water, food, and heat. According to the functionalist theory, inequality occurs in this toy society because it is vital to reward Ay highly to ensure that someone will always be able and willing to make air. But conflict theorists point out that Ay is also a monopolist and therefore has immense power. Ay can set a very high price for air, limited only by the fact that if the price is too high, the others will die for lack of food, water, or heat (having given too much to Ay) and therefore will be unable to pay

Ay anything at all for air. It follows that Ay can set a higher price on air than would be needed simply to motivate air making. In fact, Ay can get more for air than the minimum price at which he or she would be willing to make air. The difference between the price that Ay actually gets and the minimum price at which Ay would sell air is **exploitation.**

When we look around at real societies, we frequently see examples of such exploitation. The OPEC nations, for example, banded together to monopolize oil supplies to inflate the price of oil far beyond the level needed to motivate people to drill, refine, and sell oil. Similarly, the earnings of physicians would probably have to decline substantially before the number and qualifications of students seeking entry to medical school would also fall. The functionalist theory can explain why doctors earn more than orderlies do, but it requires conflict theory to explain why the actual income gap between these two occupations is as large as it is.

The politics of replaceability

Looking once more at our toy society, we can discover another major omission. A monopoly like Ay's is unlikely to occur naturally. Such monopolies usually cannot exist unless power is being exerted to prevent others from competing. Members of the medieval nobility, for example, were able to monopolize the ownership of all land and therefore set the rents that peasants had to pay only because the nobility also monopolized military force. Their monopoly of military force did not occur because they were the only able-bodied men in medieval societies or because they were so much stronger and braver than all other men. It arose because they were the only ones able to possess the most advanced military technology—armor, war horses, and weapons—against which other men were helpless. The nobility prevented other men from receiving military training. Indeed, when the crossbow was invented, it was outlawed because it enabled people with little training and no expensive equipment to attack the noble knights. Thus, coercion was the basis of the knighthood's monopoly. And coercion underlies most (if not all) forms of monopoly.

The implications of this fact are important because they suggest that the principle of replaceability, so central to the functionalist theory, is also subject to distortion—that power may be used to control and manipulate replaceability artificially. This means that political power may be used to exaggerate or minimize the degree of stratification in societies. To examine this possibility, consider two examples of how groups can use power to decrease a position's replaceability artificially: professions and unions.

Professions first attempt to establish their positions as irreplaceable and then make their members irreplaceable in the position (Freidson, 1973). The claim to irreplaceability is based on some form of expertise that no other position can perform. This tendency to monopoly is a natural outgrowth of the proficiency a position develops (or is thought to have developed).

Consider the medical profession. In the nineteenth century, medical doctors were not very proficient. Not until about the turn of the century were people better off to go to a doctor than not to go, by some estimates. Most treatments and medicines used in the nineteenth century were useless, and some were quite harmful. During this period of limited proficiency, the position of doctor faced serious competition from other positions in performing the function of healing. Other healing practitioners such as osteopaths, homeopaths, food faddists, faith healers, patent medicine sellers, and the like claimed to be able to perform the needed medical function as well as or better than medical doctors could. Eventually physicians could demonstrate that their ability to heal was greater than that of people in these other positions. Demands for consumer protection against health frauds intensified, and in the end medical doctors were given a monopoly on the right to prescribe drugs and perform surgery (later the osteopaths joined with the medical doctors).

Once they have a monopoly on expertise and are thus highly irreplaceable, professions tend to seek control over who can fill their positions. In part this is because only they possess the essential knowledge and skills of the position, so they alone can pass them on to others. This, of course, makes it possible for professions to control who and how many enter the professions—and thus to control supply and increase their rewards beyond what successful recruitment would require. That is, doctors can limit the supply of doctors. They can also limit the freedom of nondoctors to perform medical tasks. To the extent that they are successful in limiting supply and preventing competition, doctors increase their irreplaceability, and like Ay, they can force others to pay higher prices for their services.

Unlike the medieval knights, however, professions such as medicine do not possess the means to force other people to do as they are told. Therefore, the monopolies created by professions are always subject to external checks. The government, which has a monopoly on the means of force, may refuse to protect a medical monopoly on prescriptions, for example. Or political power may be used to standardize or reduce fees charged by a profession. Or political power may force an increase in the supply of trained members admitted to the profession. If the rewards for being a doctor get too low, then the quality and supply of physicians will decline. But if the rewards rise too high, then they may be reduced by political decisions that the profession cannot control.

<u>Unions</u> are also efforts to create monopolies—to use power to decrease replaceability. To see how unions do this, let us return to our toy society. Suppose our simple four-person society were greatly enlarged and that there were many more Cees and Dees than Ays and Bees. Let us also assume a democratic political process so that the wishes of the Cees and Dees count. It is easy to see that these "lower-class" persons might use their collective political power (or even coercive force) to make better bargains with the Ays and Bees. Again, the key to an improved bargaining position depends on how positions can be made less replaceable.

The standard union tactic is to use contracts and laws to prevent other positions from performing the main function of their own position. That is, if Dee can prevent the other three members of our four-person society from producing heat, despite the fact that they could produce it, then his or her position is equal to Ay's.

Craft union rules have precisely this effect. In construction work, for example, union contracts clearly specify what tasks belong to which position, and other positions are barred from performing such tasks. In extreme instances, a crew of carpenters and a crew of plasterers may wait all day for an electrician to come and turn on a switch that any normal adult could have managed. In this way, the actual high replaceability of a position is converted into an artificial state of very low replaceability.

As with professions, the second goal of unions is to control the conditions for entering positions. This is accomplished by mandatory union membership—the closed shop—and entrance and apprenticeship procedures governing membership.

As we shall see in Chapter 10, unionization has been a major force in reducing the degree of stratification in industrialized democracies. For example, the difference in average pay between blue-collar and white-collar workers has been drastically reduced. Thus, the politics of replaceability work not only for business monopolies and the professions but also for factory workers. Indeed, the business monopoly has been subjected to the strictest regulation.

Conclusion

In Chapter 4, I suggested that although there are a number of distinctive theoretical schools in macro sociology, to me they seem quite compatible. Here we have seen that each of these theoretical approaches explains something important about stratification that the others leave unexplained. Functionalist theory explains why various occupational specialties are differentially rewarded—because some workers are much less replaceable than others. Evolutionary theory explains how specialization arises in societies and thus supplements the functionalist theory. Conflict theory adds a vital point—that power will be exploited to increase or

decrease stratification, and thus stratification will reflect the outcome of conflicts among groups in a society.

Because the aim of this chapter is to present the conceptual and theoretical tools sociologists use to analyze stratification, it has necessarily been quite abstract. To apply this material to concrete issues, Chapter 10 examines how stratification systems operate in a variety of human societies.

Review Glossary

means of production Everything, except human labor, that is used to produce wealth. (p. 236)

bourgeoisie Marx's name for the class made up of those who own the means of production; the employer or owner class. (p. 236)

proletariat The name that Marx applied to the class made up of those who do not own the means of production; the employee or working class. (p. 236)

lumpenproletariat Literally, the ragamuffin proletariat; the people on the very bottom of society whom Marx labeled "social scum." (p. 236)

class consciousness The concept Marx used to identify the awareness of members of a class of their class interests and enemies. (p. 237)

false consciousness A term that Marx applied to members of one class who think they have common interests with members of another class. (p. 237)

property The term many sociologists use to identify what Weber called *class*. Property includes all economic resources and opportunities owned or controlled by an individual or a group. (p. 239)

prestige Social honor or respect; synonymous with Weber's term *status*. (p. 240)

power The ability to get one's way despite the opposition of others. (p. 240)

status inconsistency A condition in which a person holds a higher position (or status) on one dimension of stratification than on another. For example, an uneducated millionaire displays status inconsistency. (p. 241)

status inconsistency theories Theories built on the proposition that persons who experience status inconsistency will be frustrated and will, therefore, support political movements aimed at changing the stratification system. (p. 241)

structural mobility Mobility that occurs because of changes in the relative distribution of upper and lower statuses in a society. (p. 245)

exchange mobility Mobility that occurs because some people fall, thereby making room for others to rise in the stratification system. (p. 245)

utopian One who tries to design a perfect society. (p. 247)

anarchists Followers of a political philosophy that regards the state as inevitably repressive and unjust and who, therefore, propose to destroy the state and live without laws or government. (p. 247)

functionalist theory of stratification A theory that holds that inequality is built into the roles of any society because some roles are more important and harder to fill, and to ensure that the most qualified people will seek to fill the most important positions, it is necessary to reward these positions more highly than others. (p. 250)

replaceability A measure of the functional importance of a role based on the extent to which other roles can substitute for or take on the duties of that particular role. For example, a doctor can easily substitute for an orderly, but the reverse is not so. (p. 251)

evolutionary theory of stratification A theory that holds that because culture accumulates in human societies, eventually it happens that no one can master the whole of a group's culture. At that point, cultural specialization, or a division of labor, occurs. Since some specialties will be more valued than others, inequality, or stratification, will exist. (p. 253)

conflict theory of stratification A theory that holds that individuals and groups will always exploit their positions in an effort to gain a larger share of the rewards in a society, and therefore societies will often be much more stratified than functionalism can explain. Put another way, this theory holds that the stratification system of any society is the result of conflicts and compromises between contending groups (p. 254)

exploitation All profit in an exchange in excess of the minimum amount needed to cause an exchange to occur. (p. 254)

professions Occupational organizations that can prevent their functions from being performed by those not certified as adequately trained and qualified in an extensive body of knowledge and technique. (p. 255)

unions Occupational organizations that can prevent their functions from being performed by others on the basis of contractual rights. (p. 255)

■

Suggested Readings

Bell, Daniel. 1973. *The Coming of Post-Industrial Society.* New York: Basic Books (especially Chapter 1).

Bendix, Reinhard, and Seymour Martin Lipset, eds. 1966. *Class, Status, and Power,* 2nd ed. New York: Free Press.

Dahrendorf, Ralf. 1959. *Class and Class Conflict in Industrial Society.* Palo Alto: Stanford University Press.

Freidson, Eliot, ed. 1973. *The Professions and Their Prospects.* Beverly Hills: Sage Publications.

Lenski, Gerhard. 1966. *Power and Privilege.* New York: McGraw-Hill.

Comparing Systems
of Stratification

10

IN AN OLD comedy routine, one man asks another, "how's life?" "Compared to what?" is the reply. This piece of foolery reveals the basis of all scientific investigations. Virtually every important question sociologists ask requires comparisons. Suppose we ask, "How stratified is Mexico?" The first reply must be, "Compared to what?" To answer that question requires us either to compare Mexico as it was at several points in its history (thus permitting an answer such as "less stratified than it used to be") or to compare several societies (thus permitting an answer such as "less stratified than India is").

This chapter examines stratification systems by comparing different kinds of societies. In this way, the concepts and theories of stratification covered in the previous chapter can be applied and illustrated.

Chapter Preview

We shall examine stratification and social mobility in three major types of societies. First, we shall examine the simplest form of human society: the small band of hunter-gatherers. Next, we shall examine the more complex agrarian societies and see why they are so much more stratified than simple societies. Finally, we shall examine stratification in modern

industrial societies, focusing on the United States and Canada.

The way societies are ordered in this chapter—from the least to the most modern—implies social evolution. It is true that agrarian societies developed out of simple hunting and gathering societies and thus appeared later. It is also true that industrial societies grew out of earlier agrarian societies. However, such an evolutionary process is neither inevitable nor uniform. Many, probably most, simple societies did not evolve into agrarian societies—indeed, hunting and gathering societies still exist. Most agrarian societies did not become industrialized—indeed, some began to industrialize and then lapsed back into agrarianism (Chirot, 1976; Wallerstein, 1974). In Part Five we shall examine social change and consider why and how societies evolve or fail to do so. For now, simply keep in mind that the concept of social evolution is surrounded by uncertainties.

Simple Societies

Societies covering large areas and containing large populations are relatively recent. For most of human history, societies were very small—usually having only about fifty members (Mur-

Albania	1.8	Netherlands	274.0
Portugal	76.0	France	274.0
Greece	127.0	Switzerland	285.0
Romania	138.0	West Germany	306.0
Yugoslavia	161.0	East Germany	309.0
Bulgaria	176.0	United Kingdom	317.0
Spain	185.0	Denmark	323.0
Ireland	192.0	Sweden	363.0
		Finland	363.0

Poland	198.0
U.S.S.R.	217.0
Italy	220.0
Austria	236.0
Hungary	236.0
Czechoslovakia	254.0
Belgium	268.0
Norway	270.0

Figure 10-1 ■ **Television sets per 1,000 population.** Even modern industrial societies differ greatly in the standard of living the average citizen enjoys. Here we see variations among European nations in the number of television sets per 1,000 population, one of many measures used for comparative studies of economic development and affluence. In Albania there are fewer than 2 TV sets for each 1,000 persons, while in Sweden and Finland there are 363 sets per 1,000. As a comparison, there are 428 TV sets per 1,000 in Canada and 571 per 1,000 in the United States.

dock, 1949). Indeed, the largest simple societies rarely exceeded several hundred members and then only in extremely favorable environments (Kroeber, 1925). These simple societies often wandered over large areas, but the territory they inhabited at any given moment was small.

There were several kinds of simple societies, if we classify them by how they made their living. (I shall use the past tense in describing these societies, but keep in mind that some still exist.) The majority were **hunting and gathering societies.** Rather than living in a fixed spot, they moved in search of game and edible plants. Slightly more advanced simple societies lived by herding animals. They, too, moved about as their animals required new grazing areas. Other simple societies mastered elementary gardening and thus tended to be less nomadic than the herders or the hunter-gatherers were. Nevertheless, they tended to stay in one spot just long enough to grow one crop and then moved on. Only about 10 percent of simple societies managed to live in a fixed location (Lenski, 1966).

Both the herding and gardening societies were wealthier than the hunter-gatherers and had a slightly more complex division of labor. Therefore, they also tended to be more stratified. However, because the hunter-gatherer societies represent the most primitive level of human existence, they reveal the most elementary forms of stratification. For this reason, we shall look at them closely.

The major fact of life in hunting and gathering societies was the threat of death. These societies had few members because they could not support more. Traveling on foot, they could not cover much distance in a day. Hence they could only feed the number of members who could survive on the food found within so restricted a range.

They were not very deadly hunters. Most of them probably lacked weapons even as primitive as the bow and arrow and relied instead on stones, clubs, spears, and traps. In part this was because they lacked enough production to support specialists who could develop better weapons (Lenski, 1966). Furthermore, edible vegetation is usually seasonal and in most places not abundant. Because they could not preserve

■ Nomadic societies lack possessions because of the constant need to move on. If you cannot own more than you can carry with you, you will never have very much. Here we see the women and children of a nomadic African society moving across a barren waste. They own nothing but what they are wearing on their backs and balancing on their heads.

food very well, if at all, they experienced chronic famines and only occasional feasts. Even when meat was abundant, it spoiled quickly, leaving the group again without food. Colin Turnbull (1965) has reported that Pygmies in the dense jungle of the Congo deplete an area of fruit and game (scaring away more than they catch) within about a month and then move on.

These simple societies frequently lost the battle to survive. This is evident when we consider how slowly the population of humans on earth grew until historical times. Recent archeological discoveries in Africa indicate that humans existed more than 3 million years ago. Yet only 10,000 years ago, after at least 3 million years of reproduction, it is estimated that there were fewer people on earth than live in New York City today (Davis, 1971; Harris, 1979). Ten thousand years ago the human population was still growing so slowly that it would have taken another 60,000 years to double in size. Today the world's population is doubling about every thirty-seven years, and our problem is not too few but too many people. Population growth was the result of increased food production, which widened the margin of survival enough to ensure against constant crises and an appalling death rate. For most of our time on earth, however, the constant problem was simply to survive.

Under such circumstances human societies were not very stratified in terms of property (Harris, 1979). Possessions were limited to what could be carried from place to place. Because there was never much more than enough wealth to go around, the wealthiest could accumulate little more than could the poorest. Furthermore, with almost no role specialization—no full-time leaders, for example—power was also greatly equalized (Fried, 1967; Harris, 1979). Indeed, the ability to coerce others was quite limited and thus provided little basis for power. If, for example, some hunters began forcing others to give them their game, then there was little to prevent those being exploited from deserting the band. Nor could the strongest hope to live merely by taking from others, because unless everyone worked hard at getting food, survival was jeopardized. If you cannot produce

■ Eskimos on the move to a new campsite along Coronation Gulf in northern Canada, during the winter of 1911. All hunting and gathering societies are very small, but environmental conditions caused Eskimo societies to be tiny. Danish explorer Knud Rasmussen explained: "It took a large stretch of ground to provide the single individual with the necessities of life; the fewer the hunters the better were the chances, so they migrated along the coasts in little flocks."

more than enough for yourself, then you cannot be exploited easily.

However, hunting and gathering societies were nevertheless stratified to a significant degree. Usually the primary bases of stratification were age and sex (van den Berghe, 1973). Adults held power over children, and men dominated women.

However, *within* age and sex groups, simple societies were not very stratified. Men were essentially equal in terms of possessions and political power, as were women. Stratification within each sex was based mainly on achievement. Some men dominated others because they were bigger or smarter, better hunters or braver fighters, or more persuasive in group decision making. These distinctions showed up as differences in prestige and power rather than in material inequalities. Similarly, among women, prestige differences on the basis of skill at

domestic tasks, wisdom, persuasiveness, fertility, and perhaps physical appearance undoubtedly existed.

The rule seems to be that the smaller, poorer, and less secure a human society is, the less it is stratified. Universal poverty was the basis of equality among hunters and gatherers. But as soon as humans became more productive and better organized, their societies became more unequal. Herding societies and simple horticultural (gardening) societies were more stratified than were hunter-gatherer societies. When humans finally settled in one place and began to grow crops, inequality increased enormously (Harris, 1979; Cohen, 1977). Suddenly gaps in status appeared as great as those between slaves laboring in a field and emperors living opulently in palaces.

Table 10-1 shows the immense impact of settlement on stratification. The data are based

Table 10-1 ■ Fixity of residence and stratification.

Degree of Stratification	Fixity of Residence		
	Nomadic	Sedentary	Permanent
Low	89.8%	74.3%	46.1%
Medium	10.2%	25.7%	24.5%
High	0.0%	0.0%	29.4%
	100.0%	100.0%	100.0%
N =	(49)	(35)	(102)

Source: Prepared by the author from the Standard Cross-Cultural Sample selected by Murdock and White (1969).

on 186 societies selected by Murdock and White in 1969 from the more than 1,000 included in Murdock's *Ethnographic Atlas* (1967b). These societies are commonly referred to as the Standard Cross-Cultural Sample. No industrialized societies are included, and pains have been taken to make sure that all variables for any given society are from the same time period. As the data show, nomadic societies are not very stratified—only 10 percent are classified as having a medium level of stratification. Unlike nomads, sedentary societies are not constantly on the move, but neither do they stay in one place. Some rotate seasonally through a regular set of fixed locations. Some create semipermanent settlements only to be forced frequently to leave them for ecological or ritual reasons (the death of a headman, for example). Sedentary societies also aren't apt to be highly stratified. But when societies have a permanent location, many of them develop medium and high levels of stratification.

■

Agrarian Societies

The development of agriculture changed the world (Pfeiffer, 1977). No longer did humans wander the earth eking out a hand-to-mouth existence. They were able to settle in permanent locations and therefore could construct better shelters and accumulate possessions. More importantly, life ceased to be a constant struggle to find food.

As time passed, the technology of agriculture improved. With each improvement, human society became more complex. The basis for this growing complexity was *surplus food production*. When a family could produce enough food to feed others as well as themselves, two new social phenomena became possible: *specialization* and *cities*.

So long as everyone had to take part in the quest for food, no one could devote full time to other pursuits. Thus, during most of human existence, there were no full-time priests, political leaders, or other specialists. But when farmers could produce some surplus, others could be supported who made their shoes, forged their tools, conducted their religious ceremonies, and guided their political affairs. Furthermore, people not needed for food production could congregate in a central place and thus create cities.

Productivity

With the invention of plows and effective animal harnesses, agricultural productivity became so great that some people were freed from farming. At that point **agrarian societies** appeared, some of which became great empires and per-

Table 10-2 ■ Agricultural development and warfare.

Frequency of External Wars	Level of Agricultural Development			
	None	Low	Medium	High
Constant	33.3%	57.1%	56.0%	66.6%
Common	23.8%	7.1%	12.0%	16.7%
Occasional	42.9%	35.8%	32.0%	16.7%
	100.0%	100.0%	100.0%	100.0%
N =	(21)	(14)	(25)	(24)

Source: Prepared by the author from the Standard Cross-Cultural Sample and from Ross (1983).

haps the first real human civilizations. However, the number of persons who didn't farm, even in the most advanced agrarian societies, was small. Gideon Sjoberg (1960) estimates that no agrarian society had fewer than 90 percent of its members engaged in farming, and usually 95 percent were needed. Still, even by freeing one in twenty from farming, people could pursue a great variety of specialized tasks and produce an elaborate social structure.

It is important to realize that the famous cities of historical agrarian societies were not large by modern standards (see Chapter 19). In fact, even by 1800, when industrialization was already well under way, fewer than fifty cities in the world had more than 100,000 residents (Davis, 1955). Nevertheless, they were cities, not farming villages, because their residents did not grow their own food. Until agriculture became relatively efficient, there were no cities.

Warfare

Improved agriculture produced something else new in human affairs: warfare. Hunter-gatherers sometimes chased others off their hunting territory or raided other bands for wives, but such conflicts were infrequent because nobody had much of anything worth taking. Even the fighting that did occur was usually very styl-

ized and had only limited goals, such as causing the other side to run away. The number of fighters involved was small, and casualties were light. Many groups placed more importance on "counting coup"—touching an enemy during battle—than on killing.

With the rise of agrarian societies, all this changed. Such societies were worth raiding after harvest time to steal their crops, and many nomadic bands adopted a way of life based on raiding agricultural societies. Agricultural societies were also worth raiding to take their land or to seize control of the surplus their peasants produced.

Agrarian societies lived in a chronic state of warfare. In a historical survey of eleven European nations during their centuries as agrarian societies, Pitirim Sorokin (1937) computed that they had been at war 46 percent of the time. Lenski (1966) reports that Sorokin's figures are probably too low because he ignored many minor conflicts. Marc Bloch (1962) characterized agrarian European history as "the state of perpetual war."

Table 10-2 lets us take a more global view of agricultural development and external warfare. Ross (1983) coded levels of external warfare for eighty-four of the societies included in the Standard Cross-Cultural Sample. Societies have been rated as constantly at war if they are at war at least part of every year. Warfare is scored as common if a society gets into a war at least every five years. Societies having wars less often were rated as having occasional warfare. More than 80 percent of the fully agrarian societies have a war at least once every five years, and two-thirds of them fight every year. Only one-third of the societies lacking agriculture are constantly at war, and nearly half of them fight only occasionally. Constant warfare contributes greatly to the extreme stratification of agrarian societies.

Surplus and stratification

In the agrarian society we can first apply Marx's notions about the ownership of the means of production. In simple societies the means of production were primarily physical and therefore personal. But when the means of production are material things, they can be conceived of as property. Fields are different from land that is simply out there to travel over in search of game; fields must be cleared, planted, cultivated, and harvested. Thus, the question arises: Whose field? The answer to that question determines who is rich and who is not. In addition to land, many other forms of potential property existed, such as farming tools, livestock, seed, permanent houses, and the food stored from the last harvest. Because wealth was substantial, some people became much wealthier than others (Harris, 1979).

The increased wealth of agrarian societies combined with (and permitted) a complex division of labor that produced even greater stratification. We have seen that it is hard for one hunter to be much wealthier than another. But, as Chapter 9 demonstrated, persons in a particular occupation can have bargaining advantages over persons in other occupations. Because durable wealth existed in agrarian societies, bargaining advantages could be stored up to produce increasingly greater inequalities.

Indeed, because human labor in agrarian societies was so productive, other humans could be exploited. When people can barely produce enough to feed and clothe themselves, others cannot live off their labor. But in agrarian societies, a few could live off the labor of many. This

■ Even very primitive agriculture made human societies incredibly richer than before. Here we see people in Senegal grinding wheat in a way similar to that used thousands of years ago by the earliest agrarians. In addition to giving them a reliable food supply, agriculture makes it possible for them to have the large houses that can be seen in the background and a great many possessions beyond the means of hunting and gathering societies.

capacity for labor to produce surplus—that is, for peasants to grow more food than they required to live—was the basis for the marked inequalities found in such societies.

The ability to produce a surplus raises the possibility of *humans becoming property.* When labor produces little or no surplus, there is no profit in owning another person. But when labor produces surplus, then by owning another person one can possess all of the surplus that the

Table 10-3 ■ Agricultural development and stratification.

Degree of Stratification	Level of Agricultural Development			
	None	Low	Medium	High
Low	86.8%	78.5%	63.5%	38.6%
Medium	13.2%	17.9%	31.7%	15.8%
High	0.0%	3.6%	4.8%	45.6%
	100.0%	100.0%	100.0%	100.0%
N =	(38)	(28)	(63)	(57)

Source: Prepared by the author from the Standard Cross-Cultural Sample as selected by Murdock and White (1969).

other person can produce. In fact, when people are sufficiently productive, they can support those whose task is to keep them enslaved. With the emergence of slavery, the human being became a means of production (Patterson, 1982).

The production of surplus also makes government possible. Full-time specialists who coordinate the activities of societies can be supported. Thus, at the apex of every agrarian society was a ruling elite whose members "neither spin nor reap" but who lived by extracting surplus production in the form of taxes and tributes from the peasants.

Table 10-3 presents the strong link between agricultural productivity and stratification. No societies lacking agriculture have a high degree of stratification, while nearly half of the fully agrarian societies are highly stratified. Conversely, nearly 90 percent of societies that have not yet developed agriculture are rated as having a low degree of stratification as compared with about a third of the most agrarian societies.

Military domination

In agrarian societies, the elite held power by dominating the military force. The production of surplus also made this possible by enabling some members of society to become soldiers and to specialize in developing and using military technology. As these specialists began to

appear, a gap opened between the military capacity of the average man and that of the specialist soldier. Marc Bloch (1962) pointed out that so long as the average male citizen is a potential soldier who lacks nothing "essential in his equipment," he can resist being exploited. In simple societies, the weapons of war were much like those used for hunting, and all able-bodied adult males were therefore armed and capable of battle.

But with surplus production the means of warfare became specialized and differed from hunting weapons. Soon a special group of men existed who had been trained from childhood in the tactics and techniques of fighting and who possessed superior weapons and equipment for war. The medieval peasant, armed with a hayhook, an axe, or a knife, was simply no match for the heavily armored knight. A great deal of wealth was needed to equip one knight with armor, lance, long sword, and an adequate horse (see Special Topic 5). Thus, surplus provides the conditions necessary for a ruling class to monopolize military capacity (Lenski, 1966).

Because agrarian societies were based on military rule, they also tended to be expansionist. Armies are expensive to maintain, even when they are not fighting. Rulers therefore often paid for their armies by having them seize or plunder neighboring people—hence the chronic warfare found in such societies. Moreover, chronic warfare also centralized power within the ruling

■ Soon agrarian societies produced sufficient wealth so that ruling elites could live in immense splendor. In medieval society feasting was a major social activity for the wealthy, and the amounts sometimes consumed seem extraordinary. For example, when a new Prior of Canterbury was installed in 1309, his guests consumed 36 oxen, 100 hogs, 200 piglets, 200 sheep, 1,000 geese, 793 chickens, 24 swans, 600 rabbits, 9,600 eggs, and huge amounts of bread and wine. Needless to say, the Prior's peasants had to tighten their belts that winter while their flocks and herds recovered.

elite, who surrendered power to a king or an emperor (Lenski, 1966).

Culture and ascriptive status

Often ruling elites did not evolve within agrarian societies but were imposed from without. As the Mongols did in China, frequently a group of nomadic raiders, who lived by repeatedly plundering a farming region, would decide to settle down and become permanent exploiters of the region by ruling over it and gathering taxes. For this reason, ruling elites in agrarian societies were often of a different ethnic background and occasionally spoke a different language from that of their subjects. Thus, cultural differences reinforced stratification: Those on

the bottom had to cross a cultural as well as an economic barrier to rise in the system.

Moreover, even if the ruling elite was not a different ethnic group, cultural differences between members of the elite and their subjects soon appeared. A major difference between any elite and the masses is leisure. The rise of civilization—the development of an elaborate culture—is rooted in the existence of a leisure class (Veblen, 1899).

People who tilled the fields or dug in mines from dawn until dusk had little time to study the heavens, compose poems, pursue theology, or invent new tools. Such activities require spare time, which can only be provided by surplus production that frees people from labor. The elite alone had leisure and were therefore the primary creators of culture. Because they created culture, the ruling elites developed a culture much more elaborate than the culture of those whom they ruled.

The most visible cultural differences between the elite and the masses involved speech, etiquette, protocol, and even body language (Braudel, 1981). Thus, the leisure of the elite was translated into a huge array of interaction cues that strongly influenced how prestige was displayed, protected, and passed on. A peasant who donned fine clothes and attempted to impersonate a gentleman had little chance of succeeding. He would talk wrong, walk wrong, and act wrong. The cultural barrier between the elite and the masses made it virtually impossible for a person not born and raised in the elite to fit in, even if she or he somehow managed to achieve high rank. This cultural wall not only severely limited upward mobility but also restricted contact between the elite and the masses, thus widening the gap between them. Indeed, in agrarian societies the elite often came to believe that it belonged to a superior human species.

As a result of these factors, agrarian societies were extraordinarily stratified. The overwhelming majority toiled endlessly and had but the barest necessities of life. Braudel (1981) reported that in agrarian societies around the world the peasants were (and are) physically stunted by their meager diets. These usually consisted of nothing but boiled grain (rice, wheat, oats, or corn) or bread and vegetables in season. Meat and dairy products were the rarest luxuries. Indeed, the dramatic change in diet resulting from industrialization was the primary reason for the marked changes in the size and age of maturation of humans, discussed in Chapter 5. Peasants in agrarian societies had to work very hard and received very little, and their lives were restricted. Sometimes they were slaves. Usually they were bound by law and custom to remain on the land where they were born and accept their lot.

Above the huge mass of peasants in agrarian societies were artisans and merchants, who were well off by comparison but who had little power, property, or prestige compared with the nobility—the actual ruling elite. The elite was a tiny proportion of the overall population, rarely more than 2 percent and usually much less (Lenski, 1966). At the apex of the elite was a king or an emperor, surrounded by a splendid court, who possessed immense power and incredible wealth. The ruler took as much as one-fourth of the society's production, and the ruling elite as a whole may have had as much as half (Lenski, 1966). Thus, while poor people in industrial societies are far richer than average people in agrarian societies, the most powerful people in agrarian societies are far wealthier than the richest members of industrial societies. No person in North America has the wealth that an average Egyptian pharaoh took with him to his tomb, to say nothing of the many palaces staffed by thousands of servants he left behind. And Catherine the Great of Russia personally owned about 27 million serfs—peasants held in virtual slavery who farmed her immense estates. The most successful agrarian societies of history—ancient Egypt, Rome, Byzantium, Persia, China, the Inca and Aztec empires, and the nations of medieval Europe—were the most highly stratified societies in the history of the world.

Industrial Societies

The historical succession of human societies clearly shows that whenever human beings are able to produce more, their societies become more unequal. The hunting and gathering nomads had almost nothing and were relatively egalitarian. Simple gardening technology increased the degree of stratification. As fields grew larger and life became more secure, the gap between those on the bottom and those on top became immense. Undoubtedly the conditions of life of the average person improved as societies became more complex; even though most of their crop was taken from them, medieval peasants ate and lived better than hunter-gatherers (Braudel, 1981). But the life of the average person became progressively inferior to the life of the powerful. Ironically, the more productive human labor became, the more that laborers could "pay" someone to oppress and exploit them.

Thus, it is not surprising that nineteenth-

■ The productivity gains made possible by the invention of agriculture had the ironic consequence of making possible extreme levels of exploitation, including slavery. Egyptian slaves, like these depicted in a pharaoh's tomb, could be held in bondage because they could produce an economic surplus—a surplus that made it possible and worthwhile to enslave them.

century scholars expected that the staggering increases in productivity made possible by industrialization would make societies even more stratified. Marx, for one, predicted that the ruling class would become ever smaller and ever richer, while everyone else was crushed into the proletariat. He believed that wages would fall to the lowest possible level and lead to industrial slavery: masses of workers forced to toil at their machines in return for only the barest essentials. But it didn't turn out that way.

The trend toward greater stratification in response to greater productivity suddenly reversed itself. Instead of all but a few being crushed into the lowest working class, the middle classes expanded rapidly, and unskilled labor jobs began to disappear. The gap in the standard of living between the top and bottom levels of society narrowed. Welfare programs were insti-

tuted to place a "safety net" under society to prevent privation. Social mobility greatly increased. Thus, status was based much less on ascription than on achievement.

Table 10-4 lets us see this pattern in global perspective. The data are based on the fifty most populous nations of the world. Some of them are highly industrialized; some are still primarily agrarian societies. We can measure the degree of stratification in each society as the percent of total national income that goes to the richest 10 percent of families. That is, the more stratified the society, the larger the portion of income the elite will receive. Notice the very strong, *negative* correlations between this measure of stratification and five measures of industrial development and modernization. These measures show that, in effect, where there is more wealth to be had, it is being shared more equi-

Table 10-4 ■ Correlations between stratification and industrialization.

	Percent of Total National Income Going to Richest 10 Percent of Families
TV sets per 1,000	− .64
Percent of labor force employed in industry	− .53
Per capita electricity consumption	− .60
Daily average calorie supply	− .58
Average life expectancy	− .61

Source: Prepared by the author from ShowCase Presentational Software, *World: The Fifty Most Populous Nations,* data selected and supervised by Robert Szafran (Seattle: Cognitive Development, Inc., 1987).

tably. For example, in nations where more people own TVs, a smaller share of national income goes to the richest 10 percent. The same holds where a larger proportion of the labor force is employed in industry, where per capita electricity consumption is higher, where there is more to eat, and where people live longer.

Why did these patterns emerge? Why did stratification decline as societies industrialized? And what does the stratification system look like in modern industrial societies? To answer these questions, we shall examine the Canadian and American stratification systems, partly because they have been the most exhaustively studied and partly because the basic aspects of stratification in democratic nations are similar.

Industrialization and stratification

To explain why industrialization led to less stratification, we must combine insights from functionalist and conflict theories of stratification, as summarized in Chapter 9. Industrialization caused two major social changes that reduced stratification.

The first change is that industrialization raised the level of skill and training required to perform the average job (Lipset and Bendix, 1959; Wallerstein, 1974). Or, as Peter Drucker (1969) put it, **industrial societies** are not based on getting people to work harder, but to "work smarter." Laborers with picks and shovels undoubtedly work much harder to build a road than bulldozer operators do, but by working smarter rather than harder, one bulldozer driver does the work of hundreds of hand laborers. This is what the term **industrialization** means: using technology to make work much more productive.

However, industrialization changed more than tools and work techniques. It also changed the skills needed to do the work. For example, illiterates can do an excellent job of shoveling dirt. Nor do shovelers need to know any arithmetic. They also need no special training to use their tools or maintain them. This is not true for bulldozer operators. They need to be able to read and follow directions on how much dirt to remove and where to put it. They need training to operate their machines skillfully and to maintain and repair them.

To the extent that occupational positions require education and training they are *less replaceable.* Laborers employed to shovel dirt

■ In modern industrial societies there has been a rapid trend toward more complex and skilled jobs, while unskilled jobs have been disappearing. The result has been to make the average worker *less replaceable* and therefore to decrease the wage differentials across jobs.

can easily be substituted for those employed to hoe fields, but a bulldozer driver cannot be replaced so easily by operators of modern farm machines. It follows from the functionalist theory of stratification that as positions become less replaceable, their relative rewards increase.

In the long run, industrialization has made the average worker less replaceable. Compared with workers in agrarian societies, a much greater investment of time and money must be expended to prepare the average industrial worker for his or her job. Not until industrialization changed the nature of work did any society attempt to teach everyone to read, write, and do arithmetic. Indeed, technological soci-

eties can exist only with an educated labor force. As a result, the average worker can produce much more than before. More importantly, the training necessary to do most jobs has enabled workers to demand a higher level of reward.

This leads to a second consequence of industrialization: The average worker is more powerful and thus more able to resist coercion. As a result, wages and profits are determined by bargaining rather than by force. In agrarian societies, force or the threat of force could be used to get people to work hard. For example, overseers with whips could keep slaves busy digging ditches. But it is much more difficult to force people to work smarter—slaves did not seek ways to be more productive. Moreover, as members of a society are educated and trained, it becomes increasingly costly to coerce them, because education inevitably increases awareness and raises aspirations (Lipset and Bendix, 1959). For this reason, it was illegal to educate blacks in many parts of the American South before the Civil War (Sowell, 1978).

Industrialization has gone hand in hand with the rise of democracy. As we shall see in Chapter 17, some social theorists argue that economic exploitation by the ruling elite had to be curtailed for industrialization to occur; thus, democratization caused the Industrial Revolution. Even if this argument is not valid, industrialization clearly caused the proliferation of democracy—for example, it greatly expanded the proportion of the population allowed to vote. As the gap in skill and training required of average jobs and the most demanding jobs has decreased, so have the differences in power between the members of these occupations.

According to conflict theory, people exploit their power to influence their rewards. Thus, as large sectors of the population in industrialized societies became more powerful, they demanded a larger share of the economic pie. Let us recall the toy society discussed in Chapter 9. There we saw that under conditions of political freedom, the Cees and the Dees could use their numbers to obtain a better bargain with the Ays and the Bees. Thus, the decrease in stratification in industrialized societies can be seen as the outcome of ongoing conflict over who will get what. For example, automobile factory workers receive a lower wage than they would like but higher than management would like to pay. Both sides compromise on the basis of the relative costs of a strike.

To sum up, industrialization could yield incredible levels of production only by changing the nature of work. Thus, it not only led to an immense rise in the possible level of living for the average person but it also made such a rise necessary. Because in order for the average worker to become so much more productive, he or she had to receive far more education and training. This, in turn, made the average worker much less replaceable and hence more power-

ful. Therefore, it became necessary to satisfy workers' demands for a larger share.

Keep in mind that this does *not* mean that industrialized societies are unstratified. The rich and the poor, the powerful and the weak, the famous and the unknown exist in all societies. Two things distinguish industrialized from agrarian societies. First, industrialized societies are less stratified—there is a smaller gap between the top and the bottom; second, even the poor in industrialized societies are better off than rather well-off people in agrarian societies. With the rise of industrial societies, for the first time since humans settled down and began to build complex civilizations, the trend toward increased social inequality was reversed.

Industrialization did more than simply reduce stratification; it also dramatically changed the *rules* governing stratification. Status was no longer primarily ascriptive, but came to depend more on achievement. This change stimulated (and was stimulated by) social mobility. Indeed, to really understand stratification systems in industrial nations, the best thing to study is social mobility: How common is it for people to rise or fall in the stratification system, and why and how do they do so?

Social mobility in industrialized nations

Historically, North America has been regarded as the land of opportunity, where hard work could lead to success regardless of family background. Alexis de Tocqueville, a French aristocrat who visited the United States during the 1830s and wrote the classic study *Democracy in America* (1835), was surprised not only that Americans frequently achieved great wealth and power despite humble beginnings but also that they were proud to have done so. In Europe, Tocqueville noted, upwardly mobile people tried to hide their humble origins. Tocqueville, like nearly all other observers, assumed that upward mobility was unusually common in the United States compared with other industrializing nations.

■ Alexis de Tocqueville.

During the 1930s and 1940s, American sociologists began research on social mobility and found that indeed many Americans did rise above their social origins, while others were downwardly mobile. But was this a high rate of mobility? Any answer required a *comparison*, and studies comparing social mobility in America with that in other countries were lacking. Let us watch as two sociologists pioneered comparative studies of social mobility, thereby opening issues to which an immense amount of research has been directed ever since.

Lipset and Bendix: comparative social mobility

 In the 1950s Seymour Martin Lipset and Reinhard Bendix, two sociologists at the University of California at Berkeley, set out to see how much social mobility there was in the United States compared with other industrial nations. Such a study had only just become possible because of the spread of public opinion polling to many industrial nations after World War II. Often these studies asked respondents their occupation and sometimes the question "What was your father's occupation?" (Until very recently, because so many women did not work or held only short-term employment, mobility studies covered only males.)

Lipset and Bendix (1959) collected opinion poll studies from a number of industrialized nations and calculated for each nation the proportion of sons whose occupations were of higher status than the occupations of their fathers and vice versa. This allowed them to compare the rates of upward and downward mobility for these nations.

They found a great amount of social mobility in *all* the industrialized democracies studied. In fact, the total amount of social mobility was virtually identical (see Figure 10-2.) These findings seemed to refute the widespread belief that the United States has an unusually open stratification system. Thus, Lipset and Bendix concluded that the interesting question was not why there was so much social mobility in the United States but why there was so much mobility in all of these societies despite great differences in their cultures and social histories.

Lipset and Bendix argued that status based on individual achievement is inherent in the technological demands of industrial societies. Efficiency is the dominant concern in these societies, and therefore inept offspring of successful parents are necessarily displaced downward by more talented people moving up from below.

Also, a great deal of the upward mobility Bendix and Lipset observed in these societies is *structural mobility*. That is, industrialization has greatly increased the proportion of higher-status occupations and has correspondingly decreased lower-status occupations. As we saw in Chapter 9, when this occurs, many people must be upwardly mobile just to fill the demand. Figure 10-2 reveals that in the societies studied by Lipset and Bendix, a much larger proportion of people had risen than had fallen in occupational status.

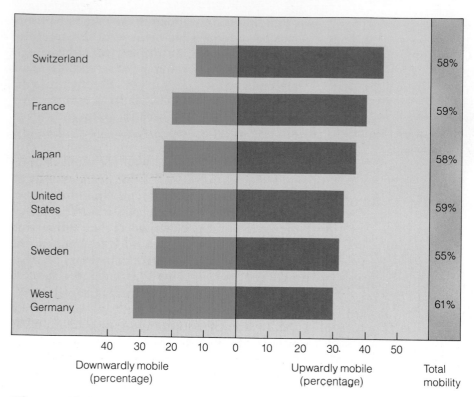

Figure 10-2 ■ **International comparisons of mobility.** These data, gathered and published by Lipset and Bendix (1959), show why they concluded that high rates of mobility are characteristic of industrialized nations in general, not just the United States. There is little difference in the total amount of mobility they found in these six nations, but there are significant differences in the amount of downward mobility, with West Germany being higher than others and Switzerland being lower. Later research showed, however, that the United States does differ from other industrial nations in its rate of long-range (rags-to-riches) upward mobility.

When structural change forces a great deal of upward mobility, people's attitudes are likely to change. That is, when upward mobility is common and not at the expense of people born into high-status families, it is hard to oppose it or to discriminate against those who have risen.

As pioneers, Lipset and Bendix had to conduct their research with serious limitations. Lacking large samples, they were limited to very crude measures of social mobility. They were forced to define mobility as movement between only two general levels of occupations: persons holding white-collar (or nonmanual) jobs and those holding blue-collar (or manual) jobs. A

man was scored as upwardly mobile if his father had been a factory worker and he was an office clerk. Thus, small differences between the occupations of a father and his son could register as upward mobility. These crude measures also prevented Lipset and Bendix from assessing dramatic changes in status.

A decade later much better data became available on social mobility. Although these confirmed Lipset and Bendix's conclusion that mobility is high in all modern, industrial societies, they also showed that, compared with Europe, there was something unusual about social mobility in the United States. **Long-dis-**

tance mobility involves huge upward or downward shifts in status—as when an unskilled laborer's child becomes a brain surgeon or president of a large corporation. Blau and Duncan (1967) reported that 1 out of every 10 sons of manual workers in the United States ends up in an elite managerial or professional occupation. By comparison only 1 Italian in 300 makes such a leap, 1 Dane in 100, and 1 Frenchman in 67. Thus, what separates Americans of humble origins from their European counterparts is not upward mobility per se but rather the much greater chance of going all the way.

Blau and Duncan: the status attainment model

 Aside from the question of *how much* social mobility goes on in modern societies, for decades sociologists sought answers to a second important question: What determines an individual's chances of achieving upward mobility? Then two sociologists realized that this wasn't quite the right question to ask.

Peter M. Blau and Otis Dudley Duncan (1967) pointed out that the answer to this question is so simple that it isn't meaningful. They wrote:

The lower the level from which a person starts, the greater is the probability that he will be upwardly mobile, simply because many more occupational destinations entail upward mobility for men with low origins than for those with high ones.

That is, people's odds of rising are greater the lower their origins, and their odds of falling are greater the higher they start. The folks on the bottom can't go down; the folks on top can't go up. But, Blau and Duncan pointed out, this trivial answer reveals that the wrong question is being asked. No one would really think that the best way to get a high-status position would be to be sure to start out on the bottom. So, Blau and Duncan argued, the question is not how are people mobile, but how do people attain their statuses? Put that way, we can see how people acquire a status with or without being mobile.

Blau and Duncan conducted a landmark research study to provide answers to their revised question, and ever since then their results (and other work of this kind) have been known as the **status attainment model.** The study was based on interviews with a national sample of 20,700 selected American men, 20 to 64 years of age. The U.S. Bureau of the Census conducted the interviews in 1962, using questions prepared by Blau and Duncan.

Not surprisingly, Blau and Duncan found that it's better to start at the top than at the bottom of the stratification system. Men whose fathers held high-status jobs had increased odds of holding a high-status job too. However, the correlation was considerably weaker than many would have expected. Moreover, the primary mechanism linking the occupational status of fathers and sons turned out to be education.

The higher a man's status, the more years of education his son is likely to receive. And there is a very strong correlation between education and occupational status: Many high-status jobs such as doctor and lawyer have advanced-degree requirements. With education controlled, Blau and Duncan found that the influence of family background (father's occupation) on status attainment is rather modest.

Blau and Duncan's work prompted many other sociologists to study status attainment. An interesting twist was added by Christopher Jencks and his colleagues (1972), who sought to measure the effects of family background on occupational achievement by comparing sets of brothers. Jencks found that brothers were nearly as different in their levels of status attainment as were randomly selected pairs of men from the general population. For men drawn at random and paired, their average prestige scores (see Chapter 16) differed by 28 points on a 97-point scale. For brothers, the average difference was 23 points. Similarly, random pairs of men had an average difference in annual income of $6,200 a year, while the average for brothers was $5,600—nearly as great. Thus, brothers who grow up in the same home, raised by the same parents, end up nearly as different in terms of status attainment as do unrelated men who grow up in different homes.

A more recent study collected data on all members of a large sample of families over a ten-year period and traced the status attainment of family members as they left home and found their place in the occupational structure. The study included an extra large sample of very poor families. Yinon Cohen and Andrea Tyree (1986) were therefore able to gain an unusually detailed basis for comparing factors governing upward mobility among the very poor with those operating among people from more favorable backgrounds. Once again the data confirmed a lot of mobility: Two-thirds of the children from the poorest families escaped from the bottom 20 percent income group, and over one-third made it to the upper 40 percent income group. Although we have long known that education is a key to status attainment, Cohen and Tyree found that education has greater importance for status attainment for people from poor homes than it does for others. Finally, Cohen and Tyree's data forced sociologists to recognize something new: Marital status is the main determinant of family income, regardless of a person's background. Getting married and staying married has more to do with family income than any other factor because affluence today is mainly the result of two-earner families, as Special Topic 2 will show. Or, as Cohen and Tyree put it, "The probability of escape from poverty for single men and women, especially the latter, is considerably less than for married men and women."

John Porter and colleagues: status attainment in Canada

 During his lifetime, John Porter (1921–1979) was regarded by many as Canada's leading sociologist. He was born in Vancouver and spent most of his career at Carleton University in Ottawa. During the early 1960s Porter grew determined to establish nationwide survey research as a component of Canadian social research. Moreover, he was especially interested in launching studies of

mobility and status attainment in Canada, for he had concluded that his nation had a needlessly rigid stratification system.

In 1964 Porter finally succeeded in raising the funds needed to conduct interviews with a nationwide sample of Canadians. To help carry on the research, Porter recruited Peter C. Pineo, who then took the lead in writing up the results (Pineo and Porter, 1967). Their initial study focused on perceptions of occupational prestige (see Chapter 16). But it also set the stage for a full-scale Canadian replication of Blau and Duncan's American study of status attainment. For as soon as the first articles by Blau and Duncan appeared in 1965, Porter set his sights on doing a Canadian version. He at once began a campaign to raise funds—an effort that took him nearly a decade. Porter's target was to collect data from 44,000 Canadians over the age of 17. As the project grew, Porter and Pineo recruited others to aid them: Frank E. Jones, Monica Boyd, John Goyder, and Hugh A. McRoberts. In 1973 the study was launched, under the auspices of Statistics Canada (Pineo, 1981; Vallee, 1981).

The Canadian study was much more than simply a repeat of Blau and Duncan's work. A most important step was the inclusion of women. As noted, mobility and status attainment studies had been limited to male respondents because so many women were not employed outside the home; many women who were, worked only from time to time and did not pursue long-range occupational goals. But as the baby boom began to ebb, patterns of female employment began to change, and by the 1970s it was both feasible and important to include women in such a study.

Porter and his colleagues expected that their results would be very different from Blau and Duncan's. Canadians, including many nonsociologists, had long believed that there was much less social mobility in Canada than in the United States—that opportunities for occupational advancement were much more restricted in Canada than in most other industrialized nations. As Porter wrote in his major work, *The Vertical Mosaic* (1965), "Canada has not been a mobility oriented society," a situation that he blamed partly on a lack of educational opportunities. In addition, Porter—along with most Canadian observers—believed that ethnicity and immigrant status played unusually prominent roles in the Canadian stratification system. Indeed, he used the term *vertical mosaic* to suggest a stratification system constructed of distinctive ethnic strata.

The results of the massive 1973 survey produced some stunning surprises (Pineo, 1976, 1977; Boyd et al., 1981). Canada was *not* an exception to Lipset and Bendix's proposition that social mobility is high in all industrialized nations. Canada's rate of social mobility is almost identical to that of the United States. Moreover, the Blau and Duncan status attainment model for the United States is duplicated in Canada. Table 10-5 compares the correlations between father's occupational prestige and son's occupational prestige for Canada and the United States. It is exactly .40 in both national studies. The table also shows the correlations between an individual's education and his occupational prestige. The results are .60 for the United States and .61 for Canada.

Now notice something else in Table 10-5. For Canada the correlations are repeated for various subgroups, letting us examine the impact of ethnicity—long thought to be so potent in Canadian stratification. Thus native- and foreign-born men can be compared, as can English- and French-speaking men. This reveals that the father-to-son transmission of status is the same within all four groups and so is the correlation between a man's education and his occupational prestige. This does not mean that these groups are equal in terms of their occupational prestige (although the differences in average occupational prestige scores turned out to be small); it does mean that the process of status attainment is very similar for all four.

How did John Porter react to evidence that some portions of his most famous book were wrong or at least overstated? Like a scientist. Peter Pineo (1981) recalls:

I began writing up the material and sent advance copies of everything to Porter. He reacted quite cheerfully to it all and . . . volunteered that he would like to collaborate [in writing final drafts of the findings].

Table 10-5 ■ **Status attainment in the United States and Canada.**

Father's Occupational Prestige	
Son's Occupational Prestige	(Correlation)
United States	.40
Canada	.40
Native-born	.40
Foreign-born	.45
English-speaking	.40
French-speaking	.41

Son's Education	
Son's Occupational Prestige	(Correlation)
United States	.60
Canada	.61
Native-born	.62
Foreign-born	.63
English-speaking	.62
French-speaking	.61

Source: Blau and Duncan (1967); Boyd et al. (1981).

Subsequent status attainment studies in Canada have confirmed the findings of the 1973 research project. Thus, in a detailed study of men in Ontario, Ornstein (1981) found that ethnicity as such plays a very slight role in status attainment, especially if one takes into account generational differences in education and language acquisition. He also demonstrated that the statistical model that most closely fits status attainment in Canada is extremely similar to the model for the United States.

Female status attainment

When the Canadian sociologists analyzed their data on female status attainment, they also found some surprising results (Boyd et al., 1981). First of all, native-born Canadian women with full-time jobs come from higher-status family backgrounds than do their male counterparts. On the average, their fathers have nearly a year more of education and hold higher-status occupations. Secondly, the average native-born Canadian working woman has a higher-status occupation than do similar males. Finally, the correlations between women's occupational prestige and their fathers' education (.26) and occupational prestige (.22) are much *lower* than for men. Moreover, these same findings have turned up in American studies; it has now become standard practice to include women in status attainment research (Featherman and Hauser, 1976; Treiman and Terrell, 1975). How can these patterns be explained?

First of all, women are less likely than men are to hold full-time jobs and are especially unlikely to work, the lower their job qualifications. For many married women, especially those with young children, low-paying jobs offer no real economic benefits; the costs of working (including child care) are about equal to the wages paid. In consequence, low-paying, low-status jobs are disproportionately held by males. This fact accounts for women having jobs of higher average prestige. But, women also are underrepresented in the highest prestige jobs. As a result their occupational prestige is limited to a narrower range than that of men, which reduces correlations with background variables. That the average working woman's father has more education and a better job than the father of the average employed male can be understood in the same terms. More-qualified women come from more-privileged homes; the daughters of the least-educated and lowest-status fathers aren't in full-time jobs. In fact, the *husbands* of working women have occupations with higher than average prestige. This is because of a very high correspondence in the occupational prestige of husbands and wives, when both are employed full-time (Hout, 1982). People who marry tend to share very similar levels of education and similar family backgrounds. Indeed, as we shall see in Chapter 13, divorce and remarriage contribute to the similarity of husbands and wives in terms of occupational prestige (Jacobs and Furstenberg, 1986).

These findings must not cause us to overlook the fact that women long were excluded from many occupations and are still underrepresented in elite managerial and professional careers. What they do show, however, is that within the special conditions outlined above, female status attainment does not differ much from that of men.

The primary results of status attainment research in the United States, Canada, and subsequently in many other nations sustain the arguments first developed by Lipset and Bendix. High rates of mobility and a decline in ascribed status do appear to be inherent in the technological demands of industrialized societies, therefore making performance rather than connections primary in occupational attainment. Indeed, Tepperman (1976) has been able to create a formal model of shifts in social mobility as societies undergo industrialization, predicting the shape of stratification systems and of mobility rates over time.

But, if status tends to depend more on achievement than on ascription in all industrialized societies, not all persons in North America (or elsewhere) have been freed of ascriptive status rules. Until recently, racial and ethnic discrimination has excluded some groups of North Americans from most of the better jobs. In the next chapter we examine this matter in depth.

Conclusion

Chapter 9 presented the basic concepts and theories sociologists use to understand stratification. In this chapter we have used these concepts and theories to examine how stratification systems work in different societies. We have seen that the relative lack of stratification among primitive hunter-gatherers was an equality of poverty. The rise of civilization and the rise of social inequalities went hand in hand. As societies became more productive and complex, the masses of humanity were increasingly exploited by a tiny elite. But this trend was reversed with the advent of modern industrial societies, despite expectations that these would become the most stratified societies in history.

We have also seen that industrialization

increased the skills required for most occupations and therefore decreased the replaceability of the average worker. This improved the bargaining position of the average worker and led to a reduction in inequalities. Moreover, the development of democracy in industrial societies has severely limited the ability of the elites to use force to exploit others. In this way, status based on ascription has given way to status based on achievement in industrial societies.

But these changes have not affected everyone in these societies, at least not at the same time. Thus, while some people can achieve high status, others continue to be ascribed a low status, especially those who belonged to certain racial or ethnic groups. In the next chapter we shall apply principles of stratification and an understanding of stratification systems in modern industrial nations to analyze ethnic and racial conflict.

Review Glossary

hunting and gathering societies The most primitive human societies; their rather small numbers of members (often less than fifty) live by wandering in pursuit of food from animals and plants. (p. 259)

agrarian societies Societies that live by farming. Although these were the first societies able to support cities, they usually require that about 95 percent of the population be engaged in agriculture. (p. 263)

industrial societies Societies with economies based on manufacturing in which machines perform most of the heavy labor. (p. 270)

industrialization The process by which technology is substituted for manual labor as the basis of production. (p. 270)

long-distance mobility Mobility that occurs when an individual or group rises from the bottom to the top of the stratification system. (pp. 274–275)

status attainment model The process by which individuals achieve their positions in the stratification system. (p. 275)

Suggested Readings

Blau, Peter M., and Otis Dudley Duncan. 1967. *The American Occupational Structure.* New York: Wiley.

Bloch, Marc. *Feudal Society.* 1962. Chicago: University of Chicago Press.

Boyd, Monica, John Goyder, Frank E. Jones, Hugh A. McRoberts, Peter C. Pineo, and John Porter. 1981. "Status Attainment in Canada: Findings of the Canadian Mobility Study." *Canadian Review of Sociology and Anthropology* 18: 651–673.

Giddens, Anthony. 1975. *The Class Structure of Advanced Societies.* New York: Harper & Row.

Patterson, Orlando. 1982. *Slavery and Social Death: A Comparative Study.* Cambridge, Mass.: Harvard University Press.

Aspects of Income Inequalities in America

The past two chapters have attempted to classify stratification systems and to explain how they function. Our attention has focused on the "big picture," on societies as systems. However, macro sociological perspectives sometimes tend to divert attention away from individuals. In this instance, our efforts to understand stratification systems may have led us to ignore how individuals actually experience stratification. What is life like for people in various strata within a society? As a corrective, we pause here to explore survey data on groups of Americans with different levels of annual family income. Keep in mind that this is not an essay on poverty, but is intended as a statistical portrait of class contrasts.

The 1986 General Social Survey asked a national sample of 1,470 Americans 18 and over to report their total annual family income. This total is a better estimate of wealth than an individual's income is. For example, based on their lack of any personal income, many housewives and students might appear to be penniless, but might in fact be affluent because of other family members' earnings. Similarly, two people with the same salary could enjoy rather different economic positions if only one of them has an employed spouse.

Figure ST2-1 shows the income distribution of adult Americans. Notice the shape of the income levels; it is typical of stratification systems in advanced industrial democracies. Recall that in agrarian societies stratification systems are shaped like a pyramid—a huge base of very poor people topped by increasingly smaller lay-

ers of the more affluent. But the shape we see here is more like a diamond, having a smaller base of lowest income families, a wide layer in the middle-income level, tapering to small layers of upper-income families. Admittedly, the figure is based on somewhat arbitrary judgments about how families ought to be grouped. For example, had I decided that all families with incomes less than $20,000 a year were equally poor, then the figure would form a pyramid with 45.5 percent of the nation on the bottom. I used two criteria for selecting these divisions. The first was to have enough people in each cate-

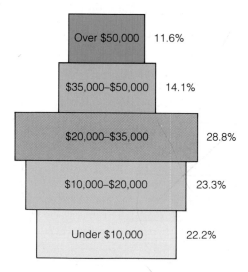

Figure ST2-1 ■ **Annual family income.**
(*Source:* Prepared by the author from National Opinion Research Center, General Social Survey, 1986).

Table ST2-1 ■ **Income and class identification.**

Class Identification	Annual Family Income					
	Under $10,000	$10,000– $20,000	$20,000– $35,000	$35,000– $50,000	Over $50,000	Total
"If you were asked to use one of four names for your social class, which would you say you belong in?"						
"Lower"	21.4%	5.1%	0.8%	0.5%	0.6%	6.3%
"Working"	41.7%	55.4%	53.4%	31.7%	12.3%	43.5%
"Middle"	34.9%	39.2%	43.5%	65.7%	71.6%	47.0%
"Upper"	2.0%	0.3%	2.3%	2.1%	15.5%	3.2%
	100.0%	100.0%	100.0%	100.0%	100.0%	100.0%

Source: Prepared by the author from National Opinion Research Center, General Social Survey, 1986.

gory to provide a reasonably stable basis for calculating and comparing the percentages that appear in the many tables included in this Special Topic. The second is a matter of effective conceptualization and operationalization. If our intention is to group people who are similar in terms of their economic position and hence to separate groups that hold substantially different positions, then these groups ought to display substantial differences in other closely related aspects of stratification. Put another way, the best way to assess these income groupings is to see how well they work.

Table ST2-1 offers evidence that people in these groups tend to be well aware of their relative position in the American stratification system. Respondents were asked to identify their class position—often called a person's subjective class—and were offered four class names to choose from. The patterns of selection reveal marked differences among these five income groups. Very few Americans identify themselves as lower class, but those who do are overwhelmingly found among those with incomes of less than $10,000. Americans are even more reluctant to identify themselves as upper class, but those who do are overwhelmingly in the over $50,000 group. Many Americans identify themselves as in the working class, but this shifts substantially as we read across the table from the lowest to the highest income group.

Table ST2-2 provides a second test of using these income levels. Overall, Americans are relatively satisfied with their present financial situation—even 19.1 percent of those earning less than $10,000 said they were "pretty well satisfied." But satisfaction levels jump upward between each income level, with 57 percent of those earning over $50,000 giving this response. About a quarter of Americans said they were "not satisfied at all" with their financial situation. Nearly half of those earning less than $10,000 were not satisfied, and this drops systematically as income levels rise.

In light of these clear differences, the lower half of the table may surprise you. Employed Americans are amazingly satisfied with their jobs at all levels of income. Granted that the upper-income groups are more apt to say they are very or moderately satisfied, but only 18.6 percent of those under $10,000 report any dissatisfaction, while 7.7 percent of those over $50,000 also are a little or very dissatisfied. In part, this is because people without jobs are not included in this table. And this helps us understand the greater contrasts that show up in Table ST2-3.

Can money buy happiness? Only to some

Table ST2-2 ■ Income and satisfaction.

	Annual Family Income					
	Under $10,000	$10,000–$20,000	$20,000–$35,000	$35,000–$50,000	Over $50,000	Total
"How satisfied with present financial situation?"						
"Pretty well satisfied"	19.1%	21.1%	32.0%	36.7%	57.0%	30.2%
"More or less satisfied"	35.9%	43.1%	47.9%	47.3%	35.3%	42.5%
"Not satisfied at all"	45.0%	35.8%	20.1%	16.0%	7.7%	27.3%
	100.0%	100.0%	100.0%	100.0%	100.0%	100.0%
"How satisfied with the work you do?"						
"Very satisfied"	41.0%	45.6%	48.1%	55.4%	65.0%	49.7%
"Moderately satisfied"	40.4%	39.7%	42.4%	39.2%	27.3%	39.0%
"A little dissatisfied"	11.5%	11.9%	8.0%	5.4%	6.3%	8.8%
"Very dissatisfied"	7.1%	2.8%	1.5%	0.0%	1.4%	2.5%
	100.0%	100.0%	100.0%	100.0%	100.0%	100.0%

Source: Prepared by the author from National Opinion Research Center, General Social Survey, 1986.

Table ST2-3 ■ Happiness and hard times.

	Annual Family Income					
	Under $10,000	$10,000–$20,000	$20,000–$35,000	$35,000–$50,000	Over $50,000	Total
"How happy would you say you are?"						
"Very happy"	21.9%	29.0%	38.3%	34.8%	42.2%	32.5%
"Pretty happy"	55.9%	60.6%	53.9%	59.4%	54.5%	56.7%
"Not too happy"	22.2%	10.4%	7.8%	5.8%	3.3%	10.8%
	100.0%	100.0%	100.0%	100.0%	100.0%	100.0%
Percent who ever have been unemployed for at least a month						
	39.1%	38.2%	28.9%	23.3%	17.3%	31.2%
Percent who have ever been on welfare						
	42.8%	22.6%	13.1%	6.9%	3.2%	19.9%

Source: Prepared by the author from National Opinion Research Center, General Social Survey, 1986.

■ Not so many years ago, when a man kissed his wife good-bye after breakfast, he headed for the office while she did the dishes and then began to clean the house or do the laundry. But that's not what this woman is going to do. Soon after her husband has left, she will back her car out of the garage and head for *her* office. That this is a two-earner family is a major factor in their ability to afford this splendid home.

extent. Those earning over $50,000 are twice as likely as those earning less than $10,000 to say they are "very happy." However, unhappiness is not widespread at any income level. This seems all the more remarkable when we examine the sharp differences among these income groups in terms of their experience of economic hardships. About four out of ten people with incomes below $10,000 have been unemployed at least once for as long as a month, and four out of ten have also been on welfare. In contrast, virtually none of those earning over $50,000 has ever been on welfare.

Table ST2-4 displays many aspects of individual life-styles. The majority of Americans own the house or apartment in which they live, and even 40 percent of those earning less than $10,000 a year do so. Many of these are elderly people whose home was paid for prior to their retirement. Nearly all in the upper-income bracket own their dwellings.

About 7 percent of Americans live in mobile homes, and they are concentrated among the lowest-income categories, illustrating how mobile home parks often serve as low-income suburbs.

Whatever else they may do, lower-income Americans are not given to drowning their troubles in drink. The proportion of people who drink alcoholic beverages rises with income. Lower-income people are less likely to read a newspaper daily, but they are more apt to watch TV more than an hour a day.

Perhaps surprisingly, upper-income people are more than twice as likely as lower-income people to belong to a nationality group. These are organizations for persons sharing a particular ethnic background such as Sons of Norway or the German-American Association. Upper-income people also are much more likely to belong to a sports group. In fact, the more people earn, the more likely they are to belong to organizations of all kinds.

Different patterns also show up in social

Table ST2-4 ■ Life-styles.

	Annual Family Income					
	Under $10,000	$10,000–$20,000	$20,000–$35,000	$35,000–$50,000	Over $50,000	Total
Percent who own their dwelling						
	40.5%	52.3%	68.6%	78.4%	85.9%	61.9%
Percent who live in a mobile home						
	10.4%	10.2%	5.4%	2.6%	0.0%	6.6%
Percent who drink alcoholic beverages						
	56.2%	67.5%	68.6%	77.2%	84.0%	68.6%
Percent who read a newspaper daily						
	41.5%	48.4%	55.4%	63.5%	69.9%	53.5%
Percent who watch TV more than an hour each day						
	82.9%	85.1%	76.2%	69.5%	70.5%	79.0%
Percent who belong to a nationality group						
	3.0%	3.8%	5.4%	5.3%	7.1%	4.7%
Percent who belong to a sports group						
	10.0%	21.0%	25.5%	25.9%	35.3%	22.2%
Percent who belong to two or more clubs or organizations						
	30.8%	41.7%	54.1%	59.8%	65.3%	48.2%
Percent who at least once a week spend a social evening with a:						
Relative	46.5%	38.9%	34.6%	30.7%	26.9%	36.8%
Neighbor	40.9%	33.4%	23.7%	19.1%	15.4%	28.1%
Friend outside the neighborhood	26.1%	25.1%	20.4%	15.9%	21.8%	22.3%
Percent living in same city or county in which they grew up						
	50.5%	42.4%	45.1%	34.9%	30.1%	42.5%
Percent who are self-employed						
	11.2%	14.0%	10.4%	15.7%	21.9%	13.5%

Source: Prepared by the author from National Opinion Research Center, General Social Survey, 1986.

Table ST2-5 ■ Beliefs about human nature.

	Under $10,000	$10,000– $20,000	$20,000– $35,000	$35,000– $50,000	Over $50,000	Total
			Annual Family Income			
"Do you think most people would try to take advantage of you if they got a chance, or would they try to be fair?"						
Percent "take advantage"	46.2%	34.7%	29.6%	32.8%	19.2%	33.7%
"Generally speaking, would you say that most people can be trusted or that you can't be too careful in dealing with people?"						
Percent "can't be too careful"	72.9%	63.4%	54.9%	53.4%	44.2%	59.4%
"Would you say that most of the time people try to be helpful or that they are mostly just looking out for themselves?"						
Percent "out for themselves"	48.2%	45.9%	33.8%	36.5%	26.3%	39.3%

Source: Prepared by the author from National Opinion Research Center, General Social Survey, 1986.

activities. Lower-income people are much more likely than others are to socialize with relatives and with neighbors. The differences are much less marked or consistent when it comes to spending social evenings with friends who live outside of one's own neighborhood.

Lower-income people have been more likely to stay put geographically, while upper-income people tend to have moved away from the city or county in which they grew up. Finally, we see that although most Americans are employees, the self-employed are concentrated in the upper-income brackets.

Clearly, then, people with quite different incomes tend to live quite different lives—and not all of these differences reflect differences in purchasing power. Upper-income people *could* socialize a lot with their neighbors, but they don't. They also could watch more television than they do.

Now let's see if income differences are connected with what Americans believe about human nature. Table ST2-5 makes it clear that lower-income people think human beings are basically selfish and exploitative, while upper-income people think others are basically generous and trustworthy. Two opposite conclusions could be drawn from these data. The obvious one is that people judge life on the basis of their own experiences and perceptions and that lower-income people have experienced many disappointments and frustrations and so have learned to be suspicious. Keep in mind too that low-income urban neighborhoods have far higher crime rates than do upper-income neighborhoods. In contrast, upper-income people typically are being rewarded by others and have thereby learned to trust people. A less obvious conclusion is that when people answer these questions they tell as much about themselves as they do about their perceptions of others. If so, perhaps people with these attitudes are much less likely to succeed because higher-status occupations require people to operate on the

Table ST2-6 ■ Politics.

	Under $10,000	$10,000– $20,000	$20,000– $35,000	$35,000– $50,000	Over $50,000	Total
			Annual Family Income			
Percent who voted for President Reagan in 1984						
	42.6%	57.8%	61.9%	67.5%	77.6%	60.9%
Percent who regard themselves as conservatives						
	22.7%	28.3%	33.5%	41.3%	51.9%	33.1%
Percent who say they think of themselves as Democrats						
	62.3%	52.6%	50.8%	47.1%	34.6%	51.3%
Percent who think "the government should do something to reduce income differences between rich and poor"						
	40.4%	42.4%	29.2%	22.8%	10.9%	31.0%
Percent who think the government spends too *much* money on						
Welfare	27.8%	44.7%	41.5%	50.5%	46.2%	40.8%
Space program	56.3%	46.0%	35.9%	27.3%	20.0%	40.2%
Percent who think the government spends too *little* money on						
Fighting crime	69.0%	62.7%	69.7%	58.6%	49.2%	64.3%
Social security	59.9%	60.5%	58.0%	47.6%	41.7%	55.6%

Source: Prepared by the author from National Opinion Research Center, General Social Survey, 1986.

basis of mutual trust. At issue here is time order. Did status differences create differing views of human nature or did the attitudes lead to the status differences? Perhaps both processes occur.

It has been said that in democratic societies, politics is class warfare pursued by nonviolent means. Table ST2-6 offers some support for this position. Ronald Reagan won the 1984 presidential election by a three-to-two margin. Here we see that he would have lost the election by a three-to-two margin had only people with incomes below $10,000 gone to the polls. Support for the president rose significantly with each step up the income ladder.

One-third of Americans identify themselves politically as conservatives (and 22.7 percent say they are liberals). People who earn more than $50,000 are twice as likely to be conservatives

than are those who earn less than $10,000. This same pattern shows up in party identification. Almost two-thirds of the lowest income group say they are Democrats, but only one-third of those in the highest group are Democrats.

Income also greatly influences what people want from government. Although most Americans do not believe the government should attempt to redistribute income, support for government intervention is much more popular in the lower-income categories. Similarly, higher-income people judge that the government spends too much on welfare, while lower-income people object to spending on the space program. Most Americans think the government spends too little money to fight crime, but half of those over the $50,000 level do not. Lower- and upper-income Americans also disagree on social secu-

Table ST2-7 ■ **Family.**

	Annual Family Income					
	Under $10,000	$10,000–$20,000	$20,000–$35,000	$35,000–$50,000	Over $50,000	Total
Percent with four or more children	25.0%	18.8%	16.0%	14.2%	16.6%	18.8%
Percent with four or more siblings	63.9%	45.6%	44.5%	39.1%	23.1%	45.9%
Percent who married before the age of 19	34.0%	24.1%	18.1%	14.5%	10.0%	21.3%
Percent whose family income when they were 16 was below average	40.4%	33.5%	25.8%	21.1%	19.3%	29.4%
Only women who have been married: Percent currently divorced or separated	34.3%	24.7%	11.7%	7.2%	4.7%	19.4%
Women only: Percent who gave their current occupation as homemaker	44.8%	28.4%	29.6%	31.5%	25.4%	33.4%
Married men only: Percent whose wives are employed full-time outside the home	7.1%	29.0%	36.7%	45.5%	40.8%	35.6%

Source: Prepared by the author from National Opinion Research Center, General Social Survey, 1986.

rity expenditures. To sum up: Class interests play a consistent and marked role in political behavior and attitudes.

Now let's consider how various aspects of the family relate to income. Table ST2-7 shows that people in lower-income groups tend to have more children. They also tend to come from larger families: About two-thirds of those in the under $10,000 group report having four or more siblings, which means they come from families with five or more children. Lower income also is associated with early marriage. A third of those in the lowest-income group married before they turned 19, while only 10 percent in the highest group married this young.

We have seen that although there is a great deal of social mobility in the United States there still is a significant correlation between the sta-

tus of parents and their children. This shows up here as well. Forty percent of those in the lowest-income category reported that they came from families with below-average incomes as compared with about 20 percent in the highest-income groups.

The next item in the table displays a major factor in creating low-income households—female-headed households created by divorce or desertion. One-third of the under $10,000 respondents fit this description as compared with only 4.7 percent of those in the over $50,000 group. The next line in the table helps us see one reason why so many of these women have very low family incomes: they are much less likely than are other women to be employed outside the home. Here's another glimpse of the impact of female employment on income: Few

Table ST2-8 ■ Employment and income of women.

Annual Family Income	Employed Full-Time		Full-Time Homemakers	
	Married	Separated or Divorced	Married	Separated or Divorced
Under $10,000	1.5%	21.3%	15.2%	87.1%
$10,000–$20,000	17.2%	33.3%	25.0%	9.7%
$20,000–$35,000	38.8%	29.3%	32.9%	3.2%
$35,000–$50,000	20.9%	12.0%	16.5%	0.0%
Over $50,000	21.6%	4.1%	10.4%	0.0%
	100.0%	100.0%	100.0%	100.0%

Source: Prepared by the author from National Opinion Research Center, General Social Survey, 1986.

married men (7.1 percent) in the lowest income group have wives employed full-time outside the home, while more than 40 percent of men in the two highest brackets have working wives. The single most important determinant of high family income in the United States is the two-earner family.

Table ST2-8 lets us examine this factor more directly. Let's look first at women who are employed full-time outside the home. The married women have a noticeable advantage in gaining the two highest brackets of family income, and that is almost entirely because theirs are two-earner families. Conversely, married women who work full-time rarely fall into the lowest-income group. Next, let's compare separated and divorced women who work full-time with married women who are full-time homemakers. The differences are much less, for now we are comparing families with only one earner. The married women are somewhat more likely to be in the higher brackets, which simply reflects that men typically earn more than women do, as we shall explore in detail in Chapter 12. Finally, look at the separated and divorced women who are full-time homemakers. Nearly all of them are in the lowest-income bracket and rely primarily on welfare for their support. Why don't these women take jobs? A primary reason is that they are not qualified for jobs that would support them after they paid

the costs of child care. That is, most low-income divorced and separated women who are full-time homemakers are high school dropouts.

Table ST2-9 lets us see how education critically influences income. Of those in the lowest-income category, 54.5 percent did not complete high school, and only 6 percent have graduated from college. In contrast, only 5.1 percent of those earning over $50,000 are high school dropouts, while nearly half have graduated from college. Chapter 16 explores the link between income and education more fully.

Finally, as an introduction to Chapter 11, let's confront the issue of race and income. Table ST2-10 shows that blacks are much more likely than whites are to report family incomes under $10,000 and that whites are more than twice as likely as blacks are to be in the over $50,000 category. In Chapter 11 we will examine many factors, including discrimination, that enter into this picture, but a major factor is one we have just seen—the family. For reasons that will be clarified in Chapter 12, the black family is much less likely than the white family to have two earners and is much more likely to be headed by a woman who does not work outside the home. Thus, while more than 40 percent of all black families in the sample fall into the category of under $10,000 a year, no black family with two earners has an income this low, and 13 percent of these families earn over $50,000 a year.

Table ST2-9 ■ Education.

	Annual Family Income					
	Under $10,000	$10,000–$20,000	$20,000–$35,000	$35,000–$50,000	Over $50,000	Total
Percent who did not complete high school	54.5%	32.5%	19.6%	12.2%	5.1%	27.6%
Percent who graduated from college	6.0%	14.7%	18.3%	30.7%	46.5%	19.6%

Source: Prepared by the author from National Opinion Research Center, General Social Survey, 1986.

Table ST2-10 ■ Race and income.

Annual Family Income	White	Black
Under $10,000	19.5%	41.6%
$10,000–$20,000	23.0%	25.3%
$20,000–$35,000	29.5%	19.9%
$35,000–$50,000	15.2%	8.4%
Over $50,000	12.8%	4.8%

Source: Prepared by the author from National Opinion Research Center, General Social Survey, 1986.

Intergroup Conflict: Racial and Ethnic Inequality

11

THE YEAR IS 1862. The scene is the outback of Australia. Two tiny bands of natives have crossed paths. No one sees familiar faces in the other group, and everyone is tense. Then spokesmen for each group begin to discuss their ancestry, examining the family trees of both groups minutely. This is not a ritual form of greeting; its outcome may decide the fate of all present. Everyone hopes desperately that some mutual relatives will turn up in the examination, for only if the groups are related can they be friends. If they are not relatives, then they are strangers. Their language does not distinguish between the word for stranger and the word for enemy: Strangers *are* enemies. If the bands are strangers, then there is nothing to be done but flee or fight. The only good stranger is a dead one.

Fear and loathing of strangers are not peculiar to the culture of Australian aborigines. They are almost universal human traits. The outsider, the foreigner, the stranger has always provoked anxiety, suspicion, hatred, and dread in human beings (Williams, 1947). Such responses are especially likely *when the strangers are noticeably different because of cultural or physical differences*. Inventing social and cultural means to neutralize conflict between groups with noticeable differences has been one of the major tasks modern societies have faced (Lofland, 1973).

Let's return to 1862, to the western prairies of North America. Many Indian tribes still move across their ancestral hunting grounds in pursuit of the great buffalo herds. Each tribe is small, often having no more than 1,000 members. Each small tribe holds strongly negative beliefs about the other tribes, and conflicts among tribes are

frequent. However, all of the Plains tribes reserve their greatest contempt and hatred for the Utes, who live in the foothills of the Rockies. The Utes have darker skins than the other tribes, and they are universally loathed and described as ugly. Everyone thinks it natural to kill Utes whenever possible. Meanwhile, white settlers are moving onto the plains. They cannot tell one tribe from another, and to them all Indians are savages, thieves, drunkards, and dangerous killers. In time they begin to say that the only good Indian is a dead Indian.

Also in 1862, the Chinese and Japanese are just beginning to have extensive contact with Europeans. They find this contact unpleasant. European customs seem barbaric, and, to make matters worse, Europeans are very ugly. (Asians also complain that Europeans smell extremely bad. Asians bathed regularly, while Europeans almost never did so.) Because of large, protruding noses and long, narrow faces, Europeans are called "dog faces." Europeans, in turn, find the faces of Asians oddly flat, and they describe the Asians as "slant-eyed."

Nor is 1862 a banner year for brotherhood elsewhere in the world. In the United States the Civil War rages. Nearly 400,000 Yankees and Confederates will be killed, and the list of atrocities will be long. In part, this war is fought to determine whether blacks will continue to be held in slavery. Yet even if the majority of Northerners want to free the slaves, they do not intend to accept blacks into their society. Free blacks are not permitted to vote or to testify in court in most northern states, and schemes to ship all blacks back to Africa or to relocate them in Indian territory are popular.

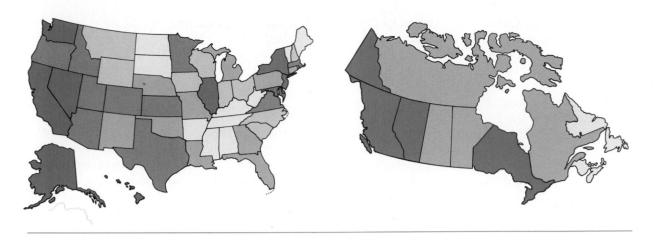

1980: Asians per 1,000 Population

Alabama	2.5	Idaho	6.3
South Dakota	2.5	Kansas	6.4
Maine	2.6	Minnesota	6.5
Vermont	2.7	Arizona	8.1
West Virginia	2.7	Texas	8.5
Kentucky	2.7	Massachusetts	8.6
Mississippi	2.9	Utah	10.3
Arkansas	2.9	Colorado	10.4
Tennessee	3.0	Virginia	12.4
North Dakota	3.1	Oregon	13.2

New Hampshire	3.2	Illinois	14.0
Montana	3.2	New Jersey	14.1
North Carolina	3.6	Delaware	15.2
Indiana	3.7	Maryland	15.4
South Carolina	3.8	New York	17.7
Wisconsin	3.9	Nevada	18.0
Iowa	4.0	Alaska	20.0
Wyoming	4.2	Washington	24.8
Ohio	4.4	California	53.0
		Hawaii	604.4

Nebraska	4.5
Georgia	4.5
Missouri	4.7
New Mexico	5.2
Pennsylvania	5.4
Rhode Island	5.6
Louisiana	5.7
Oklahoma	5.7
Florida	5.8
Connecticut	6.1
Michigan	6.1

1980: Asians per 1,000 Population

Newfoundland	1.4	Yukon	12.0
Pr. Edward Island	1.8	Ontario	19.2
New Brunswick	2.1	Alberta	23.8
Nova Scotia	2.5	British Columbia	44.7

N.W. Territories	5.8
Quebec	5.8
Saskatchewan	9.7
Manitoba	11.1

Figure 11-1 ■ **Persons of Asian descent per 1,000.** For much of the twentieth century the United States and Canada imposed minute quotas on immigration from Asia. During the 1930s, for example, Canada admitted only 150 Japanese a year, while the United States limited Japanese immigration to 102 per year. In recent years, however, prejudice against Asians has subsided greatly in both nations, the restrictions have been relaxed, and substantial new immigration from Asia is taking place. In both nations the population of Asian descent is concentrated on the Pacific Coast. There seems to be a nearly universal tendency for immigrants to cluster in locations closest to home (hence, people from eastern Europe cluster on the East Coast). Perhaps this is because the first arrivals lack money and experience to push inland from their point of arrival. Then, when others follow, they settle where they already have friends and relatives, thus amplifying the "closest-to-home" pattern.

Meanwhile, in Canada the American Civil War has caused a momentary halt to the flood of French-speaking Canadians leaving Quebec for the United States. The exodus, which eventually will total nearly a million people, is a direct result of political and economic repression imposed on the French by a government entirely controlled by English-speaking Canadians—a government installed by military force in the aftermath of a revolt aimed at establishing Quebec as an independent republic. Many decades will pass before French-speakers regain political equality. As soon as the American Civil War ends, the French-Canadian exodus will begin again—a barometer of bitterness between the "two Canadas."

In Europe, the Austrians hate the Slavs. The French hate the Germans. The Germans look down on the Poles. And the English look down on everyone, treating even the Scots and the Welsh as inferior foreigners. The Irish flee to America to escape the harsh conditions of life the English impose on them, but the Irish find they are not particularly welcome in America, either.

In 1862 Charles Darwin's new theory of evolution arouses the greatest intellectual excitement. It argues that complex biological species evolved from simple, primitive forms of life. The horse, for example, was once the size of the jackrabbit (and about as numerous), and apes and humans are cousins. The theory of evolution seems to answer a problem that has long vexed Europeans. Over the previous three centuries, Europeans explored the globe, and they now are poking into the last uncharted regions. Everywhere they go they find human societies with a lower level of technology than theirs. Indeed, they find society after society still living in the Stone Age. Why is ignorance so widespread? Why are Europeans so much more advanced? Evolutionary theory is used to support supremacist notions: The white race is at a higher stage of human evolution, and non-whites are more primitive species of humans. Europeans have long believed in their racial superiority; now they think they have a scientific basis for it. And if whites are more advanced biologically, should they not be careful to pre-serve their heritage and not dilute it by cross-breeding?

Chapter Preview

This chapter examines the causes of intergroup conflicts due to noticeable cultural or physical differences, particularly conflicts within rather than between societies. Specifically, it explores racial and ethnic differences as the basis for ascribed low status—how factors such as race, religion, language, and customs generate inequalities among members of a society. Indeed, this chapter will argue that *inequalities in property, power, and prestige among different racial and ethnic groups in a society are the basis of intergroup conflict.* We shall see how such inequalities make particular groups into strangers, thereby provoking the unreasoned reactions typical of humans confronting strangers. We shall also see that as status inequalities between groups disappear, so do prejudice and hatred.

Intergroup Conflict

Chapter 2 introduced the basic concepts that sociologists use to examine intergroup conflicts, but some additional comments will prove useful here. This chapter discusses *intergroup* conflict rather than *interracial* conflict, since much of the hatred, prejudice, and discrimination among groups is not based on race. Antagonisms between Protestants and Catholics in the United States during the nineteenth and twentieth centuries were not interracial, nor is the deadly and festering conflict in Northern Ireland today. Two centuries of conflict between English- and French-speaking Canadians have not involved racial differences. Nor was the recent bloody civil war in Nigeria a matter of race. All of these conflicts were between groups of the same race, but with different *cultures*.

The term **intergroup conflict** encompasses all such disputes, whether they are over culture or over skin color. However, this chapter is not concerned with intergroup conflict between two groups with an identical cultural and racial heritage, who may battle over politics or wealth. Our concern is only with intergroup conflicts based on noticeable physical or cultural differences.

Race

A **race** is a human group with some observable, common biological features. The most prominent of these is skin color, but racial groups also differ in other observable ways such as eyelid shape and the color and texture of hair. They also differ in subtle ways that are not visible, such as blood type. Although race is a biological concept, racial differences are important for intergroup relations solely to the extent that people attach cultural meaning to them (van den Berghe, 1967). Only when people believe that racial identity is associated with other traits such as character, ability, and behavior do racial differences affect human affairs. Historically, racial differences have typically been associated with cultural variances as well, because persons of different races were usually members of different societies. Race, then, has usually been an accurate indicator of who is and who is not a stranger.

Major trouble arises when different racial groups exist within the same society and people still assign cultural meanings to these physical differences. For one thing, members of one racial group usually cannot escape prejudice by "passing" as members of another racial group, although many light-skinned blacks can and do pass as whites. While an Italian could change his name to Robert Davis, join the Presbyterian Church, and deny his true ancestry, people cannot as easily renounce their biology.

This does not mean, however, that racial differences must always produce intergroup conflict. Biological differences may be unchangeable, but by themselves they are not important. It is what we *believe* about these differences that matters. And what we believe can change. The notion of a society that is color blind simply refers to a society in which no cultural meanings are attached to human biological variations.

Ethnic groups

Ethnic groups are groups whose cultural heritages differ. We usually reserve the term for different cultural groups within the same society. By themselves, cultural differences are not enough to make a group an ethnic group. The differences must be noticed, and they must bind a group together and separate it from others. As Michael Hechter (1974) put it, an ethnic group exists on the basis of "sentiments which bind individuals into solidarity groups on some cultural basis."

For example, nearly 13 million North Americans today are the descendants of persons who came here from Italy. Some of them can speak Italian, many cannot. Some like Italian food, some do not. Some are Roman Catholic, some are not. But the existence of an Italian-American or Italian-Canadian ethnic group does not simply depend on such cultural factors. What is important is that some of these people *think of themselves* as sharing special bonds of history, culture, and kinship with others of Italian ancestry. This makes them members of an ethnic group.

Wsevolod Isajiw (1980) has pointed out that ethnic groups are "involuntary" groups in that people don't decide to join one as they might decide to join a fraternity or sorority. People are born into an ethnic group. However, unless they live within the confines of a relatively strict caste system, people often make a voluntary choice about *continuing* to belong to an ethnic group. In fact, as noted in Chapter 2, a substantial proportion of North Americans of Italian ancestry are not part of an Italian ethnic group (Alba, 1985).

Cultural pluralism

For a long time, people believed that intergroup conflicts in North America would be resolved through *assimilation*. As time passed, a given ethnic group would surrender its distinctive cultural features and disappear into the dominant American or Canadian culture. At that point, people would no longer think of themselves as ethnic, nor would others continue to do so.

Today many once formidable intergroup conflicts have been resolved in North America. Yet the ethnic groups in question, mostly Europeans, did not disappear. True enough, their ethnic identity differs from that of their forebears. Typically, they have lost their native language and their bonds with the old country. Their present culture retains some elements of the old—religious affiliation, for example—plus a new heritage based on the special experiences of the group in the United States or Canada (Glazer and Moynihan, 1970). The important point is that conflict vanished without the disappearance of noticeable differences; conflict ended because the differences became unimportant. Such conflict resolutions are called *accommodation*, not assimilation. The growth of mutual interests between conflicting groups enables them to emphasize similarities and de-emphasize differences.

When intergroup conflict ends through accommodation, the result is ethnic or cultural pluralism—the existence of diverse cultures within the same society. That the United States is no longer a Protestant nation, but a nation of Protestants, Catholics, and Jews, as well as followers of other faiths (plus nonbelievers), demonstrates cultural pluralism.

Obviously, accommodation and assimilation are not the inevitable outcomes of intergroup conflict. Conflict has sometimes been resolved by the *extermination* of the weaker group, as happened with the Jews in Nazi Germany, Catholics in Elizabethan England, Indians in the Caribbean and on the North American frontier, Armenians in Turkey, and various tribal minorities in black Africa today. Intergroup conflicts have also led to the *expulsion* of the weaker group.

Jews have often been expelled from nations, and Europeans were expelled from Japan in the sixteenth century. Following World War II, Pakistan expelled Hindus, India expelled Muslims, and Uganda recently expelled both Pakistanis and Indians, while Vietnam has driven out several hundred thousand Chinese. Intergroup conflicts have also been stabilized by the imposition of a **caste system,** whereby weaker groups are prevented from competing with the stronger, and through *segregation*, whereby a group is inhibited from having contact with others.

The history of the New World contains all of these methods of resolution: Groups have been assimilated, accommodated, exterminated, expelled, and placed in a low-status caste. This variety, plus the persistence of intense intergroup conflicts, makes the United States and Canada extremely important in the study of intergroup relations. North America is a huge natural laboratory for examining the dynamics of such conflicts and useful means for overcoming them.

Such an examination inevitably arouses our emotions. When we examine the history of prejudice and discrimination in North America, we cannot—nor should we—avoid anger and frustration. However, it would be tragic if we let these feelings prevent us from appreciating the extent to which hatred has been over-

■ On July 8, 1853, Commodore Matthew Perry led a squadron of four American warships into Tokyo Bay in defiance of Japan's laws excluding foreign contacts. After a period of negotiations, Japan agreed to treaties opening its ports to western shipping. A Japanese artist drew these portraits of Perry (far right) and his senior officers. The Asian reaction to the facial features of Westerners is clearly displayed in this set of drawings: The "dog face"—the protruding face with a large nose—is evident in each. Moreover, other than for minor details such as glasses and whiskers and variations in age, *all Westerners looked alike!* Notice, however, that the Japanese artist depicted all of these men with eyelids of typical Asian shape.

come, for the erosion of bigotry is also a prominent feature of North American history. The study of this erosion can teach us much about how present problems may be resolved.

■

Preoccupation with Prejudice

Until very recently, social scientists regarded prejudice as the *cause* of intergroup conflict. Hostile actions against some racial or ethnic minority were believed to reflect the underlying hostile beliefs or prejudices groups had about one another. Therefore, the urgent questions were, Why do people become prejudiced? and What can be done to cure them of their preju-

dice? Little attention was paid to social and economic relations among groups that might give rise to mutual hostility. Instead, prejudice was blamed on personality defects or ignorance. For a long time, social scientists searched the heads and hearts of people to discover what was wrong with them that caused them to be prejudiced. This search culminated in the mid-1960s.

An immense number of theories have been advanced to explain why people develop prejudices toward people of different racial or ethnic backgrounds. For several decades the most influential of these was the theory of the *authoritarian personality* (Adorno et al., 1950). Its proponents argued that some people are, in effect, oversocialized, so that they accept the norms and values only of their own group and reject any variations. When such people are confronted with others whose norms and values differ from theirs, they become very anxious. To resolve this anxiety, they adopt the belief that all who differ from them are inferior, sinful, inhuman, or otherwise objectionable. Prejudice, then, was seen as a defense mechanism against having to question one's own cultural heritage. Another theory blamed prejudice on feelings of personal inadequacy or low self-esteem; that is, people adopted prejudices in order to have someone else to look down on (Ackerman and Jahoda, 1950).

Many sociologists, myself included, reacted against the notion that prejudice was entirely in the head. Consequently, a huge number of studies were done to link prejudice to social influences on the individual, especially to channels by which prejudice might be learned or unlearned. Again and again, researchers found that the more education and income a person has, the less likely a person is to be prejudiced against other racial and ethnic groups (Selznick and Steinberg, 1969; Quinley and Glock, 1979). Other studies found that the more religious a person is, the more likely that person is to be prejudiced against members of other faiths; however, religion had no effect on prejudice against persons of other races or ethnic groups of the same religion (Glock and Stark, 1966; Stark et al., 1971).

Yet despite immense effort over several decades, prejudice researchers failed to explain compellingly why people are prejudiced. Moreover, it began to seem likely that prejudice was not the fundamental cause of intergroup conflict. Instead, it became increasingly evident that intergroup conflict causes prejudice. Thus, the proposition that curing prejudice will relieve conflicts reverses cause and effect. To the contrary, sociologists became convinced that only by resolving conflicts will prejudices subside.

In the remainder of this chapter, we shall examine why sociologists came to accept the proposition that racial and ethnic conflicts are rooted in status inequalities between groups and generate prejudice. As we shall see, this approach contradicts many popular beliefs about intergroup relations. For example, if prejudice were the result of ignorance and a lack of understanding, an obvious solution would be to break down the barriers that isolate one group from another. According to this view, strangers need to get to know one another. Thus, intergroup relations are improved by more frequent intergroup contact.

For decades that sounded like very good advice, and innumerable programs were instituted to "bring people together."

Today sociologists think that such efforts are doomed so long as real grievances between groups exist. In fact, increased contacts between groups can increase conflict, hostility, and prejudice. To see why, let's watch as several social scientists first began to develop this new theoretical approach.

Allport's theory of contact

Research in the 1940s and 1950s on prejudice seemed to support the popular belief that prejudice thrives in isolation and thus getting people together will overcome prejudice. However, some social scientists began to doubt this conception of the problem. Foremost among them was Gordon W. Allport of Harvard, one of the world's most distinguished social psychologists at the time.

If contact is the answer to the problems of prejudice, Allport reasoned, then why didn't racial prejudice in the American South disappear long ago? One might argue that northern racists have simply never had a chance to get to know black people, but in the South blacks and whites have long been in close contact. Many white southerners, for example, grew up having much closer relations with a black servant than with their own parents. In small southern towns, blacks and whites had been in close, regular, daily contact for generations. Yet antiblack prejudice was as strong in these towns as anywhere in North America. Why?

In 1958 Allport proposed his answers in a classic book, *The Nature of Prejudice*. Contact won't necessarily make relations between two groups better, he argued; often it will make relations worse, depending on the conditions under which that contact occurs.

According to **Allport's theory of contact,**

■ Contact between groups will decrease prejudice when it occurs under conditions of equal status and cooperation as illustrated by these American soldiers assigned to duty at Arlington National Cemetery.

prejudice will decrease if two groups with equal status have contact. But prejudice will increase or remain high if it occurs under conditions of *status inequality*, in which one group is dominant and the other subordinate. This accounts for the failure of race relations to improve in the South until recently. White merchants had contact only with black customers, not with black merchants. White children had contact primarily with black servants, not with black teachers or black fellow students. Such contacts reinforced white people's views of themselves as superior. The inequality of the situation forced blacks to submit and caused whites to perceive blacks as submissive.

This view of the effects of contact was supported by studies of the U.S. Merchant Marine. The prejudice of white seamen against blacks did not decrease as a result of repeated voyages with black cooks and mess stewards aboard. But it changed significantly after President Harry S Truman ordered the merchant marine to become integrated and white seamen voyaged with black seamen of equal rank (Brophy, 1945).

However, even contact between groups of equal status does not always improve relations, Allport pointed out. *Prejudice will intensify if the groups are engaged in competition* (poor whites competing with poor blacks for unskilled jobs, for example), *but will decline if the groups cooperate to pursue common goals*. Thus, when white policemen work with black policemen, their prejudice decreases (Kephart, 1957).

Since Allport's work was published, considerable research has supported his views (Ford, 1973). Contact overcomes prejudice only when people meet on equal terms to cooperate in pursuing common goals. Contact accompanied by inequality and competition breeds contempt. It can even turn former friends into strangers.

The Sherif studies

 In the 1950s, Muzafer and Carolyn Sherif of the University of Oklahoma conducted a series of studies of young boys at summer camp. Their results vividly demonstrate how easily prejudice arises among groups. The Sherifs assigned young boys to living groups when they arrived for a two-week stay at summer camp and then manipulated their activities to test how prejudice arose and declined between groups. Posing as the camp janitor, Muzafer Sherif was able to wander about the camp at will in a nearly invisible role and eavesdrop on the boys.

In one experiment, the Sherifs (1953) broke up existing friendships by assigning boys who were friends to different living groups. Living groups were then made the basic camp units for activities, and each living group was treated as a separate team in sports competition. During activities requiring frequent competition among living groups, the Sherifs found that hostile stereotypes characteristic of intergroup prejudices arose within several days. For example, one group soon labeled another as "cry-babies," another as "cheats," and another as "sissies." These harsh feelings arose even when many boys in one group had close friends in another. When the Sherifs altered the contact so that the groups performed cooperative tasks, the negative stereotypes quickly subsided.

If such hostilities can be produced in a few days among young boys of similar background and with long-standing friendships, then is it any wonder that antagonism arises so easily in the real world between groups of strangers who are separated by truly noticeable differences and different experiences?

Based on the important theoretical work by Allport and the amazing experimental results the Sherifs obtained, a new approach to intergroup conflict began to spread among social scientists. Sociologists were especially attracted by the ways that Allport's theory could be applied to large social structures. For example, because prejudice among groups of unequal status is likely, most groups of new immigrants coming into contact with the established groups in a society are likely to encounter prejudice.

As sociologists began to make these theoretical applications, many widely accepted beliefs were called into question. People had, for example, long assumed that racist attitudes led to slavery in the United States. Now it suddenly seemed more likely that slavery was the cause of the unusually virulent racist beliefs that had flourished in the American South. Before we discuss how economic inequalities or status differences cause prejudice, let us briefly examine the institution of slavery.

■

Slavery and the American Dilemma

Two hundred years ago, the American Founding Fathers risked their lives and fortunes by signing the Declaration of Independence from British rule. The second paragraph of that document begins, "We hold these Truths to be self-evident, that all Men are created equal." It is beyond dispute that these American patriots meant this statement. It is also beyond dispute that many of them, including Thomas Jefferson,* who wrote these words, also owned slaves (see Figures 11-2 and 11-3).

The doctrine of equal opportunity and the sanctity of individual freedom have long been fundamental American values. Yet these beliefs were maintained in the face of continuing slavery and later through decades of harsh discrimination against blacks. How could Americans square their ideals with their practices?

In 1944 Gunnar Myrdal, a Swedish economist, published the results of a monumental study of American race relations. In it he focused on the stunning contradiction between democratic ideals and racist practices. The title of his famous book termed this contradiction as *An American Dilemma*.

Many Americans dealt with **the American dilemma** between democratic values and racism by rejecting racism. The Puritan descendants of New England were as opposed to slavery as they were to English colonialism, and they provided the grass roots support for the Abolitionist movement that culminated in the Civil War and Lincoln's Emancipation Proclamation. But most Americans found another way out of this contradiction. They did not regard human slavery as proper, but they did not consider blacks fully human. If black people are not fully human, then the ideal that "all men are created equal" does not apply. (The humanity of black *men* was at issue. That *women* were omitted from this phrase was not then embarrassing.) As a result, slavery in America was perhaps as much a *cause* of prejudice as a consequence of it.

But how could seemingly intelligent people become convinced that just because people have a dark skin they are not fully human? It wasn't just skin color. Nor was it just that blacks came

---

*Jefferson made many efforts to outlaw slavery and once nearly succeeded in doing so in Virginia. However, he felt it irresponsible to free his slaves within a slave society because he believed that they would only suffer worse fates.

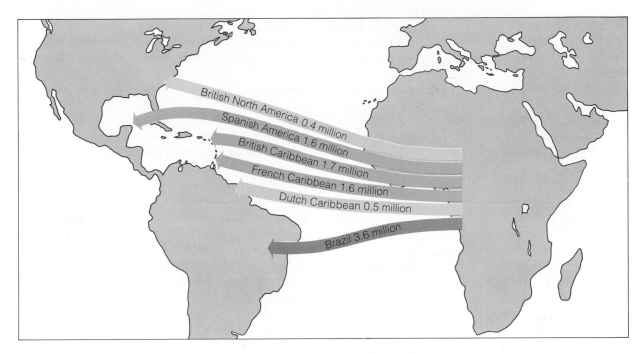

Figure 11-2 ■ **Patterns of the slave trade, 1500–1870 (numbers in arrows are in millions).** About 10 million black slaves were transported to the New World between 1500 and 1870. Here we see the primary destinations of the slavers. Notice that only a small proportion, perhaps 500,000, were taken to North America. This is surprising because the first U.S. Census, taken in 1790, recorded 700,000 slaves plus some free blacks, and by 1820 there were 1.5 million slaves in America. Indeed, by 1825 the United States had by far the largest slave population in the western hemisphere, because compared with slaves in the Caribbean and South America, slaves in the United States had low death rates and high birth rates. Historians attribute this to "better diet, shelter and general material conditions" (Patterson, 1982). Nevertheless, the United States was among the last western nations to outlaw slavery. (*Source:* Adapted from Curtin, 1969.)

from exotic, primitive cultures. It was the nature of the institution of slavery and the contact between slave and master that enabled whites to see slaves as inhuman: Blacks were required to behave as if they were, in fact, not fully human (Patterson, 1982).

Recall the conditions under which Allport believed contact would worsen prejudice, and then consider slavery. There is no greater status inequality than that between master and slave. No group can be more dominant over another than slave owners over slaves. Slaves were not educated, and they rarely had been anywhere except on the plantation where they were born.

They were traded and sold like prize livestock, and because they were black, they could not easily run away and blend into the free population. They were required to be subservient to whites, who dealt with their resistance severely. Because blacks had no choice but to be wholly dependent, most blacks appeared to be childlike to their masters. Whites denied them experience, knowledge, and literacy, thus keeping them ignorant.

If you regard people as livestock, raise them to act in such a fashion, and prevent them from acting in other ways, it is no surprise that they then reinforce your belief that they are live-

Percent of Population Who Are Slaves, 1790

Massachusetts	0.00	North Carolina	25.55
Vermont	0.00	Maryland	32.22
Maine	0.00	Georgia	35.52
New Hampshire	0.11	Virginia	39.14
Pennsylvania	0.85	South Carolina	42.99

Connecticut	1.18
Rhode Island	1.45
New Jersey	6.19
New York	6.26
Delaware	15.06

Figure 11-3 ■ **American slaves, 1790.** Here we see the proportion of slaves in the population of the fifteen United States in 1790. There actually were seventeen slaves in Vermont that year (too few to raise the population percentage above 0.00), but there were none in Massachusetts or Maine—slavery was against the law there. Not surprisingly, the proportions are highest in the South, where South Carolina was nearly half slave. But note that there also were substantial slave populations at this time in many northern states such as New York and New Jersey. (*Source:* U.S. Census, 1790.)

stock. Centuries of slavery had made blacks and whites complete strangers. And the harsh racist prejudice employed to justify slavery has lived on to infect black-white relations in our own time.

■

Status Inequality and Prejudice

Sociologists currently view status inequality as the cause, not the result, of prejudice and discrimination. Now we shall examine this line of reasoning in depth.

When two groups obviously differ on some cultural or physical characteristic (religion or race, for example) and encounter one another, these differences will dominate their initial perceptions. Each group will tend to magnify the differences and to attribute unflattering traits to the other. However, whether these initial reactions subside or intensify depends upon the conditions under which their contact continues.

When both groups live in the same society, contact is hard to avoid. According to Allport's theory, future relations between the two groups depend on whether the two groups are of equal status and whether the benefits of cooperation outweigh those of competition. When such groups are (or come to be) of equal status and when they benefit from cooperation, relations ought to improve rapidly, regardless of initial negative reactions. *But if their status is unequal (and so long as it remains unequal), then contact between these groups will worsen feelings.* Moreover, when two such groups are of unequal status, economic competition between them is virtually unavoidable.

From this line of reasoning, several conclusions follow. First, contact between culturally and racially distinctive groups of unequal status will increase prejudice and probably discrimination as well. Second, this prejudice will not subside until after the status inequality and economic competition have been eliminated. Finally, within any society, noticeable physical and cultural differences will produce prejudice only if they are associated with status inequality or with competition.

If these conclusions are correct, then efforts

■ Black slaves plant sweet potatoes on a plantation on Edisto Island, South Carolina, in April 1862. The picture was taken during a period of occupation by the Union Army (which explains why some of the men wear parts of U.S. Army uniforms). Eight months later, the Emancipation Proclamation went into effect. But by then the Union troops had withdrawn, so these people remained slaves until the war's end.

to overcome prejudice before overcoming status inequality are bound to fail. Instead, effort should be directed at eliminating the inequality; then prejudice should subside.

To see how these processes work, let's consider the relations between Catholics and Protestants over the past century in the United States. For contrast, we shall also examine relations between Protestants and Catholics in Northern Ireland today.

As discussed in Chapter 2, the arrival of large numbers of Catholic immigrants into the United States during the latter nineteenth century provoked bitter reactions among American Protestants. Like most immigrants, the Catholics arrived with little money or education and took unskilled labor jobs. For several generations, Catholics were at or near the bottom of the American stratification system. Indeed, the average income of Catholic families lagged considerably behind that of Protestants until well into this century. This inequality fueled the bitter prejudices Catholics and Protestants held toward one another.

Economic inequality and discrimination placed Catholics in direct conflict with the

■ Young Catholics in Belfast, Northern Ireland, taunt British troops. The soldiers are on patrol to prevent riots and terrorism between Catholics and Protestants. This intergroup conflict illustrates that cultural differences can produce as much bitterness and prejudice as can racial differences.

Protestant majority. For Protestants, Catholic efforts to achieve economic parity represented a threat of loss, for Catholic gains would come at the expense of Protestant privilege. As we shall see later in this chapter, the exclusionary immigration laws the United States adopted in the 1920s were imposed by the Protestant majority in an effort to protect their relatively high wages from being undercut by Catholic immigrants willing to work for less.

Eventually, Catholics did gain economic parity with Protestants (Greeley, 1974). When that happened, the basis for conflict subsided. Catholics were no longer of lower status than Protestants; the competition over privilege had ended in a draw. It was then, not before, that

bitter anti-Catholic and anti-Protestant prejudices began to subside. Indeed, they subsided so rapidly that few college-age Protestant and Catholic Americans today even know of them, although they were still widespread when their parents were young. As recently as the 1950s, books attacking Catholics as pagans and the enemies of democracy became best-sellers. Nonetheless, in 1960 a Catholic was elected President of the United States.

During the days of Catholic-Protestant conflicts in the United States, observers were convinced that these conflicts were caused by cultural differences—specifically, by differences in religion. Because these differences were unlikely to disappear, it was thought that prejudice would remain as well. However, because these religious differences do not provoke prejudice today, they must not have been the cause. Rather, the religious differences were used as indicators, or **"markers,"** of underlying conflicts over status. With the conflict resolved, these markers lost their ability to inflame antagonisms.

In his recent major work on intergroup relations, Stanley Lieberson (1980) explained how cultural and racial markers are made potent by status conflict:

I am suggesting a general process that occurs when racial and ethnic groups have an inherent conflict [competition over status between unequal groups]. Under the circumstances, there is a tendency for the competitors to focus on differences between themselves. The observers (in this case the sociologists) may then assume that these differences are the sources of the conflict. In point of fact, the rhetoric involving such differences may indeed inflame them, but we can be reasonably certain that the conflict would have occurred in their absence.

He then suggested a "thought experiment." Because Protestants in Northern Ireland refer to themselves as "Orangemen," while Irish Catholics identify with the color green, let's suppose that the Protestants in Northern Ireland had orange skins and the Catholics green skins. Clearly these marked physical differences would become part of the rhetoric of hatred and prejudice in Northern Ireland, serving as additional markers of difference. Lieberson even suggested that such physical differences would play a secondary role in fueling conflict. However, it would be silly to credit the orange and green "racial" differences as the real cause of the conflict, because a bitter, murderous conflict over economic opportunity and status already exists without such differences. In similar fashion, Lieberson argues, physical differences between blacks and whites, both real and imagined, enter into the rhetoric of interracial conflict in the United States, but they are not the cause.

Lieberson (1980) concluded that fear of blacks as economic competitors is the real cause of racial stereotypes. This means

that were the present-day [economic] conflict between blacks and dominant white groups to be resolved, then the race issue could rapidly disintegrate as a crucial barrier between the groups just as a very profound and deep distaste for Roman Catholics on the part of the dominant Protestants has diminished rather substantially.

Keeping in mind this overview of how economic inequality generates prejudice, let us now examine these matters in detail.

Economic Conflict and Prejudice

The roots of ethnic and racial antagonism usually lie in economic inequality and conflict. This is primarily because subordinate racial and ethnic minorities represent an economic threat to many members of the dominant majority. That is, the presence of a disadvantaged racial or ethnic group in a society makes available a supply of persons who can be hired for wages lower than those paid to majority group workers for the same job. Such persons will work for less—either because they lack the power to demand wages as high as those of the dominant group or because they have different economic motives for working.

Edna Bonacich (1972, 1975, 1976) has examined the relationship between labor market conflict and racial and ethnic antagonism in considerable detail. She has identified four factors that often cause or require members of subordinate racial and ethnic groups to work for substandard wages.

The first factor is a very *low standard of living.* Often enough, such groups migrate from a region with so low a standard of living that wages considered substandard by members of the dominant group are very attractive to them. Illegal Mexican workers in the American West and Southwest work for much less than the going wage paid to American citizens, but they earn far more than they could in Mexico. Similarly, blacks who migrated from the rural South in the 1930s and 1940s improved their standard of

■ This photo of a country store, taken in Gordonton, North Carolina, by Dorothea Lange in 1939, reveals the poverty and isolation of the rural South, which in comparison with other parts of the United States, made the South like a foreign land. Here we can glimpse some of the complexities and contradictions of southern race relations at that time. The white store owner, standing in the doorway, seems to be on friendly terms with the black men sitting on his front porch. Yet, while these men are free to enter the store and buy whatever they like, they may not sit down and relax inside: They can buy soda pop inside but must return to the porch to drink it, because both whites and blacks shop at this store. Had the store been for blacks only, then they could have sat down inside. The poverty of the black customers (several wear no socks) is evident, but so is that of the white owner of this dilapidated store. While whites enjoyed many social privileges denied blacks, most whites as well as blacks suffered from the economic and social deprivations that marked life in the rural South until recent times. Some of these young black men may have migrated north. If so, their journey was more like that of immigrants coming through Ellis Island than like that of people moving from one northern state to another.

■ Farm families from Oklahoma, bankrupted by the Dust Bowl and the Great Depression, loaded their remaining belongings onto old cars and pickups and set out for California. Despite being white, Anglo-Saxon Protestants, they were greeted in the Golden West as undesirable foreigners—as "dirty Okies"—and many Californians tried to keep them out or drive them away.

living even though they were paid well below union wages (and often were employed as strikebreakers) in northern mines, mills, and factories. The same was true of Chinese and Japanese workers arriving on the West Coast at the turn of the century. Indeed, white, Protestant "Okies," who fled the farms of the Southwest for California in the 1930s, during the years of the Dust Bowl and the Great Depression, found substandard wages in California to be a great improvement over the abject poverty they faced when they lost their land.

A second impediment to high wages pointed out by Bonacich is a *lack of information.* Immigrants from a very poor country may be recruited without knowing that they are being exploited. Or members of a subordinate group may not know about minimum wage laws, legal recourses

for unpaid wages, and the like, often because they do not speak the language.

A third factor that limits the ability of ethnic and racial minorities to secure high wages is their *lack of political power.* They may lack citizenship and thus have no voting power or may be too few in number to force favorable reforms. In contrast, workers of the dominant group may have substantial political power and strong unions that enable them to demand high wages, which in turn makes them vulnerable to wage competition from groups unable to unionize or to wield political power. This is especially true for unskilled jobs. As we saw in Chapter 9, unskilled positions have high replaceability, which always depresses wages unless political power can be used to create artificial conditions that lower replaceability.

Because most immigrant workers in America were not skilled, they had little power, and their ability to strike was limited by the ease with which they could be replaced.

A contrasting case makes the point. Jewish workers founded some of the first successful unions in the United States in the late nineteenth century. They rapidly won contracts for better pay and shorter hours, conditions most industrial workers did not enjoy at that time (Howe, 1976). The key to the power of the Jewish trade union movement lay in the special skills of the Jewish workers, especially those in the garment industry. Factory owners lacked an alternative supply of skilled tailors and seamstresses. Interestingly enough, the employers from whom Jewish unions won their settlements also tended to be Jews. This success in one industry shows that Jews arrived in the United States already possessing the skills needed to make rapid economic progress.

The *economic motives* of subordinate racial and ethnic groups are also a factor in their low wages, according to Bonacich. Often they only intend to be temporary workers. As a result, they often accept low wages and poor working conditions, knowing they need not endure them forever. In addition, temporary workers have little to gain and much to lose by strikes or by refusing bad jobs in hopes of getting better ones. For workers with short-term economic goals, poor wages are a greater advantage than prospects of better wages.

Many Italian immigrants came as sojourners to North America. They were young men who came to earn and save their wages and then to return to rural Italy, where the much lower standard of living made their savings worth much more. For them to participate in a long strike over an unpleasant work environment or to go unemployed while searching for a higher-paying job conflicted with their goal: to save money as fast as possible and return home.

Similarly, H. A. Millis (1915) reported that Japanese workers in California displaced other workers not only because they accepted low wages but also because they worked twelve to fourteen hours a day and on weekends. They did this so that they could save money faster and return to Japan sooner. In Africa, workers from the villages will often work very cheaply because they plan to work just long enough to afford the price of a bride, a rifle, or a bicycle (Berg, 1966). Furthermore, as Bonacich pointed out, it is against the interests of management to pay high wages to sojourners, lest the workers achieve their short-term goals faster and leave that much sooner.

Clearly, then, the presence of racial and ethnic groups willing to work for substandard wages threatens the economic well-being of other workers and is likely to cause strong antagonism toward the subordinate group. Cheap labor threatens to make *all* labor cheap. Workers belonging to the dominant group must either work for less or lose their jobs to members of the subordinate racial or ethnic group, unless such economic competition can be prevented.

Two strategies have commonly been employed to prevent a subordinate group from competing with the dominant group by providing cheap labor (Bonacich, 1972). The first is *exclusion*. Members of the subordinate group are denied entry into the society or driven out if they have already entered. The second is to establish a *caste system* that limits the subordinate group to certain occupations, often the most menial and undesirable ones.

Exclusion

The influx of cultural and racial groups who are perceived as a threat to the dominant group's wages often causes a nativistic reaction: a demand that foreigners be kept out. As already mentioned, massive immigration of Catholics during the late nineteenth century led to nativistic policies in American politics, often justified by vicious racial and ethnic prejudice. Italians and eastern Europeans were seriously discussed as "inferior racial stocks" whose immigration threatened the "racial purity and superiority" of North Americans (Grant, 1916). Following World War I, Protestant opposition to the resumption of immigration led to immigration quotas designed to prevent Catholics and Asians from entering the country in significant numbers. American workers won these tight quotas over the opposition of big business, which wanted to keep its historic supply of cheap labor.

Similarly, a workingman's party spearheaded the drive to exclude Asians from the West Coast. As the socialist Cameron H. King, Jr., wrote in 1908, this party swept California "with the campaign cry of 'The Chinese must go.' Then the two old parties woke up and have since realized that to hold the labor vote they must stand for Asiatic exclusion" (in Bonacich, 1972).

Laborers and farmers patrolled California and tried by illegal means to prevent Okies from entering the state during the 1930s (McWilliams, 1945). And it has almost always been white workers who have tried to drive out blacks moving into the industrial regions of the North from the rural South.

Caste systems

Total exclusion has often not been possible. Under such conditions, dominant-group members have often tried to create a caste system that would restrict minorities to certain occupations, thus preventing them from competing for places in other occupations (Hechter, 1978). As previously discussed, heredity is the basis of stratification in caste systems and ascription determines status. Each caste group has exclusive access to certain occupations and positions in the society. Only those born to the highest caste are permitted to perform the most important occupations and hold the most powerful positions. Those born to the lowest caste must perform the most unattractive and servile work.

India is a classic instance of a very elaborate caste society. However, elements of a caste system can exist even in a society in which status is generally based on achievement rather than ascription. Within the dominant group of such societies, status may be based primarily on achievement, but one or more racial or ethnic group may be ascribed a uniformly low status and thereby constitute a lower caste.

A low-caste status prevents a racial or ethnic group from competing with the dominant group for wages. A caste system may be created directly by strict rules about which positions a subordinate group may or may not hold or indirectly by excluding the subordinate group from entering unions or schools or from performing certain activities required to obtain better positions. For example, taboos against using drinking fountains or restrooms used by an upper caste may confine lower-caste members to a few limited physical locations and thereby to a narrow range of jobs. These subtle caste systems—long typical of race relations in the United States—constitute what Hechter (1974) has called a **cultural division of labor,** whereby cultural or racial differences among members of a society are used as the basis for occupational placement.

Middleman minorities

It is important to realize that a cultural division of labor need not place an ethnic or racial minority on the bottom of a stratification system. Often minorities have been used as "middlemen" in societies, serving as both links and buffers between the upper and lower classes. As Blalock (1967) and Bonacich (1973) have pointed out, **middleman minorities** often defuse potential class conflicts by becoming the focus of frustration and anger. In times of stress or unrest, Blalock noted, elites and the lower class often form a coalition against the middleman minority and vent their frustration on it. For example, many nations in feudal Europe permitted Jews to perform only certain middleman roles, such as moneylender, tax collector, and merchant. Thus, they were always potentially in conflict with both the nobility and the peasants. In hard times, the nobility blamed Jewish tax collectors for decreased revenues, but let them be the targets of peasant anger about high taxes. And in hard times, both the nobility and the peasants were in debt to the Jewish moneylender or the Jewish merchant. Often enough, killing or expelling the Jews proved a most attractive way for both nobles and peasants to cancel their debts.

Chinese and Indian minorities frequently have formed middleman minorities in societies in Africa and Southeast Asia. They, too, have often been scapegoats for social conflicts within the dominant group (Blalock, 1967).

Identifiability

Status conflicts always cause bitterness. For example, it is common in high schools for groups to be clearly distinguished on the basis of school performance, popularity, and, often, athletic skill and for there to be strong negative feelings between higher- and lower-status groups (Coleman 1961). This is true even when the groups are of precisely the *same* race, ethnic background, and religion—in French Catholic high schools in Quebec, for example. Indeed, we have seen how rapidly such barriers arise among little boys at summer camp.

When the conflicts truly affect one's life, and when conflicts occur between easily identifiable groups, they are even more bitter. For example, when people lose their jobs to strikebreakers or to those willing to work for lower wages, they are, of course, bitter. When the offending group is not set apart by cultural or racial differences, the anger must focus on the offending group as individuals, and their behavior is explained as the result of personal flaws. However, when the offending group has a clear group identification, bitterness can be directed toward *the group as a whole.* Then it is not a case of Harry, Marty, Mary, or Beth taking jobs but of those "dirty Swedes" taking them. In this manner, racial and cultural differences are infused with the passionate hatreds status competition and conflict generate—what is merely different is made contemptible, and strangers are transformed into enemies.

Racial and culturally identifiable "enemies" frequently acquire derogatory names reflecting prejudice, hatred, and contempt directed toward them. In North America, these names have included such terms as Wops, Hunkies, Micks, Krauts, Dagos, Gringos, Prots, Frogs, Breeds, Polacks, Rednecks, Kikes, Greasers, Wogs, Mackerel Snappers, Japs, Chinks, Chukes, and Niggers.* Indeed, as discussed earlier, one such group was known as Okies—people who moved west to California from the Oklahoma Dust Bowl during the 1930s. The prejudices against Okies were no different from those typically held against other racial and ethnic minorities (McWilliams, 1945). They were said to be dirty, to breed like rabbits, and to be superstitious, shiftless, sly, and ignorant. Yet the Okies were all white Anglo-Saxon Protestants, most of whom could trace their ancestry back to early colonial settlers. What made these people Okies? First, economic conflict did, because they would take any job at any wage to feed their hungry families. Second, they had easily identifiable cultural traits: a rural southern dialect and country ways.

Equality and the Decline of Prejudice

Today, many of the richest farms in California are owned by people who arrived as Okies during the 1930s. Nobody calls these people Okies anymore, although they sometimes call themselves Okies as a way of taking pride in how successful they have become.

If status competition and conflict fuel prejudice, then status equality causes the tank to run dry. With status equality, there is no longer anything to fight about. Once a subordinate group has achieved economic equality, for example, it no longer threatens as a source of cheap labor. And it no longer makes inroads into skilled occupations or into upper-status professional and managerial fields. The inroads have already been made.

Contact rapidly reduces prejudice under status equality, because it occurs among equals with a mutual interest in improving society—in cooperating to make the economy more productive or the environment more pleasant. Under these conditions, old hatreds and fears dissolve. This process is accelerated as younger

---

*Many readers will be unable to connect some of these names with the ethnic or religious group to which they were applied. Good. You are living evidence of how rapidly prejudice can subside once status conflicts have been resolved. Most people over 50 could easily recognize these group epithets; they did not pass some of these words on to their children. Perhaps you will let your children be ignorant of the rest.

generations with no experience of past conflicts become adults. Let's examine a recent example in detail.

The Japanese experience in North America

The history of Japanese immigrants and their descendants in North America is of special interest because both cultural and racial differences set them apart from the majority. Moreover, the Japanese immigrants were primarily farm laborers, literate but lacking education when they arrived; for decades they were the targets of intense prejudice and discrimination, especially in the Far West. How the Japanese overcame these barriers and achieved greater economic success than many immigrant groups of European origin provides an excellent foundation for the rest of the chapter. Although the stories of the Japanese in the United States and in Canada differ only slightly, it will be useful to recount each separately.

Japanese-Americans

The Japanese never made up more than a tiny portion of the great tide of immigration to America. In 1907, their peak year of entry, only 30,000 arrived, making up just 3 percent of all immigrants for that year. However, the Japanese immigrants located mainly in Hawaii and California, causing great local upset about a "yellow peril."

In California, an alien land law was passed to prohibit Japanese from owning land. For a time, the Japanese easily evaded this law by putting the land in the name of white neighbors or their American-born children. In 1920 a referendum was placed before California voters that attempted to close these loopholes and to exclude all aliens who were ineligible for citizenship from owning land. At that time only Asian aliens living in the United States were ineligible to become citizens. The law passed by a three-to-one margin, indicating the degree of public hostility to the Japanese. In time, court decisions and new evasion tactics defeated the intent of the law.

Meanwhile, in 1924 federal law prohibited immigration from Japan and other Asian nations—an action that caused great offense in Japan and played a role in decisions leading to World War II. The immediate consequences of this Asian exclusion policy were a halt to immigration and a rapid transformation of the Japanese-American population from being primarily foreign born to being primarily American born. This, in turn, led to rapid upward mobility by the Japanese, because no new, poor, unskilled immigrants arrived to depress the average status of the group.

Rapid Japanese economic success was not limited to farming, although that was the usual occupation of the first generation. Early on, the Japanese discovered a great demand for their gardening skills, a form of self-employment requiring little more capital investment than a truck, mowers, and various hand tools. As early as 1928, there were 1,300 self-employed Japanese gardeners in southern California (Kitano, 1969). The Japanese also set up produce markets in the cities to sell their vegetables and fruits, and in 1929 there were more than 700 such markets in Los Angeles alone (Light, 1972). As late as 1940, the majority of Japanese men in America were farmers. That same year about one-third of all commercial truck farm crops grown in California were produced by Japanese-American farmers (Kitano, 1969; Petersen, 1971, 1978; Sowell, 1981). The Japanese also excelled in running other small businesses where unskilled labor, especially the labor of children, could be most productive. For example, by 1919 Japanese-Americans owned almost half of the hotels and a fourth of the grocery stores in Seattle (Light, 1972).

The first generation of Japanese-Americans worked hard to establish their own farms and small businesses. They were aided in this by the creation of their own credit associations, in which they pooled their savings and used them to finance one another in starting businesses or buying property (Miyamoto, 1939). But the first generation did something else equally important: They sent their children to school.

Table 11-1 ■ **Percent enrolled in school at various ages, 1930.**

Age	Native-Born Whites	Japanese-Americans
7–13	96.1%	97.2%
14–15	90.0%	97.3%
16–17	61.0%	88.8%
18–20	24.4%	51.8%

Source: Adapted from Hirschman and Wong, 1986.

Table 11-1 compares the proportions of Japanese-Americans enrolled in school at various ages in 1930 with native-born white Americans. (Alaska and Hawaii were not states then and are not included in these statistics.) Among children age 7 through 13, nearly everyone is in school. But by age 14 a clear difference appears: 97.3 percent of the Japanese-Americans are in school, while only 90 percent of native-born whites are attending. At age 16 the gap has grown very large—88.8 percent versus 61 percent in favor of Japanese-Americans. And when we examine people of college age, the Japanese-American advantage is slightly more than two to one.

By 1940 these patterns had resulted in the average Japanese-American male having gone to school about a year beyond high school, while the average white American male had attended school only slightly beyond the eighth grade! Later this education would pay huge occupational dividends (Hirschman and Wong, 1984, 1986).

But first we must consider the war. On December 7, 1941, carrier aircraft of the Japanese Imperial Fleet made a massive surprise attack on the American fleet lying at anchor in Pearl Harbor. At the same time, Japan launched invasions of many parts of Southeast Asia and many Pacific islands. The war inflamed public emotions. Most Americans at that time agreed with President Franklin D. Roosevelt that December 7, 1941, was a "day that will live in infamy."

In the immediate aftermath of Pearl Harbor, concern mounted about the allegiance of the Japanese-American population. Many American leaders expressed the belief that they remained loyal to Japan and posed a threat as saboteurs and spies. Initially, 1,500 Japanese who had been outspoken supporters of Japan were arrested as potential security risks. Building upon the already substantial public prejudice against the Japanese, war hysteria led to the rounding up of 100,000 Japanese-Americans living on the West Coast—men, women, and children. They were relocated in a number of internment camps, to the applause of political leaders and writers across the political spectrum. All seemed united in the belief, expressed by General J. L. DeWitt, who directed the roundup, that "a Jap's a Jap, and it makes no difference whether he's a citizen or not." The blind prejudice of such views was later exposed by the tens of thousands of Japanese-Americans who fought in Europe during World War II, including the legendary 442 Regimental Combat Unit, whose heroics made them the most decorated unit in the U.S. Army.

Internment brought economic disaster to the Japanese living on the American mainland (oddly enough, only they were interned, while the 150,000 Japanese-Americans in Hawaii, living close to Pearl Harbor, were not). Thousands of farms and small businesses were lost forever, while many others were sold for next to nothing by desperate people forced to leave for a camp. And bigotry flourished. A Gallup Poll conducted on the West Coast in December 1942, a year after Pearl Harbor, found that an overwhelming majority of white Americans in that region said they would never again hire Japanese or shop in stores owned by Japanese after the war was over.

At war's end, the Japanese resumed their efforts to find a place for themselves in American life. The immediate postwar American economy was booming, and there was great demand for highly educated people, especially those with technical or financial training. Now the huge educational advantages achieved by the Japanese before the war translated into occupational achievement. By 1959, seventeen years after their internment and terrible finan-

■ Irwin Yoshimura stares into the camera while his father attempts to set up an oil stove to heat the barracks to which the Yoshimura family and other Japanese-Americans have been assigned at a temporary assembly point in Puyallup, Washington, in 1942. Notice that mattresses for the cots have not yet arrived. From Puyallup this group was sent to Moses Lake in eastern Washington where a more permanent detention camp was established for Japanese-Americans. Persons of Japanese ancestry also were forced to leave the West Coast of Canada. In both nations, families like the Yoshimuras suffered severe financial losses as well as humiliation.

cial losses, the family income of Japanese-Americans had caught up with that of the white population (Petersen, 1971). Ten years after that, the average income of Japanese-Americans was higher than that of white Americans (see Table 11-2)! Part of this was due to the concentration of the Japanese-American population on the West Coast, where wages were higher. But even among the population there, the average income of Japanese-Americans was higher.

And educational achievements are the basis of these income gains. Table 11-3 shows that by 1980 Asian-Americans as a group were much more likely than other Americans to have col-

Table 11-2 ■ Comparative earnings ratios, in constant U.S. dollars (based on employed males).

	Ratio to White Earnings		
	1960	1970	1976
Whites	100	100	100
Japanese	91	102	112
Chinese	84	91	87
Filipinos	60	71	93
Hispanics	63	73	72
Blacks	49	59	67

Source: Hirschman and Wong, 1984.

Table 11-3 ■ Race, ethnicity, and education in the United States, 1980 (based on population age 25 and older).

	College Graduates (Percent)	Less Than Nine Years of Schooling (Percent)
Asians	32.9	16.4
Whites	15.5	14.7
Blacks	8.8	24.7
Hispanics	7.8	40.6
American Indians, Eskimos, and Aleuts	7.7	25.0

Source: Statistical Abstract of the United States, 1985.

■ Japanese-American children in California in about 1910 with their book bags suspended from a carrying pole. Although Japanese immigrants were not well educated and primarily worked in agriculture, from the very start they sent their children to school. Within a few decades they far surpassed the average level of education of other Americans.

lege degrees. Equally important, their degrees are concentrated in fields such as engineering, science, medicine, law, and business administration (Sowell, 1981)—degrees that offer direct entry to the highest-paying occupations.

As the Japanese-Americans overcame economic inequality, attitudes toward them shifted rapidly. This can be demonstrated in several ways. The first is intermarriage. Perhaps nothing emphasizes the stress in relations between a majority and a disliked minority more than the question, Would you want your son or daughter to marry one? The answer is always a resounding no. In the 1920s, only about 2 percent of all Japanese-American marriages involved a non-Japanese spouse. By the 1950s this had climbed to about 20 percent (Levine and Montero, 1973), and now is about 50 percent (Kihumura and Kitano, 1973; Heer, 1980). High rates of intermarriage dramatically show that attitudes on both sides have changed.

Japanese-Canadians

In Canada, too, the Japanese were only a small group—the 1901 census counted about 20,000, nearly all of them living in British Columbia. Also in Canada, even this small number caused a panic about a "yellow peril." In 1895 Japanese were denied the right to vote. They also were excluded by law from most professions, from employment in the civil service, and from teaching positions. In 1907 white mobs rampaged through the Japanese district in Vancouver intent on driving out "heathen Orientals." Soon after, the Canadian and Japanese governments reached an agreement to allow only 400 new immigrants to come to Canada each year. In 1928 a new agreement cut the quota to 150 a year.

As in the United States, many of the Japanese took up farming. Others settled in small fishing villages where they continued to sustain themselves—even though, during the 1920s, the government severely limited the number of Japanese granted licenses to fish. Also as in the United States, Japanese-Canadians went to school. By the 1930s, the average Japanese born in Canada probably had more years of schooling than did most other Canadian ethnic groups (Ujimoto, 1976).

In the wake of the bombing of Pearl Harbor, Canadian authorities moved against Japanese residents—demanding that they immediately withdraw more than 160 kilometers from the Pacific Ocean. About 20,000 were crowded into the livestock barns on the exhibition grounds in Vancouver, and from there they were taken to inland camps to spend the war years in ramshackle barracks, built almost overnight.

In the United States the Japanese suffered great financial damage from having to sell their property in haste or abandon it. In Canada the government confiscated Japanese-owned farms, homes, businesses, fishing boats, and the like and sold them. After the war the Canadian government attempted to deport about half of those interned, but was prevented from doing so by public protests. Finally, in 1949 Japanese-Canadians were granted the right to vote.

Yet after all this the Japanese-Canadians achieved immense economic and social prog-

■ Officers of the Royal Canadian Navy confiscating the boat of a Japanese fisherman in Esquimalt, British Columbia, shortly after Pearl Harbor. The area within 160 kilometers of the West Coast of Canada was made off-limits to Japanese-Canadians during World War II. Since this was where most of them lived, they were placed in detainment camps inland, and the government seized and sold their farms, businesses, homes, and property.

ress over the past thirty years (Ujimoto, 1976). Making use of their educational advantages and newly granted freedom of occupational choice, they flocked into universities, the professions, the arts, and business administration. Today Japanese-Canadians have an average income higher than that of most white ethnic groups. And just as there has been a very rapid shift in attitudes toward the Japanese in the United States, so too have they gained social acceptance in Canada—as indicated by an intermarriage rate that is well above 50 percent (Sunahara, 1981; Adachi, 1978).

Thus, we see that despite deep prejudice, despite clear racial and cultural markers, despite the added hysteria caused by war with Japan, the Japanese in the United States and Canada suddenly ceased to be strangers and enemies as they achieved status equality.

Let us now analyze how groups succeed in North America. How did Italians, Poles, Irish, Japanese, and the other immigrant groups rise from poverty to equality and acceptance?

Mechanisms of Ethnic and Racial Mobility

In the course of North American history, a great many different ethnic and racial groups have been on the bottom of the stratification system. Nearly without exception, while each was on the bottom, it was widely believed that their future was hopeless and that they would always be on the bottom. For example, at the time of the American Revolution, Benjamin Franklin wrote that the Germans who had recently settled in Pennsylvania would never fit in or contribute to American society.

But time and again these prophesies have been wrong, as group after group has escaped an ascribed low status to achieve equality and thereby eliminate prejudice. The proper Bostonians "knew" that the "drunken, lazy, superstitious Irish" would never amount to anything. But today their average income is slightly higher than that of Protestants of English origin in the United States (Greeley, 1974).

The waves of immigrants from southern and eastern Europe who began arriving after 1880 caused one of America's leading sociologists of the time, E. A. Ross, to write in 1914 that they were so racially inferior that they would drag the nation down, intellectually and morally:

It is fair to say that the blood now being injected into the veins of our people is "sub-common." [Many of these new kinds of immigrants] are hirsute, low-browed, big-faced persons of obviously low mentality. . . . Clearly they belong in skins, in wattled huts at the close of the Great Ice Age.

That the mediterranean peoples are morally below the races of northern Europe is as certain as any social fact. Even when they *were dirty, ferocious barbarians, these blonds [northern Europeans] were truthtellers.*

The Northerners seem to surpass southern Europeans in innate ethical endowment . . . but they will lose these traits in proportion as they absorb excitable mercurial blood from southern Europe.

The year Ross published this book, he served as president of the American Sociological Society and as professor of sociology at the University of Wisconsin. Ironically, in 1959 Ross's pioneering essays on social control were rescued from obscurity, edited, and republished by two leading American sociologists, Edgar F. Borgatta and Henry J. Meyer—an Italian and a Jew! Presumably, eastern and southern Europeans had biologically evolved an incredible amount in only fifty years, if one were to take Ross's 1914 judgments seriously.

If many groups have made it in North America, then how have they done so? Through what tactics or mechanisms have groups achieved their upward mobility? Three basic elements seem crucial. First is geographic concentration. The second is internal economic development and occupational specialization. The third is development of a middle class (Wirth, 1928; Glazer and Moynihan, 1970; Sowell, 1981; Portes, 1987).

Geographic concentration

Discrimination has often forced subordinate ethnic, racial, and religious minorities to live in enclaves segregated from the surrounding dominant group. However, in addition to discrimination, the tendency for racial and ethnic minorities to concentrate in certain neighborhoods has been encouraged by the needs and desires of subordinate groups: to band together for self-help, to maintain familiar features of their native culture (such as churches, festivals, and traditional foods), and to use their own language in daily life (see Chapter 19.)

Geographic, or neighborhood, concentration is often denounced as a barrier to better intergroup relations. Yet Allport's theory suggests that, at least in the early days of a subordinate

■ In part, this scene from San Francisco's Chinatown at the turn of the century reflects the hostility and discrimination against Asians that was typical of the time and place. But Chinatown stood for more than segregation; it also helped the Chinese concentrate the economic and political resources of their community, which, in time, helped them escape from poverty and prejudice. The same pattern has governed the history of many racial and cultural minorities in Canada and the United States.

group's American experience, concentration may help to minimize the negative consequences of contact. But geographic concentration may have additional benefits as well: *When a group is concentrated in a few locations, its economic and political power is maximized.*

Consider the Irish. Today they make up about 8 percent of the U.S. population. Suppose that when they arrived in this country, they had scattered across the landscape. If they had spread

out evenly, then everywhere they would have constituted 8 percent of the population, and nowhere would they have been more numerous. But the Irish congregated in a few major cities and in particular neighborhoods within those cities. As a result, they quickly became a majority or a sizable minority of the local population. Hence they soon exerted maximum pressure on local affairs affecting their interests. The Irish soon ran the governments of many cities and used their power to further their economic and social interests.

In similar fashion, the Japanese and Chinese congregated on the West Coast, where their numbers mattered. Indeed, from 1976 through 1980, three U.S. senators were Japanese-Americans, although Japanese make up less than 0.4 percent of the U.S. population. In both Canada and the United States, Jews have achieved political influence beyond their numbers because they are geographically concentrated.

The importance of geographic concentration is perhaps nowhere so clear as in the case of French Canada. Far from being a state of mind or an ethnic subculture, the French in Canada are a virtual society. The great durability of French culture and the present political power of French-speaking Canadians are rooted in geography—in the existence of Quebec.

Internal economic development and specialization

Geographic concentration also facilitates a group's ability to develop its own economic resources and institutions, which can then be used to finance further upward mobility. In the beginning, most subordinate groups have difficulty getting credit to finance business or agricultural enterprises, and they desperately need financial resources not subject to outside control. To meet this need, the typical first step of immigrant groups is to pool their funds to provide start-up capital for purchasing or opening small stores and businesses within their own neighborhoods. Then, *by buying within their own community and by reinvesting the profits, immigrant groups gain economic freedom.*

Here geographic concentration can be vital. If a group is not concentrated in particular neighborhoods, then it will be difficult to shop only in stores run by group members. But when a group is concentrated, then economic self-interest is reinforced by the convenience of shopping close to home.

Here, too, language may play a role. Unlike most groups, the Irish did not start their rise to equality by first acquiring neighborhood businesses. This may have been because the Irish

spoke English. Polish or Japanese housewives were often willing to pay higher prices at small groceries run by Poles or Japanese, because they wanted to shop where clerks understood their language. However, Irish housewives lacked this inducement to patronize Irish grocers.

This factor may also pose a major difficulty for blacks attempting to run small shops in black neighborhoods. Unlike Puerto Ricans and other Spanish-speaking groups in America, blacks, like the Irish, have not tended to run small businesses. Although Spanish-speaking consumers may be reluctant to shop in larger stores where clerks do not speak Spanish, black consumers have no language barrier hindering them from going where prices are lowest (Glazer, 1971).

A major step forward for most subordinate groups has been the founding of their own financial institutions. We have seen that the Japanese-Americans created small credit associations and eventually founded their own banks. In Chapter 2 we traced the history of a small neighborhood bank that began as a source of loans for the Italians in San Francisco and eventually grew into the Bank of America. The small, local savings bank was also a typical feature of Irish communities. In fact, Joseph Kennedy, father of President Kennedy, began his remarkable financial empire by opening such a small savings bank.

In addition to seeking economic development and independence, many racial and ethnic minorities have taken advantage of the particular occupational opportunities existing when they arrived. As a result, they have often been (and continue to be) highly overrepresented in certain specialized occupations. We have already seen how the Japanese-Americans specialized in a few occupations: truck farming, gardening, and running small hotels and grocery stores. Today they are greatly overrepresented in engineering, optometry, medicine, and dentistry (Lieberson, 1980; Sowell, 1981). Such specialization maximizes the ability of self-help: People already in an occupation can aid friends and relatives by showing them how to gain entry to the occupation (and perhaps even hiring them); indeed, such people can be the primary source of training for that occupation (Hechter, 1978).

Such occupational specialization has been typical of subordinate groups. For example, the Irish used their control of city governments to enter civil service occupations. As late as 1950, the Irish in the United States were 3 times more likely than other whites to be policemen and firemen. In similar fashion, in 1950 Italians were 8 times overrepresented among barbers, Swedes were 5 times overrepresented among carpenters, Greeks were 29 times overrepresented among restaurant operators, Jews were 17 times overrepresented among tailors, and nearly all diamond cutters were Jewish (Lieberson, 1980).

Recently, this line of analysis has led to the formulation of an **enclave economy theory.** Most closely associated with Alejandro Portes and his colleagues (Portes, 1981, 1987; Portes and Bach, 1985; Portes and Manning, 1986), the theory stresses that ethnic and racial minorities can make more rapid, initial economic progress when they create an enclave economy. Portes (1981) describes such economies as consisting of:

immigrant groups which concentrate in a distinct spatial location and organize a variety of enterprises serving their own ethnic market and/or the general population. Their basic characteristic is that a significant proportion of the immigrant work force works in enterprises owned by other immigrants.

The advantage of this situation is that it creates an increasingly successful group of entrepreneurs within the ethnic community and that ties of ethnic solidarity force these business-owners to give their workers a better deal than would employers from outside the enclave. Moreover, in an enclave economy, firms will promote members of the minority to supervisory positions from which they would tend to be excluded outside (Portes and Bach, 1985).

Development of a middle class

Progress by subordinate groups requires leadership and expertise. To create financial institutions requires group members who know how to run them. To use a concentrated population to influence local politics requires political leadership.

We saw in Chapter 2 that some immigrant groups arrived with a large middle-class contingent—Jews and, later, Cubans are examples. Both groups made extremely rapid economic progress because they already had the skills needed for effective community building. Moreover, both groups used higher education to provide their children with a rapid route for entering upper-income occupations not requiring much capital investment. Unlike buying a store or starting a bank, no initial investment is required for a person to earn a high salary as a scientist, physician, engineer, or accountant. The person need only obtain the appropriate education. That the Jews rapidly became the most highly educated group in North America accounts for the fact that they also have the highest average family income of any racial, religious, or ethnic group (Greeley, 1974; Heaton, 1986). As we have seen, the Japanese also used higher education to improve their status quickly.

We already have seen that initially the concentration of a racial or ethnic group helps to create internal economic resources, and one important use of these resources is to educate the next generation. However, there comes a time when a racial or ethnic minority must begin to achieve substantial assimilation if it is to continue its upward mobility. As Sanders and Nee (1987) have demonstrated in their study of Cuban and Chinese immigrants, ethnic solidarity and concentration are favorable to the growth of business and financial firms and thus to the self-employed, but group members earn higher salaries when they are employed outside the enclave, if they have achieved sufficient levels of cultural assimilation to compete. Here mastery of language is of primary importance.

What can this analysis of how various immigrant groups succeeded in North America tell us about the prospects for today's subordinate groups? At first glance, our analysis might seem of little relevance. Although many of these groups are not recent immigrants, they remain in low-status positions and are the targets of prejudice. Thus, they must face problems unlike those faced by the immigrant groups just discussed. As we shall see, blacks, for example, may have special barriers to overcome, but it still is useful to consider blacks as *recent immigrants* and to analyze their recent, rapid upward mobility in terms of this same model.

Today's Minorities as "Immigrants"

Although some racial and ethnic minorities arrived in the United States and Canada only recently, many others are not recent immigrants. For what it's worth, "native" peoples such as American and Canadian Indians and Eskimos immigrated here about 25,000 years ago from Asia. Although most Canadian blacks are recent immigrants, most American blacks can trace their ancestry in the New World back more generations than can any white group. As early as 1680, most blacks in North America were native born, and by 1776 nearly all of them were (Fogel and Engerman, 1974; Patterson, 1982). Similarly, Hispanics have lived in the American West and Southwest for centuries; these regions belonged to Spain and then to Mexico until the middle of the last century.

Hence, it may seem silly to apply to these groups our model of how new immigrants succeeded in only two or three generations, since these groups remain disadvantaged after many generations. However, a number of sociologists (Lieberson, 1973, 1980; Sowell, 1981) have rejected this conclusion. They argue instead that, in the ways that count, blacks, Hispanics, American and Canadian Indians, and Eskimos have, until recently, been nearly as isolated from the mainstreams of American and Canadian society as they would have been had they lived in another country. In analyzing their situations, then, it makes sense to regard these groups *as if* they were recent immigrants. Moreover, because of the legacies of slavery and their long history of suffering, black Americans offer the most significant and theoretically strategic case. So, let's take a sociological look at American black history.

Going North: Black "Immigration" in the United States

Even today, about half of the black population in the United States lives in the South. Until the 1940s, the overwhelming majority of blacks lived in the South. In addition, the black population was not merely southern but was also very heavily rural.

World War II propelled a great wave of black migration north. Recruiters for northern industries toured the South, sending trainloads of blacks north to work in the defense industries. After the war, the movement north continued, eventually involving millions of people. As a result, while only a few decades ago most blacks lived in rural areas, today most live in cities. More blacks now live in Chicago than in the whole state of Mississippi, and more live in New York City than in any southern state.

Admittedly, blacks crossed no national border when they journeyed from Tupelo to Chicago or from Macon to New York. But because of the conditions of life in the South until very recently, going north for blacks was more like a journey from rural, southern Italy to America than a journey from Chicago to Detroit.

Recent industrial development and population growth have transformed the American South so greatly that even many younger southerners are unaware that only a few years ago this region was mired in grinding poverty and backwardness. Indeed, while the legacy of slavery lived on in the discrimination against blacks (they could not attend schools with whites or even drink from the same public water fountains as whites), the most severe deficiencies of southern life affected *both* blacks and whites.

Table 11-4 attempts to show the misery of the American South by contrasting conditions in Mississippi with those in Iowa—both highly agricultural states settled somewhat later in American history. Data for New York State offer an additional contrast.

Notice that in 1850 the majority of persons living in Mississippi were black slaves, while Iowa and New York were, by then, free states.

■ All packed and waiting for her transportation to arrive, this young black woman is fleeing the poverty of the rural South in 1940 to begin a new life in the North. Although technically she was not an immigrant, her journey crossed cultural gaps as great as those crossed by people who came from overseas.

Few Americans anywhere went to college in 1850, but in the whole state of Mississippi that year, there were eleven college students. In Mississippi most animals used for traction (to pull wagons and farm equipment) were mules or oxen, not horses—a clear indication of backward agricultural technology.

By 1880 the majority of Mississippi citizens were free blacks, but the state remained mired in ignorance and poverty. Nearly half of the population was illiterate—and the average grade school operated only seventy-seven days a year. Kids in Iowa went to school twice as long. Forty years later Mississippi's poverty was still acute. In 1920 the average farm in Iowa was worth more than *twelve times* as much as the average farm in Mississippi. Nearly all the farms in Iowa had phones; most farms in Mississippi did not. The school year had lengthened greatly in Mississippi, but it still lagged behind Iowa and New York.

By 1940 blacks made up a slightly smaller percentage of Mississippi's population and a larger proportion of New York's. Yet infant mortality was still almost twice as high in Mississippi as in Iowa and New York. With the Great Depression not yet fully abated, farm values and family incomes were low everywhere but were much, much lower in Mississippi. That year, nearly all homes in northern states had radios. But in Mississippi more than a third could not listen to Jack Benny or The Lone Ranger. By 1960 the poverty gap between Mississippi and the two other states had narrowed some. But still, while most of the nation watched football and old movies on TV, a third of those in Mississippi could only stare at the wall. By 1980 the gap had narrowed yet again, and nearly half of the state's residents were urban. The rate of high school graduation was about as high as New York's, although still well behind Iowa's.

The decline in the black population of Mississippi and the increase in the proportion of blacks living in New York reflect the massive northward migration of southern blacks in the past few decades. And these historical data help us understand what blacks were *leaving* and what they *brought with them* from the South— experience only as subsistence farmers and field hands, with little schooling (which was of low quality); no technical training or modern job skills, not even any experience of living in large cities. In these important respects they were truly going off to a new country. Only their ability to speak English set them apart from most other immigrant groups.

Table 11-4 ■ Southern poverty, 1850–1980.

	Mississippi	Iowa	New York
1850			
Population (in 1,000s)	607	192	3,097
Slaves	51%	0%	0%
Urban	2%	5%	28%
College students per 1,000	0.02	0.52	0.86
Mules or oxen among traction animals	54%	38%	28%
1880			
Black	52.2%	0.6%	1.3%
Illiterate	41.9%	2.4%	4.2%
Number of days in school year	77	148	179
1920			
Average farm value	$2,903	$35,616	$7,376
Farms with autos	5.5%	73.1%	35.2%
Farms with telephones	10.4%	86.1%	47.6%
Automobiles per 1,000	27.2	150.1	38.5
Number of days in school year	122	174	188
1940			
Black	49.2%	0.7%	4.2%
Infant mortality per 1,000 live births	61	37	37
School spending per pupil	$25	$78	$147
Median annual family income	$386	$746	$1,048
Average farm value	$1,632	$12,614	$6,180
City homes with a radio	61.5%	93.7%	96.7%
1960			
Black	42.0%	8.0%	9.3%
Income per capita	$1,208	$2,010	$2,718
Homes with a telephone	45.3%	89.2%	82.3%
Homes with a television set	66.5%	89.2%	90.7%
1980			
Black	35.2%	1.4%	13.7%
Median family income	$14,922	$20,243	$20,385
18-year-olds who graduate from high school	63.7%	88%	66.7%
School spending per pupil	$1,610	$2,264	$3,180
Urban	47.2%	58.6%	84.6%

Black progress

Stanley Lieberson (1973, 1980) has severely criticized sociologists assessing black progress for failing to take into account the fact that blacks are so newly arrived from the South. When sociologists analyze the progress of other racial and ethnic groups, they automatically control for the number of generations in this country. For example, when we compare the educational achievement or the income of Italian-Americans with German-Americans, we first sort the data to eliminate differences resulting from the fact that one group has been in America longer. Thus, we are trying to compare first-generation Italians with first-generation Germans, and so on.

Until recently, sociologists compared northern blacks with northern whites without such generation controls. In fact, only in recent years have a substantial number of blacks been born in the North, and relatively few blacks are the children of parents born in the North. When such generational controls are taken into account, many black-white differences are greatly reduced. The more generations that blacks have lived in the North, the higher their education and the better their jobs (Lieberson, 1973, 1980; Sowell, 1981).

The fact that most blacks lived in the South for so long has been a major impediment to their success. That many southern whites have recently followed the blacks north emphasizes this point, for these white migrants have displayed many of the same disadvantages. Recall from Chapter 5 that southern whites and blacks have scored equally poorly on IQ tests. Thus a great deal that has been attributed to racial differences and racial problems might be explained much more adequately as a more common phenomenon: the problems faced by new immigrants from less developed societies.

A second important matter in assessing recent black progress is age. Because blacks have had a higher birth rate than whites in recent decades, the black population is somewhat younger than the white population. For this reason, comparing the average family income of blacks and whites is also comparing the average income of younger and older families. Because people usually earn more as they get older, such comparisons can misleadingly suggest racial and ethnic differences in success that are merely due to age differences (Sowell, 1981).

All these matters aside, blacks have been making rapid progress in education and income. Table 11-2 compares the average earnings of employed men of various racial and ethnic heritages. Examining the data for black and white males reveals a very rapid closing of the income gap. In 1960, the average employed black man earned only 49 percent as much as the average employed white man. In 1976, the black average had risen to 67 percent that of whites. When allowances are made for age and educational differences (the average white worker is older than the average black worker), the differences are mostly accounted for (Hirschman and Wong, 1984). Indeed, the educational advantages of Japanese-Americans shown in Table 11-3 also are translated into income advantages. Table 11-2 shows that the average employed Japanese-American male earns 112 percent as much as the average white male.

The portrait of rapid black economic gains must be qualified, however, due to a sharp rise in the proportion of black families lacking an adult male. In 1950, only about a tenth of black families with children below the age of 18 were headed by a woman. In 1980, 47 percent of these black families lacked a father. Families headed by a woman, black or white, are much more likely to be poor than are families headed by a man. Because of the dramatic increase in female-headed black families, a substantially higher proportion of black than white families are poor. (Only 14 percent of white families with children below 18 were headed by women in 1980.)

Conversely, the primary cause of affluence is the two-earner family, as we saw so clearly in Special Topic 2. In Chapter 12 we will attempt to understand why these sudden changes in family composition have so recently afflicted the black family in America. We shall discover that a major cause is a shortage of black men, especially young adults. Black women greatly outnumber black men. And that means, of course, that for many black women, the two-earner family is impossible.

But even with the poverty experienced by

■ To truly understand the American experience of blacks, it is necessary also to understand the economic and social history of the American South—to know that until recently most southern whites as well as blacks lived in rural poverty, received inferior educations, and suffered from poor nutrition. When white southerners like these little Georgia boys grew up, many of them also went North. And there, they too resembled immigrants and encountered many of the problems faced by blacks from the South.

female-headed families, the economic situation of black Americans has improved greatly in recent decades. If we accept the notion of blacks as immigrants, then they began to arrive in large numbers only forty years ago, and many came much more recently. Viewed this way, their record of achievement compares very favorably with that of most earlier ethnic and racial groups. This observation is in no way intended to minimize the centuries of black suffering in North America or the continuing poverty of many black citizens. But it does demonstrate the immense achievements of millions of black Americans, achievements that are overlooked by the news media, which tend to portray recent black history as marked by unrelieved poverty, frustration, and helplessness.

Indeed, Thomas Sowell (1981) has bitterly attacked the common political rhetoric that

racism prevents black progress and that only a massive reformation of society can enable blacks to gain equality as propaganda that dishonors and demeans blacks. To accept such a position, he wrote, means that "some of the longest and hardest struggles for self-improvement must be denied—which is to say, history itself must be denied."

However, an accurate portrait of the situation of black Americans must also consider the many impoverished black families and the special barriers that blacks must overcome.

Integration

The image of race relations that the American national news media projects is one of extremely

Table 11-5 ■ Region and integrated neighborhoods.

Whites only: "Are there any blacks living in this neighborhood now?"	East	Midwest	South	West	Nationwide
Yes, on this block	17.9%	16.0%	28.1%	19.5%	20.8%
Yes, within 1 to 3 blocks	15.9%	10.6%	11.7%	25.0%	14.8%
Yes, within 4 to 8 blocks	6.9%	9.7%	10.4%	8.5%	9.1%
No	59.3%	63.7%	49.8%	47.0%	55.2%
	100.0%	100.0%	100.0%	100.0%	100.0%
Percent black	12.2%	9.7%	19.3%	5.1%	12.5%

Source: Prepared by the author from National Opinion Research Center, General Social Survey, 1986.

segregated residential neighborhoods, that with the exception of a few token black residents in some areas, American cities and towns consist of all-white and all-black districts. We shall see in Chapter 19 that this image is fully sustained by the largest cities of the East and upper Midwest: New York, Chicago, Philadelphia, Washington, Detroit, and Boston, for example. These are also the cities in which the national media are concentrated. But this image is not sustained by the cities further west. Nor is it sustained by the data shown in Table 11-5.

In 1986 nearly 21 percent of white Americans said that blacks lived on their block. Should they be believed? Consider that they were interviewed in their own homes by an interviewer whom the respondents knew was familiar with the neighborhood. Another almost 15 percent said that while there were no blacks on their block, blacks lived within three blocks of them. Hence, more than a third of white Americans have black neighbors, and only 55 percent live in neighborhoods without black residents.

To interpret these findings we must keep in mind that in some parts of the nation most whites would lack black neighbors even if every black family lived on an otherwise all-white block. In Boise, Idaho, for example, less than 0.5 percent of the population is black, which is also true in Laredo, Texas, and Glendale, Cali-

fornia. The bottom line of the table therefore reports the percent of the population that is black in these regions (based on this survey).

Many will be surprised to find that southern whites are much the most likely to live on the same block as blacks. This reflects several things. First, the South never had neighborhood segregation as marked as the North had; instead, an elaborate culture of subordination, rather than physical separation, kept blacks "in their places" in the South. Second, the black population is relatively larger in the South, thus increasing the arithmetic possibilities of whites having black neighbors. Finally, southern cities have been growing very rapidly over the past decade, during a time when racial attitudes have been shifting rapidly too. As a result, southern cities have not faced the need to integrate previously segregated neighborhoods, and much integration has occurred through growth. And several of these patterns apply to the greater integration of the West, also an area of new cities that have grown mostly after racial barriers had weakened.

Back in the early 1960s, 11 A.M. to 12 noon Sunday often was described as the most segregated hour in American life. No more. Table 11-6 shows that more than 40 percent of white church members claim that blacks attend their local church. Moreover, half of the black church

Table 11-6 ■ Integrated churches.

White church members only: "Do blacks attend the church that you, yourself, attend most often, or not?"				
	East	**Midwest**	**South**	**West**	**Nationwide**
Percent yes	47.5%	32.1%	38.8%	59.7%	42.8%

	Liberal Protestants	**Conservative Protestants**	**Roman Catholics**
Percent yes	33.6%	39.8%	53.2%

Black church members only: "Do whites attend the church that you, yourself, attend most often, or not?"				
	East	**Midwest**	**South**	**West**	**Nationwide**
Percent yes	59.7%	52.2%	42.5%	84.6%	49.3%

	Liberal Protestants	**Conservative Protestants**	**Roman Catholics**
Percent yes	56.9%	43.8%	78.8%

Source: Prepared by the author from National Opinion Research Center, General Social Survey, 1987 (including the black oversample).

members report that whites attend their local church. Among white Protestants, those who attend more conservative denominations are more likely to report blacks in their congregations, and blacks overwhelmingly belong to conservative Protestant bodies.

Note, however, that Roman Catholics are much more likely than Protestants to report blacks in their congregations. This reminds us that there are a substantial number of black Catholics—as the appointment of the first black American Archbishop in 1988 reflected.

Blacks and whites are least likely to attend integrated churches in the South, which no doubt reflects the historic strength of all-black denominations in that region. Black Protestants are more likely to attend an integrated congregation if they are affiliated with a liberal denomination—because these are predominately white denominations. Because the all-black denominations fall into the conservative Protestant category, it is natural that these are the black Protestants least likely to attend an integrated church. Three-fourths of black Catholics attend an integrated church.

Thus, while the big cities of the East reveal a lack of residential integration, this is not typical of the nation as a whole. Moreover, a rather surprising level of integration has taken place in the nation's churches.

■ Between 1960 and 1980, the proportion of American blacks with professional occupations more than doubled from 4.8 percent to 12.7 percent, while the proportion of whites in the professions increased only from 12.1 percent to 16.5 percent. Meanwhile, the proportion of blacks in managerial positions also rose rapidly from 2.6 percent to 5.2 percent.

Barriers to black progress

Every racial and ethnic minority that began at the bottom of the American status structure had unique features that influenced how rapidly and easily it was able to rise. Although the general model of how groups make it in America applies to each, we have also paid attention to these special features. Blacks have been making considerable progress, but it is important to consider their special handicaps.

■ **The legacies of slavery** Earlier in this chapter, we saw how the existence of slavery in America and the American ideal of individual freedom created a special American dilemma that gave rise to ardent racial prejudice. While all disadvantaged minorities in America were hampered by prejudice, none has faced such harsh prejudice and discrimination as have blacks. That antiblack prejudice has waned so substantially in the past twenty years reflects rapid black economic and educational achieve-

ment. But prejudice and discrimination have also placed much greater burdens on blacks than on other groups.

Moreover, centuries of slavery severed blacks from all but traces of their traditional cultures and limited their sense of common identity. To a crucial extent, in recent decades blacks have had to rediscover their cultural roots and construct a cohesive group sense to give them a common cause (Carmichael and Hamilton, (1967).

■ **No homeland** American blacks also lack a homeland, in the sense of having a specific nation or society of origin. This is because blacks came from many different parts of Africa; moreover, until recently these areas were not independent nations but colonies ruled by European powers. This has had major practical as well as symbolic consequences.

Most immigrants to the United States and Canada based their decisions about when and whether to immigrate on calculations about opportunities here versus opportunities in their homeland. Thus, immigration into North America fluctuated sharply in response to economic conditions, rising when the economy boomed and jobs were plentiful and falling during times of recession. Blacks never chose to come to America, nor did they choose when to become free and thus when and where to start to earn a living. In fact, blacks had to scrape for their first jobs in the aftermath of the Civil War, in a South ravaged by defeat. While their migration north often reflected the desire for greater opportunity, here, too, blacks were less able than were other immigrants to respond to fluctuations in opportunity.

As pointed out in Chapter 2, ethnic and racial immigrants could go back to their homelands if things did not turn out well for them here. During the Great Depression of the 1930s, about 500,000 immigrants went back to Europe (Handlin, 1957). Blacks lacked this option.

Finally, the homeland governments often aided many immigrants after they were here. For example, many governments provided clergy to staff churches in North America for immigrants from their nations. Other governments officially intervened with the U.S. or Canadian government to influence the treatment of immigrants from their countries. Nothing of the sort was available for blacks in North America (Lieberson, 1980).

■ **Visibility** Although the stereotypes of prejudice associated distinctive physical traits with many ethnic groups (that Jews could easily be recognized by their noses, for example), most members of these groups lacked such traits. For example, a study of Jewish men in New York revealed that only 14 percent had what was regarded as a "Jewish nose" (Fishberg, 1911). Moreover, while many immigrant groups had a distinctive culture and quite distinctive names, these traits could easily be changed, thus concealing one's origins and diminishing **visibility**. That Tony Curtis, Michael Landon, Karl Malden, Sandra Dee, Hal Linden, Woody Allen, Joan Rivers, and Kirk Douglas were once known as Bernard Schwartz, Eugene Orowitz, Malden Sekulovich, Alexandra Zuck, Hal Lipshitz, Allen Konigsberg, Joan Molinsky, and Issur Danielo-

vitch demonstrates the point. A Pole or an Italian could learn to speak unaccented English, change his or her name, join a Protestant church, and claim to be a WASP. Most blacks are native speakers of English, have Anglo-Saxon names, and are Protestant, but they're still black.

Racially different groups cannot pass as members of the majority, which may present a more difficult barrier. However, Japanese and Chinese have achieved equality despite being racially different, and most eastern and southern European immigrants did not discard their names, religions, or many of their distinctive cultural patterns en route to acceptance and equality.

■ **Numbers** Perhaps one of the greatest problems faced by blacks is simply that they greatly outnumber all other previously disadvantaged racial and ethnic minorities. Thus, while several hundred thousand Japanese and Chinese sufficed to cause a "yellow peril" on the West Coast, black migration north has involved millions of people. Moreover, sheer numbers prevent blacks from adopting some of the tactics other groups used. Occupational specialization is one of these. As Lieberson (1980) put it, "Imagine more than 22 million Japanese-Americans trying to carve out initial niches [in the U.S. economy] through truck farming!"

Thus, given that economic conflict is the primary factor in prejudice and discrimination, the large size of the black population has made blacks a greater threat to whites, especially in earlier times when blacks constituted a huge source of cheap labor. When changes in the immigration laws stemmed the tide of cheap labor from abroad in the 1920s, blacks became the only significant competitive threat to whites, especially whites holding unskilled labor jobs. Thus, the antagonism that once was spread across many groups—Italians, Poles, Japanese, as well as blacks—focused primarily on blacks; race, not religion or ethnicity, became the burning concern of organized hate groups.

Of course, the size of the black population also presents opportunities. Once barriers to black voting were removed, for example, blacks became a potent political bloc, which, in recent years, has been reflected by a sharp increase in the number of blacks holding elected office in the United States.

None of these barriers to black progress seems so effective as to limit blacks to economic and social inequality. Indeed, each has been substantially overcome, if with great pain and difficulty. Yet we need to see how each has made the road upward unusually difficult.

Of course, blacks are not the only group still suffering inequality in North America; they are simply the largest of these groups and the one whose North American experience constitutes the most shameful, painful chapter in American history. Thus, it is instructive to see the extent to which blacks have fulfilled the dream expressed in the anthem of the Civil Rights Movement, "We Shall Overcome." If blacks can retrace the steps taken by so many other disadvantaged groups in North American history, then there should be no doubt that other racial and ethnic minorities can do it too.

◼ ▬▬▬▬▬▬▬

Conclusion

The primary purpose of this chapter was to show that prejudice, discrimination, and conflict caused by racial and cultural differences are not recent phenomena or limited primarily to North America. These problems are best understood not on the basis of peculiar historical circumstances or even white bigotry, but on the basis of sociological theories having universal application. Intergroup conflict fueled by racial and cultural markers is as old as human existence. So are the processes by which these conflicts are overcome.

That these conflicts cause such agony is reflected by the intensity with which social scientists have sought to understand and prevent them. In my judgment, the contents of this chapter demonstrate that this search has been fairly successful. Current sociological theories of intergroup conflict have dispelled much of the fog shrouding these hostilities. We can now say with some certainty why and how strangers become enemies and how and why these antagonisms will pass.

As we have seen, the key to intergroup conflict is status inequality. Contact between groups who are unequal in status and competing for status produces prejudice. Prejudice does not subside until status equality has been achieved. Keep in mind that two groups being of equal status does not mean that all members of each group must be of the same status. Italians have not achieved status equality with WASPs because all Italians have become rich. Rather, groups are of equal status when the distribution of their members in the status structure is the same. Thus, when a person's race does not reliably indicate his or her status, then racial equality has been achieved. At that point, members of different races are equally likely to be rich or poor.

Review Glossary

intergroup conflict Conflict between groups that are racially or culturally different. (p. 293)

race A human group having some biological features that set it off from other human groups. (p. 293)

ethnic groups Groups that think of themselves as sharing special bonds of history and culture that set them apart from others. (p. 293)

caste system A stratification system wherein cultural or racial differences are used as the basis for ascribing status. (p. 294)

Allport's theory of contact A theory holding that contact between groups will improve relations only if the groups are of equal status and do not compete with one another. (p. 296)

the American dilemma Term used by Myrdal to describe the contradiction of a society committed to democratic ideals but sustaining racial segregation. (p. 298)

markers (cultural or racial) Noticeable differences between two or more groups that become associated with status conflicts between the groups. (p. 303)

cultural division of labor A situation in which racial or ethnic groups tend to specialize in a limited number of occupations. (p. 308)

middleman minorities Racial or ethnic groups restricted to a limited range of occupations in the middle, rather than lower, level of the stratification system. (p. 308)

enclave economy theory Proposes that the spatial concentration of an ethnic group permits it to create its own business enterprises, thus speeding the economic progress of the group. (p. 318)

visibility The degree to which a racial or an ethnic group can be recognized—how easily those in such a group can pass as members of the majority. (p. 327)

Suggested Readings

Cobas, José A., ed. 1987. *The Ethnic Economy: Special Issue of Sociological Perspectives* 30:339–472.

Driedger, Leo, ed. 1978. *The Canadian Ethnic Mosaic: A Quest for Identity.* Toronto: McClelland and Stewart.

Lieberson, Stanley. 1980. *A Piece of the Pie: Blacks and White Immigrants Since 1880.* Berkeley: University of California Press.

Petersen, William. 1971. *Japanese Americans: Oppression and Success.* New York: Random House.

Sowell, Thomas. 1981. *Ethnic America: A History.* New York: Basic Books.

Wilson, William Julius. 1987. *The Truly Disadvantaged: The Inner City, the Underclass and Public Policy.* Chicago: University of Chicago Press.

Winks, Robin W. 1971. *The Blacks in Canada: A History.* Montreal: McGill-Queen's University Press.

Minorities and Stardom

The majority of players on every team in the National Basketball Association are black. White boxing champions are rare. A far greater proportion of professional football players is black than would be expected based on the size of the black population. Furthermore, blacks began to excel in sports long before the Civil Rights Movement broke down barriers excluding them from many other occupations. This has led many people, both black and white, to conclude that blacks are born with a natural talent for athletics. How else could they have come to dominate the ranks of superstars?

The trouble with this biological explanation of blacks in sports is that it ignores an obvious historical fact: It is typical for minorities in North America to make their first substantial progress in sports (and, for similar reasons, in entertainment). Who today would suggest that Jews have a biological advantage in athletics? Yet at the turn of the century, the number of Jews who excelled in sports far exceeded their proportion in the population. And late in the nineteenth century, the Irish dominated sports to almost the same extent as blacks have done in recent decades.

By examining an encyclopedia of boxing, for example, we can draw accurate conclusions about patterns of immigration and at what period which ethnic groups were on the bottom of the stratification system. The Irish domination of boxing in the latter half of the nineteenth century is obvious from the names of heavyweight champions, beginning with bareknuckle champ Ned O'Baldwin in 1867 and including Mike McCoole in 1869, Paddy Ryan in 1880, John L. Sullivan in 1889, and Jim Corbett in 1892. The list of champions in lower weight divisions during the same era is dominated by fighters named Ryan, Murphy, Delaney, Lynch, O'Brien, and McCoy.

Early in the twentieth century, Irish names became much less common among boxing champions, even though many fighters who were not Irish took Irish ring names. Suddenly, champions had names like Battling Levinsky, Maxie Rosenbloom, Benny Leonard, Abe Goldstein, Kid Kaplan, and Izzy Schwartz. This was the Jewish era in boxing. Then Jewish names dropped out of the lists, and Italian and eastern European names came to the fore: Canzoneri, Battalino, LaMotta, Graziano, and Basilio; Yarosz, Lesnevich, Zale, Risko, Hostak, and Servo. By the 1940s, fighters were disproportionately black. Today, black domination of boxing has already peaked, and Hispanic names have begun to prevail.

The current overrepresentation of blacks in sports reflects two things: first, a *lack of other avenues to wealth and fame* and, second, the fact that minority groups can overcome discrimination most easily in occupations where

■ Yankee Sullivan was the first great Irish-American prize fighter. In 1853 he lost the American heavyweight championship in a bareknuckle bout lasting 37 rounds. The first American to win the world heavyweight championship was also named Sullivan (John L.) and held the title from 1882 until 1892 when he lost it to another Irish-American named James J. Corbett, who in turn was succeeded by an Irish-American named Bob Fitzsimmons. In the late nineteenth century nearly every famous boxer in every weight class was an Irish-American.

the quality of individual performance is most easily and accurately assessed (Blalock, 1967). These same factors led to the overrepresentation of other ethnic groups in sports earlier in history.

It is often difficult to know which applicants to a law school or a pilot training school are the most capable. But we can see who can box or hit a baseball. The demonstration of talent, especially in sports and entertainment, tends to break down barriers of discrimination. As these fall, opportunities in these areas for wealth and fame open up, while other opportunities remain closed. Thus, minority groups will aspire to those areas in which the opportunities are open and will tend to overachieve in these areas.

In an important theoretical contribution to racial and ethnic relations, H. M. Blalock (1967) was one of the first to explain why minorities more rapidly overcome discrimination in sports. Let's consider several of his propositions.

First, Blalock argued, work groups differ in the extent to which an outstanding individual can bring success to the whole group. A worker on an assembly line, for example, does not increase the earnings of other workers by working faster. But a great quarterback or a great hitter can transform an average team into champions. Thus, Blalock theorized, the more an individual can increase the benefits of all work group members, the less that group will discriminate against minority members. This will be particularly so when it is easy to judge how much a person could add to the group's success.

To illustrate Blalock's point, consider a baseball team. All the players are white, and many of them are prejudiced against blacks. However, they also want to win the pennant and the World Series, but they need a better power hitter to do so. Such a team will be inclined to ignore their prejudice against blacks if they have a chance to get a star hitter who is black.

Blalock also suggested that when employers compete intensely for talented people, they will be much less likely to discriminate. Because such competition is the essence of management in sports, highly talented minority players will be an irresistible temptation for owners and managers. Discrimination should cease in sports long before it does in most other high-status occupations. Blalock's proposition also implies that less successful teams would take the lead in ending discrimination, while the most successful teams would resist it. In fact, during the many years when they routinely won the pennant and the World Series, the New York Yankees were the least integrated team in baseball.

Thus, the overrepresentation of an ethnic or racial minority in sports often signals that group's early progress in struggling up from the bottom of society. However, the real signal that a group is making it comes when their overrepresentation in sports begins to decline, for it means that young people of this racial or ethnic background have other possible roads to success. This is not to suggest that it is better for people to become lawyers or dentists than to become linebackers. (I much prefer to watch a linebacker fill a hole than a dentist.) But no group should face such limited opportunities that playing sports is their only escape from poverty and prejudice. The overrepresentation of a racial or ethnic minority in sports does not reflect inborn athletic talent any more than their underrepresentation in science reflects an inborn lack of academic talent. Instead, both reflect limited opportunities.

These same principles apply to overrepresentation in the entertainment world. The early success of blacks in music, for example, led to the belief that they were born with a "natural sense of rhythm." Again, when opportunities are few, people will concentrate their efforts. Blacks who could play musical instruments, dance, sing, or write music dedicated themselves to perfecting their skills, as did other ethnic groups when their opportunities were limited. Like athletic talent, entertainment skills are very visible and easily demonstrated. Bill "Bojangles" Robinson could have become a star just by dancing on a street corner (which he often did even after he was world famous). Louis Armstrong's trumpet playing was as obviously inspired as Michael Jordan's dunk shots. To claim that Fats Waller couldn't play the piano would have been as silly as to say Joe Louis couldn't punch. As in sports, barriers of discrimination tend to fall early in the entertainment industry.

Schollaert and Smith: Do White Fans Reject "Too Black" Teams?

 If the visibility of outstanding individual talent is the key to minority stardom, then fans should rapidly come to place much greater value on ability and performance than on race or ethnicity. But in recent years there has been much media concern about the negative consequences for fan support of teams that have become "too black." The argument is that although sports fans readily embraced the first black superstars, they have grown increasingly restive as teams began to have substantial numbers of black players.

These worries have become quite vocal as professional basketball has turned into a black-dominated sport. By the late 1960s blacks made up more than half of the players on the average National Basketball Association team, and today the average team is about 75 percent black (Schollaert and Smith, 1987). This has led both white (Halberstam, 1981) and black (Edwards, 1982) observers to suggest that problems loom for the future of the NBA, and perhaps American basketball in general, because white fans can't identify with teams that are nearly all-black.

Through it all, however, as the NBA teams have grown increasingly black, average attendance has risen. So what's the truth? Recently, two researchers who specialize in the sociology of sport decided to find out.

Paul T. Schollaert and Donald Hugh Smith of Old Dominion University, famous for its powerhouse women's basketball teams, decided to see if the racial composition of NBA teams influenced attendance. To do so, they gathered data on the percent of black players and total attendance for all NBA teams annually over fourteen years, from 1969 through 1982. Their aim was to see if shifts in racial composition correlated with shifts in attendance. But to do this they also had to gather data on other factors as a guard against spurious findings. They argued that fan support is affected by winning. So they collected data on the won-loss record. They also hypothesized that star players might boost attendance even when a team was not having an outstanding season. They measured this by the number of each team's players named to the All-Star Game each year. They also included data on annual ticket prices for each team.

In addition, Schollaert and Smith proposed that attendance may be influenced by the location of the arena (suburban or central city) and by its seating capacity, because this determines the number of tickets a team could possibly sell. They found they had to remove Portland from the analysis because it has a small arena that has been sold out for every game for years—hence there has been no variation in Portland's attendance.

Characteristics of the metropolitan area within which teams are located might also affect attendance. Schollaert and Smith included data on the population, reasoning that where there are more people there are more potential ticket-buyers. Data on median income for the area also were included on the basis that fans with more money can buy more tickets. The percent of blacks in each area's population was noted to make sure that as a team increased its proportion of black players, a rise in attendance of black fans didn't offset and therefore hide a loss of white support. Finally, the number of other local major league sports franchises was included because these offer competition for fan support. (The Portland Trailblazers attribute their annual sellouts in part to the fact that they are the only major league franchise in town.)

So what were the results of this study? *The racial composition of teams did not influence attendance.*

The major determinant of attendance in a given year is how many games the team is winning that year. The next most important factor is arena size. A close third is a winning record the year before. Next is the total population from which the team draws. Fifth is the number of All-Star players. Finally, median income of the area and ticket prices had weak effects on attendance. The percent of the population that is black, number of competing franchises, and location of the arena didn't matter.

Schollaert and Smith concluded that the widespread belief that white fans resent black dominance of basketball is itself a myth rooted in "racism"—in this case a racial stereotype of whites as bigots.

Whatever the case, the fact remains that these results are consistent with the acceptance of blacks in entertainment long before there even was an NBA. For example, whites flocked to hear the famous all-black big bands of the swing era, such as those led by Count Basie, by Duke Ellington, and by Lionel Hampton. In fact, these bands performed primarily in front of white audiences.

Gender and Inequality

12

ONE EVENING IN the mid-1970s, Marcia Guttentag and her 16-year-old daughter attended a performance of Mozart's *The Magic Flute*. It was the first time she had heard this opera sung in English rather than in the original German, and as she listened to the lyrics she had one of those rare moments of insight that every scientist dreams of and few ever experience.

Guttentag noticed that the male leads sang again and again about the same thing—their urgent desire to find a wife and their determination to cherish her forever. The emphasis on lasting relationships immediately reminded her of the lyrics of songs popular in her youth, when Big Band singers crooned "Our love is here to stay."

After the opera, Guttentag asked her daughter if she had noticed anything odd about the music. "She said that the lyrics were strange because the men sang about wanting to make a lifelong commitment to one woman—a wife" (Guttentag and Secord, 1983). Both agreed that this was in sharp contrast to current popular music, which stresses "brief liaisons and casual relationships between men and women," a theme of "love 'em and leave 'em."

"Why?" Guttentag asked herself. Why such a shift in attitudes toward women? Then inspiration struck. Is it possible that suddenly there has been *a shift in the supply of women?* Could it be that in recent decades "a shortage of men" has developed? In the past, did men typically face a shortage of eligible women? Are Papageno and Tamino in *The Magic Flute* facing an unfavorable **sex ratio** so that there are far too few women to provide each man with a wife?

Could sex ratios lie behind the immense differences in relations between the sexes from one society to another and one era to the next?

Guttentag recognized this as the germ of a potentially immense theoretical breakthrough. So she devoted herself entirely to working out the theoretical implications of her insight and, at the same time, to collecting appropriate data from such diverse times and places as ancient Greece, medieval Europe, among Orthodox Jews in nineteenth-century Russia and Poland, for eighteenth- and nineteenth-century America, and, finally, among white and black Americans in recent decades. And as she went forward, everything began to fall into place. Sex roles and relationships have long been immensely influenced by the ratio of males to females.

Chapter Preview

In Chapter 6 we explored sex roles and sex-role socialization. Now it's time to come to grips with underlying questions of *why?* Why do societies typically socialize their members to accept unequal sex roles that oppress women? And why have some societies sometimes been much more equitable in terms of sex roles?

In this chapter we will use Guttentag's work as the framework for a wide-ranging assessment of inequalities between men and women. Other important studies will, of course, be woven into the narrative. But this chapter will be shaped by one piece of scholarship far more

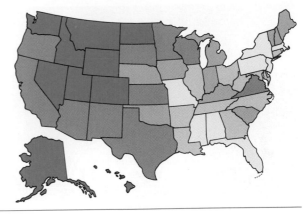

1981: Males per 100 Females

Ontario	97.4
Quebec	97.4
Manitoba	97.8
Nova Scotia	98.2

Newfoundland	101.5
Alberta	104.7
N.W. Territories	110.1
Yukon	110.4

New Brunswick	99.0
British Columbia	99.3
Pr. Edward Island	99.4
Saskatchewan	101.2

Figure 12-1 ■ **Sex ratios—males per 100 females.** For most of their histories, the United States and Canada had populations in which men outnumbered women, especially among young adults. Recently this has reversed, and in 1980 there were only 94.5 American males for every 100 females, while in Canada in 1981 there were 98.6 males per 100 females. However, overall rates such as these often can hide large variations from one region to another. Hence, American men in the Northeast are outnumbered by about 10 to 9, while in North Dakota, Nevada, Wyoming, Hawaii, and Alaska men outnumber women. Similar contrasts occur in Canada. In the Yukon and the Northwest Territories there are 11 men to every 10 women (as there are next door in Alaska), while in the urban East men are outnumbered in Ontario and Quebec. In this chapter we shall see that sex ratios can have profound effects upon sex roles and the status of women in societies.

1980: Males per 100 Females

New York	90.5
Massachusetts	90.8
Rhode Island	91.0
Pennsylvania	91.9
Florida	92.2
New Jersey	92.2
Alabama	92.5
Missouri	92.7
Mississippi	92.9

Kansas	95.9
Virginia	96.0
Wisconsin	96.0
Minnesota	96.1
Texas	96.8
Arizona	96.9
Oregon	97.0
California	97.2
New Mexico	97.2
South Dakota	97.3

Delaware	93.1
Connecticut	93.1
Tennessee	93.3
Arkansas	93.5
Georgia	93.5
Ohio	93.5
Maryland	94.0
Illinois	94.0
West Virginia	94.1
Louisiana	94.2
North Carolina	94.3

Utah	98.4
Colorado	98.5
Washington	98.7
Montana	99.6
Idaho	99.7
North Dakota	101.3
Nevada	102.4
Wyoming	105.0
Hawaii	105.2
Alaska	112.8

Indiana	94.4
Maine	94.4
Iowa	94.6
South Carolina	94.7
Vermont	94.9
New Hampshire	95.0
Michigan	95.2
Nebraska	95.3
Oklahoma	95.4
Kentucky	95.6

■ Francisco Araiza sings the part of Tamino in the San Francisco Opera Company's production of *The Magic Flute* in 1987. Hearing this opera sung in English led Marcia Guttentag to ask herself how societies would differ depending on whether they had a shortage or an abundance of women.

combines so much theoretical scope with such creative research that it presents the opportunity to use it not only to illuminate gender relations but also to provide a mid-book review of the sociological process as we have encountered it thus far. I thought you might find it helpful to see the entire sociological forest again, before moving on to look at more big trees in this forest. Finally, in this instance it seems more important to thoroughly understand a big idea about gender relations than to be exposed briefly to a flock of little ones, many of which also appear in the mass media frequently.

■
_____

Sex Ratios and Sex Roles: A Theory

Sad to say, three years after she began working out the connections between sex ratios and gender relations, Marcia Guttentag died suddenly in 1977. She left a book only half written. All might have been lost but for the fact that in 1972 she had married Paul F. Secord, who is also a well-known sociologist. As a memorial to his wife, Secord set out to finish her work. In addition to his wife's drafts and notes, Secord was able to draw upon countless discussions they had as she worked on the book. Eventually, however, Secord's contributions went far beyond simply writing up chapters Guttentag left unwritten. For he became as absorbed in the topic as she had been, and so he worked over the theory and added substantially to the supporting research. Finally, in 1983 the book appeared: *Too Many Women? The Sex Ratio Question*, by Marcia Guttentag and Paul F. Secord. The next year it received the American Sociological Association's Award for Distinguished Contribution to Scholarship.

Sex ratios

To examine the Guttentag and Secord theory, let's begin by imagining a world in which one gender greatly outnumbers the other in the age groups during which people usually marry and have children. Based on ordinary economic

than is true for any other chapter—for several reasons. First of all, I could not resist the opportunity to let you watch the birth of a really important idea, see it grow into a sophisticated theory, and then look on as it is confronted with stringent empirical tests. This opportunity was especially irresistible because the theory is so purely *sociological*. Sex ratios are not traits of individuals; they are *social structures*. When individuals move from a society with an excess of males to one with an excess of females, their lives change even though their gender does not.

My second reason is that Guttentag's work

principles of supply and demand, we can assume that the gender in short supply has an advantage, that it can impose premium costs on members of the other gender in return for assenting to marriage.

Now assume that eligible females are the ones in short supply. How will they benefit from their advantage in the marriage market? Doesn't it make sense that when women have the advantage that they can more easily resist male efforts to restrict their choices? For example, isn't it logical that a woman in this position could play one suitor off against another and thereby obtain great latitude in what she was allowed to say and do? Couldn't such a woman expect to have considerable sexual freedom where men greatly outnumber women—freedom, for example, to take a series of lovers, moving on whenever she got bored or disappointed?

Now, think about the reverse situation, in which women greatly outnumber men. Here men have the advantage, so women will have to pay the premiums. Isn't it likely that women in this situation will have to vie with one another to be pure, faithful, submissive, maternal—all the "virtues" associated with traditional female sex roles?

In fact, Guttentag and Secord's theory of sex ratios and sex roles predicts sex-role patterns *opposite* to those just outlined! And reality seems to agree with them: As we examine societies around the world, women are clearly much more subject to the limits of traditional sex roles in societies where there is an excess of men. Table 12-1 shows that in nations where men outnumber women, female status tends to be low (women trail men in primary school enrollment, literacy, and voting rights). The table also shows that where men outnumber women, women are less likely to be employed outside the home, the divorce rate is low, and the birth rate is high. How can this be? As we shall see, there are important constraints on the bargaining position of individuals other than the relative supply of persons of their sex.

But before we see how the Guttentag and Secord theory clarifies these issues, let's consider a question that you may already be wondering about: How does it happen that societies

Table 12-1 ■ **Correlations between sex ratios and sex roles for the 50 most populous nations.**

	Males per 100 Females
Index of Women's Status*	−.52%
Percent of women in labor force	−.58
Divorce rate	−.50
Birth rate	.52

*Based on female primary school enrollment, female literacy, and female voting rights (Estes, 1984).

Source: World ShowCase, data selected and supervised by Robert Szafran (Seattle: Cognitive Development, Inc., 1987).

have too many men or too many women? Aren't sex ratios purely a function of biology?

Causes of imbalanced sex ratios

In most human populations, for every 100 female births there are from 105 to 106 male births (Matras, 1973). However, since males have higher rates of infant and child mortality, the sex ratio soon evens out if nothing else intrudes. But in most times and places, other things have intruded. Usually these intrusions have produced an excess of men; throughout history most human societies have had a shortage of women. Sometimes, however, the intrusions produce a shortage of men.

■ **Geographic mobility** Extremely imbalanced sex ratios often are caused by periods of rapid and large-scale migration or immigration. In the typical instance young men depart in pursuit of economic opportunity, leaving the young women behind. In consequence, there is an excess of women in the place from which the men are moving and a shortage of women in the place they are moving to. For example, the 1850 census found that in California men outnumbered women by more than twelve to one (or 1,222 men per 100 women). The cause?

■ In the summer of 1897 word reached the West Coast cities of Canada and the United States that gold had been discovered on the Klondike River in Canada's remote Yukon Territory. Within hours a Gold Rush was on. Here we see a pier in Seattle where hundreds are crowding aboard anything afloat headed north. Notice that there are virtually no women among them. Rapid migrations such as this typically create situations with extreme sex ratios. However, when these crowds of prospectors reached the Yukon and created Dawson City at the site of the gold strike, they did not find themselves in a community *without* women but in one where men outnumbered women by more than 100 to 1. Even in extreme cases of rapid migration such as a gold rush, some women go, too. Notice the group of women in the foreground. They also were waiting for passage to the Yukon.

■ Here we can see a basic aspect of sex roles in Dawson City as two elegantly dressed women stand among more than two dozen men at the bar of the Monte Carlo Saloon. Here miners showered Margie Newman with gold nuggets as she danced on stage, and Roddy Conners once spent $50,000 to dance with Jacqueline and Rosalinde, two sisters who, like the women in the photograph, charged $1 for each circuit around the small dance floor. Here too a miner once paid $20 a bottle for enough wine to fill a bathtub so Cad Wilson, famous for her rendition of "Such a Nice Girl, Too," could bathe in it. Others, including Oregon Mare, Sweet Marie, and Flossie de Atley, expected to be treated to $60 pint bottles of champagne to sit at a man's table—and one miner spent $1,700 in a single night in this manner. Whether they were superstars or just saloon hostesses, the women in Dawson City were sex objects in the most literal sense. Lavished with gifts and attention, they were nevertheless treated like property. Cecile Marion, one of the most popular singers, was auctioned off to Chris Johansen for her weight in gold.

■ "I'm Only a Bird in a Gilded Cage" was a favorite song performed in frontier saloons by female singers, like this star of Dawson City at the height of the Gold Rush. Although the song lamented the lost chance for true romance by a young woman who had surrendered to "a rich man's gold," the lament is shared by *most* women in times and places with a great excess of males. For, although their cages may be gilded, women in these circumstances tend to be locked into highly restrictive sex roles. Indeed, the saloon owner may have sold this young woman to one of the city's instant millionaires for her weight in gold—more than $60,000 at that time, or over $500,000 today.

The California Gold Rush that began in 1849. The Forty-Niners, as the prospectors were called, were nearly all younger men, most of them single. Meanwhile, back East the absence of these young men was clearly felt. In Massachusetts in 1850 the census counted only 96.5 men per 100 women. That may not sound like much of an imbalance. But it was concentrated in the

prime marriage age group, so that for every ten women between age 15 and 30 there were fewer than nine men. Worse yet, as we shall see, shortages of men typically are greatly increased when only the unmarried population is examined. Hence, young women in Massachusetts in 1850 probably had only about three chances in five of finding a spouse. And as the American West continued to attract young men, the sex ratios in many states became even more imbalanced. Figure 12–2 shows that by 1880 there were fewer than 93 men per 100 women in Massachusetts and Rhode Island, while out West there were 258.7 men per 100 women in Montana, 231.1 in Arizona, and 215.2 in Wyoming. And again the imbalance was concentrated among younger adults.

■ **Female infanticide**   The major cause of imbalanced sex ratios is female **infanticide.** *Most* human societies have systematically killed a substantial proportion of female infants— sometimes through selective neglect, but most often by smothering them or by abandoning them to die from exposure and dehydration (Petersen, 1975). In China, for example, census takers found sex ratios as high as 430 boys for every 100 girls in some areas as late as 1870 (Ho, 1959). In India in 1846, a British enumeration in the Punjab found *not one* female child in 2,000 upper-status Bedi Sikh families with children (Dickeman, 1975).

Nor was female infanticide limited to non-Western societies. Female infanticide and abandonment were widespread in Europe even quite recently. Langer (1972) reports, "In the eighteenth century it was not an uncommon spectacle to see the corpses of infants lying in the streets or on the dunghills of London and other large cities." In 1835 the French government officially recorded the abandonment of more than 150,000 infants. Although this total included only those found still alive, most died. Many male French infants were abandoned too, but the majority were females (Langer, 1972).

■ **Health and diet**   Not only do males have higher infant and childhood mortality rates but they also are subject to a higher rate of fetal deaths—female fetuses are more robust and have a higher rate of survival in the womb. This becomes especially significant among populations suffering from inadequate nutrition and lack of medical care. In such circumstances there will be little difference in the ratio of males to females at birth, and an excess of females will emerge in childhood—in the absence of female infanticide. Later in this chapter we will see that male fetal deaths have played a major role in producing the marked shortage of males among black Americans. This is also reflected in the disproportionate number of black infants suffering from a low birth weight, as we saw in Chapter 5.

Another aspect of diet also must be noted: Societies that practice female infanticide often tend to provide a less adequate diet for women and girls, and this shows up in their mortality rates (El-Badry, 1969; Kennedy, 1972).

■ **Differential life expectancy** Because of the high mortality rates associated with childbirth, in many societies men have outlived women, adding to the excess male population. Today, however, in most societies women outlive men. Hence, even in populations that have a well-balanced sex ratio in early adulthood, a shortage of men begins to build up as age cohorts mature. In their later years, women greatly outnumber men in all advanced industrial nations. In the United States today, there are only two

Figure 12-2 ■ **Sex ratios in 1880.** In 1850 Horace Greeley, editor of the *New York Tribune*, wrote "Go West, young man, and grow up with the country." Clearly that's exactly what many young men did, whether or not they ever heard of Greeley. As the map shows, in 1880 there were really two Americas—at least in terms of gender. The West was male territory, the East was female. West of the Missouri River was a land of cowboys and miners where women were in short supply. Along the eastern seaboard, women outnumbered men. Moreover, these ratios were even much more extreme when only young, single adults were counted. (In 1880 the area that was to become Oklahoma was officially designated as Indian Territory; its population was not enumerated by the census.)

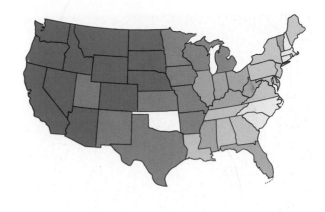

1880: Males per 100 Females

Rhode Island	92.7	Wisconsin	107.0
Massachusetts	92.8	Utah	107.2
Connecticut	96.5	Arkansas	107.8
New Hampshire	96.6	Missouri	108.3
North Carolina	96.6	Iowa	109.2
South Carolina	97.1	Texas	111.1
		Michigan	111.3
		Minnesota	115.9
		Kansas	116.8
New York	97.2	New Mexico	117.1
Virginia	97.2		
Alabama	97.3		
Maryland	97.8		
Georgia	97.9	Nebraska	122.6
New Jersey	98.0	Oregon	144.8
Louisiana	99.5	California	149.6
Tennessee	99.5	South Dakota	155.6
Pennsylvania	99.6	North Dakota	155.6
Maine	99.8	Washington	157.7
		Colorado	198.0
		Idaho	201.9
		Nevada	207.9
Mississippi	100.5	Wyoming	215.2
Vermont	100.9	Arizona	231.1
Ohio	101.9	Montana	258.7
Kentucky	102.0		
Delaware	102.2		
Florida	102.5		
West Virginia	103.5		
Indiana	104.4		
Illinois	106.4		

■ Vincent de Paul, a Catholic priest, devoted much of his time and effort to rescuing infants abandoned in the streets of Paris in the seventeenth century. The religious society he founded, and which today bears his name, established and sustained the first shelters in Europe for foundlings—as abandoned babies came to be known. He was canonized as Saint Vincent de Paul in 1737.

males to every three females over age 65, and over age 85 women outnumber men by well over two to one. As a result, most men over age 65 are living with a wife (78 percent do), while only 40 percent of women over age 65 have husbands—51 percent of the women are widows compared with 14 percent of the men. In Special Topic 4, immediately following Chapter 13, we will see how imbalanced sex ratios cause serious problems for the elderly.

■ **War**   Many societies have experienced periodic shortages of young adult males because of heavy wartime casualty rates. In Chapter 18 we will see that France suffered from a lack of young men following World War I. The Soviet Union had an acute lack of younger males following their heavy losses in World War II. During these periods sex-role norms often are relaxed until the usual sex ratio is restored.

■ **Sexual practices**   It now appears likely that the extreme excess of male births among Orthodox Jews—which probably has persisted since Biblical times—is the result of strict norms governing *when* intercourse occurs in relation to the woman's menstrual cycle. Because Talmudic law forbids intercourse during and for seven days following menstruation, intercourse is most likely to occur just prior to ovulation and there is some evidence that this is a time when the conditions in the woman's reproductive tract are most favorable to Y sperm and hence to a higher proportion of males being conceived (Guttentag and Secord, 1983). Similar patterns may exist, or have existed, in other cultures.

In the long run, of course, our concern in this chapter is not with *why* unbalanced sex ratios occur, but with how they shape sex roles and gender inequality. However, before we examine the way Guttentag and Secord's theory explains these connections, it will be helpful to deal with concrete examples. So let's contrast two societies having similar cultural roots but very different sex ratios: the ancient Greek city-states of Athens and Sparta.

Ancient Athens: too few women

As with most premodern societies, Athens in its classic period (500 to about 300 B.C.) had a great excess of males, except for brief periods of heavy military casualties. The cause? Female infanticide—practiced by rich and poor families alike. Moreover, girls received little or no education and were raised to be quiet and submissive. Typically, Athenian females were married at puberty, but their husbands were much older. Hence, quite aside from inequalities built into sex roles, marriages began with one partner having much greater maturity, experience, and education than the other.

Although women were celebrated in poetry and drama as romantic love objects, under Athenian law women were classified as children, regardless of age, while males obtained adult standing in law at age 18. Hence an Athenian woman was at all stages in her life the *legal property* of some man—first of her father, then of her husband, and, should her husband die, of her son. If a man wanted a divorce, he needed only to order his wife from his household. If a woman wanted a divorce, she had to have her father or some other man bring her case before a judge. Women were denied all participation in politics—they could not hold office, vote, or serve on juries. Instead, the Athenian woman's role was that of mother and manager of the household (Finley, 1982; Pomeroy, 1975).

Three aspects of Athenian sexual patterns also are typical of societies with too few women. First, "respectable" women were isolated by extremely protective sexual norms. They were secluded from the sight of all men other than close relatives. They wore clothing designed to conceal. Virginity was expected of brides and absolute chastity of wives; unchaste wives could be sold into slavery, as could an unmarried woman who had lost her virginity. If a woman was seduced or raped, her husband was compelled to divorce her, while also having the legal right to kill the man who had violated his property rights (Pomeroy, 1975; Lacey, 1968).

The second aspect of sexual patterns in societies with a high ratio of males to females is the highly visible presence of "disreputable" women—running the gamut from cheap prostitutes to the courtesans and mistresses of the rich and powerful. The prostitutes of Athens wore provocative and revealing gowns and some solicited openly on the streets. Males, of course, were not expected to be chaste and were thought to need additional sexual outlets (Pomeroy, 1975). The third aspect of sex in societies with an excess of males is male homosexuality. There was a good deal of this in Athens too (Dover, 1978).

Ancient Sparta: too few men

The ancient Greek city-state of Sparta offers a mirror image of Athens. Far smaller than Athens or other leading Greek cities, Sparta was nonetheless the dominant power in Greece for centuries. Why? Because of a standing army of unparalleled skill and tenacity, an army that for centuries observed "unfailing obedience to the rule never to retreat in battle" (Finley, 1982). Spartan mothers bidding good-bye to sons going off to battle always advised them to either come home with their shields or upon them—win or die.

Upon reaching age 18, all able-bodied male Spartans went off for twelve years of full-time military service, after which they remained liable for recall until age 60. The army had two primary missions. The first was to defeat any and all other armies that challenged it. But the second, and more important, mission of the Spartan army was to maintain control over a subjugated peasantry known as helots. Because all male Spartans took up the same occupation—soldier—their society depended on outsiders to grow the food and perform the other needed domestic tasks. And with most of the men off in army camps, it often fell to Spartan women to manage the estates and oversee the helots.

Sparta practiced infanticide, but without sexual preference—only healthy, well-formed babies were allowed to live. However, because males are more subject to birth defects and more apt to be sickly infants, the result was a slight excess of females from infancy, a trend that accelerated with age because of male mortality—including mortality from war.

If Sparta put similar value on male and female infants, it took a radically sex-differentiated approach to child rearing. At age 7 all Spartan boys left home to be raised by the state in public, all-male dormitories—the toughest military boarding schools in history. This system made Sparta a highly sex-segregated society. Although men could marry at age 20, they could not live with their wives until they left the army after age 30. That meant that Spartan men had very limited contact with Spartan women from age 7 through 30 and were, understandably,

■ This fourth-century B.C. terra-cotta figurine of a Greek woman portrays the very concealing style of clothing worn by women in cities such as Athens where males greatly outnumbered them. In this same era, however, in the Greek city of Sparta, where women outnumbered men, women's dresses came only to the knee and often were sleeveless and low necked.

■ This classic Greek statue depicts the goddess Diana dressed like a Spartan woman. The contrast with the statue of the Athenian woman reveals the extent to which women's fashions are influenced by sex ratios. Where women outnumber men, they tend not to hide their bodies under many layers of clothing.

inclined to prefer the social company of men thereafter. However, Spartan men who did not marry were ridiculed in public and suffered legal penalties.

As is typical of societies where women outnumber men, Sparta offered girls as much education as boys. They spent much less time than Athenian women learning traditional women's work (cooking and sewing were consigned to slaves), while Spartan women received a substantial amount of physical education and gymnastic training.

And a Spartan woman did not belong to anyone. If she divorced her husband, she took all of her own property and half of the produce of the household. If her husband was at fault, he was fined. Spartan women not only controlled their own property but they also had the right to dispose of their husband's in his absence, and if a father failed in his duties concerning his children's property, control was transferred to his wife or mother. Indeed, it was thought that women had special abilities with financial matters, and it is estimated that women were the sole owners of at least 40 percent of all land and property in Sparta (Pomeroy, 1975).

Given their good educations and their economic power, Spartan women were not known for their reticence or submissiveness. In fact, they were famous throughout Greece for being outspoken and witty. Not one of the many women poets remembered in classical Greek literature came from Athens, but many were from Sparta.

Although Spartan culture emphasized childbearing (the army always needed more soldiers), sexual patterns in Sparta were the opposite of Athens. The women were not hidden away. In contrast to the heavy, concealing gowns worn in Athens, women in Sparta wore short dresses and went bare legged. When women are in oversupply men tend to regard them in much less romanticized terms and place considerably less emphasis on virginity and chastity. Hence, while Athenian parents married off their daughters at puberty, in part for fear they might lose their virginity, Spartan women usually did not marry until they were 20 or older. Also illustrative of the more casual Spartan approach to sexuality, rape and adultery carried only monetary fines, and a husband would have been scorned for deserting a wife who had been raped. Moreover, there were too few men to provide a sufficient number of husbands and no males their own age around for Spartan women from age 7 through 30. No doubt many older men took advantage of this situation to demand casual sexual relations, as men have in modern times. Indeed, societies with an excess of women tend to be sexually permissive for both men and women. Another aspect of sexuality in societies with insufficient males also must be noted: It is from Sparta that we first learn of openly lesbian relationships, particularly between older women and young girls (Guttentag and Secord, 1983). These may even have been recognized by

the state. There is no similar evidence of homosexuality among females in Athens.

To sum up: Where women are scarce they are treated as precious property, but without rights of their own. Where women are in excess supply there is much less gender inequality, but men are inclined to be less dependable as spouses and lovers. Now let's try to discover why.

Sex ratios and power dependency

Guttentag and Secord's theory has both a micro and a macro level. At the micro level it is an *exchange* theory and begins with the fundamental rational choice premise introduced in Chapter 1 and elaborated in Chapter 3: *People will seek to maximize their rewards and minimize their costs.* In other words, as people interact with one another, they keep score. Suppose a man and a woman are involved in a dyadic, or two-person, relationship in which they are exchanging affection, among other things. Although they may put it in more romantic terms, from time to time each must ask: Is this relationship paying off? Am I getting back as much as I am giving? How can I obtain more in return for less? Could I do better by finding a different exchange partner? From that last question, we see that no exchange between two humans is limited to them alone—social circumstances always intrude, limit, define, or otherwise affect their options. And sometimes social circumstances greatly influence the *relative power* of members of a dyad.

■ **Dyadic power** The capacity of each member of a dyad to impose his or her will on the other member is called **dyadic power.** A social circumstance that can greatly influence dyadic power is the sex ratio within which a dyad is located. As Guttentag and Secord (1983) explained:

When one sex is in short supply, all relationships between opposite-sexed persons are potentially affected in a similar way: The individual member whose sex is in short supply has a stronger position and is less dependent on the partner because of the larger number of alternative relationships available to him or her *[emphasis added].*

When women are in short supply, each can select from among several suitors who must vie for her favor. When men are in short supply, they can pick and choose from among several available women.

The concepts of **power** and of **dependency** allow us to isolate the key elements in dyadic relationships. Let us consider a dyad made up of A and B, or Alan and Betty. Each will have certain goals they wish to achieve within this relationship—perhaps each will be seeking to satisfy sexual and emotional desires. Recall that we have defined *power* as the ability to get one's way over the resistance of others (see Chapter 9). Thus if one member of a dyad has superior power, he or she will be more successful in achieving personal goals within the relationship. And a member of a dyad with inferior power can be identified as the *dependent* member. Or, to put this more formally: The dependence of one member of a dyad upon the other is equal to their inability to achieve their goals *outside* the dyad (Emerson, 1962).

An unfavorable sex ratio causes power dependencies in dyadic relationships for members of the sex in excess supply. From this it follows that men will experience power dependency in their dyadic relations with women when women are in short supply; this unbalances their relative abilities to achieve their goals outside the dyad. This imbalance shows up in the romanticized and idealized images of women typical of societies with a shortage of women. But then why do women appear to be worse off when they are scarce and better off when they are in excess? To answer this question we must move outside dyadic relations.

■ **Structural power**   We have seen that a social structure—sex ratios—can shape power relations within dyads. Other social structures can play a similar role. Among these are organized activities by gender groups. Dependent members in dyadic relations may seek to improve their bargaining positions in a number of ways, as Guttentag and Secord pointed out. They

may seek to develop techniques and cultural means to make themselves unusually attractive to the opposite sex. For example, where women are in short supply, men may pursue such romantic approaches to courting as serenading beneath their "fair damsel's" window or by sending her poetry. Or men may fight duels or tatoo their bodies to gain female admiration. When men are in short supply, it will be women who will seek male admiration, and this often proves to be a very good thing for the cosmetics industry.

Another response by the gender in excess supply is to attempt to reduce their reliance on dyadic relations with the opposite sex, spending more of their time in same-sex dyads. Or they may withdraw from dyadic relationships, seeking their satisfaction in solitary activities as artists, writers, or religious ascetics. But if the imbalance between the sexes continues for a substantial period, "an appreciable number of individuals from the gender lacking dyadic power may well get together and organize various types of actions to correct the situation" (Guttentag and Secord, 1983).

Here Guttentag and Secord have used insights from *conflict* theories to explain macro level responses to sex ratios. Recall from Chapter 4 that conflict theories emphasize the ways that various groups in societies attempt to utilize their power to *shape social structures to serve their own interests.* Historically, men have usually lacked dyadic power, so they have been motivated to shape the rules governing status to favor them. Moreover, in this circumstance men also have the power of greater numbers on their side. Thus as men seek to offset the greater power of women at the dyadic level, their organized efforts lead to the elaborate culture of traditional sex roles. That is, men have combined to create social structures based on norms governing appropriate sex-role behavior, norms that serve to limit the dyadic bargaining power of women by limiting their ability to form additional dyadic relations. Chief among these norms are:

1. Brides shall be virgins. This reduces the margins within which women can form alternative dyads.

2. Wives shall be chaste. This reduces a woman's options to find alternatives outside the dyad, once it is formed.

3. Women shall devote themselves to the roles of wife and mother. This tends to discourage both divorce and pursuit of careers outside marriage. This typically leads to:

4. Defining women as temperamentally unsuited to positions of power and authority, which facilitates male control of laws as well as customs.

Keep in mind that men do not need to send thought police around to enforce these norms. Instead, both males and females will be *socialized from birth into a culture in which these norms are taken for granted and seen as self-evident truths.* That is, as Chapter 7 clarified, most men and women will *internalize* these norms. Hence women will be as quick as men to criticize people who depart too far from standards of behavior appropriate to their gender, and parents will do their best to raise their daughters to be properly feminine and their sons to be properly masculine.

But what about societies with an excess of women? Typically these societies have a long history of excess males, so when an excess of women develops, it does so within a culture sustaining traditional sex roles providing for male superiority. Initially, an excess of women will combine with a male-biased culture to cause a "sexual revolution." That is, when *both* structural and dyadic power favor men, they respond by exploiting their advantages to the fullest, discarding one dyadic partner for another, giving little to any one partner, and demanding the maximum benefits from each. Hence norms valuing virginity disappear, and soon norms of chastity do, too. Moreover, as men seek more from women, it is to their immediate benefit if wives can provide economic as well as emotional and sexual rewards. Norms restricting women's roles begin to erode.

Meanwhile, women will be reacting to their new conditions and reassessing their options. As they gain less satisfaction and security from traditional sex roles—as wives and mothers find themselves cast aside to support themselves and to raise their families alone—and as they gain more exposure to the "man's world" of careers and decision making, women can be expected to exert organized effort to restructure sex-role culture.

Initially this effort probably will take the form displayed by women's movements in modern societies—a demand for social, legal, and economic equality. But what will happen once this is fully achieved *if* an acute shortage of males continues? Will women eventually evolve and impose an elaborate new sex-role culture to limit the dyadic power of men? Could there be societies with a mirror image of traditional sex roles, with men enclosed by norms of virginity and chastity? Could househusband be the primary male role in societies of the future—especially since it no longer is necessary to breast-feed infants? No one knows.

Testing the Sex-Ratios and Sex-Roles Theory

Once Guttentag and Secord had worked out their theory of sex ratios and sex roles, they set out to test it against appropriate empirical evidence. Keep in mind that we can never prove a theory—we never run out of future opportunities to which it applies and hence of opportunities for it to fail. So scientists assess theories by doing their best to *disprove* them. Turning to history, Guttentag and Secord tested their theory against evidence from ancient Greece. As we have seen, they found that Athens displayed the patterns their theory predicts for societies with an excess of males, while Sparta was as predicted for societies with an excess of women.

Next, they asked whether the significant shifts in sex ratios that occurred in medieval Europe had produced the predicted shifts in sex roles. They found that they had. When men greatly outnumbered women early in medieval times, women were highly prized and norms defining traditional sex-role relations were strong. In late medieval times the excess of men gave way to an excess of women. Soon men were

Table 12-2 ■ Males per 100 females: United States 1790–1980.

	White	Black
1790	103.8	
1800	104.0	
1810	104.0	
1820	103.2	103.4
1830	103.8	100.3
1840	104.5	99.4
1850	105.2	99.1
1860	105.3	99.6
1870	102.8	96.2
1880	104.4	97.7
1890	105.4	99.5
1900	104.9	98.6
1910	106.6	98.7
1920	104.4	99.2
1930	102.9	97.0
1940	101.2	95.0
1950	98.9	94.3
1960	97.3	93.3
1970	95.3	90.8
1980	94.8	89.6

Source: U.S. Bureau of the Census, 1975, *Historical Statistics of the United States,* and *1980 Census of the Population, General Population Characteristics,* Part 1, (Washington, D.C.: U.S. Government Printing Office).

reluctant to marry and sexual permissiveness flourished. A medieval women's movement also appeared on schedule, in parallel versions inside and outside religious institutions. As Guttentag and Secord reported: "Women struggled to gain economic, religious, and social places for themselves outside the traditional roles of wife and mother."

But the bulk of their efforts to test the theory rests on modern times, especially on modern developments in Europe and North America. These societies have recently produced an enormous amount of research and writing on contemporary sex roles, sex-role socialization, the feminist movement, and gender inequality. Does the evidence fit together as the theory would predict? To find out, let's take an in-depth look.

Trends in North American sex ratios

Table 12-2 shows trends in sex ratios in the United States over the past two centuries: a marked shift from an excess of men to an excess of women and a shift even more dramatic among blacks than whites. Among whites, in 1910 there were almost 107 men for every 100 women. In 1980 there were slightly fewer than 95 men for every 100 women. For black Americans, an excess of females appeared by the middle of the nineteenth century, and by 1980 there were fewer than 90 black men for every 100 black women.

A similar shift has occurred in Canada but much more recently. In the 1961 census men still outnumbered women in Canada (102.2 to 100). But the 1981 Canadian census reported only 98.6 men per 100 women. Meanwhile, Mexico remains a society with a slight excess of men, having 101.5 to 100 in 1985, but the ratio there has declined, too.

The reason for excess male populations in Mexico until recent times was a high female mortality rate associated with childbirth, while in Canada and the United States the primary cause was immigration. Thus while males congregated in the West of Canada and the United States, more males than females were arriving in the flood of immigration reaching both nations during the nineteenth and early twentieth century. Indeed, Canada's sex ratio remained male dominated later than did the U.S. sex ratio because of later patterns of heavy immigration.

Sex ratios based on total population do not reveal the full story. A primary aspect of the Guttentag and Secord theory has to do with sex ratios within the ages at which people desire to marry. Moreover, in most societies women tend to marry men somewhat older than themselves, which probably is a response to the fact that females pass through puberty sooner than males do (see Chapter 5). In Canada and the United States, brides average nearly three years younger than their husbands. So Guttentag and Secord computed the ratio of men age 23 through 27 to women 20 through 24. The results are seen in Table 12-3 (with added data from the 1980 census).

■ Geographic mobility was a major cause of the great oversupply of men in Canada and the United States until recently, because it is young men who are most apt to move from one nation or region to another. This picture (circa 1890) of passengers crowding on deck to catch their first glimpse of Ellis Island captures a common sight—not a woman to be seen.

From the data we see that the sex ratios are much less favorable to women in their prime marrying years than the overall ratios would suggest. In 1980 there were 87 white males, age 23–27, for every 100 white females, 20–24. Among blacks, the ratio was only 72 males per 100 females in these age groups. The second thing we see in the table is the "marriage squeeze" American women faced during the 1960s and 1970s because of the baby boom. When a population grows rapidly, younger cohorts are always larger than the ones born before them. Since women from younger cohorts tend to marry men from older cohorts, women baby boomers faced an acute shortage of slightly older men to marry. In contrast, men their own age had an abundance of slightly younger women to choose among.

In recent years, this pattern has been reversed. With a declining birth rate, cohorts entering adulthood are smaller than the cohorts preceding them, so the sex ratio in 1980 was much less unfavorable to young women than it had been a decade earlier.

Thus far we have been dealing with national sex ratios. But humans experience life locally, not nationally. For example, although the United States still had more males than females in 1880, local sex ratios—those that determined the relative supply of husbands or wives individuals faced—usually differed greatly from the national average. Recall that in that year many states on the eastern seaboard had a substantial excess of women, while many western states had huge excesses of men. And these local conditions are the ones most pertinent to the Guttentag and

Table 12-3 ■ Sex ratios faced by young, unmarried American women.

Year of census	White			Black
	1960	1970	1980	1980
Unmarried men 23–27 per 100 unmarried women 20–24	93	67	87	72

Source: Guttentag and Secord (1983) and the 1980 census.

Secord theory. Keeping that in mind, let us assess the shifting nature of sex-role relations in North America over the past century to see if it supports or contradicts predictions from the theory.

Gender and social movements

Guttentag and Secord predict that when one gender group faces a substantial lack of dyadic power for an appreciable time, they will organize to seek ways to remedy their problem. According to the theory, the elaborate sex-role culture by which women are prevented from fully exercising their options was created by organized male efforts to remedy the lack of dyadic power inherent in the oversupply of men. Similarly, when men have the greater dyadic power, based on their inferior numbers, women can be expected to organize to change the balance of power. Guttentag and Secord found support for their prediction among Spartan women and in a women's movement in late medieval Europe. But what about modern times?

Recall the unfavorable sex ratios women faced in many eastern states throughout the nineteenth century. Shouldn't they have become activists? According to the theory, they should have. According to history, they did.

■ **The "woman movement"**   On July 19, 1848, a group of women gathered in Seneca Falls, a village in upstate New York, "to discuss the social, civil, and religious rights of women." Led by Elizabeth Cady Stanton and Lucretia Mott, the group issued a "Declaration of Sentiments," modeled on the Declaration of Independence, proclaiming that "all men and women are cre-

ated equal." Thus was born what was known throughout the latter half of the nineteenth century as the "woman movement," an effort to end the subordination of women. "Men, their rights and nothing more; women, their rights and nothing less!" was the motto of the weekly newspaper published by the National Woman Suffrage Association.

Although there were many factions and conflicting points of view within the woman movement, two somewhat contradictory positions were widely shared: (1) there was no difference between man and woman and (2) woman possessed a superior moral nature from which the whole of society stood to gain. Hence many of those active in the movement combined the drive for women's rights with a call for more general social reform and proposed that the one would result in the other. As Jane Frohock expressed this: "It is woman's womanhood, her instinctive femininity, her highest morality that society needs now to counteract the excess of masculinity that is everywhere to be found in our unjust and unequal laws" (Cott, 1987). The tension between these two positions grew as time passed. In her superb historical study of American feminism, Nancy F. Cott (1987) summed up the situation thus:

By the close of the century the spectrum of ideology in the woman movement had a see-saw quality: at one end, the intention to eliminate sex-specific limitations; at the other, the desire to recognize rather than quash the qualities and habits called female, to protect the interests women already had defined as theirs and give those much greater public scope.

■ At the turn of the century, San Francisco had more than 130 males for every 100 females, and the imbalance was far greater among single persons between 18 and 35. This led to organized efforts to import brides. These women came all the way from England aboard the liner *California*, by way of the new Panama Canal. Each had a fiancé waiting at the pier—an engagement arranged by mail. Since women were so scarce in San Francisco and the whole North American West, these women could expect to be idealized and pampered. But according to the theory of sex ratios and sex roles, they could also expect to be excluded from many occupations and spheres of power and decision making.

However, underlying ideological ambiguities were submerged as the woman movement gave rise to the suffragette movement, dedicated to obtaining the right to vote for all American women. As Cott observes, this issue served as "a platform on which diverse people and organizations could comfortably, if temporarily, stand." And this unity produced a rapid swelling of the ranks during the decade from 1910 to 1920, culminating in final ratification of the Nineteenth Amendment on August 26, 1920:

The right of citizens of the United States to vote shall not be denied or abridged by the United States or by any State on account of Sex.

Congress shall have power to enforce this article by appropriate legislation.

During the last few years of the drive for suffrage, women all over the nation took part. But in keeping with the Guttentag and Secord theory, the woman movement began and achieved greatest prominence in the northeastern states

■ On November 9, 1912, these women posed on a New York City rooftop before joining twenty thousand other women in a march for suffrage. *The New York Times* described the event: "As for the parade itself, it was a line, miles long, of well-dressed, intelligent women, deeply concerned in the cause they are fighting for." Each of these women carries a lantern, as did the other thousands; when these were lighted at sundown, they created a spectacle that the *Times* described as "a rolling stream of fiery lava."

with their long-standing shortage of men. And it was also there that the next major development took place.

■ **The feminist movement**   It has become an article of faith among contemporary writers on the status of women that the suffrage movement derailed the woman movement. Once women received the vote, it is claimed, their efforts to achieve full equality and to reform

basic sex-role relationships died out, not to reappear until Betty Friedan's *The Feminine Mystique* (1963) aroused a revival of feminine militancy (Epstein, 1976; Rothman, 1978; Rapp and Ross, 1983). In fact, what had died out by the time women gained the right to vote was the "woman movement," and what replaced it was not apathy or quietude, but something called *feminism*.

The word seems to have first appeared in

■ Back in 1913 the young suffragettes above formed a pep band to publicize a rally in support of "VOTES for WOMEN," as their banners proclaim. As was typical of small town life in those days, the rally was held outdoors in front of the courthouse. Preceded by a band concert to help assemble a crowd, a series of speakers proclaimed the cause of female suffrage—and in these days before amplifying equipment, public speakers had to have strong voices. On the right is a poster advertising a feminist mass meeting in New York City, 1914.

English usage around 1906. Before long, it became a popular new buzzword. In 1913 a leading campaigner for women's rights wrote that the word *feminism* was "something so new that it isn't in the dictionaries yet" (Cott, 1987). By 1914 Henrietta Rodman, a militant New York City teacher, had organized the Feminist Alliance.

What did the word mean? Why did it suddenly become so popular? Cott (1987) points out that "woman movement" is ungrammatical and implies an agenda limited to matters of concern only to women, whereas the term *fem-*

WHAT IS FEMINISM?
COME AND FIND OUT

FIRST FEMINIST MASS MEETING
at the PEOPLE'S INSTITUTE, Cooper Union
Tuesday Evening, February 17th, 1914, at 8 o'clock, P. M.

Subject: "WHAT FEMINISM MEANS TO ME."
Ten-Minute Speeches by

ROSE YOUNG	GEORGE CREEL
JESSE LYNCH WILLIAMS	MRS. FRANK COTHREN
HENRIETTA RODMAN	FLOYD DELL
GEORGE MIDDLETON	CRYSTAL EASTMAN BENEDICT
FRANCES PERKINS	EDWIN BJORKMAN
WILL IRWIN	MAX EASTMAN

Chairman, MARIE JENNEY HOWE.

SECOND FEMINIST MASS MEETING
at the PEOPLES' INSTITUTE, Cooper Union
Friday, February 20th, 1914, at 8 o'clock, P. M.

Subject: "BREAKING INTO THE HUMAN RACE."

The Right to Work.—
RHETA CHILDE DORR
The Right of the Mother to Her Profession.—
BEATRICE FORBES-ROBERTSON-HALE.
The Right to Her Convictions.—
MARY SHAW.
The Right to Her Name.—
FOLA LA FOLLETTE.
The Right to Organize.—
ROSE SCHNEIDERMAN.
The Right to Ignore Fashion.—
NINA WILCOX PUTNAM.
The Right to Specialize in Home Industries.—
CHARLOTTE PERKINS GILMAN.

Chairman, MARIE JENNEY HOWE.

ADMISSION FREE.   NO COLLECTION.

inism implies much broader intentions and the involvement of both women and men in fashioning new relationships.

Cott defines **feminism** as an ideology having three essential features: (1) opposition to all forms of stratification based on gender, (2) belief that biology does not consign females to inferior status, and (3) a sense of common experience and purpose among women to direct their efforts to bring about change.

Feminism sprang from the woman movement and the suffrage movement in the second decade of the twentieth century and has never gone into decline or suspension since then. The feminism of the 1960s was a direct outgrowth of the movement that began to attract women in New York and Boston fifty years before (Cott, 1987). What misled so many observers was that in the beginning the feminist movement was very small, its early appeal being limited to women of two different and unusual backgrounds. The first were women active in leftist politics and union organization, often women employed in the garment industry. The second were young female intellectuals and artists ready to explore bohemian life-styles—like the avant-garde women who were frequenting the Greenwich Village scene by the 1920s. These women typically were well educated, often at women's colleges, and frequently their mothers had been active in the woman movement. Hence, while the suffragette movement rapidly attracted a massive, popular base, feminism began as a movement among small, often elite, groups and grew but slowly. When the suffragettes ceased their huge marches, it seemed as if all organized interest in gender inequities had disappeared, too. Instead, the feminist movement continued to grow, fueled by two other major trends changing the circumstances of American women.

Women in the labor force

When men are in short supply, women increasingly find they need to become self-supporting. Early in the nineteenth century, as many young men headed West (in those days, the "Wild West" was in western New York State and Ohio), many young women in New England supported themselves in their homes by spinning wool into yarn. This became so widespread that the term *spinster* soon ceased to mean a female spinner and instead identified any unmarried woman over a certain age (Guttentag and Secord, 1983). But as the proportion of males declined and the number of women needing work increased, new inventions made it possible for huge textile mills to spring up in New England— drawn there partly because of the supply of young women workers. "New England textile factories from the start employed a vastly greater proportion of women than men" (Cott, 1977). Thus began a trend that in the course of a century has drawn the majority of North American women from their homes to hold regular jobs.

Table 12-4 shows this trend. In 1890 only 18.2 percent of American women were employed full-time outside the home. Over the next ninety-five years female labor force participation (as the census calls it) increased regularly until now more than half of all women in the United States and Canada hold full-time jobs. Table 12-5 shows an even more dramatic and recent trend, the tendency for mothers of young children to go off to work every day. In 1950, with the baby boom in full flower, slightly fewer than 14 percent of women with children under age 6 held jobs. Today almost 54 percent do.

Not only has the traditional division of labor between husband as earner and wife as housekeeper given way to the two-earner household, but occupations also have become much less gender segregated than they once were—although substantial differences persist. As recently as 1970 women made up only 33.9 percent of persons employed in the top jobs, those classified by the census as managerial and professional occupations, but held 41.6 percent of those jobs by 1984 and the trend continues upward. Within this category, men dominate the fields of engineering (6.2 percent are women), architecture (10.8 percent are women), and law (16.2 percent female). Among those fields most dominated by women are nursing (96 percent), elementary school teaching (84.6 percent), and librarianship (85.9 percent).

Women still dominate the occupations of secretary (98.3 percent) and typist (95.7 percent), and men still dominate the skilled blue-

■ The scores of textile mills that sprang up in New England during the nineteenth century depended on a labor force of young, single women like these. The English novelist Charles Dickens reported in his 1841 *American Notes*, an account of his travels in America, that "these girls, as I have said, were all well dressed; and that phrase necessarily includes extreme cleanliness. . . . They were healthy in appearance, many of them remarkably so, and had the manners and deportment of young women; not of degraded brutes of burden. . . . I am now going to state three facts which will startle readers this side of the Atlantic very much. Firstly, there is a piano in a great many of the boarding houses. Secondly, nearly all of these young ladies subscribe to circulating libraries. Thirdly, they have got up among themselves a periodical:" What Dickens saw was the massive entry of young women from "respectable" backgrounds into the New England labor force in response to a marked shortage of eligible young men. Note how nicely they are dressed and groomed, and that each is wearing an apron to protect her skirt.

■ Many women entered the labor force during World War II, often taking jobs that previously had been done only by men. Here three women are being taught to weld at a shipyard in Tacoma, Washington, in 1943. Some have suggested that this wartime experience caused a rapid shift in female employment patterns—that once out of the home earning good pay, women refused to go back to the role of housewife. But most of them did go back, and their increased fertility rate created the baby boom. Consequently, Table 12-4 shows no unusual spurt in female employment between 1940 and 1950. The really rapid increase has taken place since 1960, as the baby boomers began to come of age and young, single American women greatly outnumbered eligible men.

Table 12-4 ■ Percent of American females employed full-time outside the home, 1890–1985.

1890	18.2%
1900	20.0%
1920	22.7%
1930	23.6%
1940	25.8%
1950	29.9%
1960	35.7%
1970	41.4%
1980	51.5%
1985	54.5%

Source: U.S. Bureau of the Census, Historical Statistics of the United States: Historical Times to 1970 and U.S. Statistical Abstract, 1987.

Table 12-5 ■ Percent of American mothers with children under age 6 employed full-time outside the home, 1950–1985.

1950	13.6%
1955	18.2%
1965	25.3%
1975	38.9%
1980	46.6%
1985	53.5%

Source: U.S. Bureau of Labor Statistics.

■ In periods of rapid social change, some things change faster than others. Here we see the Becker sisters branding cattle on their ranch in the San Luis Valley in 1894. They could demonstrate that "cowgirls" were able to do jobs long reserved for "cowboys." But they weren't ready to dress like cowboys. Instead, they had learned to rope and tie steers while dressed in the demure women's fashions of the time.

collar crafts such as auto mechanic (less than 1 percent are women) and carpenter (1.3 percent).

Although the majority of women now work outside the home, they bring home significantly less money than men do. This is a familiar newspaper feature story, but the "facts" usually are presented in a very crude and misleading way. The typical story is content to report that the average annual income for American women in a recent year was between $8,000 and $9,000 while for men it was between $18,000 and $19,000 and to conclude that men are paid more than twice as much as women. But that figure includes the millions of women who are full-time homemakers and earn no income of their own. Sometimes the reporters are careful enough to base their figures only on men and women who worked year-round, full-time. In 1984 that would show women earning only 64 percent as much as men—better, but still a depressing pic-

ture of inequity. But this too is what Cynthia M. Taeuber and Victor Valdisera (1986) call a "simplistic" use of statistics. They point out that such a comparison neglects the fact that the women and men are not doing the same kinds of work. While women have entered many occupations once closed to them, they still are concentrated in the relatively lower-paying occupations such as secretary and typist and remain very underrepresented in some high-paying jobs, especially the highly unionized, skilled, blue-collar occupations, such as mechanic, plumber, electrician, or machinist.

There can be no doubt that discrimination and false notions about women as the "frail" sex are involved in these patterns. However, many additional factors must be considered to really understand male/female income comparisons. One is that because female employment rates have risen rapidly, the average working woman is considerably younger than the average working man. That means the average male benefits from greater seniority and a longer opportunity to have accrued raises. When Taeuber and Valdisera analyzed 1984 income data, they found that among persons employed full-time, year-round, age 18–24, women's income was 86 percent that of men—and most of the remaining difference could be explained by differences in types of jobs. Another aspect of the gender wage-gap is turnover. Women change jobs more often than do men and take time out from the labor market more often. Again this influences seniority and experience. Of employed persons, one out of every nine men has worked at the same occupation for twenty-five years or more, while only one woman in twenty has done so. One reason for higher rates of female job turnover is maternity and child rearing. Another is the tendency of families to move when this benefits the husband's career, thus causing wives to quit jobs and seek new ones. Ironically, this move usually is the wise financial choice for individual families because the husband's sal-

■ In the summer of 1920, only weeks before final ratification of the Nineteenth Amendment gave American women the right to vote, something brand new began: beauty contests, known initially as "bathing beauty contests." Suddenly the American woman went from floor-length skirts (when men ogled pretty ankles) and similarly concealing beachwear to bare legs and figure-hugging fabrics. Here we see the contestants in the first Annual Bathing Girl Parade held at Balboa Beach in 1920. A

ary is higher, but it tends also to cause husbands' salaries to remain higher.

A final consideration is sex-role socialization. One aspect of this is that women still tend to shun some of the activities that lead to high incomes. For example, women remain far less likely to enroll in majors that lead to the highest income professional and managerial jobs, spurning the sciences and engineering while greatly over-enrolling in the humanities and education (Taeuber and Valdisera, 1986). In addition, cultural definitions of the character-

istics needed to be an effective leader are traits regarded as masculine—traits such as ambitious, aggressive, tough, confident. In contrast, traits associated with femininity such as being sensitive and understanding are seen as inappropriate in leaders (Hollander, 1985). Women are less likely to be selected as leaders to the extent that people are socialized to perceive that women lack appropriate leadership traits. Note too that among men there has long been a significant bias in favor of selecting tall men for leadership slots (Deck, 1971). If short men are

year later the Miss America Beauty Pageant began at Atlantic City. If you look closely at the photograph, you will be able to detect many signs of the sudden revolution in women's wear and, of course, in the norms governing standards of female modesty.

Clearly, many of these young women had never appeared in such revealing suits before, and they don't know how to pose in them to look their best. Instead, they look nervous, awkward, and very self-conscious. The photo also reveals that no customs

seen as lacking leadership, women also probably suffer from their smaller stature.

All these factors help to account for the fact that when men and women have similar education and training and are employed in the *same* occupation, the men are more apt to hold managerial and supervisory positions and hence to earn higher salaries (Taeuber and Valdisera, 1986). Ironically, when people are asked to name traits they would prefer in a manager they would like to work *for*, they tend to favor more feminine traits, but reverse themselves and stress mas-

culine traits when asked to describe a manager they would like to have working *for them* (Cann and Siegfried, 1987).

The sexual "revolution"

In 1900 in New England, about one in every four first births was to an unwed mother or to a woman who had married after becoming pregnant (Smith and Hindus, 1975). Fifty years earlier only about one birth in ten involved

had yet been established about what "bathing beauties" should wear with their swimsuits. Many of these young women wear hats, but some don't. Many have on high heels; others are in flats or are

barefoot. Some wear hose; others wear socks. One of the many ironies explained by Guttentag and Secord's theory is that women marching for equal rights and women parading in scanty costumes tend

an unwed or premarital pregnancy. What was going on?

What was *not* going on is what the suffragette Christabel Pankhurst had proposed with her "notorious" slogan: "Votes for Women and Chastity for Men!" With an abundant supply of eligible women, men grew increasingly less concerned about sexually monopolizing one woman and became more interested in easy sexual access to several. Sexual norms began to change, and premarital sex became more common, as the data on first births demonstrate.

As always with changes in basic cultural patterns, at first the changes are slow and accompanied by a great deal of controversy as people who have been effectively socialized into the old norms seek to enforce and defend them. Thus, in the early years of the century, there was a lot of organized effort to stem the "rising tide of immorality." These efforts were directed not so much at people who broke sexual norms as at people who advocated doing so or who made a "public display" of sexuality through art, literature, or drama. "Banned in Boston"

to go hand in hand. In the most sexist societies women are romanticized, but male tendencies to regard them as sex objects are greatly muted by strictly enforced norms of modesty, virginity, and

chastity. It is when women enjoy much greater freedom from male-imposed limits on their behavior that they also are, at least initially, most subject to being overtly paraded as sex objects.

■ The young women on the left model fashionable beachwear at the turn of the century. Bare arms were considered daring in those days, so it is likely that very few women actually bought suits like the one worn by the woman on the right. Twenty years later women suddenly appeared on the beach in suits that bared not only their arms but also their legs. A lot of people were very upset by this. When significant norms are challenged, bitter conflicts usually break out between those who want to preserve old norms and proponents of the new. Thus, in July 1922, two years after bathing beauty contests introduced "revealing" swimsuits, the women above were arrested for indecency and escorted from Chicago's Lake Michigan beach by police—including the policewoman who is between the two women in the foreground.

Table 12-6 ■ American attitudes toward premarital sex.

"If a man and woman have sex relations before marriage, do you think it is always wrong, almost always wrong, wrong only sometimes, or not wrong at all?"				
	1969*	1972	1977	1982	1985
Always wrong	—	35%	30%	29%	28%
Not wrong at all	21%	26%	35%	40%	42%

*Only two categories (wrong, not wrong) used.
Source: Data for 1969 from the Gallup Poll, other years from the National Opinion Research Center, General Social Survey.

became a common phrase reflecting that city's strict censorship. And, in the center of the controversy stood the feminists. For unlike the woman movement before them, they did not advocate ending the double standard of morality by restricting males. Instead, they advocated complete sexual freedom for women. And they did so in writing and in public speeches. As Cott (1987) characterized the sexual views of the early feminists:

Seeing sexual desire as healthy and joyful, they assumed that free women could meet men as equals on the terrain of sexual desire just as on the terrain of political representation or professional expertise.

Today these views seem commonplace (see Table 12-6), but in the America of the early 1900s they were condemned as a dangerous, reckless advocacy of "free love" and an attack on basic institutions such as marriage and family. And there is a certain amount of truth behind these charges. For there is a darker side to the moral stance of the early feminists—*the sexual exploitation of women.* As Cott (1987) put it:

Feminists were far from acknowledging publicly the potential for submergence of women's individuality and personality in heterosexual love relationships, or the potential for men's sexual exploitation of women who purposely broke the bounds of conventional sexual restraint. In private they saw, inevitably, travesties of their ideal.

And here was a tragic irony. As women battled to free themselves of dehumanizing limits—for example, to be allowed to wear comfortable and appropriate gym clothes and beachwear—they unleashed forces that tended to impose new forms of dehumanization. The new styles of the 1920s freed women from painful corsets and floor-length skirts, but they also put women on parade. In similar fashion, as women struggled to be free of the sexual double standard, they made themselves increasingly vulnerable to being divorced, deserted, and used by husbands and lovers.

Feminists today have made a major issue of the many ways in which women are treated as sex objects, especially in the mass media, and dehumanized and sexually exploited by such recent innovations as the singles bar. But this state of affairs is the very transformation in sex roles and sexual norms Guttentag and Secord predicted. Although it may be possible to change current patterns in gender roles and relations, these patterns are not simply accidents of history.

Sex ratios and the black family

In the 1920s the great black composer and performer Fats Waller popularized a song he wrote to tell women how to hold onto their men: "Find Out What They Like." The opening lines advise, "Find out what he likes and how he likes it, give it to him just that way." Meanwhile, the famous Bessie Smith replied for black women with her bitter "Why don't you do right, like some other

■ In 1900 Captain William T. Shorey, his wife, and their two children posed for this family portrait in Oakland, California. Shorey was master of a whaling ship and the only black captain on the Pacific Coast at this time. But if Shorey was exceptional in his occupational achievement, the Shorey family was typical in its composition—it included a father as well as a mother and children, as did *most* American families at this time, black or white. Although today more than half of black children are growing up in a female-headed family, this has been a recent development, not a cultural holdover from slavery days.

men do?" What these songs reflected was *not* a tradition of matriarchy and of female-headed families in black culture, as too many have suggested. What Fats Waller and Bessie Smith were singing about was a trend that was influencing dyadic power relations between black men and women—a trend that sixty years later has resulted in the majority of black American children living in a fatherless household. That trend was a growing shortage of black men, especially of younger, single black men. To conclude this chapter we will examine how many of the current family-related problems that afflict blacks in America today are the result of their extremely imbalanced sex ratio.

Recall from Table 12-2 that by the middle of the nineteenth century there already were more black women than men. During this century the trend has continued, so that each year the sex ratio among blacks reflects more women and fewer men. Moreover, this shortage is even more acute among young black adults—Table 12-3 showed that there were 72 single black males age 23 through 27 for every 100 black women age 20 through 24. But even this fails to show how severe the shortage of black males is. The availability of black men is further reduced by the gender imbalance of interracial marriage patterns. Black men are at least twice as likely as black women to marry someone of another race.

■ Why are black men in short supply?

The shortage of black males begins at birth. Rather than having from 105 to 106 males born for every 100 females, the sex ratio is nearly even at birth for blacks in North America. The primary reason for this is a considerable gender imbalance in fetal deaths among blacks, which probably reflects poor nutrition and health care, especially in previous generations (see Chapter 5). The next factor in black sex ratios is infant mortality. Because blacks have a substantially higher infant mortality rate than whites have, and because male infants are more likely to die, by the end of the first year of life the number of males had dipped below the number of females. As black children grow up, the proportion of males continues to drop due to higher black mortality rates and the especially high

■ Thomas "Fats" Waller (1904–1943) was one of the most prolific and influential composers of American popular music during the 1920s and 1930s. He turned out scores of hits, including "Honeysuckle Rose," "Ain't Misbehavin'," and "Squeeze Me." His tunes often were included in Broadway shows, and, equally gifted as a pianist and singer, he was a pioneer of early radio—seen here during a 1934 broadcast on CBS. Although there is no reason to suppose Waller knew that black women substantially outnumbered black men in the 1920s, the lyrics of his songs often reflected the greater dyadic power of men—that it was up to women to hold onto men.

mortality of young black men from accidents, drugs, and violence.

■ Consequences for the black family

One of the earliest consequences for black women faced with an acute shortage of men was the need for employment. By 1900, when only 20 percent of all American women were employed outside the home, 43.2 percent of black women were in the labor force compared with 14.6 percent of native-born white women.

■ In 1939, when John Phillips took this picture for *Life* magazine, this young bride had overcome a substantial shortage of potential grooms. In Georgia at that time there were only 91.3 black men per 100 black women, and the sex ratio was even more imbalanced when only young, single adults were counted. At this moment, as her mother adjusted her veil, this young woman was not thinking about statistics. But she may well have noted that many of her friends, waiting in the church, were having trouble getting the local men to marry and settle down.

But the primary consequence has been to make the father-mother-children family a receding memory among black Americans. Superficial scholarship to the contrary, the fact is that the black family was not broken up by slavery, and sexual promiscuity was not the norm among blacks on southern plantations. Indeed, the stable nuclear family and long-lasting marriages seem to have been typical, and black slave families took a very protective attitude toward the chastity of their daughters (Fogel and Engerman, 1974; Guttentag and Secord, 1983). The signs of severe disruption displayed by the black family are recent. Less than twenty years ago, in 1970, only 28 percent of black families including minor children were headed by a woman, and two-thirds of black children lived with both of their parents. In 1985, 44 percent of black families with children were headed by women, and fewer than half of black children lived with both parents. In 1960 the **illegitimacy ratio** (the percentage of all births that occur out of wedlock) was 22 percent among American blacks; in 1983 it was 58 percent. Here is another way to see what has been happening to the black family: I have calculated from the National Opinion Research Center General Social Survey for 1987, which included a substantial additional sample of blacks, that only 56 percent of blacks, compared with 80 percent of whites, lived with both their father and their mother at age 16.

■ **Sexual norms**   Guttentag and Secord's theory would predict not only that men would be less willing to marry when faced with a great excess of women but also that they would expect women to grant sexual privileges readily. The data on the black family make it evident that sexual norms have shifted among blacks in precisely the direction the theory anticipates. Clearly, when most infants are born to women without husbands there is reason to suppose that a lot of sex is going on among people who are not married. Moreover, a growing literature indicates the pressures black women feel from black men to provide sex without commitment (Washington, 1975; Guttentag and Secord, 1983).

The strains between black men and women over sexual norms are clear in the national survey data shown in Table 12-7. Black men are much less opposed to extramarital and premarital sex than are black women. In contrast, married black men are much more likely (61.7 percent) to rate their marriage as "very happy" than are black women (40.7 percent).

To sum up: The recent history of gender relations within the black community displays the links between changes in sex ratios and changes in sex roles postulated by Guttentag and Secord.

■

Conclusion

Our understanding of the problems created by imbalanced sex ratios is only in its infancy. After all, not until 1983 had more than a handful of social scientists even heard of Guttentag and Secord's theory. But already it has caused a flurry of research on a wide range of topics, including the involvement of women in crime. Where men

Table 12-7 ■ Contrasting attitudes of black American men and women.

	Black Men	Black Women
What is your opinion about a married person having sexual relations with someone other than the marriage partner?		
Always wrong	59.5%	73.7%
If a man and woman have sex relations before marriage, do you think it is always wrong, almost always wrong, wrong only sometimes, or not wrong at all?		
Always wrong	12.3%	33.6%
Not wrong at all	56.9%	39.5%
What if they are in their early teens, say 14 to 16 years old?		
Always wrong	46.2%	69.7%
Taking things all together, how would you describe your marriage? Would you say your marriage is very happy, pretty happy, or not too happy? *		
Very happy	61.7%	40.7%

* Asked of married people only.

Source: Prepared by the author from the National Opinion Research Center, General Social Surveys, 1986 and 1987.

■ Moslem nations today exemplify how cultural rules traditionally have enclosed and oppressed women in response to extremely imbalanced sex ratios. This Arab husband and his son wear western clothes; the wife still must wear a veil and hide her figure under a billowing robe while in public. Where women are in short supply, men tend to define them as too valuable to be seen, let alone to be free.

greatly outnumber women, the latter are much less apt to commit crimes and the police are more successful in solving cases of rape (South and Messner, 1986).

As we've seen, the purpose of research is to test theories. But the purpose of a theory is not to give researchers work. Theories are created to answer questions, to explain to us how some aspects of the world work. The major achievement of the Guttentag and Secord theory of sex ratios and sex roles has been to offer an *expla-*

nation to an immense puzzle: Why do men so often wrap women up in oppressive social structures? Before their work, the answers available amounted to little more than accusations. For example, to say women are oppressed because men are sexists is simply to rephrase the mystery in new language, to ask why are men sexists? Moreover, to seek the causes of gender inequalities in some sexist psychological traits of men is to ignore the great *variations* in the positions of women around the world and through history. Otherwise, we are forced to such unlikely explanations as to propose that the psychological processes of men in Sparta were different from those in Athens.

My aim in this chapter has been to reveal one of sociology's most powerful recent accomplishments to let you better understand major aspects of your social world. Keep in mind, of course, that theories never can be proved. So as researchers continue to test this theory, evidence may turn up that will cause us to greatly revise it or even to reject it. But there can be no doubt that Marcia Guttentag's trip to the opera will have lasting results. By calling our attention to the fact that societies often have a great excess of one gender, she has identified a matter of basic interest. All future attempts to understand gender relations must take sex ratios into account.

Finally, this chapter was never intended to be a chapter about women's issues. There are none. All issues of gender are reciprocal—male sex roles, for example, are incomprehensible except as they fit with female sex roles. The elimination of gender inequalities has implications for men as much as for women. This is underscored by the fact that gender inequalities are *fundamentally* different from inequalities between racial or ethnic groups. Gender inequalities occur *within* families, not between them. And it is to arrangements within the family that we must look as we seek to understand and to alter the culture surrounding relationships between men and women.

Review Glossary

sex ratio The number of persons of one gender relative to the number of persons of the other gender, usually expressed as the number of males per 100 females. (p. 334).

infanticide The practice of killing infants soon after birth, often done by simply abandoning them out of doors. (p. 340)

dyadic power The capacity of each member of a dyad to impose his or her will on the other member. (p. 345)

power dependency The dependency of one member of a dyad upon the other is equal to their *in*ability to achieve their goals *outside* the dyad. (p. 346)

structural power Power based on statuses within social structures. (p. 346)

feminism An ideology having three essential features: (1) opposition to all forms of stratification based on gender, (2) belief that biology does not consign females to inferior status, and (3) a sense of common experience and purpose among women to direct their efforts to bring about change. (p. 354)

illegitimacy ratio The proportion of all births that occur out of wedlock. (p. 366)

Suggested Readings

Cott, Nancy F. 1987. *The Grounding of Modern Feminism*. New Haven, Conn.: Yale University Press.

Guttentag, Marcia, and Paul F. Secord. 1983. *Too Many Women? The Sex Ratio Question*. Beverly Hills, Calif.: Sage.

Pomeroy, Sarah B. 1975. *Goddesses, Whores, Wives, Slaves: Women in Classical Antiquity*. New York: Schocken Books.

Taeuber, Cynthia M., and Victor Valdisera. 1986. *Women in the American Economy*. Bureau of the Census, Current Population Reports, Special Series P-23, no. 146. Washington, D.C.: U.S. Government Printing Office.

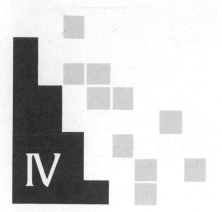

Social Institutions

IV

Human societies contain internal clusters of people and culture devoted to fulfilling primary social needs—clusters called *institutions*.

The cluster devoted to coordinating the activities of a society, to leadership and decision making, is called the political institution. All societies have political institutions, but in less complex societies political institutions tend to blend into other basic institutions, such as the family and religion. When societies do not have full-time political specialists, they tend to allow the average adult a good deal of say in political decisions. But when some people devote themselves full-time to leadership roles, they tend also to monopolize political power. Indeed, as we saw in Chapter 10, with the emergence of the state, societies become far more stratified and oppressive.

Here we see the extremes to which political institutions can be monopolized by a hereditary ruling class. In this 1902 photograph, the woman seated on her portable throne is Tz'u-hsi, the Dowager Empress of China. She is surrounded by the Imperial eunuchs, who served as her bearers as well as her advisors.

The Empress was not merely a symbolic ruler like the current Queen of England. A mere nod from her could cause anyone or everyone else in this photograph to have his head chopped off, and it required little more effort on her part to send armies into battle or to outlaw "foreign" religions. Moreover, even as great famines raged through China, killing millions, the Imperial Court dined on rare delicacies.

In 1908 Tz'u-hsi died under mysterious circumstances and was succeeded by Pu Yi, a very young boy, whose life was the subject of the Academy Award-winning film *The Last Emperor.*

The next four chapters assess the five primary social institutions.

Chapter 13 concentrates on the most intimate of institutions, the family. Why do all societies have families? Is it true that the family faces hard times in modern societies, that families today are less closely knit and less durable than before?

Chapter 14 asks why societies have religious institutions. What do people get from religion? Has religious belief and participation been declining in recent times? Where do cult movements thrive, and why?

In Chapter 15 we shall examine political institutions and see why political elites so typically oppress other members of societies. How can this be prevented? On what does political freedom depend?

Chapter 16 examines the interplay between educational and occupational institutions. Does education really pay off? Are American students learning less than they used to? Is it true that schools let poor kids to fall farther and farther behind?

The Family

13

SOCIOLOGICAL WRITING ON the family has long been dominated by two themes: *universality* and *decline*. The theme of universality asserts that the family exists in all human societies. For a number of compelling reasons, people cannot live as solitary creatures, nor can human females raise their young by themselves as mother cats do. Hence, humans always live in groups containing adults of both sexes as well as children. Moreover, within any society, people form small clusters, called families, containing males and females, adults and children. Membership in these clusters usually is determined by common ancestry and sexual unions.

This definition of **family** is vague because sociologists and anthropologists have had much difficulty framing a more specific definition, given the amazing variety of social forms called families in different societies. Again and again, more specific definitions of the family have been found not to apply in one society or another, thus destroying the claim that the family is universal. Yet it seems clear that all societies *do* have families.

The second theme in modern sociological writing on the family is that, despite the universality of the family, in modern societies the family is in *decline*. Some claim that, thanks to modernization, the family has eroded dangerously: Families are now shrunken and unstable, and the modern family is increasingly unable to provide for the well-being of its members. Indeed, recent textbooks typically end discussions of the family with the question: Will the family survive? The usual answer is maybe.

Despite the problems of definition, a great deal of historical, anthropological, and cross-cultural evidence supports the universality theme. The family *is* a fundamental social institution occurring in all societies, although its particular forms differ substantially from place to place. Even the radical utopian communes of the nineteenth century did not succeed in eliminating the family as the basic unit of social relations (Nordhoff, 1875).

The theme of decline has seemed equally well supported by evidence. Statistics show that in all of the most modernized nations, the divorce rate has risen rapidly. This would seem to reflect the weakness of fundamental family bonds today. However, to know whether the modern family is really less able to fulfill its functions, we need to know whether the family in traditional societies fulfilled them better. For a long time, social scientists thought it self-evident that the traditional family did function better, and so they didn't bother to seek pertinent evidence.

Recently, however, much has been learned about families in the "good old days." This evidence seriously challenges the theme of decline. It can be argued that the family has become more important than ever during the past century and much better able to provide strong emotional attachments between its members than did families in traditional societies.

■

Chapter Preview

In this chapter, we shall first wrestle with the problem of what the family is. Once we can

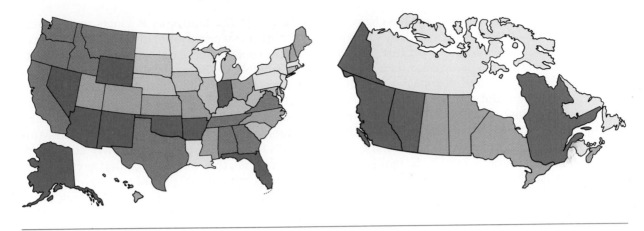

United States, 1980

State	Rate	State	Rate
Massachusetts	3.0	California	5.9
New Jersey	3.2	Montana	6.5
North Dakota	3.2	Tennessee	6.6
Pennsylvania	3.4	Georgia	6.7
New York	3.7	Texas	6.7
Wisconsin	3.7	Washington	6.7
Minnesota	3.7	Virginia	6.8
Louisiana	3.7	Oregon	6.8
Rhode Island	3.8	Alabama	6.9
		Idaho	6.9

State	Rate	State	Rate
Iowa	3.9		
South Dakota	3.9	Florida	7.4
Nebraska	4.0	Indiana	7.6
Maryland	4.0	Arizona	7.6
West Virginia	4.4	Oklahoma	7.7
Kentucky	4.4	Wyoming	7.8
Vermont	4.5	New Mexico	7.8
Connecticut	4.6	Alaska	8.6
Illinois	4.6	Arkansas	9.0
South Carolina	4.7	Nevada	15.4
Michigan	4.8		

State	Rate
Delaware	5.2
North Carolina	5.2
Hawaii	5.3
Kansas	5.4
Mississippi	5.4
Utah	5.4
Maine	5.5
Ohio	5.5
Missouri	5.7
New Hampshire	5.8
Colorado	5.8

Canada, 1981

Province	Rate	Province	Rate
Newfoundland	1.0	Quebec	3.0
N.W. Territories	1.4	Yukon	3.2
Pr. Edward Island	1.5	British Columbia	3.5
New Brunswick	1.9	Alberta	3.8

Province	Rate
Saskatchewan	2.0
Manitoba	2.3
Ontario	2.5
Nova Scotia	2.7

Figure 13-1 ■ **Divorces per 1,000 population.** In both Canada and the United States the divorce rate has risen considerably during the twentieth century. Back in 1920 there were 1.6 divorces per year for every 1,000 Americans, while in Canada the rate was 0.06 divorce for every 1,000 Canadians. Today, there are more than 5 divorces per 1,000 Americans and nearly 3 per 1,000 Canadians. Both nations have substantial regional variation. In Canada the far western provinces and the Yukon Territory have much higher divorce rates than do the eastern provinces—with the perhaps surprising exception of Quebec. In the United States the western states also tend to have a higher rate than those in the east. Nevada's rate is extremely high because tourists still use that state's very simple divorce procedures.

define the family, we will see how it has changed in response to modernization and then we will be able to assess the theme of decline. To do this, we shall examine what the family was like in Europe several hundred years ago. How did families live? How did family members treat one another? How did they feel about one another? How distinct was the family from the larger community? Against this benchmark, we shall assess the modern family. Is family life better or worse than it used to be?

Defining the Family

Perhaps the most consistent efforts to define the family have drawn on the functionalist approach to sociological theory. A number of anthropologists and sociologists have started from the premise that if the family is a universal social institution, then it must do something vital for human beings, something not done as well or as easily by other institutions. In seeking to define the family on the basis of *what it does*, functionalists have attempted to specify a list of functions the family performs.

In 1949, George Peter Murdock formulated what may be the most influential of these definitions. He defined the family as "a social group characterized by common residence, economic cooperation, and reproduction." He added that the family "includes adults of both sexes, at least two of whom maintain a socially approved sexual relationship, and one or more children."

Murdock then spelled out four primary functions of the family: sexual relationships, economic cooperation among members, reproduction, and the educational function, by which he meant the socialization of infants and children. Murdock admitted that agencies and relationships outside the family may share in the fulfillment of these functions, but "they never supplant the family."

However, Murdock's definition soon came under critical attack. On the one hand, much of the criticism pointed out examples of a society or two that seemed exceptions to one or more of Murdock's functions. For example, many claimed that economic cooperation is not an element of the family as it exists in a typical kibbutz (rural commune) in Israel. Instead, economic cooperation exists among all members of the kibbutz (Reiss, 1980). Among the Nuer of East Africa, some families contain no adult males—an older woman can adopt a younger woman and her children (Gough, 1974). On the other hand, some critics complained that Murdock's functions were too narrowly conceived. For example, they pointed out that sexual intercourse is but a small part of the emotional life husbands and wives share, and Murdock's sexual function completely ignores all the other strong, but nonsexual, relationships among family members.

Eventually, most sociologists of the family solved the problem by adopting a definition based on the notion of kinship and limited to the single function of child care. Other functions, such as those Murdock identified, are treated as necessary to *individual* well-being, but not as necessary parts of the family. For example, while humans need emotional support and frequently rely on their families as their primary source, in some societies this function is fulfilled primarily from outside the family. This revised approach lets us see that the connections between the family and various functions are problematic. In fact, a major activity of family sociologists is to examine changes over time or variations from one society to another in which functions the family fulfills and how well it does so.

The standard definition of the family as a universal human institution is *a small kinship-structured group with the key function of nurturant socialization of the newborn* (Reiss, 1980). This definition attempts to specify both *who belongs* to a family and *what the family does*—its primary function. Let's examine each element of this definition in greater detail.

The phrase "kinship-structured group" is more satisfactory than one invoking "biological ties" because many societies define kinship on the basis of such things as common residence rather than biological relationship—indeed, some preliterate societies have rather mistaken notions about biology. But, as Ira Reiss (1980) put it, "The tie of kinship is a special tie in every society of which we have any record." Yet if we define the family as a kinship cluster, then how can we justify that additional element of the definition which asserts that the key function of the family is "nurturant socialization of the newborn?" Is it always so? What about some future society that consigns all reproduction to government laboratories where eggs from female donors are fertilized with sperm from male donors and develop in a mechanical womb—a society where the infants are raised by trained nurses? Where's the family? And what happens to the universal applicability of this definition?

Here's the answer Reiss (1980), a leading family sociologist, gives:

Kinship, as we have defined it, is not dependent on biological connections, but rather is dependent on socially defined connections. In a society that assigned nurses to rear newborn infants, the ties between the nurse and the infants given to her/him would be defined as distinctive and special. Such ties of nurse and children, because they begin from infancy and last a period of years, would possess special emotional significance and would invest both the nurse and the children with special rights and duties relative to each other. What would such a small group of nurse and children be but a kinship group or a family? . . . The feeling of belonging to or "descending" from one another is the heart of the kinship notion. . . . The earliest memories of a child are of those who nurtured that child, and these memories are what comprise the feelings of descent.

Research might show that children raised in these "nurse and children" families did not do so well as children raised by a father and mother, but that finding would not change the designation of both forms as families.

The facts of human reproduction and maturation, and the extent of human culture, seem to require families to fulfill the nurturant socialization of infants. Human infants are born so helpless and take so long to mature that they require an immense amount of nurturance. A colt can stand within an hour, run before it is a day old, and race in the Kentucky Derby at the age of three. A human infant can learn to walk during its second year and takes many years to achieve physical and mental maturity. Moreover, even in the most primitive societies, there is a great deal to learn before one is an adequate adult. It is easier to supply such a large amount of nurturance if more than one adult is available to provide it—which is why it is so common to find families that include couples united in **marriage,** a formal commitment to maintain a long-term relationship involving specific rights and responsibilities.

Thus far our efforts to define the family have been quite abstract. So let's look at some specific aspects of family life in societies unlike our own.

Table 13-1 lets us examine variations in marriage and family patterns in premodern societies. The data are based on a set of 186 societies that make up what is known as the Standard Cross-Cultural Sample, which is a subset of the societies included in the *Ethnographic Atlas* described in Chapter 4. No modern industrialized societies are included in the sample, and even the most advanced societies in this set are relatively undeveloped agrarian societies. Indeed, the vast majority of these societies are small tribal groups—including several dozen North American Indian and Eskimo societies. More than 75 percent have no written language and many are seminomadic. Although many of these societies still exist, their value here is to offer us a view of cultures during earlier stages of civilization.

The first line in the table reveals that most premodern societies are not monogamous—three-fourths permit men to have more than one wife. Most are patrilocal—newlyweds take up residence with or near the groom's parents. In all of these societies marriages are arranged by parents, but many give the male greater say in the selection, and it is rare to find women with the greater say.

In two-thirds of these societies women have the final word when it comes to the care and discipline of young children. In half, men do no domestic chores at all. However, this is *not* because they are busy providing the necessities of life for their families: In only 16 percent of these societies (and only in those with the most developed agriculture) do men devote more time and effort than do women to subsistence activities. In most societies both men and women are equally involved in these activities, while in one-quarter women devote the greater time and effort.

Male dominance is the rule. In 84 percent of these societies *only* males hold leadership roles in kinship groups, and there is no society in which only women hold these roles. In two-thirds men and women share an explicit view that husbands ought to dominate their wives. Four of five condone wife beating. Nearly half value a woman's life less than a man's life. Finally, in close to half there exists a double standard concerning premarital sex—it's okay for men, wrong for women. These data suggest that we need not look to the simple life to discover how to base marriages on more equitable relations between husbands and wives.

None of these societies has the kind of family that is typical of modern nations—a family containing only one adult couple. Recall from Chapter 4 that such families are called **nuclear families.** Because of the very high mortality rates and short life expectancy of persons in premodern societies, one or both parents frequently die before their children are mature. These factors encourage the formation of families containing more than one adult couple. That is, in societies such as these nuclear families do not live apart from other relatives. Rather, the basic family unit includes several nuclear families; these are called **extended families.** Extended families can be composed in many different ways. For example, they can consist of an adult couple (the grandparents), their children, and the spouses and children of their children. Because people in some cultures often die before they become grandparents, the extended family often contains several brothers, their wives and children, and sometimes unmarried siblings.

Regardless of its composition, the extended family is larger than the nuclear family and always contains more than one adult couple. Extended families would seem able to provide more effective and attentive child care and socialization than nuclear families can simply because more adults are available for these tasks. For example, one adult can watch the infants while the others go out to pick fruit or gather eggs. Consequently, sociologists have long

Table 13-1 ■ **Variations in family life in premodern societies.**

Percent in which men may have more than one wife	77%
Percent in which newlyweds settle closer to groom's family	69%
Do women or men have greater say in selecting a spouse?	
Men do	39%
Equal	57%
Women do	4%
Percent in which women have the final authority over care and discipline of infants (4 years old and younger)	66%
Percent in which males do no domestic chores	51%
Do men or women devote more time and effort to subsistence activities?	
Men do	16%
Equal	61%
Women do	23%
Percent in which only males hold leadership roles in kinship groups	84%
Percent with explicit view that men should and do dominate their wives	67%
Percent in which it is acceptable for husbands to beat their wives	80%
Percent placing low value on women's lives	48%
Percent with a double standard on premarital sex	44%

Source: Prepared by the author from the Standard Cross-Cultural Sample as selected by Murdock and White (1969).

believed that the extended family fulfills its basic functions better than the nuclear family does.

■

Families and Functions

We have noted that many functions once assigned to the definition of the family now are seen as problematic. In many (even most) societies, these functions are fulfilled primarily by the family, but there always are many excep-

■ This little girl is finding out about where babies come from. She is learning more than the physiology of reproduction, however. She is also learning the essential sociological truth that people come from families. Around the world families function not simply for reproduction but for child rearing as well.

tions. Consequently, sociologists have found it useful to regard the link between various functions and the family, in particular times and places, as an appropriate question for research. For example, we can ask the question, Is the family in North America providing as much emotional support to members as is the family in Japan or as did the North American family of 1800? Because such questions and comparisons will form a major part of this chapter, let's spell out some functions usually associated with the family institution.

Sexual gratification

All societies have norms governing sexual behavior. Some impose very narrow limits on who may engage in sex, with whom, when, and how. Others have few restrictions. Within societies, families tend also to play a role in sexual norms. Wherever the institution of marriage exists, the norms define sexual rights of partners. In general, the family provides for sexual intercourse between certain members and typically prohibits it between certain other members—a prohibition often referred to as the **incest taboo.** But beyond these broad parameters, the link between the family and sexual gratification is incredibly various. Moreover, as we saw in Chapter 12, sexual norms often change rapidly.

Economic support

In most societies families serve as the primary economic units. Families contain **dependents**—such as infants, children, the elderly, and the disabled—who cannot support themselves. By sharing in a common economic unit, some family members provide care for their dependent kin. In primitive societies, able-bodied adults will hunt and gather food and then feed the rest of the family. In modern societies, some family members earn money to support the others. Moreover, in most societies decisions about the distribution of resources among family members are made within the family.

Obviously, the family's role as a source of economic support can vary across societies and through time. As mentioned, the family is not the basic economic unit for residents of a kibbutz. And in modern society, pension plans, insurance, welfare programs, and a variety of charitable and service agencies have assumed responsibility for supporting many dependents who once were the responsibility of their families.

Emotional support

In many societies families serve as primary groups for their members, giving people a sense of emotional security, a sense of belonging and of personal worth. For North Americans, the question might be posed: If our families won't love us, who will? When we are young we expect our parents, brothers, sisters, and other relatives to appreciate us. Later we expect this from spouses and even from our children. Of course, not all families fulfill these needs for their members—as divorce, child abuse, extramarital affairs, runaways, and other such situations suggest. And in different times and places, there has been much less reliance on the family for emotional support.

These functions of the family are, of course, intertwined. Sexual unions and the rearing of children both cause and reflect emotional attachments. Similarly, these attachments underlie economic relations within societies: Some family members work to support others at least partly because of their feelings toward them. Moreover, parents often rear large families because of the economic security children provide when they become adults.

However, not all families are equally able or willing to fulfill these primary functions. Children can be neglected, incest can occur, family members can be brutal to one another, and families can fail to support their dependents. Usually only a few families in a society function poorly, in most cases because of defects of particular members. Sometimes families in a society fulfill basic functions relatively poorly

because of social forces. Indeed, the theme of family decline asserts that modern conditions have forced families to function less well than they used to. To assess this claim, we shall examine how well the family functioned in Europe a few centuries ago.

Life in the Traditional European Family

Not until quite recently did social historians and sociologists of the family begin to dig out reliable data on family life in times past, and not until the late 1960s and the 1970s did substantial reports on these efforts begin to appear (Laslett, 1965, 1977; Rosenberg, 1975). Up to that time, our notions about family life in, for example, seventeenth-century Europe came from novels, letters, diaries, and autobiographies written at the time. The trouble with these sources is that they reflect a narrow stratum of society—the wealthy and literate. Although they may shed light on how the privileged few lived and felt, they tell us very little about the lives of the vast majority.

Europe's peasants and urban laborers left no literary traces. To discover what the life of an average family was like in past times and places, scholars have had to laboriously reconstruct the period from tax records; lawsuits; parish records of baptisms, weddings, and funerals; and even information on gravestones. These labors proved to be worthwhile. The picture of traditional family life is far from the warm, intimate, loving, caring extended family that we have long celebrated.

For many sociologists, the first real fruits of these historical searches came with the publication of Edward Shorter's *The Making of the Modern Family* in 1975. In it Shorter combined the research of many scholars to depict the traditional family and contrast it with the modern family. Shorter's book has changed sociologists' views about the family. Let's see what Shorter found out about the traditional European family.

Household composition

The first step in assessing family life is to know who is living with whom—that is, what the usual composition of a household is. From many studies of different parts of Europe, Shorter discovered that the extended family living in a single household was not typical except for the wealthy, both urban and rural. As we shall see, the typical household did include more than a nuclear family, but the additional members were often only temporary members, such as lodgers and hired hands. Moreover, the traditional household was much smaller than had been assumed. While wealthy households often included ten or more people, most households had only five or six members (see Table 13-2).

We know that in those days women gave birth to many children, often as many as eight or ten. How, then, could the normal household be so small? One reason was high infant and child mortality. One of every three infants died before the age of one, and another third died before reaching adulthood. Another reason is that children typically left the household to take full-time employment at ages that seem incredibly young to us.

In the eighteenth century, for example, children in western France left home to work as servants, shepherds, cowherds, or apprentices at the age of 7 or 8! By the age of 10, virtually all children had gone off on their own. In England at this same time, children did not begin to leave home until the age of 10, but by age 15 nearly all of them had left. Keep in mind that people physically matured later in this period (see Chapter 5). These were little kids who were having to go it alone.

Of course, not all the children left. Eldest sons stayed home or returned home after a period of working elsewhere, and one day took over the farm. In some places, daughters remained home until they married. Nevertheless, the traditional household is remarkable for the small number of children living in it, especially given the large number who were born.

In addition, the traditional household contained fewer adults than one might expect. High mortality meant that there were few elderly in

Table 13-2 ■ Average household size in preindustrial societies.

Nation	Year	Number of Persons in Average Household
British North America	1689	5.85
England	1599	4.75
France	1778	5.05
Germany	1687	5.77
Italy	1629	4.50
Japan	1746	5.50
Poland	1720	5.40
Scotland	1779	5.25
Serbia	1733–34	4.95

Source: Laslett (1977).

the households, and many homes lacked either a father or a mother. In fact, female-headed households were as common in the past as they are today. The primary cause of such households today is divorce, and thus the father often continues to see the children and to send financial aid. Back then, the cause was death. The average married couple had only about ten years together before one died. As a result, many people remarried; therefore, many children grew up with a stepparent and with half sisters and half brothers. Perhaps you've wondered why so many fairy tales involve wicked stepmothers: because she was such a common part of life back when parents weren't especially nice even to their own children.

Thus, the image of the large extended families of preindustrial societies is based on wealthy households. These households were large because their rate of mortality was lower (the rich were much more likely to live to see their grandchildren, and more grandchildren survived), because their children were not pushed out to fend for themselves at young ages, and because many servants were considered part of the household.

■ New historical research has found that preindustrial households contained many fewer children than had been supposed because children were sent off on their own at a young age. Three centuries ago in France, for example, children began to leave home to work as shepherds, servants, and apprentices at age 7 or 8, and by 10 nearly all children had left home.

Crowding

Although the average traditional household was not large, even compared with modern households, it was crowded. The overwhelming majority of traditional European families lived in one room, where all indoor family activities took place. Rural families usually shared their one-room houses with livestock and poultry, while urban families frequently had a lodger or some other nonfamily member sharing their living space. Usually the one room wasn't even very large. At night, beds were arranged on the floor, and when people had mattresses, the beds were often crowded: Adults and children, males and females, family members and outsiders huddled together for warmth.

As late as the 1880s, when good census data were first recorded, half of the people in Berlin and Dresden still lived in one-room households. This situation seemed to be much more common throughout Europe earlier in the century. In Chapter 19, we shall see that far less crowding in households can cause serious strains among family members. When American families have more than one person per room, husband-wife and parent-child relations become strained. With whole families crowded into one room, family relations in preindustrial times were simply terrible, as we shall see.

"Outsiders"

Though much smaller than had been believed, many traditional households contained non-

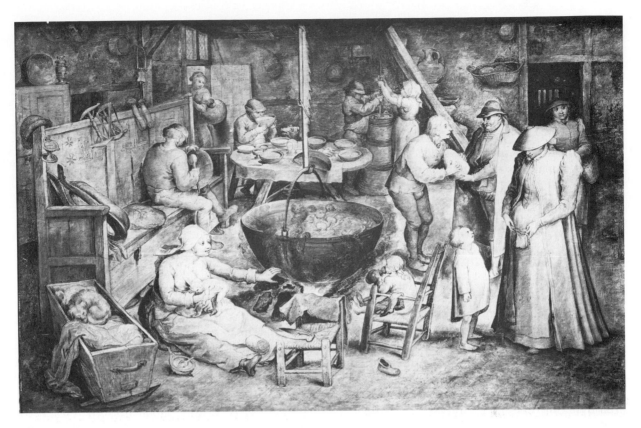

■ There was no privacy in preindustrial households; most dwellings had but a single room in which all activities took place. Often more than one family shared a one-room home. Imagine yourself growing up in this Flemish household painted by Pieter Brueghel (1525–1569).

family members. Many rural households contained male and female teenagers who served as hired hands. Such outsiders were particularly common during the peak of the farming season. Urban households frequently included lodgers who paid to eat and live with a family. Often, several unrelated families shared one-room urban homes, forced into a common residence by poverty. Moreover, there was a considerable coming and going by these live-in outsiders. Families tended to have people they did not know well living temporarily in their midst.

Clearly, the traditional family lacked privacy and a well-defined boundary. Family members ate, slept, gave birth, engaged in sex, and argued not only in full view of one another but also in full view of a changing audience of outsiders. And the traditional family was under close

observation by neighbors, too. Even rural families did not live far apart, each on their own farm as in Canada and the United States, but in cramped farming villages. As we shall see, these crowded living conditions undermined feelings of family unity.

Child care

We have seen that the traditional family was quick to send kids out on their own. This reflected more than mere economic necessity or the fact that unskilled children could perform productive labor in preindustrial economies. It also reflected an indifference toward children and neglectful child care practices.

Shorter put it bluntly: "Good mothering is an invention of modernization."

A good index of neglect and indifference is found in journals kept by local doctors. All of these doctors complained about parents leaving their infants and young children alone and untended for much of the day. Rashes and sores from unchanged swaddling clothes afflicted nearly all infants. Repeated accounts tell of children burning to death because they were left too close to an open hearth, and reports of unattended infants being eaten by barnyard pigs are frequent. In the part of France where silkworms were raised, a peasant proverb acknowledged that children were neglected during the busy season: "When the silkworms rise, the kids go to paradise." Indeed, throughout Europe, rural infants were most likely to die during the harvest season, when they were most neglected.

Even when parents were around their infants, they ignored them. Mothers rarely sang or talked to their infants when they tended them, nor did they play games with them as the children grew older. In fact, mothers didn't even refer to children by name, calling a child "it" or, in France, "the creature."

Mothers frequently were unsure of their children's ages (Shorter reports a mother who said her son was either 11 or maybe 14), failed to recall how many children they had given birth to, and often gave the name of a child who died to the next one born.

Because of the high rates of infant mortality, it might be understandable that parents were somewhat reluctant to form intense emotional bonds with their babies. But in some parts of France, parents typically did not attend funerals for children younger than 5, and there is widespread evidence that infant deaths often caused little if any regret or sorrow. Instead, parents often expressed relief at the deaths of children, and many proverbs reflected this attitude. Moreover, dead and even dying infants were often simply discarded like refuse and were frequently noticed "lying in the gutters or rotting on the dung-heaps."

Large numbers of legitimate infants whose parents were still living were abandoned outside churches or foundling homes. Some scholars suggest that as many as half of the children abandoned in parts of France during the eighteenth century were abandoned by intact families. Additional indifference and neglect is evident in the large numbers of infants sent off to wet nurses, despite the well-known fact that such children faced much higher probabilities of death. Indeed, wet-nursing became a high cottage industry outside of major cities in the eighteenth and nineteenth centuries, as families, especially the poor, sent away infants so that the mother would not be tied down by nursing and child care responsibilities. It is estimated that at least one-sixth of all babies born in Paris in 1777 were shipped out to wet nurses.

Once at the wet nurse's, infants were often not nursed at all but fed a paste of grain and water and given little attention. In truth, these homes were baby barns, crowded with infants. Parents seldom, if ever visited. Deaths were often covered up so that payments could still be collected. But staggering numbers of these babies were never seen again. Nor, it seems, were they missed.

The extraordinary infant death rates in preindustrial Europe now become easier to understand. The general conditions of life and public health practices alone would have produced high rates. But the actual rates were pushed even higher because of neglect and indifference. Indeed, as late as the 1920s, a government study in Austria attributed about 20 percent of infant deaths to "poor care."

Obviously, infants usually gained little emotional support from the preindustrial family. But what about other family members? What Shorter found seems as alien to us today as the idea of parents engaging in sex while sharing their bed with children and a lodger.

Relations between husbands and wives

Only in modern times have most people married for love. In the good old days, most married for money and labor—marriage was an economic arrangement between families. How much land or wealth did the man have? How large a dowry would the bride bring to her spouse? Emotional attachments were of no

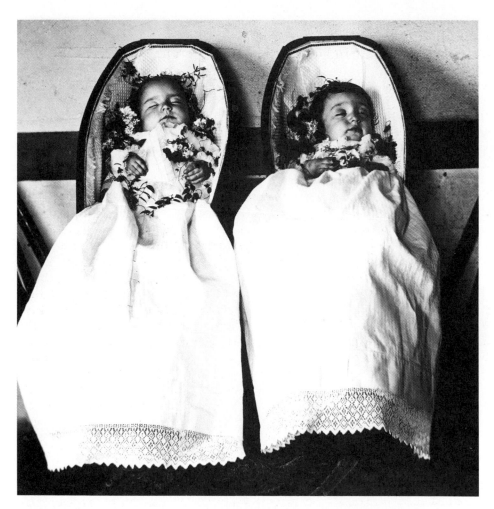

■ This poignant photograph of twins in their coffins, taken in Wisconsin in the 1890s, stands in dramatic contrast to the typical attitudes toward children in preindustrial families. Funeral portraits like this showed the determination of grieving parents to remember their lost children. In preindustrial times parents often were little interested in the death of a child—and sometimes simply reused its name for a later child.

importance to parents in arranging marriages, and neither the bride nor the groom expected emotional fulfillment from marriage.

Shorter (1975) noted an absence of emotional expression between couples and doubted that more than a few actually felt affection. The most common sentiments seem to have been resentment and anger. Not only was wife beating commonplace but so was husband beating. And when wives beat their husbands, it was the husband, not the wife, who was likely to be punished by the community. In France, a husband beaten by his wife was often made to ride backward through the village on a donkey, holding the donkey's tail. He had shamed the village by not controlling his wife properly. The same practice of punishing the husband was frequently employed when wives were sexually unfaithful.

The most devastating evidence of poor husband-wife relations was the reaction to death and dying. Just as the deaths of children often

■ Had photography existed three hundred years ago there would have been very few pictures like this one. Only in modern times has it become typical for parents to be deeply attached to their children.

caused no sorrow, the death of a spouse often prompted no regret. Some public expression of grief was expected, especially by widows, but popular culture abounded with contrary beliefs. Shorter reported the following proverbs:

The two sweetest days of a fellow in life,
Are the marriage and burial of his wife.

Rich is the man whose wife is dead and
horse alive.

Indeed, peasants who rushed for medical help whenever a horse or cow took sick often resisted suggestions by neighbors to get a doctor for a sick wife. The loss of a cow or a horse cost money, but a wife was easily replaced by remarriage to a younger woman who could bring a new dowry.

Bonds between parents and children

Besides the lack of emotional ties to infants and young children, emotional bonds between parents and older children were also weak. First, most of the children left the household at an early age. Second, when they did so, it was largely a case of "out of sight, out of mind." If a child ventured from the village, he or she was soon forgotten, not just by the neighbors but by the parents as well. All traces were lost of those who moved away. According to Shorter, a French village doctor wrote in his diary in 1710 that he had heard about one of his brothers being hanged but that he had completely lost track of the others.

Finally, even the children who stayed in the village did not come to love their parents. Instead, they fought constantly with their parents about inheritance rights and about when their parents would retire, and they openly awaited their parents' deaths. Shorter concluded that dislike and hatred were the typical feelings between family members.

Peer group bonds

Surely people in traditional societies must have liked someone. Unfortunately for our image of traditional family life, the primary unit of society and attachment was not the family but the peer group. The family provided for reproduction, child rearing (such as it was), and economic support (often grudgingly), but emotional attachments were primarily to persons of the same age and sex *outside* the family.

Wives had close attachments to other wives, and husbands to other husbands. Social life was highly segregated by sex and was based on childhood friendships and associations. For example, a group of neighborhood boys would become close friends while still very young, and these friendships remained the primary ties of these people all their lives. The same occurred among women. While this no doubt provided people with a source of intimacy and self-esteem, it hindered the formation of close emotional bonds within the family.

A woman would enter marriage expecting to share her feelings not with her husband but with her peers. Men reserved intimate feelings for their peers, too. In this way the weak boundaries defining the household were perforated by primary relations beyond the family. Thus, outsiders determined much that went on within a household. Husbands and wives often acted to please their peers, not one another.

Of course, sometimes people loved their children, and some couples undoubtedly fell in love. But most evidence indicates life in the preindustrial household was the opposite of the popular, nostalgic image of quiet, rural villages where people happily lived and died, secure and loved, amidst their large families and lifelong friends. It was instead a nasty, spiteful, loveless life that no modern person would willingly endure. Indeed, as industrialization made other options possible, the family changed radically because no one was willing to endure the old ways any longer.

Modernization and Romance

In Part Five we shall examine the why and how of the immense social changes that have resulted from modernization. Here we shall point out that life in modern societies is not simply better than in preindustrial societies but *it is also different.*

Nowhere is this clearer than in the transformations in family life. Where once a "happy couple" meant an absence of mutual antagonism, today that phrase is reserved for people who feel strong positive sentiments. We do not hope for a tolerable marriage; we seek love. Nor do we think it enough that parents do not hate, abuse, or neglect their children; we expect parents to love, nourish, and encourage them. We expect people to grieve when their parents die, not to be relieved that they are out of the way. In short, we assume that families foster deeply felt emotional attachments. How did this transformation come about?

Quite simply, modernization radically changed the conditions of life, giving people the opportunity to seek individual happiness. Shorter has sketched a number of these changes. First of all, industrialization freed individuals from depending on inheritance for their livelihoods. Eldest sons no longer had to wait for their fathers' land; daughters no longer had to wait for a husband with land. Both sons and daughters could seek wage-paying work, especially in the rapidly expanding urban industries. Soon young people were heading off to the cities in droves.

This change allowed people to make their own marital choices, free from both parental approval and concern about keeping property in the family. People no longer had to delay marriage until their parents died or retired, and property concerns no longer dominated the choice of a spouse. As these matters became

■ The industrial age made romantic love possible. Of course, people in earlier centuries sometimes fell in love, but it was not typical, and certainly rarely was love the basis for deciding whom to marry. Although modern people are determined to fall in love, they also have discovered the pains of falling out of love.

less important, other concerns emerged. And as men and women began to select their marriage partners, they began to seek people who appealed to them. Romantic attraction rapidly became the basis for marriage. "I love you" became the precondition for asking, "Will you marry me?"

Of course, notions of romantic love were not discovered in modern times. Greek and Roman poets and dramatists wrote of love—indeed, the Trojan War was thought to have been fought because of Paris's all-consuming love for Helen. And love was a major theme of court poets and minstrels in the days of chivalry and knighthood. But until relatively modern times few could afford to let love be the basis for marriage selection. The Puritans in England were among the first to stress the importance of romantic sentiments between husbands and wives, and this reflected their status as members of a newly

affluent middle class who could afford to marry for love.

In fact, affluence explains much of modern family life. The average modern family is wealthy beyond the dreams of preindustrial families. One of the first fruits of this affluence was space and privacy. As rapidly as economic circumstances permitted, families sought sufficient household space to gain privacy from one another and to shield themselves from outsiders. While married couples today routinely and openly express affection in ways unthinkable in the past, they are able to keep their most intimate relations private.

Moreover, the rise of romantic love in marriage redirected the primary attachments of the individual to within the household. Husbands and wives now expect their relationship to take priority over attachments to peers. A popular song at the turn of the century proclaimed, "Those wedding bells are breaking up that old gang of mine." With modernization came the expectation that husbands would not remain "one of the boys."

This redirection of primary attachments to family members was facilitated by mobility. People now seldom remain in the same place throughout their lives. As people become adults, they move away and break ties to their peers. Even if an individual does not go away, most of the peer group does. A common observation today is that if you want a lifelong friend, you had better marry one. Husbands and wives have become the only consistent, permanent emotional attachments.

Romantic love between spouses has also affected parent-child relationships. We now commonly believe that children must be wanted or they should not be engendered. By the late nineteenth century, books on child care and good parenting became a major topic in publishing (Zuckerman, 1975). Attitudes toward children have changed so dramatically that it is now against the law to treat children in ways that were once customary.

Modernization and Kinship

One of the widely noted "symptoms" of the decline of the family in modern times is the erosion of kinship bonds. We have seen that these perceptions are based in part on nostalgic illusion—the preindustrial family was not the nest of warmth and security we once thought it was. Yet for many North Americans and Europeans, the extended family remains an ideal standard against which the nuclear family is seen as wanting. Reiss (1980) has noted the irony that this should be so even though most of these same people do not want to live with their parents or with their grown children.

Nevertheless, the question persists: Has kinship really taken on less importance among people in modern societies? To answer the question, we shall have to distinguish between the *quantity* and the *quality* of kinship bonds.

There can be no doubt that most Americans are much less likely to have as many close bonds to brothers and sisters, cousins, aunts and uncles, and nephews and nieces than was the case several generations ago. This is a simple result of the *decline in fertility*.

The preindustrial household contained relatively few people despite widespread impressions about family life in that period. However, in the nineteenth and early twentieth centuries, especially in the United States and Canada, the average woman had many more babies than she does today and, even with mortality considered, the average family was much larger. The result is that several generations ago the average person in the United States and Canada had many more relatives (Pullum, 1982). A simple example will make the point.

At the turn of the century, the average North American woman gave birth to more than three children, and when only those women who married are counted, their average was four children. So put yourself in an average family. If all members marry and each couple has the average number of children, then if you gave a party and invited your relatives, the gathering would include your two parents, twelve aunts and uncles (six by marriage), twenty-four cousins, three siblings, twelve nieces and nephews, and four children—a total of fifty-seven people. In contrast, put yourself in an average family when the birth rate is two per female. Now your family reunion will draw two parents, four uncles and aunts (two by marriage), four cousins, one sibling, two nieces and nephews, and two children—a total of fifteen people. And that's part of what has happened to kinship bonds in modern life—there simply are far fewer of them. Other things being equal, a person born at the turn of the century had *six times* the probability of forming a close bond with a cousin, for example. So modernization has greatly reduced the *quantity* of kinship bonds and, in that way, may have reduced the quality as well. But then, again, maybe with so many kinship bonds the chances were reduced of having any one of them become really close.

Table 13-3 offers a gauge of the *quality* of family relations based on the frequency of

Table 13-3 ■ Family ties.

Persons with living parents only: How often do you spend a social evening with your parents?	
Almost daily	9.8%
Several times a week	21.6%
Once or twice a month	25.8%
Once or twice a year	32.3%
Never	10.4%

How often do you spend a social evening with relatives?	
Almost daily	9.7%
Several times a week	26.8%
Once or twice a month	31.9%
Once or twice a year	26.4%
Never	5.2%

Persons with siblings only: How often do you spend a social evening with a brother or sister?	
Almost daily	6.5%
Several times a week	14.1%
Once or twice a month	27.5%
Once or twice a year	40.8%
Never	11.1%

Married persons only: Taking things altogether, how would you describe your marriage? Would you say that your marriage is	
"Very happy"	63.1%
"Pretty happy"	33.5%
"Not too happy"	3.4%

Source: Prepared by the author from National Opinion Research Center, General Social Survey, 1986.

socializing by family members. Of American adults who have a living parent, one in ten spends nearly every evening with his or her parents, while another two of ten spend a social evening with their parents several times a week. Indeed, more than half of Americans with living parents see them at least once or twice a month. Another third only sees their parents once or twice a year—they probably live a long distance apart—and only one in ten seems to have broken off ties.

Americans are even more active in spending social evenings with relatives (often their sons and daughters). Those with siblings also see them often, although less frequently than they see parents and other relatives.

Finally, almost two-thirds of married Americans rate their marriage as "very happy," and less than 4 percent said it was "not too happy."

The picture that emerges here is not one of weak family ties. The American family has grown much smaller, but it seems to have stayed rather tightly knit. Most Americans spend frequent social evenings with relatives, and most are happily married.

But, you may be asking, if people are so happy with their marriages, why are there so many divorces? Don't high divorce rates suggest a breakdown in ties between wives and husbands?

■

Modernization and Divorce

Ironically, a high divorce rate probably indicates that the marital relationship has become much *more important than it used to be.* Back when most couples had weak emotional ties at best, they seldom divorced; now, although couples marry for love, they often divorce in anger and disappointment. Let's explore why divorce occurs and what it means for family life.

Divorce means the end of a marriage, but it does not necessarily mean the end of a family, because two-thirds of divorces occur between people who have children. One parent (usually the father) leaves the household, but a family remains. Moreover, divorce does not mean that many people experiment with marriage and then opt for a single life. Fewer than 5 percent of

North American adults at any given moment report their current marital status as divorced; more than 80 percent who divorce remarry. Thus, millions of couples give up on their marriages but not on marriage. These statistics offer an important insight into *why* people get divorced.

Most people who get divorced report that their marriage ceased to provide adequate emotional satisfaction—that is, their relationship was no longer happy. That might mean that the current high divorce rate indicates a lot of unhappy marriages, but it could also mean that at any given moment the great majority of marriages are happy ones. How is this possible?

Over the past eighty years, divorce laws have become much less restrictive. The intention behind this legislation was to strengthen the family by permitting intolerable marriages to dissolve. The rationale was that if the bad marriages are ended by divorce, most marriages will be good ones. Today, when many marriages end in divorce, it seems unlikely that people are enduring bad marriages to the same extent as when only a few got divorced. Indeed, it seems likely that people today become dissatisfied with marriages that people would have deemed acceptable fifty years ago.

Marital satisfaction is partly a matter of comparison. In days when few people divorced, a couple comparing themselves with their friends might have rated their marriage as good. Today the same couple might find theirs to be a poor marriage by comparison because the standard has risen: Marriages must be better to qualify as satisfactory when more unsatisfactory marriages are eliminated by divorce. Thus, as divorce rises, the average level of satisfaction in existing marriages should rise also. We have reason to suspect, however, that a substantial part of this perceived satisfaction is simply a "newness" or "variety" effect. That is, as people divorce and remarry, many may not actually find someone who suits them better but simply a replacement for a partner who had become too familiar.

How much divorce?

Although divorce tends to be higher in the more modernized nations, the divorce rate has been rising in most nations of the world, just as it has been in the United States. However, no one can say for certain how much increase in divorce actually has taken place because measuring the divorce rate in an accurate and valid way is very difficult.

The usual method, used in Figure 13-1, is to divide the number of divorces that occur in a given year by the population, to reflect the number of divorces per 1,000. That measure reveals that in the United States in 1900 there was 0.7 divorce per 1,000 population, while in 1980 there were 5.2 divorces per 1,000. That comparison is valid, however, *only* if the age and marital status of the population did not change during that eighty-year period. Other things being equal, a population having a large proportion of children must have fewer marriages and fewer divorces than one having a small proportion of children. Because 44.4 percent of Americans in 1900 were under 20, compared with 32 percent in 1980, the divorce rate per 1,000 probably *overestimates* the amount of increase. But by how much? Similarly, comparisons among nations are biased by differences in age and marital status—where large numbers of people never marry, there will be less divorce, too.

A second way to compute a divorce rate is to divide the divorces that take place in a year by the number of marriages. But, of course, the divorces that occur one year nearly all involve marriages that took place in earlier years. Hence this measure also is subject to distortion by population shifts. A more accurate measure would be based on the final *outcome* of all marriages occurring in a given year. But then we would have to wait until the last couple died or divorced before we could compute the rate—by now we would almost be ready to produce a divorce rate for 1910. We would have a very accurate rate but not a very timely one.

However, there is a way to estimate these outcomes without waiting to see how each marriage turns out (Preston, 1975). But the computation is highly complex, and thus far the only available rates based on this method apply to the United States alone. What do they show? A dramatic increase in divorce. Of all weddings held in 1923, 19 percent ended in

Table 13-4 ■ **Percent who have married and divorced, 1972–1986.**

Persons who have been married only: Have you ever been divorced or legally separated?	1972	1986
Percent "yes"	14.1%	18.7%

Source: Prepared by the author from National Opinion Research Center, General Social Surveys, 1972, 1986.

divorce. For weddings held in 1975 the projection is that 50 percent will result in divorce. Projections for more recent years (Weed, 1980) suggest a slight decrease—which also shows up in the rate of divorces per 1,000 population, down to 4.9 per 1,000 in 1984.

As sociologists examined the more accurate divorce rate, everyone's worst suspicions were confirmed. Marriage clearly has become a very unstable institution if half of all marriages end in divorce. For this fact was interpreted to mean that half of all Americans who get married will eventually get divorced. *But it wasn't so!*

In the spring of 1987, Louis Harris, the well-known public opinion pollster, touched off a controversy when he pointed out something that had long been turning up in survey studies but had gone ignored. Maybe half of all *marriages* break up, Harris noted, but the vast majority of *people* never get divorced. How could that be?

Because some people get married and divorced again and again, they contribute again and again to the statistics on broken marriages. Imagine four college roommates. Upon graduation each marries. Three never get divorced. But one marries and divorces three times. Hence this group produced six marriages and three divorces—so half of all marriages of this group ended in divorce. Although this is correct, it also is true that 75 percent of these people never divorced.

In an unusually silly display of professional jealousy, demographers in the U.S. Census Bureau rejected Harris's point, claiming that marriages, not people, are the proper basis for computation—thus, the significant fact is that

half of all marriages end in divorce. But for sociologists interested in whether the family is coming unglued, what matters is people. If most people marry only once, then that is a very different picture from one in which only half of them do.

Table 13-4 lets us look at survey data similar to those Harris was talking about. In 1972, the first year a General Social Survey was conducted, only 14.1 percent of Americans who had ever been married reported that they had ever been divorced or legally separated. By 1986 this percentage had crept up to 18.7 percent. There are two problems to deal with in interpreting these data. First, *some* of these people will eventually divorce. So the final figure will be higher than either of these percentages. Second, we can't just subtract the figure for 1972 from the one for 1986 and conclude that the ever-divorced population grew by 4.6 percentage points between 1972 and 1986. The adult U.S. population was substantially younger in 1972 than it was in 1986, so the average person in 1986 has had a longer opportunity to get divorced than did the average person in 1972.

Sociologists may be able to create age-specific divorce rates based on the percentage of ever-married persons who divorce for various recent years and use these to more accurately gauge the trend. But, whatever the results, already it is clear that recent assessments of family instability were exaggerated. Perhaps someday most people who marry will get divorced. But that's far from the case today. Nevertheless, the fact remains that a substantial number do divorce. Sociologists suggest two additional reasons why they do: (1) romance is a highly perishable commodity and (2) the opportunities to get divorced have increased.

When romance fades

We have seen that romance has become the basis for marriage in modern times. People now expect deep romantic sentiments to lead them into marriage and to sustain their marriages. Unfortunately, these feelings can fade and be difficult to revive. Because so many adults rely on their spouses for their deepest emotional ties, immense weight is placed on these romantic feelings. Even small tensions are easily magnified, for any discontent or threat to this primary attachment provokes anxiety. Indeed, romantic sentiments may suffer from too frequent assessment, and the slightest doubts can easily shatter that "special feeling." So, too, can the simple passage of time—especially when sexual attraction is the focal point of romance.

Studies suggest that sexual attraction, in and of itself, is based partly on novelty and tends to decline with time (Pineo, 1961). If this is an intrinsic feature of sexual attraction and not just a temporary aspect of current sexual patterns, then a decline in sexual attraction and satisfaction will permanently threaten marriages based on sexual attraction. That is, if sexuality is a primary basis for emotional attachment between husbands and wives, then marriages will tend to weaken as familiarity causes a loss of fervor. In this sense, a good deal of divorce may reflect a form of swapping sexual partners.

Clearly, however, most people do not equate love with sexual thrills. While a decline in sexual novelty may be at the root of many divorces, many other couples find that their relationships improve the longer they live together. Research shows that marital satisfaction is higher the longer a couple has been married (Campbell, 1975). Once again, this finding could partly reflect a bias of selection. As time passes, more of the less-satisfied couples get divorced. However, many couples report that their marriages have become more satisfying over time and that they are happier now than when they were just married.

Increased opportunities for divorce

In contrast with preindustrial societies, modern societies make it much easier for people to get divorced. Today, geographic mobility allows people who get divorced to do so in relative privacy. During or following a divorce, many couples do not have to face all of their relatives and old friends or even one another. They have long since moved away from where they grew up, and after a divorce they often move to new places and make new friends.

Female employment and small families also make divorce more likely in modern societies. A major impact of the massive entry of women into the labor force has been to decrease the dependence of wives on their husbands for economic support. This change has had many beneficial effects. For example, a woman need no longer cling to a brutal or drunken husband merely because she has nowhere else to turn. But it also encourages some women to give up on a relationship more quickly. Similarly, husbands have greater economic freedom to divorce wives who work, because working wives are seldom granted substantial alimony. The conditions that have enabled people to seek marriages based on romance have also enabled them to continue that search if a marriage fails to satisfy (Booth et al., 1984).

In addition, the increase in the number of women who work increases the opportunities for extramarital affairs. Wives who work have a much greater opportunity than housewives for regular contact with men other than their husbands. Similarly, with so many women at work, husbands have more contact with other women than did their fathers or grandfathers.

The huge recent influx of women into the labor force both reflects and contributes to a low birth rate. This too makes divorce easier because it reduces the burdens of being a single parent. And female labor force participation recently has produced another phenomenon: *the mature mother*. This designation is applied to women who are age 30 and older when they give birth to their first child. As recently as 1970 such women produced only 4 percent of the first births in the United States. In 1982 they accounted for 11 percent—an increase from 57,000 to 165,000 mature mothers. Mature mothers are overwhelmingly "career women" who delayed their families while completing their educations and getting established in an occupation. Seventy percent of them have been to college, and almost 40 percent earn more than $35,000 a year (Langer, 1985). Survey findings suggest that these women also waited to make sure they had a stable marriage before they bore children—many are married for the second time.

The One-Parent Family

The primary concern raised by high divorce rates is not broken marriages but broken families. How does divorce affect children? In recent years, researchers have devoted a good deal of study to this question. The results are somewhat inconsistent, but in general they indicate that divorce usually has little impact on children if they are not subsequently raised in a one-parent home (Rosenberg, 1965; Landis, 1965). It is important to see, however, that many one-parent homes are not the result of a divorce. Some are caused by the death of one parent, and a rapidly growing number occur when single women become mothers.

Over the past several decades in most industrial nations there has been a substantial increase in the proportion of children born to unwed mothers—the *illegitimacy ratio.* In 1960, 5.3 percent of all births in the United States and 4.3 percent in Canada were to unwed mothers. Today in the United States the ratio is about 20 percent. That is, of every 100 babies born in America, 20 percent are born to women who are not married. In a few cases the couple live together, although they are not legally married. But most of the time these women live alone or with their parents. In times past many illegitimate children were put up for adoption. Today most unwed mothers keep their children. Furthermore, in 90 percent of divorces, the children remain with the mother, and the combined result is a substantial number of *female-headed households*—households having children under age 18 and headed by a woman.

In Chapter 12 we saw that in addition to divorce, a shortage of eligible men has contributed to the increase in female-headed families, especially in the black community. But the primary consequence of female-headed families is poverty. Thus Special Topic 2 showed that the lowest-income families are very disproportionately made up of mothers raising children on welfare. Moreover, even when female-headed families are not poor, they are much less likely than are other families to be affluent, for the major source of high family incomes is *two earners.*

Lack of income can have many negative effects on family life (McLanahan, 1985). But sociologists are increasingly concerned about another shortage that besets the one-parent family: *time.* When there is only one parent rather than two, supervision of children may be reduced greatly. In the case of divorce, when children must split their loyalties between parents, the result may be weaker attachments to each in comparison to attachments in two-parent families.

From Chapter 7 it should be clear that if one-parent families cannot sustain the same level of supervision and the same strength of attachments as can two-parent families, then research ought to find that the one-parent family is in greater risk of having delinquent children. Research on this hypothesis has produced mixed results over the years. Recent studies suggest that children in one-parent families are more prone to various forms of delinquency, but that the differences are not great (Wilkinson, 1980).

Research does find that *poor parenting,* regardless of the structure of the family, *is a primary cause of deviant behavior among children.* Put another way, it isn't how many parents a child has at home that matters, it's how effective they are at being parents that is of primary importance in how a child turns out. Because this new line of research is so important, let's watch over the shoulder of Gerald Patterson as he demonstrated the link between poor parenting and childhood deviance and see how he made progress in training parents to become more effective at parenting.

Gerald Patterson: Incompetent Parents and Problem Kids

 Since the early 1970s, Gerald Patterson and his colleagues at the Oregon Social Learning Center have studied and attempted to treat young children (many not yet of school age) who frequently engage in acts of deviant and antisocial behavior. These are not just kids who throw tantrums and act up; many of them are already serious offenders— kids who constantly steal and even commit arson.

Initially, Patterson and his colleagues adhered to the standard approach recommended by behavior modification psychology: The way to get rid of undesirable behavior is to not reward it and to instead make sure to reward desirable behavior. As time passed, however, Patterson noticed that much undesirable behavior simply did not disappear no matter how much others ignored it. Indeed, by studying very young children of 2 and 3 Patterson found that little kids engage in a great deal of antisocial behavior, such as pushing and shoving and yelling. Moreover, they have no understanding of property rules and simply take anything they want if they can reach it, whether it might be a cookie, their sister's doll, or their father's car keys. Having established "normal" rates for these forms of antisocial behavior for 2- and 3-year-olds, Patterson soon discovered that his problem children were simply continuing to behave in a way that was normal for much younger children. This discovery led to an important conclusion: Kids will not cease these forms of misbehavior unless they are forced to. In effect, *kids continue to act in such ways unless parents effectively use punishment to teach them not to.*

Thus, Patterson and his group learned that there is solid scientific evidence for what our grandmothers always believed: Parents are to blame when their children misbehave. By the late 1970s, Patterson and his group had turned their fullest attention to the parents of problem kids. What did they fail to do or do wrong? Could they be trained to do better?

Eventually, Patterson (1980) described adequate parenting skills in terms of seven tactics:

1. Notice what the child is doing.

2. Keep track of the child's behavior over long periods.

3. Act in ways you want the child to act (and don't act in ways you do not want the child to act).

4. Clearly state the rules the child is expected to obey.

5. Consistently apply reasonable punishments for violations of the rules.

6. Consistently reward conformity.

7. Negotiate disagreements so that they get settled rather than escalate.

Patterson himself has described these procedures for dealing with children as obvious and mundane. But, he pointed out, increasing numbers of parents have not had the kind of experiences with younger brothers and sisters that helped people in the past learn how to parent. Moreover, for several reasons some parents simply are unwilling or unable to use these procedures.

One major problem is lack of attachment. Throughout this book, we have seen the power of attachments to shape behavior, and Chapter 7 emphasized how attachments to parents resulted in young people's conforming to the norms. But Patterson has drawn attention to the other side of that coin—the attachment of parents to their children. He found that many parents of the problem children treated by his center didn't really like their kids, feel obligations toward them, or even want to be parents. It was very hard, and often impossible, to teach such people to be adequate parents. And it surely is no surprise that kids are not strongly attached to parents who reject them.

A second major impediment to good parenting is that people often refuse to "see" what their children are doing. Many parents of children who were chronic stealers simply denied all charges of theft unless they had personally seen the child steal. Indeed, many of these parents applied the word *steal* only when an act of theft could be proven, as if it weren't stealing if you could get away with it. Pursuing this insight, Patterson and his colleagues found that the parents of chronic stealers had deviant views of misbehavior; in fact, they had attitudes most similar to those of delinquent adolescents. Thus, while these parents probably seldom went so far as to reward stealing behavior in their children, they often did not punish it because it did not really offend them.

Parents of problem children repeatedly fail to punish them for failing to obey. Such parents frequently will ignore everything the child does until or unless it irritates them sufficiently to take action. As a result, even when they do punish an offense the punishment often fails to cause the misbehavior to diminish. First, the child has learned that he or she can often get away with the misbehavior; second, the punishment is generally without any lasting consequences. As Patterson put it, "These parents yell, scold, threaten, and occasionally physically assault the child." The adequate parent, on the other hand, backs up threats and scoldings, and even spankings, by withdrawing privileges or assigning extra household chores.

Having concluded that parents are a primary cause of problem children (that when an 8-year-old child steals or hits other kids, he or she has been allowed to do so), Patterson and his group have set out to attempt to treat problem kids by training their parents how to control their children's behavior. The results so far are promising. While some parents simply will not or cannot be helped, many others have been helped to improve their children's behavior.

The Oregon project is the first delinquency prevention program that has produced some signs of success. For this reason, Patterson and his colleagues can claim to have made a truly major scientific breakthrough. That does not mean, however, that this program can be put into practice across the country with major benefit. For one thing, it has proven to be extremely time consuming (and thereby expensive) to teach parents to deal more adequately with their children. Moreover, even when parents have learned to manage their kids, they will often slide back into their old neglectful ways, especially if they encounter difficulties in their own lives. A great deal more experimentation and study are required to see whether lasting improvements can be achieved in enough cases to justify the immense expense needed to apply Patterson's techniques nationally.

Remarriage

As mentioned, more than 80 percent of Canadians and Americans who divorce remarry. Recently, several major studies have focused on questions of *whom* people choose the second time around. First, do they select differently after having a first marriage result in divorce? Second, how do second marriages work out? And, third, what is the impact of children from a previous marriage on adjustments in a new marriage?

To answer questions like these, sociologists have begun to collect data on what Furstenberg and Spanier (1984) have called **conjugal careers.** Sociologists have long studied occupations in terms of careers—the pattern of employment individuals follow over the course of their working lives. Why not treat marriage the same way? Let's watch two recent sociological studies of conjugal careers as they shed light on the three questions we've posed.

Jacobs and Furstenberg: second husbands

 It is well known that first marriages involve women and men of quite similar social status. For example, Michael Hout (1982) found that couples who both work full-time are very likely to hold jobs similar in prestige. That is, women who work in factories tend to be married to other factory workers; women professionals tend to have husbands who also have a profession. This is not surprising because the two most usual places for married couples to have met is at school or at work. People who met in school tend to have the same levels of education and hence to qualify for the same levels of jobs. And people who meet at work tend to be doing the same sort of work. But what happens the second time around?

To find out, Jerry A. Jacobs and Frank F. Furstenberg, Jr. (1986) of the University of Pennsylvania collected data from a national sample of American women over ten years. In 1967 two groups of women were interviewed. One sample was limited to women 30 to 45. The second included only women 14 to 25. Ten years later these same groups were interviewed again. Then the data were assembled to form a marital or conjugal career for each woman up to 1978. By then, 743 of the older women had been divorced or widowed and had remarried, as had 413 of the younger women. Jacobs and Furstenberg focused on these two groups in their study.

At first glance it appeared that women bettered their economic situation by remarriage—second husbands had a higher average occupational prestige and income than did first husbands. But this was an illusion. Women are older when they remarry and therefore second husbands are older at remarriage than are first husbands. When the *current* economic position of first and second husbands was compared, the average turned out to be the same. On average, then, women marry second husbands who are no more, and no less, successful than their first husbands. Within this overall finding for the average remarriage, however, there were some distinctive patterns applying to certain subsets of women. The sooner women remarried, the greater the similarity in the social status of their first and second husbands. When older women remarried they more often married men noticeably more or less successful than their first husbands; the older a woman is when she remarries, the smaller is the pool of available husbands, because of the much lower life expectancy of men.

Children also play an important role in the economic success of second husbands. That is, a woman with children under age 10 is usually unable to marry a second husband who is as successful as her first husband. As Jacobs and Furstenberg put it, women "who bring children with them into the second marriage are at a distinct disadvantage. The negative socioeconomic consequences of bringing children into the second marriage are substantial." Put another way, men will prefer a family of their own to assuming another man's family, ready-made. Other things being equal, the more financially successful the man, the more options he will have in choosing a wife, and he will tend to use those options to marry a woman without younger children.

White and Booth: stepchildren and marital happiness

 If women pay a price for bringing children into a marriage, what happens after that? How do stepchildren influence relations between a couple following remarriage? To find out, Lynn K. White and Alan Booth (1985) of the University of Nebraska interviewed a national sample of married adults under age 55 in 1980. Then in 1983 they reinterviewed them—a total of 1,673 people.

White and Booth were aware of research showing that the divorce rate is higher in remarriages than in first marriages. So they were especially interested in measuring aspects of the marital relationships of their respondents—how happy they were, how much fighting they did, and the like. And because they had interviewed people twice over a three-year period they could contrast those who separated or divorced during this period with those who did not—and 7 percent had done so.

When they examined their results, the first and most striking thing they discovered was that couples who remarry do not have a higher rate of divorce than people who are marrying for the first time if there are no stepchildren in the home or if it is the first marriage for the other partner. When it is a remarriage for both partners and when one or both bring children from a prior marriage to live in the home, the odds of divorce are increased by 50 percent. And not surprisingly, couples with stepchildren in the home report a lot more tensions and problems with children than do couples with only their own biological children in the home. Apparently the children feel it too. White and Booth found that stepchildren leave home at a younger age than do biological children. Summing up their findings, White and Booth wrote:

A comparison of parents with stepchildren and those without shows a strong and consistent pattern: parents with stepchildren more often would enjoy living away from their children, perceive their children as causing them problems, are dissatisfied with their spouse's relationship to their children, think their marriage has a negative effect on their relationship with their own children, and wish they had never remarried.

Conclusion

The modern family has many imperfections. Many families abuse or neglect their children. Arrest statistics show that family fights are common and that homicides frequently occur within families (see Chapter 7). Many of today's marriages will end in divorce. Yet these problems do not demonstrate that family life is deteriorating or that the family is less able to fulfill its functions. We have seen what the good old days were like, and as far as family life is concerned, they should be called the "miserable old days."

I have emphasized a historical view in this chapter not to minimize concern about current family problems, but to put them in perspective. It's not helpful to run in search of answers to why the world is going to pot if that is not really what's happening. Here the decades of sociological concern about the decline of the family seem instructive. For example, for years sociologists asked why marriage no longer worked without asking if a high divorce rate might reflect unceasing efforts by individuals to find marriages that do work. Preindustrial marriages may have lasted, but did they work? If we rate them by current standards, then they seldom did.

Review Glossary

family A small kinship-structured group with the key function of nurturant socialization of the newborn. (p. 372)

marriage A formal commitment between a couple to maintain a long-term relationship involving specific rights and duties toward one another and toward their children. (p. 375)

nuclear families Families made up of only one adult couple and their children. (p. 376)

extended families Families made up of at least two adult couples. (p. 376)

incest taboo Prohibition against sexual relations between certain members of the same family. (p. 377)

dependents Family members unable to support themselves. (p. 377)

conjugal careers The histories of individuals in terms of marriages. (p. 394)

Suggested Readings

Collins, Randall. 1988. *Sociology of Marriage and the Family.* Chicago: Nelson-Hall.

Laslett, Peter. 1977. *Family Life and Illicit Love in Earlier Generations.* London: Cambridge University Press.

Patterson, G. R. 1980. "Children Who Steal." In *Understanding Crime: Current Theory and Research,* edited by Travis Hirschi and Michael Gottfredson. Beverly Hills, Calif.: Sage Publications.

Reiss, Ira L. 1980. *Family Systems in America.* New York: Holt, Rinehart and Winston.

Rosenberg, Charles E., ed. 1975. *The Family in History.* Philadelphia: University of Pennsylvania Press.

Shorter, Edward. 1975. *The Making of the Modern Family.* New York: Basic Books.

The Older Family

Until modern times most human beings never got old—they didn't live that long. Even at the beginning of this century, the average life expectancy of people born in the United States was only 47 years, 46.3 for men and 48.3 for women; among black Americans, the figures were 32.5 and 33.5, respectively. Today, nearly ninety years later, life expectancy in America is 74.7 years—71.1 for men and 78.3 for women (67.3 for black men and 75.2 for black women). As a result, the proportion of Americans over age 65 has nearly tripled over the past ninety years. This fact, combined with an overwhelming preference for nuclear families, means that not only are there more older individuals but there are also a lot more older families.

Our images of older families are contradictory. The media stress the poverty that so often accompanies the "graying" of the family. Yet one gains a very different image by traveling the highways of the nation, an image of the older family on an endless vacation in the passing streams of recreational vehicles and trailers. Or nonstop Congressional hearings on problems of senior citizens produce endless testimony on the need for improved retirement and social security benefits, but polls show that younger people, not those over 65, think the government spends too little on social security. Or in one section of the newspaper we can read of the serious health problems of the elderly, while in another section we can read about how active most older Americans remain.

Which of these images is true? Probably *all* of them. The older American family is as varied as are younger families. Some older couples live on yachts, some live in shacks; some run in marathons, some are bedridden. Nevertheless, comparisons between older and younger families can reveal interesting contrasts. This Special Topic will inspect some of these comparisons based on national survey data. I think you will find many surprises here.

Happiness

I must admit that Table ST4-1 really surprised me. Older Americans are the happiest Americans. People over 65 are significantly more likely than younger people to say they are "very happy." Moreover, the big difference is between those over 65 and everyone else—a pattern that held up in comparison after comparison. So we need not examine the full set of age categories in the remainder of this analysis, but can simply compare groups over and under 65.

These data on happiness call up the image of the older American family rolling down the highway in a Winnebago looking for adventures. Of course, many over 65 did not say they were very happy. Moreover, while men and women age 65 and under were equally likely to say they were happy, among those over 65, men were significantly more likely than were women to say they were very happy. Let's see why this gender difference exists.

Table ST4-1 ■ **Age and happiness.**

	Age: 18–29	30–39	40–49	50–65	Over 65
Percent who are "very happy"	29.4%	29.1%	31.5%	32.7%	38.8%

Source: Prepared by the author from National Opinion Research Center, General Social Survey, combined samples for 1986 and 1987.

Table ST4-2 ■ **Marriage and happiness for people over 65.**

	Married		Unmarried	
	Men	Women	Men	Women
Percent who are "very happy"	50.9%	53.8%	29.4%	29.2%

Source: Prepared by the author from National Opinion Research Center, General Social Survey, combined samples for 1986 and 1987.

Marriage

Look at Table ST4-2. Here men and women over 65 have been further separated into those who are or are not currently married. Within each group the relationship has effectively vanished—showing that the gender effect is spurious. It isn't that older women are less happy than older men, it is that married people are much more likely than unmarried people to be happy.

But what the gender difference in happiness reveals is perhaps the single most important thing about the older family: Frequently, it includes only *one* member. And because of longer female life expectancy, combined with the tendency of wives to be younger than their husbands, the one-member family is very disproportionately female. In 1984, of the nearly 11 million American men over 65, 78 percent were currently married. But of the more than 15 million American women over 65, only 40 percent were currently married. This marriage gap continues to grow with age. Of people 75 and older, 70 percent of the men still have wives, but only 24 percent of the women still have husbands.

Another way to look at this is through sex ratios. In 1910, among persons over 65, there were 101 men for every 100 women. In 1984 there were only 67.5 men. The average older American wife faces the burden of a lengthy widowhood—which is precisely what these findings on greater male happiness reflect. Now, let's look at a second aspect of happiness.

Finances

In light of what we know about the financial plight of many older Americans, Table ST4-3 offers another surprise. People over 65 are almost twice as likely as younger people to be "pretty satisfied" with their present financial situation.

■ This photograph of a bridge tournament for senior citizens displays a major problem facing older Americans: widowhood. That is, the great majority of men over age 65 are married, while the great majority of women that age are widows. In addition to loneliness, many women face a substantial decline in income when their husbands die.

Undoubtedly, some of this greater satisfaction stems from older people no longer having to strive for future occupational status. If many find the work world a "rat race," for most older Americans that race is ended. Hence their assessment of their present financial situation sums up how they did, and a lot of them think they did pretty well. But here again there is a sex difference, and again we see that this is largely a function of marriage. Married men and women are much more likely than the unmarried to be pretty satisfied, and the only significant sex difference is the one among the unmarried. Table ST4-4 lets us see why.

People over 65 are much more likely than younger people to report a family income of less than $10,000 a year; more than four out of ten have incomes this low. However, only about one in five among married older Americans have incomes below $10,000. In contrast, over one-third of unmarried men and two-thirds of unmarried women have low incomes. So if unmarried women are less likely to be satisfied than are married people or unmarried men, they have less to be satisfied about.

The unmarried are in greater risk of poverty because even in retirement, married people often constitute two-earner households. Unmarried women run a greater risk of poverty than do unmarried men because they are much less likely to have been employed outside the home and therefore they are less likely to be qualified for social security (except for widow's benefits from their husband's social security) or to have an independent pension.

Family ties

The image of the older American family as isolated from children and kin undoubtedly fits some people, but in fact most older Americans frequently see their children (Shanas, 1973), and Table ST4-5 shows that people over 65 see rel-

Table ST4-3 ■ Satisfaction with finances.

So far as you and your family are concerned, would you say that you are pretty well satisfied with your present financial situation, more or less satisfied, or not satisfied at all?	Percent Who Are "Pretty Satisfied"
65 and under	26.5%
Over 65	46.1%
Married men over 65	57.9%
Married women over 65	60.0%
Unmarried men over 65	45.6%
Unmarried women over 65	33.6%

Source: Prepared by the author from National Opinion Research Center, General Social Survey, combined samples for 1986 and 1987.

Table ST4-4 ■ Low incomes.

Annual Family Income under $10,000	
65 and under	16.5%
Over 65	44.4%
Married men over 65	19.6%
Married women over 65	23.2%
Unmarried men over 65	39.7%
Unmarried women over 65	67.7%

Source: Prepared by the author from National Opinion Research Center, General Social Survey, combined samples for 1986 and 1987.

atives as often as younger Americans do. The second item in the table also may come as a surprise. Older Americans overwhelmingly reject the idea of sharing a home with their grown children. In contrast, younger people are much more inclined to see that as a good idea.

Leisure

So what do older Americans do with their time? Do older and younger people tend to spend their leisure time differently? Table ST4-6 offers some answers.

Older people are more apt to read a newspaper every day. However, this is not because they have more time. Americans now over 65 were more apt to read newspapers when they were 30 than are people that age today. Consequently, newspaper circulation has been declining, relative to population size, for decades. For example, in 1950, per capita newspaper circulation was .35. Today it is only .26.

Perhaps as a result of their newspaper reading, older Americans are more apt to know the name of their local representative in Congress.

Older people are also more likely to watch TV for more than two hours a day than are younger people. That undoubtedly does reflect their greater amount of free time, as may the fact that older people are more apt to spend frequent social evenings with neighbors than are younger people.

Younger people are less likely than those over 65 to attend church weekly—even though for many older people transportation can be a problem. More available time would not seem to be the relevant factor because, despite having lower incomes, people over 65 are substantially more likely to contribute more than $300 a year to a church.

Indeed, despite having more spare time, older people are extremely unlikely to spend any of it in a bar or tavern; only 6 percent do this as often as once a month, compared with about 30 percent of those under 65. Older people are much more likely to drink at home (46.4 percent) than to drink out, but are not as likely to do so as younger Americans, 72.2 percent of whom drink. Older people are not inclined to go out to X-

■ This couple belongs to the happiest group of Americans, married couples over 65. And, giving substance to the adage "Youth is wasted on the young," the group least apt to say they are very happy are single people between 18 and 30.

rated movies either. But older people are as likely as those 65 and under to say that they find life to be "exciting."

Health and mortality

Table ST4-7 shows that older Americans are less likely than those under 65 to rate their health as excellent, but the difference seems smaller than one might expect. In fact, only 11 percent of those over 65 rated their health as poor, as did 4 percent of the younger group. More than half of those over 65 report having been hospitalized during the past five years, but so have more than one-third of those younger.

However, older Americans are much more likely to experience the death of loved ones. Half of those over 65 have lost a spouse, compared with only 7.6 percent of those 65 and under. More than one-third have lost a brother or sister within the past five years, compared with 11.2 percent of those under 65. Indeed, one in ten have lost a child during the past five years—a grown child, not an infant. Finally, about 60 percent have lost another close relative during the past five years, as have one-third of younger Americans.

One major lesson to be learned from these data is that the older American family has high levels of contentment and satisfaction. But there is a second, and darker, lesson to be learned here as well. The older family is, of course, a couple's household—although high levels of contact are maintained, the children and grandchildren live elsewhere. And herein lies a major vulnerability of the older family. Eventually, the couple becomes a one-person household, and the loss of what was the survivor's most intimate relationship too often also is accompanied by a very substantial decline in income. When discussions of poverty among older Americans arise, they are primarily discussions of the poverty of widows.

This aspect of what some have called the "feminization of poverty" may be only temporary. Because of the rapid expansion of the proportion of females in the labor force, younger women are much less likely to have spent their married years as full-time homemakers. Hence, as each new age cohort of women reaches retirement age, each year a larger proportion of older women have been employed outside the home for a substantial number of years. These women qualify for social security benefits in their own right, and many have earned other pension benefits. As a result, they are not nearly so vulnerable to financial distress if their spouse dies. The emotional distress of widowhood may prove much more intractable.

Table ST4-5 ■ Family ties.

	65 and Under	Over 65
Percent who spend a social evening with relatives once or twice a week	36.8%	34.3%
Percent who think it is a *good idea* for older people to share a home with their grown children	43.8%	23.8%

Source: Prepared by the author from National Opinion Research Center, General Social Survey, 1986.

Table ST4-6 ■ Social and leisure activities.

	65 and Under	Over 65
Percent who read a newspaper every day	50.4%	67.9%
Percent who can name their congressional representative	35.4%	43.5%
Percent who watch TV more than 2 hours a day	49.4%	60.8%
Percent who spend a social evening with a neighbor once or twice a week	26.3%	35.5%
Percent who attend church weekly	33.3%	50.2%
Percent who contribute more than $300 a year to a church	27.7%	38.5%
Percent who go to a bar or tavern at least once a month	29.2%	6.0%
Percent who drink alcoholic beverages	72.2%	46.4%
Percent who have attended an X-rated movie in the past year	29.4%	3.0%
Percent who find life "exciting"	45.0%	42.3%

Source: Prepared by the author from National Opinion Research Center, General Social Survey, 1986.

Table ST4-7 ■ Health and mortality.

	65 and Under	Over 65
Percent who rate their health as excellent	36.8%	19.8%
Percent who have been hospitalized in the past 5 years	35.9%	53.4%
Percent who have had a spouse die	7.6%	51.7%
Percent who have had a brother or sister die in the past 5 years	11.2%	37.7%
Percent who have had a child die in the past 5 years	1.8%	9.6%
Percent who have had another close relative die in the past 5 years	31.5%	59.3%

Source: Prepared by the author from National Opinion Research Center, General Social Survey, 1987.

Religion

14

NOBODY KNOWS WHEN humans first possessed religion. Unlike tools chipped from stone, cultural ideas do not lie secure for millions of years, awaiting the archeologist's pick. So while we know that humans living over a million years ago made tools, we can only guess about their religion. However, there can be no doubt that our Neanderthal ancestors had religion at least 100,000 years ago, because evidence of their faith has been unearthed. The Neanderthal buried their dead with great care and provided them with gifts and food for use in the next world. And deep in their caves, the Neanderthal built small altars out of bear bones. These relics make it clear that the Neanderthal believed in life after death and conducted ceremonies to seek the aid of supernatural beings. Such beliefs and practices are properly called religion, and all human societies since the days of the Neanderthal have had religion.

Chapter Preview

In this chapter we shall try to understand why religion is a vital part of human societies. What does religion do for people? How does it influence social life? Then we will explore the concept of a **religious economy**—the marketplace of competing faiths within a society. Although societies often claim to have only one faith (and sometimes use military force to keep competing faiths out), this is never really true. We shall see why not, why "underground" faiths exist even in the most repressive nations, and why

these tend to erupt into significant movements whenever repression eases. Viewing the religious sector of societies as economies of faith permits us to examine how religious organizations influence one another. We shall see that in time the most successful religious organizations become increasingly worldly, a process called **secularization.** As this occurs, conditions become favorable for new organizations to break away and restore a less worldly form of the conventional faith, a process known as **revival.** We shall also see how wholly new religions can arise in societies, a process called **religious innovation** or cult formation.

We shall use our model of religious economies to examine current conditions and trends in the United States. Then we shall apply the model to Canada and the nations of western Europe.

The Nature of Religion

A most difficult problem facing sociologists of religion has been to define their subject matter. An adequate definition must include the vast array of faiths found in the world without including too much. As Georg Simmel urged in 1905, a general definition of religion must apply "alike to the religion of Christians and South Sea Islanders." It must isolate the common elements in Buddhism, Islam, and other faiths of modern times, as well as the faiths of our primitive ancestors, such as the Neanderthal.

For a few decades, this problem was solved

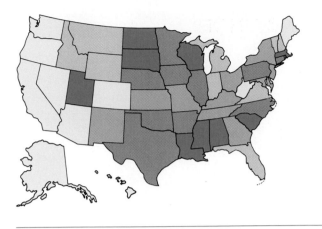

1980: Church Members per 1,000 Population

Nevada	311	North Carolina	606
Alaska	315	Texas	607
Washington	317	Oklahoma	614
Hawaii	337	Iowa	620
Oregon	365	Illinois	632
California	368	Arkansas	634
Colorado	378	Connecticut	649
Arizona	404	Nebraska	650
West Virginia	408	Minnesota	658
Maine	411	Pennsylvania	659

Florida	438	Wisconsin	668
Wyoming	442	Massachusetts	669
Montana	443	South Dakota	672
New Hampshire	445	South Carolina	674
Indiana	474	Alabama	681
Michigan	478	North Dakota	742
Vermont	479	Utah	756
Delaware	479	Louisiana	769
Virginia	494	Mississippi	771
Idaho	501	Rhode Island	775

Maryland	503
Ohio	539
Kansas	561
New York	565
Kentucky	578
Missouri	589
Georgia	598
New Mexico	601
Tennessee	604
New Jersey	605

1981: Percent Claiming a Specific Religious Affiliation on Census Form

British Columbia	79.5	New Brunswick	97.2
Yukon	80.5	Pr. Edward Island	97.4
Alberta	88.5	Quebec	97.9
Manitoba	92.7	Newfoundland	99.0

Ontario	92.9
N.W. Territories	93.6
Saskatchewan	93.8
Nova Scotia	96.0

Figure 14-1 ■ **The social geography of religious affiliation.** Church membership in the United States reveals a very marked "unchurched trench" running along the West Coast. All of the states in the Pacific region have membership rates below 40 percent (400 per 1,000); of the remaining forty-four states, only Colorado falls below that level. Nor does this regional pattern stop at the border. In Canada, British Columbia and the Yukon also are noticeably lower in religious affiliation than are other provinces and territories. The U.S. data reflect membership statistics for Christian and Jewish denominations. The Canadian data are based on what people marked on their census form. This makes Canada look more religious than the United States—in both nations many people who are not official members of a church will state a denominational preference. In fact, the membership rate is virtually the same on both sides of the border.

by recognizing that all religions had one feature in common. They always involve answers to **questions about ultimate meaning,** such as, Does life have a purpose? Why are we here? Is death the end? Why do we suffer? Does justice exist?

It is characteristic of humans to ask such questions. Indeed, these questions must have troubled the Neanderthal, for they had accepted answers to some of these questions. Hence, religion has been defined as socially organized beliefs and activities offering solutions to questions of ultimate meaning. But that definition is too broad. It applies to communism as well as Catholicism. And it applies to a philosophical system that denies that there can be answers to questions of ultimate meaning. It is inconvenient to have a sociological concept that ignores differences between what are widely regarded as religious and antireligious positions.

In the end, most sociologists agreed that the term *religion* ought to be applied to only particular kinds of answers to questions of ultimate meaning—those that posit the existence of the *supernatural.* Defined this way, *religion can invoke the power, wisdom, authority, and aid of the gods, a capacity that nonreligious philosophies lack* (Spiro, 1966; Berger, 1967; Stark, 1981; Stark and Bainbridge, 1985).

The gods

If we closely examine the ultimate questions that humans keep asking, many of them clearly require a very special kind of answer. People do not usually ask if life has meaning; they ask, What is the meaning of life? Why does the universe exist? Why do I exist? For life to have meaning, in this sense, history must be guided by intention. For this to be true, a consciousness capable of imposing intention on history must exist. In other words, if the universe is to have purpose, then it must have been created and directed by a conscious agent—a being capable of making plans and having intentions. Such a being has to be of such power, duration, and scale as to be beyond the natural world. That is, such a being must be supernatural.

Many questions of ultimate meaning, therefore, can only be answered by referring to the

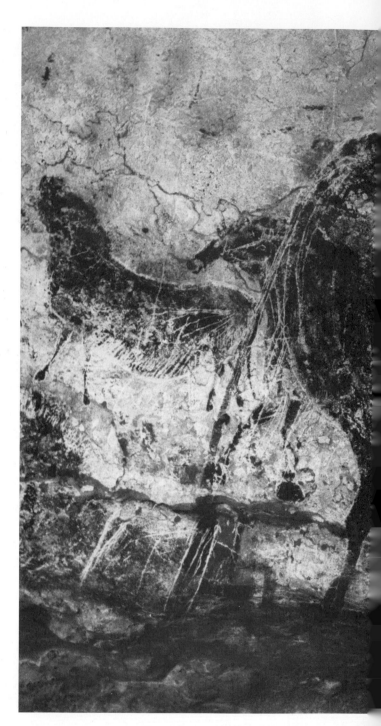

■ Thousands of years ago our ancestors created sacred chambers by painting superb animal figures like this on the walls of natural caverns. Even modern visitors are awed within these exotic confines and immediately sense the sacred intentions of those who used to come here at times of special religious significance.

Table 14-1 ■ Percent who believe in God* and in life after death.

Nation	Believe in God		Believe in Afterlife	
	Percent Yes	Percent No	Percent Yes	Percent No
United States	94	3	69	20
Canada	89	7	54	29
Australia	80	15	48	40
Great Britain	76	14	43	35
France	72	23	39	48
West Germany	72	20	33	48
Italy	88	7	46	36
India	98	2	72	18

Source: International Gallup Polls as reported in Lee P. Sigelman (1977).

*Or in a "higher spirit." Percentages do not sum to 100 percent because of those who answered "don't know" or "undecided."

supernatural—to beings or forces beyond nature who are able to suspend, alter, ignore, and create physical forces. To believe, for example, that there is life beyond death is to accept the supernatural. To believe that earthly suffering is compensated in the world to come also requires belief in the supernatural. Some things that humans greatly desire cannot possibly be attained in this world but can come only from the gods.

By defining **religion** as socially organized patterns of belief and practices that concern ultimate meaning and assume the existence of the supernatural, sociologists can isolate the essential element that sets religion apart from other aspects of social life and accounts for its universal appeal.

Systems of thought that reject the supernatural cannot satisfy the concerns of most people. Atheists can search for explanations of how the universe functions, but they cannot say that these functions have underlying purpose. Communists can promise to reduce poverty, but they cannot offer an escape from death. In any society, some people can accept the beliefs that the universe has no purpose, that what we gain in this life is all we shall receive, and that death is final. But as we shall see throughout this chapter, for most people this is not enough—only religion can fulfill their needs, their hopes, their dreams (see Table 14-1).

Legitimization of norms

Religions do more for humans than supply them with answers to questions of ultimate meaning. The assumption that the supernatural exists raises a new question: *What does the supernatural want or expect from us?*

Let us return to the Neanderthal. They believed that life has purpose and that the individual survives death. They also believed that the supernatural controls events in this world. How should they prepare for the next life? How could they enlist the aid of the supernatural in this world? The Neanderthal were greatly concerned about escaping the anger of the supernatural. All around them were signs of the terrible wrath of the gods: lightning bolts, violent winds and storms, deadly forest fires, floods, droughts, sickness, and injury. As demonstrated by their altars and their burial customs, the Neanderthal had beliefs about what the gods required. Like other primitive peoples, they undoubtedly observed elaborate codes of behav-

■ These Roman Catholic children are taking part in the sacrament of Holy Communion—a ritual that illustrates the unique capacity of religions to answer questions of ultimate meaning. Communion, also known as the Lord's Supper among many Protestants, symbolizes their belief that all may be saved in Christ and gain everlasting life.

ior meant to please the unseen spiritual forces that surrounded them.

By specifying what the gods require of humans, *religions* in effect *regulate human behavior by formulating rules about how we must and must not act.* Such rules of behavior, of course, are social norms. Religions explain why certain norms exist and why they should be obeyed.

For norms to be obeyed, most members of a society must believe that the norms are proper and right. Sociologists have long recognized the important role of religion in legitimizing norms. Why shouldn't we steal? Because the gods forbid it. Why should we obey our parents? Because

the gods demand it. Why should we obey the king? Because he was chosen by the gods to rule over us.

Thus, religious institutions can be a major force in holding societies together, providing legitimacy and reason to the norms, and giving divine sanction to other social institutions, such as the family or the state. Indeed, as we have already seen in Chapter 4, religion fosters conformity to the norms primarily by creating moral communities, not simply by influencing individuals' beliefs and practices. Recall that religious teenagers were less delinquent than nonreligious teenagers only in communities where the majority belonged to a church. The power of religion to create moral communities is also demonstrated by research showing that cities with high church membership rates have considerably lower rates of crime, suicide, venereal disease, and alcoholism than do cities with low church membership rates (Stark et al., 1983; Stark, Doyle, and Rushing, 1983).

Of course, religion is not the only reason why people observe norms. In Chapter 3 we saw that norms also arise from interaction. Many people who lack religious beliefs accept social norms and obey them (Hirschi and Stark, 1969). For many people in all societies, however, religion has served as the ultimate justification for norms.

Religious Economies

Early religions were local affairs. A tribe or very small society and its religion were one. A person was born into a religion as part of being born a member of his or her group. Although religion constantly changed even in small, primitive societies, the idea of choosing a religion was as alien as the idea of choosing one's tribe or family.

As societies became more complex, they began to include several cultures and religions. Larger cities of ancient Egypt, Greece, and the Roman Empire contained a variety of different religions (Johnson, 1979; Meeks, 1983). In such cities, people could compare religions, worry about which one was best, and regard religion as a matter of choice. Such a religious situation is best described as a *religious economy.* Just as commercial economies consist of a market in which different firms compete, religious economies consist of a market (the aggregate demand for religion) and firms (different religious organizations) seeking to attract and hold a clientele.

The notion of religious economies underscores the dynamic interplay of different religious groups within a society. This interplay accounts for the religious makeup of societies at any given time and explains why and how religions change.

As with commercial economies, a key issue is *the degree to which a religious economy is regulated by the state.* To what extent do free market conditions prevail and to what extent is the religious economy distorted toward monopoly by coercion? For reasons explained below, the natural state of a religious economy is **religious pluralism,** wherein many religious "firms" exist because of their special appeal to certain segments of the market (or population). However, as for a commercial organization, it is always in the interest of any particular religious organization to secure a monopoly. This can only be achieved, and even then to just a limited extent, if the state forcibly excludes competing faiths.

In medieval Europe, states used coercion to create a monopoly for Catholicism. Anyone who deviated from orthodoxy was subject to punishment, including execution. However, even at its most powerful moments, the medieval Catholic Church was beset by dissent and heresy from all sides and never achieved full monopoly. Whenever and wherever state coercion wavered, competing faiths burst forth and prospered (Johnson, 1979). Nevertheless, regulation often made it difficult and dangerous for competing faiths, thus greatly reducing religious choice. Yet even medieval society is best understood in terms of its religious economy.

To understand why religious economies incline toward pluralism, we need to understand the major processes at work within them. We shall explore these processes by first seeing why a virtually endless supply of new and competing organizations exists in any religious economy.

Church-Sect Theory

In 1929 H. Richard Niebuhr published *The Social Sources of Denominationalism.* In this book he tried to explain why Christianity was fractured into so many competing denominations. Why weren't Christians content with one church? Why did they constantly form new ones?

The answer he proposed combined two concepts developed by Max Weber with elements of conflict theory. Weber had distinguished two kinds of religious organizations: churches and sects. **Churches** intellectualize religious teachings and restrain emotionalism in their services. They offer an image of the gods as somewhat remote from daily life and the individual. **Sects** stress emotionalism and individual mystical experiences and tend toward fundamentalism, rather than intellectualism, in their teachings. They present the gods as close at hand, taking an active interest and role in the lives of individuals.

Perhaps prayer provides the best contrast between church and sect. Churches favor formalized prayers, often recited from memory or read from prayer books. Sects favor extemporaneous, informal prayers. Church prayers imply gods who are very far away: "Our father, who art in Heaven." Sect prayers imply gods who are nearby: "Yes, Lord, we feel you present. Bless this poor sinner kneeling here before you now."

Niebuhr argued that churches and sects differ greatly in their ability to satisfy different human needs. Sects provide for the religious needs of people low in the stratification system—the masses. Churches provide for the religious needs of the middle and upper classes (McKinney and Roof, 1982). Class conflict, according to Niebuhr, underlies the religious conflicts that split Christianity into many different denominations.

Niebuhr stressed the unique ability of religion to make life bearable, even for those in misery. This is achieved by turning one's thoughts away from this world and stressing the primacy of the spiritual world. The more we believe that this life is only a brief prelude to afterlife and that we shall find relief from our pains in the more perfect world to come, the more easily we can bear life's burdens. Indeed, religions commonly teach that if you spurn material pleasures in this life, you will increase your rewards in the everlasting life to come—that the social order will be turned upside down in the next life, where "the first shall be last, and the last, first."

To make these views convincing, however, religions must resist the pleasures of the material world. A religious organization filled with members, especially its leaders, enjoying material pleasures is hampered in its efforts to serve the religious needs of the deprived.

When members of a congregation actively participate in the services as this woman is doing—when members seem to be really enjoying themselves—chances are that the group is one that sociologists would classify as a sect. Groups with more formal and sedate services usually are classified as churches.

The key to Niebuhr's theory is the proposition that *successful religious organizations always shift their emphasis toward this world and away from the next.* He argued that as religious organizations grow and become more popular, the proportion of middle- and upper-class members will increase. These members have much less need than the deprived to reject this world in favor of the next. Indeed, they will want to harmonize their religious beliefs with their own worldly success. In time, these members will prevail, and the religious organization will cease to preach that material success in

■ Members of this Protestant congregation, located in a tiny Inuit village far above the Arctic Circle, belong to a Protestant sect. As is typical of sects, members are expected to devote a lot of time to their religion—most attend three times on Sunday, and on Wednesday and Friday evenings, too. What the Glad Tidings Mission lacks in terms of a building is made up for in the excitement and emotional intensity of the services, which stress salvation and personal religious experience. According to church-sect theory, the poor and dispossessed seek the comforts of an intensely otherworldly religion, while the more affluent prefer a religion more accommodated to this world. Out of this tension comes a succession of sect movements.

this life will be punished in the next. These faiths will cease to emphasize the spiritual and will portray the supernatural in ever more remote and less vivid terms. That is, the religion will become progressively worldly.

However, such a shift will erode the ability of the religious organization to satisfy the religious needs of the lower classes. This will lead to growing discontent. Eventually *the masses will defect to form a new religious organization,* a sect, which emphasizes the original otherworldliness of the former organization.

Thus, Niebuhr proposed a dynamic cycle. Religions originate as sects designed to serve the needs of the deprived. If they grow and flourish, then these sects increasingly serve the interests of the middle and upper classes and are transformed into churches, thereby making them less effective in satisfying the needs of the poor. Then the conditions that prompted the original **sect formation** are re-created, a split occurs, and a new sect is formed. In time this sect, too, is transformed into a church, whereupon a new sect is born—thus, there is an endless cycle of the birth, transformation, and rebirth of new religious organizations. Niebuhr explained the existence of the huge array of Christian denominations as the result of countless cycles of this church-sect process.

In the nearly sixty years since Niebuhr first sketched his **church-sect theory,** it has been much refined and elaborated (Wilson, 1959, 1961, 1970; Wallis, 1975). Niebuhr's definitions of church and sect were not clear or efficient, and in 1963 Benton Johnson proposed better ones. He suggested that church and sect are opposite poles on an axis representing the degree of tension between religious organizations and their sociocultural environment (see Figure 14-2). Tension, as Johnson defined it, is a manifestation of deviance. To the degree that a religious organization sustains norms and values different from those of the surrounding culture, it is deviant and tension will exist between its members and the outside world. In the extreme case, tension is so high that the group is hunted down by outsiders. Religious groups whose norms and values resemble those of the larger society have no tension. *Churches* are religious bodies with relatively low tension; *sects* are religious bodies with relatively high tension.

Niebuhr tended to limit this application of church-sect theory to religious organizations. But the theory is even more useful when it is

Degree of Tension with Sociocultural Environment

Low   Medium   High

Figure 14-2 ■ **Degrees of tension between religions and society.** Clergy who "fit right in" illustrate that some religious groups are wholly accommodated to their social environment. Clergy who demonstrate in protest against pornography or abortion reflect that some degree of tension exists between their religious group and the social environment. Clergy who are jailed for refusing to submit to state regulation of church-sponsored grade schools show that religious bodies can exist at a level of high tension with their environment. The higher the tension between a group and its environment, the more sectlike it is.

applied to whole societies. Let's see how church-sect theory has recently been linked with the concept of religious economies.

■ Secularization and Revival

Social scientists and modern intellectuals have generally paid close attention to only one aspect of church-sect theory: They have noted the movement away from traditional Christian teachings by many of the largest and most respected denominations. Projecting these trends into the future, they have predicted that religion is in its last days, that soon religion will disappear. Noting that these denominations continue to retreat from a vivid, active conception of the supernatural, many social scientists have concluded that this is because supernatural beliefs cannot be maintained in an increasingly scientific age, and therefore human societies will soon, to paraphrase Freud (1927), be cured of the infantile "illusion" of religion.

The process by which religion will disappear has been called *secularization* to indicate a turning away from religious to secular explanations of life. This process is regarded as far along and irreversible. Indeed, the distinguished anthropologist Anthony F. C. Wallace (1966) spoke for the majority of modern social scientists when he wrote:

The evolutionary future of religion is extinction. Belief in supernatural beings . . . will become only an interesting historical memory. To be sure, this event is not likely to occur in the next generation; the process will very likely take several hundred years. . . . But as a cultural trait, belief in supernatural powers is doomed to die out, all over the world, as a result of the increasing adequacy and diffusion of scientific knowledge.

Besides overwhelming religion, many scholars have thought that science might provide a substitute for religion—people might perform solemn rituals patterned on those of religion but with an explicitly antisupernatural thrust (see the photo on p. 414). In fact, the French philosopher Auguste Comte, who coined the term

■ A Soviet couple is married in a "socialist wedding palace" in Kiev, complete with an altar and a bust of Lenin. This is part of the latest effort in a seventy-year government campaign to eradicate religion in the USSR. But according to the Soviet press, vast numbers of the Soviet people remain committed to religious organizations (many of them illegal). Sociologists of religion argue that religion without the supernatural is no religion at all and therefore that efforts like this cannot succeed.

sociology, intended that sociology serve as the scientific substitute for religion. Thus, the assumption that religion is both false and doomed has been widespread among social scientists from the start. This assumption has led them to discover terminal symptoms in every sign of decline in religion but to ignore or be perplexed by every sign of vigor. For 150 years or more, social scientists have predicted the triumph of secularization. Whenever they have

confronted broad-based religious revivals, they have dismissed them as dying spasms.

I must confess that as a young sociologist I largely shared these views. But as I did research on religious groups, from Moonies to major denominations, I found it very difficult to square these views with what I saw. For millions of people, faith was alive and well. Many sophisticated scholars appeared to have no problem in reconciling science with a belief in the super-

■ Compare this picture of the extraordinary interior of Montreal's Notre Dame Cathedral with the socialist wedding palace to see the vital difference between organizations based on religion and those based on secular philosophies. Both buildings can serve as a site for ceremonial behavior. But no one at a wedding conducted before a bust of Lenin can suppose that Lenin is actually looking down upon them, blessing their union, and promising them everlasting life. Yet that is exactly how many people in this cathedral respond to the depictions of Jesus on the Cross and of the host of saints—not as reminders of the heroic dead, but of the sanctified and eternal.

natural. Could the secularization thesis be flawed? By 1980, I had concluded that it was—that secularization was but one aspect of religious change (Stark, 1981; Stark and Bainbridge, 1980, 1985). Other sociologists began to express similar views (Bell, 1980; Martin, 1981). Together, we began to apply church-sect theory to religious economies and to argue that the secularization thesis rested on a misperception—that social scientists had mistaken the obvious decline of once powerful religious organizations for a general decline of religion. In this sense, they had seen only the transformation of some religious organizations into states of ever lower tension, but had failed to note the reactions to this trend elsewhere in religious economies. A more comprehensive view of religious economies suggests that *secularization is a self-limiting process that leads not to irreligion but to a shift in the sources of religion.* One of the ways this occurs was already implicit in church-sect theory.

Church-sect theory suggests that many religious bodies are always in the process of becoming very worldly. That is, secularization should occur in all religious economies. But we must also expect the trend toward secularization to produce religious reactions: the formation of sects. We can call this process *revival.* As secularization weakens some organizations, new ones split off to revive less worldly versions of the faith. This not only helps to explain why some religious bodies have declined as the secularization thesis predicts they should but also why religion refuses to fade away: why, for example, a religious body like the Church of God in Christ can grow at an extraordinary rate in contradiction of the secularization thesis. The Church of God in Christ has moved into the market vacuum created by the secularization of once dominant Protestant bodies. The result is a change in the source of religion—a shift in what religious group people turn to—not the demise of religion.

But there is a second response to secularization besides revival. Sometimes people do not revive the conventional faith by embodying it in new organizations. Sometimes they turn to new faiths altogether.

Innovation: Cult Formation

Sects are not new religions; they are new organizations reviving an old religion. They claim to have returned to a more authentic version of the traditional faith from which its parent organization has strayed. Thus, a set of churches and sects will form a single religious tradition. For example, most churches and sects in the United States and Europe are part of the conventional Christian religious tradition.

Sometimes, however, organizations appear that are based on religions outside the conventional religious tradition. This may occur by *importing* a faith from another society—Hinduism in the United States and Christianity in India are examples. New faiths also appear through *cultural innovation.* Someone may have new religious insights and then succeed in attracting followers. New religions, whether imported or the result of innovation, are deviant and thus elicit unfavorable reactions from others. Like sects, they are in a high state of tension with surrounding society. But unlike sects, new religions cannot claim cultural continuity with conventional religious beliefs and practices.

The hostility usually directed at new religions is reflected in the name applied to them: cults. Sociologists use this term without prejudice to distinguish new religions from sects arising out of old religions. **Cults** are religious movements that represent a new or different religious tradition, while churches and sects represent the prevailing tradition in a society. The negative connotations of the word *cult* reflect the unusually high tension between these movements and their social environment.

All religions begin as cult movements. All of today's great world faiths once were regarded as weird, crazy, foolish, and sinful. How Roman intellectuals in the first century would have laughed at the notion that a messiah and his tiny flock in Palestine, an obscure corner of the empire, posed a threat to the mighty pagan temples. But from obscure cult movements have risen not only Christianity but also Islam,

Buddhism, and other faiths that today inspire hundreds of millions of faithful.

Given their current rate of growth, the Church of Jesus Christ of Latter-Day Saints, the Mormons, may be repeating this pattern of a meteoric rise from obscurity to world significance. In 1830 this faith began with six members: the three Smith brothers, the two Whitmer brothers, and Oliver Cowdry. Today there are more than 5 million Mormons, and even if they continue to grow at a somewhat slower rate, there will be at least 265 million Mormons worldwide a century from now (Stark, 1984).

New religions appear constantly in all societies (Stark and Bainbridge, 1985). Nearly all of them fail. To succeed, many things are required, but the primary necessity involves *opportunity*. That is, for new firms to make their way against large, long-established firms in a religious economy, the older firms must be failing to serve the needs of a significant number of people. People do not abandon a faith that satisfies them to embrace a new faith: *New faiths prosper only from the weaknesses of old faiths.*

Sometimes new faiths find opportunity because of great social crises that overwhelm conventional faiths. For example, plagues or natural disasters may cause a sudden loss of confidence in conventional faiths (Wallace, 1956). Wars can have the same effect, especially on the losing side: New faiths repeatedly swept through the Indian tribes of North America as their efforts to resist white encroachments failed (Mooney, 1896), and many new religions have flourished in Japan since World War II (McFarland, 1967; Morioka, 1975).

But a major opportunity for new faiths results from *the excessive secularization of the old.* That is, after many cycles of the church-sect process, an entire religious tradition may lose its ability to provide a plausible faith for a substantial portion of the population. Such moments are rare, but when they occur, new faiths quickly rise in influence, just as Christianity overwhelmed a highly secularized and complacent paganism.

Thus, secularization prompts two reactions that restore religion: revival and innovation (**cult formation**). Rather than being a symptom of the death of religion, *secularization provides the impetus for religious change.*

■■

Charisma

We saw in Chapter 3 that people join new religious movements primarily because of their attachments to members of those movements; when a sufficient proportion of a person's attachments are to members of some religious group, the person is likely to accept that religion. That tells us something not only about how religious movements recruit and grow but also about *how they begin.*

Suppose a young electrical engineer in Korea believes he has received a revelation from God. He then believes he has a divine mission to launch a new religious movement that will create an era of great religious vigor and purity and unite the many religions of the world into One Truth Faith. Is this the birth of a cult movement? Not yet.

As long as only one person accepts a new religious message, no religious movement exists. To launch a social movement, this engineer must convince other people to share his beliefs and join him. Many people each year believe they have discovered a new faith, but only a few of them can convince others to join. What characterizes those who can attract followers? What was it about a Korean electrical engineer, famous today as Reverend Sun Myung Moon, that enabled him to attract ardent followers and to found a major cult movement (the Unification Church, known as the Moonies)?

Pondering the special gifts of religious founders, Max Weber credited them with charisma. **Charisma** is a Greek word meaning "divine gift." Weber used it to indicate the ability of some people to inspire faith in others, to get others to believe their message. For contemporary sociologists of religion, *the basis of this gift is an unusual ability to form attachments with others.* Just as people join religions out of attachments to members, in the beginning people accept the claim of a founder of a new faith because they develop very strong attachments

Table 14-2 ■ **American denominations enrolling at least 1 percent of the population.**

Denomination	Percent of U.S. population
Roman Catholic Church	22.3
Southern Baptist Convention	6.1
United Methodist Church	4.0
National Baptist Convention of the United States	2.4
Evangelical Lutheran Church in America	2.3
Church of Jesus Christ of Latter-Day Saints	1.6
The Church of God in Christ	1.6
United Presbyterian Church	1.4
The Episcopal Church	1.2
National Baptist Convention of America	1.2
Lutheran Church, Missouri Synod	1.2
Jewish*	1.0
African Methodist Episcopal Church	1.0
More than 1,200 other denominations	14.7
Total	62.0

Source: Prepared by the author from the *Yearbook of American and Canadian Churches,* 1987, and from Stark (1987b). These statistics include a number of religious bodies not included in the rates shown in Figure 14-1.

*Includes all Jewish congregations.

to the founder. All studies of new religions report that the founders possessed remarkable gifts for interpersonal relations (Wallis, 1982).

Moreover, founders of new faiths typically turn first to those *with whom they already have strong attachments in their quest for converts.* Joseph Smith, the founder of the Mormon Church, first converted his two brothers and three close friends. Jesus, likewise, numbered his own brothers among his early followers. In founding Islam, Mohammed's first convert was his wife Khadîjah, the second was his cousin Ali, the third was his servant Zeyd, and then his old friend Abû Bakr joined and brought his family and his slaves into the new faith.

Having outlined the dynamic character of religious economies and the processes by which sects and cults form, we can now analyze religion in the United States. Then we shall see how the same dynamic patterns occur in a variety of other nations.

■

The American Religious Economy

Europeans have long marveled at both the diversity of religions and the high levels of participation in religious activities in the United States. Max Weber, for example, noted that Americans gladly contributed sums of money to their churches that would shock people in Europe. Others wondered how so many faiths could exist side by side.

It is true that the American religious economy is very diverse. Over 1,200 religious denominations exist in the United States (Melton, 1978). Church attendance is high—in any given week, about 40 percent of Americans attend services. Moreover, almost two-thirds of Americans (62 percent) are official members of a local congregation (Table 14-2).

However, the American religious economy is unique only in that it is an exceptionally free market with little regulation. Within this economy, the three major processes of secularization, revival, and innovation are well developed and related.

Secularization and revival

Many major religious bodies in the United States have become highly secularized in the sense that they no longer present traditional versions of their faith or emphasize the supernatural. Table 14-3, based on the General Social Surveys for 1984, 1985, and 1987, shows one indicator of this shift. I was able to combine these three national samples because the very same question was asked about the Bible in each year. Combining the samples provided enough cases to characterize the beliefs of members in the larger denominations. Looking at the table, we see that only small minorities of members of the United Church of Christ, the United Presbyterian Church, the Episcopal Church, the United Methodist Church, and the newly merged Evangelical Lutheran Church in America expressed their belief that "the Bible is the actual word of God and is to be taken literally, word for word." A century ago most members of these denominations would have affirmed this statement. But to find majorities holding this traditional tenet of Christian doctrine today, we must look to the lower half of the table to groups that are best described as sects.

If secularization weakens the holding power of religious organizations, then those denominations at the top of Table 14-3 ought to be showing signs of decline. On the other hand, if secularization is inevitable as science triumphs over faith, then the denominations holding to Bible literalism ought to be the ones in decline.

Table 14-4 offers compelling evidence for the notion that as religious bodies deemphasize the supernatural, they seem less able to satisfy religious needs. The United Church of Christ, Presbyterians, Episcopalians, Methodists, and Lutherans all have experienced substantial losses in their shares of church membership. But in the middle of the table the sign turns from negative to positive, reflecting growth rather than decline. Beginning with the Southern Baptists, denominations are on the rise. Indeed, the higher the proportion of members who take the Bible as the literal word of God, the higher the group's rate of growth.* What we see happening here is the interplay between secularization and revival.

Table 14-3 ■ **American denominations and literal faith in the Bible.**

Percent of members who agree that "the Bible is the actual word of God and is to be taken literally, word for word"	
United Church of Christ	15%
United Presbyterian Church	28
Episcopal Church	15
United Methodist Church	33
Evangelical Lutheran Church in America	34
Southern Baptist Convention	60
Church of the Nazarene	47
Seventh-Day Adventist Church	62
Jehovah's Witnesses	61
United Pentecostal Church	81
Assemblies of God	76
Church of God in Christ	90
All Protestants	47
Roman Catholics	23

Source: Prepared by the author from National Opinion Research Center, General Social Surveys, 1984, 1985, 1987.

As some denominations are eroded by secularization, new sects erupt and seize the opportunity to attract members to a less secularized faith, thus reviving and revitalizing the religious tradition.

Sect formation is very common in the United States. At least 417 American-born sect movements currently exist, and probably hundreds of others have existed in times past (Stark and Bainbridge, 1981). Most sects are very small: 28 percent have fewer than 500 members today. However, some are very large: The Southern Baptists, with more than 13 million members, are the largest Protestant body in the nation.

---

* The correlation (*r*) is .76 and is .87 with the Church of God in Christ omitted from the calculation.

Table 14-4 ■ Some growing and declining American denominations.

| | Members per 1,000 U.S. Population | | |
	1960	1983	% Change
United Church of Christ	12.5	7.3	− 42%
United Presbyterian Church	23.2	14.0	− 40
Episcopal Church	19.2	12.0	− 38
United Methodist Church	55.1	40.3	− 27
Evangelical Lutheran Church in America	29.2	22.6	− 23
Roman Catholic Church	234.7	223.4	− 4
Southern Baptist Convention	54.3	60.7	+ 12
Church of the Nazarene	1.7	2.2	+ 29
Seventh-Day Adventist Church	1.8	2.7	+ 50
Jehovah's Witnesses	1.4	2.8	+100
United Pentecostal Church	1.0	2.0	+100
Assemblies of God	2.8	8.5	+204
Church of God in Christ	2.2	15.9	+623

Source: Prepared by the author from the *Statistical Abstract of the United States,* 1962 and 1986.

Sect formation revives the conventional religious *tradition* and reflects efforts by church members to remain church members: Those committed to the religious tradition but who find their church has become too worldly form sects to restore the otherworldliness of that tradition.

This analysis suggests that membership in conventional religious groups will be highest where sects are most active. This is precisely what contemporary data show. Sect movements are clustered in those states where membership in Christian churches is highest. Sects are very underrepresented in parts of the country where overall church membership and attendance are low (Stark and Bainbridge, 1980). That is, sects move not into market openings where there is general religious inactivity but only into those where people are active but dissatisfied. I shall expand on this point as we examine the contrasting patterns of cult success.

Secularization and innovation

If sects represent efforts by the churched to *stay* churched, then cult movements represent efforts by the unchurched to *become* churched. That is, cult movements arise where both sects and churches fail to satisfy the religious market. To see this more fully, let's examine the geography of religion in contemporary America.

■ **The "unchurched" belt**   The American South is frequently called the "Bible Belt," where religion, especially evangelical Protestantism, is unusually strong. In many of our recent studies, however, Bainbridge and I have failed to find evidence of such a belt (Stark and Bainbridge, 1985). The South does not differ from most other regions of the nation in terms of church membership rates, church attendance rates, belief in God, or belief in life after death.

Although the South may not be a Bible Belt,

the Far West is certainly an "unchurched" belt. As is clear in Figure 14-1, church membership is far lower in the Pacific region than in any other region. Moreover, Figure 14-1 shows that church membership is uniformly low among Far Western states: Nevada, Alaska, Washington, Hawaii, Oregon, and California are the bottom six states in terms of church membership.* The Far West also has low rates of church attendance. Clearly, the conventional churches have failed to take root along the shores of the Pacific. However, it is church membership, and not religious belief, that is missing in the Far West. Westerners are nearly as likely to have faith in God and believe in life after death as people elsewhere in the country. Thus, the average westerner believes in the supernatural, but lacks a church affiliation that gives form and expression to his or her beliefs. This should provide an ideal market opportunity for cult movements able to form attachments with unchurched West Coast "believers."

■ **The geography of cult movements** It should be no surprise that religious innovation is far more common and successful in the Far West than elsewhere in the nation. Figure 14-3 shows the distribution of the headquarters of 501 cult movements active in the United States today. The states of the Far West tower above the rest. Moreover, Nevada, the state with the lowest church membership rate, leads the nation in cult headquarters. These patterns match those shown in Figures 1-6 and 1-8. Recall that the Pacific region is also where the subscription rate for *Fate* magazine and the rate of astrologers with listings in the *Yellow Pages* are the highest. Nor is the West's affinity for novel religion and mysticism a recent development, as Figure 14-4 demonstrates. Data collected in a special 1926 U.S. census tally of religious groups showed

that even then church membership was comparatively low in the Far West and cult membership very high. This was true even as long ago as 1890 (Stark and Bainbridge, 1985).

A major cause of low church membership rates on the West Coast is constant and rapid population movement (Welch, 1983). When people move frequently, as has always been common in the West, they abandon attachments to all social organizations—not just churches but also fraternal clubs, hobby groups, veterans organizations, PTAs, political groups, and the like. Arriving in a new place, they also find it difficult to reestablish such connections in communities where many others are also newcomers and transients. Instead, they are likely to form attachments to people who are not attached to such organizations. Recall from Chapter 3 that after moving to San Francisco, the Moonies only began to grow again when they discovered how to locate and build attachments with other newcomers to the city. In places where unattached newcomers abound, new movements have a much greater opportunity to grow than in places where the population is settled and attached. And unlike most of the conventional churches in the Far West, cults go out in search of members.

In a sense, the disorganization of the Far West caused by population instability is somewhat like that created in times of crisis, when religious changes are likely to occur. Wars and natural disasters result in dramatic social disorganization. Constant population movement provides a less obvious but persistent form of the same thing.

However, the fact that cults attract members in all parts of the nation shows that secularization itself, even when not assisted by disorganization, produces a market for new faiths. Indeed, data on who joins cult movements demonstrate this factor.

■ **Who joins cults?** The belief that secularization is leading to the demise of religion assumes that people who discard conventional faiths have embraced rationalism and no longer find supernatural beliefs plausible. Thus, sociologists have interpreted increases in the pro-

---

* The rates used in Figure 14-1 underestimate church membership. They have been corrected so that they accurately reflect regional differences in church membership, but the figures are somewhat depressed because of omissions in reporting. If these rates were summed, they would produce a national church membership rate of 56 percent, whereas the correct rate for the United States is about 62 percent.

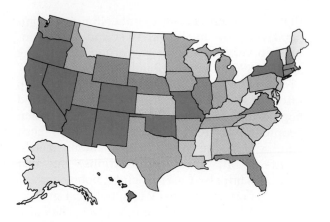

Alaska	0.0
Montana	0.0
Mississippi	0.0
West Virginia	0.0
Delaware	0.0
South Dakota	0.0
North Dakota	0.0
Vermont	0.0
Maine	0.0

Connecticut	1.6
Virginia	1.6
Utah	1.7
Massachusetts	1.9
Nebraska	2.0
Florida	2.4
New Hampshire	2.5
Wyoming	2.5
Washington	2.9
Illinois	3.0

Kentucky	0.3
Louisiana	0.3
Kansas	0.4
South Carolina	0.4
Georgia	0.4
Maryland	0.5
North Carolina	0.6
Alabama	0.6
New Jersey	0.7
Wisconsin	0.7
Ohio	0.8

Missouri	3.1
New York	3.3
Hawaii	4.4
Oregon	4.8
Arizona	5.9
Colorado	6.0
Oklahoma	7.0
California	7.9
New Mexico	9.1
Nevada	10.0

Indiana	0.9
Rhode Island	1.0
Minnesota	1.0
Iowa	1.0
Tennessee	1.0
Arkansas	1.0
Michigan	1.1
Texas	1.2
Idaho	1.3
Pennsylvania	1.5

Figure 14-3 (left) ■ **Cult movement headquarters per million population.** These rates are based on the location of the headquarters of each of 501 cult movements listed in J. Gordon Melton's (1978) *Encyclopedia of American Religions.* This measure understates the strength of new religious movements in America because several of these movements are very large and have centers in many states, but only the state where they are headquartered gets credit. No state has no cult centers, but a number do lack a headquarters. Nevertheless, these findings are consistent with those already shown in Figures 1-6 and 1-8, for here too the Far West excels. New Mexico's high rate, however, is more a measure of its abundant sites for rural communes than it is a measure of social climate.

Figure 14-4 (right) ■ **Occult practitioners per 100,000 in the labor force, 1920.** For more than 100 years the census has asked each adult his or her occupation. Here we see rates for 1920 based on persons who reported that their occupation was some form of occult practitioner (psychic reader, fortune-teller, astrologer, and so forth). Sixty years makes surprisingly little difference. Then, too, Nevada was number one, with California second. *Note:* Alaska and Hawaii were not states in 1920.

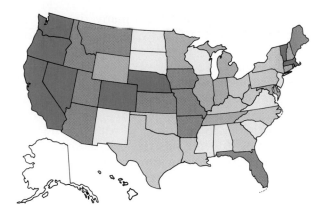

South Dakota	0.00		Montana	2.80
New Jersey	0.53		Kansas	2.88
South Carolina	0.74		Iowa	3.03
Alabama	0.77		Maine	3.23
New Mexico	0.82		Idaho	3.26
Virginia	0.84		Arkansas	3.31
North Dakota	0.97		Florida	3.37
Wisconsin	1.10		Missouri	3.57
Mississippi	1.11		Arizona	3.83
			Utah	4.02

Kentucky	1.17			
New York	1.24		Nebraska	4.16
West Virginia	1.43		Oregon	4.34
North Carolina	1.45		Massachusetts	4.45
Oklahoma	1.47		Washington	4.49
Louisiana	1.47		Rhode Island	4.73
Texas	1.51		Vermont	5.05
Pennsylvania	1.52		Colorado	5.18
Georgia	1.68		California	5.62
Ohio	1.82		Nevada	10.67

Michigan	1.83
Illinois	1.98
Tennessee	2.05
Delaware	2.19
Connection	2.20
Wyoming	2.45
Indiana	2.51
Minnesota	2.54
New Hampshire	2.59
Maryland	2.65

■ The spread of religious movements imported from Asia, such as this Zen Buddhist Center, permits an unbiased assessment of the comparative receptivity of European and North American nations to new religions. In computing rates for these nations, congregations of Asian immigrants were not counted. Instead, the rates were based only on congregations made up primarily of Westerners—as the picture shows this group to be.

■ Contrary to conventional wisdom, those who join new religious movements (or what sociologists call cult movements) are not mostly a bunch of maladjusted or deprived people from an intensely religious family. If this Hare Krishna member is typical, he is well educated and from an affluent background. It also is very likely that his parents are irreligious or at least religiously inactive and that he grew up without participating in any religious group.

portion of people who say "none" when asked their religious affiliation as very significant evidence of the trend to irreligion.

I also long assumed that people who claimed no religious affiliation were primarily nonbelievers. I was extremely surprised, therefore, when one of my studies showed that far from being secular humanists or rationalists, people who say they have no religion are those most likely to express faith in unconventional supernatural beliefs (Bainbridge and Stark, 1980,

1981a). These people were many times more likely to accept astrology, reincarnation, and various psychic phenomena and to value Eastern mysticism.

Subsequently, my colleagues and I obtained the results of surveys of members of various contemporary cult movements: the Moonies, Hare Krishnas, Scientologists, witches, and several groups studying yoga. In each case, we found extraordinary overrepresentation of persons who had grown up with parents claiming no religious affiliation. Most of the other members had parents who were not active members of any faith, although they had a nominal affiliation (Stark and Bainbridge, 1985).

Thus, *to the extent that large numbers of people grow up in irreligious homes* (that is, in times and places where large numbers have drifted away from the conventional faiths), *large numbers of potential converts to cult movements will exist.*

■

The Canadian Religious Economy

A comparison of the Canadian and American religious economies reveals striking similarities and differences. In both nations, church membership is relatively high—62 percent in the United States and 63 percent in Canada. But, in Canada this membership is spread across far fewer religious bodies. In the United States, the thirteen largest denominations enroll 47.3 percent of the population (see Table 14-2); in Canada, the three largest enroll 54.4 percent of the population (Table 14-5). Clearly, the Canadian religious economy is less diverse than that of the United States.

Harry W. Hiller (1978) has suggested that one reason for less diversity is that the close ties between church and state in Canada produced policies and institutional arrangements designed to "discourage religious experimentation." But another reason there is less apparent diversity in Canadian religion is due to a merger of Canadian Presbyterians, Methodists, and Congregationalists into the United Church of Canada back in 1925, while these remain separate denomi-

Table 14-5 ■ Canadian denominations enrolling at least 1 percent of the population.

Denomination	Percent of Canadian Population
Roman Catholic	41.9
United Church of Canada*	8.8
Anglican Church of Canada	3.7
Jewish**	1.2
More than 200 other denominations	7.4
Total	63.0

Source: Yearbook of American and Canadian Churches, 1985. The statistics refer to actual membership and therefore are lower than the census data shown in Figure 14-1, which are based on claimed religious preference.

*Created in 1925 by a merger of the Presbyterians, Methodists, and Congregationalists, plus some independent congregations.

**Includes all members of the Jewish community whether or not they actually belong to a local congregation.

nations in the United States. In part it is also because the large black population of the United States tends to belong to separate denominations (the National Baptist Convention of the United States, for example). And partly it is because the Roman Catholic Church enrolls nearly twice the proportion of Canadians as Americans. Moreover, Canada's Catholics are more highly concentrated. As Kenneth Westhues (1976) has pointed out, only 9 percent of American Catholics live in a neighborhood where they make up a majority of the population, while almost 60 percent of Catholic Canadians live in an overwhelmingly Catholic neighborhood.

In Canada, too, the more secularized denominations have been getting smaller, while the more sectlike groups have been growing. For example, between 1971 and 1981, according to census figures, the United Church and the Anglicans showed a decline, while the Baptists,

Pentecostals, and other evangelical Protestants registered substantial gains. Table 14-6 shows the proportion of persons in each denomination who were classified as highly religious by Reginald Bibby (1979). This order corresponds with the trends in their growth rates. Hence in Canada as in America, secularization prompts revival. When people don't find sufficient otherworldliness in one church, they go to another.

While the Canadian religious economy displays less diversity within the conventional end of the spectrum, it does not lack for variety at the unconventional end. In 1946 William Mann (1955) found that nine cult movements active in the United States had congregations in Alberta. When Bainbridge and I examined the listings for cult movements in the *Yellow Pages* for all Canadian cities in 1980, we found that every group having any substantial success in the United States also was active in Canada. Moreover, Canadians have founded many new religious movements, including the Latter Rain Movement, Kabalarian Philosophy, the Apostles of Infinite Love, and Emissaries of Divine Light (Hexham, Currie, and Townsend, 1985).

Table 14-6 hints that the association between cult growth and secularization found in the United States holds in Canada too. Members of evangelical Protestant groups were much less likely to express interest in various cult movements. The same patterns hold up when the Canadian map shown in Figure 14-1 is compared with those in Figures 1-7 and 1-8. In Canada, too, religious affiliation is lower in the West and it is there that one finds more cult movements and more *Fate* readers. In fact, after Bainbridge and I completed our studies of secularization and cult movements in the United States, our next step was to repeat the research in Canada (Bainbridge and Stark, 1982). We found the results were, if anything, even stronger.

Table 14-7 presents some correlations between secularization and various measures of the strength of cult movements. Secularization is measured as the percent of the population of a province or territory who told Statistics Canada their religion was "None." Overall, the greater the degree of secularization, the more successful are unconventional faiths. Recall that the closer a correlation comes to 1.0, the greater the

Table 14-6 ■ Orthodoxy and interest in cults among members of Canadian denominations.

	Percent Highly Religious*	Percent Interested in Cults**
United Church of Canada	10	13
Anglican Church of Canada	23	11
Evangelical Protestants†	45	4
Roman Catholic Church		
English speakers	22	14
French speakers	20	16

Source: Reginald W. Bibby (1979).

*People who expressed firm belief in God and the divinity of Jesus, who said they had at least once felt they were actually in the presence of God, who prayed frequently, and who could correctly identify Peter as the disciple who denied Jesus three times.

**Who expressed strong interest in one or more of the following groups: Children of God, Hare Krishna, Zen, yoga groups, satanism, gurus, or Transcendental Meditation.

†Includes various Baptist and Pentecostal groups and a number of other small Protestant sects.

correspondence between two variables. These are very high correlations. Let's examine them in greater detail.

The first measure of cult strength is the same as shown back in Figure 1-7, a count of cult centers based on the *Yellow Pages*. The correlation between it and percent "None" is getting close to perfect. The same huge correlation exists between secularization and the *Fate* magazine subscriber rate (see Figure 1-8). The third measure is based on members of various tiny and unusual religious groups who Statistics Canada lumps together and calls "para religious" groups. Again the correlation is positive and strong. Pagans are persons who say they are pursuing religions found in England and Wales before the arrival of Christianity. They also refer to themselves as witches and ritual magicians. Where there are more "Nones," there are more pagans. Theosophy was founded in India in the 1880s by a member of the Russian nobility, Helen Petrovna Blavatsky. She combined various Western occult practices, including the use of séances to contact spirits, with elements of Hinduism. Returning to Europe she gained a

following in England and her movement was brought to North America in the 1890s. Theosophical membership also is concentrated in the more secularized Canadian provinces. Finally, the same pattern holds for spiritualists, who also focus on séances and communication with the "spirit world."

The final correlation in Table 14-7 shows that in Canada, too, the West has weak conventional faiths because of a lack of population stability. Where people frequently move, creating communities of newcomers, all organizations, including churches, are weakened. Moreover, in such communities people tend to lack the attachments to others that would limit their freedom to form new attachments that link them to a cult movement.

As noted by Bibby and Weaver (1985), correlations like these must not be interpreted as showing that the majority of people who drift away from conventional religions soon rush off and join a novel religious movement. Most do not. The membership figures attributed to new religious groups in the media usually are wildly exaggerated, and most new religious movements are, and remain, very small. For example, a Toronto magazine recently estimated that there were about 10,000 Hare Krishna members in that city. In fact, there were but 80 full-time members (Hexham, Currie, and Townsend, 1985). The census figures for membership of each group shown in Table 14-7 reveal them to be quite small. For example, there are 835 Canadian Theosophists.

The theory that secularization produces religious innovation does not predict that cult movements snap up all the slack left by a weakening of conventional faiths. It merely predicts that where there is more secularization there one also will find the most active efforts to start and build up new faiths. It also predicts that, over the longer historical run, this is where one or more new movements will achieve substantial success (Stark and Bainbridge, 1987).

■

Secularization, Revival, and Innovation in Europe

Although the thesis that secularization is a self-limiting process that prompts revival and cult formation seems very congruent with data for North America, many have claimed that Canada and the United States are simply oddities— that the trend toward secularization is far along in northern Europe, while no corresponding rise in cult movements exists (Wallis and Bruce, 1984; Wilson, 1975, 1979, 1982).

Clearly, Europe is the acid test of the thesis. In many European nations church attendance is very low indeed: In Denmark and Finland only about 5 percent attend weekly, and in Sweden only about 9 percent do. If secularization leads to innovation, then these nations should be awash with new religions. Yet most observers agreed that they weren't and that these movements were doing best in North America, where conventional religion remains strong.

As it turns out, however, Europe is not lacking in cults, only in scholarly interest in them. Contrary to popular wisdom, North America is not the land of cults. Cults are much more plentiful and successful in most of northern Europe

Table 14-7 ■ **Correlations between secularization and cult strength in Canadian provinces and territories.**

	Secularization*
Cult centers**	.85
Fate magazine subscriptions**	.85
"Para religious" group membership†	.58
Pagan membership†	.57
Theosophy membership†	.60
Spiritualist membership†	.60
Newcomers per 1,000 population†	.55

* Percent giving their religious affiliation as "None" on 1981 census form.
** Bainbridge and Stark (1982).
† Statistics Canada, 1981 census.

and Great Britain than in the United States or Canada. Indeed, this is even true of groups that originated in the United States (Stark and Bainbridge, 1985).

The most telling comparison is based on groups that did not originate in either North America or Europe but which have attempted to gain converts on both continents. The success of these groups reveals the receptivity of some nations to the same alien faiths. Table 14-8 shows the rates of Indian and Eastern cult centers for the United States, Canada, and the nations of western Europe (Norway, Ireland, Portugal, and Switzerland are omitted for lack of data). These centers represent various Eastern faiths, from Hinduism to Zen Buddhism, that have recently been brought to Western nations and whose followers are largely Western converts. The statistics do not include Indian and Eastern faiths sustained by congregations of Indian and Eastern immigrants. The results are very revealing.

Overall, the rate of cult centers per million people is higher for Europe than for the United

Table 14-8 ■ Indian and Eastern cult centers per million population.

Country or Area	Centers per Million Population
Denmark	3.1
United Kingdom	3.0
Finland	2.8
Sweden	2.5
France	2.5
Austria	2.1
Netherlands	2.0
Federal Republic of Germany	1.4
Belgium	1.0
Italy	0.7
Spain	0.6
Western Europe*	1.8
United States	1.3
Canada	1.5

Source: Stark and Bainbridge (1985).

* Figure based only on nations listed above.

States or Canada. But even this is misleading, because the European figure includes the populations of Italy and Spain, large nations that are not greatly secularized and that should not have many cults. (The weekly church attendance rates for Italy [53 percent] and Spain [78 percent] exceed that of the United States.) Thus, the truly interesting comparisons are between nations. These reveal that most European nations shown in Table 14-8 have considerably higher rates of Indian and Eastern cult centers than does the United States. And what nations are these? Primarily those with the lowest church attendance rates.

Clearly, secularization is producing religious innovation in Europe as well as in the United States and Canada. Moreover, areas where Indian and Eastern religions are having the greatest success in Europe have also been receptive to Scientologists and Hare Krishnas. But this pat-

tern is reversed for sect movements, as our theory predicts.

Initially, it seemed impossible to find good data on sect movements for the nations of Europe. It turns out, however, that hundreds of American and Canadian Protestant sects maintain very active missionary programs in Europe. These groups periodically submit reports on their work, which are collated and published in the *Mission Handbook.* These data show that North American sects have had no impact in the most secularized nations of Europe. While Sweden has three Hare Krishna Temples and well over 100 full-time Scientology staff members, it has only one congregation founded by Protestant missionaries from North America. This is not for lack of effort—in 1979, there were 55 such missionaries stationed in Sweden. On the other hand, in Italy, where no Scientology staff members are stationed and where Indian and Eastern cult centers are scarce, there are 1,624 Protestant mission congregations. Thus, sects do best where they tap into a strong religious tradition. Cults abound where the conventional religious tradition is weak.

A new study based on Canada suggests the need to qualify this generalization slightly. David A. Nock (1987) found that only certain kinds of Canadian sect movements do best where religious affiliation is highest, while other kinds seem to need a more secularized environment. He found that conventional Protestant sects, such as the Church of God, Church of the Nazarene, and various Baptist groups, were strongest in provinces where the people were least likely to say they had no religion. But less conventional sects, such as the Jehovah's Witnesses and Christadelphians, were more successful in the provinces where cult movements were doing best. Nock suggests that within the context of Canadian religion, these groups are on the borderline of what is a sect or a cult because, while claiming to be Christian bodies, they have added a great deal of unconventional culture to this religious tradition. However they may see themselves, Canadians tend to view these groups as so distant from traditional, conservative Christianity that the groups are forced to attract members more from the ranks of the unchurched than from the conventional churches. This may also be true in Europe, because Jehovah's Witnesses generally are doing better in the secularized north than in the well-churched south.

The Universal Appeal of Faith

At the start of this chapter, we examined the unique capability of religion to satisfy basic human needs. So long as people want to know what existence means, so long as they are prone to disappointment, suffering, and death, the religious impulse will not be stilled. Only religions, only systems of thought that include belief in the supernatural, can address problems of this magnitude.

From this line of analysis, we can see that Niebuhr left a vital element out of his church-sect theory. In stressing the needs of the deprived and the lower classes for an otherworldly faith, he failed to note that in the face of some of life's greatest questions, all human beings are deprived. No one, neither the rich nor the poor, can achieve immortality in the natural world. And both rich and poor seek to find meaning in existence. The rich as well as the poor join religions. Granted, the rich tend to prefer more worldly churches, but there comes a point at which a religion can become too worldly, too emptied of supernaturalism, to serve either rich or poor. Thus, rising, vigorous, otherworldly religions attract the rich as well as the poor. Although well-educated and successful people tend not to join sects that are in a very high state of tension with the environment, they are often overrepresented among cult converts. In fact, the average cult convert these days is not a social outcast lacking education and good job prospects. The average convert is unusually well educated with excellent career potential (Stark and Bainbridge, 1985).

Conclusion

For more than a century, social scientists have confidently predicted the end of religion. Each

Because religion serves to answer questions of ultimate meaning, its appeal is not limited primarily to the poor, as many sociologists long have believed. For the fact is that all humans are subject to some of life's greatest tragedies and mysteries. Thus rich and poor, young and old, male and female are found in the rank of pilgrims such as these at Fatima, Portugal.

new generation of social scientists has expected that their children, or surely their grandchildren, would live in an irreligious society.

Yet religion has not gone away. Granted, many of the great religious organizations of today may be fated to slide into oblivion. But to notice only their decline and to ignore the vigor of new religious organizations and of new religions in general is to look only at sunsets and never at the dawn. In the long course of human experience, many religions have come and gone, but religion has remained.

Oddly enough, while social scientists have

awaited the end of religion, they have been content to teach that religion has been a universal social institution, found in all societies. They attribute this universality to the ability of religion to serve worldwide human needs. Thus, to expect religion to vanish meant that such needs would vanish or at least that a new institution such as science would replace religion.

However, this implication ignores the unique aspect of religion and the fundamental differences between religion and science. As discussed early in this chapter, some things that humans seem to desire can come only from the gods. So long as such desires exist, religion will exist to satisfy them. Moreover, the supernatural claims of religion are, in their purest form, immune to scientific disproof. Scientists can send cameras and detection equipment through space to inspect the planets for signs of life, but they cannot send probes to test for life after death.

Review Glossary

religious economy The set of competing faiths, and their adherents, within a given society or geographic area of a society. (p. 404)

secularization The process by which particular religious organizations become more worldly and offer a less vivid and less active conception of the supernatural. (p. 404)

revival Movements within religious organizations, or the breaking away of new organizations, to reaffirm less secularized versions of a faith (see *sect formation*). (p. 404)

religious innovation The appearance of new religions in a society either by founding of a new faith (see *cult formation*) or by importing a new faith from another society. (p. 404)

ultimate meaning, questions about Questions about the very meaning of life, the universe, reality—for example, Does life have purpose? Is death the end? Why do we suffer? (p. 406)

supernatural That which is beyond natural laws and limits. (p. 408)

religion Any socially organized pattern of beliefs and practices concerning ultimate meaning that assumes the existence of the supernatural. (p. 408)

religious pluralism The existence of several religions in the same society. (p. 410)

churches Religious bodies in a relatively low state of tension with their environment. (p. 411)

sects Religious bodies in a relatively high state of tension with their environment but which remain within the conventional religious tradition(s) of their society. (p. 411)

sect formation The breaking off of a group from a conventional religion in order to move into a higher degree of tension with the environment. (p. 412)

church-sect theory The proposition that, in time, successful sects will be transformed into churches, thereby creating the conditions for the eruption of new sects. (p. 412)

cults Religious movements that represent faiths that are new and unconventional in a society. (p. 416)

cult formation The process by which a person or persons with new revelations succeed in gathering a group of followers. (p. 417)

charisma The unusual ability of some religious leaders to influence others. (p. 417)

Suggested Readings

Barker, Eileen. 1984. *The Making of a Moonie: Brainwashing or Choice.* Oxford: Basil Blackwell.

Bibby, Reginald W. 1987. *Fragmented Gods: The Poverty and Potential of Religion in Canada.* Toronto: Irwin.

Glenn, Norval D. 1987. "The Trend in 'No Religion' Respondents to U.S. National Surveys, Late 1950s to Early 1980s." *Public Opinion Quarterly* 51:293–314.

Hadden, Jeffrey K., and Theodore E. Long, eds. 1983. *Religion and Religiosity in America.* New York: Crossroad.

Meeks, Wayne A. 1983. *The First Urban Christians: The Social World of the Apostle Paul.* New Haven: Yale University Press.

Stark, Rodney, and William Sims Bainbridge. 1985. *The Future of Religion: Secularization, Revival and Cult Formation.* Berkeley: University of California Press.

Politics and the State

15

IN MEDIEVAL ENGLAND tenants could freely use all uncultivated land of a lord's estate as pasture for their livestock. This pasture land came to be known as the "commons," because it was used by the common people, and their right to use the land was known as the "freedom of the commons." For centuries this arrangement worked well, and its fatal design flaw remained unnoticed. Freedom of the commons worked only as long as wars, disease, and natural disasters greatly limited the number of common people on an estate—thereby keeping down the size of the herds put to graze on the commons. However, when the rural population of England began to grow rapidly in the eighteenth century (see Chapter 18), a crisis suddenly arose. To see why, let's examine the situation from two points of view: that of each individual herd owner and that of the common people as a whole.

With free access to the commons, each individual herd owner always faces a decision of whether to add more animals to the herd. Operating as a rational human being, each herd owner asks, "Will I be better or worse off by adding more animals?" Suppose it is a question of adding another dairy cow to a herd of ten. Adding an eleventh cow will mean more milk, cream, and butter for the herd owner—who gets all of the benefits from the herd. Of course, adding a cow increases the demand placed on the commons to provide adequate feed. However, because all herd owners use the commons, this additional cost will be *shared equally*. Because a herd owner receives all of the profits from an expanded herd while paying only a portion of the costs of additional grazing, an individual

herd owner will always benefit by adding animals even though this causes overgrazing. Thus we can predict that when herders share a commons they inevitably will follow a strategy in which each adds animals as often as possible, making each individual herd as large as possible. So long as external constraints limit population and grazing, the system will not proceed to its tragic outcome. But when limits on expansion are removed, the result will be destruction of the commons and the ultimate economic ruin of all herd owners.

This analysis was first published in 1833 by William Forster Lloyd, an English mathematician who was trying to explain the crisis that had arisen in England over freedom of the commons (Hardin, 1964). For by then "the tragedy of the commons" had been recognized. The individual herd owners, unleashed by population growth, had overgrazed the commons to the point of massive erosion and destruction of the land's productive capacities. No matter how reduced the pasturage, any individual herder still was better off with more animals, no matter how skinny, than with a smaller number of equally skinny livestock.

What happened then? The lord of the estate, often joined by his most affluent tenants, enclosed the commons and withdrew free access. Thenceforth, grazing rights were strictly controlled and, in fact, most common people lost access to the commons. Because the same people now owned both herds and lands, the basis for computing self-interest was changed. When they opted to increase the size of their herds they also bore the full cost. Hence decisions had

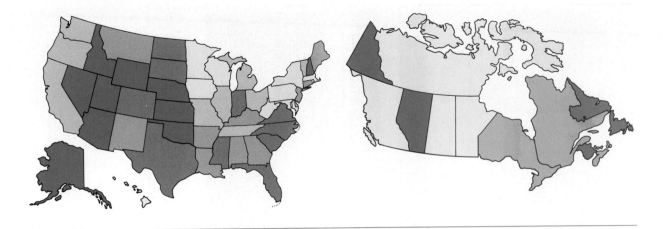

1984: Percent of the Two-Party Vote Won by President Reagan

Minnesota	49.9	North Carolina	62.0
Massachusetts	51.4	Indiana	62.1
Rhode Island	51.8	Mississippi	62.3
Maryland	52.8	Virginia	62.7
Pennsylvania	53.7	South Dakota	63.3
Iowa	53.7	Texas	63.8
New York	54.0	South Carolina	64.1
Wisconsin	54.6	Colorado	64.4
West Virginia	55.3	Florida	65.3
Hawaii	55.7	North Dakota	65.8

Oregon	56.1	Kansas	67.0
Illinois	56.5	Arizona	67.1
Washington	56.8	Nevada	67.3
Tennessee	58.2	New Hampshire	68.9
California	58.2	Oklahoma	69.1
Vermont	58.7	Alaska	69.1
Ohio	59.5	Nebraska	71.0
Michigan	59.5	Wyoming	71.4
Delaware	59.9	Idaho	73.3
Missouri	60.0	Utah	75.1

Georgia	60.2
Kentucky	60.3
New Mexico	60.3
New Jersey	60.5
Connecticut	61.0
Maine	61.1
Arkansas	61.2
Alabama	61.3
Montana	61.3
Louisiana	61.4

1984: Percent of Vote Won by Progressive Conservatives

N.W. Territories	41.3	New Brunswick	53.6
Saskatchewan	41.7	Yukon	56.8
Manitoba	43.2	Newfoundland	57.6
British Columbia	46.7	Alberta	68.9

Ontario	48.0
Quebec	50.2
Nova Scotia	50.8
Pr. Edward Island	52.2

Figure 15-1 ■ **Conservative landslide victories in 1984.** In 1984 President Ronald Reagan was returned to office by one of the largest margins in U.S. election history. His opponent, Walter Mondale, carried only his home state of Minnesota. Some observers suggested that Reagan's landslide was due in part to the fact that the Democrats' vice presidential candidate was a woman. In Canada in 1984 the Progressive Conservative Party also won a landslide victory, taking 211 of 282 seats in the House of Commons. Until then, the Conservatives had been in power for only nine months during the previous twenty-one years. No one blamed the downfall of the Liberal Party on a female candidate. In fact, the proportion of women serving in the House was doubled by the 1984 election. Still, women are underrepresented in elective office on both sides of the border. Later in this chapter we will review some good research on how Canadian and American voters respond to women candidates.

■ A century before this aerial photo was taken, there were no tree-lined fence-rows crisscrossing this English landscape. Instead, this was one huge pasture known as the commons because the common people had the right to graze their herds here. When rapid population growth began, the problem of administering "public goods" was revealed by the overgrazing of the commons. In response, the landowner put up fences, planted trees, and henceforth denied his tenants the right to graze their herds here.

to reflect the need to preserve the pastures. Under these conditions, the pastures recovered. Once again there was an abundance of dairy products and meat. Those with grazing rights grew rich and powerful—at the cost, however, of much individual freedom of choice. Freedom of the commons was replaced by their enclosure and control by an elite.

■

Chapter Preview

In this chapter we shall examine the great contradiction in human affairs revealed by what has come to be called "the tragedy of the commons." Many things vital to humans as *social* beings conflict with things vital to humans as *individuals*. To provide for the common or col-

lective good, people often are forced to surrender considerable control over their lives to leaders and governments. Unfortunately, as we shall see, this surrender often results in much misery, when leaders use their power and authority to repress, exploit, and even enslave their people. Indeed, through most of history the state has been an institution of repression. Thus we confront one of the oldest dilemmas of political philosophy: how to have a state and keep it tame. As we examine theories for limiting the state's power and increasing individual freedom, we discover two fundamental kinds of state: the elitist state, which tends toward tyranny, and the pluralist state, which tends to permit considerable freedom.

We approach these matters by watching a famous equity experiment that assessed aspects of the tragedy of the commons problem. Then we move to the more macro level and assess an application of the same logic to the problem of *public* or *collective* goods. We then see how the state provides for public goods and explore means for preventing the state from being captured by a repressive and exploitative "power elite." The latter part of the chapter is both less macro and less theoretical. It concentrates on political behavior in democratic nations, especially the United States and Canada. We examine the rise of opinion polling and its implications for political decision making. Then we watch two creative studies of voter reactions to female candidates for elective office. Finally, we assess the role of ideology in forming individual political opinions.

The "Tragedy of the Commons" in the Laboratory

 Several years ago a group of researchers at the University of California, Santa Barbara, figured out how to re-create the situation of the freedom of the commons in a social experiment. Led by David M. Messick and Henk Wilke (Messick et al., 1983), the team recruited undergraduate students as subjects. When the subjects arrived at the laboratory in groups of six, each was placed in a semiprivate booth containing a computer terminal. Then Messick and his colleagues explained that the group would participate in a "harvesting" game in which each person would remove points from a common pool. Each would receive a dime for every point he or she harvested. After each turn, the pool would be replenished at a variable rate, but would never rise above 300 points—the level of the pool at the start of the game. Players could harvest from zero to ten points whenever it was their turn. They could continue to take points as long as any remained in the pool.

Subjects were told that the game had two goals. First, players should try to accumulate as many points as possible; the group of six with the highest total would receive a cash bonus at the end of the experiment. The second goal was to make the resource last as long as possible, to maximize the number of turns during which points still could be harvested. The parallel with the real world was spelled out as the experimenters told subjects that the game involved a choice between "taking all that one can or wants at the moment—at the risk of using up the resource—or taking a little on many occasions, with the possibility of getting more in the end because the pool is able to replenish itself." Finally, subjects were told they would be able to watch each player's choices as they occurred; these would appear on their monitor screen.

The game began with each player in the situation of herd owners in the days of freedom of the commons. Just as each herd owner had to choose whether to take a larger share of the commons' grass, these subjects had to choose between sustaining the pool by taking fewer points or maximizing their sure winnings by taking a dollar's worth of points every time they got a chance, since the cost of depleting the pool would be equally shared by all. The computer recorded what each subject did on each turn.

However, the players weren't really interacting. Instead, the computer was in control, and so the feedback each player got about what others were doing and the condition of the pool was manipulated experimentally. Two *independent variables* were manipulated in this experiment. The first was *level of harvest*. One-third of the subjects were led to believe that so much was being taken in each turn that the size of the pool was dwindling rapidly. This was the *overuse* condition. The second third of subjects were informed that so little was being taken in each turn that the pool was growing. This was the *underuse* condition. The final third were shown results in which the pool remained of constant size. This was the *optimal* condition.

The second independent variable was *equity*. Half of those in each of the three harvest level groups were shown that members of the group were taking relatively similar numbers of points each turn; this was the condition of high equity. Those in the inequitable condition were shown that members were taking very different numbers of points, that some were taking a lot more than others on each turn.

After ten turns the subjects were informed that the first part of the experiment was over. Each was told that in the past some groups had suggested that they could have done better if they had a leader who took points for the whole group and who then allocated points to each group member. Subjects were given the choice of continuing to withdraw points individually, as they had been doing, or electing a leader to control point withdrawals and distribution. No matter how the vote actually went, the subjects next were informed that the majority had voted to elect a group leader. So each subject was asked to rank all six group members in terms of their preferences for who became leader. Each player had been identified as a color during the first part of the experiment, and so colors were the identifications used in the voting procedure. Of course, the election was rigged. *Every* subject was told she or he had been elected leader. So for another ten trials each subject took points from the pool and awarded a share to each player—unaware that all the others were doing the same.

What were the results? First, subjects in all groups tended to increase their harvests over time. The longer they played, the more they moved to maximize individual gain. Second, subjects took larger harvests and increased their harvests more rapidly when they believed there was great inequity across players—when they thought some players were taking a lot more than others. Third, players increased their harvests more in the underuse than in the overuse condition.

The independent variables also greatly influenced voting behavior. The overwhelming majority of those in the overuse condition voted to put harvesting in the hands of a leader—to opt, in effect, for government regulation. Only minorities in the other use conditions voted to have a leader. Equity also influenced vote—people in the highly inequitable groups were much more anxious to have a leader.

Finally, how did subjects behave once they became leaders? First, they decreased the size of the harvests to the level of optimal use—taking only the rate at which the pool was being replaced. So just as the landowners in England restored the productive capacity of the commons, so did the leaders in this experiment. Second, they were quite equitable in assigning shares to the other five players. Third, just as did the English lords, the leaders in the experiment gave themselves larger shares than they gave others. That is, given leadership power they moved to translate their advantage into cash—even at a dime a point.

In this remarkable experiment we see why humans accept leadership and create governments, and we also see the risks entailed in doing so. For, just as conflict theories of stratification anticipate (see Chapter 9), *human beings will tend to use power to exploit others.*

Public Goods and the State

Mancur Olsen (1965) has argued that governments are unavoidable features of human societies. His conclusion rests on the simple point illustrated in the tragedy of the commons: To provide for the best interests of the group, coercion (the use of force) is necessary. In order to create public or collective goods, the interests of the individual and the interests of the group collide.

It wasn't sufficient for the English landlords to inform their tenants that they were overusing the commons. They knew it. But how could the overuse be stopped? Not by persuasion, for it will always be in the interests of each individual to let the others be persuaded while he or she continues as before. So the lords had to put up fences, drive out tenant herds, and keep them out. In the end, the English government had to enforce the property rights of the lords against the demands of the evicted herd owners.

There are many **public** or **collective goods** vital to the survival and welfare of human societies. First, we must be secure from harm from other members; we can't risk living together if we constantly must fear for our lives and possessions. Second, we must be secure against harm from external dangers—from being attacked or looted by members of another society.

■ Any military cemetery demonstrates the inherent problem of creating public goods. If a society is to remain safe from external attack, some members must be induced to serve in the armed forces. Here, what's best for the group collides with what's best for the individual. For any individual, the best choice is to benefit from the protection provided by others while he or she remains out of danger. Just as long as their side won the war, men like Bill Cooper, John P. Okun, and Charles M. Magee would have been better off enjoying civilian life and keeping their names off monuments like these. But if they had all stayed home, North America might be under Nazi rule today.

Third, certain resources and services must be provided that cannot be supplied by voluntary individual actions. For example, a dam to prevent floods requires that many people contribute wealth, time, and energy.

The crucial aspect of public goods is, of course, that the best deal for any individual is to reap the benefits without sharing the costs—that is, to be a "freeloader." This problem remains chronic because so often it is impossible to withhold the benefits of a specific public good selectively. When an enemy attack is beaten off, all members of a society benefit, but a warrior profits more if, while the others go off to battle, he stays home and avoids the risk of death or injury. Were such a strategy possible, public goods

would not be created because (to pursue the example) *all* the warriors would stay home.

Olsen concluded that because it is always against an individual's self-interest to contribute to the public good, there will be no public goods unless means exist to *force* individuals to do their share. Often this force need not be used, but its use must always be a credible threat.

The **state** or government is the organized embodiment of political processes within a society—the means by which decisions are made and social life directed and regulated. The state arises in human societies because of the need to provide a credible threat to force the creation of public goods. As we shall see, such threats require that the state organize and *monopolize*

■ The great dilemma of human societies is the need to create a state and the frequency with which the state then turns upon its citizens—most states in most human history have exploited and repressed their citizens. These citizens of Prague, Czechoslovakia, watch as troops roll into the city bringing to an end their nation's brief experiment with a less repressive regime.

the use of coercion. Indeed, Max Weber defined the state as consisting of such a monopoly: "One can define the state sociologically only in terms of the *means* peculiar to it . . . namely the use of physical force" (Weber, trans. 1946).

Only through organized coercion can people assure themselves of public goods. And therein lies the greatest of all social dilemmas. We must have certain kinds of public goods in order to exist. To get them, we must create organizations capable of coercing us. By doing that, however, we set up the possibility, even the probability, that those who control the means of coercion will act in their own interest rather than for the public good. As a result, political leaders may use the government monopoly on coercive force for their personal benefit. Thus, peasants driven to create a government capable of defending them from bandits have often found themselves victims of a ruling elite. Members

of this elite turn the coercive powers of the state against the peasants and tax them severely so the elite can live in luxury.

■

Functions of the State

As we have seen, Max Weber argued that the essence of a state or government is that it "claims the monopoly of the legitimate use of physical force" within its boundaries. Robert Nozick (1974) has developed this definition more fully:

A state claims a monopoly on deciding who may use force when it says that only it may decide who may use force and under what conditions; it reserves to itself the sole right to pass on the legitimacy and permissibility of any use of force within its boundaries; fur-

thermore it claims the right to punish all those who violate its claimed monopoly.

To understand why the state's monopoly on force arises, it helps to see how the state uses this monopoly to secure certain public goods. In some cases, the government must use coercion to prevent coercion by individuals. For example, one primary collective good is security against being the victim of coercion by other individuals, such as robbers.

Indeed, precisely here is where anarchist proposals to dispense with the state break down. Without a collective good such as security against harmful actions by other group members, people would not be able to remain within the group. That is, without organized coercion to prevent private coercion, humans would live in a condition that Thomas Hobbes described as "the war of all against all." In his book *Leviathan*, published in 1651, Hobbes tried to describe what life would be like in a condition of anarchy:

Hereby it is manifest, that during the time men live without a common power to keep them all in awe, they are in that condition which is called war . . . where every man is enemy to every man. . . . In such condition, there is no place for industry; because the fruit thereof is uncertain: and consequently no [agri]culture . . . no society; and which is worst of all, continual fear, and danger of violent death; and the life of man, solitary, poor, nasty, brutish, and short.

Hobbes argued that there could be no freedom where there was no security of person or property. An individual's freedom to live and to benefit from his or her efforts requires that limits be placed on the freedom of others. I am not free to live unless you are not free to kill me. I am not free to create unless you are not free to take my creations from me. When the attempts of individuals to coerce each other are not held in check, the possibility of preserving group life is destroyed.

Thus, a primary function of the state is to preserve internal order, to make life predictable and secure. However, the state also exists to provide the collective good of external security.

In fact, the state serves to provide all collective goods—things its members could not individually provide for themselves, from irrigation ditches to armies to legal codes.

These functions of the state were clearly understood by those who wrote the preamble to the U.S. Constitution:

We the People of the United States, in Order to form a more perfect Union, establish Justice, insure domestic Tranquility, provide for the common defense, promote the general Welfare, and secure the Blessings of Liberty to ourselves and our Posterity, do ordain and establish this Constitution of the United States of America.

Rise of the repressive state

According to our definition, all societies, even the tiniest and most primitive hunting and gathering societies, have a state. However, in small, simple societies, the state is no more than a loosely organized authority structure based on kinship and age—the "ruler" is more like the head of a large family than like a king or a president. That is, in small, preliterate societies some persons hold the authority to settle disputes and to oversee the creation of public goods. But there are no full-time leaders. Relations between the individual and those having authority are direct and personal. When someone is seriously deviant, the person or persons having authority administer punishment, usually by physical force. Because of these features, many anthropologists and sociologists refer to these as "stateless societies," applying the name state only when there are full-time specialists who exercise the functions of the state.

In reality, however, the dividing line between stateless societies and those having states is somewhat hazy. So societies included in the Standard Cross-Cultural Sample have been classified in terms of the *span* or the *scope* of their internal political authority. Eighty-two of the 186 societies in the sample are classified as having only local political control. That is, political authority is limited to one place or social unit, such as a specific village, rather than being

The most famous contemporary symbol of the repressive state is the Berlin Wall, built to prevent people from leaving East Germany. The more repressive a state, the more effort required to keep people from fleeing.

exercised over several such units. These societies best fit the definition of a stateless society, although a few of them do support full-time leaders. An additional seventy-five of these societies can be called semistates, for they sustain political leaders with a span of control that extends over multiple units and which may consist of two levels of administrators—that is, one set of leaders who, in turn, have superiors. Finally, twenty-nine of these societies qualify as fully developed states.

The existence of states, as with the existence of all specialization within societies, rests on the development of agriculture. For it is only the capacity to produce surplus food that allows people to specialize in work unrelated to obtaining food; in stateless societies the leaders must provide for their own subsistence. Table 15-1 shows this relationship. In societies lacking agriculture, 81.6 percent have only local political structures. This decreases sharply as the level of agricultural development rises; and where there is relatively well-developed agriculture, just 22.8 percent of the societies have only local political structures.

The emergence of political specialists is accompanied by the emergence of military specialists, who provide the monopoly on force that is the essence of the state. And when military specialists exist, they tend to be busy. Table 15-2 shows that even societies with local political structures generally are quite warlike— nearly half fight a war every year. But the typical agrarian state, with its cohorts of military specialists, is hardly ever at peace—and in none is war a rarity.

Not only does the agrarian state use its military power against its neighbors but the state's monopoly on force is a constant threat to its citizens as well. A king, for example, will use his soldiers to provide for the common defense and to ensure public order, but he will also use them to exploit his subjects. Table 15-3 shows that the amount of stratification is low in 93.9 percent of societies with only local political authority, and none of these societies has a high degree of stratification. No agrarian state has a low degree of stratification and 69 percent are highly stratified. This is the feature of the state that has long driven people to despair. How can the state be made bearable?

Taming the State

For more than 2,000 years, a dominant question in political thought has been how to limit the powers of the state. The nature of the problem seems clear enough. The state must exist. This means that the state will always have the potential to use its coercive powers to exploit and repress its citizens. How can the abuse of these coercive powers be limited without weak-

Table 15-1 ■ Agricultural development and the scope of political structures.

Scope of Political Structure	Level of Agricultural Development			
	None	Low	Medium	High
Local only	81.6%	57.1%	34.9%	22.8%
Semistate	18.4%	39.3%	57.2%	36.8%
State	0.0%	3.6%	7.9%	40.4%
	100.0%	100.0%	100.0%	100.0%
N =	(38)	(28)	(63)	(57)

Source: Prepared by the author from the Standard Cross-Cultural Sample as selected by Murdock and White (1969).

Table 15-2 ■ The state and warfare.

Frequency of External Warfare	Scope of Political Structure		
	Local Only	Semistate	State
Constant	46.2%	57.9%	71.4%
Common	15.3%	15.8%	14.3%
Occasional	10.3%	2.6%	14.3%
Rare	28.2%	23.7%	0.0%
	100.0%	100.0%	100.0%
N =	(39)	(38)	(7)

Source: Prepared by the author from the Standard Cross-Cultural Sample as selected by Murdock and White (1969).

Table 15-3 ■ The state and stratification.

Degree of Stratification	Scope of Political Structure		
	Local Only	Semistate	State
Low	93.9%	53.4%	0.0%
Medium	6.1%	33.3%	31.0%
High	0.0%	13.3%	69.0%
	100.0%	100.0%	100.0%
N =	(82)	(75)	(29)

Source: Prepared by the author from the Standard Cross-Cultural Sample as selected by Murdock and White (1969).

ening the ability of the state to fulfill its necessary functions?

The Greek philosopher Plato thought the solution was creating a special class of philosopher-kings—persons trained to be fair and restrained in their use of state power. However, it seems too much to expect people placed in positions of immense power to practice self-restraint. Indeed, as Lord Acton claimed in a widely quoted maxim, "Power corrupts, and absolute power corrupts absolutely."

Rejecting hopes that the state could be tamed by putting people of high character in power, political theorists searched for social arrangements that would limit the power of leadership positions, regardless of the character of the leaders. By the eighteenth century, political thinkers had concluded that two things were necessary to tame the state. First, *a clear set of rules* (procedures and laws) had to be established that defined the limits of state power and the manner in which that power could and could not be exercised. But rules by themselves mean nothing. Some of the most repressive regimes on earth have model constitutions that guarantee all sorts of rights and freedoms to citizens. Such guarantees do not mean anything unless they are embodied in a structure designed to ensure that the rules are observed. What kind of structure can have this effect?

This leads to the second requirement for taming the state: *a structure in which power is widely dispersed among many powerful groups.* In this way, no one group can pursue its own interests without regulation; every group is checked by the other powerful groups acting to preserve their own interests. This aspect of taming the state was not so much discovered as it was something that just slowly evolved by trial and error. In fact, only after a considerable dispersal of power had occurred in England did political theorists recognize the principle involved. So let's see what happened and how it works.

The evolution of pluralism

English democracy evolved from a single principle, the right to private property. The English believed that the essential feature of state repression was the use of coercion to deprive people of their property. If this could be prevented, then the state could be brought under control. In particular, if the king could be prohibited from taking any person's property without that person's permission, then the king could not squeeze all the economic surplus out of the people to provide for his luxuries. Nor could the king afford to go to war unless he had the support of the people, for he would lack the needed funds. Thus, the English believed that the state could be tamed if taxes could not be imposed or collected without the approval of those being taxed.

This view is in direct conflict with the Marxist theory of the state, which holds that private property is the root of all repression and exploitation by the ruling class. Marxists argue that the right to private property and the state's use of coercion to protect private property are the means by which the ruling class becomes and remains rich and exploits the masses. Marx claimed that only if property rights are abolished can the masses be liberated (see Chapter 9). Yet the fact remains that in Marxist states there is very little individual freedom, while in all nations with free elections and substantial individual liberties, the state guarantees the property rights of individuals.

This contrast between capitalist and Marxist states would not surprise those who helped to create democracy in England or those who wrote the American Constitution. Long observation of European feudalism had convinced them that when property rights are not secure, the masses, not the rich, suffer most. They recognized that the repressive state mainly confiscates the property of the powerless—the peasants, small merchants, and artisans—because the wealthy rule the state and receive the wealth seized by the state. There was, in fact, a second quite workable solution to the tragedy of the commons—to place ownership of herd and land in the same hands *by dividing the commons* into pastures, each owned by one of the herd owners. In this way the ecology of the commons would also have been restored, because now the full costs of herd expansion would fall on the herd owner. Of course, this division would have violated the property rights of the land-owners. But enclosure also violated a property right in the sense that, for centuries, the decision to labor in the lord's fields had been calculated on the basis of the value of grazing rights on the commons. Enclosure was unilateral withdrawal of a valuable portion of this exchange relationship and, furthermore, destroyed the value of the evicted herds. With whom did the government side? With the wealthy and powerful. Had *all* property rights been accorded protection, the common people would have gotten a much better bargain. Guaranteeing the property rights of everyone offers greater protection to those with the least property.

But the pressing question was, How could property rights be protected from the state? The solution is not simply a law or a constitution, but a particular kind of social structure in which a number of powerful factions, or elites, restrict one another's ability to use the state's coercive power. The state can be tamed only when political power is dispersed among groups with diverse interests. Such a situation is described as **pluralism.**

Pluralism developed in England partly by accident. In 1215 King John found himself unable to control the nobility. To remain on the throne, he was forced to sign the Magna Carta, a contract in which he agreed to impose no taxes on the nobility except when they freely agreed to be taxed. This led to the creation of the House of Lords, wherein the nobility gathered periodically to vote on tax requests from the king.

In time, the right to have one's property secure against seizure by the king was extended to property owners who were not members of the nobility. They began to send elected representatives to the House of Commons, where they also gave or withheld approval of the king's tax requests. The power to control the king's revenues proved to be the power to control the government. If the House of Lords or the House of Commons did not like a policy, it could withhold funds until it was changed.

Moreover, neither house of Parliament was dominated by a single group with identical interests. Policies favorable to some nobles often affected others adversely; policies good for merchants were often bad for shopowners or farm-ers. Thus, besides English kings having to depend upon the two houses for their revenues, decisions within each house required *a coalition of groups* and therefore *a compromise of competing interests.* Governmental decision-making processes involved increasingly diverse groups and interests.

Of course, English rulers occasionally attempted to destroy these limits on their power and restore the absolute power of the throne. However, these efforts were always thwarted because too many people had too much to lose should the king regain control. Therefore, if one faction of nobles wanted to restore an unlimited monarchy, others combined to block them.

The American Revolution occurred primarily because the English failed to extend their principle of no taxation without representation to their North American colonies. The English tried to levy taxes on the colonies, but they did not grant the colonies representation in the House of Commons, where they could influence tax policies.

Once free of English rule, the Americans had to create their own system of government. By this time, however, political philosophers, especially the Scottish rationalists, had analyzed why and how the English system worked. Thus, the men who wrote the American Constitution did so with considerable understanding of the essential issues.

James Madison, the principal designer of the American Constitution, believed that democracy always faces two threats. The first is *a tyranny of the minority*—the historic danger that a privileged few would capture the state and use its coercive powers to repress and exploit the many. This classic problem of taming the state had given rise to the English form of democracy. But Madison was also concerned about *the tyranny of the majority*—the danger that a majority of citizens would use the machinery of representative government to exploit and abuse minorities. Here, Madison was mindful that even the English democracy persecuted religious dissenters and that coalitions of interest groups sometimes exploited weaker groups. Indeed, Madison was concerned that people who achieved great wealth be as secure in their property rights as anyone else, and he feared that the mass of citizens might use their superior numbers to impose discriminatory taxes on the rich and thereby escape paying taxes themselves. Put another way, Madison believed the poor could be as selfish as the rich.

To block both kinds of tyranny, Madison developed a system of government in which powers were widely distributed and procedures made somewhat cumbersome. Each of the three branches of our federal government—the executive, legislative, and judicial—has the power to nullify actions taken by the other two. This is called the system of checks and balances in government. Madison hoped to make it possible for minorities to block actions against them, at least for a long period, and for substantial majorities to be required to take any action, thereby blocking minorities from controlling the government.

The system of checks and balances has dominated the American political process for more than 200 years. It has not always produced ideal results, and sometimes the United States has been less democratic than Madison had hoped. Despite these defects, the state has remained relatively tame. Moreover, many of the worst violations of individual liberty have been corrected within the system.

The important point, however, is that the U.S. Constitution, like all constitutions, is meaningless without support from political institutions and, indeed, without a general willingness to play by the rules. Some of the most repressive regimes on earth have magnificent written constitutions that solemnly guarantee all sorts of freedoms, while the British have provided a model of democracy without ever having written down most of their constitution. And Canada has sustained democracy both with and without an extensive written constitution. For a long time, aside from various acts of the British Parliament defining some aspects of Canadian governing principles, Canada primarily relied on the "unwritten" British constitution. In 1981 the Canadian government secured the right to frame and amend its own constitution without the approval of the British Parliament—a process referred to as "patriation." That same year the Canadian Supreme Court noted a number of documents and acts as parts of the constitution, and then in April 1982 Queen Elizabeth II came to Ottawa to sign the new Constitution Act—which begins with a very detailed list of rights and freedoms guaranteed to all Canadians.

Thus far we have seen how the dispersal of power plays a fundamental role in taming the state through the process wherein one powerful faction is played off against another. Now let's more clearly develop the underlying theory.

Elitist and pluralist states

States are of two essential types: elitist and pluralist. In an **elitist state,** a single elite group rules. Sometimes power struggles go on within this elite, for example, when there is a dispute over who is to be the new head of state or the new party leader. But power resides almost totally with this single elite, which controls the state and can therefore use its coercive powers as it sees fit.

The elitist state is the most common type. The agrarian societies examined in Chapter 10 were elitist states, and most societies today are elitist states, regardless of what their constitutions say. Whenever only a single political party is permitted and rule is passed on by power struggles within the one-party elite, that state is elitist, even if it calls itself a democracy or a people's republic.

It is almost impossible for an elitist state to avoid being tyrannical. Plato's hypothetical unselfish philosopher-kings have not appeared. In short, the elitist state is an untamed state wherein the state's coercive powers are used to repress and exploit people.

In a **pluralist state,** rules governing state power are maintained by the existence of many competing elites. The pluralist state has been tamed. That does not mean that all persons living in such a state have an equal amount of power in decision making. No such society exists. Indeed, the word *pluralist* refers to several (plural) elites. The state is tamed because power is dispersed among many contending minorities, or elites, each of which can secure some, but not all, of its desires.

The elitist state is ruled by a single minor-

■ The Soviet Union is an example of an elitist state, ruled by a small circle of Communist Party officials. The party has attempted to eliminate all other power centers in Russian society—centers that might give rise to competing elites.

ity; the pluralist state is ruled by shifting coalitions of many minorities. Robert Dahl (1956) explains the difference this way:

If there is anything to be said for the processes that actually distinguish democracy from dictatorship, it is not discoverable in the clear-cut distinction between government by a majority and government by a minority. The distinction comes much closer to being one between government by a minority and government by minorities.

Thus, Dahl conceded that in no states do majorities rule directly. Rather, in democratic states numerous minorities or interest groups represent the interests of most citizens: business interests, labor interests, religious interests, racial and ethnic interests, regional inter-

ests, and so on. The constant struggles and shifting coalitions among these groups prevent any one from imposing its will on the others. Should business become too powerful, labor unions and consumer groups may unite to hold it in check. Or should labor become too powerful, consumer groups may side with business. If the eastern states seek to exploit other regions, these regions will unite to protect themselves. And so it goes.

However, democracy is not the cause of pluralism. Rather, *pluralism is the mechanism that sustains democracy* as each of many political blocs acts to preserve its right to influence decision making. Indeed, in some nations that do not claim to be democracies, the existence of pluralism limits the power of the state—a pattern often found in Latin American countries

■ In Poland, as in other Communist bloc nations, all newspapers are strictly controlled by the government. Oddly, the government also makes it hard for citizens to get these papers. This long line of people in the main market square in Krakow, Poland, waits to buy a morning paper from the vending truck.

ruled by military governments. In some nations that do claim to be democracies, the absence of pluralism results in little freedom for the individual; nations in the Soviet bloc are examples.

Pluralism or power elites?

The pluralist thesis has been hotly contested by some sociologists, especially by Marxists. They claim that the democracy of Western nations is mostly an illusion, that there really aren't a variety of independent elites contending with one another. Instead, behind the superficial appearances of pluralism, these nations are, in fact, really being run by a tiny ruling elite.

The most forceful and famous proponent of the ruling elite thesis was C. Wright Mills (1916–1962), who taught at Columbia University. In his book *The Power Elite* (1956), Mills charged that the United States is effectively ruled by a small set of influential people who, together, hold the preponderance of power. Mills identified these people as a **power elite** rather than as a "ruling class," because their power often is not based primarily on their economic positions. Instead, their power derives from the positions they hold in three major kinds of organizations that, according to Mills, dominate American life: the military, the government bureaucracy, and the large corporations. These leaders don't actually get together and plan and conspire to run the nation, but, Mills argued, they serve the same interests. Moreover, Mills claimed that these people tend to have such similar social

■ Direct democracy is possible only for very small groups, such as this group of New Englanders gathered for a town meeting. For larger groups, representative democracy is required.

backgrounds that they almost intuitively come to the same conclusions about what ought to happen. The power elite, said Mills, is male, Protestant, of old East Coast families, and educated in the Ivy League; its members tend to belong to the same set of clubs and organizations. They also serve together on many corporate boards and government commissions.

The Power Elite was a very controversial book and has been the focus of much conflict among sociologists. From the beginning many, such as David Riesman (1961), argued that Mills missed the variety of significant conflicts of interest among those said to form the power elite. What's good for the banks often is bad for manufacturing firms. Price controls on oil may be good for the auto industry but bad for oil companies. Or high oil prices may be great for Texas and Alberta and bad for Michigan and Ontario.

Despite such criticisms, much empirical research also demonstrates that those in the highest reaches of government and business do tend to be people with similar backgrounds and many social ties to one another (Domhoff, 1980). Does that mean they constitute a single elite? The debate continues. The more widely accepted view seems to be that no single elite dominates in Western democracies, but neither do "the people" make most of the decisions.

■

Democracy and the People

The essence of popular democratic political theory is that government should be of the people, by the people, and for the people. But how can this be accomplished, and would it really be in the public interest? Clearly, it is impossible to run even a modest-sized city along the lines of the New England town meeting, where citizens gather to speak their piece and, by majority vote, make all town government decisions. Such a direct democracy requires tiny populations. Moreover, a substantial number of citizens do not take part in town meetings, and thus government is not by all the people. Even if those who fail to attend were rounded up and forced to take part, it is not clear that government would be conducted more wisely or even with greater concern for the interests of all. Many people seem too little interested in politics or too uninformed to make any responsible contributions to decision making.

For both of these reasons, practicality and indifference, democracies rest on the principle of representative government. Free elections are held to select persons to govern on behalf of the rest. Should these elected officials stray too far from the public will, they can be turned out of office at the next election. But even this solution is not perfect if the concern is to represent everyone, because many citizens do not vote or otherwise participate in the political process. As a result, they give disproportionate political influence to those who do participate. And many who take part appear to have only the vaguest impression of what is going on and therefore may be better served politically by doing nothing.

In the remainder of this chapter, we shall explore political participation and political opinion in Canada and the United States to see how democratic political processes shape the state. However, before turning to these matters, it will be useful to see how the recent development of public opinion polls made it possible to determine how the people feel about major issues and to discover who takes part in the political process.

George Gallup: The Rise of Opinion Polling

Modern democracies are founded on the belief that those elected to represent the people will actually do so. This does not mean that they ought to be rubber stamps for public opinion. In fact, political leaders often earn great respect when they risk popularity to abide by their principles. Nevertheless, in a representative government, elected officials should at least know the people's feelings on various issues. Obtaining this knowledge does not seem difficult today, when it is hard to open a newspaper or watch the nightly news on TV without learning the results of the latest opinion poll.

Nevertheless, until recently most elected officials could only guess about public opinion, even on major issues, and often their guesses were wrong. Those representing a minority viewpoint can often instigate massive letter-writing campaigns, public demonstrations, and editorial support so that they appear to be representing the majority. Before public opinion polling, it was very difficult to see the contrivance of such campaigns. In fact, some of the earliest polls were as misleading as publicity campaigns in support of particular points of view.

In 1936 Franklin Delano Roosevelt ran for his second term as President of the United States. His opponent was Alfred Landon, the Republican governor of Kansas. In order to have advance knowledge of the election results, the *Literary Digest*, one of the leading magazines of the time, conducted a huge poll of public opinion. They sent postcards (which could then be mailed for a penny) to millions of Americans, asking them how they planned to vote. Based on more than 5 million responses, they confidently predicted that Alf Landon would win in a landslide with more than 60 percent of the vote. In fact, Roosevelt won with more than 60 percent of the vote.

Where had the *Literary Digest* gone wrong? One problem was that they did not select a random sample of the population (see Special Topic 1). Having no national list of the American public, the *Digest* editors used telephone books and automobile registration lists to get names and addresses for their poll. Unfortunately, people having telephones and automobiles in the depths of the Great Depression were much wealthier than the millions without such luxuries. As we saw in Special Topic 2, social class has a substantial impact on voting; the *Literary Digest*'s poll was defective because it overrepresented the voting intentions of a wealthy minority, not

■ U.S. Senator Nancy Landon Kassebaum (Republican, Kansas) poses with her father, Alf Landon, former governor of Kansas. In 1936 Landon was the Republican candidate for president of the United States and ran against the incumbent, Democrat Franklin Delano Roosevelt. A misconceived opinion poll by the *Literary Digest* predicted an easy Landon victory. Instead, Roosevelt was reelected by a large margin, as had been predicted by the Gallup Poll in its first-ever election forecast. In 1987, several years after this picture was taken, Alf Landon died, shortly after celebrating his 100th birthday.

the voting population as a whole. However, even this flaw would not have caused them to pick the wrong winner had it not been for a second bias. For reasons no one knows, people favoring Landon were much more likely to return their postcards. That is, despite having a biased selection of voters, if everyone contacted by the *Literary Digest* had sent back his or her card, "the

magazine would have, at least, correctly predicted Roosevelt the winner" (Squire, 1988). As it was, the magazine was mortally wounded. Stephen Birmingham (1973) reported that:

The Literary Digest, *which had a few days earlier been a great and trusted American institution, was suddenly a national laughingstock, and all over the world "Literary Digest jokes" proliferated.*

The magazine began to lose circulation rapidly, and in two years was forced into bankruptcy.

Meanwhile, in 1936 another poll on the election appeared in a number of newspapers. Unlike the *Literary Digest's* poll, it was not based on millions of respondents, but on fewer than 2,000; yet it correctly predicted an easy Roosevelt victory. This poll was conducted by the American Institute of Public Opinion (AIPO). AIPO had begun in 1935, and on October 20 of that year its first weekly report on public opinion about current issues appeared in several newspapers. It proved to be a very popular feature, and soon it was carried by scores of leading papers across the country. A year later, AIPO's correct prediction of the election made it an authoritative source of information on public opinion. The name of the president and founder of the American Institution of Public Opinion soon became well known: George Gallup.

George Gallup received a doctorate from Northwestern University in 1928 and was head of the department of journalism at Drake University from 1929 to 1931. He returned to Northwestern for a year as professor of journalism and advertising, but then went to New York to become director of research for Young and Rubicam, a leading advertising agency. In 1935 he founded the polling organization that has come to be known as the Gallup Poll.

Gallup's aim was to provide frequent reports of public opinion on major political, social, and moral issues. As he put it in his first newspaper report in 1935, his was a "nonpartisan fact-finding organization which will report the trend of public opinion on one major issue each week. . . . The results of these polls are being published for the first time today in leading newspapers—representing every shade of political preference."

Gallup's first report demonstrated the difficulties of gauging public opinion without conducting a poll. In 1935 most of the world was in the midst of the Great Depression. Millions were out of work, many banks had failed, factories were closed or running at very reduced levels, and thousands of homeless people had taken to the highways in search of a livelihood. In the United States, after three years in office, Franklin Delano Roosevelt's "New Deal" had made little progress toward economic recovery. As a result, a widespread campaign was begun to greatly increase government spending to feed and clothe the needy and to stimulate the economy. Countless public speakers claiming to represent the public demanded that Roosevelt increase federal spending. Many members of Congress joined in these demands, and press accounts frequently echoed the cry that "the people demand action now."

Along came the Gallup Poll. The first Gallup Poll ever published reported national responses to the question: "Do you think the expenditures by the Government for relief and recovery are too little, too great, or just about right?" Only 9 percent of Americans thought the government was spending too little. Sixty percent thought it was spending too much. Thirty-one percent thought the current level of spending was about right. Whether or not increased public spending would have helped recovery, clearly those who supported it as representing the will of the people were incorrect.

This was only the first of many instances in which Gallup findings revealed widespread misperception and misrepresentation of public opinion. Two months later, Gallup reported that despite the fact that most members of Congress, encouraged again by many organized political groups, wanted to decrease military appropriations, the public overwhelmingly wanted them increased. For example, 7 percent of the American public wanted a smaller budget for the Army Air Force, while 74 percent wanted a larger budget. Apparently, the public was more concerned about the massive armaments programs then under way in Nazi Germany than were members of Congress.

In time, political leaders and the mass media learned how hard it was to judge public opinion without taking a poll, and polling became a major industry. But the Gallup Poll, which now has affiliates in more than fifty nations, remains the most influential source of information on political and social issues.

Female Candidates

The nomination of Geraldine Ferraro for vice president of the United States in 1984 brought out many conflicting points of view. There seemed to be widespread agreement among Americans that it was a welcome step toward the full participation of women in positions of power and influence. In fact, 78 percent of Americans told Gallup interviewers they approved of the nomination. Still, there was a lot of disagreement over the net effects of Representative Ferraro's candidacy on voters. Many suggested that it would make little or no difference. Others claimed it might well get Walter Mondale elected. And others saw negative effects on voters. Then in the aftermath of President Reagan's landslide victory, many grumbled that lots of people hadn't really voted for him but simply had rejected a woman for so high an office.

Clearly, however, voters in some other democracies will vote women into high office, as the careers of Margaret Thatcher, Indira Gandhi, Golda Meir, and others attest. Are American voters unusually sexist? If so, how do some American women get elected to high office? And what about voters in other Western democracies, such as Canada and Australia? Do they vote against women? As it happens, an excellent research literature already exists on these matters. So let's watch while researchers in Canada and the United States investigate how voters in those nations respond to female candidates. First we will watch a study based on statistical analysis of election results in Canada and note similar findings for the United States and Australia. Then we will see how two American sociologists used an experiment to try to determine if gender influences a candidate's chances.

■ Geraldine Ferraro, the first woman to be nominated for vice president of the United States, poses with presidential nominee Walter Mondale at the podium of the House Chamber of the Minnesota Legislature. After the Mondale-Ferraro ticket was resoundingly rejected by the voters, some commentators blamed the defeat on prejudice against women candidates. Research shows, however, that voters do not discriminate against women running for office.

Do Canadian voters reject women for Parliament?

 Canadian women received the right to vote in 1918 and the right to stand for elected office at the federal level in the following year. In 1921 the first woman was elected to the House of Commons. For decades, very few women served as M.P.s (Members of Parliament). In 1980 only 5 percent of the 282 M.P.s were female. This number was doubled by the 1984 election, which sent a record of 28 women to the House. (In comparison, women make up 5 percent of the U.S. House of Representatives.)

Why so few female M.P.s? Do voters reject them? Examinations of election results seem to show that they do. In the election of 1979 the average male candidate for the House received 8,494 votes, while the average female candidate received only 4,493. In the election held the next year, the average male received 7,967, and the average woman received 3,500. Overall, women seeking election to the House received only about half as many votes as their male opponents. Moreover, male candidates were three times as likely as female candidates to win elections when women ran against men. But these figures hide most of what really keeps women out of the House.

Alfred A. Hunter and Margaret A. Denton

■ Only a few Canadian women have walked the corridors of power here in the Parliament Buildings in Ottawa. In the 1984 election a record number of women were elected to the House of Commons—28 of 282 members. Studies of election returns show, however, that it is not voters who discriminate against female candidates. Their difficulty is getting nominated by their party.

(1984) of McMaster University noted that many uncontrolled variables raise the possibility that these gender effects are *spurious*, that something other than gender is producing these results.

Because of the existing underrepresentation of women in the House, a much higher proportion of the male candidates are *incumbents* trying for *reelection*. In any election, incumbents have many advantages—including name familiarity and the fact that voters already have responded favorably to them. A second impor-

tant factor is that in recent years Canadian political parties have shown a tendency to be more likely to nominate women during times when the party has been less successful at the polls—in other words, parties that have been losing nominate women for office. The time order is important here. The data do not show that parties start losing because they nominate women but that *after* they have been losing they increase their rate of female nominations. Candidates representing losing parties will tend to lose—another factor in the low number of votes

■ Agnes Campbell Macphail became the first woman elected to the Canadian House of Commons when she won a seat representing a rural Ontario district in the election of 1921—the first federal election in which Canadian women had the vote. Macphail first sat as a member of the Progressive Party but later became an independent. She also was the first woman appointed a member of the Canadian delegation to the League of Nations. Macphail served as an M.P. until 1940, when she was defeated, partly because of her reluctance to support Canada's entry into World War II.

women receive. To make matters worse, all parties in Canada disproportionately nominate women to run for "lost cause" seats where voters have a record of overwhelming support for another party.

To see if these factors could be the real causes of the low voter support for women, Hunter and Denton undertook an analysis of all House races in the 1979 and 1980 elections. For each race they noted the gender of each candidate, the party, and whether one candidate was an incumbent. They also examined the voting rec-

ord for this seat in the previous three elections in order to construct a measure of "competitiveness"—the odds in favor of any candidate based on votes his or her party gained in the past.

Hunter and Denton found differences in the vote-getting abilities of male and female candidates "disappeared entirely" when the candidates were equated in terms of party, incumbency, and competitiveness. The apparent link between gender and votes is in fact spurious, as Hunter and Denton had suspected. It's not the voters who are keeping the proportion of women in the House so low. But if not them, who? Party political elites. As Hunter and Denton put it:

The problems which women aspiring to elected federal office experience largely occur before election day, most notably in their difficulties in securing nominations in the first place and, beyond this, in gaining nominations which carry a reasonable prospect of victory.

Their findings parallel those found in the United States. Having controlled for incumbency and party in recent elections to the U.S. House of Representatives, R. Darcy and Sarah Schramm (1977) reported:

The evidence indicates that the electorate is indifferent to the sex of congressional candidates. . . . Why then are so few women serving? The answer lies in the recruitment and nomination processes.

And, from Australia, comes the same story. Voters do not discriminate against women, but the parties do (MacKerras, 1977).

However, not long ago the overwhelming majority of Americans, both men and women, *would not* vote for a woman running for president. Table 15-4 shows the trend from 1937 through 1986. In 1937 the Gallup Poll found that only one-third of Americans would vote for a female presidential candidate. Twelve years later it was still less than half. Today 84 percent say they would vote for a qualified woman for president.

An interesting facet of the most recent data is that although not everyone would be willing to vote for a woman, Table 15-5 shows that men

Table 15-4 ■ **A woman for president, 1937–1986.**

If your party nominated a woman for president, would you vote for her if she were qualified for the job?*	
Year	Percent Yes
1937	34%
1949	48
1955	52
1967	57
1972	70
1977	77
1986	84

Source: Prepared by the author from the Gallup Poll and National Opinion Research Center, General Social Surveys, 1972, 1977, 1986.

*Several slightly different wordings of the question were used prior to 1972.

Table 15-5 ■ **Gender, age, and voting for a woman, 1986.**

Percent Who Would Vote for a Woman for President	
Men	86.7%
Women	82.1%
Men 65 and under	88.7%
Women 65 and under	87.2%
Men over 65	74.7%
Women over 65	63.5%
Men 75 and over	72.4%
Women 75 and over	55.7%

Source: Prepared by the author from National Opinion Research Center, General Social Survey, 1986.

are slightly more likely than are women to say they would do so. In fact, the difference is statistically significant. How can this be? The table shows us that among people age 65 and under, there is not a significant difference but that among those over 65 the gender difference is substantial: Three-quarters of the men over 65 say they would vote for a female presidential candidate, while less than two-thirds of women over age 65 would do so.

What do these patterns suggest? First, the great increase in the proportion willing to support a female candidate is not due only to people changing their minds about things. Rather, younger people have adopted new outlooks, and the overall change reflects a passing of generations. Older Americans remain less willing to vote for women. However, an age difference does not account for the gender difference among those over 65, despite the fact that the average age of women over 65 is greater than the average age of men over 65 (because women live longer). Even when the comparison is limited to people 75 and older, women are much less willing to support a member of their gender for president.

A reasonable explanation has to do with the different experiences of elderly men and women. The great majority of the latter devoted their lives to being mothers and housewives. As a result, they were unlikely to get to know women pursuing careers. Knowing only housewives, these women sincerely believe that men are more qualified to lead—more than 60 percent of women over 65 agreed that "Most men are better suited emotionally for politics than are most women." In contrast, fewer than half of men over 65 agreed. Why? Because, while relatively few women in this generation pursued careers outside the home, it was men, not housewives, who were likely to encounter them. The best way to meet career women in those days was in the course of business or professional activities, not through the social activities housewives pursued. So, having met or worked with career women whom their wives did not know, these men were more likely to think at least some women could fully compete with men.

Gender and vote: an experiment

 The Canadian and American studies of women candidates used statistical procedures to test whether the correlations between gender and voting were spurious—finding that they were. But the best way to test a hypothesis is to use an experiment. Unfortunately, as I pointed out in Chapter 3, often sociologists can't conduct an experiment. For example, sociologists can't ask political parties to use random procedures to nominate candidates, nor can we change the gender of politicians. Nevertheless, two social scientists employed by private research firms figured out a way to do an experiment on candidate gender and voter responses. Moreover, they also were able to see if gender, race, religion, and residence of voters make a difference in their reactions to male and female candidates.

Laurie E. Ekstrand and William A. Eckert (1981) created campaign leaflets for each of two candidates for governor of the state. These leaflets presented pertinent information on qualifications for office and three issue statements, on environment, unemployment, and taxation. These statements were written to clearly indicate that one candidate was a liberal, the other a conservative. No party affiliation was stated on either leaflet. By randomly varying the name of the candidate on each leaflet, the researchers could, in effect, change the gender of candidates while keeping everything else the same. They created three gubernatorial races. The first had two men running against each other—to see the effect of one leaflet versus another. In the second race the liberal candidate was a woman, the conservative a man. In the third, the liberal was a man, the conservative a woman.

To conduct their experiment, Ekstrand and Eckert recruited 732 college students from four universities in Florida and Georgia to be subjects. Each student was presented with one of the leaflet pairs and asked to vote for one or the other candidate for governor of the state. Random procedures were used to determine which pair any student got—this means the groups seeing each pair should be alike. In addition, students completed brief questionnaires indicating their sex, race, political party preference, religious affiliation, size of hometown, and frequency of church attendance.

The results of the experiment powerfully support those based on real election data. The student subjects strongly favored liberal candidates, but the gender of a candidate didn't matter (see Figure 15-2). Neither did the char-

acteristics of the students. Women candidates did as well with male as with female subjects; with blacks and whites; with Republicans, Independents, and Democrats; with Catholics and Protestants; with subjects from farms, small towns, and big cities, and with frequent and infrequent churchgoers.

Note that these subjects were not all typical of the voters of Florida and Georgia. Liberals do not win the governor's office by landslides in either state. However, these students may well reflect voter attitudes toward women candidates. For these results are in strong agreement with the statistical analyses of voter behavior. Indeed, as Ekstrand and Eckert noted in reporting that their results are supported by the nonexperimental findings, when quite different methods produce the same outcomes, our confidence in each result must increase.

Many of you may be surprised that the underlying political positions of these students, as measured by such things as their religion and party preference, did not influence their reactions to candidate gender. We know that spokespersons for various political and religious groups strongly disagree on many matters, including sex roles. Yet nothing of the sort turned up in this experiment. So we come to a final topic, the role of ideology in the political judgments of the general public.

Ideology and Public Opinion

As I mentioned at the start of this book, all social scientists have the advantage of intimate familiarity with their objects of study; no astronomer can be a comet, but every sociologist is a person. Ironically, this familiarity is also the source of much frustration to social scientists because too often we expect everyone else to function as we do. Nowhere is this more evident than in the area of research on public attitudes and opinions. Time and again a researcher has framed a hypothesis linking some set of beliefs or opinions—a linking that seemed obvious—only to have the data offer little or no support. Some examples from a recent survey

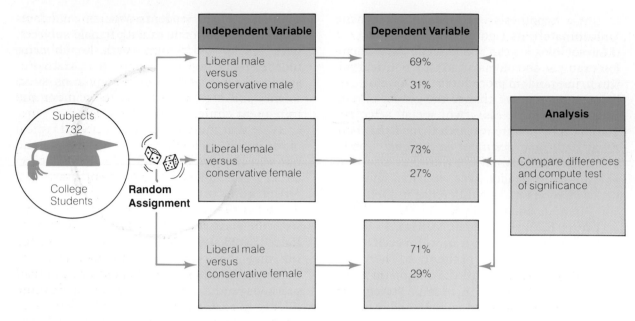

Figure 15-2 ■ **The gender and voting experiment.** By randomly determining which of these three races for governor their subjects were asked to vote on, Ekstrand and Eckert (1981) were able to eliminate other factors that influence elections. Notice that while the liberal won by a huge margin in each race, the sex of the candidate did not influence voting behavior.

based on my own students in introductory sociology will illustrate the point.

Among the many opinion questions I asked the students were these two developed by Robert Wuthnow (1976):

If one works hard enough, one can do anything.

____Agree strongly

____Agree somewhat

____Disagree somewhat

____Disagree strongly

The poor simply aren't willing to work hard.

____Agree strongly

____Agree somewhat

____Disagree somewhat

____Disagree strongly

Wuthnow not only thought people who agreed with one would agree with the other (and vice versa) but he also thought the statements formed part of a very general meaning system, or political ideology, on which people would base a

whole spectrum of their beliefs and opinions. However, among my students these attitudes were hardly correlated at all. It turned out that they weren't correlated in Wuthnow's sample of the population of San Francisco either (Stark and Bainbridge, 1985).

In the same questionnaire I asked students to agree or disagree with the following statement, also developed by Wuthnow.

It is good to live in a fantasy world now and then.

____Agree strongly

____Agree somewhat

____Disagree somewhat

____Disagree strongly

It seemed likely to me that people who agreed with this statement would be more apt to also report they liked to read novels—using reading as a way to enter a fantasy world. Not so. Nor was this item correlated with liking to read spy and detective novels. It wasn't even correlated with liking to read science fiction novels.

These examples help us see a very basic problem for social scientists. We prefer to believe that every human is, underneath it all, a philosopher. As the celebrated anthropologist Clyde Kluckhohn (1962) put it, there is a "philosophy behind the way of life of every individual and of every relatively homogeneous group at any given point in their histories." Kluckhohn identified these philosophies as "world views." Wuthnow (1976) explained it this way:

People adopt relatively comprehensive or transcendent, but nonetheless identifiable, understandings of life which inform their attitudes and actions under a wide variety of conditions.

Wuthnow called these understandings "meaning systems." When such meaning systems are very prominent in a person's thought or in the discussions within a group, they sometimes are called ideologies. An **ideology** is a connected set of beliefs based on a few very general and abstract ideas. An ideology is used to evaluate and respond to proposals, conditions, and events in the world around us. An ideology, then, is essentially a theory about life. If its content is primarily political, an ideology will consist of a few abstract assertions to explain why and how societies ought to be run. Hence, when faced with a specific issue, a person seeks to derive an answer from his or her ideological premises, not simply on a pragmatic issue-by-issue basis.

For years social scientists had not the slightest doubt that only a few people of deficient intellect lacked world views or that most people based their political reactions on an ideology. In fact, in one of my earliest papers I flatly asserted that "All men and all human groups have . . . a world view . . . furnishing them a more or less orderly and comprehensible picture of the world." Today I am equally embarrassed by my use of "men" instead of "humans" and by the claim that we all are amateur philosophers.

I was wrong because I was misled in a way that many social scientists are misled: Most of us and most of those we meet are amateur philosophers, and many have a very noticeable political ideology. However, as social scientists

have begun to do research on attitude and opinion surveys based on general populations, they have been forced to learn that although some people base their beliefs and actions on a world view, and some people base their politics on an abstract ideology, a lot of normal and competent people don't. In fact, it appears that most people don't. Moreover, a substantial part of the population in any society ignores most of the "issues," reserving attention for occasional matters of great urgency or with special personal implications.

We can see, then, why Ekstrand and Eckert found that religious affiliation or church attendance, among other factors, did not influence willingness to support a woman political candidate. It also helps us understand why they had expected to find such an influence. In framing their hypotheses, they wrote: "The tenets of religious fundamentalism seem inconsistent with support for female candidates. Fundamentalism urges a traditional role for women." Clearly, they were assuming that religious students were guided by an ideology—that each was a young Jerry Falwell. If this is so, then people who support prayer in public schools, for example, can be expected to oppose the Equal Rights Amendment, and they probably also will oppose both abortion and pornography. This set of expectations would clearly be consistent with the public position of conservative Protestant groups such as the Moral Majority.

The reasoning is cogent, but the conclusion is wrong. It is not only contrary to how student subjects acted in an experiment but it is also inconsistent with the political behavior of the general public. According to the Gallup Poll, most Americans (77 percent) want to crack down on pornography, yet most (69 percent) do not want to ban abortion. Most Americans support the Equal Rights Amendment (59 percent), and yet most support public school prayers (53 percent). Perhaps even more important, most Americans who hold this pattern of beliefs do not see their views as inconsistent or muddled, because they are not trying to remain in tune with an ideology.

A final example may clarify how willing people are to express seemingly contradictory opinions. In the 1986 General Social Survey, which asked about voting for a woman for president, respondents were also asked to agree or disagree with the following statement: "Most men are better suited emotionally for politics than are most women." One might suppose that people who agreed with that statement would be unlikely to endorse a woman for president. In fact, 67 percent of those who agreed said that they would, nevertheless, vote for a woman for president. The survey also asked people to agree or disagree with an even stronger statement about the proper political role for women: "Women should take care of running their homes and leave running the country up to men." But of those who agreed with this statement, 59 percent still insisted they would support a woman for president. Sociologists might think these attitudes form a tight little logical package, but clearly many Americans do not.

In a classic study of American voters, Philip E. Converse (1964) could classify only about 3 percent as basing their decisions and opinions on an ideology. Another 12 percent he classified as making some use of an underlying political ideology. About half of the voters took a mildly issue-oriented approach to politics, and the rest seemed to ignore all policy, issue, and ideological matters. These results imply that *some* people take a very different approach to politics than do others and that only *some* people participate in the democratic political process at all.

Elite and Mass Opinion

Converse (1964) recounts that a few years ago a young scholar became interested in the rise of the abolitionist movement in the northern United States: how antislavery, abolitionist beliefs spread and shaped political opinion, and how this in turn fostered the new Republican Party and culminated in the election of Lincoln and—soon after the Civil War broke out—in the Emancipation Proclamation. He was aware that the American Anti-Slavery Society never attracted more than 200,000 members, or about 3 percent of the adult population outside the South. So to see how support for the abolition

movement was translated into the nearly 2 million votes needed to elect Lincoln, he needed to trace the informal channels through which abolitionist sentiments had spread beyond the confines of the Anti-Slavery Society. In other words, he wanted to show how opposition to slavery had become an increasingly significant part of informal political discussion and of public opinion during the decade leading to the war. To do this, the young scholar analyzed the contents of many large collections of personal letters saved by various families in Ohio, letters written during the 1850s and 1860s. But his study never was published or even completed—because the young sociologist found no references at all to abolition in any of the letters. This forces the conclusion that mass support for Lincoln and, eventually, for the war was based on many factors, but concern about the plight of blacks in the South was not one of them (although that may have changed once the war really got going). However, a small elite committed to abolition had sufficient influence to see that antislavery policies won. Moreover, the abolitionist ideology seems to have infused this elite with a sense of singlemindedness and dedication that got results.

This example does not reflect an isolated case. Leaders of social movements and political organizations usually display patterns of opinion consistent with a basic outlook or ideology.

Elites and ideology

 Studies of opinions and attitudes not only show that ideologies and world views typically are limited to small elites within a society but they also offer some clues about why this is so. Primary among these is the pressure toward intellectual consistency placed on some people because of the special positions they occupy and the roles they play. We can best see this by watching Herbert McClosky (1964) conduct a classic study of roles and ideologies.

McClosky arranged to distribute very lengthy questionnaires to 3,020 delegates and alternates to the Republican and Democratic presi-

■ Many Americans are deeply committed to particular moral and political issues—as these antiabortion demonstrators illustrate. But many other Americans have little interest in these issues and display no consistency in their responses during survey interviews.

dential nominating conventions in 1956 (the Republicans renominated President Dwight Eisenhower while the Democrats renominated Adlai Stevenson). Then McClosky commissioned the Gallup Poll to distribute this questionnaire to a national sample of 1,500 American adults. The questionnaire included scores of items on political philosophy, positions on current national issues—the whole range of political concerns of the time. McClosky expected the answers to many of the questions to combine into distinct ideological clusters—to be very highly intercorrelated.

When McClosky began to examine his results, striking differences appeared. Among the delegates, the expected correlations held strongly. For the general public, the correlations were weak. When he separated the general public according to their levels of education, McClosky found much stronger correlations among those who had attended college. But even they displayed much lower correlations than either group of delegates.

In a now-classic paper, McClosky explained that delegates to political conventions are selected for active participation in political affairs in their home states; many of them hold state and local political office. Every day they talk about politics, often seeking to convince others to agree with them and to support them. That's part of the politician's role. But it also places their political views under constant inspection by others, many of whom disagree with them or want to change their minds. A continual part of this interactive process involves pointing out inconsistencies: "If you say you favor this, how in the world can you also favor that?" The result of this pressure is that members of political party elites will tend to have political views that are highly internally consistent. Indeed, the easiest way to accomplish consistency is to adopt a political ideology and let it guide your specific issue positions.

Even most college-educated persons do not experience the pressures toward ideological consistency felt by professional politicians, hence their lower correlations. However, because they are well educated they will be more sensitive than the less-educated to more obvious inconsistencies. Moreover, many other occupational roles associated with higher education also place their occupants under pressures to form consistent world views. The clergy are an obvious example. So too are college professors, journalists, and intellectuals generally—explaining why social scientists have had so much trouble recognizing that not everyone shares their taste for detailed world views. Better-educated persons of all occupations are particularly likely to take an active part in politics—just as the Anti-Slavery Society was highly overrecruited from among the educated. As suggested, anyone who gets active in politics will feel constraints toward being more ideological, even when being active means no more than being interested and paying attention.

Issue publics

 The most severe shock to social scientists' conceptions of public opinion occurred when **panel studies** began. In these surveys, the same sample of respondents is interviewed several times. One purpose of panel studies has been to chart the ebbs and tides in the fortunes of candidates as a campaign progresses. In a series of panel studies conducted during presidential campaigns by the Survey Research Center at the University of Michigan, some questions about political attitudes and opinions were repeated several times. As a result, the same person's answers could be compared over time. The shock came when these comparisons exposed the fact that a substantial part of the population has no political opinions. On major issues, some voters display a crystallized opinion that is stable over time. For example, if asked whether the post office should be sold to private business, they have a firm view that is the same on April 15 as on May 1. However, a very substantial proportion of respondents will give a series of utterly inconsistent responses over time. They are not constantly changing their minds. Instead, many people simply offer impulsive answers that have no significance to them and are selected on the spur of the moment. So over time their answers form a meaningless, random pattern of response. Converse (1964) summed it up this way:

Large portions of an electorate do not have meaningful political beliefs, even on issues that have formed the basis for intense political controversy among elites for substantial periods of time.

Thus, Converse found that on any given issue only a subset of the public will have opinions or interest. He coined the term *issue publics* to identify those who take interest in and who participate at least as observers in discussions of an issue. He identified issue publics in the plural, rather than define a single public who has political knowledge and interest, because people are even inconsistent in their lack of beliefs and interests. People will belong to one issue public and not another, depending on how much that issue directly affects them personally. Some take part only in issue publics devoted to retirement and old-age issues. Others attend only to agricultural issues. Still others are interested only in the space program (Taylor, 1983).

Parties and ideologies

One reason many people lack political ideologies is that rarely do people invent their own. Ideologies are intellectual creations, often involving many different authors and interpreters. Moreover, ideologies must be sustained, protected, and promulgated. In effect, only elites can create and preserve ideologies. Thus for an ideology to have general impact on a culture depends on its successful popularization by an elite. Organizations based on a specific political ideology often take the form of a political party. However, many political parties are not committed to a single or sharply defined ideology. Where parties are less ideological the public will be less ideological, but where many highly ideological parties compete for support, a larger proportion of the public will be ideological too.

Compared with Europe, successful American political parties are not very ideological. Canada's leading parties sustain more clearly defined ideologies than do parties in the United States, but they too are far less ideological than are significant parties in much of Europe. A major barrier to the highly fragmented and ideological political spectrum found in much of western Europe is the geographical basis of representation used in both Canada and the United States. In France and West Germany, for example, if a party gets 5 percent of the vote nationwide, it automatically is assigned 5 percent of the seats in the parliament. In Canada and the United States a party gets seats only by coming in first in a given congressional district or parliamentary riding. In principle, a party could get 49 percent of the votes across Canada or the United States and get no representation because in every district some other party got 51 percent of the vote. Thus there is no political future in building a highly ideological party aimed at appealing to a narrow interest group within an electorate—which has sealed the fate of highly ideological parties. Instead, a party must seek to appeal broadly. As a result, successful parties are coalitions of many internal issue publics. This feature encourages parties to make a lot of internal compromises to satisfy their disparate membership. Such parties often will try to appeal to many of the same interest publics. The result is parties that tend toward the middle of the political spectrum, and therefore they tend to resemble one another. Voters always have a choice, but their choices are always limited.

Conclusion

This chapter began with an examination of the problem of public goods, how individuals must surrender some of their freedom in order to sustain organized social life. The experiment that simulated the tragedy of the commons further illustrated this necessity. In the end, social life requires that the individual be subject to coercion by the group. The state arises as specialists appear in societies whose task is to monopolize and use the means of coercion. Unfortunately, those who control the state are apt to abuse their power and exploit the rest of the society.

Thus, *the* political question always is, How to have a state and keep it tame—how to keep it from being repressive and exploitative? We then saw how the slow diffusion of power in England offered an answer to this question. If power can be dispersed among a number of elites with conflicting self-interests, they will keep the state tame by constantly shifting coalitions to limit one another's power. This is the principle of *pluralism*. Some sociologists dispute the belief that democracy really exists in Europe and North America, claiming instead that a small interlocking power elite really decides what is going on. But other sociologists regard this claim as oversimplified.

We then looked at the role of the public in democratic societies. First we saw how the invention of public opinion polling has made it possible to discover what the public thinks about issues. Next we examined how voters in Canada and the United States react to female candidates for high office, finding that they seem entirely willing to accept them. Then we considered more closely the role of ideology in public opinion, finding that it primarily influences political discourse among members of political and occupational elites. Finally, we saw that successful political parties in North America tend to seek support from many elites and issue publics and, therefore, tend toward the middle of the political spectrum.

Review Glossary

public or **collective goods** Things necessary for group life that individual members of a society cannot provide for themselves and which require cooperative actions by many members; often synonymous with public goods. (p. 436)

state The organized monopoly on the use of force (or coercion) within a society; synonymous with government. (p. 437)

pluralism, pluralist state A system or a society in which power is dispersed among many competing elites who act to limit one another's power and therefore minimize the repression and exploitation of members. (pp. 443, 444)

elitist state A society ruled by a single elite group; such states repress and exploit nonelite members. (p. 444)

power elite A term C. Wright Mills used to identify an inner circle of military, government, and business leaders he believed control the United States. (p. 446)

ideology A connected set of strongly held beliefs based on a few very abstract ideas, used to guide one's reactions to external events; for example, a political ideology is used to decide how societies ought to be run. (p. 457)

panel studies Public opinion surveys that interview the same respondents several times. (p. 460)

Suggested Readings

Dahl, Robert. 1956. *A Preface to Democratic Theory.* Chicago: University of Chicago Press.

Gallup, George H. 1972. *The Gallup Poll: Public Opinion 1935–1971* (3 vols.). New York: Random House.

Gallup, George H. 1985. *The Gallup Poll: Public Opinion 1972–1984.* New York: Random House.

Nozick, Robert. 1974. *Anarchy, State and Utopia.* New York: Basic Books.

Olsen, Mancur. 1965. *The Logic of Collective Action.* Cambridge, Mass.: Harvard University Press.

The Interplay
Between Education
and Occupation

16

IN SIMPLE SOCIETIES, children don't go off to school in the morning and their parents don't go off to jobs. Yet children still get educated and work gets done. As with the family, religion, and politics, all human societies have educational and economic institutions. The forms often differ, but the basic functions are always performed in an organized way. In hunting and gathering societies, children are educated by their parents and older siblings. Also, by tagging after their fathers and uncles, the boys slowly learn to perform the work expected of adult males, such as fishing. The girls learn their adult tasks from helping their mothers. Yet even in such primitive circumstances, the link between education and occupation is direct and powerful. Until people are sufficiently educated, they cannot fulfill their economic responsibilities.

In modern societies, the link between education and occupation is so obvious and important that we can often guess a person's education from knowing his or her occupation and vice versa. We can be sure that lawyers and doctors spent many years in school and that unskilled laborers probably had minimal educations. Generally, the more education people have, the more they earn and the higher their occupational status. Indeed, if we know people's education and occupation, then we can often deduce many other things about them: how they vote, what kind of TV shows they watch, what kind of neighborhood they live in, their tastes in food, clothing, art, automobiles, magazines, and music, and even what kind of sporting events they attend.

Chapter Preview

Because of the interdependence of education and occupation, this chapter examines the *interplay* between these two social institutions. We shall begin by examining the dramatic shifts in the number and kinds of occupations produced by modernization. In Chapters 9 and 10, we saw that these changes resulted in a great deal of structural mobility. They also prompted major changes in the educational system, and these, in turn, led to more changes in the occupational structure. While the general connection between education and occupation is obvious, many of the links are subtle.

Occupational Prestige

Because our occupations play a central role in our lives, we have very clear and sensitive notions about which jobs are "better" and which are "worse." A long series of studies of **occupational prestige** have demonstrated these distinctions.

Back in 1947, Paul Hatt and Cecil North presented a national sample of American adults with a list of ninety occupational titles (Reiss, 1961). Each respondent was asked to rate the "general standing" of each job as excellent (a rating of 5), good (4), average (3), somewhat below average (2), or poor (1). From these numerical

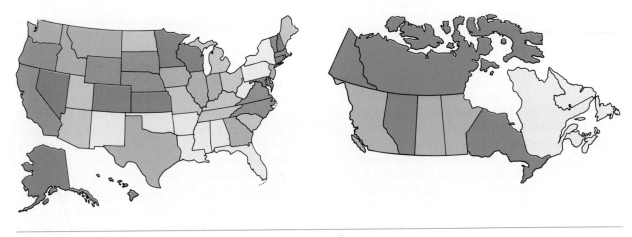

West Virginia	39.1	Oregon	53.8
Florida	45.8	California	53.8
Pennsylvania	46.6	Massachusetts	54.1
Louisiana	46.6	Nebraska	54.5
New Mexico	46.9	Virginia	54.5
Alabama	47.2	Rhode Island	54.7
New York	47.7	Vermont	54.8
Mississippi	48.5	South Dakota	55.3
Oklahoma	48.7	Wyoming	55.5
Arkansas	49.0	North Carolina	55.6

Tennessee	49.5	Connecticut	56.0
Arizona	49.8	Kansas	56.1
Kentucky	50.0	Wisconsin	56.3
Maine	50.3	Hawaii	56.7
Michigan	50.4	Maryland	57.1
Ohio	50.5	New Hampshire	57.3
Missouri	50.6	Minnesota	59.1
South Carolina	51.2	Nevada	59.1
Utah	51.6	Colorado	59.5
North Dakota	51.7	Alaska	60.6

Idaho	51.8
Montana	51.9
Delaware	52.1
New Jersey	52.3
Texas	52.3
Washington	52.3
Illinois	52.6
Iowa	52.9
Georgia	53.1
Indiana	53.2

Newfoundland	39.0	N.W. Territories	55.0
New Brunswick	44.2	Ontario	56.4
Nova Scotia	46.0	Alberta	59.8
Quebec	47.9	Yukon	67.3

Pr. Edward Island	49.5
British Columbia	52.4
Saskatchewan	52.5
Manitoba	54.6

Figure 16-1 ■ **Percent of women over age 15 in the labor force.** At the turn of the century fewer than one out of five women in North America was employed outside the home. Today more than half of Canadian and American women hold regular jobs. But there are marked regional variations in both nations. Canada's Yukon Territory has the highest rate (67.3 percent of women over 15 are employed), and next door in Alaska is the highest rate for American women (60.6 percent). Women in Newfoundland (39 percent) have the lowest rate in Canada, while women in West Virginia (39.1 percent) have the lowest rate in the United States. Overall, southern women are less likely than other American women to be employed, while in Canada eastern women are those least likely to be in the labor force.

weights an average score was computed for each occupation. Because of the computational method used, each occupation received a score between 20 and 100.

Table 16-1 shows the list of occupations and their scores. U.S. Supreme Court justice heads the list, followed by physician, nuclear physicist, scientist, government scientist, state governor, U.S. cabinet member, and college professor. At the bottom are garbage collector, street sweeper, and shoe shiner. Americans and people in other nations have rated this list of occupations many times, and the results are very stable over time and place. Notice how many of the higher prestige positions require a college education or even postgraduate study.

In 1962 the Hatt and North study was repeated. The results were identical—the correlation was .99 (Hodge, Siegal, and Rossi, 1964). In a follow-up study these same researchers measured the occupational prestige of an expanded list of occupations, 200 in all. This study prompted John Porter to seek funding for a replication in Canada, as mentioned in Chapter 10.

Having secured the needed funding and recruited Peter C. Pineo as his collaborator, Porter adapted the list of occupations to suit Canadian respondents. Most of the occupational titles needed no adjustment (biologist, airline pilot, or musician). A few others needed minor editing: "state governor" was changed to "provincial premier" and "member of the United States House of Representatives" to "member of the Canadian House of Commons." In the end, Pineo and Porter (1967) used 174 occupational titles common to the two nations. They added several more to assess regional variations within Canada ("whistle punk" and "cod fisherman" were two of these). Finally, they added two nonexistent occupations to see if people would respond "don't know" or just go ahead and rank them: "biologer" and "archaeopotrist." At this point Pineo and Porter had the list translated into French, using elaborate procedures to attempt to make the lists equivalent.

What were the results? First of all, the correlations between the American and Canadian results were a resounding .98; people on both sides of the border have the same ideas about

what constitutes a good or a bad job. Second, expected differences between French- and English-speaking Canadians did not show up. "In spite of the stereotype of French Canadians as placing greater value on artistic pursuits than on others," they did not rank artistic occupations higher than did English-speaking respondents. Finally, substantial numbers did respond "don't know" rather than rank "biologer" or "archaeopotrist." The majority, however, assigned them above-average ranks, probably because both made-up names clearly suggest scientific professions and are easily associated with biologist and archaeologist. One must wonder if made-up names sounding like manual-labor jobs would have done so well ("deltahumper" or "snoodkelper," for example).

Not only do Americans and Canadians agree about occupational prestige but people all over the world also appear to do so. Similar results have been reported for Germany, Great Britain, Japan, New Zealand, the Soviet Union, Ghana, Guam, India, Indonesia, the Ivory Coast, and the Philippines (Hodge, Siegal, and Rossi, 1964; Hodge, Treiman, and Rossi, 1966).

Because of these similarities, sociologists suspect that people of all nations are familiar with the occupations found in industrial societies and the relative importance of these occupations.

Further research has determined why people rate various occupations high or low. Peter Blau and Otis Dudley Duncan (1967) found that if they took the average education of persons in a particular occupation and combined that with the average income of those persons, they could accurately predict the occupational prestige score that people would give that occupation. In other words, the more training an occupation requires and the more pay it offers, the greater its public prestige. This suggests that people rate a job by its importance. They seem to assume that no one will put in many years to prepare for a job that is unimportant and that society will not pay high salaries to get people to do unimportant work.

That prestige ratings reflect education and training indicates that the process of obtaining a particular occupational status begins when we are young. How much and what kind of edu-

Table 16-1 ■ Occupational prestige scores.

Score	Occupation	Score	Occupation
94	U.S. Supreme Court justice	72	Policeman
93	Physician	71	AVERAGE
92	Nuclear physicist	71	Reporter on a daily newspaper
92	Scientist	70	Bookkeeper
91	Government scientist	70	Radio announcer
91	State governor	69	Insurance agent
90	Cabinet member	69	Tenant farmer who owns livestock and machinery and manages the farm
90	College professor	67	Local labor union official
90	Member, U.S. Congress	67	Manager of a small store in a city
89	Chemist	66	Mail carrier
89	U.S. Foreign Service diplomat	66	Railroad conductor
89	Lawyer	66	Traveling salesman for a wholesale concern
88	Architect	65	Plumber
88	County judge	63	Barber
88	Dentist	63	Machine operator in a factory
87	Mayor of a large city	63	Owner-operator of a lunch stand
87	Board member of a large corporation	63	Playground director
87	Minister	62	U.S. Army corporal
87	Psychologist	62	Garage mechanic
86	Airline pilot	59	Truck driver
86	Civil engineer	58	Fisherman who owns his own boat
86	State government department head	56	Clerk in a store
86	Priest	56	Milk route man
85	Banker	56	Streetcar motorman
85	Biologist	55	Lumberjack
83	Sociologist	55	Restaurant cook
82	U.S. Army captain	54	Nightclub singer
81	Accountant for a large business	51	Filling station attendant
81	Public school teacher	50	Coal miner
80	Building contractor	50	Dock worker
80	Owner of a factory that employs about 100 people	50	Night watchman
78	Artist whose paintings are exhibited in galleries	50	Railroad section head
78	Novelist	49	Restaurant waiter
78	Economist	49	Taxi driver
78	Symphony orchestra musician	48	Bartender
77	International labor union official	48	Farmhand
76	County agricultural agent	48	Janitor
76	Electrician	45	Clothes presser in a laundry
76	Railroad engineer	44	Soda fountain clerk
75	Owner-operator of a printing shop	42	Sharecropper who owns no livestock or equipment and does not manage farm
75	Trained machinist	39	Garbage collector
74	Farm owner and operator	36	Street sweeper
74	Undertaker	34	Shoe shiner
74	City welfare worker		
73	Newspaper columnist		

Source: Hodge, Siegal, and Rossi (1964).

cation we receive is the primary factor determining our occupational opportunities. This touches on the matter of differential socialization discussed in Chapter 6. There we saw that much of socialization is geared to the specific roles a person is expected to play. One of the most important roles is the child's future occupation. Thus, from an early age, children tend to receive socialization appropriate to certain occupations. Children who display little academic aptitude tend to be placed in educational tracks that end with high school and lead to manual occupations. More academically talented children are tracked into college preparatory courses and groomed for technical and professional occupations. Education and occupation are thus intimately associated, and the interplay between them begins early in life.

The Transformation of Work

Peter F. Drucker (1969) examined how changes in work dramatically increased productivity to make modern standards of living possible. He pointed out that such achievements are not the result of harder work. Surely, modern workers do not work harder than their grandparents and probably they do not work as hard. They get better results from their work because, as Drucker put it, "they work smarter."

Technological innovations have made it possible to work smarter. In times past, ten laborers may have worked a week to dig a hole for the foundation for a new house. Today, one operator with an earth mover digs the same hole in a few hours. This operator is obviously not working harder than those who dug with shovels. Having a machine and the technical knowledge to use it, one modern worker possesses the strength of many manual laborers.

However, more than machines let us work smarter. Applying any knowledge to work produces smarter work. Consider the accomplishments of Frederick W. Taylor, who originated time and motion studies of work. Taylor applied scientific principles to increase the efficiency of even very unskilled tasks.

One of Taylor's most famous experiments, conducted in 1899, involved teaching a group of unskilled laborers to shovel sand efficiently. He selected a man named Schmidt and began to work on increasing the rate at which Schmidt could shovel sand. The first thing Taylor did was to experiment with shovels of different sizes. He argued that the shovel should not be too big, or else workers would tire rapidly; then the amount of rest time they would need would offset the extra amounts they shoveled while they worked. On the other hand, if the shovel was too small, the work would be inefficient. Through trial and error, Taylor selected the right-sized shovel for Schmidt. Taylor then experimented with Schmidt to find the best technique for using it—the goal was to find the technique maximizing the sand shoveled and minimizing the energy expended. Finally, Taylor determined the most efficient intervals for rest periods. He found that it was better for men to rest frequently for short periods than to rest occasionally for long periods.

Soon Schmidt was able to shovel more sand per shift than the combined amount shoveled by the two strongest men not prepared by Taylor. As a result of his increased production, Schmidt earned more than twice as much as the other workers. Then the whole shoveling team was on the new method, and each laborer earned a much higher salary than before. Not only did they shovel much more sand but they were also much less tired at the end of the day. All of this resulted not from using machinery but from what came to be known as **scientific management**—the application of scientific techniques to improve work efficiency.

Although today a host of experts is still carrying on Taylor's approach to the study of work, his attempts to revolutionize manual labor were short lived. Unskilled manual work has been taken over almost entirely by machines. As machines have replaced people in the most repetitive, dirty, and sweaty jobs, people have turned more and more to "knowledge" work—including using knowledge to design, maintain, and operate these machines.

Consequently, the *kind* of work people are most likely to perform in industrial nations has changed remarkably. In 1900, fewer than 20 per-

■ These farmers were already working smarter back in the 1890s. Using horse-drawn wagons and a newly invented shucking machine, this crew picked and piled 10,000 bushels of corn. Nevertheless, today one farmer driving a modern harvester could outwork several crews this size.

cent of North Americans had white-collar jobs; most people did manual labor on farms and in factories. Today there are more white-collar than blue-collar workers, and fewer jobs involving manual labor are available each year.

Whereas manual workers manipulate "things" for a living, white-collar workers manipulate information. In Drucker's judgment, we are changing from a primarily industrial economy to a "knowledge" economy. In fact, the most rapidly expanding job categories over the past century have been at the top—professional, technical, and managerial occupations. Today, one out of four working Americans holds a job of this type. We are working smarter all the time, and this has changed *who* is working and *why* they work.

■

The Transformation of the Labor Force

In highly industrialized economies, not only has what people do for a living changed but the proportion of people who are employed also has dramatically altered. In 1870, about 40 percent of North Americans over the age of 16 were in the **labor force.** In 1980, 64 percent were in the labor force. This expansion of the proportion of Americans and Canadians in the labor force occurred despite the fact that much smaller proportions of both young people and old people are working today. Today most North Americans finish high school or college before entering the labor force, and most people must retire at age 70 (most retire before then). In 1870, few went to high school or college, and therefore most started work young; people rarely retired so long as they could continue to work. How did an enormous expansion of the work force occur despite these changes? Women joined the labor force.

Women in the labor force

In 1900 few women in North America or anywhere else were employed outside the home. Today women make up a large part of the labor force—42 percent in the United States and 40.6 percent in Canada. This increase of women in the labor force is likely to continue until as many women as men are working.

Why have so many women gone to work? There are probably many reasons. As we saw in

■ Spring housecleaning at the turn of the century included hanging all of the bedding out to air. This housewife in Seattle is pumping a pail of water for scrubbing. If she wants it to be hot, she will have to heat it on her kitchen range. On laundry day she will have to carry many pails of water into the house and heat them. After scrubbing the laundry by hand, she will carry it out to hang on the lines to dry. It will take her most of the next day to do the ironing.

Chapter 12, the rapid expansion of female labor force participation first occurred on the East Coast, where a highly unfavorable sex ratio forced many women to support themselves. This factor, in turn, attracted industries able to use this newly available work force.

A second reason women went to work is reduced fertility. Freedom from long years of pregnancy and child rearing has given women more opportunity to pursue a career. A third reason is increased freedom from housework. Women in 1900 made their own soap, spent Monday washing clothes, and needed most of Tuesday to iron them. The modern home has a washer and drier and commercial detergents, and clothes need little or no ironing. Reduced demands in the home have enabled women to take outside jobs.

However, another key reason for the massive entry of women into the labor force has been a change in the kinds of work available.

The shift to knowledge work has lured many women out of the home. Modernization has eliminated muscle power as a major requirement for jobs and a major source of energy; many jobs today are entirely "mental." In Chapter 19 we shall examine how technology revolutionized farming. Here we need only note that farming today requires a great deal of sophistication but only a modest amount of strength. In fact, few jobs today require more strength than the average woman possesses.

The impact of modernization on female participation in the labor force is most easily seen in the international comparisons like those in Figure 16-2. In less industrialized nations such as Spain, Ireland, Yugoslavia, and Greece, fewer than 25 percent of the women are employed outside the home. In the more industrialized nations, female participation in the labor force is much higher. The fact that women marry younger (see Chapter 13) and have more children (see Chapter 18) in the less industrialized nations also influences their remaining at home.

A final reason women work is obvious: for money. The old cliché "Two can live as cheaply as one" was probably never true. But as we saw in Special Topic 2, it surely is true that two can live better when they both have jobs. Today, in most North American upper-income families, both adults are employed. In fact, the average two-wage family has an income about 40 percent higher than the average family in which only the husband works. Of families with incomes in the top 20 percent, only one in four depends on just one salary.

However, the rapid entry of women into the labor force has placed an even greater premium on education for getting and holding jobs. With millions of talented and well-educated women in the labor force, it is increasingly difficult for less-educated people to find employment. This has especially affected minority groups with relatively high rates of dropping out of school.

Unemployment

The term **unemployed** is applied not to everyone who is not employed but only to those of legal working age who are without jobs and seeking work. There are several ironies about unemployment that news reports often overlook. Unemployment sometimes rises when jobs are more plentiful and declines when jobs are more scarce. This is because people frequently decide to look for work when they believe they are more likely to find a job.

When many jobs are available, people are drawn into the labor force. Rapid increases in the number seeking jobs but who have not yet found them cause the unemployment rate to rise. Conversely, when jobs are thought to be scarce, many people cease looking and thus are not counted in the unemployment rate. Some of this volatility in the supply of persons seeking work is due to married women and young people who are still living at home; both groups tend not to look for work when jobs are hard to get.

An important component of unemployment bears little connection to the health of the econ-

Spain	18.1	Finland	41.9
Ireland	21.3	Sweden	43.0
Yugoslavia	22.9	Romania	45.1
Greece	23.4	Poland	45.4
Italy	26.6	Czechoslovakia	46.7
Netherlands	26.9	Denmark	47.8

Austria	32.2
Switzerland	34.4
France	34.5
West Germany	34.6
Portugal	35.9
Hungary	39.9
Norway	40.9

Figure 16-2 ■ **Percent of women in the labor force.** The immense shift in the proportion of American and Canadian women employed outside the home is mirrored in patterns for European nations. In the less industrialized nations with higher fertility rates, such as Spain and Ireland, female participation in the labor force is about as low as it was in North America eighty years ago. In the more industrialized nations, such as Denmark, the rate approaches that of North American women today. *Note*: No data are available for Albania, Belgium, Bulgaria, East Germany, the United Kingdom, and the USSR.

omy—several percent of the population are always seeking their first job or in the process of switching jobs. If people spend several weeks or more to get a first job, or find a new one, then they will contribute to the unemployment rate. In addition, some of the unemployed are people who routinely cease working so that they can collect unemployment benefits. That is, some workers take periods of unemployment as planned vacations.

These kinds of unemployment do not cause much social concern, because the time without a job is brief and often voluntary. It is the long-term, chronic unemployment of many North Americans that causes concern, because it results in poverty. Moreover, this unemployment is concentrated in certain areas, such as the Appalachia region of the United States or the Atlantic provinces of Canada, and in certain segments of the population, especially minority groups. For example, unemployment afflicts a higher proportion of blacks than whites, and urban black teenagers in the United States often have shockingly high rates of unemployment—sometimes as high as 40 percent.

Why are rates of unemployment higher among blacks? Undoubtedly, discrimination plays a role, especially in skilled manual occupations (Lieberson, 1980). But a major cause is the dwindling supply of unskilled labor jobs. This is particularly evident in teenage unemployment, for only teenagers who are high school dropouts can be counted as unemployed—people enrolled in school are not counted as unemployed no matter how hard they seek work. Unfortunately, school dropouts are not qualified for most available jobs.

In Chapter 11 we examined the remarkable increases in black education over the past several decades. Blacks today are about as likely as whites to enter college. But they remain more likely than whites to drop out of high school.

Today most young Canadians and Americans graduate from high school, and only a minority in each nation has fewer than nine years of schooling. Even forty years ago this would have been regarded as a spectacular achievement. But changes in the nature of work make it likely that the million or so Americans and Canadians who drop out each year before

■ These children pledging allegiance to the flag in Hampton, Virginia, around 1890 were among the minority of black children in the South enrolled in school at that time.

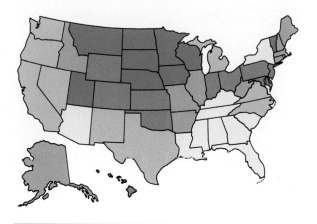

Louisiana	57.2	Indiana	78.3
Mississippi	63.7	Colorado	79.2
Tennessee	65.1	Oklahoma	79.6
Florida	65.5	Pennsylvania	79.7
Georgia	65.9	Maryland	81.4
South Carolina	66.2	Wyoming	81.7
New York	66.7	Hawaii	82.2
Alabama	67.4	Ohio	82.2
Arizona	68.4	Kansas	82.5
Kentucky	68.4	New Jersey	82.7

North Carolina	69.3	Montana	83.1
Texas	69.4	Wisconsin	84.0
New Mexico	71.4	Nebraska	84.1
Oregon	73.0	Utah	84.5
Michigan	73.4	South Dakota	85.0
Nevada	74.6	Vermont	85.0
California	75.1	Iowa	88.0
Rhode Island	75.2	Delaware	88.9
Washington	75.5	Minnesota	90.7
Virginia	75.7	North Dakota	94.8

Arkansas	76.2
Missouri	76.2
New Hampshire	76.5
Maine	76.6
Illinois	77.1
West Virginia	77.4
Massachusetts	77.5
Alaska	77.8
Idaho	77.9
Connecticut	77.9

completing high school will have trouble finding and keeping jobs in the years ahead (see Figure 16-3). There simply are fewer jobs for people lacking education. Hence, although in the past new immigrants could get started in North America by doing unskilled labor, there is little opportunity to do so today; in fact, modern immigrants tend to be well educated. Any group that has difficulty keeping its teenagers in school carries a special burden.

The Transformation of Education

Clearly, no society can shift from an economy based on manual labor to one based on knowledge unless its people are educated—illiterates cannot process information. The vast transformation of work in industrial societies was based, in part, on vast changes in educational systems and practices.

Even a century ago, nowhere in the world did most people get a chance to go to school. Schooling was reserved for an elite few. However, the Industrial Revolution not only made mass production possible but also led to policies of mass education. And perhaps nowhere did the notion that *all* children should go to school catch on faster than in the United States. Nevertheless, not until well into this century did most people attend high school. In 1920, 42.9 percent of all Americans aged 16 or 17 were enrolled in school. That is, fewer than half of those of high school age were still students.

Figure 16-3 ■ **Percent of 18-year-old age cohort who completed high school in 1983.** The dark area of the upper Midwest reveals where high school graduation rates are the highest. In 1983, nearly all 18-year-olds in North Dakota earned a high school diploma. Next highest were young people in Minnesota, where slightly more than 90 percent graduated. The historic educational deficiencies of the South still show up strongly today. In Louisiana just over half of the 18-year-olds graduated, and only about two-thirds finished high school in most other southern states.

Table 16-2 ■ High school enrollment in selected U.S. cities, 1920.

City	Percent Age 16–17 in School in 1920	City	Percent Age 16–17 in School in 1920
Salt Lake City	63.9%	Houston	40.2%
Spokane	61.4%	St. Paul	40.1%
San Jose	59.9%	Nashville	40.1%
San Diego	56.7%	Charlotte	39.7%
Portland (Oregon)	56.1%	Memphis	39.4%
Portland (Maine)	55.9%	Cincinnati	39.3%
Sioux Falls	55.5%	Albany	39.1%
Butte	55.5%	Atlanta	37.4%
Seattle	55.2%	Charleston	37.4%
Oakland (California)	55.0%	Cleveland	37.3%
Los Angeles	54.0%	Pittsburgh	36.8%
Des Moines	54.0%	San Antonio	36.1%
Wichita	53.7%	Wheeling	36.0%
Phoenix	53.1%	Savannah	35.7%
Tulsa	52.6%	Richmond	35.4%
Denver	51.1%	New Haven	33.7%
Columbus	51.0%	Indianapolis	32.9%
Minneapolis	50.9%	Kansas City (Kansas)	32.8%
Milwaukee	50.8%	Detroit	31.9%
San Francisco	50.7%	Providence	31.8%
Oklahoma City	49.5%	Buffalo	30.9%
Little Rock	47.7%	Louisville	30.5%
Dallas	46.2%	New Orleans	30.3%
Kansas City (Missouri)	44.9%	Philadelphia	30.1%
Washington, D.C.	44.8%	Wilmington	29.6%
Omaha	44.1%	Chicago	29.1%
Boston	43.2%	St. Louis	28.3%
Birmingham	43.1%	New York City	27.0%
Miami	42.1%	Baltimore	25.8%
Syracuse	41.7%	Newark	25.1%

Source: Prepared by the author from *Abstract of the Fourteenth Census of the United States, 1920.*

Females (45.5 percent) were more likely than males (40.3 percent) to stay in school, and regional variations also were marked. More than half of teenagers in the Mountain (57 percent) and Pacific regions (55.4 percent) were still in school. The Middle Atlantic states were lowest (32.3 percent), closely followed by New England (39.0 percent).

Table 16-2 lets us compare cities on this same measure. In Salt Lake City in 1920, nearly two-thirds of people 16 or 17 were still enrolled in school. And western cities dominate the top of the list. Although southern cities tend to have low rates of enrollment, much the lowest are the industrial cities of the East. Why? Two major factors are involved. Cities such as New York, Newark, Baltimore, St. Louis, and Chicago had low high school completion rates seventy years ago because they had very large foreign-born populations. Foreign-born teenagers were only about half as likely (23.5 percent) as native-born whites (44.7 percent) to stay in school. The sec-

Portugal	30.0	Denmark	81.5
Hungary	39.0	Netherlands	81.5
Albania	60.0	Norway	82.5
Italy	66.0	East Germany	84.0
Austria	67.5	Finland	84.5
Spain	67.5	Belgium	86.0
Greece	68.5	Sweden	86.5
		West Germany	91.5

Bulgaria	69.0
Czechoslovakia	69.0
Switzerland	69.5
United Kingdom	77.0
Yugoslavia	78.0
France	78.5
Ireland	79.5
USSR	79.5

Figure 16-4 ■ **Percent of appropriate age group enrolled in secondary schools.** Although Europe is highly affluent and industrialized compared with most of the rest of the world, there is considerable variation among European nations in these respects. These variations also are reflected in educational patterns, with lower rates of secondary school enrollment in the less affluent and industrialized nations. Fewer than half of Portuguese and Hungarian young people attend secondary schools, while in the industrialized northwest of Europe, more than 80 percent do so. Highly educated populations not only reflect the opportunities provided by affluence but also are a significant resource for producing wealth: Educated people can perform work that uneducated people cannot.

ond factor is southern poverty. There were virtually no foreign-born teenagers in the South in 1920. There were, however, an immense number of poor families, many of them black.

It was not until after World War II that the majority of Americans began to finish high school—the Class of 1948 included 52.9 percent of its age group. The Class of 1984 included 73.9 percent of its age group.

Figure 16-4 shows secondary school enrollment statistics for most nations of Europe. Secondary schools are the equivalent of what North Americans usually call high school. In the most industrialized nations, such as West Germany and Sweden, nearly every person of high school age is in school, as are more than 90 percent in Canada and the United States. (Japan and Korea also have rates above 90 percent.) However, in the less industrialized European nations such as Portugal and Hungary, most teenagers do not enroll in secondary schools. In the rest of the world, secondary school enrollment usually is much lower. For example, in Ethiopia 12 percent go to high school; in Uganda, 5 percent; in Kenya, 19 percent; in India, 26 percent; in Bolivia, 15 percent; in Mexico, 64 percent. Peru, where 71 percent attend secondary schools, has the highest rate in Latin America.

If industrialization has led to mass education, it has not yet led to the great emphasis on *higher* education that has developed in the United States and Canada. In both nations public universities were founded in the nineteenth century with the aim of making college educations available to more citizens. And in both nations private and denominational institutions also play a substantial role in higher education. But in both nations the real explosion in higher education has occurred over the past forty years. In 1950, 1,863 American colleges and universities enrolled 2.2 million students. By 1980 more than 12 million students were attending 3,231 American colleges and universities. Today the majority of Americans start college and nearly one-third earn degrees. In Canada today more than a quarter of a million students attend nearly 300 colleges and universities and about 20 percent of all persons 18 to 24 are enrolled. These college attendance rates are far higher than those for European nations.

A Decline in Quality?

As increasingly large proportions of young people attend schools at all levels, concern has grown that the quality of education has been declining—that students today learn less in school than students used to. It is difficult to prove or disprove such claims. The evidence suggests that these claims are part truth, part illusion. Let's explore the illusion first.

The average high school graduate of 1900 probably would have scored much higher on academic proficiency tests than the average high school graduate today. Indeed, it would be astounding if that were not the case. Why? Because only good students went to high school then. Since it was unusual to graduate from high school in 1900, the schools could impose very strict standards, and students who lacked the talent or motivation to meet these standards could be flunked out without being condemned to a life of poorly paid jobs. Therefore, those who graduated in 1900 were probably a very select academic group.

As the mission of high school shifted from educating a small, motivated, and talented elite to educating virtually everyone, average achievement had to decline. Thus, it is both unfair and unrealistic to expect the achievements of students in a mass system to equal the achievements of students in an elite system.

It would be much more reasonable to compare the top 6 percent of high school graduates today with the graduates of 1900, although we will never know what that comparison would show. But even today's top graduates might well fall below the levels of achievement high school students attained in 1900. Schools providing mass education must also teach slow students. Because schools in 1900 could gear their curricula to their uniformly gifted students, the average high school graduate in the top 6 percent today is probably not as well educated as the average graduate of 1900. But at the same time, the average American is probably much better educated today than the average American in 1900, when most people quit school before the end of the eighth grade.

We can apply a similar line of reasoning at the college level. Because colleges formerly trained only a tiny intellectual elite, the average graduate in those days would have tested higher than the average graduate today, when colleges train a much higher proportion of young people. When a much larger proportion of people attend college, their average aptitude will be lower, just as the average height of police officers would decline if the minimum height were reduced.

However, not all concerns about a decline in the quality of education can be dismissed as a function of a change in the basis of comparison. Many studies in the United States and elsewhere have suggested declines in student achievement in recent years (Peaker, 1971). But the major focus of interest and anxiety has been the long downward slide in the average scores of American high school seniors on the **Scholastic Aptitude Test (SAT)**. Each year many high school students planning to enter college take the SAT because many of the better colleges and universities give great weight to the exam scores in deciding whom to admit. Throughout the 1950s, the national average of the SAT rose, and those who took the exam in 1963 set an all-time high. But then scores began to drop. Every year the average was lower. By 1981 the combined mathematical and verbal average SAT score was 893 (out of a possible 1,600 points), which was 80 points lower than in 1963 (Powell and Steelman, 1984). In the late 1970s a national commission was convened to determine why the scores were falling. It concluded that part of the decline was due to a change in who took the exam—in earlier periods only better students tended to take the exam. But much of the decline was regarded as reflecting real changes in the educational achievements of Americans. Why had this decline occurred?

Many people blamed the decline on a corresponding decline in the quality of teachers. Thus Samuel Preston (1984) noted that the average SAT scores of education majors had declined even more than had those of students generally. By 1982, education majors averaged 82 points below the national average. Moreover, Preston found that those who enter teaching *and then leave it* have an average SAT score of 42 points higher than the scores of people who remain in teaching. As a result, the average teacher has an SAT score 118 points below that of college graduates who have never taught. The obvious conclusion is that students are getting progressively poorer educations because the quality of their teachers is getting progressively worse.

Preston blamed the decline in teacher quality on a decline in the real incomes of teachers over this same period. He argued that because of a decline in pay, "a disproportionate number of the brightest teachers (who get the best results) left the field and many potentially good teachers avoided the field altogether." But quite apart from the impact of current salary trends, a decline in teacher quality also can be explained by the recent, rapid changes in sex roles. Not so long ago, women had few occupational choices; among these teaching was one of the most attractive. Thus the teaching profession could tap a vast pool of very talented candidates. Today, the most talented women are unlikely to become teachers and, in fact, the proportion of elementary and secondary teachers who are women has fallen rapidly.

However, just as sociologists became convinced that teachers were to blame for the SAT decline, this explanation was challenged by events, for suddenly the test scores began to rise. In 1983 and 1984 they inched upward. Then in 1985, the combined SAT score rose by nine points. Perhaps of even greater note was the fact that Hispanic and black students made the biggest gains. But while the scores rose, there was no indication that teachers had improved in any way. So another explanation was needed. Whatever caused the trend in SAT scores must not only have begun to shift at the start of the decline but must also have reversed its trend coincidental with the rise in SAT scores. Thus a new explanation suggested itself. The SAT scores fell for the very first time in history the year that the *first* of the *baby boomers* took the test—the kids born in 1946 were seniors in 1964 when scores fell. If we allow the baby boom a duration of eighteen years, then we see that scores began to rise again as soon as the last boomers had been tested in 1982. Special Topic 6 suggests some reasons why the baby boomers may have

been less well educated than earlier or later generations. Among these are the strains placed upon the schools by having to deal with so many students.

Do Schools Really Matter?

Concern over the quality of education reflects the assumption that schools play an important role in what students learn. It might seem self-evident that schools are critical to the educational process. However, beginning in the 1960s, many critics, including many prominent social scientists, started to argue that schools had little effect on what people learned or on preparing people for jobs.

Some critics pointed out that a great majority of people in colonial times could read, write, and do arithmetic even though few attended school, even grade school. Others noted that schools seem unable to overcome differences in background—students from privileged homes do well in school, while those from disadvantaged backgrounds do poorly. They concluded that schools simply certify the educational advantages or disadvantages that students bring to school (Jencks et al., 1972).

These views of the ineffectiveness of schools were lent some support by a huge study conducted by James Coleman and his associates (1966). The U.S. Congress commissioned Coleman to assess the nation's schools and determine which aspects of schooling were the most valuable. As he began his research, Coleman expected to find that blacks suffered from attending poor-quality schools, and he hoped to prompt massive federal aid to correct the inequity (in Silberman, 1971).

What he found was startling. First, there was little difference in the quality of schools blacks and whites attended in terms of expenditures per student, age and quality of the buildings, libraries, class size, and teacher training. Second, these aspects of school quality had no detectable impact on student achievement scores. Thus, lavish expenditures during the 1950s and early 1960s to upgrade schools had accomplished nothing in terms of actual education. Whether students went to school in ramshackle buildings or nice ones, attended large classes or small ones, or had fancy labs or makeshift equipment didn't matter. Nor did it matter if their teachers had advanced degrees or just two-year teachers college certificates.

Coleman could only conclude that school was simply a place where students learned in proportion to the educational qualities of their homes, neighborhoods, and peer environment. Still, Coleman's report contained one finding often overlooked in subsequent discussions. How well students from any background did in school was correlated with the scores that their teachers made on a vocabulary test. This suggests a link between declines in student achievement scores and a corresponding decline in the quality of teachers as measured by test scores.

So the questions persist: Do the schools actually accomplish anything? Do kids actually learn in school? For most social scientists, it seemed evident that people do learn in school, for even children from the most privileged homes are usually not taught at home to read, write, or do arithmetic. Most kids must be learning these things in school, if they learn them at all. Yet good evidence of the effectiveness of schools was lacking.

Barbara Heyns: the effects of summer

 How can we see if schools have a real impact on learning? The most obvious way would be to randomly assign some children to attend school and others to stay home and then to compare the results. But that would be both illegal and immoral. Because schooling at the elementary level is universal in the United States and Canada, we can't seek out students who do not go to school and compare their achievements with those who do. Faced with this problem, Barbara Heyns (1978) came up with a brilliant solution.

Kids don't go to school all year. Why not compare the learning that occurs during the school year with that occurring during summer vacation? In this way, summer learning can serve

as a basis for estimating what children might learn if they did not go to school.

Heyns gave verbal achievement tests to 2,978 students enrolled in Atlanta schools. They were tested at the start of the fifth grade, at the end of the fifth grade, at the start of the sixth grade, and again at the end of the sixth grade.

Heyns's results gave strong evidence that school matters but that it matters much more to some kinds of children than to others. On the average, children in Atlanta learned much less during their summer vacation than they did in an equivalent time period during the school year. Their verbal achievement scores rose much more rapidly on a monthly basis over the school year than over the vacation. However, children from higher-income families learned about as much during vacation as during the school year. Children from the most deprived backgrounds actually lost ground during the summer—their scores were not as high in the fall as they had been the spring before vacation began.

What Heyns found means that, rather than merely maintaining differences children bring to school, schools greatly improve the situations of poor children. Differences in the rates of learning between blacks and whites and between higher- and lower-income children were very small while school was in session, but when school was out, the kids from privileged backgrounds sprinted ahead. Schools therefore minimize initial background advantages by enabling the disadvantaged to keep up. However, schools can only accomplish this during the school year. The long summer vacations characteristic of most American schools undo much that is accomplished with underprivileged children during the winter. In the summer, the academic effects of students' backgrounds reassert themselves. Moreover, these summer effects accumulate, so that as children advance through the grades, the children of more advantaged families get further and further ahead of the others.

Surprisingly, Heyns found that attending summer school did not prevent summer learning losses. Atlanta has a massive summer school program (a fourth of the students enroll), and children from disadvantaged backgrounds are especially likely to enroll. However, attendance at summer school had no influence on summer learning. Heyns concluded that this was because the summer school programs were oriented toward recreation rather than the regular curriculum. Students overwhelmingly said they went to summer school because it was fun.

What did the kids from the more advantaged homes do during the summer that caused them to continue to learn? Heyns examined many possibilities, including vacation trips and participation in organized summer activities such as sports or camps. But only one activity had real impact: reading. As Heyns (1978) put it:

The single summer activity that is most strongly and consistently related to summer learning is reading. Whether measured by the number of books read, by the time spent reading, or by the regularity of library usage, reading during the summer systematically increases the vocabulary test scores of children.

Heyns estimated that every four books read over the summer produced an additional right answer on verbal achievement tests.

She also discovered that a major factor affecting reading, independent of a student's background, was the distance from the student's home to the nearest public library. Eighty percent of the students who lived within seven blocks of a library used it regularly. Among children living more than seven blocks from a library, library visits fell rapidly. Thus, in showing that schools matter, Heyns showed that libraries do, too.

Heyns's findings also suggest that schools might be much more effective if the school year were extended. The long summer vacation was instituted back when most kids were needed to help on the farm, and it has persisted long after this need has vanished. Indeed, children in Japan and many other industrial nations attend school throughout the year with short breaks.

Heyns's study was a major breakthrough. First, it showed how to study school effects. Second, it demonstrated conclusively that school does affect how well educated students become. Moreover, Heyns's study prompted others to try other ways to assess the impact of schooling.

■ Recent research suggests that these girls will make as much educational progress during the summer vacation as they would during a similar period of attending school—because they are reading books while school is out. Children who don't read fall behind during the summer.

Karl Alexander, Gary Natriello, and Aaron Pallas (1985) set out to extend Heyns's analysis to high school students by comparing the cognitive development of those who remained in school with those who dropped out. They tested a sample of 30,000 sophomores from 1,000 high schools and retested them two years later, when those who had remained in school were in the last months of their senior year. Then the sociologists computed the increase (or decline) in cognitive test performance for all respondents over the two-year period. They found that dropouts had a much smaller increase than did those

■ A couple poses with their son after taking part in graduation exercises at Harvard University. Clearly, this man and woman will benefit from holding their degrees from such a high-prestige school, but, as John Meyer has pointed out, the more important thing is not what school they graduated from but that they have a college degree from somewhere.

who remained in school. Moreover, consistent with Heyns's findings, dropping out had the most severe negative effects on students from the most disadvantaged backgrounds.

Heyneman and Loxley: school effects worldwide

 Because most sociological research takes place in a few of the most industrialized nations, many findings are based on a quite limited range of variation. Studies of school effects conducted in the United States, Canada, Great Britain, or France are restricted to a narrow range of variation in school facilities and quality. There probably isn't a public school in any of these nations without a blackboard, a filmstrip projector, a tape recorder,

or even a TV set. In addition, although none of these nations is without poverty, even the poor are affluent compared with most people in many other nations. Hence, Canadian, American, or British children may not be so dependent on schools for their learning as are children in less developed nations—which is consistent with the finding within the United States that schools do the most for the kids from the more disadvantaged homes.

This line of reasoning recently led Stephen P. Heyneman and William A. Loxley (1983), sociologists on the staff of the World Bank, to analyze data on school effects by using a series of studies of school effects in twenty-nine nations. In all, over 300 different researchers were involved, working in more than a dozen languages, with a total sample of more than 10,000 schools, 50,000 teachers, and 260,000 students.

Denmark	16.3	West Germany	32.3
Belgium	18.3	Portugal	33.3
Norway	19.0	Czechoslovakia	33.3
Sweden	19.5	Spain	34.1
Finland	20.0	Albania	34.5
Italy	21.4	Ireland	34.7

France	22.9
East Germany	23.3
Netherlands	24.1
Austria	24.3
United Kingdom	26.8
Greece	30.7

Figure 16-5 ■ **Average number of students per teacher in primary classes.** A good measure of school quality and educational resources is the size of classes—the ratio of students to teachers. This ratio is especially significant for students in the early grades. Here we see the huge contrasts in average class size across the nations of Europe. In Ireland, Albania, and Spain teachers have more than twice the number of students as does the average elementary school teacher in Denmark. *Note*: No data are available for Bulgaria, Hungary, Poland, Romania, Switzerland, the USSR, and Yugoslavia.

What did they find? First, kids in the wealthier, more industrialized nations learn more during the same number of school years. In part this difference in learning may be because of better schools. It probably also reflects the whole "package" of benefits that comes with a much higher standard of living.

Second, the poorer the nation, the less that student backgrounds influence their school performances, probably because education is a scarce resource in these nations. As Heyneman and Loxley pointed out: "Scarcity creates competition for school places from the onset of grade 1, and at a level of intensity unknown in wealthy countries until college or, in the case of the United States, until graduate school. This scarcity is well understood within both rich and poor families." Thus family background tends to be cancelled out in the process of gaining a place in school—only the better students get in or remain.

Third, the effects of school and teacher quality are comparatively greater in the poorer nations. As suspected, where there is much greater range in facilities and teacher training, much bigger impacts on students are observed. Figure 16-5 hints at some international educational differences. The average teacher-to-student ratio reveals much about the affluence of school systems and the amount of individual attention available to each child. Here we see that in Denmark's primary schools there is one teacher for every 16.3 students. But in Spain, Albania, and Ireland, there are more than 34 students for each primary teacher.

Finally, the poorer the nation, the greater the economic returns for getting an education. While there is a positive correlation between education and income in all nations, the correlations are higher in the poorer countries, where it remains relatively unusual to obtain many years of schooling.

■

Does Education Pay?

We have just noted the economic benefits of education, especially to people in less developed nations. Moreover, in Chapter 10 we saw

■ Like most children, this boy probably wonders from time to time whether homework is worth it. Getting a lot of education won't guarantee him a good job, but lack of education would exclude him from most of the better-paid occupations.

the immense role education plays in the occupational achievement of Canadians and Americans. And a look at Table 16-1 will reveal the obvious connection between education and occupation: It is impossible to enter most of the highest-prestige occupations without attending college and often graduate school as well. In this sense, education may not guarantee success, but it tends to be necessary for it. Without enough education, many opportunities simply are unavailable.

Nevertheless, a number of people recently have begun to question whether education really pays off. Caroline Bird (1975) has argued that most people would come out ahead if they skipped college, invested the money saved thereby, and went right to work after high school. Why is there doubt about the economic value of education?

One reason is the rapid rise in the relative earnings of skilled blue-collar workers, such as plumbers, electricians, long-distance truckers, and tool and die makers. Many college graduates end up in lower-paying occupations than

these, and college is of no advantage for entry into these skilled trades. In fact, going to college would be a waste of earning years for people planning to enter these occupations. But perhaps the primary reason why people question the economic importance of education is simply that in advanced industrial nations a college degree is not worth as much as it used to be.

When relatively few people earned college degrees, they possessed a scarce occupational qualification. Now many people can earn degrees, and therefore a degree is not a certain ticket to success. When 5 percent graduate from college, then only 5 out of 100 people can compete for a job requiring a college degree. But when a third earn degrees, 33 people out of 100 compete for those jobs requiring degrees. Hence, the decline in the value of a college education is the result not of colleges ceasing to prepare people for careers but of colleges preparing so many people for careers.

As the level of education has risen in the industrial nations, the relative advantage of completing a given level of education has

Table 16-3 ■ Education and income for married persons age 40 through 65.

Annual Family Income	Less Than High School	High School Graduate	Some College	College Graduate	Graduate School
Less than $10,000	15.1%	4.3%	2.7%	0.0%	0.0%
$10,000 to $20,000	27.7%	13.2%	7.1%	4.7%	3.1%
$20,000 to $35,000	32.7%	37.2%	32.1%	18.8%	9.2%
$35,000 to $50,000	17.0%	24.8%	25.0%	26.5%	29.2%
Over $50,000	7.5%	20.5%	33.1%	50.0%	58.5%
	100.0%	100.0%	100.0%	100.0%	100.0%

Source: Prepared by the author from National Opinion Research Center, General Social Surveys, 1986 and 1987.

declined. If people today want to have the same educational advantage that their parents had, then they must stay in school longer than their parents did.

French sociologist Raymond Boudon (1974) has created elegant mathematical models of this process of educational "deflation." As he pointed out, however, we must realize that such deflation applies to all educational levels, not just the top. That is, not only is a college degree of less value than it used to be but so is an eighth grade education. The child of a school dropout who also drops out of school will have a harder time finding and holding a job than the dropout parent did.

Table 16-3 reveals the immense impact of education on income in the United States today. Here, samples from the 1986 and 1987 General Social Surveys have been merged to supply sufficient cases for a more focused look at the link between education and income. Usually, such a table includes all adults. The trouble with that inclusion is that the group without high school degrees includes a disproportionate share of people over 65 whose incomes have declined substantially because of their retirement. Similarly, the categories of those who have completed college and graduate school include a disproportionate share of young people who have just entered the labor force and whose incomes have yet to catch up with those of skilled blue-collar workers who have been employed and gaining seniority since leaving high school. For

this reason, Table 16-3 has been restricted to persons in the prime earning years, 40 through 65. Moreover, as we saw in Special Topic 2, family income is greatly increased when there are two earners. So the table has been limited to married people.

The results present the true extent to which education determines income. It is almost impossible for people in this age and marital bracket who have completed graduate school to earn less than $35,000 a year. In fact, nearly 60 percent of these families have incomes over $50,000 a year. In contrast, slightly fewer than one-quarter of those who did not complete high school have family incomes above $35,000, and only 7.5 percent receive more than $50,000 a year. While 15.1 percent of those without a high school diploma earn less than $10,000 a year, *not one person* in these samples with a college degree or more has a family income of less than $10,000.

The very tight connection between income and education, on the one hand, and the very rapid rise in the average level of education, on the other, has had unfortunate side effects for several disadvantaged groups, especially blacks and Hispanics. As Randall Collins (1979) has noted, the "inflation" of academic credentials has partly offset the economic value of gains in educational attainment these groups have made. Let's see how that happened.

In 1970, 11.3 percent of whites, 4.4 percent of blacks, and 6.0 percent of Hispanics were college graduates. Over the next fourteen years, blacks and Hispanics increased their levels of education dramatically. So in 1984, 10.4 percent of blacks and 8.2 percent of Americans of Hispanic origin were college graduates. But they didn't catch up much, if at all, because by 1984 19.8 percent of white Americans were college grads. By the time blacks and Hispanics were about as likely as whites were in 1970 to have a college degree, the market value of that degree had declined.

Ironically, Collins pointed out, it is really doubtful that the immense inflation in higher education means that colleges actually impart training vital for performing many of the jobs that now demand that applicants have degrees. Obviously, colleges impart needed skills to engineers, physicians, accountants, and scientists. But it is not at all clear that anything learned in college bears directly on performance in many other jobs for which college graduates are hired but then must be given substantial additional training—most sales positions, for example. Many of the specific job skills that colleges do provide probably could be acquired more rapidly and effectively through on-the-job training.

Collins therefore describes the expansion of higher education in America as the creation of a *"credential society"*—because of what he regards as a misplaced stress on limiting many occupations to those possessing specific occupational credentials or licenses. For example, it is impossible to obtain a college teaching position in the United States nowadays without a master's degree and very difficult to do so without a doctorate. Either requirement would have excluded Albert Einstein. Conversely, even the most famous faculty members of the best universities are prohibited from teaching in high schools unless they go back to college to earn a teaching certificate.

Why so much stress on credentials? Collins noted the way in which credentials serve as a sort of currency through which occupational positions are allocated. As the systems of educational credentials expanded, Collins argued:

the value of any particular kind and level of education came to depend less on any spe-

cific content that might have been learned in it, and more and more upon the sheer fact of having attained a given level and acquired the formal credential that allowed one to enter the next level [or ultimately to pass the requirements for entering a monopolized position].

Put another way, the point of a teaching credential is not so much to provide classroom skills as to control entry to the teaching profession. By getting state legislatures to make it illegal to teach without an authorized teaching credential, education departments of universities seized control of the replaceability of teachers. Recall from Chapter 9 that power can be used to make positions much less replaceable than they really are, thus inflating their status and rewards. In similar fashion, credentials such as barber, beautician, and real estate licenses can be used to limit the numbers of people in a given occupation.

A considerable debate has raged among sociologists about the extent to which schools are used to educate as opposed to being used to *allocate status*. Many Marxist sociologists claim that the primary function of schools in American society is to re-create the class structure in each generation by designating people as successes or failures on the basis of racial, cultural, or class characteristics and hence assigning each individual to a status level (Illich, 1970; Bowles and Gintis, 1976). Proponents of these **allocation theories** of education claim that educational requirements and credentials are meant to screen out those lacking the opportunity to attend college or those who rebel against the prevailing rules governing status allocation.

Because there is some justification for suspecting that educational credentials do not simply certify that one has received vital training, allocation theories speak to a significant question: What is the function of education in our society? However, the extremist rhetoric in which allocation theories typically are stated tended to deafen sociologists to this underlying question. Then in the late 1970s a sociologist at Stanford University drew upon allocation ideas to formulate a more general theory of the functions of education as a social institution.

Meyer's Theory of Educational Functions

John W. Meyer (1977) began his theory by accepting the traditional view of educational socialization—that, through schooling, individuals increase their knowledge and competence, which in turn increases their abilities to perform adult roles. But he then added the insight that *levels of education, in and of themselves, are social statuses.* That is, aside from any other status individuals hold, they have a distinct status based on their amount of formal education: high school graduate, college graduate, Ph.D., and the like. Schools, then, can be seen as institutions empowered, or chartered, by society to grant statuses to individuals.

Moreover, a major aspect of schools as socializing agents is to encourage individuals "to adopt personal and social qualities appropriate to the positions [or statuses] to which their schools are chartered to assign them." As with all positions in society, educational statuses come equipped with roles. A major effect of education is that *people learn to play the role appropriate to the status that their school confers on them.*

This proposition allowed Meyer to explain why variations in school quality seem of little or no importance in the attitudes, values, opinions, and behavior of graduates. Research shows that the amount of formal schooling a person completes has a great effect on a wide variety of personal qualities and characteristics: from the way people vote to their religious commitment. If this is a consequence of the content of actual instruction, than people who attended very high quality schools ought to differ from those who attended low-quality schools. However, research has failed to turn up such differences (or they are extremely small). Instead, graduates of elite colleges resemble graduates of obscure schools much more closely than they resemble people who did not graduate from college.

According to Meyer's theory, this finding is to be expected if the real impact of schools is to admit people to a particular educational status. For then, all schools chartered to convey that status ought to have similar socializing effects. Indeed, Meyer pointed out that school quality is seldom of much importance in assessing a person's claim to a given status. Graduates of all North American high schools, for example, have the occupational rights reserved for high school graduates—no one asks if their high school was a good one. By the same token, a college degree satisfies the requirements to claim the status of college graduate, whether the degree was from Harvard or North Dakota State College in Valley City.

Thus, Meyer argued that the most powerful socializing property of schools is the ability to confer statuses that are recognized in society at large, and that people who acquire a given status tend to perform the role attached to it in similar fashion. Indeed, Meyer cited research showing that people adopt personal qualities appropriate to a given educational role upon admission to a school chartered to grant that status: They often begin to do so upon acceptance to such a school, before they have even attended (Benitez, 1973; W. L. Wallace, 1966).

Meyer also argued that socialization into these roles does not stop when people leave school. Instead, *people continue to act out the role attached to their educational statuses throughout their adult lives, regardless of their occupation.* Occupational success often varies over time, as do family relations and even geographic location, but a "college graduate" or "high school dropout" is an unchanging status once school is done. People continue to respond to an individual's educational status, and the individual maintains the role appropriate to that status. Indeed, John Irwin (1970) found that educational statuses even count among inmates in prison, where people with college degrees or postgraduate training are frequently sought out for advice and information.

Meyer was not content to view educational institutions as allocating status only to the degree the occupational system allows. Allocation theorists have argued that educational institutions simply allocate people into positions determined by the occupational system—

for example, medical schools are chartered to produce doctors only insofar as the occupational structure has recognized this occupation and the occupational group (doctors) has granted this power to schools.

Meyer argued instead that *the educational system has the power to create new occupations, even elite occupations, and to control the placement of these occupations in the occupational structure.* This is possible because educational institutions, especially universities, play a leading role in defining new knowledge, developing new techniques and technologies, and giving these techniques legitimate occupational standing.

In other words, many of the most highly paid, highest-status occupations in contemporary society exist because universities invented them, defined their occupational worth, and determined the conditions under which people could enter these occupations. There were no economists until universities established the science of economics and legitimized its claim to special competence. Nor were there sociologists, geneticists, or even football coaches until universities created a special body of knowledge and began training people to use it.

In this way, Meyer undercut the narrow view of allocation theories—that education is a passive servant of the stratification system. Instead, "education helps *create* new classes of knowledge and personnel which then come to be incorporated in society." That is, the expansion of the education system increases the "number of specialized and elite positions in society."

As educational achievement has risen, the occupational structure has rapidly expanded at the top (more professional, managerial, and technical positions) and contracted at the bottom (fewer unskilled labor jobs). Meyer's theory helps explain how industrial nations have increasingly become "knowledge" economies.

Finally, Meyer argued that the rising level of mass education has expanded the proportion of the population regarded as having citizenship responsibilities, capacities, and rights. The larger the proportion of the population who are educated, the harder it is for elites to exclude them from decision making or to ignore their economic demands. Here Meyer parted company with the allocation theorists, who argue that education serves only elite interests. Instead, Meyer noted, the primary emphasis in modern education is on mass education—on providing the maximum number of people with the opportunity to be educated and to gain entry to elite occupations.

Meyer's theory offers a more comprehensive and intelligible view of the way in which educational institutions fit into society. Because schooling is largely confined to childhood and early adulthood, sociologists have tended to view educational institutions as only having early socialization effects, in much the same way that the cultural determinists (see Chapter 6) attempted to attribute adult personality wholly to child-rearing patterns. By recognizing how educational statuses continue to have socializing effects throughout a lifetime, Meyer was able to explain why these effects endure. It is not that what we learn in school lasts forever. Rather we take with us from school an educational status that continues to influence our chances and experiences in life.

■

Conclusion

Education remains crucial to occupational achievement, but as more people get more education, a given level of education becomes less valuable. This is because educational and occupational institutions remain somewhat independent. Although a shift to a knowledge economy can only occur with an increase in the supply of educated people, such an increase does not automatically create more knowledge jobs for them to fill. Nevertheless, as John Meyer pointed out, schools can create new occupations, including new elite occupations. But the number of people aspiring to these occupations can still exceed the supply of positions available. A person may have the training and desire for a given occupation, but that alone does not create a position for that person to fill. On the other hand, as Raymond Boudon has pointed out, aptitude and motivation often suffice to gain an education. Thus, the supply of college-educated people, for example, may increase beyond the positions available in the economy, or at least beyond the level of upper positions.

In the nineteenth century, high school graduates qualified for most teaching jobs. Until the 1930s, a person who attended a teachers college for two years was well qualified to teach. Today, most elementary and high school teaching jobs are reserved for people with master's degrees. The primary reason for this change has been an increase in the proportion of educated people.

We also have seen that, despite research casting doubt on the contribution of schools to the learning process, schooling does matter. The effects of schooling are greatest for students from the most disadvantaged homes and those living in the poorer nations.

Finally, we have seen that the connections between educational institutions and the rest of society are neither simple nor restricted to in-school instructional effects. Education has strong and lasting socialization effects because it creates permanent statuses. Consequently, people tend to perform roles appropriate to their educational status, even when they follow an occupation that is above or below the occupational status usually associated with their level of education. The school dropout millionaire never fully sheds that dropout status and is likely to continue to enact that role in some ways. Similarly, the person with a doctorate who drives a cab, will often be "Doc" to the other drivers. That people with the same amount of formal schooling hold the same educational status helps to explain why variations in school quality have little or no effect on behavior—these people are equal in the way that continues to matter most in their lives.

The educational structure does not simply allocate people among occupational categories. It often creates new occupations and alters the occupational structure. The power of universities to determine the social significance of a body of knowledge is so great that Meyer speculated about what might happen if universities began to offer accredited courses and degrees in astrology: Companies would soon begin to hire staff astrologers (perhaps placing them in the economic forecasting department), and government grants for research in astrology would soon be forthcoming. Professional astrologers have failed to achieve high prestige despite their ability to attract large numbers of clients because they have been unable to convince universities that they possess a body of valid knowledge.

Clearly, then, educational institutions are not passive servants of elites and the occupational structure. Perhaps this is most easily illustrated by a norm among faculty at major research-oriented universities. They never list their occupation as "teacher," even though they teach. Instead, they call themselves chemists, economists, or sociologists—people who pursue a creative, technical profession. In this way, they claim an occupational status in the world beyond the classroom—in the world of adults, not students. Because the modern university does not simply prepare people to perform various professions, but discovers and analyzes the knowledge on which these professions are based, faculty members feel justified in treating their teaching functions as secondary.

■

Review Glossary

occupational prestige The respect people receive on the basis of their job; often refers to a score on a standard system for rating occupations. (p. 464)

scientific management The application of scientific techniques to increase efficiency. (p. 468)

labor force Those persons who are employed or seeking employment. (p. 469)

unemployed Persons of legal working age who are not enrolled in school, who do not have a job, and who are actively looking for one. (p. 471)

Scholastic Aptitude Test (SAT) A standardized test taken by many high school seniors planning to go to college. (p. 477)

allocation theories Argue that the primary function of schools is to allocate status, to place students in the stratification system, rather than to train them. (p. 485)

■

Suggested Readings

Boudon, Raymond. 1974. *Education, Opportunity, and Social Inequality: Changing Prospects in Western Society.* New York: Wiley.

Collins, Randall. 1979. *The Credential Society: An Historical Sociology of Education.* New York: Academic Press.

Heyns, Barbara. 1978. *Summer Learning and the Effects of Schooling.* New York: Academic Press.

Hodge, Robert W., Donald J. Treiman, and Peter H. Rossi. 1966. "A Comparative Study of Occupational Prestige." In *Class, Status, and Power,* edited by Reinhard Bendix and Seymour Martin Lipset. New York: Free Press.

Meyer, John W. 1977. "The Effects of Education as an Institution." *American Journal of Sociology* 83:55–77.

Change

V

Societies constantly change, often in response to inventions in technology. On December 17, 1903, in Kitty Hawk, North Carolina, Orville and Wilbur Wright made the first successful airplane flight. They had worked for several years in their bicycle shop to build their flimsy Dayton Flier. Once they discovered it really would fly, they had to spend the next two years teaching themselves to fly. So it wasn't until 1905 that the public actually discovered that air travel was possible.

Airplanes aroused immense interest and soon lots of people were learning to fly. Here we see one of the first women to take lessons in a Wright brothers' airplane. Identified only as "Miss Todd," she was photographed in 1909 getting ready for takeoff. From the look on her face, it seems certain that she was determined to soar with eagles.

After the outbreak of World War I in 1914, thousands of people became fliers, and in only a decade, Orville Wright had risen from being a bicycle mechanic to being a world-famous pilot—and then to being head of a major company manufacturing fighter planes. (Wilbur died unexpectedly in 1912.)

Airplanes produced many changes in modern life. Perhaps the most important is to have made the world much smaller. Not long ago few people ever traveled to distant places—Edgar Rice Burroughs wrote dozens of Tarzan novels without ever having been in Africa. Today, when millions of tourists cross the Atlantic and Pacific each year, it almost seems as if everyone has been everywhere. At the time this picture was taken, a trip from New York to Los Angeles aboard the fastest and most expensive trains took over five days. From New York to London aboard the most expensive ocean liner took a week.

The last five chapters of this book deal with aspects of social change.

Chapter 17 examines some general models of social change and then assesses sociological explanations of the major recent change—modernization. It addresses questions such as: Why are some nations able to send satellites into space while others have not yet learned how to make metal? Can all nations one day be fully modernized?

Chapter 18 looks at patterns of population growth and decline and traces the links between modernization and population explosions. Are we in danger of producing a population too large for the planet to support?

Chapter 19 explains why modern societies are also urban societies—in which most people live in cities rather than in farming villages or rural areas. Among the questions addressed: Is city life dangerous for our mental health? Are cities becoming more dangerous and polluted?

Chapter 20 links the rise of large formal organizations to modernization. And Chapter 21 examines human reactions to change—how people band together to cause or to resist change.

Social Change
and Modernization

17

MY FATHER GREW up in a world without airplanes, radios, or refrigerators. I grew up in a world without TV or polio vaccine—some of my classmates died and others were crippled by this dread disease that students today hardly know about. In your own lifetime, computers have shrunk from multimillion-dollar giants housed in air-conditioned, sealed environments to tiny, inexpensive gadgets found in millions of homes, and many of these microcomputers are much more powerful than the huge machines of a decade ago.

Once it was difficult to convince people that anything in life changed—for the pace of change was so slow that change was not apparent in one lifetime. Today, at least in modern societies, it is difficult to convince people that some things haven't changed and that some kinds of social change are not likely.

Yet many previous chapters have stressed continuity as well as change in social life, suggesting that some forms of societies are probably impossible. For example, Chapters 7 and 8 suggest that we shall never create societies without crime and other forms of deviance. Chapter 9 concluded that unstratified societies are impossible. Chapter 13 proposed that the family will persist and that the nuclear family has been made more important by the rise of urban, industrial societies. Chapter 14 examined the dynamics of religious change, which make it seem unlikely that religion will dis-

appear from societies despite the periodic decline of some religious organizations.

Basic elements of social life limit the scope of social change—not all changes are equally likely or even possible. And social conditions influence the pace of change. For most of human history, change took place very slowly. In the past few centuries, change has been very rapid—but only in some parts of the world. While some societies launch space rockets, others have not yet learned to make tools from metal. These observations lead us to the central sociological questions about social change: Why does it occur? What factors stimulate or retard change?

Chapter Preview

In the first part of this chapter, we shall examine general principles of social change. First, we shall assess internal sources of change—things that occur inside societies that cause them to change. Then we shall see how external forces can produce change within societies.

Then we will apply these general principles in examining the truly dramatic changes that have taken place in the world during the past several centuries—social and economic changes that are summed up by the term *modernization*. **Modernization** is the process by which agrarian societies were transformed into indus-

Albania	5
Romania	51
USSR	89
Poland	95
Yugoslavia	96
Hungary	118
Portugal	138
Bulgaria	141

West Germany	463
Belgium	468
Finland	496
United Kingdom	497
Netherlands	509
Denmark	636
Switzerland	725
Sweden	796

Ireland	187
East Germany	189
Czechoslovakia	206
Greece	289
Spain	310
Italy	337
Austria	398
Norway	453
France	459

Figure 17-1 ■ **Telephones per 1,000 population.** Sociologists who study modernization often use rates such as the number of telephones per 1,000 people to compare nations in terms of their economic development. The immense variations among European nations help us to see that not all parts of that continent are highly modernized. For example, telephones are scarce in Albania, where the 5 phones per 1,000 people are probably nearly all in government offices such as police stations. In fact, phones are relatively uncommon in most of eastern Europe. Southern Europe also shows a low ratio of telephones to population, Spain and Italy having only about a third as many phones as people. The most industrialized nations of northern and western Europe possess telephones on a par with North America. (Canada's rate is 671 and the United States has 837 phones per 1,000.) In this chapter we explore causes of modernization and try to understand why people in some parts of the world have several telephones per household while people in some other areas have never even heard one ring.

James Watt's steam engine revolutionized Western civilization. This drawing of his "double-acting" model incorporated the latest developments through 1791.

trial societies (see Chapter 10). Each of the remaining chapters in this book deals with particular aspects of modernization: the relationship between modernization and population trends, the rise of urban societies, new forms of organizations required to cope with and direct modernization, and the role of collective behavior and social movements in resisting and speeding modernization.

In the latter half of this chapter, we shall try to see how modernization occurred. We will assess four basic theories of what caused the rapid changes that transformed Europe and North America into modern societies. Why did so many other societies fail to modernize? What are the prospects that all societies will eventually be modernized?

Internal Sources of Social Change

In Chapter 4, we examined societies as social systems. In a system, connections exist among the parts so that changes in one part cause reactions in other parts. Because social systems consist of self-conscious, active human beings, internal changes are always taking place, and often a particular change will have far-reaching consequences, which people frequently fail to anticipate. Let us examine certain kinds of common activities within social systems to see how they produce changes.

Innovations

The most obvious thing that happens inside societies is that people have new ideas and change how they do something. When the Quakers implemented the idea of using prisons as a substitute for physical punishment (see Chapter 8), many other aspects of society were affected, including the criminal justice system, which expanded greatly. Three basic kinds of new ideas, or innovations, frequently cause social change.

■ **New technology** New technology is a major source of social change. Chapter 10 traces the immense social changes produced by the invention of agriculture. Chapter 19 will explain how the automobile revolutionized the structure of cities and the character of urban life. Some historians suggest that the major revolutionary event in 1776 was not the rebellion of the American colonies against Great Britain but the perfection of the steam engine.

Note that new technology does not change societies by itself. It is the *response* to the technology that causes change. Often, new technology appears and goes unused for a very long time. For example, the Romans fully understood how to use windmills and waterwheels to replace muscle power for various kinds of work but they made no use of this technology. Similarly, the Chinese had gunpowder centuries before Europe, but did not exploit its mili-

■ Plans to import modern technology often go astray. A rail line was laid near the village in which these women live. But so long as the rails serve only as a path and basket-carriers continue to serve as the primary means of transportation, these people have made no progress toward modernization.

tary potential. And the Aztecs put wheels on many children's toys but did not use the wheel for transportation; they carried goods on their backs rather than pulling them in wagons.

■ **New culture** Not only machines change the world. Beliefs and values can also produce dramatic social change. Indeed, many sociologists and historians have argued that rapid technological changes in Western societies were stimulated by acceptance of the **idea of progress** (Nisbet, 1980). That is, unlike most societies

that did not expect technological progress and often turned away from it, in Europe during the seventeenth and eighteenth centuries people widely accepted that such progress was not only possible but also certain. Such confidence inspired ever more determined efforts to achieve technological and scientific progress, and as these efforts bore fruit, they inspired even greater confidence and effort. To a considerable extent, Europe made progress because it believed in progress and underwent rapid social change because Europeans wanted change.

■ For a long time anthropologists wondered why civilizations as sophisticated as those of the Incas and the Aztecs had failed to discover the wheel. Then toys like this one were discovered in Aztec ruins in Mexico—little dogs on wheels so children could pull them. Suddenly the mystery deepened: Given that these civilizations did know about wheels, why did they use them only on toys and not to move heavy loads?

■ **New social structures** New forms of social structure can also be the result of invention. Chapter 20 is devoted to understanding the invention, application, and evolution of formal organizations as a new mode of social structure designed to cope with and direct modernization. Indeed, in the twentieth century, the search for technological innovation has been substantially directed by formal organizations such as the corporation, government, and the university.

Because roles are a basic social structure, changes in roles and the creation of new roles often cause other social changes. Changing sex roles have stimulated many changes. For example, the fact that the majority of women now work has changed the family (see Chapter 13), and the fact that women can now choose from a wide range of occupations has greatly increased the proportion of men teaching the lower grades. Likewise, the development of full-time specialists in combat was a major factor in the repressive character of government in agrarian societies (see Chapter 10).

Conflicts

Innovation is not the only major internal source of change. Much change is produced by conflicts among groups within societies. Chapters 9, 10, and 11 discussed many such conflicts among classes, racial and ethnic groups, and different regions. Thus, the Civil Rights Movement of the 1950s and 1960s not only removed many barriers to black participation in the mainstream of American society but also changed many other aspects of society. Indeed, the end to official southern racism may have been essential to the rapid economic growth now taking place in the South. Or, in an earlier time, conflict among the many Protestant denominations seems to have been the basis for making separation of church and state part of the U.S. Constitution, with the consequence of creating a competitive religious economy that generates high rates of church membership.

Growth

As we shall see in the remaining chapters in this book, population growth has been a major engine driving modern social change. Large populations present new problems that demand new modes of social organization. For example, as pointed out in Chapter 15, small populations may permit direct democracy in which all citizens may participate in decision making. However, such procedures are impossible for large populations, which require new models of democracy such as representative government.

Similarly, large cities must be constructed very differently from small cities (see Chapter 19). The simple growth of cities has produced great social change. As we shall see in Chapters 18 and 19, the earliest stage of modernization—industrialization—caused rapid population growth, which in turn spurred even more rapid industrialization.

Change and Cultural Lag

Social change involves complex patterns of response, because a change in one part of society forces changes in other parts. For example, a sharp decline in the birth rate during the 1960s soon caused a crisis in American schools. Suddenly there were too many teachers and classrooms for the number of students. Many teachers had to be let go, and many schools had to be closed. Ex-teachers had to find new occupations, and some use had to be found for unneeded school buildings. In addition, colleges reacted to the lower demand for teachers by cutting back their number of education majors. Thus, some students who had planned to become teachers had to rethink their career plans.

Beyond changing the schools, the reduced birth rate forced many readjustments elsewhere in society. Industries and stores that specialized in products for infants and young children had to respond to rapidly declining sales. A leading baby food company launched new products designed for the elderly, for example; TV stations reduced the amount of children's programming. More recently, the lower birth rate has been reflected in smaller numbers of teenagers, with a corresponding decline in sales of records and tapes and of acne medications.

This is but a sketch of the most direct effects of the reduced birth rate (which resulted from changes in the family and in female employment). But none of these reactions was immediate. The schools did not readjust as soon as the number of births declined. In fact, they took no action until the number of elementary school students had seriously dropped. And the colleges did not reduce the number of new teachers they trained until massive unemployment confronted their graduates.

There can be considerable delay before a change in one part of a society produces a realignment of other parts. During such a period of delay, parts of a society can be badly out of harmony—such as when education depart-

ments continue to pump out waves of new graduates after there are no employment opportunities for them. William F. Ogburn (1932) described such periods as **cultural lags.** According to Ogburn, cultural lags are times of danger for societies because severe internal conflicts can result.

Cultural lag and the Iranian revolution

The recent history of Iran illustrates the explosive potential of times of cultural lag. During the 1960s and 1970s, the Shah of Iran made an immense effort to rapidly modernize his country. Thousands of young people were sent to the West for advanced technical educations. Many new industries were founded, and many foreign experts were brought in to train Iranians to operate them. Indeed, the Shah encouraged the importation of Western culture generally—movies, music, books, clothing, and the like. For these reasons, most Western observers regarded Iran as the most modern and Western of Middle Eastern societies and a model of development for other nations in the region. The Shah received unqualified praise for realizing that he had only a few years to modernize his country's economy before Iranian oil reserves were exhausted. Instead of spending the huge oil income of Iran on importing luxury goods (as many other less developed nations have done), the Shah was thought to be using it to build a modern society, able to provide a high standard of living for Iranians after the oil wells were pumped dry (Halliday, 1979).

But the Shah fell victim to cultural lag. Beneath the gleaming surface of rapid modernization, which was all Westerners could see of this society, the majority of Iranians remained deeply committed to their traditional culture and to an unusually strict form of Islam. From their perspective, Western clothing and manners, especially for women, were intolerably evil. Because Islamic doctrine prohibits the making of images (which is why Islamic art excels in floral and geometric designs, but does not depict humans), movies and TV were regarded as blasphemous. In short, the mass of Iranian society

■ Sharp contrasts between the modern and the traditional were greatly reduced in Iran after the Ayatollah Khomeini and his fundamentalist Muslim followers took over the government. Much Western culture was outlawed, including Western clothing styles for women.

was not readjusting to the rapid modernization fostered by the Shah and was instead increasingly scandalized and angry.

This anger led to constant opposition. Sometimes the opposition was mainly symbolic, such as shunning women in Western dress. At other times, acts of terrorism occurred—several times angry Muslim fundamentalists chained the doors of movie theaters during a movie and then burned down the buildings, killing those inside. Of course, the opposition produced countless conspiracies to overthrow the Shah. In response, the Shah resorted to increasingly repressive

measures, using his growing secret police forces to uncover and punish his enemies. These measures aroused opposition among many of the most Westernized Iranians, who, educated in the United States, Canada, and Europe, aspired to greater democracy.

The Shah was caught between two irreconcilable forces, one reflecting cultural change and the other cultural lag. He could not democratize without the society exploding in civil war. But as protest in demand of increased democracy attracted support from Western governments, he was forced to try. Despite these efforts, civil unrest rapidly increased.

In hopes of regaining the support of the most Westernized citizens, the Shah appointed the opposition leader Shapur Bakhtiar to the premiership on December 29, 1978. Still the public protests continued, and riots broke out between traditionalist and modernist factions. On January 16, 1979, the Shah and his family left the country on an extended "vacation," hoping to give the new government a chance to gain support.

But then on February 1, 1979, the Ayatollah Khomeini, the most militant Muslim opponent of the Shah, returned from years of exile in France. The Ayatollah directed a civil war against the Shah's supporters and, in less than two weeks, seized the government.

Now the Westernized opponents of the Shah faced a day of reckoning, for the Ayatollah was a much more deadly enemy. Music broadcasts were prohibited as "no different from opium." Women were commanded to don veils or at least the *chador* (a large head scarf). Swimming pools and movie theaters were shut down (Ismael and Ismael, 1980). Firing squads began the bloody task of purging not only former supporters of the Shah but also all "blasphemers and servants of the devil" who opposed the Ayatollah.

In the midst of this terrible purge, a mob stormed the United States embassy and took American citizens hostage. It took more than a year to secure their release and safe return. Meanwhile, war broke out between Iran and Iraq and has continued ever since. The oil has not run dry, but a breakdown of Iranian industry has reduced exports to a trickle.

Looking back, analysts now agree that the

Shah failed because he tried to do too much too rapidly, creating intolerable internal strains. Iranian culture had no time to adjust to major changes.

■
External Sources of Change

Unlike the solar system, social systems exist not in a vacuum but within a social and physical environment. Interaction with that environment is a major cause of change within societies as well as a major factor limiting the kinds of changes that occur.

Assume that a number of small societies exist in close proximity, such as the many small societies of American Indians that once existed side by side. Assume that change is going on within each. Each change causes other parts within the societies to adjust in response to cultural lag.

But here internal changes can have external implications. That is, some cultural or social arrangements may weaken the ability of a society to withstand external threats, either from other societies or from the physical environment. Thus, some changes that may have been effective adaptations to internal social needs can be maladaptive to external demands. Societies that change in such directions are not likely to survive, as, indeed, many societies have not.

What has just been outlined is the process of *social evolution* (see Chapter 4). All theories of social change imply evolutionary mechanisms such as this. All social change is subject to external constraints, and external factors frequently produce internal changes.

Diffusion

We have seen that innovation is a major source of change. But innovations, whether in the form of new weapons, new customs, or new religions, are more often imported from other societies than developed independently within a society. As the famous anthropologist Ralph Linton (1936) put it:

The number of successful inventions originating within . . . any one . . . society . . . is always small. If every human group had been left to climb upward by its own unaided efforts, progress would have been so slow that it is doubtful whether any society by now would have advanced beyond the level of the Old Stone Age.

More rapid progress has been possible because societies borrow innovations from each other. This transfer of innovations is called **diffusion.** Anthropologists and many other scientists have specialized in tracing the routes by which innovations have spread, or diffused, from their point of origin to other societies. Special Topic 5 traces the diffusion of the stirrup from Asia to Europe and the role this played in the rise of feudalism. When Marco Polo returned to Italy from his journey to China, he brought back (among other things) the noodle, which was the basis for the development of the many forms of pasta popular in Italy and elsewhere in the West today. The horse was brought to the Western Hemisphere by Spanish explorers and spurred immense changes in American Indian societies. Corn, tomatoes, turkeys, and peppers diffused from the Americas back to Europe and Asia. Gunpowder was invented in Asia and then spread around the world. And central to this chapter is the rapid diffusion of modern European culture and technology throughout the world and the impact of this diffusion.

Conflict

Threats from other societies frequently are sources of social change. The rapid evolution of firearms and artillery in Europe, once gunpowder reached there from Asia, occurred because Europe was divided into scores of feuding societies, each needing to match or exceed the military capacity of its neighbors. In contrast, the relative lack of conflict within the vast Chinese empire did not stimulate the development of similar innovations.

As we saw in Chapter 14, grave external threats often prompt religious innovation. For example, as repeated efforts by American Indian tribes to fend off westward development by European settlers failed, often they concluded that their difficulties stemmed from a faulty religion, from worshiping the wrong gods, or from worshiping them in the wrong way, and new religious movements flourished.

Ecological sources of change

Changes in the physical environment often produce social change. Concerns about depleting natural resources and polluting the environment have caused many recent changes in the United States. Droughts and natural disasters have often prompted massive social changes. Similarly, more favorable ecological changes have also prompted change.

The interplay between environment and society is well illustrated by the great Viking expansions that began about A.D. 900. The Vikings conquered or colonized Russia, large sections of northern Europe, Ireland, parts of England and Scotland, Iceland, and Greenland. This Viking "explosion" was probably caused primarily by several centuries of unusually warm weather (Mowat, 1965; Sawyer, 1982). Warm weather meant much more abundant crops in Norway and Sweden, and more food meant population growth. Soon this larger population lacked land, and younger sons who could expect no inheritance set out to seek their fortunes by raid and conquest. As it happened, they had the fighting skills and seamanship to succeed. And the good weather made it possible to voyage successfully in the North Atlantic to such places as Iceland, Greenland, and even North America.

In time, the weather turned cold once more and the population declined. The North Atlantic was once again shrouded in fog, battered by storms, and filled with icebergs. The Viking ships stopped going to Iceland and Greenland. The Vikings in Iceland adjusted to the new conditions and survived centuries of isolation, but the Viking settlements in Greenland slowly died out. By the time new explorers from Europe visited Greenland again, only ruins and graves remained. Yet the Greenland Eskimos, who had been there long before the Vikings came, sur-

vived the shifts in the climate and still live in Greenland today. Their culture was able to readjust to the frigid climate that made farming impossible for the Vikings (McGovern, 1981).

In summary, both internal and external forces produce social change, and both can cause societies to break down. Europeans in the eighteenth century were probably correct in believing that change was inherent in all societies. They were probably wrong, however, in their faith that change always means progress. Surely, the North American Indians, despite gaining the horse, firearms, and other new technology from European settlers, did not find that change meant progress. In the end, change destroyed their societies. Nor did northern and western Europeans find that improved weather brought only progress, for it also brought fleets of Viking raiders down upon them.

Keeping in mind these principles of social change, we may now assess the causes of the dramatic set of social changes known as modernization.

The Rise of the West

In the eighteenth and nineteenth centuries, European intellectuals found it easy to accept the idea of progress, because rapid economic and technological changes were transforming their societies. Looking back over their history, Europeans saw a long period, now called the Dark Ages, when change had been very slow. During that time, Europe had been technologically backward compared with the nations of the Middle East and Asia. Then, beginning in the sixteenth and seventeenth centuries, came an immense step forward. Within a few centuries, European technology had raced far ahead of that of the rest of the world.

In the midst of this period of great progress, Europeans had set out to explore, colonize, and trade with the rest of the world. Everywhere they went they found themselves possessed of superior technology. Indeed, when Western fleets began to voyage to China, long known in the West for its advanced civilization, they found a

■ These Eskimo boys in northern Greenland (about 1900) demonstrate the survival advantages of hunter-gatherers in the frozen north. When a shift in the climate made it impossible for the Vikings in Greenland to farm, they perished. Meanwhile, the Eskimos continued to get their clothing from animal hides and their food from hunting and fishing.

backward nation unable to defend itself against a few ships armed with cannon (Mendelssohn, 1976; McNeill, 1982).

Thus, the questions arose: *Why had China not kept pace? Why had social change been so rapid in Europe?* Indeed, why was so much of the world so little advanced—why were some societies still huddled in the Stone Age, while in Europe machines were replacing human labor?

These were and continue to be dominating questions in the study of social change. Moreover, new questions have arisen: *Why has continued exposure to Western technology had so little effect in some parts of the world? Can all societies become modernized? If not, why not? If so, how?* You will recognize that these ques-

tions not only preoccupy sociologists interested in modernization and social change but also are among the leading international political questions of our time.

There are four major bodies of theory about why the West suddenly produced the Industrial Revolution and sprinted ahead of the rest of the world. Because these theories range from Marxism to free market economic theories, they stand in vigorous, basic disagreement. Yet, perhaps surprisingly, they agree on their initial assumption. Each attributes modernization, the rise of industrialized Europe, to the same basic source: the development of a particular pattern of economic relations called *capitalism*. Indeed, no conservative economist has ever heaped more praise on capitalism as the source of modernization than did Karl Marx, even though he devoted his life to planning for the overthrow of capitalism. So it is fitting to begin our assessment of modernization by seeing why Marx thought it was the result of capitalism. Then we shall closely examine the nature of capitalism itself.

Marx on Capitalism

Marx wanted a new world in which all people could enjoy a good life, where no one would be hungry or homeless, and where everyone would have freedom, dignity, and security. Throughout the ages, many people have longed for such a world. But in the mid-nineteenth century, Marx believed such a thing had become possible for the first time. In earlier times, equality could exist only as the equality of poverty. Humans simply were not sufficiently productive to provide themselves with comfort. But as Marx surveyed the immense flow of products from Europe's new and booming industries, he was convinced that societies were finally capable of providing everyone with a good life. The potential wealth was there; it had only to be shared.

Marx did not believe that the Industrial Revolution itself caused Europe's new explosion of productivity. Instead, he thought that this new technology was the result of something more basic: a new mode of economic arrangements that unleashed the full productive potential of human beings. He called these economic arrangements *capitalism.*

Before the rise of capitalism, Marx wrote, humans had been victims of their own "slothful indolence." That is, people tried to avoid work and did not try to find ways to be more productive. In fact, many historians have been struck by the short work days of medieval society and the careless farming methods of medieval peasants (see Braudel, 1981; Thomas, 1979). Similarly, anthropologists have long noted the casual attitudes toward work among primitives, as compared with modern work norms. Marx believed that Europe's great leap forward occurred because people suddenly began to work harder and smarter as a result of the inducements of capitalism. Capitalist society, he wrote in *The Communist Manifesto* (1848), was

the first to show what man's activity can bring about. It has accomplished wonders far surpassing Egyptian pyramids, Roman aqueducts, and Gothic cathedrals; it has conducted expeditions that put in the shade all former Exoduses of nations and crusades.

Moreover, capitalism cannot help but produce endless technological innovation: It must be "constantly revolutionizing the instruments of production." This is because capitalism has stripped away the traditional bases of relationships and left only one "nexus between man and man," that of "naked self-interest."

Here we encounter a great irony. Marx believed that the reason capitalism could be so productive was precisely the reason it ought to be destroyed. He believed that capitalist economies produced their economic miracles by degrading and alienating humans, both from one another and from themselves. By pursuing self-interest alone, humans ruthlessly exploit one another, according to Marx. Thus, he argued, capitalist societies not only were the first with the productive capacity to overcome poverty and exploitation but also were incapable of doing so. Indeed, Marx believed that capitalist societies could only become increasingly unequal, eventually consisting of tiny ruling elite (the bourgeoisie), possessed of incredible wealth and power, and a huge mass of "wage slaves" (the proletariat), sweating out their lives in dismal factories. Thus, Marx proposed communist revolutions, in which the masses would seize collective ownership of all means of production and turn the immense capacities of modern industrial societies to the benefit of all (see Chapters 9 and 10).

Although Marx believed capitalism had been the cause of modernization, he believed *the benefits of modernization could be separated from this initial cause*—that communism could replace capitalism, once modernization was sufficiently developed. But what is capitalism? And what is the secret of its economic power?

Capitalism

Current dictionaries define **capitalism** as an economic system based on private ownership of the means of production and a system by which people compete to gain profits. Such a definition fails to reveal the feature of capitalism that differentiates it from other kinds of economies. For example, there was much private ownership of the means of production (farms, tools, and ships) in ancient Rome and medieval Europe, and there was competition for wealth. But these were not capitalist economies. What is unique about capitalism is its reliance on a *free market.*

In a free market, freely made choices of individuals set prices and wages. That is, people decide for themselves what price they will charge or pay. They cannot be forced to buy or to sell, to hire or to become employed. Each is free to make the best possible bargain.

Prices and wages are set by supply and demand. When many people sell some commodity, competition among them forces prices down. Competition among people wanting to buy something in limited supply forces prices up. Competition among people wanting to be employed forces wages down. Competition among persons wanting to hire forces wages up. *The essence of this system is that everyone seeks to maximize personal gain and that such gains can be accumulated in the form of private property, secure from arbitrary seizure by the government.*

In a free market, individuals benefit by being more productive. If one farmer works longer hours in his fields, then at the end of the year he will have more wealth than his neighbors who worked less. Moreover, the free market rewards innovation and the reinvestment of wealth. A farmer who finds a way to plow better or faster will become richer. A farmer who saves some of his profits and uses them to buy more land, more cattle, or better machinery will become richer. In this way, capitalist economies motivate everyone to try to become wealthier, and these collective efforts increase production; when there is more to be had, standards of living rise. Marx believed that capitalism had

unleashed such productivity in Europe that it would soon be possible to eliminate all poverty.

Precapitalist command economies

Precapitalist societies do not rely on free market principles and individual economic self-interest. Instead, they are **command economies.** That is, some people decide what work is to be done and command others to do it. The lord of a medieval estate decided which fields were to be plowed, when, and what to plant and then ordered his peasants to do it. An emperor decided to build a road and ordered workers to be assembled and set to their tasks. The weakness of command economies is that *those doing the work have nothing to gain by doing it well.* A slave may avoid the overseer's whip by doing just enough, but a slave will not eat better or gain possessions by working harder or discovering ways to become more productive. Lack of worker motivation caused Marx to scorn the slothfulness of such economies.

The goal of command economies is consumption. Everyone tries to consume what they can before someone else takes it away from them. Thus, there is no motive to produce surplus. Indeed, as we saw in Chapter 10, when individuals lack secure property rights, their surplus production is simply taken from them and used to support others who suppress and exploit them. *The secret of capitalism is to reward surplus production.* Permitting people to keep their wealth encourages them to seek wealth and to curb their consumption so that they can reinvest their wealth to create more wealth.

An episode from ancient China clearly reveals the productive superiority of capitalist over command economies. In the late tenth century, an iron smelting industry rapidly developed in the central Chinese province of Hunan. By 1018, these iron smelters were producing more than 35,000 tons a year, an incredible achievement for the time. This iron industry was not the result of royal command. Instead, private individuals had recognized the great demand for iron and the good supplies of ore and coal in Hunan, and they realized that the smelted iron could easily be transported to distant markets over an existing network of canals and navigable rivers.

Having invested in foundries, these Chinese industrialists were soon reaping huge profits from their enterprises, much of which they reinvested to build more foundries. Production rose rapidly. The availability of large supplies of iron soon led to the introduction of iron agricultural tools, which in turn rapidly increased food production in China. Thus, China began to industrialize many centuries before Europe's great leap. Then as suddenly as it had begun, it all stopped. By the end of the century, only tiny amounts of iron came down the rivers from Hunan, and soon the foundries were forgotten ruins.

What happened? The imperial court had noticed that some commoners were getting rich by manufacturing iron and considered this undesirable. So the government taxed away their earnings, declared a monopoly on the sale of iron, and took over the smelters. Workers had flocked to work in the smelters, where they earned more than they could as peasants, but now work was commanded of them. The motive for working died out, as did the fires in the smelters (McNeill, 1982).

If capitalism caused the rise of the West, what caused capitalism? Here Marx was relatively silent. He argued that it was invented by the bourgeoisie, who used it to overthrow the old medieval nobility. But he said very little about why and how the bourgeoisie developed capitalism. Thus, it was left to Max Weber to attempt the first general explanation of the rise of capitalism.

The Protestant Ethic

The goal Weber set for himself was to explain why capitalism developed where and when it did and why it failed to appear (except for the brief instance cited in ancient China) in other societies that had achieved a stage of economic development similar to that of precapitalist Europe. In Weber's judgment, the essential question was, How had Europeans gained the self-discipline to cease unrestricted consumption while increasing production? Many societies have learned to curb consumption. Ascetic religions, for example, have led many people to spurn material things. But this has been accomplished by destroying their interest in *creating* material things. In Europe, however, people curbed their consumption while working all the harder to produce. How was this possible?

Weber believed the answer lay in the Protestant Reformation. In his famous book *The Protestant Ethic and the Spirit of Capitalism,* he argued that the religious ideas produced by Protestantism had motivated people both to limit their consumption and to pursue maximum wealth. People soon discovered that reinvestment was the fastest road to wealth.

The **Protestant Reformation** began in Germany when Martin Luther (1483–1546) asserted that the church was not needed to mediate between a person and God. Rather, each person should seek his or her own salvation through direct relations with God. In Switzerland, John Calvin (1509–1564) carried this notion much further. He argued that God was entirely unknowable. Therefore, no person could achieve salvation by appealing to God or by obeying the commandments. Who would be saved and who would be damned had been decided by God at the beginning of time and could not be altered. This doctrine was called predestination: Our futures were predestined by God.

But then how could one be sure of being saved? Indeed, what motive was there not to sin? Calvin provided an answer that put extreme pressure on the individual to lead an exemplary life: You can never be certain you are saved, but there are clues that indicate who is elected by God for salvation—persons whose lives are above reproach and who succeed in life.

No longer was work merely a calling to be endured; now it was seen as a glorification of God and more of an end in itself. The successful worker was the successful servant [of God], and money became a metric for the measurement of grace [Demerath and Hammond, 1969].

In addition, Calvinist Protestants condemned the most conspicuous forms of consuming

■ John Calvin.

wealth as sinful. They believed that you could not show the world that you were rich by a great display of your wealth (and therefore you could not display that you were one of God's chosen). You could show your success only by visible productive activities. And because you could not consume much wealth, why not plow it back to gain even greater wealth and that much greater certainty that you would go to heaven?

Strict predestinarian views of salvation did not last long as a dominant theme in Protestantism, but the actions they set in motion did. It soon became popular Protestant doctrine that one could actually earn one's way into heaven. Economic zeal became the road to heaven.

From these cultural developments, Weber argued, capitalism blossomed. Soon the religious roots of capitalism were no longer needed, for capitalism became a secure ideology in its own right—the **spirit of capitalism.** The spirit then spread through both Protestants and Cath-

olics and stimulated the Industrial Revolution. Weber quoted at length from Benjamin Franklin to show how deeply belief in the importance of saving and reinvestment had become imbedded in Western cultures.

Weber did not argue that the **Protestant Ethic** was the sole cause of the rise of capitalism. Nor did he ignore interaction between developing commercial activities and developing religious doctrines. He merely argued that the development of these religious and economic ideas gave rise to the Industrial Revolution. Today, many sociologists think that Weber emphasized religious values too much and economic changes too little. Nevertheless, a majority agrees that a shift in how people regarded wealth was an important part of the development of industrial capitalism.

The State Theory of Modernization

A third line of social theory suggests that Marx and Weber were both correct, but both views are limited. Proponents of this perspective agree with Marx that capitalism led to the rapid modernization of Europe, but they agree with Weber that the rise of capitalism itself must be explained if we are to account for modernization. They disagree with Weber that Protestant ideology led to the development of capitalism, arguing instead that both Protestantism and capitalism were produced by something more basic in European history: the taming of the state.

Building on classical economic theories, these social scientists propose that capitalism could develop *only as the state became tamed;* moreover, capitalism *will always develop* when the state is tame (North and Thomas, 1973; Nozick, 1974; Chirot, 1985). Because of the centrality of the state in this explanation, it is called the **state theory of modernization.**

The state theorists argue that the critical event in European history was the limitation of government power in several European nations, especially England and Holland. This resulted in capitalist economies, which in turn gave rise to the Industrial Revolution, or modernization.

The argument is very simple. When a repressive state exists, so will a command economy. Few persons in such societies benefit by being more productive, for the state supports itself by confiscating all surplus production, which is then consumed by the ruling elite. Under these conditions, as Marx recognized, it would be foolish to curb consumption or try to produce more because of the state's insatiable appetite. The most powerful religious ideas could not cause people to act like capitalists in such societies. Even if some people do, they will soon find their work is in vain, as did the Chinese iron makers.

Daniel Chirot (1985) has pointed out that the untamed state is incapable of not stifling economic development because *it is incapable of not overtaxing.* Ruling elites always overreproduce themselves and therefore need "to extract increasing amounts from their subjects." Comparing agrarian ruling elites with parasites, Chirot noted that they could not long resist the temptation to expropriate the wealth of merchants and any other visible source of funds to support their always-expanding numbers. Periodically, of course, these practices led to bankruptcy; they never lead to industrial development.

However, if the powers of the state are limited so that private property is secure from seizure and people are free to pursue their economic self-interest, capitalism becomes attractive and possible. For then, the more that people work and save, the better off they will be. Thus, whenever the state is prevented from seizing property, a free market, or capitalism, will develop. Rapid economic and technological progress then becomes very likely. When people are more productive, more wealth exists. In seeking to be more productive, huge numbers of people will seek more effective technology.

Marx was inclined to take technological progress for granted, seeing it as the natural result of human curiosity. The state theorists do not. They point to the historical fact that for long periods little, if any, technological progress occurred, while at other times new technology rose rapidly. Why is this? The answer they offer is that in some times and places, it is not worthwhile for people to develop new technology because they will not benefit from it. Why build a windmill so you can grind much more grain than you have been grinding by hand if your increased production will simply provide more flour for the nobility and no more for yourself?

Chirot explained it this way:

Economic rationality means that economic actors are willing and able to make reasonable predictions about their return on investments. Social and political systems which are arbitrary, or which do not guarantee property rights, or which do not protect key economic actors, are not conducive to economically rational behavior. This hardly means that in nonrational circumstances most people behave foolishly or illogically, only that predictability becomes so difficult that, to protect themselves, economic actors take measures which have little bearing on maximizing the productive power of their investments.

Since patent records have been kept, inventions have not been developed at a steady rate; many more patents are applied for during economic booms than during recessions (Schmookler, 1966). This suggests that people tend to invent things when it is profitable to do so. Historians of technology argue that it was the creation of patent laws that truly spurred invention during the Industrial Revolution (Jewkes, Sawers, and Stillerman, 1969). Patent laws protect an inventor's right to profit from his or her invention. Neither individuals nor firms would risk years of effort and the large investments needed to perfect many inventions if others could then simply steal their results.

Once the state had been tamed in parts of Europe, free markets sprang up, and, the state theorists argue, from then on the development of modern industrial societies was virtually certain (North and Thomas, 1973). Moreover, some state theorists claim that the taming of the state was the primary cause of the Protestant Reformation (Walzer, 1963).

In Chapter 14 we saw that religious pluralism is the natural state of religious economies—that different kinds of people have different religious needs, so that the market is served best by a variety of faiths. When the state does not try to create a monopoly for one faith, many faiths will exist. Thus, religious variety sprang forth in those European nations where the power of the state was restricted. However, state theorists go further than attributing religious pluralism to the taming of the state. They suggest that the rise of capitalism prompted specific Protestant doctrines, thus reversing Weber's argument. When people pursue their own economic self-interests, their sense of individualism is heightened. As a result, people want to deal with God directly rather than through a religious hierarchy. The stress in Protestantism that each person must seek his or her own understanding of God and his or her own salvation was thus compatible with daily economic activities.

■

Dependency and World System Theory

Each of the three explanations of modernization just examined seeks the causes of the Industrial Revolution within societies. That is, each points to social changes within a society. Marx believed that the development of capitalism within nations led to the Industrial Revolution. Indeed, Marx denied that nations could achieve communism without first passing through a capitalist phase. Similarly, Weber tried to show that capitalism arose only where the Protestant Reformation had first planted an ethic promoting hard work, saving, and reinvestment. State theorists argue that capitalism arose only in nations that had first tamed the state. But a fourth body of modernization theory looks not to changes within a nation but to changes in relationships among nations as the causative force. This explanation is called **world system theory.**

Most advocates of world system theory claim to be Marxists, although the first extended statement of this view was written not by Marx but by J. A. Hobson, an English economist. In his *Imperialism*, published in 1902, he charged that industrial European nations looted their colonies by forcing them to sell their raw materials too cheaply and to buy manufactured goods at too high a price. In 1915 V. I. Lenin, who soon

was to lead the Russian Revolution, borrowed Hobson's argument (as well as many of his statistics) and published them in a book called *Imperialism, the Highest State of Capitalism*. Ever since then, communist writers have claimed that Western capitalist nations not only exploit the less developed nations of the world but actually prevent them from modernizing. A few years ago this approach gained serious advocates among American sociologists. The man most responsible for recruiting sociologists to world system theory is Immanuel Wallerstein.

Elements of a world system

In *The Modern World System*, Wallerstein (1974) elaborated on the view that modernization of the West was paid for by its less fortunate neighbors. That is, the causes of the Industrial Revolution are to be found not within individual nations but in the *relations among nations that unite them into a single social system*. He therefore set out to examine in detail the world system existing in the sixteenth century, during which Europe began to develop capitalism and to industrialize.

In Wallerstein's judgment, the crucial development in the sixteenth century was the growth of an international economy that was not politically united. Through this economy, some nations extracted wealth from other nations without having to resort to military force. Wallerstein argued that this was different from all previous forms of international relations. In the past, nations had extracted wealth from other nations by plunder or by forcing them to submit to political control as part of an empire. Thus, for a long period Rome and before it Egypt dominated huge empires in which the threat (and often the use) of coercion extracted taxes and tributes.

Such empires were inefficient. They were command economies incurring great military and administrative costs. These costs were so great that they probably lowered the standard of living of all but the ruling elite. Any border troubles or internal rebellions raised the costs of maintaining an empire and strained available resources. When these costs could no longer be met, the empire became unstable and eventually collapsed.

What was unique about developments in Europe, according to Wallerstein, was that economic relations developed among nations whereby some could exploit others without paying the huge costs of running an empire. Thus, a few nations in western Europe were able to finance their rapid industrial development by extracting wealth from their neighbors without the need to plunder or dominate them through military force. Wallerstein called this international economy in sixteenth-century Europe the "modern world system," even though it was far from worldwide in scope. His term emphasized that this was an international social system.

Within this world system, Wallerstein argued, *stratification exists among nations.* A few nations form an upper class, some a lower class, and a few a middle class. A nation's class position is determined by its place in a geographic division of labor.

The dominant, or upper class, nations in a world system Wallerstein calls **core nations.** They have very diversified economies and are the most modern and industrialized. Core nations also have the strongest internal political structures marked by stable governments and little internal class conflict. As did Lenin, Wallerstein argues that core nations are stable because they can provide a very high standard of living for their workers and thus, in effect, buy their cooperation. Core nations also have a large middle class and permit considerable political freedom and individual liberty.

At the bottom of world systems are nations that Wallerstein identifies as **peripheral nations.** Many are located far from core nations. Typically, they have weak internal political structures and a low standard of living for workers. Because of their high potential for political instability and class conflict, they are ruled by repressive governments. Peripheral nations have highly specialized economies, typically relying on the sales of a narrow range of raw materials (such as food, ore, fiber, petroleum, or timber) to core nations.

A few nations in a world system may display features of both core and peripheral nations. Their economies are more diversified than those of peripheral nations, but are more specialized than those of core nations. Wallerstein calls these **semiperipheral nations.**

Dominance and dependency

To explain the relations among nations in a world system, Wallerstein applied a Marxist analysis of class relations within nations. Thus, he argued, the core nations act as an upper class exploiting the peripheral nations, which are the lower class. Core nations are wealthy like upper classes because they extract all surplus production from the periphery. They do this by dominating trade relations with the peripheral nations, making them dependent and distorting their economies so that peripheral economies cannot develop into modern societies.

Wallerstein used this model to explain the unevenness of modernization and industrialization in Europe. He admitted that he could not explain why some nations in western Europe initially got the jump on others and became core nations. But once some had done so, he claimed, they forced the nations of eastern Europe to accept a peripheral position. In this fashion, he explained why nations such as Poland and Hungary began to industrialize, then stopped and regressed to agricultural nations that lived by exporting food to western Europe in return for manufactured goods. Because of their late start, Poland and Hungary could not successfully modernize against western European competition and thus became dependent upon the West.

Although Wallerstein's book dealt with Europe during the sixteenth century, his real interest (and the main interest of many other sociologists now using world system theory) is in current international relations. The two primary questions are these: (1) Why is so much of the world so little modernized despite centuries of trade and contact with more advanced nations? (2) Can modernization ever become worldwide? Proponents of world system theory answer that trade with advanced nations has prevented the less developed nations from developing and that unless these nations escape

■ Proponents of world system theory argue that these Bulgarian peasants must toil with old-fashioned methods because the developed nations prevent industrialization in the less developed nations.

the control of advanced capitalist societies, they can never develop properly.

Mechanisms of dependency

The world system theory specifies a number of mechanisms by which less developed nations are made dependent on and are dominated by the advanced nations (Frank, 1969; Galtung, 1971; Wallerstein, 1974; Chase-Dunn, 1975; Chirot, 1977).

The fundamental mechanism is that the less developed nations are *dominated by foreign firms and investors that control their economies*. This, in turn, has several consequences. First, profits flow back to the developed nations

rather than being reinvested in the local economies: Foreign firms and investors spend or invest their profits back home. This denies the underdeveloped economies the capacity to grow.

Second, foreign firms and investors control what economic activities take place in underdeveloped nations. Generating manufacturing capacity is not in their interest; rather, they profit more by selling manufactured goods to underdeveloped nations and extracting raw materials from them. Therefore, foreign domination means that a peripheral nation remains a supplier of raw materials unable to become industrially self-sufficient.

Third, nations that specialize in exporting raw materials must remain poor. World demand for raw materials is relatively inelastic due to

■ Harbor scenes like this in Cotonou, Benin, in West Africa, encourage belief in the dependency hypothesis—that when a nation is a primary exporter of unprocessed food and raw materials, its modernization is retarded. That nations lacking industry do not export manufactured goods is hardly surprising.

the small or negligible population growth in the advanced nations (so their need for raw materials does not increase). So a nation cannot increase its wealth by increasing the amount of raw materials it exports. Also, world prices for raw materials are subject to manipulation by speculators in the advanced nations and often fall so low as to create economic depressions in supplier nations.

According to the world system theory, nations that specialize in the export of raw materials also develop very distorted economies. Their development tends to be limited to small enclaves of workers employed in the export industries, while the rest of the nation remains undeveloped. The result is a dual economy that confines all modernization to the export sector, while providing neither incentives nor resources

for modernizing the rest of the country (Frank, 1969; Paige, 1974; Chase-Dunn, 1975).

■

Delacroix: Testing the Dependency Theory

 Intellectuals and many political leaders in the less developed nations find the world system theory of great appeal. It tells them that the lack of progress in their nations is not their fault but is imposed upon them by the developed nations. However, many social scientists, especially those in the advanced nations, have rejected these views.

Although the world system theory offers an elegant model of international economic rela-

■ Scenes like this in the Port of Seattle, where huge grain ships line up to take on loads of wheat, call the dependency thesis into question. Similar scenes occur in all major American and Canadian ports because these two nations export more unprocessed foodstuffs than the rest of the world put together. Yet, contrary to dependency theory, the United States and Canada are not "underdeveloped" nations.

tions, many critics have argued that the real world is much more complex. The world system theory neatly divides the world into poor, underdeveloped nations that export raw materials and rich, modernized nations that export processed manufactured goods. However, critics point out that exceptions to this scheme abound. The United States and Canada are rich, modernized nations, yet they export more raw, unprocessed foodstuffs than the rest of the world combined. Taiwan's economy is dominated by foreign investors, yet rather than specializing in the export of raw materials, nearly 90 percent of its exports are manufactured goods (Barrett and Whyte, 1982). Moreover, research designed to support the dependency claims of world system theory was either unsuccessful or poorly designed and executed. Thus, a young graduate

student at Stanford University in the mid-1970s saw an opportunity to do some important sociology.

Jacques Delacroix (1977) wanted to test the dependency portion of world system theory: *that specialization in the export of raw materials prevents modernization.* His first task was to select valid measures of the major concept: modernization. He selected two measures that reflect slightly different aspects of modernization. The first of these is per capita **gross national product (GNP),** the value of all economic activities within a society during some specific period, usually a year. When this total is divided by the total population the result is per capita GNP, or the amount of GNP per person. Per capita GNP lets us compare the economic development of nations of very different size. For example, India's

Table 17-1 ■ Per capita GNP for selected nations, 1983.

	Per Capita Gross National Product in Dollars		Per Capita Gross National Product in Dollars
Switzerland	$15,552	Portugal	$2,208
United States	13,492	Mexico	1,997
Sweden	11,850	Brazil	1,987
Canada	11,535	Chile	1,886
West Germany	10,903	South Korea	1,870
France	9,896	Peru	984
Netherlands	9,581	Philippines	734
Japan	9,149	Egypt	674
Austria	8,908	Uganda	407
Great Britain	8,693	China	376
Belgium	8,505	Pakistan	373
Czechoslovakia	7,511	Kenya	339
Soviet Union	6,490	India	248
Italy	5,924	Burma	173
Poland	5,580	Ethiopia	147
Spain	4,774	Bangladesh	124

Source: Prepared by the author from *Statistical Abstract of the United States, 1986.*

GNP is much larger than Switzerland's, but India is a less developed, poor nation while Switzerland is highly developed and wealthy. This is obvious when you compare their per capita GNPs in Table 17-1.

For his second measure of modernization, Delacroix selected high school enrollment rates. A nation's level of school enrollment, especially above the grade school level, represents both an investment in modernization and modernization itself. Only educated populations can deal with technology and modern culture.

Table 17-2 lets us examine the correlations between Delacroix's two measures and some other common measures of modernization. The data are based on the fifty most populous nations in the world. Because all of these factors are supposed to measure modernization, it is reassuring that all of the correlations are very high.

Next, Delacroix formulated two hypotheses derived from the dependency portion of world system theory: (1) If dependency theory is correct, then we ought to discover that per capita gross national product increases more slowly in nations to the extent that they specialize in exporting raw materials, and (2) by the same token, we ought to find that dependent nations—those specializing in exporting raw materials—lack the resources to expand their educational systems, especially above the primary grades. In effect, the rich nations should be increasing per capita GNP and high school enrollments while the poor nations remain stagnant or advance much less rapidly.

Delacroix knew that the dependency hypothesis could not be tested properly at only one point in time. No one disputes that some nations are less developed than others. The issue is whether these nations are catching up in terms of modernization. Clearly, changes over time must be examined. So Delacroix obtained data for 1955 and 1970 for fifty-nine nations. He then examined changes in his dependent variables: changes in per capita GNP and changes in secondary school enrollment as these were related to his independent variable, the proportion of a nation's exports that are unprocessed raw materials.

What did he find? No relationships. Nations specializing in raw material exports showed as

Table 17-2 ■ Per capita GNP and high school enrollment as measures of modernization.

	Correlations with Per Capita GNP	Correlations with High School Enrollment Rate
Telephones per 1,000	.98	.68
TVs per 1,000	.92	.79
Per capita electricity consumption	.92	.70
Radios per 1,000	.86	.69
Percent attended college	.83	.66
Percent of labor force employed in industry	.65	.71
Percent of labor force employed in agriculture	−.71	−.80

Source: ShowCase Presentational Software, *World: The 50 Most Populous Nations*, data selected and supervised by Robert Szafran (Seattle: Cognitive Development, Inc., 1987).

much increase in per capita GNP as did nations specializing in the export of manufactured goods. Secondary school enrollment grew as greatly in the nations exporting raw materials as in those exporting manufactured goods. Delacroix found no support for the dependency hypothesis.

But he did find something else. Secondary school enrollments and increases in per capita GNP were strongly correlated. This led Delacroix to suggest that modernization is influenced primarily by internal processes rather than external processes of the world system. That is, nations that devoted substantial effort to educating their populations improved their standard of living, no matter what role they played in the world import-export system. Educational policy is decided within nations, not imposed upon them by their trading partners. Indeed, Delacroix concluded that even the least developed nations retain considerable "freedom to maneuver" in determining domestic policies and thus retain substantial opportunity, as well as responsibility, to establish their own patterns of modernization.

Since Delacroix's landmark study a great deal

of additional research has been done (Semyonov and Lewin-Epstein, 1986). The results have been somewhat mixed. Some studies have reported moderate support for the claim that dependency retards development. Others have contested these claims, reporting results similar to Delacroix's. At the moment, although considerable controversy exists, the best conclusion is that there probably are dependency effects but that they are small and limited to an over-reliance on agricultural exports. Bradshaw (1987) found that when nations rely almost entirely on agricultural exports, this "has a negative impact on economic growth, suggesting that underdeveloped countries should diversify their agricultural export structure." Hence, when Delacroix looked at the effects of exporting all kinds of raw materials he found no dependency effects, but when agricultural exports are separated from other raw materials such as ore, timber, and petroleum, small effects can be seen. The quote from Bradshaw indicates a marked shift in discussions of dependency. Few sociologists now describe dependent nations as helpless victims at the mercy of an exploitative world

■ Delacroix's research showed that a major source of modernization is secondary school enrollment. To the degree that a nation invests in its young people by keeping them in school, its modernization is speeded up. These Ivory Coast children are their nation's primary asset.

system. Instead, with Delacroix, they trace the primary control over economic development to factors within these societies and therefore, like Bradshaw, suggest strategies that nations might adopt to develop more rapidly.

Conclusion

However capitalism arose and modernization occurred, the fundamental fact remains that some nations are much more modernized than others and that the less developed nations desire the quality of life that modernization provides. To achieve this quality of life, they may have to develop "modern" values of thrift and rein-

vestment, as Weber proposed; develop capitalist economies, as Marx believed; and tame their states, as state theorists argue. And they may have to pay close attention to their opportunities in the world trade economy, as world system theorists suggest.

Yet in all of this discussion of change and modernization, a primary element has been omitted. The first effect of modernization on the less developed nations has been an immense population explosion in recent decades. As rapidly as many of these nations have been increasing their wealth, they have been increasing their populations even faster. Thus, a pressing issue has been whether this rapid population growth can be halted before it results in catastrophe. The answers to this question have often been blurred by doomsday pronouncements based on distorted evidence and political rhetoric. Nevertheless, the answers remain vital for the world's future. The next chapter is devoted to the sociology of population and will deal with many of the issues raised in this chapter.

Review Glossary

modernization The process by which societies develop advanced industrial technology and the political, cultural, and social arrangements appropriate to sustaining, directing, and using that technology. (p. 492)

idea of progress The philosophical doctrine that technological and social progress is inevitable. (p. 495)

cultural lags Periods of delay following a change in one part of a society when other parts of the society have not yet readjusted. (p. 497)

diffusion The process by which innovations spread from one society to another. (p. 499)

capitalism An economic system based on free-market exchanges and individual property rights with the result that any individual can benefit from becoming more productive. (p. 503)

command economies Economic systems wherein property rights are not secure and much productive activity is based on coerced labor. (p. 503)

Protestant Reformation The separation of Protestant Christians from the Roman Catholic Church during the sixteenth century; usually associated with the founding of the Lutheran Church in Germany. (p. 504)

spirit of capitalism According to Weber, a nonreligious version of the Protestant Ethic; values favoring hard work, thrift, and the importance of economic success. (p. 505)

Protestant Ethic According to Weber, doctrines holding that economic success reflects God's grace. (p. 505)

state theory of modernization Theory that wherever the power of the state to seize private property is curtailed, free markets will appear, capitalism will develop, and modernization will occur as a result of mass efforts to become more productive. (p. 505)

world system theory (or dependency theory) Theory stating that some nations become modernized by exploiting other nations and that their continuing exploitation prevents less developed nations from becoming fully modernized. (p. 507)

core nations According to Wallerstein, those most modernized nations, having diversified economies and stable internal politics, that dominate the world system. (p. 508)

peripheral nations According to Wallerstein, those nations in the world system that are forced to specialize in the export of unprocessed raw materials and food to the core nations and that must import manufactured goods. This makes them dependent on the core nations, which in turn force them to adopt economic and social policies that prevent them from modernizing. (p. 508)

semiperipheral nations Wallerstein's term for nations that fall in between core and peripheral nations, being more industrialized than the latter and less industrialized than the former. (p. 508)

gross national product (GNP) The total value of all economic activities within a society. When GNP is divided by the total population of a society, the result is per capita GNP. (p. 511)

Suggested Readings

Chirot, Daniel. 1977. *Social Change in the Twentieth Century*. New York: Harcourt Brace Jovanovich.

Chirot, Daniel. 1985. "The Rise of the West." *American Sociological Review* 50:181–195.

McNeill, William H. 1976. *Plagues and Peoples*. New York: Basic Books.

North, Douglass C., and Robert Paul Thomas. 1973. *The Rise of the Western World: A New Economic History*. Cambridge: Cambridge University Press.

Wallerstein, Immanuel. 1974. *The Modern World System*. New York: Academic Press.

Weber, Max. 1958. *The Protestant Ethic and the Spirit of Capitalism*. New York: Scribner's.

White, Lynn, Jr. 1962. *Medieval Technology and Social Change*. London: Oxford University Press.

Stirrups and
Feudal Domination

Stratification in agrarian societies arose from the ability of the elite to monopolize military capabilities. As Chapter 10 explained, when the weapons of war are like those for hunting, and when the average man has both the training and the essential equipment for going to war, the ability of the elite to coerce him is very limited. The immense inequalities of agrarian societies arose as a group of specialists in waging war emerged. In medieval European societies, this military monopoly developed as the unexpected consequence of a very small technical innovation—the stirrup.

After the fall of the Roman Empire, western Europe was a collection of tribal kingdoms that were not very stratified. One such tribe was the Franks, whose territory included most of modern France. Like the other tribal kingdoms, Frankish society was composed largely of free and independent farmers. When war came, all able-bodied men took their shields, swords, and spears and formed a huge host of infantry. They wore no armor and depended on their number and high morale to gain victory. They were part-time farmer-soldiers. As such, they could resist not only invaders but also their king.

Then came the stirrup. Until the seventh century, horse saddles did not have stirrups. Without stirrups, a mounted soldier is handicapped; he can use only the strength of his arm, not the full weight of rider and horse, to deliver a blow. Thus cavalry was little used. The Romans, for example, used mounted soldiers only for scouting duties and the pursuit of fleeing enemies. With stirrups, however, a rider is much more securely seated and can smash a lance into a target with the full force of a galloping horse.

Late in the sixth century, the stirrup reached Europe from China (White, 1962). Soon a few mounted Franks began to show up for battle armed with long lances. As these mounted tactics evolved, defenses also evolved. For protection against the lances, riders began to wear heavier armor. This required them to ride very big, strong horses. Soon the knight in armor had arrived, but only in limited numbers.

During the seventh century, a few of the richest Franks began to report for military duty wearing armor and mounted on horses. The rest came on foot as always. Possibly the first charge by knights took place in a battle between the Franks and the Saxons in 626 (Montgomery, 1968). But another century passed before the real military superiority of the knights was recognized. In 733 Charles Martel led the Frankish host against the invading Saracens, Moslems who had conquered Spain and sought to push their rule north. At the Battle of Tours, the Franks routed the Saracens and pushed them back across the mountains into Spain. The turning point in the battle came when the Saracen ranks collapsed under the weight of a thundering charge by mounted knights. Lacking stirrups, the mounted Saracens could not withstand the lance attack. Victory convinced Charles Martel that knights held the key to military supremacy. He began to transform the Frankish host from an army of foot soldiers to an army of armored cavalry.

This ended the importance of farmer-sol-

■ As depicted here in the Utrecht Psalter, the Frankish host was formed of all able-bodied males. The host was a mass of lightly armed infantry. Agathias, a historian who wrote during the middle of the sixth century, gave this description of the Frankish host:

The arms of the Franks are very rude; they wear neither mail-shirt nor greaves, and their legs are only protected by strips of linen or leather. They have hardly any horsemen, but their foot-soldiery are bold and well practised in war. They bear swords and shields, but never use . . . the bow. Their missiles are axes and barbed javelins. These last are not very long, they can be used either to cast or to stab.

diers in Frankish military operations. They could not afford to arm as knights. History records that in 761 a Frank named Isanhard "sold his ancestral lands and a slave for a horse and a sword" (White, 1962). To buy weapons and a suit of armor in the eighth century cost the equivalent of twenty oxen, enough for ten plow teams, at a time when only well-to-do farmers owned such a team. Moreover, a knight needed an unusually big, fast, well-trained horse—a horse, as Field Marshal Bernard Law Montgomery (1968) put it,

strong enough to carry him when fully-armed, sufficiently trained not to bolt or panic in battles, and fast enough to take part in a charge at full gallop. Such a horse had to be specially bred and trained.

The famous breeds of huge horses that appear today in ads pulling beer wagons were not developed to pull loads but to carry knights wearing armor so heavy that they had to be hoisted up by a derrick and lowered onto the saddle. Moreover, a knight could not go off to war with only one horse; he needed spare mounts. He also needed someone to hold his spare mounts during the battle, to help him get into his armor, to hoist him onto his horse, and to transport his supplies. Thus, each knight needed a retinue of aides and servants. These people also had to have mounts and some weapons. Furthermore, horses must be fed grain, not just grass. To feed one war-horse for a year required the grain crop of several peasant farms. Finally, to fight as a mounted knight took years of training. Knights had to be free to dedicate their lives to military training from early childhood, freedom only a few could have (White, 1962).

To have an army of knights required the transformation of Frankish society. Few could afford to be knights, and even a king could not afford to equip and support many. But the peasants could. So each knight was given title to a

■ As you can see in this classic statue, the Roman cavalry had no stirrups. A mounted soldier like this one could strike only with the strength of his arm. Had he tried to charge with a lance, he would have been vaulted off his horse because he could not brace his feet.

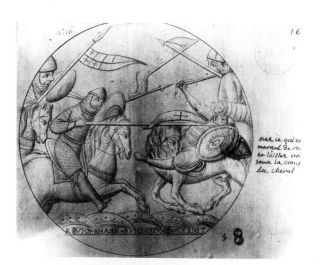

■ Here Frankish knights, braced in their new stirrups and wearing protective chain-mail armor, sweep over Saracen horsemen, as shown in the stained-glass choir windows of St. Denis Abbey. The Saracen rider on the right has no stirrups; his sword and shield are useless against the long lance of the Frankish knight.

■ Knighthood in full flower: Both horse and rider wear heavy, elaborate armor in this display of authentic equipment used in the late Middle Ages. Some military historians regard such horses and riders as forerunners of the modern tank. They were virtually immune to spears and arrows, and they could overtake infantry and literally run over them.

tract of land and the authority to tax all who lived on it in return for his service as a knight when called upon. This is the political system known as *feudalism.*

In feudal societies, land ownership is based on military obligations. The ruler grants title to large areas in return for the fulfillment of a military quota. A great lord, for example, might have been obligated to provide several hundred knights when called upon. To do so, he assigned portions of his estate to lesser nobles in return for promises to provide some portion of this force. They, in turn, could assign land to others for a pledge of service. The result is that the great mass of society was taxed to support a relatively small number of knights who ruled the people. The people could be greatly exploited because they did not possess the essential equipment and training necessary to resist the knights. With the rise of the knight, the average Frank became a heavily taxed peasant, subject to coercion. Knights held their control of land as a hereditary right, but only so long as they fulfilled their military obligations, for knighthood was not a ceremonial title. War was chronic, and woe unto him who failed to fulfill his obligations to his lord when ordered to duty. Excerpts

from a summons sent by Charlemagne, the great emperor of the Franks, to his nobles in 806 suggest how Frankish society had changed since the days of the infantry host and hint at the seriousness of the feudal system of obligations:

You shall come to Stasfurt on the Boda, by May 20th, with your "men" prepared to go on warlike service to any part of our realm that we may point out; that is, you shall come with arms and gear and all warlike equipment of clothing and victuals. Every horseman shall have shield, lance, sword, dagger, a bow and a quiver. On your carts you shall have ready spades, axes, picks and iron-pointed stakes, and all other things needed for the host. The rations shall be for three months. . . . On your way you shall do no damage to our subjects, and touch nothing but water, wood, and grass. . . . See that there be no neglect, as you prize our good grace [quoted in Montgomery, 1968].

Of course, as the Franks used their knights to extend their rule over new territory, their neighbors soon followed their example. For centuries, feudalisms held all Europe in thrall.

Population Changes

IN 1066 WILLIAM, Duke of Normandy, landed in England with a small army and, having defeated King Harold in the Battle of Hastings, seized the English throne. After a few years he began to suspect that his new subjects were not paying their proper amount of taxes. So William the Conqueror, as he now was called, decided to find out what his conquest really consisted of. As described by a resentful, Anglo-Saxon chronicler:

He sent his men all over England into every shire and had them find out how many hundred hides there were in the shire, or what land and cattle the king himself had in the country, or what dues he ought to have in twelve months from the shire. Also he had a record made of how much land his archbishops had, and his bishops and abbots and his earls, and . . . what or how much everybody had who was occupying land in England, in land or cattle, and how much money it was worth. So very narrowly did he have it investigated, that there was no single hide nor a yard of land, nor indeed (it is a shame to relate but it seemed no shame to him to do) one ox nor one cow nor one pig was there left out, and not put down in his record: and all those records were brought to him afterwards [quoted in Hallam, 1986].

This massive document came to be known as the *Domesday Book* (pronounced "doomsday") because it made William's English subjects think of the accounting at the Last Judgment, described in the Bible. Today, historians consider the **Domesday Book** unsurpassed in medieval history for its thoroughness and for the speed at which it was assembled.

William was not the first ruler to count his population and their property. The pharaohs of Egypt began doing so as early as 2500 B.C. The Old Testament records that once the Israelites were safely out of Egypt, "The Lord spoke to Moses, saying 'Take a census of all the congregation of the people of Israel, by families.' " The emperors of Rome also counted and assessed their subjects frequently—Augustus ordered a count of the entire empire in 28 B.C., in 8 B.C., and again in A.D. 14. Why all this interest in counting people? To estimate tax revenues and military manpower.

To know how much revenue a tax can produce, a government needs to know how many people will be paying it. Moreover, only by knowing how many people live in a particular district can the central government be sure that local officials are not embezzling. For example, a local tax official might report to the imperial government that there are 5,000 tax-paying families in his district when there are, in fact, 8,000, thus enabling him to pocket the taxes paid by 3,000 families.

By the same token, only by knowing the number of able-bodied males of military age can a ruler estimate how large an army he can raise. In the days of tiny hunting-and-gathering societies, it was easy to count noses and know that fourteen warriors were available for battle. But when societies grew to include tens of thousands of people, counting noses became a major task.

Thus, from ancient times, governments

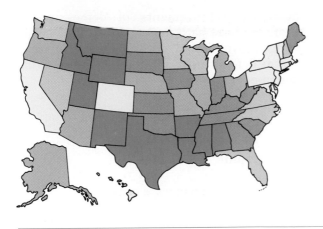

Massachusetts	1.11	Maine	1.36
Rhode Island	1.14	Kansas	1.36
Connecticut	1.18	South Carolina	1.36
New York	1.19	Tennessee	1.36
Hawaii	1.19	Iowa	1.37
Colorado	1.20	Indiana	1.39
New Jersey	1.21	West Virginia	1.39
Maryland	1.22	Georgia	1.39
Vermont	1.23	Oklahoma	1.39
Pennsylvania	1.23	South Dakota	1.40
California	1.23	Kentucky	1.40

New Hampshire	1.24	Texas	1.41
Virginia	1.24	Alabama	1.42
Delaware	1.26	Montana	1.42
Florida	1.26	Wyoming	1.46
Minnesota	1.28	New Mexico	1.46
Washington	1.28	Louisiana	1.48
North Carolina	1.29	Mississippi	1.51
Wisconsin	1.30	Arkansas	1.51
Nevada	1.30	Idaho	1.56
		Utah	1.64

Nebraska	1.31
Oregon	1.31
Ohio	1.33
Illinois	1.33
Missouri	1.33
Michigan	1.34
North Dakota	1.34
Arizona	1.34
Alaska	1.35

British Columbia	2.23	New Brunswick	3.05
Yukon	2.26	Pr. Edward Island	3.17
Ontario	2.33	N.W. Territories	3.46
Alberta	2.37	Newfoundland	3.48

Manitoba	2.60
Quebec	2.63
Nova Scotia	2.76
Saskatchewan	2.85

Figure 18-1 ■ Fertility, 1981. The *fertility rate*—the number of infants born to the average woman age 15–44—has been declining in North America over the past two decades. In the United States the fertility rate now is below that needed to replace the population. In Canada the rate is still high enough to sustain growth. But in both nations there is considerable variation across states and provinces. In Canada fertility is highest in the Atlantic provinces, while just to the south this is the region of the United States with the lowest fertility rates. The data also destroy another stereotype: Quebec, the most Catholic province in Canada, has only an average fertility rate, while the three states with the highest proportions of Catholics have the three lowest fertility rates. This chapter will explore the sociological explanations of why populations grow or decline. We will discover that variations in fertility rates often are *not* the reason.

instituted a **census:** a population count, often broken down into useful categories such as sex, age, occupation, marital status, and the like. The *Domesday Book* was a census. But even though William's agents conducted what was probably the most efficient census taken in medieval times, it took them two years to assemble the *Domesday Book*, and gathering the information was costly. Moreover, the *Domesday Book*, like any census, soon became outdated.

As we shall see, populations often change rapidly. Therefore, it may be necessary to redo a census frequently to have accurate information. However, because censuses are very expensive, governments are reluctant to conduct them. Generally, that has meant muddling along with badly outdated information. But over time, ways have been found to gauge population changes between censuses. And because populations so often fluctuate in size, governments encouraged inquiry into why this occurs. Thus was born the science of *demography*.

Chapter Preview

The word *demography* is formed from the Greek word *demos*, meaning "people," and *graphy*, meaning "description." Doing **demography** means describing the people. Whenever you read in the newspaper about such things as the marriage rate, the divorce rate, or population decline, you are reading about the work done by demographers.

In this chapter we shall examine fundamentals of modern demography, a major area of specialization within sociology. We shall also see the important role of population shifts in prompting or impeding social change. The chapter's primary object is to assess theories of population change.

Historically, human population trends have undergone *four* dramatic shifts, and a *fifth* major shift seems to have just begun. These shifts are the main subjects of the major theories of demography. Thus, we shall examine historical population patterns while assessing the major

theoretical achievements of demographers. Before we trace patterns of population change, however, we should understand a few basic technical tools used to monitor and describe human populations.

Demographic Techniques

As a population changes, a census becomes out of date. For a long time, governments often lacked accurate information on the size and composition of their populations. Then one day some unremembered bureaucrat hit upon an ingenious way to keep track of what was going on. It became the law to record all births and all deaths with the government. This procedure became common among societies, and governments created bureaus of vital statistics to keep an accurate count of these registrations. These records made it possible to update the census each year. (In many countries, birth and death registration was facilitated by the clergy, who had kept local records for religious purposes.)

Let us consider a hypothetical nation that has just conducted a census showing that it has 10 million citizens. The next year 500,000 babies are born and 400,000 people die. By subtracting deaths from births, we determine that the population has undergone a net increase of 100,000. Adding this to 10 million, we know that this nation now has 10,100,000 citizens. Furthermore, by dividing the year's growth (100,000) by the total population of a year before (10 million), we can see that the population grew by 1 percent in a year. By making these computations each year, we can find out the size of the population and its rate and direction of change without taking a new census.

Suppose that each year 100,000 more people are added to this nation's population. Is this rate of growth the same year after year? No. As the population grows, each year 100,000 people constitute a smaller percentage of the existing population and thus represent a smaller percentage increase. We therefore know that population growth is slowing down. Because it is often vital to governments to know how fast their populations are growing, they pay great attention to the percentage of annual growth, or the **growth rate,** of the population.

Even what appear to be small growth rates can cause populations to grow at a breathless pace. For example, a population that is growing by 3 percent per year will double in size in twenty-three years and increase tenfold in only seventy-seven years. The growth rate is computed in this way:

$$\frac{\text{Net population gain (or loss)}}{\text{Size of population}} = \text{Growth rate}$$

For any given year, the net population gain (or loss) takes three variables into account: (1) the increase (or decrease) in births, (2) the increase (or decrease) in deaths, and (3) the increase (or decrease) due to migration.

A record of all births and deaths permits some crude insight into why a population changes in size. A population can grow because births are increasing, because deaths are decreasing, because people are migrating into a region, or all three reasons. Similarly, a population can shrink because of a decline in births, an increase in deaths, a loss of people who move away, or all these reasons. Assuming that migration is constant, suppose a government wants a larger population. It would need to know whether encouraging more births or combating disease is the more appropriate course.

Obviously, in answering this question, simply knowing the numbers of births and deaths over several years would not help much. To compare, say, births for two years, we need to take into account the fact that the total population for these years is different, making a direct comparison between the number of births meaningless. Again the solution is to compute a percentage—the ratio of births to the population total for each year. Such percentages are called *rates*.

Rates

We can compute a **crude death rate** by dividing the total number of deaths for a year by the total population for that year. A **crude birth rate** can be computed by dividing the total number of births for a year by the total population for that year. By using rates, we can make meaningful comparisons between years in which the total population differed in size. For example, in 1910 there were 2,777,000 live births in the United States; in 1970 there were 3,731,000 live births. Although there were almost a million more births in 1970, fertility was much higher in 1910—there were fewer than half as many people in 1910 as there were in 1970 to produce those births. Thus, newborns added only 1.8 percent to the total population in 1970, in contrast to 3 percent in 1910.

Crude birth and death rates give only limited information. They do not take into account some important factors: For example, most members of a society cannot bear children. Males cannot, nor can prepubescent or postmenopausal females. What will happen if the proportion of fertile females in a population changes? A change in the crude birth rate will occur even if fertile women are reproducing at exactly the same rate as before. Therefore, demographers try to avoid using crude birth rates. Instead, they prefer a **fertility rate,** which is the total number of births, divided by the total number of women within a certain age span. Most nations, including the United States and Canada, base their fertility rates on women 15 through 44.

The importance of using a fertility rate rather than a crude birth rate is demonstrated by the immense contrasts between the two rates in Canada (see Figures 18-1 and 18-2). Table 18-1 compares the correlations between the crude birth and fertility rates and a number of important independent variables. Use of the crude birth rate would lead to the conclusion that people have more kids where incomes are higher, where religious affiliation is lower, and where there are more men than women. One also would conclude that neither telephones per 1,000 people nor the abortion rate influences births. But this would be absolutely incorrect. When we actually measure *fertility*—how many infants the average woman is having in various provinces—we discover that affluence, as measured by income and by phones, has a huge negative impact, as does the abortion rate, while religion has an immense positive effect. That the proportion of males doesn't really correlate with

Quebec	14.1	Saskatchewan	18.3
Ontario	14.5	Alberta	20.1
Nova Scotia	14.6	Yukon	22.8
New Brunswick	15.2	N.W. Territories	30.3

British Columbia	15.6
Manitoba	15.7
Pr. Edward Island	15.8
Newfoundland	16.2

Figure 18-2 ■ **Canada's crude birth rate, 1982.** Here we see the crude birth rate—the number of infants born in a year per 1,000 population—for the provinces and territories of Canada. If you compare these rates with those shown in Figure 18-1, you will see how very different they are. Thus, for example, the Yukon shifts from the second highest on the crude birth rate to second lowest on the fertility rate. Alberta also jumps from a low position on fertility to a high one on crude births. This shows how important it can be to base fertility on women of child bearing years rather than on the total population. There are a lot of births in the Yukon because a very large proportion of women there are in their child bearing years. However, the average woman in the Yukon also is having fewer babies than are women anywhere else in Canada except those living in British Columbia (by a tiny margin). The correlations in Table 18-1 show further examples of how misleading crude birth rates can be.

Table 18-1 ■ Contrasting Canada's crude birth rate and fertility rate (correlations based on provincial rates).

	Crude Birth Rate	Fertility Rate
Median income	.61	−.52
Percent of population with religious affiliation	−.28	.71
Telephones per 1,000	−.09	−.90
Percent of population that is male	.91	.10
Abortions per 1,000 live births	.12	−.80

Source: ShowCase Presentational Software, *Family and Socialization in North America* (Seattle: Cognitive Development, Inc., 1986).

fertility underscores that only women bear children.

Just as not all members of a society can reproduce, not all members of a society are equally likely to contribute to the death rate in a given year. It is crucial to know who is and who is not contributing to the death rate. The *crude death rate* does not reflect these subtleties; it is simply the number of deaths per 1,000 in the general population. Demographers are mainly interested in **age-specific death rates.** These are computed by separating the population by age categories and computing the number of deaths per 1,000 of each age group.

Obviously, everyone dies. However, *when* people die greatly affects future population growth—and virtually every aspect of society. A comparison of crude death rates tells us that in 1900 nearly twice as many Americans per 1,000 (17.2) died as in 1970 (9.5). But an examination of age-specific death rates reveals that a massive shift occurred in the age at which people died. In 1900, 162.4 infants (age 1 year and younger) per 1,000 died. In 1970, only about an eighth as many infants (21.4 per 1,000) died. Furthermore, in 1900, 19.8 out of every 1,000 children age 1 to 4 died, whereas in 1970 fewer than 1 (0.8) per 1,000 of these children died. In 1900, the birth rate was much higher than in 1970; however, as we have seen, far fewer of those born grew up to reproduce. The birth of 1,000 infants had less of a long-range impact on the population in 1900 than it does today.

Demographers concern themselves with a great many other rates. You have already seen a number of these in previous chapters. For example, we have discussed rates of crime, marriage, divorce, disease, and illegitimacy. All of these are constructed in the same way as fertility and death rates. Crude rates are based on units of 1,000 (or sometimes 10,000) persons in the total population. Other rates are specific to certain relevant groups within the population. For example, the crude rape victimization rate was 10.1 per 10,000 Americans in 1979. However, the specific rates for women 20 to 24 were 63.3 for whites and 99.2 for blacks.

Cohorts

One of the main uses of demographic data is to provide a basis for long-term planning. A government may project future conditions by saying, "If the present birth rate holds steady, then we will have a population twice as large thirty years from now. We must make provisions to house, employ, and feed these additional people." A critical unit in such planning is the birth cohort, or age cohort. A **birth cohort** consists of all of the persons born in a given time period, usually one year. The interesting feature of cohorts is that although they may get smaller as time passes, they never get any larger. At the end of 1990, there will be no more people born in that year. Therefore, if we know the number of persons included in the 1990 birth cohort, and if we have accurate age-specific death rates for our population, then we can predict the size of that cohort as it passes through all the stages of life, from infancy to old age. For example, by subtracting the figure based on mortality expected by age 6, we know the total number of children who will be entering first grade in 1996. Our society thus has some time to adjust the number of classrooms and teachers accordingly. Likewise, by subtracting the figure based

■ In the eyes of his proud father, this baby boy is the newest member of the family. In the eyes of the neighbors, he is the newest resident of this mining village. In the eyes of the British census department, he is another member of the birth cohort made up of all infants born in Wales that year.

on the probable mortality between birth and 18 years, we know how many 18-year-olds there will be in 2008. If we can predict what percentage of these people will choose to attend college, then we can predict the size of the freshman class of 2008 at the end of 1990.

When fertility and mortality abruptly shift, governments often become obsessed with the future implications of a birth cohort. The fact that the size of the cohort cannot be increased caused grave concern among French military planners. In 1870 France was totally defeated by Germany. For the next forty years, the French were determined to gain revenge. But while France and Germany had approximately the same-sized populations in 1870, Germany had 65 million to France's 40 million by 1914. In part this came about because Germany annexed

■ French troops rushing to take part in the great battle at the Marne River where the German invasion was halted in 1914. Although the French eventually were on the winning side, their losses in World War I resulted in tiny birth cohorts for the next generation.

new territory during this period. But in part it was because France had a lower—and declining—birth rate.

Thus, where it mattered, in the age cohorts of males suitable for military service, the Germans had nearly twice the number as France had in 1914 (7.7 million to 4.5 million). According to Shirer (1969), "Gloomy prophets in Paris did not see how France could escape another military debacle if the Germans chose to attack again." In 1914 the Germans did attack and just failed to win the war in the first six weeks. Finally, in 1918, the Germans were defeated, but only because millions of Russian, British, Canadian, Italian, and American troops came to the support of France.

From a demographer's point of view, France's revenge on Germany for having been defeated in 1870 was gained at dire future cost. Of French men between 18 and 28, three of every ten died

in the war and did not make their expected contribution to future fertility. More than a million more came home from war badly maimed and disabled and also did not reproduce to the extent they might have. In addition, there were at least 1,400,000 fewer births between 1915 and 1919 in France than there would have been had the young men not been off in the trenches. Thus in 1933, when the birth cohort of 1915 was old enough for military service, nearly half a million potential new soldiers came of age in Germany, while fewer than 190,000 did so in France. Worse yet, the depressed level of the number born during World War I led to a depressed number of women of child-bearing age in the 1930s. It was clear that Frenchmen of military age would be in even shorter relative supply by the late 1940s. Furthermore, the French fertility rate continued to drop throughout the 1920s and 1930s, while the German rate stayed high. In terms of potential manpower, France faced an ever-deteriorating military disadvantage with Germany.

In 1940 the Germans attacked again, and this time they did defeat France in the first six weeks. The small French birth cohorts of 1915 to 1922 were overwhelmed as French military planners had long feared and as German military planners had anticipated for years.

Age and sex structures

Small birth cohorts occurring in France had two major effects on population size. First, *they were too small to replace their parents' cohorts*, and the size of the population declined as older cohorts died. Second, when these smaller cohorts reached reproductive age, *they produced fewer children than a larger cohort would have*.

This limit on population size directs our attention to another important demographic factor: the distribution of people of various ages and sexes within a population. Obviously, a population in which the majority are elderly or are males has a far lower potential for growth than a population in which the majority are females of reproductive age. Therefore, to predict future trends in a population, we need to know not only fertility and mortality rates but also the **age structure** and **sex structure** (or distribution) of that population.

Normally, populations fall into one of three age and sex structures, depicted in Figure 18-3. The first structure is an **expansive population structure** and is characteristic of present populations in the underdeveloped nations. The expansive structure is shaped like a pyramid—each younger cohort is progressively larger. Such a population grows very rapidly. At any given moment, there are many more people who have not yet begun to reproduce than there are who have. This situation has serious implications for growth, even if fertility suddenly falls. For even if couples suddenly limit their families to only enough children to replace themselves, the population will continue to grow until each of the increasingly larger, younger cohorts has gone through the reproductive period.

That is what is causing population growth today in the United States and many other industrialized nations. Fertility in these nations has fallen to levels that will eventually cause a population decline, but the population continues to grow while the massive birth cohorts of the post–World War II "baby boom" pass through their reproductive years. Growth will not stop until the relatively smaller birth cohorts of the 1970s take over reproduction. When that happens, the age and sex structure of the United States may resemble the **stationary population structure** shown in Figure 18-3. The base of this structure is in proportion to the other cohorts. Thus, there are only enough infants and children to make up for early mortality, and each cohort entering the reproductive period is the same size as previous cohorts. Therefore, the population does not grow.

Finally, the third drawing depicts a **constrictive population structure**. The bottom of this structure is smaller than the middle, indicating that in the future fewer people will enter reproductive ages. Such a structure reflects a declining population, now typical of many European nations.

Armed with these elementary demographic concepts, we can now examine the history of human population trends.

Preindustrial Population Trends

Primitive societies often had difficulty maintaining their populations. Women had to bear many children to make sure that several would survive to have children of their own. Historians believe that, in primitive groups, about 50 percent of all children died before the age of 5 (Petersen, 1975). For over several million years, the human population of the earth grew so slowly that only a few more people were added every 100,000 years. Kingsley Davis (1976) estimates that only 10,000 years ago, after at least 3 million years of human reproduction, there were about 5 million human beings on the face of the earth, a figure about equal to the population of Chicago. For most of human existence, we were an endangered species.

Figure 18-3 ■ **Population structures.**
(a) Expansive population structure, with fertility of
four children per couple. (b) Stationary population
structure, with fertility of two children per couple.
(c) Constrictive population structure, with fertility
of one child per couple.

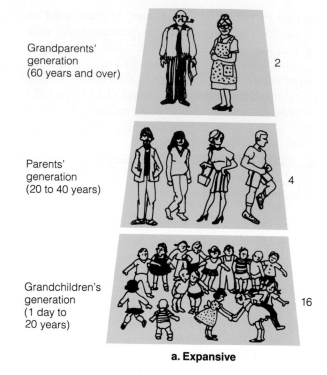

Grandparents'
generation
(60 years and over)   2

Parents'
generation
(20 to 40 years)   4

Grandchildren's
generation
(1 day to
20 years)   16

a. Expansive

But then came the *first great shift* in human population trends: Beginning about 10,000 years ago we began to increase our numbers rapidly. This was caused by the development of agriculture. As humans ceased being nomadic hunters and gatherers and settled in one place to grow crops, life became more secure. There was a lot more food, and it was regularly available. With a better diet, we became healthier, and our reproductive rates finally began to outstrip death rates. More babies lived to maturity, and the population began to grow more rapidly. Davis (1976) estimates that 8,000 years later, by the year A.D. 1, the worldwide human population was about 300 million. That means 295 million more people (or 60 times as many) had been added in 8,000 years than had been amassed over the previous several million years. (In the past 2,000 years, the population has increased by more than 1,300 times, to a world total of about 5 billion.)

Nevertheless, although the human population began to grow rapidly, growth was not continuous. The population trends of agrarian societies fluctuated, as rapid growth was followed by rapid decline. By 1700, the world population was only about twice as large as it had been in the year A.D. 1. What caused these periodic declines in the population? A sudden increase in the death rate. Every so often, human populations were laid waste by famine, disease, or war.

Famine

Though the invention of agriculture permitted a rapid increase in the human population, agrarian societies were extremely vulnerable to crop failures caused by drought, storms, or blight (plant disease). Famine could cause an immense number of deaths directly through starvation and indirectly through undernourishment, making people more vulnerable to disease. Europe suffered from severe periodic famines until the twentieth century. Often these famines were confined to one country or to one section of a country, but they sometimes affected most of the continent, as they did from 1315 to 1317, in the 1690s, and again from 1708 to 1709 (Petersen, 1975). Mortality rates soared and the

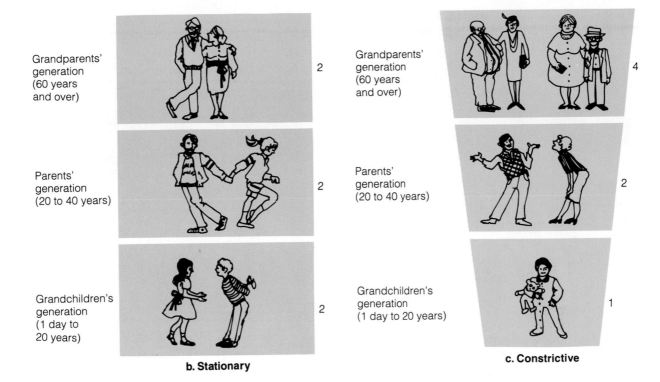

Grandparents'
generation
(60 years
and over)   2

Parents'
generation
(20 to 40 years)   2

Grandchildren's
generation
(1 day to
20 years)   2

b. Stationary

Grandparents'
generation
(60 years
and over)   4

Parents'
generation
(20 to 40 years)   2

Grandchildren's
generation
(1 day to 20 years)   1

c. Constrictive

population was seriously reduced. The last great famine in Europe took place when blight destroyed the potato crops in Ireland in 1845. As Chapter 2 pointed out, millions of Irish immigrants fled to the United States to escape starvation, but perhaps a million others, unable to flee, died as a result of the blight.

Nevertheless, Europe was much less vulnerable than Asia was to this cause of widespread death. In part, this may have been because European agriculture was less productive. In good times, European agriculture could not support great population growth; therefore, in bad times there were fewer people in danger of starvation. Asian farming, on the other hand, was very efficient but was vulnerable to the highly variable and unpredictable monsoon rains. Asia suffered more than Europe from severe droughts, but had more plentiful crops between droughts. Famine was chronic in Asia (Petersen, 1975), and Walter Mallory (1926) found that a serious famine has been recorded in some part of China almost yearly for the past 2,000 years.

William Petersen (1975) reported on one of China's more recent and severe famines:

One of the worst famines of modern China struck four northern provinces in 1877–78. Communications were so poor that almost a year passed before news of it reached the capital. Cannibalism was common, and local magistrates were ordered "to connive at the evasion of laws prohibiting the sale of children, so as to enable parents to buy a few days' food." The dead were buried in what are still today called "ten-thousand-men holes." From 9 to 13 million, according to the estimate of the Foreign Relief Committee, perished.

Similarly, Davis (1951) calculated an immense loss of life due to famine in India during the 1890s by contrasting the rates of population increase for several decades:

In the previous decade [India's population] grew 9.4 percent, and in the following decade 6.1 percent. If the 1891–1901 decade had experienced the average rate of growth shown by these two decades, it would have grown by 7.8 percent instead of 1 percent. The difference is a matter of some 19 million persons,

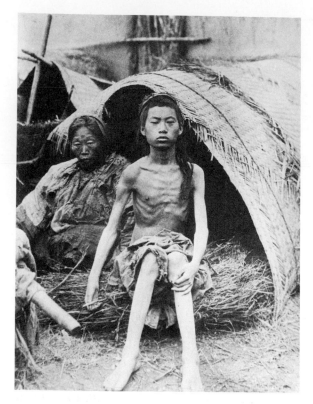

■ A famine victim in China's Honan Province at the turn of the century. Famine was a chronic cause of high mortality rates in China for more than 2,000 years and struck again in the 1960s when the Cultural Revolution disrupted farming and food distribution.

■ This drawing is from a manuscript published by Henri de Mondeville in 1314, the first book on human anatomy that was based on actual dissections. Lacking such research, physicians could make little progress in understanding disease, because they had virtually no knowledge of how the body functioned.

which may be taken as a rough estimate of loss due to famines.

Davis also pointed out that a great deal of food was shipped to India to help overcome the famine. Had this famine occurred in premodern times, millions more would have died.

Disease

A second major cause of a sudden rise in mortality is the outbreak of deadly, contagious diseases. One of the worst was bubonic plague, known as the Black Death, which often thinned the populations of agrarian societies in Europe and Asia. The worst outbreak began in Con-

stantinople (today known as Istanbul, Turkey) in A.D. 1334. In less than twenty years, the Black Death mowed down millions in Europe and Asia; some estimates of plague deaths run as high as 40 percent of the total population of Europe and Asia (see Figure 18-4). After the plague, thousands of villages in Europe and Asia stood completely uninhabited and were never resettled (McNeill, 1976).

Smallpox was another epidemic killer. In 1707, 31 percent of the population of Iceland died of smallpox. Shortly after the first Spanish expedition reached the New World, smallpox and measles epidemics wiped out as many as three-fourths of the inhabitants of Mexico and the West Indies (McNeill, 1976).

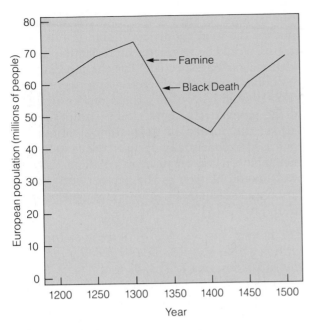

Figure 18-4 ■ **Population of Europe, A.D. 1200–1500.** Famine and plague reduced Europe's population by nearly 40 percent from A.D. 1300 to 1400.

War

Throughout recorded history, innumerable societies have been ravaged and even destroyed by war. A case in point is the Thirty Years' War, which embroiled the nations of northern Europe from 1618 to 1648. The war was fought partly as a result of the Protestant Reformation, and religious antagonisms made it especially savage. By the end of the struggle, only 6,000 of 35,000 peasant villages survived in Germany, and an estimated 8 million Germans had perished (Montgomery, 1968). An even more devastating war was the Taiping Rebellion in China (1851–1864), in which prisoners were slaughtered and farms were burned (Ho, 1959). In one area of 6,000 square miles, no trace of human life remained. Earlier estimates that 20 to 30 million people were killed are now considered too low! A century later the populations in the four provinces that fought the war were estimated to be still 14 percent below the number living there when the fighting began (Petersen, 1975).

Malthusian Theory

Modern social science was born in the eighteenth century with the publication in 1776 of Adam Smith's economic treatise, *An Inquiry into the Nature and Causes of the Wealth of Nations.* This book not only was the start of economics but also led to the first demographic theory. In attempting to account for economic changes, Smith found it necessary to consider population patterns. This led him to a famous proposition: "Men, like all other animals, naturally multiply in proportion to the means of their subsistence." In other words, human populations grow or decline according to *the availability of the necessities of life, especially food.* Eighty years later, Charles Darwin adopted this proposition of Smith's to help formulate the theory of evolution. Long before then, however, Smith's proposition prompted Thomas Robert Malthus to construct the first theory of population change.

Malthus was born in 1766 and, like Smith, he was a Scot educated in England. At 22, he became a clergyman in order to realize "the utmost of my wishes, a retired living in the country." However, he soon became fascinated with Smith's economic theories, especially in using them to explain the growth and decline of human populations. In 1798, he published a short book, *Essay on the Principle of Population.* For the rest of his life, he continued to revise and expand this book through seven editions. The last edition was published after Malthus died in 1834.

Although the book eventually became very long, its central arguments are brief and easy to follow. Surveying the population patterns in Europe over many centuries, Malthus detected a repetitive cycle of rapid growth followed by rapid decline. He set out to explain this cycle.

His first clue came when he noticed that human (and animal) populations have the capacity for rapid exponential growth. That is, they need not show an **arithmetic increase** (1-2-3-4-5) but easily can show an **exponential increase** (2-4-8-16-32). For a human population to double every generation, all that is necessary

■ Thomas Malthus.

is for every couple to raise four children. This is not difficult for people to achieve. Indeed, in Malthus's day, the average North American woman gave birth to more than seven children during her lifetime.

If a population doubles each generation, it grows at an astonishing rate. For example, suppose we start with a single human couple. If they doubled their number (produced four children), and if each successive generation did so, then in only thirty-two generations a population of 8.4 billion would be achieved (well above the present world total). If we assume that a generation takes twenty-five years to grow up and reproduce, then in 800 years the population could have gone from an Adam and Eve to far more than today's world population.

Considering these figures, Malthus realized that something prevented the population from doubling every generation. For it was obvious that "in no state that we have yet known, has the power of population been left to exert itself with perfect freedom." Nowhere did humans exist in the numbers that would have resulted from unchecked doubling.

But what checks population growth? Smith had suggested available subsistence, and Mal-

thus concluded Smith was right. He reasoned that for the food supply to double in one generation would be "a greater increase than could with reason be expected." For the food supply to double again over the following twenty-five years "would be contrary to all our knowledge of the properties of land." Thus, unlike population, the means of subsistence cannot be increased exponentially. Here Malthus found an inevitable tension. He made calculations to show what would happen to the gap between population and subsistence if both grew at the optimum rates.

The human species would increase as the numbers 1, 2, 4, 8, 16, 32, 64, 128, 256; and the subsistence as 1, 2, 3, 4, 5, 6, 7, 8, 9. In two centuries, the population would be to the means of subsistence as 256 to 9; in three centuries as 4,096 to 13, and in two thousand years the difference would be almost incalculable.

A shortage of subsistence, or famine, is always the ultimate check on population. But famine was not the only thing that kept the population down. As populations became denser, they were more vulnerable to epidemics: first, because greater contact among people made it easier for disease to spread and, second, because people weakened by hunger are less resistant to disease. Furthermore, increased populations taxed resources, which often led to war over land and resources. Malthus identified the limits to growth we discussed—famine, disease, and war—as **positive checks** that kept populations proportionate to the food supply.

From these insights, Malthus created a theory that accounted for the population cycles occurring in agrarian nations. Essentially, his theory says that populations will always rise to the level of subsistence. Thus, when a new farming method is introduced, when there is a period of good crops, or when new land is cleared and put into production, population will grow. However, *the population growth will always tend to rise slightly above the supply of food.* This happens because initial food shortages causing poorer diets will not be sufficient to slow growth. Eventually, however, population pressure will activate one or more of the posi-

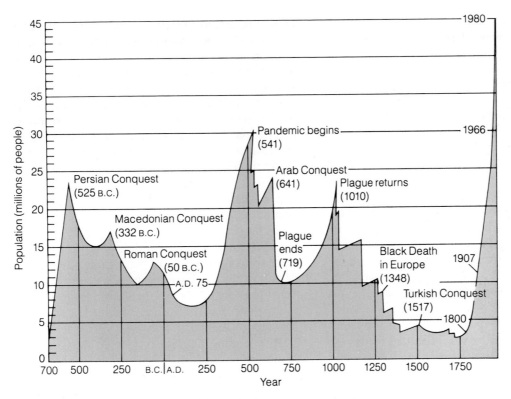

Figure 18-5 ■ **Population of Egypt, 700 B.C.–A.D. 1980.** The characteristic sawtooth population pattern on which Malthus based his theory of population is revealed by centuries of Egyptian demographic history. A rapidly growing population repeatedly and rapidly shrank as external conquests caused agricultural shortages or when plagues broke out. By 1800, as Malthus worked on later editions of his theory, the Egyptian population began a long, unbroken rise.

tive checks "until the population is sunk below the level of the food; and then the return to comparative plenty will again produce an increase" in the population, and the pattern will be repeated (Figure 18-5).

Malthusian theory regards mortality as the fundamental variable determining population size. When mortality declines, populations grow. When mortality increases, growth slows or is reversed. You may wonder why Malthus was not concerned with fluctuations in fertility, since populations obviously grow or decline if the birth rate rises or drops. More to the point is the question of why rational and self-conscious people don't see the cause of their periodic misery—runaway population growth—and thus limit their fertility. Malthus believed that fertility could not be controlled. He granted that some-

times "vice" in the form of abortion or birth control can briefly reduce fertility. He also granted the possibility of "moral restraint," or chastity, as a check to fertility. But he doubted that humans could control their sexual natures sufficiently to prevent rapid population growth whenever the food supply permitted it. He therefore did not consider changes in fertility significant in determining changes in population patterns. From his reading of the past, he believed that human fertility *was always high* and that only mortality rose and fell.

Although the **Malthusian theory of population** predicts that populations will follow cycles of growth and decline, these cycles do not prohibit a long-range upward, or even downward, trend. If the supply of food is increasing, then at the end of each cycle the population will be slightly larger, or just above what the new, larger food supply can support. Conversely, if the long-term trend is a reduced food supply, then the population will be smaller after each cycle.

Malthusian theory seemed to explain the facts of early agrarian societies quite well. The population had grown over the long run, as had the food supply. Yet the population remained subject to the cycle of ups and downs, and humans suffered from the activation of the positive checks of famine, disease, and war, just as Malthus had postulated. But even as Malthus was writing, the *second great shift* in population trends was under way, which seemed to defy Malthusian theory. The Industrial Revolution was taking place. It was accompanied by extraordinary population growth in Western nations without activating the positive checks Malthus predicted. A new optimism grew. Most people began to believe that by mastering technology humans could overcome the forces of fertility and mortality. Soon many social scientists considered Malthus's views outdated and pessimistic.

Modernization and Population

To most people, the phrase "Industrial Revolution" suggests machines and factories. But the Industrial Revolution first affected agriculture. Indeed, the age of the factory and the growth of large industrial cities were possible only because of the modernization of agriculture. Recall from Chapter 10 that in agrarian societies about 95 percent of the labor force is needed on the farms in order to grow enough food. Today, although fewer than 4 percent of Americans and Canadians farm, they grow enough food not only to feed all the rest of us but also to make North America by far the largest exporter of food in the world. As we shall examine in Chapter 19, the industrialization of agriculture caused this dramatic change. With machines replacing draft animals and hand labor, better plant and animal varieties, new techniques of crop rotation and field design, and the use of chemical fertilizers,

food production soared. As Malthus would have predicted, so did the population.

In England, where the Industrial Revolution began, the population was three times larger by 1841 than it had been in 1700. As modernization spread across northwestern Europe, so did rapid population growth. In 1650, Europeans (including those living overseas) made up 18 percent of the world's population. In 1920, they made up 35 percent (Davis, 1971).

This growth was possible only because there was enough food. Indeed, the specter of famine suddenly disappeared from Europe: People began to eat far better despite there being millions more mouths to feed. This is demonstrated by the virtual disappearance of nutritional-deficiency diseases as causes of death in western Europe. Scurvy, a dread disease produced by a lack of vitamin C, was once a major cause of death. In less than a century, it became so rare that in 1830 a leading English physician failed to recognize its symptoms (Drummond and Wilbraham, 1957). Indeed, as we saw in Chapter 5, the improved diets resulting from modernized agriculture caused a revolution in the patterns of human growth and maturation in modern societies.

In addition to providing much more food, modernization resulted in more effective protection against disease. Public health measures caused the mortality rate to drop rapidly. Vaccination and inoculation campaigns prevented huge numbers of deaths, especially among children. For centuries, smallpox was a dreaded killer. In 1980, World Health Organization officials announced it no longer existed on earth. Of perhaps even greater importance were modern sanitation measures. Sewers, sewage treatment, and the availability of safe drinking water saved huge numbers of lives (as we shall see in Chapter 19).

Thus, the increase in food and sanitation measures greatly reduced mortality. As a result, during the eighteenth and nineteenth centuries, the population grew so large and so fast that we now speak of this as the first population explosion.

In the wake of these changes, many began to regard Malthusian theory as outdated. Modernization seemed to have given societies the

■ My grandfather may have been a member of this crew threshing wheat in North Dakota's Red River Valley in the 1880s. Although the crew is very large and the machinery antiquated compared with modern harvesting methods, these men were able to produce food at a level their own grandfathers would have found unbelievable. The result of the early industrialization of agriculture was a population explosion in Europe and North America.

capacity for unlimited growth, because food supplies could expand as quickly as population grew. However, others suspected that modernization had simply postponed the day of reckoning, when Malthus's positive checks would again strike. Before this proposition could be tested, however, a *third great shift* in human population trends occurred. And this shift seemed to discredit the Malthusian theory once and for all.

The Demographic Transition

According to Malthus, population size is determined by fluctuations in mortality, because human fertility always remains high. This seemed to fit the patterns of population growth and decline observed up to Malthus's time. In the beginning, the Industrial Revolution affected mortality almost exclusively. Increased food supplies and the conquest of many diseases caused mortality to fall and therefore the population to grow. But then what Malthus said would not happen began to happen: Fertility began to decline in the more modernized nations.

We have seen that the population of England tripled between 1700 and 1841. Growth continued for a few more decades but at an increasingly slower rate, until by 1930 the population stabilized. However, growth was not halted by increased mortality. Instead, as mortality continued to decline, fertility also began to decline in the 1860s. Growth ceased by the 1930s because fertility no longer exceeded mortality.

Similar patterns were occurring on this side of the Atlantic as well. From the middle of the nineteenth century, the fertility rates of Canadian and American women also began a steady decline. By 1940, fertility in the United States was nearly at replacement level, while the average woman in Canada was having only 2.8 children. This was above the replacement level but still relatively low. **Replacement-level fertility** occurs when the number of births each year equals the number of deaths. In the most modern societies, replacement fertility occurs when the average woman has only slightly more than two children—one to replace herself, one to replace her husband, and a slight excess to make up for infant mortality. Replacement-level fertility produces **zero population growth** as soon as the age structure has adjusted.

Most industrialized nations achieved replacement-level fertility rates by the 1930s. Then, after World War II, population stability was upset by a brief baby boom (see Special Topic 6). However, fertility soon began to drop once more, and by the late 1960s it was down to replacement level in most industrialized nations. Their populations will continue to grow for a few years more, as the baby boom goes through the reproductive age.

Nevertheless, modern nations have undergone a radical change in population patterns—described as the **demographic transition.** This transition involves a change from the age-old pattern of high fertility and high but variable mortality to a new pattern of low mortality and fertility. The demographic transition seemed to prove that Malthus's theory of population was no longer valid: In the modern world, people did control their fertility and thus averted the suffering that occurs when population size is determined wholly by mortality.

■

Kingsley Davis: Demographic Transition Theory

Why had this happened? How had modernization led to a decline in fertility? In 1945, Kingsley Davis, one of the most important contemporary sociologists (and my most formidable and stimulating teacher), pro-

posed a theory of the demographic transition. Acknowledging that Malthus's theory still seemed applicable to less modern parts of the world, Davis attempted to isolate those aspects of modernization that Malthus had not anticipated.

Davis argued that modernization naturally leads to conditions encouraging low fertility. People in modern societies had fewer children because they no longer wanted large families. One reason was that with mortality so greatly reduced, especially infant and childhood mortality, families no longer needed to have many children to ensure that some lived to adulthood. Second, the economic value of children had declined. In fact, children ceased to be an economic asset and became an economic burden.

On preindustrial farms and even in preindustrial crafts and manufacture, child labor is valuable. For example, small children on preindustrial farms can more than earn their keep by feeding chickens, gathering eggs, herding animals, milking, pulling weeds, and helping with household chores. Under such circumstances, larger families tend to be wealthier than smaller families. But, as we shall examine in detail in the next chapter, a major aspect of modernization was a shift of population from farms to cities. In cities, the labor of children is of much less value than on a farm. In fact, city kids are a financial drain.

Drawing on the choice premise that is basic to all social science, Davis argued that as large families became a cost rather than a benefit, people changed their conceptions about how many children they wanted. His stress on choice is important because the great reduction in fertility in modern times occurred *before* most modern birth control devices were invented.

Indeed, anthropologists have found that techniques for limiting fertility are known and often practiced in even very primitive societies (Ford, 1952; Harris, 1979). Moreover, historical demographers have learned that Malthus was simply wrong in his belief that humans never restricted their fertility. Throughout European history, long before the Industrial Revolution, fertility was greatly controlled whenever conditions made reduced fertility a reasonable course of action. For example, fertility often fell

■ Children were an economic benefit on preindustrial farms: This New England farmer would have had a difficult time plowing with his ox team without his son to walk in front and goad the oxen. Although this picture was taken in 1899, long after the picture of harvesting in North Dakota, the farming methods in use are preindustrial. New technology was adopted much sooner in the frontier regions of the Great Plains than in the long-settled Northeast.

during economic depressions (Simon, 1981). The demographic transition did not reflect new contraceptive technology, but new conditions that influenced what people chose to do.

As outlined by Davis, the initial consequence of modernization is a sudden drop in mortality, which causes rapid population growth. This is because there is a delay before fertility begins to drop. The shifts from rural to urban living and from unskilled to skilled labor must also occur before the conditions that depress fertility prevail.

Davis's **demographic transition theory** has been subjected to a great deal of refinement and testing in the forty years since it was first published. In the current form of the theory, demographers have included a number of "thresholds" of modernization that must be crossed before fertility is substantially reduced.

A listing of these thresholds by Bernard Berelson (1978) helps clarify the theory:

1. More than half of the labor force is not employed in agriculture.

2. More than half of the persons from age 5 to 19 are enrolled in school.

3. The average life expectancy reaches 60 years.

4. Infant mortality falls to 65 deaths per 1,000 infants.

5. Eighty percent of females from age 15 to 19 are not married.

6. Per capita gross national product reaches $450.

7. At least 70 percent of adults can read.

Berelson's focus was on the less developed nations and in predicting when their rapid population growth would be halted by the demographic transition. However, the demographic transition theory offers a powerful explanation

Number of Children Born to Average Female

West Germany	1.4	Portugal	2.3
Sweden	1.5	Greece	2.3
Netherlands	1.5	Czechoslovakia	2.3
Switzerland	1.5	Poland	2.3
Finland	1.6	Spain	2.4
United Kingdom	1.6	USSR	2.4
Austria	1.6	Romania	2.5
Belgium	1.6	Ireland	3.2
		Albania	3.6

Denmark	1.7
Norway	1.8
France	1.8
Italy	1.8
East Germany	1.8
Yugoslavia	2.1
Hungary	2.1
Bulgaria	2.2

Infant Mortality per 1,000 Live Births

Sweden	6.7	Bulgaria	19.9
Finland	7.7	Poland	21.2
Denmark	8.5	Hungary	23.1
Switzerland	8.5	Portugal	26.0
Netherlands	8.6	Romania	31.6
Norway	8.8	Yugoslavia	32.8
France	10.0	USSR	36.0
Belgium	11.0	Albania	47.0

Spain	11.1
United Kingdom	11.8
East Germany	12.1
Ireland	12.4
West Germany	12.6
Austria	13.9
Italy	14.3
Czechoslovakia	16.6
Greece	18.7

Figure 18-6 ■ **Fertility and infant mortality in Europe.** The map on the left shows the most recent fertility rate for each of the major nations of Europe. In Albania and Ireland, the average woman still bears more than three children, while in most other nations of southern and eastern Europe the fertility rate exceeds two children. In the most industrial and affluent nations of northern and western Europe, fertility is well below replacement levels. The map on the right shows the infant mortality rate—the number of children who die before age 1 per 1,000 live births. Here, too, Albania is the highest and the overall close correspondence between the maps reveals that a major factor in large families is the need to "hoard" children against infant and childhood mortality.

Table 18-2 ■ Demographic transition thresholds and fertility in Europe.*

Threshold	Correlation with Fertility Rate
1. Percent not employed in agriculture	−.87
2. High school enrollment	−.49
3. Average life expectancy	−.69
4. Low rate of infant mortality	−.85
5. Low rate of teenage marriage	−.62
6. Affluence:	
TVs per 1,000	−.86
Telephones per 1,000	−.78
7. Literacy	−.75

Source: ShowCase Presentational Software, *Aspects of Social Change in Europe and Latin America* (Seattle: Cognitive Development, Inc., 1986).

*Ireland was omitted as a deviant case.

Table 18-3 ■ Demographic transition thresholds and population growth in the 50 most populous nations.

Threshold	Correlation with Population Growth Rate
1. Percent not employed in agriculture	−.70
2. High school enrollment	−.71
3. Average life expectancy	−.76
4. Low rate of infant mortality	−.75
5. Low rate of teenage marriage	−.57
6. Affluence:	
GNP per capita	−.73
TV sets per 1,000	−.75
7. Literacy	−.80

Source: ShowCase Presentational Software, *World: The 50 Most Populous Nations*, data selected and supervised by Robert Szafran (Seattle: Cognitive Development, Inc., 1987).

of variations of fertility even among more developed nations such as those in Europe. Figure 18-6, for example, shows the great similarity in the patterns of fertility and infant mortality rates. Table 18-2 offers support for each of the seven thresholds formulated by Berelson. Each is very highly negatively correlated with fertility in Europe.

Table 18-3 provides a more global test of the demographic transition theory by analyzing data from each of the fifty nations with the largest populations—including some that are quite underdeveloped and have rapidly growing populations. Instead of fertility, here the dependent variable is the rate of population growth. There is a huge, negative correlation between population growth and measures of each threshold.

When he published these thresholds, Berelson (1978) pointed out that they were not meant as precise rules, nor would a nation have to fulfill all seven in order to undergo the demographic transition. He suspected that meeting

any three or four might suffice to cause a decline in a nation's fertility.

Several years later, Cutright and Hargens (1984) showed that Latin American nations that meet the two thresholds of 70 percent adult literacy and 60-year life expectancy have declining fertility. Unfortunately, many of the nations of the world fall short of all of these thresholds.

This fact has troubled demographers and produced doomsday predictions about a "population bomb." Many dire predictions have been highly publicized during the past twenty years, each claiming that a huge new population explosion may soon reactivate Malthus's positive checks. Although many nations have failed to become sufficiently modernized to reduce their fertility, they have become modernized enough to reduce their mortality. Indeed, just about the same time that Davis published his theory, the *fourth great shift* in population trends occurred: massive, unprecedented population growth in the less developed nations.

The Second Population Explosion

As we have just seen, the first population explosion occurred in Europe and North America as a result of modernization. The industrialization of agriculture and advances in public health reduced mortality. Eventually, however, rapid population growth was halted by a decline in fertility. While the demographic transition changed basic population patterns in the modern nations, preindustrial population patterns persisted in the rest of the world: high fertility checked by high mortality. Then, suddenly, mortality quickly fell in less developed nations, thus initiating the greatest population explosion in history.

Shortly after the end of World War II, demographers noticed rapid population growth nearly everywhere on earth. Growth soon halted in the most modern nations, but elsewhere growth rates continued to rocket. Throughout the 1950s and 1960s, the population in most of the less developed nations grew by rates of from 2 to 3.5 percent a year. Such rates mean that populations double in size every twenty to thirty-five years. In other words, populations can increase enormously in a short time. For example, in the early 1970s, the world's population was growing at a rate that would double its size every thirty-seven years. If that rate were to hold for only 200 years, then instead of 5 billion people on earth, as there are now, there would be 157 billion!

Understandably, these population projections frightened demographers, as well as a lot of other people, and world population patterns received widespread publicity. For example, people were shocked when demographers pointed out that if Mexico continued to grow at the rate maintained during the thirty years following World War II, its population would increase from 63 million to 2 billion by the year 2080. Obviously, long before 2 billion people lived in Mexico, disaster would strike—if nothing else, massive starvation would set in.

In the wake of the second population explosion, predictions of world calamity received great publicity. Oddly enough, some of the most obviously faulty projections attracted the greatest attention and acceptance. A small book called *The Limits to Growth* (Meadows et al., 1972), which predicted that the world would run out of most raw materials and food in only a few years, sold over 4 million copies, despite its arguments having been dismissed as incompetent in virtually every scientific periodical (see Simon, 1981).

Still, very competent demographers and economists were influenced by the widespread anxiety about rapid population growth and warned of impending calamity. I confess that I joined in this dismal chorus. In a textbook on social problems I published in 1975, I ended the chapter on population by telling students that they would be hearing of terrible famines in the underdeveloped nations for the rest of their lives. That will not be the message of this chapter. Apparently Western social scientists forgot something important: Populations do not have babies—only people have babies. And people turn out to be a lot smarter than we sometimes assume. So let's examine the population explosion in the less developed nations to see why and how it occurred and how people have recently responded to it.

The sudden decline in mortality

Whereas the brief **baby boom** in Western nations after World War II was caused by a rise in fertility, the population explosion in the less developed nations was not. There, fertility had always been high. The population explosion was caused by a sudden and dramatic plunge in the mortality rate.

The most important feature of this decline in mortality is that it was produced primarily not by internal changes in these nations but by external forces: *Low mortality resulted from a few elements of modern technology imported from developed nations.* Thus, while the decline in mortality experienced in the West had developed slowly, in the less developed nations it came suddenly and often without significant changes in other parts of these societies. The result was a period of extreme cultural lag, as we shall see.

To grasp just how the second population explosion took place, consider the case of a single nation. At the end of World War II, Sri Lanka (then known as Ceylon) had a very high mortality rate typical of agrarian societies in warm latitudes. The average life expectancy was only 43 years, and the crude death rate in 1945 was about 22 deaths per 1,000.

Then, in 1946, the World Health Organization provided a small sum of money that Sri Lanka used to buy DDT from Switzerland and to hire some free-lance pilots with surplus U.S. Army planes to spray the country. Thus, in the most literal sense, a modern, low mortality rate fell upon Sri Lanka from the sky. Disease-carrying insects, especially the dreaded malaria-carrying mosquitoes, were nearly wiped out in a few days.

As a result, Sri Lanka's mortality rate fell by more than 40 percent within a few months. Understandably, everyone in Sri Lanka thought it was wonderful to have greatly increased life expectancy. Because this program could be continued simply and cheaply, it was continued. By 1954, Sri Lanka's crude death rate had fallen to about 10 per 1,000 per year. By 1975, it was down to 7.7—a rate lower than that of most modernized nations (partly due to Sri Lanka's very young population). As a result of its reduced mortality, Sri Lanka's population began to grow very rapidly.

In other less developed nations, similar changes took place: Insects were sprayed, swamps and stagnant pools of water were drained where insects bred, populations were inoculated against dangerous communicable diseases such as smallpox, and safe drinking water was provided. Everywhere the mortality rate plunged. From 1940 to 1965, the mortality rate fell by 59 percent in Mexico, 63 percent in Puerto Rico, 44 percent in Egypt, and 72 percent in Taiwan.

But something besides imported public health technology was involved in the second population explosion: the modernization of agriculture. Modern chemistry provides not only insect killers but also weed killers and fertilizers. Agricultural biologists have made rapid progress in breeding faster-growing, disease-resistant, higher-yielding varieties of basic food plants. The less developed nations also imported these plants, along with farm machinery and

■ A generation ago many of these children would already have been dead and others would have died before reaching adulthood. The introduction of modern sanitation and public health measures into the less developed world, during and just after World War II, caused a dramatic decline in death rates—and produced the second great population explosion.

modern irrigation techniques. Thus, the food supply increased in all parts of the world. Indeed, despite the rapid growth of population, food production increased even more rapidly; today people in most nations eat more and better food than they did twenty years ago. This change also reduced mortality.

High fertility and cultural lag

The demographic transition theory suggests that the long-term effect of modernization is population stability: Eventually fertility will bal-

■ These boats, which belong to a remote tribe of Indians in Mexico, symbolize the cultural gap responsible for the population explosion in the less developed world. When modern levels of mortality were combined with preindustrial levels of fertility, the future of these societies was placed in jeopardy. When powerful modern outboard motors were combined with primitive wooden boats, the future of the passengers was placed in jeopardy.

ance out with mortality. The question posed about the population explosion in the less developed nations is whether they will have the time to pass through the demographic transition before their populations become so huge that mass starvation results.

The demographic transition in the West was gradual, based on broad internal social changes, and the first population explosion was slow compared with the second. In the West, infant mortality fell slowly for a number of generations, and people had a long time to adjust to the changed conditions. So a gradual downward trend in fertility was sufficient to prevent catastrophic rates of growth. Some people argue that mortality has fallen so fast in the less

developed nations that people have had no time to adjust. Age-old customs favoring high fertility are necessarily slow to change, but unless they change very rapidly, runaway population growth will overwhelm these nations.

This resultant cultural lag has been the focus of the grave anxieties about the second population explosion. Indeed, hundreds of millions of dollars have been spent to popularize family planning and to reduce fertility in the less developed nations. However, for a long time, it looked as if these programs would fail and that fertility would not be checked in time. This prompted not only projections of disaster but also the frequent depiction of people in the less developed nations as virtual animals, incapable of reasonable behavior. For example, William Vogt (1948), in the first best-selling book on the population explosion, blamed it on "untrammeled copulation" by people in the less developed nations, whom he characterized as the "backward billion." Many others asserted that fertility in these less developed nations was outside the realm of decision making (Simon, 1981).

Amidst all this hue and cry, people in many of the less developed countries began to respond reasonably to their new conditions. The cultural lag began to be reduced. As happened in the modernized nations, fertility began to decline in most of the less developed nations. Thus, the *fifth great shift in population* patterns began to develop.

The Population Explosion Wanes

By the early 1970s, leading demographers began to detect a fertility decline in the less developed nations. At first the downturns seemed slight, and for a while no one was willing to announce a significant new trend. Moreover, projections were difficult because population statistics for many of the less developed nations are unreliable.

But as time passed and more statistics came in, it became clear that very substantial fertility declines were taking place in most of the less developed nations where population growth had been exploding. In fact, fertility began to go down in most of these countries at the very height of the population explosion scare in the West—in the latter 1960s.

For example, between 1965 and 1975, India's crude birth rate fell by 16 percent, China's by 24 percent, South Korea's by 32 percent, Colombia's by 25 percent, Malaysia's by 26 percent, and Sri Lanka's by 18 percent. Declines at least as great are predicted for the period from 1975 to 1985, although the figures will probably not become available until around 1990 (Berelson, 1978).

The fertility rate has not yet fallen in every less developed nation, but substantial declines have occurred in most, particularly those with the largest populations. Countries where fertility has not fallen have only 16 percent of the total population of the less developed nations.

Keep in mind that populations that have been growing rapidly will still continue to grow even after their fertility has fallen to replacement level. This is because in quickly growing populations, each new birth cohort is larger than the one before it. Thus, even when fertility falls to replacement level, the largest age cohorts have yet to pass through their reproductive years, and even if they only replace themselves, the population will increase further.

A second aspect is that even in many less developed nations that achieved really substantial fertility reductions between 1960 and 1980, the mortality rate fell just as fast so that there was no net decline in population growth. However, as Cutright and Smith (1986) point out, for many of these nations "the fall in mortality is nearly over, and future diminution of fertility should have substantial impact on growth rates."

Taken altogether, these developments invalidate the projections of huge world population totals that were considered nearly certain only a few years ago. We still cannot be sure how large the world's population will become or that overpopulation problems have been wholly averted. Some nations are likely to experience severe problems caused by overpopulation. Nonetheless, there has been a dramatic improvement in the overall picture. To conclude this chapter, let us examine this picture in greater detail.

Bernard Berelson: Stability by the Year 2000?

 Perhaps no demographer has paid closer attention to population trends and efforts to reduce fertility in the less developed nations than Bernard Berelson, who for many years served as president of the Population Council, an organization of demographers devoted to international research. Berelson was one of the first to spot the sudden decline in fertility rates in the developing nations and played the major role in assessing just where and why it was taking place. In 1978, when many scholars were still warning that population catastrophe was at hand, Berelson published a major reassessment of future growth.

Berelson concentrated his analysis on the twenty-nine largest less developed nations, each having a population of more than 10 million. The goal of his study was to predict which of these nations would be likely to reduce their annual crude birth rate to 20 per 1,000 by the year 2000. A crude birth rate of 20 translates into approximately 2.5 births per adult female. Given the probable infant and child mortality in these nations, this birth rate would be close to replacement-level fertility; at most, this would produce very little population growth.

Berelson found that the population patterns and modernization rates divided these nations into four categories. First were three nations that seemed "certain" to achieve a crude birth rate of 20 by the year 2000 and probably much sooner: South Korea, Taiwan, and Chile. Next were ten nations for whom it seemed "probable" that the crude birth rate would fall to 20 by the end of the century: China, Brazil, Mexico, Philippines, Thailand, Turkey, Colombia, Sri Lanka, Venezuela, Malaysia.

Berelson rated India, Indonesia, Egypt, and Peru as "possible." Finally, twelve nations seemed "unlikely" to succeed in bringing their fertility that low by the year 2000: Bangladesh, Pakistan, Nigeria, Iran, Zaire, Afghanistan, Sudan, Morocco, Algeria, Tanzania, Kenya, and Nepal. Fortunately, these twelve nations make up only 16 percent of the total population of the twenty-nine nations. Unfortunately, they are concentrated on the continent of Africa and thus lack close neighbors who could give them aid.

Why have some of these nations been so much more successful than others in reducing fertility? The answer lies in the demographic transition theory. Recall that the reduced fertility of the West is the result of modernization: Modern conditions of life discourage high levels of fertility.

We also saw that demographers (especially Berelson) had made the demographic transition theory more precise by stating a set of thresh-

olds of modernization that marked when fertility would decline. By the late 1960s and early 1970s, many of these nations had crossed many of the thresholds of modernization, and their fertility suddenly declined as predicted. This further supported the demographic transition theory.

In rating the chances of each of the twenty-nine larger developing nations to control their fertility by the year 2000, Berelson (1978) used the seven thresholds of modernization discussed earlier in this chapter. The nations he rated in the "certain" category have crossed nearly all of the thresholds, as have those in the probable category. Those rated as possible have crossed only a few thresholds, but are moving closer to them. The nations rated as unlikely are still well below achieving these thresholds of modernization. Their fertility has not yet begun to decline because they have not yet become sufficiently modernized.

Since Berelson's study was published in 1978, the evidence has supported his predictions that population growth would slow in many of the less developed nations. In some of them changes have been absolutely dramatic. For example, the fertility rate in *rural* China fell from 6.7 children in about 1970 to 3.0 in 1979—the most rapid decline ever recorded for a large population (Lavely, 1984). Table 18-4 lets us examine the onset of the demographic transition *within* a nation; it shows the correlations between most of Berelson's thresholds and the fertility rate, using data for each of the thirty provinces of China. The correlations are very high and negative.

Although Berelson's thresholds have proven invaluable, other demographers have been hard at work to make them even more precise.

Cutright and Smith: "second" threshold projections

Phillips Cutright and Herbert L. Smith (1986) suspected that Berelson's thresholds might be improved if they were not treated as having a single value, constant over time. For example, instead of treating gen-

Table 18-4 ■ **Demographic transition thresholds and fertility in China.**

Threshold	Correlation with Fertility Rate
1. Percent not employed in agriculture	−.66
2. Percent high school graduates	−.74
3. Life expectancy	−.67
4. Low rate of infant mortality	Not available
5. Low rate of teenage marriage	Not available
6. Affluence:	
GNP per capita	−.74
Percent of farms with TVs	−.65
Percent of farms with phones	−.74
7. Literacy	−.67

Source: ShowCase Presentational Software, *Modern China*, data selected and supervised by Xin Hun Ren and William R. Lavely (Seattle: Cognitive Development, Inc., 1987).

eral mortality simply as a single threshold of an average life expectancy of 60 years, Cutright and Smith suggested there may be a series of life expectancy thresholds, each with an accelerating impact on fertility decline. As conceived by Berelson, once a sufficient number of constant thresholds have been fulfilled, fertility will begin to drop and will continue to do so until replacement levels, or lower, have been reached. Cutright and Smith thought this unlikely and therefore set out to create a model that would compare the impact of a threshold as a single value or as one taking a succession of values.

Cutright and Smith concentrated on the effects of changes in life expectancy on fertility. They gathered data on life expectancy from eighty-three less developed nations—all of those for whom trustworthy statistics exist. The data were for three successive decades: 1950–60,

1960–70, 1970–80. They found that there are *two* major life-expectancy thresholds. Until a life expectancy of 46 years is reached, there is no correlation between life expectancy and fertility. That is, nations whose populations have a life expectancy of, say, 42 years do not have lower fertility than do nations where the life expectancy is 32 years. But, among nations with a life expectancy of 46 or higher, there is a strong negative correlation—the higher the life expectancy, the lower the fertility. There is a second threshold at 56. For nations with life expectancies of 56 or more, the correlation between expectancy and fertility is even higher. This is illustrated in Table 18-2, which reports a huge negative correlation between life expectancy and fertility among European nations—all of which are well above the 56-year threshold. (Albania, Yugoslavia, and the Soviet Union have the lowest life expectancies in Europe, 69 years.)

Cutright and Smith then used a model based on these results to project the population patterns of these less developed nations. When compared with Berelson's projections, Cutright and Smith's were a bit less optimistic about how many would achieve the goal of a crude birth rate of 20 per 1,000 or less by the year 2000. Their findings supported Berelson's on the three nations in the "certain" category. But of those Berelson classified as "probable," Cutright and Smith projected only China and Sri Lanka as reaching the goal. However, they projected four others as at or near the 20 per 1,000 fertility level by 2010. They projected crude birth rates of from 23.8 (India) to 27.4 (Indonesia) for the nations Berelson identified as "possible." Finally, their projections placed all of those Berelson classed as "unlikely" in the over 30 births per 1,000 range. While Cutright and Smith's results are less optimistic than Berelson's, they too project a much less dismal future than that taken for granted only a few years ago.

But simply because the shrill forecasts of an unstoppable population explosion turned out to be wrong, it would be equally misinformed to assume that the problems have all been solved. Clearly, the twelve nations in the unlikely category, with a current population total of 383 million, may encounter serious problems. Still, their problems should not be insurmountable

Table 18-5 ■ Infant deaths per 1,000 live births in the 50 most populous nations.

Japan	6	Vietnam	55
Canada	8	Thailand	57
France	8	China	61
United Kingdom	9	Brazil	63
Taiwan	9	South Africa	72
West Germany	10	Kenya	76
East Germany	10	Iraq	80
Australia	10	Algeria	81
United States	11	Indonesia	88
Spain	11	Morocco	90
Italy	11	Turkey	92
Czechoslovakia	14	Egypt	93
Poland	19	Peru	94
Romania	26	India	101
Soviet Union	26	Zaire	103
Yugoslavia	29	Burma	103
Sri Lanka	30	Tanzania	111
South Korea	30	Sudan	112
Malaysia	30	Nepal	112
North Korea	33	Iran	113
Argentina	35	Nigeria	124
Venezuela	38	Pakistan	125
Colombia	48	Bangladesh	140
Mexico	50	Ethiopia	152
Philippines	50	Afghanistan	182

Source: ShowCase Presentational Software, *World: The 50 Most Populous Nations,* data selected and supervised by Robert Szafran (Seattle: Cognitive Development, Inc., 1987).

with assistance from other countries, because current projections do not indicate the imminent exhaustion of raw materials or food supplies. Even in many of the nations rated as unlikely to reduce fertility soon, the food supply has greatly increased (Simon, 1981). Bangladesh, for example, the largest of the unlikely group, has recently increased its agricultural production significantly. And American agriculture remains severely hampered by overproduction despite elaborate government programs to limit planting.

Yet it would be wrong to overlook the misery that abounds in the nations where development lags while fertility remains high. Table 18-5 reveals that an infant born in Japan is thirty times as likely to live past his or her first birthday than is an infant born in Afghanistan. Cana-

dian infants are nearly eighteen times more likely to live for at least a year than are infants born in Bangladesh. And if people in nations with such high infant mortality rates continue to have high birth rates, it is partly because they are trying to beat these odds against survival.

■

Conclusion

There have been five major shifts in human population patterns during the past 10,000 years. The first of these occurred when the invention of agriculture permitted the population to begin to grow rapidly. This period of growth, however, was marked by cycles of growth and decline, as population was periodically cut back by sudden rises in mortality. This led Malthus to formulate a theory of population based entirely on fluctuations of mortality.

But no sooner had Malthus published his book than a second great shift occurred. Industrialization stimulated a long period of uninterrupted growth, sometimes referred to as the first population explosion. After several centuries of rapid population growth in the industrial countries, a third great shift occurred—one Malthus had believed impossible. Population was halted by a decline in fertility. This is called the demographic transition, which resulted in stable populations in which low mortality was balanced by low fertility.

In the aftermath of World War II, a fourth population change took place, a population explosion in the less developed nations caused by decreased mortality and increased food supplies. This growth was so rapid that many people predicted a return to Malthusian conditions, in which terrible famines would halt population growth. These predictions failed to anticipate the fifth major shift in population patterns: sharply falling fertility in most of the less developed nations as they, too, underwent the demographic transition.

This last shift in population patterns took most scholars, even expert demographers, by surprise. Perhaps the most influential book on population problems was *The Population Bomb*, published in 1968 by Paul Ehrlich, a biologist at Stanford University. In it he wrote, "The battle to feed all of humanity is over. In the 1970s the world will undergo famines—hundreds of millions are going to starve to death." In 1974 the famous novelist and scientist C. P. Snow told the *New York Times*, "Perhaps in ten years, millions of people in the poor countries are going to starve to death before our very eyes. . . . We shall see them doing so upon our television sets."

And in 1975 I wrote in a textbook for college students:

The population explosion is not just someone else's problem. It threatens every nation and every person. There will surely be global famines and mass starvation. . . . For the rest of your life, you will be hearing of terrible famines.

Despite such hysterical predictions, per capita food production continued to increase worldwide, as it had been doing for decades (Simon, 1981). We are now nearly into the 1990s, and millions have not dropped dead of hunger. Instead, the world has continued to eat even better than in the 1970s. Despite the hoopla over "Band Aid" for Ethiopia, the famine there is *not* mainly due to population pressure. The proximate cause is a long drought; the more general cause is Ethiopian government policy preventing food, even that sent by Western relief agencies, from reaching its destination.

Demographic and economic forecasting is extremely difficult and frequently very wrong. The possibility of error is maximized when current trends are projected into the future without an underlying theory about relationships among these trends. Here we see that much more attention should have been given to demographic transition theory and much less to simple projections of fertility. The less developed nations not only experienced a huge decline in mortality because of modernization but also increased their agricultural production, thus increasing food supplies. In time, modernization began to have the predicted effects on their fertility.

Reactions to the population explosion might have been more subdued had social scientists remembered that at many times in history humans have limited their fertility when necessary. If even primitive tribes have achieved low fertility when they wanted to, then we should have suspected that people in nations already somewhat modernized might possess similar abilities. And, of course, they did.

In this chapter, I have tried to explain population trends. However, after all is said and done, the key to understanding population lies in the most basic premise of micro sociology, introduced in Chapter 1. Human behavior is based on choice, and humans choose to do what they believe to be in their own best interests. When mortality is high, the reasonable family will have many children. But when mortality is low and children are not an economic asset, the reasonable family will have fewer children. And that is the fundamental thesis Davis developed in his theory of the demographic transition.

Review Glossary

Domesday Book Pronounced "doomsday" book, this was an outstanding medieval census conducted by William the Conqueror following his takeover of England in 1066. (p. 520)

census A population count, often recorded in terms of categories such as age, sex, occupation, marital status, and the like. The United States Census is conducted during the first year of each decade. (p. 522)

demography Literally, written description of the people; the field of sociology devoted to the study of human populations with regard to how they grow, decline, or migrate. (p. 522)

growth rate Population gains or losses computed by dividing the net gain or loss for a particular period by the population total at the start of that period. (p. 523)

crude death rate The total number of deaths for a year (or similar period) divided by the total population that year. (p. 523)

crude birth rate The total number of births for a year (or similar period) divided by the total population that year. (p. 523)

fertility rate The total number of births for a year divided by the total number of women in their child-bearing years (the U.S. Census bases this rate on all women from age 15 to 44). (p. 523)

age-specific death rates The number of deaths per year of persons within a given age range divided by the total number of persons within that age range. (p. 524)

birth cohort All persons born within a given time period, usually one year. (p. 525)

age structure The proportions of persons of various age groups making up a total population. (p. 527)

sex structure The proportions of males and females in a population. (p. 527)

expansive population structure An age structure in which each younger cohort is larger than the one before it; such a population is growing. (p. 527)

stationary population structure An age structure in which younger birth cohorts are the same size as older ones were before mortality reduced them; such a population neither grows nor declines. (p. 527)

constrictive population structure An age structure in which younger cohorts are smaller than the ones before them; such a population is shrinking. (p. 527)

arithmetic increase A constant rate of growth (or decline); the same number of units are added (or subtracted) each cycle, as in 1-2-3-4-5. (p. 531)

exponential increase A rate of growth (or decline) that speeds up as an increasingly larger number of units is added (or subtracted) each cycle, as in 1-2-4-8-16. (p. 531)

positive checks According to Malthus, famine, disease, and war—the primary factors that check or stop population growth. (p. 532)

Malthusian theory of population Theory stating that populations will always rise to, and then somewhat above, the limits of subsistence and then will be reduced by the positive checks, only to rise again and be checked again. (p. 533)

replacement-level fertility (sometimes called **zero population growth**) Point at which the number of births each year equals the number of deaths. (p. 536)

demographic transition A shift in population trends from high fertility, controlled by high mortality, to one of low mortality and low fertility. (p. 536)

demographic transition theory Theory stating that the demographic transition was caused by modernization, which reduced the need for and the value of large numbers of children. (p. 537)

baby boom A brief period of high fertility in many Western industrial nations immediately following World War II. (p. 540)

Suggested Readings

Berelson, Bernard. 1978. "Prospects and Programs for Fertility Reduction: What? Where?" *Population and Development Review* 4:579–616.

Cutright, Phillips. 1983. "The Ingredients of Recent Fertility Decline in Developing Countries." *International Family Planning Perspectives* 9:101–118.

Davis, Kingsley. 1945. "The World Demographic Transition." *Annals of the American Academy of Political and Social Sciences* 237:1–11.

Petersen, William. 1975. *Population*. New York: Macmillan.

Simon, Julian L. 1981. *The Ultimate Resource*. Princeton, N.J.: Princeton University Press.

Wrigley, E. A. 1969. *Population and History*. New York: McGraw-Hill.

The Life Cycle
of the Baby Boom

In May 1946, nine months after the surrender of Japan brought World War II to an end, demographers noticed that the number of births in the United States was up that month by 10 percent. The next month fertility continued to rise. By October births were up 50 percent. And by the end of the year an all-time record of 3.4 million births had been established—one baby had been born every nine seconds.

These statistics were widely publicized and prompted many jokes about returning war veterans. But no one took this surge in fertility very seriously. During 1946 the director of the U.S. Bureau of the Census explained that the U.S. population might climb as high as 163 million by the year 2000, but that the current spurt in the birth rate was a brief and freakish postwar event. Demographers agreed that the American population could never come close to the 200 million mark—for the demographic transition had already taken place, and it was final. Indeed, most of what was written about fertility in 1946 and 1947 was concerned with a fertility deficit that would cause the population to decline rapidly.

How little the experts knew. For the "baby boom" following World War II was not a brief event. The birth rate remained high for almost twenty years—not until 1965 did it drop back to the level of 1940. The unthinkable 200 million mark was passed in 1968.

Moreover, the baby boom was not limited to the United States. Canadian fertility followed the same path, shooting up in 1946 and coming back to prewar levels in the early 1960s. In some parts of Europe a baby boom took place too, but usually on a much smaller scale.

The baby boom was far more than a set of birth statistics. The reality was that nations with relatively few infants and children suddenly were filled with them. As high fertility persisted, these huge birth cohorts of infants and young children began to cause major social changes. In fact, the baby boom age cohorts, those born between the mid-1940s and the early 1960s (and who are now in their late 20s to early 40s) continue to have immense impact simply because there are so many of them. Let's retrace the impact of the "baby boomers" on North American societies and then anticipate their influence on the future.

Early Days

If academic demographers took a while to grasp the meaning of the rapidly rising fertility rates in the aftermath of the war, American business was not slow to see that radical changes were being wrought in basic consumer market patterns.

Consider the following statistics for the United States (Jones, 1980).

- Sales of baby food rose from 270 million cans in 1940 to 1.5 billion in 1953.

- Sales of toys grew from $84 million a year in 1940 to $1.25 billion by the early 1950s.

- Business boomed for companies that bronze-plated baby shoes.

- Diaper sales doubled and redoubled as did sales of washing machines.
- In June 1946, Pocket Books published *The Common Sense Book of Baby and Child Care*, by Benjamin Spock, M.D. Unadvertised, unpromoted, and unreviewed, the 35-cent book sold 4 million copies by 1952 and has now sold well over 30 million copies.

New parents were not only rushing to buy food, clothing, and toys for their infants but also were seeking a comfortable environment in which to raise them: The baby boom accompanied a massive expansion of the suburbs. Between 1950 and 1970 the suburban populations of Canada and the United States doubled. More than 80 percent of the population growth during this period was located in the suburbs, as were 85 percent of all the homes built then. Suburban life influenced other consumption patterns. It spurred automobile sales by making the two-car family necessary. Sales of lawn furniture and backyard barbecues zoomed, and hot-dog sales tripled in the decade of the 1950s.

The average American and Canadian family, now living in the suburbs with young children, changed its entertainment patterns. Mom and dad no longer went dancing, and the era of Big Bands and popular ballrooms came to a crashing end. Moreover, mom and dad stopped going to movie theaters (and during the 1950s large numbers of huge, luxurious, downtown movie palaces closed their doors). Instead, they loaded the whole family in the station wagon and went to the drive-in. In 1948 there were fewer than 500 drive-in movies in North America. A decade later there were more than 4,000, with everything from playgrounds to Laundromats. When they weren't at the drive-in, the baby boom family was beginning to sit in front of a flickering little box in their living rooms and watch television.

The baby boom kids were the first to grow up with television, the first to sing "M-I-C-K-E-Y M-O-U-S-E," the first to, in effect, live in a movie theater. From the very start television has been shaped to an extraordinary extent by and for the baby boomers. Early television was inundated with programming for little kids, and the grown-up shows mirrored the lives of the suburban baby boom family: "Ozzie and Harriet," "Father Knows Best," and "Leave It to Beaver."

Then one day the baby boom kids headed off for school. When they got there they found they were unexpected. In 1952–1953 the kids born in 1946–1947 turned six and began first grade—their group was much larger than the group a year ahead of them! As they passed through the school system, followed by even larger waves of students, they burst the seams of the system. By 1964 one of every four North Americans was enrolled in the lower grades or in high school.

Because demographers had claimed, through the first years of this population explosion, that it would be brief and unimportant, provision had not been made to provide space and teachers for these throngs who suddenly showed up at the classroom door. Many schools went to double-shift schedules, and everywhere class sizes were huge. Crash school construction programs began everywhere—during the 1950s, California opened a new school every week. Because they were in such demand, teachers found their salaries rising rapidly.

Looking back, we can see that the schools were not able to cope with the baby boom and that the quality of education that members of these cohorts received probably was seriously inferior to that of people slightly older. In 1964 the first crop of baby boomers graduated from high school and took the Scholastic Aptitude Test (SAT). Their average score was lower than that of the year before. And every year after that the average SAT score in the United States fell, until 1982 when the last boomers had graduated.

The growing baby boom kids had a major impact after school too. Their tastes registered in a series of fads (see Chapter 21). For example, in 1955 kids reacted to an episode on the Disneyland TV show, starring Fess Parker as Davy Crockett, and went out to spend more than $100 million in seven months, buying imitation coonskin caps (real coonskin prices jumped up by 3200 percent), toy muzzle-loading rifles, T-shirts, and thousands of other items with a Crockett motif. In 1958 they rushed to buy more than 20 million Hula Hoops in a few months.

Table ST6-1 ■ The baby boomers work out.

	Baby Boomers (%)	People Older Than Baby Boomers (%)
Belong to a health club	17	8
Currently in an exercise class	18	9
Do garden and lawn work	49	61
Take regular walks	56	56
Go hunting	14	10
Go fishing	29	26
Jog regularly	26	10
Swim regularly	46	23
Bicycle regularly	29	11

Adapted from: Brown (1984).

The Teen Boom

The baby boom eventually produced crops of teenagers who continued to cause dislocations and rearrangements in the world around them. The sales of skin medications skyrocketed. So did record sales. With these sales came a dramatic shift in what music was popular and in the range of music performed. Although the baby boomers did not invent rock and roll, they turned it into what was, for over a decade, the *only* popular music—the maturing baby boomers had ears for only "their" songs. An immense repertoire of popular songs suddenly disappeared. (This music began to reappear in the 1980s, often revived by country performers such as Willie Nelson.)

Of course, the baby boomers soon did to colleges and universities what they had done to the public schools. Never before had so many people attended college. More important, never before had so high a proportion of people attended. The consequence was a massive increase in the number and the size of colleges and universities and in the number of faculty members.

Moving On

Thus far we have looked only at the impact of the front end of the baby boom, but they left important consequences behind them as well. For example, the boom in elementary education turned to a bust in the 1970s as the small birth cohorts behind the baby boom left the nation with far too many schools and teachers. A similar, but less sharp, depression also hit higher education as large cohorts have been followed by smaller ones. Moreover, since the baby boom, fertility rates have fallen to all-time lows, and baby product manufacturers have struggled to survive in shrunken markets. The amount of children's television programming has declined.

In June 1984 perhaps the most symbolic event in the baby boom's passage through the life cycle came in the announcement by Levi Strauss & Co. that it was shutting eleven manufacturing plants, laying off 3,200 workers. This brought to twenty-seven the number of plants the company had closed in less than two years. What did these plants make? The famous Levi's blue jeans. Why did the plants close? Because the

Table ST6-2 ■ **The baby boomers play.**

	Baby Boomers (%)	People Older Than Baby Boomers (%)
Attend plays	18	19
Eat out	68	67
Read	63	65
Watch television	80	85
Go to movies	66	35
Attend concerts	33	16
Go to parties	66	49
Listen to records	71	46
Play video games	25	8
Do volunteer work	12	19

Adapted from: Brown (1984).

baby boomers outgrew the age for wearing blue jeans, according to company officials, and there was a sudden drop in the size of the population 18 to 24 years old, the primary jeans consumers. In the 1960s and early 1970s, the baby boomers had made Levi Strauss one of America's most successful companies. Then they left Levi Strauss with far too much production capacity.

Now other companies enjoy a huge upsurge in sales. The hot new products suddenly are those associated with anxieties about getting old— many of the baby boomers are over 40. The runaway sales figures for *Jane Fonda's Workout Book* and her exercise videotapes reflect the sudden new market for fitness. Creams to keep the skin soft and youthful have taken over the markets once dominated by acne remedies. Table ST6-1 shows that the baby boomers are twice as likely as older Americans to belong to a health club and to be currently taking part in an exercise class. However, they are much less likely to get exercise by doing garden or lawn work, they are no more likely to go for regular walks, and not much more likely to hunt or fish. But they are much more likely than older Americans to jog, swim, and ride bicycles.

In other aspects of leisure-time pursuits, the baby boomers often have distinctive patterns too. Table ST6-2 shows that they are not more likely to attend plays, eat out, read, or watch TV. But they are much more likely to go to movies and concerts, to attend parties, to listen to records, and to play video games. And the baby boomers, with a reputation as a self-centered generation, are less likely to perform volunteer work. Given the disproportionate size of the baby boomer age cohorts, these preferences continue to shape our leisure economy.

■

The Future

Of course, the wrinkle creams and the fitness programs will not work in the long run: The baby boomers will get old. When they do they will continue to shape society. Businesses and products directed at the elderly ought to thrive. But perhaps the major impact will be an overload on the economy as we find that the retired population outnumbers those who are working. How will today's cohorts of college freshmen manage to provide adequate goods and services for such a huge number of dependents? It seems likely that many of the baby boomers won't retire or won't retire as young as most people do today. For as the baby boomers begin to reach these ages a labor shortage will develop (unless increased immigration greatly expands the pop-

■ The baby boom cohorts were the first to grow up with television. In the 1950s the puppet Howdy Doody and his friends, Buffalo Bob and Clarabell the clown, had the top-rated children's show.

ulation younger than the baby boomers). Such a labor shortage will give many baby boomers a chance to stay in their jobs beyond the age of 65 or 70. But will they want to?

In future years you will hear much discussion of these issues and of what policies and programs ought to be pursued. But the reason for all these problems remains a simple one: For a few years following World War II young Canadian and American couples turned their backs on the demographic transition and produced relatively large families in a short period of time. This resulted in some immense age cohorts and, ever since, they have formed a disproportionate population bubble moving through the life cycle, distorting the system as it goes.

Urbanization

19

UNTIL VERY RECENTLY, the vast majority of human beings lived and died without ever seeing a city. The first city was probably founded no more than 5,500 years ago. But even 200 years ago, only a few people could live in cities; nearly everyone lived on farms or in tiny rural villages. It was not until this century that Great Britain became the first **urban society** in history—a society in which the majority of people live in cities and do not farm for a living.

Britain was only the beginning. Soon many other industrial nations became urban societies. The process of *urbanization*—the migration of people from the countryside to the city—was the result of modernization, which has rapidly transformed *how* people live and *where* they live. In 1900 fewer than 40 percent of Americans and Canadians lived in urban areas. Today, 74 percent of Americans and 76 percent of Canadians are urban residents, and fewer than 4 percent live on farms (the remainder live in small towns and villages).

Large cities were impossible until agriculture became industrialized. Recall from Chapter 10 that even in advanced agrarian societies, it took about ninety-five people on farms to feed five people in cities. That kept cities very small. Until modern times, cities were inhabited mainly by the ruling elite and the servants, laborers, craftsmen, and professionals who served them. Cities survived by taxing farmers and were limited in size by the amount of surplus food the rural population produced and by the ability to move this surplus from farm to city.

Over the past two centuries, the Industrial Revolution has shattered this balance between the city and the country. Modernization drew people to the cities and freed them to come by making farmers incredibly productive. Today, instead of our needing ninety-five farmers to feed five city people, one American farmer is able to feed nearly fifty nonfarmers.

Chapter Preview

This chapter examines the urbanization of industrial societies. It explores in detail why and how the shift to urban life occurred. We shall also examine the structure of cities: why and how cities have grown and changed. Finally, we shall consider the impact of urban living on people. Have big cities really worsened the quality of life, destroyed the intimacy of social relations, and undermined the health and sanity of human beings?

Before we turn to these questions, we need a basis for comparison. Let us therefore go back into history and examine what life was like in the famous cities of preindustrial times. What was it really like in ancient Athens and Rome? What was it like in London and Paris when they had only 40,000 to 50,000 residents and before they had factories or freeways, subways or suburbs?

Preindustrial Cities

Until very recently, cities were small, filthy, disease-ridden, densely packed with people, and disorderly, and they were dark and very danger-

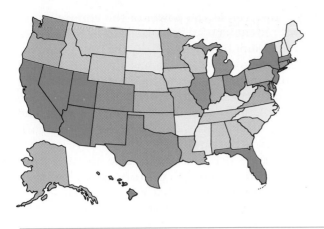

Vermont	33.7	Michigan	70.7	Pr. Edward Island	36.3	Alberta	77.0
West Virginia	36.1	Delaware	70.7	N.W. Territories	48.0	Quebec	77.6
South Dakota	46.4	New Mexico	72.1	New Brunswick	51.1	British Columbia	78.0
Mississippi	47.2	Ohio	73.3	Nova Scotia	55.2	Ontario	81.7
Maine	47.4	Washington	73.5				
North Carolina	47.9	Connecticut	78.8				
North Dakota	48.7	Texas	79.6				
Kentucky	50.8	Maryland	80.3				
Arkansas	51.5	Colorado	80.6				
New Hampshire	52.1	Illinois	83.3				

Montana	52.9	Massachusetts	83.8	Saskatchewan	58.2
Idaho	54.0	Arizona	83.8	Newfoundland	58.6
South Carolina	54.1	Florida	84.2	Yukon	64.0
Iowa	58.6	Utah	84.3	Manitoba	71.2
Alabama	60.0	New York	84.6		
Tennessee	60.4	Nevada	85.3		
Georgia	62.3	Hawaii	86.5		
Wyoming	62.6	Rhode Island	87.8		
Nebraska	62.9	New Jersey	89.0		
Wisconsin	64.1	California	91.2		

Indiana	64.2
Alaska	64.3
Virginia	66.0
Kansas	66.6
Minnesota	66.8
Oklahoma	67.2
Oregon	67.9
Missouri	68.1
Louisiana	68.6
Pennsylvania	69.3

Figure 19-1 ■ **Percent of population living in urban places.** Canada and the United States are nearly identical in terms of urbanization—three-fourths of their citizens live in places with a population of 2,500 or more. And in both nations, the extent of urbanization varies greatly from region to region. Urbanization is bicoastal in the United States; California is the most urban state, followed by New Jersey, Rhode Island, Hawaii, Nevada, and New York. Urbanization is least in Vermont, then West Virginia and South Dakota. Canada's most urban province is Ontario, followed by British Columbia, Quebec, and Alberta. Prince Edward Island is slightly more urban than Vermont. In this chapter we will see why and how nations recently became urbanized and the consequences of this shift.

Table 19-1 ■ **Population of major cities in preindustrial Europe.**

City	Population	Year
Amsterdam	7,476	1470
Brussels	19,058	1496
Berlin	6,000	1450
Geneva	4,204	1404
London	34,971	1377
Paris	59,200	1292
Pisa	9,940	1551
Rome	55,035	1526
Vienna	3,836	1391

Source: Russell (1958).

ous at night. If that description is unlike your image of Athens during the Golden Age of Greek civilization, that is because history so often leaves out the mud, manure, and misery.

Typically, preindustrial cities contained no more than 5,000 to 10,000 inhabitants (Table 19-1). Large national capitals were usually smaller than 40,000 and rarely larger than 60,000 (Russell, 1958). Few preindustrial cities, such as ancient Rome, grew as large as 500,000 and then only under special circumstances. Moreover, these cities rapidly shrank back to a much smaller size as slight changes in circumstance made it impossible to support them.

Limits on city style

A major reason why cities remained small was poor transportation; food had to be brought to feed a city. With only animal and human power to bring it, however, food could not be transported very far. Therefore, cities were limited to the population that could be fed by farmers nearby. The few large cities of preindustrial times appeared only where food could be brought long distances by water transport. Ancient Rome, for example, was able to reach the size of present-day Denver (and only briefly) because it controlled the whole Mediterranean area. Surplus food from this vast region was shipped by sea to feed the city's masses.

However, as the power of the empire weakened, Rome's population declined as the sources of food supplies dwindled. By the ninth century, the sea-power of Islam had driven nearly all European shipping from the Mediterranean, and the cities of southern Europe, including Rome, were virtually abandoned. In fact, Europe had practically no cities during the ninth and tenth centuries (Pirenne, 1925).

Disease also checked the size of cities. Even early in the twentieth century, cities had such high mortality rates that they required a large and constant influx of newcomers from the countryside just to maintain their populations. As recently as 1900, the death rate in English cities was 33 percent higher than that in rural areas (Davis, 1965). A major reason for the high mortality in cities was the high incidence of infectious diseases, which are spread by physical contact or by breathing in germs emitted by coughs and sneezes. Disease spreads much more slowly among less dense rural populations (McNeill, 1976).

Disease in cities was also caused by filth, especially by the contamination of water and food. Kingsley Davis (1965) pointed out that even as late as the 1850s, London's water "came mainly from wells and rivers that drained cesspools, graveyards, and tidal areas. The city was regularly ravaged by cholera."

Sewage treatment was unknown in preindustrial cities. Even sewers were uncommon, and what sewers there were consisted of open trenches running along the streets into which sewage, including human waste, was poured from buckets and chamber pots. Indeed, sewage was often poured out of second-story windows without any warning to pedestrians below.

Garbage was not collected and was strewn everywhere. It was hailed as a major step forward when cities began to keep a municipal herd of pigs, which were guided through the streets at night to eat the garbage dumped during the day. Of course, the pigs did considerable recycling as they went. Still, major cities in the eastern United States depended on pigs for their sanitation services until the end of the nineteenth century.

Today we are greatly concerned about pollution, especially that produced by automobile

■ The Dutch artist Pieter Brueghel demonstrated in this painting his awareness that the rise of the city depended on increased agricultural productivity. The city in the background could exist only because farmers like this plowman could produce enough surplus food to feed city people. When European peasants began to plow with horses rather than oxen, they could farm twice as much land and so cities got larger.

exhausts and factories. But the car and the factory cannot match the horse and the home fireplace when it comes to pollution. It is estimated that in 1900 horses deposited 26 million pounds of manure and 10 million gallons of urine on the streets of New York City every week.

London's famous and deadly "fogs" of previous centuries were actually smogs caused by thousands of smoking home chimneys during atmospheric inversions, which trapped the polluted air. Indeed, the first known air-quality law was decreed in 1273 by England's King Edward I. It forbade the use of a particularly smoky coal. The poet Shelley wrote early in the nineteenth century that "Hell is a city much like London, a populous and smokey city." In 1911, coal smoke

during an atmospheric inversion killed more than a thousand people in London, and this incident led to the coining of the word *smog* (Miller, 1982).

Pedestrians in preindustrial cities often held perfume-soaked handkerchiefs over their noses because the streets stank so. They kept alert for garbage and sewage droppings from above. They wore high boots because they had to wade through muck, manure, and garbage. And the people themselves were dirty because they seldom bathed. Not surprisingly, they died at a rapid rate (Figure 19-2).

Population density also contributed to the unhealthiness of preindustrial cities. People were packed closely together. As we saw in Chapter

■ Herds of municipal pigs such as these were used as street-cleaning crews in many nineteenth-century cities and even in small towns. These "road hogs" did remove some garbage, but they left more.

13, whole families lived in one small room. The houses stood wall to wall, and few streets were more than 10 to 12 feet wide.

Why was there such density when the population was so small? First of all, for most of its history, the city was also a fortress surrounded by massive walls for defense. Once the walls were up, the area of the city was fixed (at least until the walls were rebuilt), and if the population grew, people had to crowd ever closer. Even cities without walls were confined. Travel was by foot or by hoof. Cities did not spread beyond the radius that could be covered by these slow means of transportation, and thus the city limit was usually no more than 3 miles from the center (Blumenfeld, 1971).

Second, preindustrial cities could not expand upward. Not until the nineteenth century, when structural steel and reinforced concrete were

developed, could very tall structures be erected. Moreover, until elevators were invented, it was impractical to build very high. By expanding upward, people could have much greater living and working space in a building taking up no greater area at ground level. This could, of course, have meant that cities would become even more crowded at street level. They did not, however, because even modern high-rise cities have much more open space than did preindustrial cities, and, as we shall see, newer cities have expanded primarily outward rather than upward.

Preindustrial cities were not only dirty, disease-ridden, and dense but also dark and dangerous. Today we sometimes say people move to the city because they are attracted by the bright lights, and we joke about small towns where they "roll up the sidewalks by 9 P.M." The preindustrial city had no sidewalks to roll up

■ Nobody worried much about littering in cities where horse-drawn wagons were the primary means of transportation. The preindustrial city suffered from much worse problems of pollution than does the modern industrial city.

and no electricity to light up the night. If lighted at all, homes were badly and expensively illuminated by candles and oil lamps. Until the introduction of gas lamps in the nineteenth century, streets were not lighted at all. Out in the dark, dangerous people lurked, waiting for victims. To venture forth at night in many of these cities was so dangerous that people did so only in groups accompanied by armed men bearing torches. Many people today fear to walk in cities at night. Still, it is much safer to do so now than it used to be.

Why live in such cities?

Knowing what preindustrial cities were like, one must ask why anyone willingly lived there and why a large number of newcomers were attracted to cities each year from rural areas.

One reason was economic incentive. Cities offered many people a chance to increase their incomes. For example, the development of an extensive division of labor, of occupational specialization, virtually required cities. Specialists must depend upon one another for the many goods and services they do not provide for themselves. Such exchanges are hard to manage when people live far apart. Thus skilled craftsmen, merchants, physicians, and the like gathered in cities. Indeed, cities are vital to trade and commerce, and most early cities developed at intersections of major trade routes.

In addition to economic attractions, cities drew people because they offered the prospect of a more interesting and stimulating life. As

The Diseases, and Casualties this year being 1632.

A Bortive, and Stillborn	445	Grief	11
Affrighted	1	Jaundies	43
Aged	628	Jawfaln	8
Ague	43	Impostume	74
Apoplex, and Meagrom	17	Kil'd by several accidents	46
Bit with a mad dog	1	King's Evil	38
Bleeding	3	Lethargie	2
Bloody flux, scowring, and flux	348	Livergrown	87
Bruscd, Issues, sores, and ulcers	28	Lunatique	5
Burnt, and Scalded	5	Made away themselves	15
Burst, and Rupture	9	Measles	80
Cancer, and Wolf	10	Murthered	7
Canker	1	Over-laid, and starved at nurse	7
Childbed	171	Palsie	25
Chrisomes, and Infants	2268	Piles	1
Cold, and Cough	55	Plague	8
Colick, Stone, and Strangury	56	Planet	13
Consumption	1797	Pleurisie, and Spleen	36
Convulsion	241	Purples, and spotted Feaver	38
Cut of the Stone	5	Quinsie	7
Dead in the street, and starved	6	Rising of the Lights	98
Dropsie, and Swelling	267	Sciatica	1
Drowned	34	Scurvey, and Itch	9
Executed, and prest to death	18	Suddenly	62
Falling Sickness	7	Surfet	86
Fever	1108	Swine Pox	6
Fistula	13	Teeth	470
Flocks, and small Pox	531	Thrush, and Sore mouth	40
French Pox	12	Tissick	34
Gangrene	5	Tympany	13
Gout	4	Vomiting	1
		Worms	27

Christened { Males .... 4994 / Females .... 4590 / In all .... 9584 } Buried { Males .... 4932 / Females .... 4603 / In all .... 9535 } Whereof, of the Plague. 8

Increased in the Burials in the 122 Parishes, and at the Pesthouse this year 993
Decreased of the Plague in the 122 Parishes, and at the Pesthouse this year 266

Figure 19-2 ■ **Causes of death in the city of London, 1632.** In 1662, John Graunt, a London storekeeper, published the first set of vital statistics by compiling the weekly reports of deaths issued by the clerks in each London parish of the Church of England. Here we see the breakdown for the year 1632—a year in which there were no major plagues. To get some idea of health risks in an era ignorant of germs and lacking antibiotics, notice that 5 percent (470) of the deaths in London in 1632 were from infected teeth. Graunt based his volume on all death reports from 1603 to 1624. During this 20-year period 229,250 people died in London, a number larger than the total population of the city at this time. Such a huge death rate was sustained in part by the extraordinary mortality rate for infants and children—more than half of whom failed to reach the age of 6. But a large influx of newcomers each year kept the city from becoming uninhabited. Two years after Graunt's book was published, an outbreak of plague killed about a third of London's population; the year after that the Great Fire destroyed 80 percent of the city.

■ This engraving by William Hogarth (1697–1764) depicts the many perils of the London streets at night, including the chamber pot being emptied from second-story window, splattering two drunken Free Masons on their way home from a lodge meeting. The "wickedness" of cities has been a theme in literature and art through the centuries.

Gideon Sjoberg (1965) noted, "new ideas and innovations flowed into [cities] quite naturally," as travelers along the trade routes brought ideas as well as goods from afar. Moreover, simply by concentrating specialists in an area, cities stimulated innovation not just in technology but also in religion, philosophy, science, and the arts. The density of cities encouraged public perfor-mances, from plays and concerts to organized sporting events.

Cities undoubtedly also enticed some to migrate from rural areas in pursuit of "vice." The earliest writing we have about cities includes complaints about rampant wickedness and sin, and through the centuries cities have main-tained the reputation for condoning behavior that would not be tolerated in rural communities (Fischer, 1975). In part, this may be because from the beginning cities have been relatively anonymous places. Preindustrial cities may have been even more anonymous, given their size, than modern cities.

Consider that cities relied on large numbers of newcomers each year just to replace the population lost through mortality. As a result, cities tended to abound in people who were recent arrivals and who had not known one another previously. Before modern identification systems, many people in cities were not even who they claimed to be—runaway sons and daughters of peasants could claim more exalted social origins. The possibility of escaping one's past and starting anew must have drawn many to the cities. But this also meant that cities then were even less integrated by long-standing interpersonal attachments than modern cities.

In any event, it was primarily adventuresome, single, young adults who constantly replenished city populations. E. A. Wrigley (1969) has computed that in the years from 1650 to 1750, London needed 8,000 newcomers each year to maintain its population. The newcomers averaged 20 years of age, were unmarried, and came from farms. Most of these newcomers came from more than 50 miles away—at least a two-day trip at that time.

For all our complaints about modern cities, industrialization did not ruin city life. Preindustrial cities were horrid. Yet for many young people on farms, the prospect of heading off to one of these miserable cities seemed far superior to a life of dull toil. Then as the Industrial Revolution began, the idea of going off to the city suddenly appealed not just to restless young people but also to whole families. Soon the countryside virtually emptied, as people flocked to town (see Table 19-2).

■

Industrialization and Urbanization

Industrialization and urbanization are inseparable processes; neither could have occurred without the other. Industrialization made it

Table 19-2 ■ Population living on farms.

	Canada (percent)	United States (percent)
1820	*	72
1890	68	42
1911	55	34
1921	50	30
1931	46	25
1961	11	8

Source: U.S. and Canadian census reports.
*No statistic available.

possible for most people to live in cities. It also made it necessary: Industrialization requires the concentration of highly specialized workers. To understand how industrialization both caused and depended upon urbanization, let us first examine how the effects of the Industrial Revolution on agriculture made urbanization possible.

The agricultural revolution

Preindustrial farmers could support only a very small urban population and only by accepting a very low standard of living. Cities could live only by coercing peasants to surrender their crops and livestock. Industrial technology changed all that. Suddenly, farm productivity soared to undreamed of heights, and farmers became eager to sell their crops to the cities. Let us chart this change as it took place in the United States, since good records exist and since North American agriculture has become the most industrialized and productive in the world (see Table 19-3).

In 1820, when almost no modern technology had yet appeared on the farms, a full-time farm worker could produce only enough food to feed 4.1 persons (including the farm worker). That left little surplus to send to the cities after farm families had fed themselves. But by 1900, the average American farm worker could feed 7.0 people. At the turn of the century, the average

■ Modern self-propelled combines harvesting wheat near Pullman, Washington. With such a machine a single farmer can harvest more land in several hours than huge threshing crews at the turn of the century could do in a week. According to estimates, there are enough of these giant combines at work in North America so that together they could harvest an area the size of the state of Kansas in a single day.

American farmer was feeding 5.3 Americans and 1.7 persons abroad. This was just the beginning, for by the middle of the twentieth century, farm productivity began to accelerate at an incredible pace. In 1960, the average American farmer was feeding 22.3 Americans and 3.5 persons living in other nations. By 1970, one farmer fed 39.9 Americans and 7.2 foreigners. In addition, the farmer in 1970 was feeding each person more food than had the nineteenth-century farmer, despite the fact that the government, through various subsidy programs, was preventing modern American farmers from growing nearly as much as they could. Perhaps even more surprising is the fact that the modern farmer accomplishes these wonders by working far fewer hours and with much less physical exertion than did preindustrial farmers.

Back in 1800, American farmers worked 56 hours for every acre of wheat they raised (see Table 19-4). In return, they harvested an average of 15 bushels for each hard-worked acre. Today American farmers farm their wheat fields while riding in the air-conditioned cabs of huge diesel

Table 19-3 ■ **The agricultural revolution.**

Year	Number of Persons Supplied with Farm Products by One U.S. Farm Worker
1820	4.1
1900	7.0
1940	10.7
1950	15.5
1960	25.8
1970	47.1

Source: U.S. Census, *Historical Statistics of the United States,* 1975.

tractors and self-propelled combines. It takes them an average of 2.8 hours a year to farm an acre of wheat. And they average 31.4 bushels from each acre: twice as much wheat in 5 percent as many hours of work.

Similarly, corn yields have more than tripled, while only 4 percent as much labor is

Table 19-4 ■ Changes in agricultural productivity, 1800–1980.

Product	1800	1900	1980	Product	1910	1980
WHEAT				MILK		
Hours of labor per acre (yearly)	56.0	15.0	2.8	Hours of labor per cow (yearly)	146.0	45.0
Hours of labor per 100 bushels	373.0	108.0	9.0	Hours of labor per 100 pounds of milk	3.8	0.4
Yield per acre (in bushels)	15.0	13.9	31.4	Milk per cow (in pounds) yearly	3,842.0	11,000.0
CORN				BEEF		
Hours of labor per acre (yearly)	86.0	38.0	3.6	Hours of labor per 100 pounds of meat	4.6	1.3
per 100 bushels	344.0	147.0	4.0	PORK		
Yield per acre (in bushels)	25.0	25.9	95.2	Hours of labor of meat	3.6	0.5
				CHICKEN		
				Hours of labor per 100 pounds of meat	9.5	2.9

Source: U.S. Census, 1975, 1981.

required. Modern farmers give less than one-third the hours of attention to each of their milk cows as their grandparents did in 1910, but the cows now give three times as much milk. In 1910, it took ranchers 4.6 hours of labor to raise 100 pounds of beef. Today, ranchers work 1.3 hours to raise that much.

Many things have gone into this agricultural miracle: new machines, new animal breeds, new varieties of plants, weed sprays, fertilizers, crop rotation, drainage and irrigation systems—in short, the application of science and engineering to farming. But the major effect was the huge reduction in labor. Only because fewer farmers could feed greater numbers of people did it become possible for people to move to the cities and staff the great urban industries.

Recall from the previous chapter that the percentage of the population engaged in agriculture is one of the critical thresholds of modernization demographers used. Only when people are released from field work can they live in cities and pursue industrial occupations (and, as a result, begin to reduce their fertility).

If city people today were asked to name the machines vital for the existence of cities, they would probably mention automobiles, computers, telephones, and the great machines used in heavy industry. In fact, modern cities depend on machines few people see: tractors, plows, cultivators, and harvesters. Without these, our cities would be small, and most of us would spend our lives following horses across grain fields or riding them to round up herds.

Specialization and urban growth

Industrialization requires urbanization because it depends upon the coordinated activities of large numbers of specialized workers who must perform their tasks in a few central locations.

Industrialization depends on specialization—an elaborate division of labor—to simplify production. As an example, let us consider the industrialization of shoemaking. The preindustrial shoemaker was a skilled craftsman who spent several years learning the various steps in the process of making a pair of shoes. In a mod-

■ As recently as 1934 it took 225 hours of work per year to care for a flock of 100 laying hens. For every egg laid in the United States or Canada, a farmer put in more than a minute of labor. By 1970 farmers worked less than 15 seconds for each egg. Today one worker can do what it would have taken more than 100 to do in 1934—care for as many as 100,000 hens in a huge "egg factory" like this. Automatic conveyor belts keep the feeding troughs full and the cages clean, and the eggs roll out where they can easily be reached. All this farmer needs to do is drive his electric cart down the aisles and put the eggs into flats, ready for shipment.

ern shoe factory, a worker need only learn to perform one simple task in this process to be productive. By the use of machines to perform some tasks and by the concentration of labor in the most time-consuming aspects of shoe-making, many more shoes can be made for the same amount of labor expended by traditional shoemakers.

One consequence of this is that shoes became much cheaper to consumers. A second consequence is that while the traditional shoemaker could locate his shop anywhere he could find customers, industrialized shoemakers must gather in one place where each can make his or her contribution to the complex manufacturing process.

Industrialization also depends upon bringing together many highly trained specialists to achieve goals beyond the ability of single individuals. It takes many people with a variety of sophisticated skills to make computers or jet planes or to construct oil refineries. This, too, requires people to gather (Figure 19-3).

But industrialization also produces an elaborate division of labor, not just within organizations but also among them. Plant A gets parts from plant B and supplies its production to plant C. It is often efficient if these plants are close together. Indeed, in the early stages of industrialization, limited transportation made proximity vital.

If people must gather in large numbers to work, then they will also concentrate in that same area to live. This was especially true in days when most people walked to work. When people congregate in one place in large numbers and do not farm for a living, we call that place a city. Thus, urbanization and industrialization are inseparable.

■

Metropolis

Suppose a young man left his father's farm and moved to Silo, North Dakota, population forty-

Portugal	30	France	73
Albania	34	Czechoslovakia	74
Yugoslavia	46	United Kingdom	76
Romania	49	East Germany	77
Netherlands	52	Sweden	83
Hungary	54	Denmark	83
Austria	55	West Germany	94
Ireland	56	Belgium	95

Switzerland	58
Poland	59
Finland	60
Spain	64
USSR	64
Bulgaria	65
Greece	70
Norway	71
Italy	72

Figure 19-3 ■ **Percent of population living in urban places in Europe.** Urbanization is the result of industrialization and therefore occurs around the world. Most nations of Europe also have more than half of their populations living in urban places—only in Portugal, Albania, Yugoslavia, and Romania is the rural population in the majority.

three, where he got a job in a cafe. Is this an example of urbanization? Most people wouldn't think so. Even though the folks in Silo are not farmers, their way of life would not seem very urban to people used to large cities (in small North Dakota towns, people still do not lock their doors, and many leave their ignition keys in their cars). It seems we have some notion that to be urban a place must be larger than Silo. But how much larger?

There can be no "true" answer to that question: It is simply a matter of judgment. American demographers classify a locale as an **urban place** if it has a population of more than 2,500 people. The statement that nearly three out of four North Americans today live in urban places means that they live in communities larger than 2,500.

Obviously, many urban places are not cities, at least not in the sense that the term is normally used. The U.S. Census does not classify a community as a **city** unless it has at least 50,000 residents, but that standard can be very confusing. Many large communities are crisscrossed by political boundaries that separate them into many independent units—often a major city is surrounded by dozens of smaller independent communities. Suppose one of these has fewer than 2,500 people. Should we classify its residents as part of the rural population? What if most of the adults in this community commute to jobs in the heart of the major city? The political boundaries that divide large communities often have no relation to the actual social and economic boundaries. In fact, the notion of a city as a legal entity is faulty.

The word *city* once had a rather clear meaning, and a person either lived in a particular city or not. But today, two strangers meeting on a plane may say they live in Chicago and Toronto, when they are not legal residents of either city. Instead, each lives in a **suburb,** a smaller community in the immediate vicinity of a city. Yet these travelers were truthful in the real, if not legal, sense. Cities do not simply stop at their legal boundaries but extend socially and economically into many adjacent communities. That's why we often speak of Greater Chicago or Greater Toronto—to identify this larger aspect of cities.

■ New technology often requires new skills: These girls in a Brooklyn high school in about 1900 used time in gym class to develop their skills in boarding trolley cars. Their practice apparatus allows them to learn to grab a bar and swing aboard the high side step.

■ Here a fashionable New York woman boards a real trolley. Because these vehicles had no center aisle, people just slid into the seat from either side. At rush hour the outside of the car was lined with riders unable to find a seat.

Back in 1910, the U.S. Census tried to find a more suitable definition of city than is provided by legal boundaries. Recognizing that many surrounding areas are functionally part of a central city, they substituted the term *metropolitan area* for city and began to lump suburbs with their central city as a single unit: the **metropolis.**

The first metropolitan areas had 200,000 or more residents, including the settled areas around a city. In 1940 this was again revised. To be a metropolitan area, the central city had to have 50,000 people, no matter how many more lived in surrounding areas.

Still, problems persisted. As Roderick McKenzie (1933) pointed out, still "only a part of the area that is economically and socially tributary to each of these central cities was included." What was needed was a way to identify the **sphere of influence** of a city—the area whose inhabitants depend on the central city for jobs, recreation, newspapers, television, and a sense of common community.

Therefore, in 1950 the **Standard Metropolitan Statistical Area (SMSA)** was created. Around central cities with 50,000 or more people, counties are included in the SMSA if at least 75 percent of those working in the county do not hold agricultural jobs and if the county serves either as the residence or place of employment for at least 10,000 nonagricultural workers. Furthermore, at least 15 percent of the workers living in a county must commute to the central city or at least 25 percent of those working in the county must commute from the city.

Statistics Canada uses similar principles to define **Census Metropolitan Area (CMA).** CMAs must have an urban core "or continuously built-up area" with a population of at least 100,000. Surrounding municipalities are included in the CMA if at least 40 percent of their labor force is employed within the boundaries of the urban core, or if at least 25 percent of those employed in the municipality commute from residences within the urban core.

As both these names suggest, sociologists no longer use the term *city* in their technical vocabulary but speak instead of a metropolis or metropolitan area. Thus, we agree with people from Oak Park, Illinois, when they tell strangers they are from Chicago. The industrialized city is no longer a tight, tidy, compact entity, contained within defensive walls. It sprawls hither and yon across the landscape—a reality better expressed by the term *metropolis.*

But even the modern metropolis isn't completely formless. Cities exist as places to work and to live. Given these fundamental purposes, the shape and organization of cities have been determined primarily by transportation. Two basic forms of modern metropolises exist, depending on the dominant forms of transportation when the metropolises grew: the **fixed-rail metropolis** and the **freeway metropolis.**

Much concern about cities and urban policies has been generated recently because many people think cities must be like those built before cars and trucks took over transportation from fixed-rail systems. These critics dislike the new form of the metropolitan area, especially the way the older form is changing to be more like the new. This dispute helps reveal basic aspects of urban sociology, so let's examine and compare these two basic urban forms.

The fixed-rail metropolis

The preindustrial city was small and dense because people relied primarily on walking for transportation. Although industrialization caused cities to expand, the continued reliance on foot transportation meant cities were cramped and workers were housed close to their factories. The development of rail transportation made it possible for cities to expand greatly in area.

First came horse-drawn trolleys running on

rails. Then came electric- and steam-powered trolleys running on the same rails. These new modes of transportation were much faster than walking (or even than riding a horse) and were cheap enough so people could afford to live farther from work. Thus, cities began to expand outward, but they did not expand evenly. They expanded only along the rail lines. People could travel only where the rails led and could live or work only out from the center of the city along the rail lines.

Riding on these fixed-rail mass transit systems was quite unpleasant. The cars were usually overcrowded and dirty. Still, it beat walking. Moreover, it enabled large numbers of city dwellers to escape apartments close to huge, noisy, dirty factories and move out where real estate was cheaper and life less hectic. As soon as railroads appeared in the 1840s, many wealthy people fled the cities and commuted from country estates or distant, luxurious communities.

As industrializing cities began to sprawl, they began to resemble spiders. From a dense center in which business and industry were concentrated, the metropolitan area expanded along narrow corridors, where the fixed-rail lines extended (Ward, 1971). Fixed-rail transportation requires many riders going from and to a small number of stops. Thus, rail lines were extended from the city center only as the population grew at the end of the line. People were not as cramped as before, but they still had to crowd together.

Moreover, fixed-rail transportation made the center of the city the focal point. Offices and stores were concentrated here because everyone could most easily travel to the center. Industry was also concentrated in the heart of the city, usually adjacent to the business section. Factories relied on rail transportation to bring in supplies and to carry out the finished goods to market. So factory locations were also close to rail routes.

The metropolis that was built to suit fixed-rail transportation fits our image of the old industrial cities of the eastern parts of Canada and the United States and in Europe: dense cities where, in the very center, the streets are jammed with people going to shops by day and to restaurants, theaters, nightclubs, concert halls,

■ Fixed-rail transportation systems created cities with densely packed central cores. They also could create monumental traffic jams, as can be seen here at the intersection of Dearborn and Randolph Streets in Chicago in 1909. At least these trolleys were powered by electricity. In many cities coal-burning engines pulled trains to depots in the heart of the city, belching their contribution to the polluted air.

and sports arenas by night. Whether the citizens called it the Great White Way, the Loop, or the Hub, this was the heart and soul of what everyone found exciting and sophisticated about the city.

Today the central core of most such cities is in decay, abandoned by shoppers, by offices, by industry, and by nightlife. Billions have been spent to renovate and renew these central cores in hopes of luring department stores, offices, and nightclubs to return. Yet they do not recapture their old glory. And many newer cities never had such centers at all. Why?

The freeway metropolis

Compared with rail lines, streets and roads are inexpensive to build and maintain. With the mass production of automobiles and trucks, the metropolis no longer had to resemble a spider. The empty areas between the rail lines became easy to reach. Moreover, people could settle in sparsely populated areas where no rail line could afford to run but where anyone with a car could easily go. The metropolis began to spread outward evenly, shaped more by geographic barriers (such as rivers, harbors, hills, and ravines) than by rail routes. And just as the car freed people to live where they liked, the truck freed industry to decentralize.

The center of a city had always been a constrictive location for industry and business. There was always a shortage of space for expansion and considerable congestion from the dense concentration of plants. These shortcomings were offset by the urgent need to be located on a fixed-rail line and to be able to send material from one local plant to another by slow horse-drawn wagons. But the truck ended the dependence of industry on rail transport. Today more than 80 percent of all commercial transportation in North America is by truck.

Meanwhile, new technology forced industry to seek low-density locations in the suburbs. Assembly-line methods of manufacturing require long, low buildings and therefore considerable space. Machines for handling and stockpiling materials, such as forklifts, work best in one-story buildings. Thus, plants have shifted to outlying areas where land is plentiful and cheap. Indeed, with workers now commuting mainly by car (and 87 percent of American workers do so), business and industry often require parking lots that cover considerably more area than their plants and office buildings.

And so the metropolis has become decentralized. Business has moved to outlying locations, as have many residents. Not surprisingly, so have many stores and shops—the shopping mall has replaced the old central core as the dominant retail locale.

Although decentralization has caused substantial changes in cities that grew large during the era of fixed-rail transportation, it has not caused similar upheavals in many western cities. These cities grew up after the automobile and the truck had already displaced the trolley and the train. They were never high-density cities revolving around a cramped but thriving central core. They were never shaped like spiders.

For decades, literary Easterners have scoffed at the decentralized cities of the West for not being "real" cities at all. Los Angeles, for example, has been described as a dozen towns in search of a city. Why in the world, they complain, don't Westerners get their cities put together so that one need not travel 20 miles down a freeway to get from the office to the theater or from one department store to another?

This charge is accurate enough. Los Angeles does not have a "downtown"; instead, it has at least eight downtowns. Indeed, as many people in decentralized cities have discovered, the time it takes to get somewhere matters more than the actual distance traveled. By avoiding the congestion of shopping in dense, central cores, millions of North Americans have demonstrated that they would rather zip along a free-

way and find easy parking at a shopping center than take much longer to go a few blocks in heavy traffic. That brings us to the fundamental point in the dispute over what a real city is. Most people want cities to be decentralized.

Preferring a decentralized metropolis

Several signs show that people find life better in sprawling, decentralized cities than in the older, centralized cities. First of all, when the chance came to move out of the central city and to the outskirts, millions did so as fast as they could. Although the dense central core offers an exciting urban life, it also causes vast numbers of people to live in cramped, unattractive housing and their children to play in the streets.

A second sign is that people running large industrial and business firms have joined in the move to less dense areas, taking their plants and offices with them. Surely the rich can maintain luxury and privacy even in dense central cores, but they were among the first to leave. As early as 1848, approximately 20 percent of the leading businessmen of Boston were commuting to their downtown offices by train from the suburbs (Ward, 1971).

Third, large numbers of people have been migrating from the old, high-density cities to the new decentralized metropolitan areas of the South and West.

Fourth, people avoid public transportation whenever possible. Indeed, almost as many Americans walk to work (5.5 percent) as ride mass transit (6.3 percent). No public mass transit system in the nation can attract enough riders at a high enough fare to break even. People seem willing to commute long distances, but they seem to want the freedom of driving their own vehicles. Hence, they prefer a metropolis constructed with auto transportation in mind— freeway cities.

But we need not rely on these indirect signs. The Gallup Poll (1972) asked Americans: "If you could live anywhere you wanted to, would you prefer a city, a suburban area, a small town, or a farm?" Only 13 percent chose to live in a city.

■ The fixed-rail city required that large numbers of residents live in crowded, expensive housing. Whenever people have had the opportunity, most have abandoned such areas for life in the suburbs. Despite complaints that the suburbs are dull, the people who live there usually seem to be having too good a time to notice.

In contrast, a third picked the suburbs, another third said a small town, and one-fifth said they would like to live on a farm. Indeed, of people who were living in cities, only one person in five preferred living there.

This might suggest that Americans long to undo urbanization and return to the good old days of living in small towns and on farms. But that isn't true. Gallup asked those who said they would like to live on a farm or in a small town how far from a major urban area they would like to be. Three out of four said no more than 30 miles (Fuguitt and Zuiches, 1973). Thirty miles is little more than a half-hour drive from the city. That is not a retreat to the sticks. Indeed,

as Claude Fischer (1976) remarked about these findings, anyplace "within thirty miles of a large city is essentially a suburb. That seems to be what most Americans want." But not everyone who wants this has been able to get it.

■

Urban Neighborhoods

The ethnic or racial neighborhood has always been a feature of the city. In the cities of the Roman Empire, various sections of cities were named according to the ethnicity of persons living there—because members of a minority group lived in the same neighborhood. In addition to racial and ethnic divisions, class and status have always differentiated city neighborhoods, with neighborhoods ranging from the very wealthy to the very poor.

Of course, cities are constantly changing. Thus even in ancient times, what was a Jewish or a Greek neighborhood in one generation might be something else a generation or two later. And rich neighborhoods sometimes turn into slums and vice versa.

In North America, the rapid growth of cities and the huge waves of immigration produced complex neighborhood patterns. Our cities have abounded with neighborhoods occupied by a single racial or ethnic group—many cities have (or have had) a "little Italy," a "Germantown," or a "Chinatown." And all cities have their wealthy areas and their slums.

Observers of the nineteenth-century American city noticed the remarkable turnover in the ethnic identity of neighborhoods. A slum area occupied by the Irish or the Germans would suddenly change as these groups moved out and newer immigrants such as the Italians or the Jews moved in. In time, these groups also were replaced, often by blacks, Asians, or Hispanics.

Minority ethnic and racial groups concentrate in particular neighborhoods for several reasons. Members of a group are lured to the same neighborhoods in which their relatives and friends live—a place where their native language, their customs, their food, and their religion predominate. They are also pulled toward these neighborhoods because they can afford to live there. Higher housing costs in other neighborhoods and discrimination keep members of ethnic groups out of these other neighborhoods.

Recently there has been a substantial decline in discrimination, in part because it is illegal in Canada and the United States to refuse to sell property or to rent to people on the basis of race or ethnicity. However, long before these legal measures took force, many groups that once were the targets of discrimination in housing escaped their segregated neighborhoods and became integrated. In the 1920s, two of America's most famous early sociologists proposed an explanation of this process.

Park and Burgess: ethnic succession

Robert E. Park (1864–1944) and Ernest Burgess (1886–1966) proposed that ethnic and racial segregation in cities was based primarily on economic and status differences. In their famous book *The City* (Park, Burgess, and McKenzie, 1925), they proposed a **theory of ethnic succession** that closely resembles the economic explanation of prejudice and discrimination outlined in Chapter 11. Park and Burgess argued that new immigrant groups huddle together in segregated neighborhoods upon arriving in America. However, as these groups begin to rise in the stratification system, these changes "tend to be registered in changes of location." That is, as new groups succeed in America, they move out of ethnic neighborhoods. This occurs, first, because they can afford to live in better neighborhoods; second, because they no longer are so tied to their traditional culture; and third, because they have shed the stigma of low status: They are no longer regarded as undesirable neighbors.

Park and Burgess also accounted for the process of *succession*, whereby slum neighborhoods are successively occupied by the lowest-status groups of the time. For a long time, the Park and Burgess viewpoint dominated sociology. And a number of later empirical studies seemed to confirm it. Stanley Lieberson (1961, 1963) found that from 1910 through 1950, older European ethnic groups (such as the Germans) and newer ones (such as the Italians) increasingly lived together in the same neighborhoods. Karl and Alma Taeuber (1964) found similar trends.

However, in the wake of the racial confrontations of the 1960s, other sociologists suggested that the Park and Burgess model was inadequate, that it glossed over continuing ethnic inequalities, and that it did not apply to racial, as opposed to ethnic, neighborhood integration. Working with data for Toronto, Gordon Darroch and Wilfred Marston (1971) reported that individuals belonging to different ethnic groups still tended not to live in the same neighborhoods in Toronto, even when they were of equal status. Nathan Kantrowitz (1973) drew similar conclusions from New York City data, suggesting that even when ethnic groups escape the city, they tend to form segregated suburbs.

Once again, prejudice was judged the primary barrier to integration. Yet this did not square with the deemphasis on prejudice as being a major factor in race and ethnic relations, as we saw in Chapter 11. This was a serious discrepancy, and something was clearly wrong with one of these positions.

Guest and Weed: economics and integration

 In 1976, Avery M. Guest and his student James A. Weed attempted to resolve this contradiction. First, they carefully reexamined what Park and Burgess had actually argued. They discovered that Park and Burgess were discussing group, not individual, upward mobility. That is, Park and Burgess did not suggest that as soon as a few members of a low status economic group manage to become wealthy, they are welcomed in the best neighborhoods. Rather, they argued that when a particular group, such as the Italians, achieves economic parity with the majority, at that point their ethnicity will not be a barrier in choosing where to live.

This is a critical distinction. Darroch and Marston had shown only that higher-income members of a low status group do not live in integrated neighborhoods, not what would happen when groups achieve status equality. But Guest and Weed, following Park and Burgess, argued that so long as a group's overall status is low, it will reflect on all members, including the more successful ones. As an example, they suggested that, in evaluating a neighborhood in which many Poles are living, a person of German descent will not ask, "Do *these* Poles earn as much as I do?" but "Are Poles as a *group* similar in status to Germans as a group?" If the answer is yes, then the German will move into the neighborhood. If the answer is no, the German will choose to live elsewhere. Group

inequality, not individual comparisons, lies at the heart of prejudice and discrimination, Guest and Weed argued.

To test this view, Guest and Weed assembled data for Cleveland, Boston, and Seattle SMSAs. They chose these three cities because of their different histories and ethnic makeup, a choice that proved to be wise. Their first step was to determine the extent to which various racial and ethnic groups live in integrated neighborhoods.

The degree of segregation or integration of a neighborhood is measured by an **index of dissimilarity** (Taeuber and Taeuber, 1969). This index contrasts the racial and ethnic makeup of a neighborhood with the racial and ethnic makeup of the whole metropolitan area. If the racial and ethnic composition of a neighborhood is the same as that of the metropolitan area, then the neighborhood scores zero on the index—it is fully integrated. On the other hand, if a single racial or ethnic group lives in a neighborhood, while other racial and ethnic groups live in the metropolitan area, the neighborhood scores 100—it is wholly segregated. To measure the degree to which a particular racial or ethnic group is integrated or segregated in a city, sociologists compute the average dissimilarity scores for the neighborhoods in which this group lives. Guest and Weed's findings substantially supported the Park and Burgess theory and the status inequality approach to prejudice and discrimination.

Group neighborhoods differed as would be predicted from current status differences among them. Persons of British origin, the people often known as WASPs, live in the most integrated neighborhoods. Others of northern and western European descent (such as Swedes, Germans, and Irish) are virtually as integrated. Groups arriving later from eastern and southern Europe (Czechs, Poles, Hungarians, and Italians) live in only slightly less integrated neighborhoods. Persons of Mexican descent live in quite unintegrated neighborhoods in Cleveland and Boston but in neighborhoods as integrated as those of eastern and southern Europeans in Seattle. Blacks and Puerto Ricans live in the least integrated neighborhoods, but again the differences are smaller in Seattle. Finally, and importantly, Asians live in neighborhoods as integrated as those of most people of European origin.

By comparing 1960 and 1970 data, Guest and Weed found that all neighborhoods had generally become more integrated. Asians had made the greatest gains, but black neighborhoods had also become less solidly black.

These data appear to support the group mobility interpretation of Park and Burgess. Asians have recently made striking status gains, and they have become quite well integrated. Earlier status gains of eastern and southern European ethnic groups also appear in the breakup of the once solidly Italian, Polish, Hungarian, and Czech neighborhoods. Between 1960 and 1970, blacks made substantial status gains, and their neighborhoods began to reflect these gains.

However, Guest and Weed were able to test the Park and Burgess model more rigorously. Using sophisticated statistical regression techniques, they found that when the effects of income differences among racial and ethnic groups are removed, relatively little neighborhood segregation based on race or ethnicity remains. That is, status inequality between groups seems to be the primary neighborhood barrier. As status inequalities disappear, so do racial and ethnic neighborhoods. At that point, neighborhoods are identified only on the basis of class.

Guest and Weed also found that neighborhood patterns tend to persist. Hence, western cities such as Seattle are more integrated no matter which ethnic or racial group is examined. They suggest that one reason is because western cities are newer—ethnic enclaves never got established as they had in cities that were settled long ago. Consider the following example. All cities are divided into census tracts. The Census Bureau tries to keep tracts about the same size everywhere—around 5,000 residents. The city of Seattle consists of 123 census tracts. The 1980 census found that there was not a tract in the city without black residents. Although Seattle does have a black neighborhood, only four tracts are more than 50 percent black and none is more than 85 percent black.

Now look at Figure 19-4. Chicago's community areas are about eight to ten times larger than census tracts. Nevertheless, the 1980 census found that twenty-one of them had no black residents and eight more had only 1 percent. Twenty community areas in Chicago are more than 90 percent black, and eight are 99 percent black. In Chicago, most neighborhoods are either all black or all white. Indeed, Chicago is the most racially segregated city in America.

Guest and Weed suggest that cities like Chicago face the need to break down patterns of ethnic and racial neighborhoods established long ago, while cities like Seattle simply never had these patterns to contend with. In any event, Guest and Weed showed that racial and ethnic succession, from ghetto to integration, continues in accordance with current theories of intergroup conflict.

Karl Taeuber: segregation declines

In 1983, Karl Taeuber, who originated the index of dissimilarity, announced that American cities had become less segregated between 1970 and 1980. This confirmed the results of Guest and Weed's study. Taeuber's research was based on the twenty-eight American cities having more than 100,000 black residents. Using data from the 1970 and the 1980 censuses, Taeuber examined each city block by block and computed dissimilarity scores. Oakland, California, ranked as the most integrated of these cities; only 2 percent of blacks in Oakland lived on an all-black block. Surprisingly, Chicago, where a black mayor won election in 1983, was the most segregated city. Nearby Detroit, on the other hand, was one of the least segregated cities (see Table 19-5). While nearly all cities showed a decline in black neighborhood segregation, segregation in Philadelphia and Cleveland increased. Southern cities, on the other hand, showed marked declines.

Taeuber pointed out that integration was occurring primarily as blacks moved into the suburbs or into white neighborhoods. Little reverse integration was taking place—that is, whites moving into heavily black neighborhoods.

This seems an appropriate place to explain why a chapter devoted to urban sociology appears

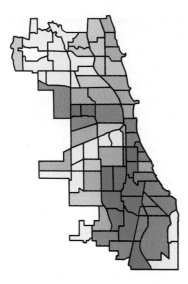

Montclare	0	Lincoln Park	9	South Chicago	48	Riverdale	97
Edison Park	0	South Lawndale	9	South Deering	55	Roseland	97
Norwood Park	0	West Town	9	Morgan Park	62	West Englewood	98
Jefferson Park	0	Rogers Park	9	Austin	74	Washington
Clearing	0	Chicago Lawn	10	Near West Side	75	Heights	98
McKinley Park	0	Edgewater	11	Pullman	76	Auburn Gresham	98
West Elsdon	0	Garfield Ridge	13	Kenwood	77	Chatham	98
Forest Glen	0	Beverly	14	Douglas	87	Fuller Park	99
Belmont Cragin	0	Uptown	15	Calumet Heights	87	Greater Grand
Archer Heights	0	Loop	19	Burnside	89	Crossing	99
Portage Park	0	New City	22	West Pullman	91	West Garfield Park	99
Brighton Park	0	Armour Square	25	Near South Side	94	Englewood	99
East Side	0	Near North Side	33	South Shore	95	East Garfield Park	99
Irving Park	0	Humboldt Park	36	Woodlawn	96	Washington Park	99
Bridgeport	0	Hyde Park	37	Avalon Park	96	Oakland	99
Avondale	0			North Lawndale	96	Grand Boulevard	99
West Lawn	0
Hegewisch	0
Hermosa	0
Mount Greenwood	0
Dunning	0

Lincoln Square	1
Albany Park	1
Gage Park	1
West Ridge	1
North Park	1
Lower West Side	1
North Center	1
O'Hare	1
Logan Square	3
Ashburn	3
Lakeview	7

Figure 19-4 ■ **Percent black in Chicago's community areas, 1980.** Chicago is the most racially segregated of major American cities, and here we can see just how segregated. These community areas are large, with an average population of about 40,000. Yet twenty-one of these areas have no black residents or so few that they do not add up to .5 of 1 percent. Another eight have only 1 percent black population. At the other end of the scale, eight areas are 99 percent black, and twenty are more than 90 percent black.

Table 19-5 ■ **Index of dissimilarity scores for twenty-eight U.S. cities with more than 100,000 black residents (the higher the score, the more segregated blacks are from whites).**

City	1970	1980
Chicago	93	92
Cleveland	90	91
St. Louis	90	90
Philadelphia	84	88
Baltimore	89	86
Atlanta	92	86
Kansas City	90	86
Memphis	92	85
Birmingham, Ala.	92	85
Dallas	96	83
Pittsburgh	86	83
Indianapolis	90	83
Jacksonville, Fla.	94	82
Houston	93	81
Los Angeles	90	81
Nashville, Tenn.	90	80
Boston	84	80
Milwaukee	88	80
Washington, D.C.	79	79
Richmond, Va.	91	79
Cincinnati	84	79
Newark, N.J.	76	76
New Orleans	84	76
New York City	77	75
Columbus, Ohio	86	75
Detroit	82	73
Gary, Ind.	84	68
Oakland, Calif.	70	59

Source: Taeuber (1983).

in the social change section of this book. A city is not an enduring physical structure, despite its permanent appearance. Instead, *a city is as much a process as a structure: It is constantly changing.* The great fixed-rail metropolis, for example, which still dominates our conception of the city, existed in all its glory for less than a century. Millions of Americans and Canadians have nostalgic memories of the ethnic neighborhood in which they grew up but which has completely disappeared.

In 1959, when I became a reporter for the *Oakland Tribune,* Oakland was a very segre-

gated city where editors did not regard a story of a black murdering another black as worth printing. Today, Oakland is the least segregated of American cities with substantial black populations, the mayor is black, and the *Tribune* now has black owners. So the next time you look around a city, keep in mind the impermanence of what you see.

To conclude this chapter, we must return to a basic question about city life raised in Chapter 1. Has urbanization harmed social relations and dulled our sensibilities?

■

Theories of Urban Impact

By the middle of the nineteenth century, educated people in Europe and North America recognized that rapid urbanization was under way—and they didn't like it. Cities were still unhealthy, squalid places. In 1841, the average life expectancy of men in London was five years less than in the rest of England. In the United States, the life expectancy of urban dwellers did not equal that of rural folk until after 1940 (Simon, 1981). As cities grew, it seemed that their problems could only grow worse. Many asked at what price people were being uprooted from their intimate, healthy, traditional lives in rural areas and crowded into impersonal, unhealthy, chaotic cities. Most people who raised this question were sure that the costs of urbanization would be devastating, even though they could see no way to stop the great migration to the cities.

One of the first social scientists to write in detail about the dangers of urbanization was Ferdinand Tönnies. In the mid-1880s, he introduced the concepts of *Gemeinschaft* (community) and *Gesellschaft* (society or association) to capture the different qualities of life in preindustrial and industrial societies.

Gemeinschaft identifies the qualities of life Tönnies thought were being lost because of urbanization. It describes small, cohesive communities such as the farming village. People know one another well and are connected by bonds of friendship, kinship, and daily interaction. In such places, people agree on the norms,

■ Street scenes like this abound in all modern cities in defiance of nineteenth-century urban sociologists, who predicted that city growth would create massive anomie, that people would become estranged from one another and thus lose their moral bearings. Most people in cities are not alone but are firmly attached to others.

and few people fail to conform. In fact, such communities serve as primary groups for most of their members.

Gesellschaft is the exact opposite. People tend to be strangers, and they are united only by self-interest, not by any sense of common purpose or identity. There is little agreement about norms and much deviance. Human relationships are fleeting and manipulative rather than warm and intimate.

If we think of people as marbles, then in the *Gemeinschaft* the marbles are glued together into a solid piece, while in the *Gesellschaft* the marbles are constantly being tossed about in a revolving drum.

Following Tönnies, a long line of social sci-entists characterized urban life in such terms. Émile Durkheim wrote in 1897 that a primary consequence of urbanization was the break-down of order: Urbanites live in a situation in which norms lack definition and force, a state he called **anomie.** In losing their attachments to others, people lose their primary source of moral judgment. As an early control theorist (see Chapter 7). Durkheim believed that con-formity to the norms is caused by attachments, and thus urbanization, by destroying attach-ments, destroys the normative order. He there-fore described the modern urbanite as adrift in a sea of normlessness (or anomie). Durkheim attempted to show that cities had much higher deviance rates than rural areas had.

Anomie theories

Early American sociologists found Durkheim's theory of urban anomie very compelling. Perhaps this was partly because the great majority of them were raised on farms and in small towns, and Durkheim's position agreed with their own personal reactions to city life. In any event, sociologists have long believed that cities are inimical to human relations and thus to the very basis of social life.

Louis Wirth (1938) made a major contribution to this position in a paper called "Urbanism as a Way of Life." In it he argued that city life forces the individual to become withdrawn from others. This occurs, first of all, because city people so often interact with complete strangers. Such interactions are necessarily impersonal, and this impersonality becomes a habit. Second, cities threaten to overload the people's senses, forcing them to shut out and ignore most of what is going on around them. We walk down streets filled with strangers, traffic flows past, store windows beckon, signs seek our attention, sirens and car horns blare, phones ring: The sights and sounds of the city would overwhelm us if we did not set up sensory buffers to filter out most of these stimuli. But in so doing, we become insensitive and unresponsive.

In 1939, two of Wirth's students published a study that convinced most American sociologists that the stress of city life caused mental illness. Robert E. L. Faris and Warren Dunham's famous book *Mental Disorders in Urban Areas*, was based on Chicago's community areas. They stated their thesis in the book's first paragraph:

A relationship between urbanism and social disorganization has long been recognized and demonstrated. Crude rural-urban comparisons of rates of dependency, crime, divorce and desertion, suicide, and vice have shown these problems to be more severe in the cities, especially the large rapidly expanding industrial cities. But as the study of urban sociology advanced, even more striking comparisons between different sections of a city were discovered. Some parts were found to be as stable and as peaceful as any well-organized rural neighborhood while other parts

Table 19-6 ■ Poverty and social pathology, Chicago 1922–1931.

	Correlations with Percent of Households Owning Radios, 1930
1930–1931: mental hospital admissions per 100,000	−.52
1922–1931: average annual hospital admissions for advanced syphilis per 100,000	−.61
1922–1931: average annual hospital admissions for alcoholism per 100,000	−.59

Source: Prepared by the author from Faris and Dunham (1939) and Burgess and Newcomb (1933).

were found to be in extreme stages of social disorganization.

And what kinds of neighborhoods are disorganized? According to Faris and Dunham, these are the poor areas, which are afflicted with high rates of population turnover and hence low rates of attachments. As they phrased it, "Any factor which interferes with social contacts with other persons produces isolation." After a long and careful examination of maps and data, Faris and Dunham concluded that when humans are exposed to high rates of social disorganization, and especially as disorganization causes them to be isolated, they become mentally ill.

Table 19-6 is based on the data Faris and Dunham provided in their book and on census data published by Burgess and Newcomb (1933). Among several measures of neighborhood affluence, Faris and Dunham used radio ownership—in 1930 just over 60 percent of Chicago

Table 19-7 ■ Sex ratios and social pathology, Chicago 1922–1931.

	Correlations with Males per 100 Females
1930–1931: mental hospital admissions per 100,000	.61
1922–1931: average annual hospital admissions for advanced syphilis per 100,000	.41
1922–1931: average annual hospital admissions for alcoholism per 100,000	.62

Source: Prepared by the author from Faris and Dunham (1939) and Burgess and Newcomb (1933).

households had a radio. Faris and Dunham did not use correlations to analyze their data—few sociologists did in those days—but the correlations shown in the table strongly support their conclusion that community areas lacking in radios were high in their rates of mental hospital admissions. Life in the poor community areas of Chicago seemed too much for many residents to bear. Here too were the high rates of advanced syphilis (then an incurable disease that often destroyed mental capacities) and the high rates of alcohol abuse. During the next several decades, Faris and Dunham's findings were confirmed in other cities (Hare, 1956; Srole et al., 1962). Moreover, studies that found poor people to have higher rates of mental illness (Hollingshead and Redlich, 1958) were thought to support these ecological findings.

Nevertheless, from the very start some social scientists rejected the claim that urban ecology causes mental illness. They argued instead that the mentally ill drift into the poorest areas of cities after they became ill and that the mentally ill also drift downward in the stratification system because of their inability to get and hold jobs. This is called the "social drift" explanation of why mental illness is concentrated in slum neighborhoods and among persons of low social class (Dohrenwend, 1966; Turner and Wagenfeld, 1967).

If we look once more at Table 19-6, we can see evidence in support of social drift. Because advanced syphilis takes many years to develop, and because these are neighborhoods marked by population instability, it seems very unlikely that these victims contracted syphilis in these neighborhoods. A more likely scenario: As the disease began to take its toll on the mental abilities of these victims, they drifted into the slums. Similarly, people usually have been problem drinkers for some time before they are committed to hospitals. It seems reasonable that they too drifted in rather than to argue that they became heavy drinkers only after they were exposed to the pressures of life in these neighborhoods. And if the alcoholics and syphilitics drifted into these neighborhoods, why not the mentally ill?

Indeed, the most striking characteristic of the most "socially disorganized" urban neighborhoods is that they are overrun by unattached male drifters. For example, there were 395 men per 100 women residents of the Chicago area with by far the highest rate of mental hospital admissions. Conversely, the community area with the lowest mental hospital admission rate had only 83 men per 100 female residents. Table 19-7 shows that the ratio of males to females is as good as radio ownership in identifying the neighborhoods with high rates of mental illness, advanced syphilis, and alcoholism. As the studies piled up, the social drift explanation dealt a fatal blow to the Faris and Dunham thesis.

Meanwhile, in the aftermath of World War II, Wirth's assertions about city life were incorporated into mass society theories to help explain why people responded to mass movements such as Nazism and Communism. Mass society theorists argued that as isolated, unattached individuals, city people were easily attracted to mass movements, especially those that promised to

■ New York City office buildings tower over St. Patrick's Cathedral. Many people would think this symbolic of the impact of cities on religious life—that people who live on farms and in small towns are much more apt to take part in religion than are people in big cities. Many social scientists have described the ways in which the "sophistication" of cities erodes faith. But, in fact, people in cities are the ones most apt to participate in religion. One reason is they don't have to travel long distances to reach a church of their choice. Another is that they have many more choices available (Finke and Stark, 1988).

restore order and provide followers with a clear sense of belonging.

In Chapter 1, we examined the fate of mass society or anomie theories when they were subjected to sociological research. These theories were correct in arguing that a lack of attachments results in deviance and anomie (see Chapter 7). Where they went wrong was in the claim that anomie was characteristic of urbanites. Research found that people typically maintain close attachments even in the largest cities. Human relations turn out to be much more

durable than the early sociologists had supposed. Indeed, as we saw in Chapter 3 and will examine again in Chapter 21, people do not join social movements because they are loose marbles bouncing randomly in normless cities, but because they are attached to persons who already belong to the movement.

This is not to say there are no lonely, isolated people in cities. There are, and many display the symptoms predicted by Durkheim and others: alcoholism, suicide, and criminal behavior. But most urbanites do not lack attachments, and the city does not have the destructive effects earlier sociologists believed it did.

Effects of crowding

What about the problem of "psychic overload"? This supposed effect of urban living was first identified by Louis Wirth, but it gained widespread attention in the 1960s as a potential hazard caused by population growth (Calhoun, 1962; Hall, 1966). Many critics of modern urban life have proposed that the population density of cities causes serious physical and mental pathologies. Noting that when rats are crowded into cages they become extremely abnormal, many sociologists have issued doomsday predictions—Peter Hall (1966) warned that increased urban density is an impending disaster "more lethal than the hydrogen bomb." Once again sociologists turned to empirical research.

Macro studies of crowding

The initial studies attempted to see whether neighborhoods with greater population density had higher rates of pathology than less dense neighborhoods had. The results did not support the psychic overload theory. People in dense neighborhoods were not more prone to alcoholism, mental illness, suicide, and other such problems than were people in less dense neighborhoods—in fact, city people were no more prone to these problems than rural people were (Fischer, 1975; Galle and Gove, 1978).

Sometimes the studies did find differences indicating crowding effects, but these proved to be spurious. That is, the kinds of people most likely to live in the most crowded places tend to have higher rates of pathologies wherever they live. Those who live in the most crowded neighborhoods also tend to be poor, without families, or elderly or to have been mentally ill before they arrived in the neighborhood. When these characteristics of residents were taken into account, no crowding effects could be detected. Thus density, viewed at the macro level, has no effect on people.

Micro studies of crowding

 Although these studies disproved the wild assertions of impending doom from urban density, several sociologists thought that a more modest proposition—that *excessive crowding of a person's immediate environment* has negative effects—might still be valid. That is, the density of a neighborhood might not matter, but the degree to which people have privacy or "personal space" might matter a good deal.

Walter Gove, Michael Hughes, and Omer Galle (1979) designed a study to see if it mattered that some people live in very crowded homes. They set out to discover whether crowding at the micro sociological level mattered. They reasoned that when a family lives in a home where there are several people to each room, it will be difficult for them to have privacy and to limit interaction with others. Therefore, people in crowded homes ought to experience a lack of privacy and an overload of demands on them from others. This might cause them to withdraw, both by staying away from home and by being unresponsive to other members of the household. Such withdrawal ought to have negative consequences for attachments and for mental health.

Gove and his colleagues selected more than 2,000 homes that varied in the number of persons per room. Analysis of the data, which were obtained by interviews with members of these households, supported their expectations. They found the following:

1. The more persons per room, the more that people complained of a lack of privacy and of too great demands on them by others.

2. People responded to crowding by withdrawing, both physically and emotionally.

3. People in crowded homes had poorer mental health.

4. Members of crowded homes had poor social relations with each other. There were more family fights, and husbands and wives were less satisfied with their marriages.

5. Child care in crowded homes was poor. Parents expressed relief at getting the kids out of the home and were much less aware of where their children were and what they were doing when they were out.

6. The effects of crowding began to show up when there was more than one person per room in a household.

Thus, we see that crowding can have negative effects. Although it doesn't seem to matter how many people live in a neighborhood or even in a single home, it does matter how much room people have to find peace and quiet. When ten family members live in a ten-room home, they will be happier than when they live in a four-room home.

Although Gove and his colleagues found support for micro effects of crowding, these effects are of little import for the more general fears about urban crowding. Few urban families live in crowded conditions, that is, with more than one person per room. In 1970 only 8.2 percent of households in America had more than 1.01 persons per room. The median household had almost two rooms per member. Moreover, crowding is declining, not increasing. In 1950, 15.7 percent of American households had more than 1.01 persons per room, and the median household had only about 1.5 rooms per member.

These changes partly reflect a decline in the average family size. But they primarily reflect the decentralization of cities and the decreased density that results. The preindustrial city was extremely crowded. The early fixed-rail industrial city was less crowded, but much more crowded than the freeway city. Transportation has always been the key to density. As transportation changes enabled people to escape crowded, centralized cities to get some elbow room, they rushed to do so. They did not wait for sociological research to tell them that it was desirable to have a large enough home so that family members could find privacy.

Conclusion

We have seen that until very recently cities were small, unhealthy, filthy, dangerous, and crowded. Little wonder, then, that when rapid urbanization began in the nineteenth century, so many regarded it as tragic. However, the very processes of industrialization that prompted migration to the cities also transformed city life itself. Granted, many mistakes have been made in the design and administration of modern cities—such errors are inevitable when experience is lacking. Yet if gloomy prophets such as Tönnies and Durkheim could visit a modern city, they would be dumbfounded—not by the errors in planning or the problems that persist, but by the comfort, cleanliness, beauty, and tranquility of our cities.

Of course, our cities have ugly, dirty, and dangerous neighborhoods. But even the worst parts of modern cities are an improvement on large sections of cities during the early days of the Industrial Revolution, to say nothing of the squalor and misery of preindustrial cities. On a walk through the most horrid urban neighborhood today, no one will see dead or dying infants lying on dung heaps—or even any dung heaps. This is hardly to suggest that there are no urgent urban problems. It is merely to give historical perspective to current concerns.

Perhaps the most important sociological lesson in this chapter is that the future is not always a simple extension of the past. Modern cities are not just big versions of older cities. As cities grew, they were greatly transformed. Indeed, in the next chapter we shall see that growth alone is enough to revolutionize social structures and organizations.

Review Glossary

urban society A society in which the majority of people do not live in rural areas. (p. 554)

urban place According to the U.S. Census, a community having at least 2,500 inhabitants, the majority of whom do not farm. (p. 566)

city According to the U.S. Census, a community having at least 50,000 inhabitants. (p. 566)

suburb An urban place in the immediate vicinity of a city. (p. 566)

metropolis A city and its sphere of influence. (p. 567)

sphere of influence (of a city) The area whose inhabitants depend on a city for jobs, recreation, newspapers, television, and a sense of community. (p. 567)

Standard Metropolitan Statistical Area (SMSA) According to the U.S. Census, a central city (with at least 50,000 residents) and all surrounding counties where 75 percent of the labor force is not in agriculture and where either 15 percent of the workers commute to the city or 25 percent of the workers commute from the city. Statistics Canada's **Census Metropolitan Area (CMA)** includes an urban core of 100,000 and surrounding communities if 40 percent of the labor force work in the urban core or 25 percent of those employed in the outlying area commute from the urban core. (p. 567)

fixed-rail metropolis A city whose form and size are determined by the routes of rail transit systems (trains and trolleys). (p. 568)

freeway metropolis A city that developed after the widespread use of autos and trucks freed city structures from rail dependency. (p. 568)

theory of ethnic succession Theory stating that ethnic and racial groups will be the targets of neighborhood segregation only until they achieve economic parity and that slum neighborhoods will therefore house a succession of ethnic and racial groups. (p. 572)

index of dissimilarity A measure of the degree to which a given ethnic or racial group lives in integrated or segregated neighborhoods; it compares the ethnic makeup of city blocks with the ethnic makeup of the city as a whole. (p. 573)

Gemeinschaft A German word meaning community and used to describe the intimacy of life in small villages. (p. 576)

Gesellschaft A German word meaning society or association and used to describe the impersonality of life in cities. (p. 577)

anomie A state in which norms lack definition and force, that is, in which people aren't sure what the norms are and don't greatly care. (p. 577)

Suggested Readings

Bourne, L. S., ed. 1971. *Internal Structure of the City.* New York: Oxford.

Fischer, Claude S. 1976. *The Urban Experience.* New York: Harcourt Brace Jovanovich.

Girouard, Mark. 1985. *Cities and People.* New Haven, Conn.: Yale University Press.

Gove, Walter, Michael Hughes, and Omer Galle. 1979. "Overcrowding in the Home." *American Sociological Review* 44:59–80.

Pirenne, Henri. 1925. *Medieval Cities.* Princeton, N.J.: Princeton University Press.

Sjoberg, Gideon. 1960. *The Preindustrial City.* New York: Free Press.

The Organizational Age

20

NAPOLEON BONAPARTE WAS the last Great Captain to exercise direct command of his army, but by the end of his career, even he failed at the task. Armies had simply become too big and the area of the battlefield too vast. Even by standing on a hill and using a telescope, Napoleon could not keep track of everything that was going on. His orders to various units began to arrive too late and often they were wrong (Chandler, 1966).

Napoleon's problems were neither unique nor limited to the commands of armies. During the nineteenth century, many human activities grew in size and complexity to the point that no single leader could orchestrate them. When he was President of the United States, George Washington personally evaluated every government employee: There were fewer than 700 of them! Today the U.S. government has more than 3 million employees, not including members of the armed forces. In fact, General Motors now employs more people than the total able-bodied adult population of the United States in 1776.

When organized human activities reached the scale of Napoleon's Grand Army of 1812 (about 600,000 troops), a crisis developed. Traditional principles of leadership and organization failed. When one of the greatest leaders in history could no longer master affairs on this scale, it was obvious that new methods were needed for directing and coordinating large-scale activities. If no one individual could manage large organizations, somehow several persons had to

share the management. But how? How could leadership and decision making be shared among people without a breakdown in coordination? When Napoleon relied on his subordinates to act on their own, the result was often chaos, as different units marched off in different directions and to defeat.

The answer was the creation of a new kind of group, the **formal organization.** Because such an organization was produced by applying reason to the problems of management, and because the key to its success lies in operations based on logical rules, it is often called a *rational organization.*

A formal organization has several characteristics that distinguish it from older forms of organization. First of all, it depends on a clear statement of goals. What is it meant to do? Second, a formal organization requires suitable operating principles and procedures for pursuing these goals. Third, leaders must be selected and trained in the use of these operating principles. Fourth, clear lines of authority and communication must be established for issuing instructions, transmitting information, and coordinating the activities of different groups. Finally, to avoid misunderstanding and error, written records and communications must be used.

These five elements of the formal organization seem familiar and obvious to us today, for we live in an age dominated by such organizations. Yet formal organizations are very new

Albania	0.00	Denmark	13.41
Romania	0.01	Netherlands	15.15
East Germany	0.02	Ireland	18.94
USSR	0.03	Finland	19.59
Poland	0.09	Sweden	23.51
Czechoslovakia	0.11	Belgium	24.93
Hungary	0.28	Norway	26.42
Yugoslavia	0.33	Switzerland	51.17
Bulgaria	0.36		

Spain	3.36
Italy	4.85
Austria	5.51
Portugal	5.64
West Germany	6.74
Greece	8.45
France	8.51
United Kingdom	9.33

Figure 20-1 ■ European circulation of *Business Week* per 100,000 population, 1983. Magazine circulation figures frequently provide a sensitive gauge of complex cultural patterns. Suppose we want to know the relative interest in worldwide economic and business trends present in various communities. An inexpensive way to measure this is by obtaining circulation figures for publications that specialize in that subject. Perhaps the most useful of these is *Business Week*, which has a circulation of nearly one million and has subscribers in almost every nation in the world. Here we see that Switzerland deserves its reputation as a business and financial capital, having nearly twice the *Business Week* circulation rate of the next highest nation, Norway. Overall, these circulation rates correlate with industrialization. But they also reflect a lack of private business organizations and investors in Eastern Europe.

human creations—so new that we still do not fully understand how to make them work effectively. Moreover, our understanding of formal organizations has been painfully gained by trial and error and in the face of urgent necessity.

■

Chapter Preview

When you complain about the government, your employer, or your college or university, chances are that your complaint is not really about shortcomings of individuals. More likely, your complaints are about typical features of large formal organizations. Everywhere you turn, you find that some aspect of your life is governed by and occurs within such organizations. That makes it important to know something about how such organizations operate and the theoretical principles behind their structure and performance. In this chapter, you will see that although organizations are created by and for humans, we are not free to create them in just any way we like.

Because large formal organizations are so new—very large organizations have existed for little more than 100 years—and because how they are created and operated has such far-reaching effects, they have been the object of intense study. From the beginning, theories of organization have influenced the structure and operations of organizations, and changes in theory and in organizations have gone hand in hand. We can therefore trace the development of both organizations and theories of organizations at the same time.

■

The Crisis of Growth: Inventing Formal Organizations

During the nineteenth century, the first large formal organizations were created, and the first social scientific attempts were made to figure out how to create and control them. These developments went forward in three somewhat independent sectors of industrializing societies: the military, business, and government.

Let's examine developments in each of these sectors before we focus on the work of the first great sociologist of formal organizations, Max Weber.

The case of the Prussian General Staff

After Napoleon's defeat at Waterloo in 1815, Europe entered a long period of peace. Armies were cut back to small professional corps, and interest in military science waned in most nations. Only in Prussia (later to become Germany) did people study the crises of command that emerged during the last stages of the Napoleonic Wars, when mass armies took to the battlefields. In Prussia they addressed the question head-on: What would happen if war broke out again and huge armies—made possible by the recent European population explosion and the mass production of arms—once again engaged in battle? Napoleon's failure had shown that such armies could not be led in the traditional way. The Prussians concluded that military command and organization had to be completely revised (Ropp, 1959).

If Napoleon was the last Great Captain of history, then Helmuth von Moltke was the first Great Manager of the modern military era. Moltke took command of the Prussian army in 1857 and rapidly built up a new system based on the principle of using *highly trained* and *interchangeable* staff officers. These elite officers were trained in a war academy. Each year 120 young officers were selected from the whole officer corps on the basis of competitive examinations. Of these, only about 40 finished the intensive scholastic course of the academy. And of these graduates, Moltke selected only the best 12 to be trained for the General Staff (Howard, 1962).

In peacetime, officers cannot get real experience in their profession, so Moltke arranged for the academy to provide the next best thing: making battle plans for a great variety of hypothetical campaigns and analyses of past battles. By fighting battles on paper, young officers were trained in Prussian strategic and tactical theories. After their academic studies, officers chosen for the General Staff spent several years with

■ Field Marshal Helmuth von Moltke.

Moltke at his headquarters and rode with him through a series of field maneuvers in which real troops participated. Then these officers were assigned a period of duty with a regiment. After that, they rotated between assignments on Moltke's staff and regimental duty (Ropp, 1959).

The point of all this training was to overcome the inability of a single commander to direct a war fought with mass armies. Because the supreme commander could not be everywhere at once, the Prussians tried to create many "duplicates" trained to act as he would act. The decision of one leader could then be carried out

through the reflexes which he had already inculcated in his subordinates through previous training: so that, even when deprived of his guidance, they should react to unexpected situations as he would wish. . . . Thus the Prussian General Staff acted as a nervous system animating the lumbering body of the army, making possible the articulation and flexibility which alone rendered it an effective military force [Howard, 1962].

Between wars, the Prussian General Staff spent time looking ahead, planning in minute detail for future wars, and agreeing on proper tactics and strategies for various circumstan-

ces. When war came, each military problem was solved according to the overall plan and the approved methods. Thus, Moltke dealt with the overwhelming scale of modern warfare by training corps of subordinate managers he could count on to be not only his eyes and ears on the battlefield but also his brain.

While Moltke was creating an interchangeable set of military managers, he also perfected another military system that gave these managers standardized units to work with: the **divisional system**. Before the Napoleonic Wars, European armies were organized by armament and function. The cavalry, the infantry, and the artillery were separate branches of service and appeared on the battlefield as separate units under separate commanders. Coordinating these units was the task of the supreme commander of the army, who arrayed these forces into a battle formation and then told infantry units where to march, cavalry units where to charge, and artillery units where to fire.

However, as armies grew, this system proved cumbersome. Under Napoleon, the French army began to break up into smaller units, each of which was an independent mini-army consisting of infantry, cavalry, and artillery and capable of doing battle on its own.

These French formations were of varying size, and their makeup was never standardized. However, Napoleon's British archrival, the Duke of Wellington (who in his long career never lost a battle), adopted this idea of mini-armies and created a standardized unit called the division. British divisions, being complete units, could be detached to fight as self-sufficient units, combined to form larger units, and interchanged. For example, a rested reserve division could replace a fatigued division in combat.

Moltke carried the standardization of Prussian divisions to the point that commanders could easily move from unit to unit. Each division was similar to the others in makeup, training, size, and structure. Indeed, Moltke's divisional system was so detailed that each division had a specified number of spoons and cooking pots.

In 1871, Moltke tested his new military managers and his divisional structure in the Franco-Prussian War. During a lightning campaign, the Prussians utterly routed the much more experienced French army. The Prussians did not win because they were better armed, had more soldiers, or were braver in battle. The French army was their equal in all these ways. But the French General Staff was only a group of messengers and clerks serving the commander, and the French commander could not control his far-flung armies.

Noting Moltke's success over the French, all major nations soon copied his methods. Later, with the advent of telephones and radios, commanders could better guide their subordinates in the field. But the principle of delegating command to officers on the spot, who are highly trained in a common military theory and in the command of standardized military units, has remained the only workable solution to the problem that overwhelmed Napoleon.

The cases of Daniel McCallum and Gustavus Swift

It seems fitting that while the key to managing huge military organizations was first found in Prussia, the key to managing huge business organizations was first discovered in the United States. For business, the rapid growth of railroads in the 1850s was the equivalent of Napoleon's Grand Army—the railroads revealed the inability of traditional organizational principles to cope with large-scale enterprises. The crisis appeared in dramatic fashion: Small railroads made profits while the big railroads lost money.

In 1855 Daniel C. McCallum, general superintendent of the Erie Railroad, pointed out that the reason his line and other large lines such as the New York Central, the Pennsylvania, and the Baltimore & Ohio were in financial distress was a problem of management. He wrote:

A Superintendent of a road fifty miles in length can give its business his professional attention and may be constantly on the line engaged in the direction of its details; each person is personally known to him, and all questions in relation to its business are at once presented and acted upon; and any system however imperfect may under such cir-

cumstances prove comparatively successful [Chandler, 1962].

These comments recall the spectacular ease with which Napoleon dealt with grave military disadvantages when he had only seventy to eighty thousand troops to maneuver on a single, compact battlefield. But, McCallum continued, when one attempts to manage a railroad "five hundred miles in length a very different state exists. Any system which might be applicable to the business and extent of a short road would be found entirely inadequate to the wants of a long one." For want of an adequate organizational system, McCallum argued, the large railroads faced financial failure.

McCallum quickly moved to install a management system to replace the overloaded manager. He broke his railroad into **geographical divisions** of manageable size. Each was headed by a superintendent responsible for the operations within his division. Each divisional superintendent was required to submit detailed reports to central headquarters, from where McCallum and his aides coordinated and gave general direction to the operations of the separate divisions. Lines of authority between each superintendent and his subordinates and between each superintendent and headquarters were clearly laid out. In sketching these lines of authority on paper, McCallum created what might have been the first organizational chart for an American business (Chandler, 1962). Soon the other great railroads copied the Erie's system, enabling the big railroads to function as effectively as small ones. As a result, railroads rapidly became the largest industrial companies of that time.

The railroads had two direct effects on other industrial firms. First, they made it possible for other firms to grow by using rail shipments to reach national rather than just local markets. Rail shipments could carry goods across the nation and bring needed supplies from far away. Second, the railroads provided a first crude organizational model for operating large firms. As other kinds of firms grew, they adopted the idea of divisions, but as we shall see, these were based on functions rather than geography. As they grew, new industrial firms created **func-**

■ A train crossing the Niagara Suspension Bridge in 1859. When trains were new, people often went out to watch them go by, as these gentlemen are doing. Notice the horse and buggy on the lower level. In those days, people knew a lot more about building and operating trains than they did about managing the railroad business. (William England, *Niagara Suspension Bridge*, 1859. Albumen print, 9½ × 11½. Collection, The Museum of Modern Art, New York. Purchase.)

tional divisions that controlled each step in production through a process called **vertical integration.** These two features of industrial firms came to dominate organizational theory for many decades.

The story of Gustavus Swift, who built a huge meat-packing firm in the 1870s and 1880s, reveals how the new industrial organizations came into being.

Swift was a wholesale butcher in New England who moved west to Chicago in the 1870s. The population was concentrated in the East, while the herds of livestock were concentrated on the Great Plains, and getting the meat to market was a cumbersome and inefficient process that depended on the uncoordinated services of small, specialized, local firms. Swift was determined to bring order and efficiency to the process by controlling each step from ranch to retail store. In 1878 he made an experimental shipment of meat from Chicago to the East, using the newly invented refrigerator car. The success of this experiment encouraged Swift and his brother Edwin to found Swift & Co. But they still faced vast problems. Shipping refrigerated meat east required refrigerated storage facilities

■ The huge stockyards founded by Gustavus Swift in Chicago, the first of many operated by his company. In Swift's new organizational scheme, stockyards not only made up a functional division of the company but also were the initial level in the vertical integration of the company—control of each step in the process of bringing beef from the range to the meat counter.

at the other end; so Swift built them. Then the meat had to be sold; so Swift hired a sales crew and set up a distribution system in each major city. Local butchers tried to prevent the sale of his western meat in eastern markets, even claiming that it was unhealthy to eat "meat killed more than a thousand miles away and many weeks earlier" (Chandler, 1962). Massive advertising was required to convince consumers that Swift meat was safe. Soon Swift built additional packing plants in St. Louis, Omaha, St. Joseph, St. Paul, and Fort Worth.

Then Swift turned his attention to making supplies of meat dependable. He organized stockyards to purchase large numbers of animals on a regular and orderly basis. Finally,

he branched out to make use of animal by-products by entering the leather, glue, fertilizer, and soap businesses.

Swift & Co. became a vertically integrated company: It controlled each step in the process of bringing meat products to the consumer. Although Swift did not raise cattle, the company took over at the point of sale and conducted each step thereafter: buying, packing, shipping, and marketing. Furthermore, each of these steps was the province of a *different division* of the company. That is, rather than creating geographic divisions, as the giant railroads had done, Swift *based its divisions on different functions*. In fact, Swift broke up its organizational divisions in the same way that the Industrial Revolution had divided the labor of workers into a few specific production steps. Just as each worker on an assembly line performed only one or a few specialized functions, each division of large industrial firms handled only one aspect of the industry.

Swift had a marketing division, a meat-packing division, a purchasing or stockyards division, a shipping division, a sales division, and an advertising division. Each of these divisions was headed by a manager to whom subordinate managers reported; each manager reported to and received directions from corporate headquarters. As Moltke's General Staff mastered large armies, vertical integration and functional divisions under centralized command made it possible to create and operate huge business firms.

The case of civil service

Armies and corporations were not the only organizations that grew to immense size in the modern world. Governments also became very large because of the rapid expansion in size and complexity of the societies they governed. As governments got big, they, too, found that they could no longer function with outdated practices.

In traditional agrarian societies, the government was nothing more than the king's household and court. Such needed functionaries as clerks, accountants, and tax collectors were servants of the king, equal in status to his cooks, grooms, and butlers. When the king needed a general, an advisor, a chief justice, or an administrator of the treasury, he asked one of the noblemen in his court to do the job. These noblemen did not regard a government post as an occupation or even as a full-time activity. Often they had no special training and little aptitude for their government duties beyond their noble birth and their social graces.

Such a system worked because governments did little governing. Beyond extracting taxes from the populace, maintaining some semblance of public order, and defending the realm against invaders, there was little for governments to do. After all, more than 90 percent of the population were peasants leading quiet lives of rural

■ A Dutch tax collector in about 1500. His filing system consists of several spikes on the wall and a ledger. If asked who he was, he would not say a government employee or a tax collector. Instead, no doubt he would say, "a gentleman." He would find modern civil service practices as strange as computerized accounting systems.

toil. No complex laws, no large regulatory agencies, and no swarms of government experts were needed. Indeed, if the central government had disappeared, people in outlying districts would not have noticed for a long while.

With the growth of population and of cities, the complex divisions of labor, and the development of technology, agrarian governments found it increasingly difficult to control their societies. Indeed, modern societies require more control than agrarian societies do.

Governments adopted much the same solutions as did armies and industries. Organizations were created specifically to perform government functions in an orderly and efficient

■ Records are the basis of bureaucratic organizations. For organizations to run on the basis of rational procedures, exact records must be kept of each transaction—only then can the operation of the system be reviewed and improved.

manner, and these organizations were staffed by persons specially trained to carry out their duties. In fact, staffing governmental positions caused the greatest conflict.

Kings were accustomed to rewarding their loyal and valued friends with government positions. Early democratic governments continued this practice—the party or political faction in control of the government appointed its favorites to office. When the government changed hands, government officeholders were also changed. Thus, when Thomas Jefferson became President of the United States in 1801, he dismissed hundreds of Federalists appointed by Presidents Washington and Adams and replaced them with his supporters. This practice is known as the **spoils system**—the spoils,

or benefits, of public office go to the supporters of winning politicians. The spoils system probably reached its height in the United States during the presidency of Andrew Jackson in 1829, when thousands of officeholders were replaced.

When government is based on the spoils system, disorganization arises from so much turnover and people are prevented from making a career of government service. The administration of government organizations is forever left in the hands of untrained novices. To combat this problem, governments adopted merit systems for government employment—a practice often referred to as civil service. Civil service systems base government hiring and promotion practices on merit. People are recruited on the basis of their educational and occupational qualifications and by successfully competing with others on a written examination. When a government wants accountants, it hires trained accountants with the highest scores on the civil service examination rather than the brother-in-law of some politician. What Moltke learned was needed for modern war and what Gustavus Swift had discovered about business, modern government also put into practice: a carefully designed organizational system operated by specially selected and trained people.

Weber's Rational Bureaucracy

At the turn of the century, Max Weber began to study the new forms of organization being developed for managing large numbers of people in far-flung and complex activities. As a German, he was very familiar with Moltke's development of the General Staff. Furthermore, Germany had been an early leader in developing a civil service. And, in Weber's day, German industry was rapidly adopting the organizational methods developed in the United States. Surveying this scene, Weber attempted to isolate the elements common to all of these new organizations.

Weber concluded that all these new large-scale organizations were similar. Each was a **bureaucracy**. Today many of us regard *bureaucracy* as a dirty word, suggesting red tape, inefficiency, and officiousness. As we shall see, bureaucracies can develop these features, especially if authority is highly centralized. Weber's purpose, however, was to define the essential features of new organizations and to indicate why these organizations worked so much better than traditional ones. Let us examine the features that Weber found in bureaucracies.

Above all, Weber emphasized that bureaucratic organizations were an attempt to subdue human affairs to the rule of reason—to make it possible to conduct the business of the organization "according to calculable rules." For people who developed modern organizations, the purpose was to find rational solutions to the new problems of size. Weber saw bureaucracy

as the rational product of social engineering, just as the machines of the Industrial Revolution were the rational products of mechanical engineering. He wrote:

The decisive reason for the advance of bureaucratic organization has always been its purely technical superiority over any former organization. The fully developed bureaucratic mechanism compares with other organizations exactly as does the machine with nonmechanical modes of production [Weber, 1946].

For Weber, the term *bureaucracy* was inseparable from the term *rationality*. And we may speak of his concept as a "rational bureaucracy."

But what were the features developed to make bureaucracies rational? We have already met them: (1) functional specialization, (2) clear lines of hierarchical authority, (3) expert training of managers, and (4) decision making based on rules and tactics developed to guarantee consistent and effective pursuit of organizational goals. Weber noted additional features of rational bureaucracies that are simple extensions of the four just outlined. To ensure expert management, appointment and promotion are based on merit rather than favoritism, and those appointed treat their positions as full-time, primary careers. To ensure order in decision making, business is conducted primarily through written rules, records, and communications.

Weber's idea of functional specialization applies both to persons within an organization and to relations between larger units or divisions of the organization. We have already seen how this applied to Swift & Co. Within a Swift packing plant, work was broken down into many special tasks, and employees were assigned to one or a few such tasks, including the tasks involved in coordinating the work of others. (Such coordination is called administration or **management**.) Furthermore, Swift was separated into a number of divisions, each specializing in one of the tasks in the elaborate process of bringing meat from the ranch to the consumer. Weber argued that such specialization is essential to a rational bureaucracy and that the specific boundaries separating one functional division from another must be fixed by explicit rules, regulations, and procedures.

For Weber, it was self-evident that coordinating the divisions of large organizations requires clear lines of authority organized in a hierarchy. That means there are clear "levels of graded authority." All employees in the organization must know who their boss is, and each person should always respect the chain of command; that is, people should give orders only to their own subordinates and receive orders only through their own immediate superior. In this way, the people at the top can be sure that directives arrive where they are meant to go and know where responsibilities lie.

Furthermore, hierarchical authority is required in bureaucracies so that highly trained experts can be properly used as managers. It does little good to train someone to operate a stockyard, for example, and then have that manager receive orders from someone whose training is in advertising. Rational bureaucracies can be operated, Weber argued, only by deploying managers at all levels who have been selected and trained for their specific jobs. Persons ticketed for top positions in bureaucracies are often rotated through many divisions of an organization to gain firsthand experience of the many problems that their future subordinates must face. (Recall how Moltke rotated his General Staff officers through various regiments.)

Finally, Weber stressed that rational bureaucracies must be managed in accordance with carefully developed rules and principles that can be learned and applied and that transactions and decisions must be recorded so that rules can be reviewed. Only with such rules and principles can the activities of hundreds of managers at different levels in the organization be predicted and coordinated. If we cannot predict what others will do, then we cannot count on them.

Moltke had to be sure that staff officers faced with an unexpected crisis would solve it as he would. To ensure that, officers had to be trained in Moltke's tactical principles and rules. Similarly, Gustavus Swift had to know that his stockyards would not buy meat faster than his packing plants could process it or that more meat would not be shipped than his eastern refrigerators could accommodate. Of course, it is impossible to spell out detailed rules to fit all contingencies. Therefore, decision makers must be highly trained and must report their decisions promptly and accurately to their superiors.

For a long time, Weber's rational bureaucracy model dominated social science thinking about large, modern organizations. If organizations did not operate quite as Weber had said a bureaucracy should, then the solution was to bring them in line with the ideal bureaucratic procedures. However, by World War II, sharp criticism of Weber's ideas began to surface. Social scientists began to argue that Weber had ignored much of what really went on in organizations—the conflicts, the cliques, and the sidestepping of rules and the chain of command. The problem, according to Philip Selznick (1948, 1957), lay in the fact that bureaucracies were not and could not be like machines because they consisted of human beings. In the final analysis, people will simply not imitate machines.

■

Rational Versus Natural Systems

Weber stressed the rationality of bureaucratic organizations; that is, organizations are created and maintained to pursue clearly defined goals, and the structure and operation of organizations are the result of reasoned, conscious efforts to attain these goals. This approach to studying organizations is called the **rational system approach**.

Alvin Gouldner (1959) described the rational system viewpoint as one in which

the organization is conceived as an "instrument"—that is, as a rationally conceived means to the realization of expressly announced group goals. Its structures are understood as tools deliberately established for the efficient realization of these group purposes. . . . Changes in organizational patterns are viewed as planned devices to improve the level of efficiency. . . . The focus is, therefore, on . . . the formally "blueprinted" patterns.

From this viewpoint, organizations that make

poor choices and fail to achieve stated goals are guilty of ignorance and miscalculation.

However, many sociologists have criticized the rational approach as too limited. They argue that many important goals of organizations are not the "announced goals" and that often not all members of an organization pursue the same goals. Critics further argue that the real lines of communication and authority in organizations are not always the same as those laid out on the organizational chart. In fact, the real lines may violate the formal structure.

Persons approaching organizations in this way focus on the natural system. They argue that the general principles of the natural behavior of people and groups apply to the behavior of bureaucratic organizations; thus, these principles, not the rational system, reveal what is really going on in the system. A fundamental principle of the **natural system approach** is that the rarely stated but overriding goal of organizations is simply to survive. The living, breathing human beings who staff an organization develop a personal stake in the life of that organization, regardless of the stated goals of the organization. For its members, the existence of an organization means the continuation of jobs, careers, and friendships. When an organization folds, its members are cast adrift. People can be expected to resist such a fate even at the expense of the formal goals of the organization. Therefore, features of an organization that appear as miscalculations from the rational perspective may reflect people's efforts to keep the organization alive.

Goal displacement

The importance of survival over other goals is well illustrated by an organization created during the 1930s to combat the dread disease of polio. The National Foundation for the March of Dimes created a huge network of volunteers in each American community who, guided by the professional staff, conducted an extremely successful annual fund drive. The funds were used to support the treatment of polio victims and research for a way to cure or prevent the disease. The March of Dimes was an extremely

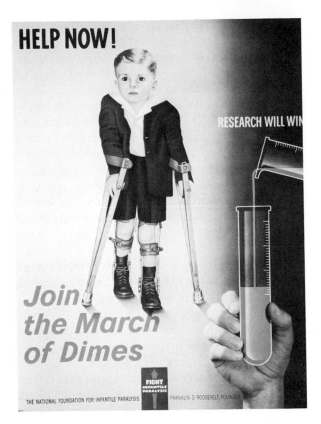

■ Posters like this were on display everywhere when I was growing up. Some of my playmates died of polio (often called infantile paralysis); many more were badly crippled. The line "Research will win" turned out not to be an empty slogan. Research paid for by March of Dimes contributions funded the discovery of the polio vaccine.

successful and well-run organization. Then, one day, it was too successful. In the 1950s, research supported by March of Dimes funds led to the discovery of effective vaccines. A massive vaccination drive soon resulted in the virtual elimination of polio. The March of Dimes had achieved its goals.

Yet this achievement was not met with an office party of gleeful people toasting to victory and going off happily to pursue new careers. Instead, there was something closer to panic as the March of Dimes staff searched for a new goal to sustain the organization. Quickly they declared war on birth defects and, as the National Foundation, continue still to raise funds and to conduct business as usual (Sills, 1957).

Organizations often change, or displace, their goals in the pursuit of survival, but not often as dramatically as did the National Foundation. Philip Selznick (1949) has documented substantial **goal displacement** by the Tennessee Valley Authority (TVA). When created during the 1930s, TVA announced broad goals to transform the whole social structure of the rural farming region served by its hydroelectric power and flood control projects. Many found these goals too radical, and opposition to the TVA grew. In reaction to threats to disband the agency, these far-reaching social goals were replaced by the more limited goals of rural electrification and resource management.

These examples illustrate the truth of a principle: When the formal goals of an organization threaten its existence, the goals will be changed.

Goal conflict

Natural system theorists also argue that different groups within an organization tend to pursue different goals, which often have nothing to do with (and may even conflict with) the goals of the larger organization. This situation is called **goal conflict**.

The official goal of corporations is to earn profits for stockholders, but the managerial revolution—whereby owners have been separated from the control of corporations—resulted in the displacement of the profit goal as the overriding goal of modern corporations. Managers as a group have goals that may *conflict* with the profit goal of a company. For example, managers may approve lavish expenses—sales meetings in posh resorts, elegant business entertainment, and company-owned jets and limousines—that cut into potential profits. They do this to reward themselves rather than a mass of anonymous, disorganized owners (stockholders).

A second reason why managers may deemphasize profit seeking is because other groups in the corporation effectively pursue goals that also conflict with the profit goal. Consider the case of labor. Maximum profits depend upon getting the greatest amount of production from workers for the lowest possible wage. While all managers seek to raise worker productivity and

to hold down labor costs, modern corporation executives do not do so without regard for their own welfare. Unions often resist changes in work procedures and the introduction of new technology and press for the highest possible wages. Therefore, management often does not seek the most profitable labor contracts, settling instead for a compromise that involves the least disruption and stress.

Management and labor are the most obvious examples of groups who strike bargains that affect the structure and operations of an organization. Many such compromises are not designed to make the organization more effective in pursuing its stated goals. Organizations often develop many competing interest groups, and various divisions of a company may strike bargains with one another over who is responsible for what. Such bargains may reflect desires for enhanced status or lesser workloads, but they may lower efficiency.

Informal relations

Formal organizations are based on clear lines of authority and responsibility. Each member is supposed to know to whom to give orders and from whom to take them. However, natural system theorists point out that people often do not adhere to the formal chain of command. They constantly construct social relations that serve as bases for authority, influence, and communication that often bear little resemblance to relations set out in the formal blueprint.

Suppose Jack in division A needs assistance from division B. He could go to his supervisor, who would then request the assistance from the supervisor of division B. He could also call his friend Sally in division B and get what he needs without either supervisor knowing what is going on. Indeed, Jack and Sally could call on each other all the time. They could thus get around the formal procedures for interdivision cooperation and override the formal system. It is well known in many organizations that you must see certain people in order to get certain things done, despite the fact that these people do not hold the formal position that is supposed to control these activities. Friendships and enmi-

■ A clear organizational chart could easily be created of this newspaper staff. Everyone has a distinct job title with specific responsibilities, and clear lines of authority state who is supposed to report to whom. But observation would reveal great differences between the chart and what really goes on.

ties may also lead to the overriding of formal operations.

But if the rational system approach overemphasizes the organizational blueprint, the natural system approach tends to forget that there is one. Although organizations are filled with informal channels of authority, influence, and communication—informal networks of social relations and groups pursuing goals other than the corporate goals—we can predict from the corporate blueprint most of what people do most of the time. Persons who are hired to work on an automobile assembly line, for example, may cooperate to keep production at the level that they think is best for them and get around their supervisors to alter procedures, but they

do not work in the accounting office sorting invoices, in the design division drawing new models, or in the showrooms selling cars. When we know the official duties and responsibilities of a particular job, we can predict a great deal about what people hired to fill that job will spend their time doing.

Consequently, neither the rational nor the natural system approach can fully explain formal organizational activities. They are complementary views. The long conflict over which approach better explains organizations is probably nothing more than an academic dispute between college departments. Those who have given the most time to study of the rational system are usually employed in the department of business administration. Those who opt for the natural system are mainly employed in sociology and psychology departments. In the competition for customers (in this case, students), each firm (or department) stresses the merits of its product. But the wise customer knows that making a choice is unnecessary; one need not choose between cereal or fruit for breakfast, but may benefit from mixing both in the same bowl.

The important point is that when people design or evaluate an organization, they must pay attention not only to what people are supposed to do but also to what they are apt to do.

The Crisis of Diversification

In the case studies examined at the beginning of this chapter, we saw some basic solutions to problems in managing large organizations: Gustavus Swift coordinated a large business firm on the basis of vertical integration of functional divisions, Moltke recognized the need for highly trained, interchangeable commanding officers holding a common military doctrine, and civil service developed to ensure experienced and competent managers in government.

As time passed, however, the solutions of Swift, Moltke, and others to the problems of operating large organizations began to fail. As organizations continued to grow and become more complex, a need arose for even better organizing and managing of principles. In part, this new crisis occurred because the rational system approach created some organizational problems that exceeded the natural human capacities of managers. There are limits to how much any one person can know and do. These new problems, and the principles they spawned, can best be understood by examining one of the first organizations in which such problems became evident and were solved.

Du Pont is one of the oldest and most successful firms in the world. It began in 1802 when Éleuthère Irénée Du Pont, an immigrant from France, built a gunpowder factory on the banks of Brandywine Creek near Wilmington, Delaware. The factory grew and prospered.

Throughout the nineteenth century, Du Pont sons attended West Point or M.I.T., the best engineering schools in the country at that time, and then went into the family business. The firm grew larger and larger. Although the product line expanded to include blasting powder and dynamite as well as gunpowder, the firm manufactured explosives almost exclusively.

Functional divisions

By the turn of the century, Du Pont displayed the same problems of bigness that many other organizations then faced. With many factories requiring massive amounts of raw materials, supplies had to come in regularly and at predictable prices, and the production flowing out of these plants had to be directed to customers in an orderly and efficient manner. When the operations of Du Pont became bogged down, the directors responded, as Gustavus Swift had done, by reorganizing the firm into functional divisions.

All personnel and facilities involved in manufacturing explosives were grouped into a single administrative unit under a general manager. All purchasing was centralized into a single unit, rather than having factories buy on their own. Sales were coordinated within a single unit, as were engineering, research and development, finance, and legal services. An effective reporting system was instituted so that a steady flow of information kept managers aware of the operations for which each was responsible. This information flowed upward to provide an accurate picture of operations on which the president and directors could base major policy decisions.

Once reorganized, the firm functioned extremely well. In 1914, World War I broke out in Europe and created a sudden, nearly inexhaustible demand for gunpowder and high explosives. To meet this demand, Du Pont undertook one of the largest expansions the world of business had ever seen. At the start of the war, Du Pont plants had a maximum capacity of slightly more than 8 million pounds of smokeless gunpowder a year. In little more than twelve months, they had expanded their factories by nearly

■ Women at work in a Du Pont factory making smokeless gunpowder during World War I. Frantic pleas from England and France for powder prompted Du Pont to undertake one of the most rapid industrial expansions in history.

twenty-five times to produce 200 million pounds a year. By 1917 they had increased production by more than fifty times, to 455 million pounds a year. Expansion of production capacities for high explosives grew almost as dramatically. Similarly, the company's payroll expanded enormously. In the fall of 1914, Du Pont employed 5,300 people. In 1918, they employed more than 85,000. And the company's investment in plants and equipment grew from $83 million to $309 million.

The new organization based on functional divisions coped very well with these terrific demands. Efficiency did not suffer, and the firm earned excellent profits on its investment. But the enormous growth presented the company with both an opportunity and a challenge. What would they do when the war ended? The demand

for gunpowder and explosives would then return to low prewar levels. Should they plan to close down the huge new plants they had built and lay off most of their employees? Or should they try to find a way to convert these new assets into peacetime production?

The Du Ponts decided to diversify by entering the growing market for chemical products, a market for which their mastery of explosives manufacture was ideally suited. Demand for early synthetics such as patent leather, synthetic silks, and plastics was growing, and Du Pont prepared during the war to enter these new markets when peace returned.

In 1919 these plans were put into operation on a huge scale. The company became a large manufacturer of paint, dyes, plastics, chemicals, fertilizers, and the host of products associated with the chemical industry today. Du Pont had immense amounts of money from its wartime profits to invest in these new activities. It had the plants, skilled labor, and highly skilled managers. The quality of its products was excellent, and sales rose rapidly. But the company almost went broke.

What happened? The principle of *functional divisions*, a hugely successful arrangement for organizations engaged in a relatively narrow set of activities, turned out to be *a disastrous arrangement for organizations engaged in a broad range of activities.*

Autonomous divisions

Before diversifying into its many new activities, Du Pont resembled Swift & Co. The company was organized to govern each step in the manufacture of explosives from the acquisition of the needed raw materials to their delivery to customers. But now they were engaged in many parallel operations. For example, before diversification, the sales division had dealt with only a few very large customers—primarily governments and manufacturing firms (for example, ammunition manufacturers). To sell paint, however, they had to deal with thousands of small retail merchants and create a demand for Du Pont paint among consumers. The same was true of their soap, glue, and finished plastic products. The sales department found itself overwhelmed by an immense array of products that had to be sold in different ways to many different kinds of customers.

The same thing was happening in the manufacturing divisions. Instead of having a number of similar factories, each engaged in similar production processes and thus facing similar difficulties, Du Pont now had factories with different concerns. The paint factories bore little resemblance to the plastics factories, the fertilizer factories, and so on. Similarly, the purchasing department no longer searched for a few raw materials but for a huge variety from many different sources.

With diversification of the firm into many businesses, executives faced demands that exceeded their capabilities. Executives in the manufacturing division could not grasp the major technical problems of so many different manufacturing processes. Nor could the sales force master knowledge about so many different products or the appropriate sales techniques for every market. In addition, as the firm diversified, upper management had too many people to supervise.

Considerable research has demonstrated that there are limits on the number of people a given person can supervise effectively. This limit is called the **span of control**. Research suggests that no executive should have more than seven subordinates who report directly to him or her. Beyond that number, confusion begins to set in, and the executive has neither the time nor the memory to serve each subordinate adequately (Drucker, 1967). But at Du Pont, the span of control imposed on senior executives was far more than seven, many having direct responsibility for thirty to forty subordinate managers.

Faced with operations of such magnitude, the organizational system began to crack and split open. Just as the large railroads had once lost money while the small railroads were highly profitable, Du Pont began to lose money while small, specialized competitors flourished. Worse yet, the more Du Pont sold of its new products, the more money it lost! Thus, when sales of paint and varnish rose from $1 million to $4 million over three years, annual losses on these products rose from $100,000 to $500,000. Even

this giant company with its huge wartime cash reserves couldn't endure such losses, which came to $2.5 million in the first six months of 1921 alone.

Unlike government agencies, business firms get very nervous when their profits fall, because unlike government agencies, they can go broke. The top managers at Du Pont sat down and carefully rethought their entire organization. They knew that they were engaged in the right business, because their products sold well. But they also knew that they were not conducting their business properly. As one of their directors put it in a memo to his fellow board members: "The trouble with the Company is right here in Wilmington, and the failure is the failure of administration for which we, as directors, are responsible" (Chandler, 1962).

After careful consideration, Du Pont management realized that the failure of their administration lay in current theories of organization: The functional division system was wrecking them. This system is fine for a firm that produces a narrow line of products or performs a few services. It is an excellent system for an explosives company or a meat company. But it is an unworkable system for a **diversified organization** that manufactures many different kinds of things.

Indeed, what the Du Pont managers suddenly realized was that they should no longer think of themselves as a single firm. They had grown so large and were in so many different businesses that they needed to reorganize themselves into *divisions organized around each business*, not around each function. Functional divisions could be retained but at a lower level of management: only within **autonomous divisions** constituted as independent firms. The larger company of Du Pont would consist of a number of divisions, each fully organized to conduct its own business.

Du Pont discovered the business version of the military divisions the Duke of Wellington created and Moltke perfected. As a military division included all essential components of an army, a Du Pont division included all components of a manufacturing company. It would purchase its raw materials (and pay the market price, even if they were purchased from another

Du Pont division), supervise its own manufacturing, conduct its own research and development, and operate its own marketing and sales organization.

Each division would be run by a general manager who had the authority to make business decisions for the division and who would answer to top management, who were primarily interested only in the success or failure of the overall operation. The top management at Du Pont stepped back from the details of the operations of its divisions and appointed or fired top division managers, decided which divisions to keep and which to dispose of, and made plans for creating and acquiring new divisions. Like Moltke, the Du Pont management planned and communicated the grand strategy of the firm but delegated the tactical decisions to commanders on the spot.

Soon most major business firms faced problems similar to Du Pont's, and they, too, solved them by establishing autonomous divisions (Fligstein, 1985). In this way, Alfred Sloan remodeled sprawling General Motors into the Chevrolet, Pontiac, Oldsmobile, Buick, and Cadillac divisions. With their separate assembly plants, their own systems of exclusive dealerships, their own advertising budgets, and their own financial resources, they competed with one another almost as fully as they did with Ford, Chrysler, and other automobile makers.

These autonomous divisions transformed single firms that had become too big and too complex to manage into a cluster of smaller, coordinated firms. This was the second step taken in a new approach to managing big organizations: **decentralization**.

■

Blau's Theory of Administrative Growth

 We have seen that the solution for managing large corporations lies in creating a division of labor among executives—parceling out administrative responsibilities so that several people perform duties too numerous for any one person to handle. A direct consequence of the growth of organizations has therefore been an even more rapid growth in the number of persons required to manage them. Peter M. Blau (1970, 1972) considered the rapid expansion of managerial positions and formulated a theory of organization. Two of his major propositions were:

1. *Organizational growth causes differentiation.* This is precisely what we have seen throughout this chapter. As organizations get larger, they must be broken down into units so that their activities can be controlled.

2. *As organizations become more differentiated, the size of the administrative component increases relative to the size of other components.* Blau argued that the difficulties of coordinating and communicating are much greater across differentiated units than *within* units. The greater the number of units, the greater the effort required to coordinate them and the greater the number of supervisors and managers needed.

From these two propositions it follows logically that *the larger the organization, the greater the proportion of total resources that must be devoted to management functions.*

By now there is considerable empirical support for **Blau's administrative theory**. Its most obvious implication is that organizations are less costly to run when they are kept smaller and that efficiency may be lost rather than gained when several organizations are combined into one huge organization. The reason for creating larger organizations has always been to achieve savings. For example, a grocery chain can undersell an independent grocer because of the great savings made possible by large-scale purchasing and marketing. However, at some point such savings must be weighed against the greater resources needed to manage the organization. These accelerating management costs are an overhead—they add to the costs of the goods and services offered by an organization. Some organizations are too small and some are too large to be efficient.

It is impossible to give a general answer to the question, How big is too big? For any given organization, the answer comes from weighing administrative costs against savings and then determining when bigness offsets efficiency. But organizational theorists now believe that any organization can get too big.

Blau's theory, therefore, once again leads to the principle of decentralization. When organizations got too big for one person to control, means had to be found to place the control in the hands of many people, that is, to decentralize authority. The various ways to cope with great size that we have examined were all meant to decentralize organizations without letting them become uncoordinated. It turns out, however, that efforts to decentralize organizations tend to run into resistance from the natural system within organizations.

Rational and Natural Factors in Decentralization

The goal of top executives in most business organizations has long been to get decisions off their desks and place them on the desks of subordinates. Thus, McCallum ceased making operating decisions for the Erie Railroad and instead asked his division superintendents to make them. Ever since, business has sought ways to push this process of decentralization further. Indeed, maximum decentralization is the main principle of current management science.

Business theorists such as Peter F. Drucker (1946, 1967, 1974) preach that companies ought to create the *smallest possible operating units* in order to give *maximum flexibility to the person on the spot.* Drucker argues that it is impossible for higher management to have firsthand experience of the specific conditions in a remote department. Let the people in charge of those departments make the decisions, because they will usually make the right ones. As long as the overall performance of a department is satisfactory, leave it alone. If performance falls, then appoint new people. But never try to run it from upstairs.

This doctrine is often called **management by objectives**, because managers and their subordinates negotiate the objectives the subordinates should reach. Then managers give subordinates maximum freedom to decide how to achieve the objectives and later judge the subordinates by how well they succeed. In this way, decision making is delegated to those in the best position to make particular decisions quickly and correctly.

The key element in the decentralization of organizations is *discretion*, the freedom to make choices and decisions. Decentralization consists of giving the maximum number of subordinates in an organization discretion in running their part of the operation. But discretion involves two closely linked elements: (1) the *responsibility* for making decisions and (2) the *authority* to carry them out. Giving people responsibility is futile unless they are also given the power to meet their responsibilities. This is more than a truism, however. Often it is very difficult to give members of organizations enough authority to allow the decentralization of decision making to be effective.

Limits on the power to implement decisions come from both within and without organizations. Internal limits come from the necessary interdependence of the many subunits of an organization. Limits can also come from having to deal with external factors, such as suppliers, markets, competitors, and regulatory agencies, which organizational members cannot control. For example, a decision to increase efforts to market a particular item may be thwarted when suppliers cannot increase their production, when competitors cut their prices or introduce an improved model, when the market fails to respond, or when the government imposes new requirements.

Reflecting on these aspects of decentralization, James D. Thompson (1967) developed a number of theoretical propositions. Several of these pertain to the conditions under which members of an organization will accept discretion. Thompson proposed that when individuals in an organization believe that they cannot adequately control conditions affecting decisions, they will try to evade discretion—they will try to pass responsibility on to someone else (usually someone higher in the organization). Thus, *the more a particular position in an organization depends on other positions in the organization, the less willing people in that position will be to exercise discretion.* Similarly, the more that a decision involves forces outside the organization, the less willing people will be to make that decision.

Second, *the more serious the potential consequences of an error are perceived to be, the less willing people will be to assume discretion.* People want to share responsibility for a decision with all who will be affected by the decision if it turns out to be wrong. A variant on this is that the more discretion assigned to a position in an organization, the more a person holding that position will seek power over those affected by his or her decisions. This approach also minimizes the negative consequences of poor decisions by limiting the power of others to retaliate.

So we see that despite efforts to impose decentralization on the formal system, forces generated within the natural system tend toward recentralization. People often seek to regain dispersed power in order to control the conditions affecting their decisions more fully. Or people seek to disperse responsibility for decisions that the organization meant to place in their hands alone.

From the viewpoint of formal organizational models, decentralization has many benefits. It places decisions in the hands of those closest to the scene. Although decentralization disperses power widely, thus diluting the power of top management, it limits an organization's dependence on any given decision maker. That is, decentralized organizations are like ships with many separate, watertight compartments. If such a strip strikes an iceberg, flooding is limited to a few compartments and the ship remains afloat. Similarly, decentralized organizations suffer only limited damage from bad choices made by any given person because each makes only a few decisions. However, Thompson's theory suggests that the natural system within an organization often thwarts these formal arrangements and cuts holes in the watertight compartments.

We have seen why Thompson stated that the natural system of organizations tends to be less decentralized than the formal system. Moreover, coalitions tend to form within an organization (see Chapter 1). Thompson postulated that whenever an individual given discretion has insufficient power to control conditions governing his or her decisions, that individual will seek added power by forming a coalition with other decision makers. For instance, consider someone empowered to decide how much of a product to produce and someone else empowered to decide how to market that product. The marketing decisions depend on supply, and production decisions depend on sales. No matter how the company is organized, the production and marketing managers are likely to get together and act jointly—to form a coalition.

Perhaps the most interesting of Thompson's propositions about coalitions pertains to attempts to control external threats to decisions. When these threats are great, people given substantial discretion will seek to form coalitions with people outside the organization. For example, marketing managers for competing firms may secretly agree to split up the potential market and thereby limit their vulnerability. Or a production manager may make secret agreements with suppliers in order to reduce uncertainties. Indeed, newspaper editors have noted that reporters assigned to cover the police form coalitions with police commanders, trading favorable coverage for special access to information. A reporter assigned to cover the police risks his or her job if the police favor competing reporters with inside information, and police commanders fear unsympathetic reports will provoke public criticism. Coalitions therefore serve the interests of both commanders and reporters, but undercut the interests of both organizations.

Although the natural system of organizations often circumvents decentralization, many organizations, especially business organizations, are much more decentralized than they used to be. This decentralization has been the major trend for formal organizations generally. The Napoleonic problem of managing large armies was solved by delegating authority. The problem of managing big railroads was corrected by breaking them up into functional units, each the size of a small railroad. And the problems of managing a huge, diversified company like Du Pont were solved by treating parts of the organization as independent companies. The adoption of management by objectives, in which

■ After spending weeks in city offices trying to get a building permit in Brooklyn, artist George Tooker painted *Government Bureau,* which now hangs in New York's Metropolitan Museum of Art. We catch but glimpses of the bureaucrats hiding behind their rules and regulations.

authority is delegated to ever smaller internal organizational units, is simply an extension of this same trend. But it would be misleading to end this chapter without noting that not all organizations have followed this decentralizing trend. Thus, while decentralization has dominated organizations in the private sector, government organizations have tended toward ever greater centralization.

Governments have grown rapidly in the twentieth century. In most modern societies, the government is by far the largest employer, and government spending makes up a very substantial proportion of all monetary transactions. But as governments have grown huge, they have become ever more centralized. Many government activities that were left wholly to local jurisdictions even twenty years ago are centralized today.

In Europe, government is even more centralized than in Canada or the United States. In most nations, local government is nearly nonexistent—the central government appoints and controls local mayors. Many colleges and universities are run by a ministry of education in the capital. The ministry not only determines how money is spent but also makes all faculty appointments, chooses textbooks, and even controls student admissions.

Governments in communist nations are even more centralized. In fact, the government in these nations attempts to administer the whole economy—industry, retailing, farming, and so on—from a central bureaucracy. The results have been detailed in dozens of studies of inefficiency and waste caused by decision makers buried in a sea of detail (Kaiser, 1976; Smith, 1976).

If so many other organizations have found that they became too big and too centralized to work, then why haven't governments, democratic and communist alike, learned this lesson too?

Bureaucracy and the Bottom Line

In everyday speech we often use the words *bureaucracy* and *bureaucrat* negatively. They suggest meddlesome people and muddled organizations. Yet as Weber noted, all modern organizations, public or private, are bureaucracies. We usually think of government agencies and personnel when we hear the terms *bureaucracy* and *bureaucrat* because government agencies generally do not work as well as private organizations. They are less efficient because they do not face the same pressures to reexamine and improve their organizational methods.

The strength of private bureaucracies is their vulnerability. They can and often do go broke. This means that they are under constant pressure to earn the right to exist, to achieve their goals, and to adapt to changing circumstances. The Du Pont executives stayed late at night in 1921 trying to figure out how to put their organization right, not because they were more conscientious than government executives but because their time was rapidly running out. If they had not found immediate effective solutions to their organizational problems, then they soon would have had to inform their creditors that Du Pont was bankrupt.

Business organizations, therefore, have a very clear standard by which to judge their performance—profit and loss. While profit is not the only goal of corporation executives, it is the ultimate one. Day in and day out, profit and loss provide a gauge indicating which operations are working better and which are working worse, which managers are doing better and which are doing worse. The bottom line is always evident. Thus, Du Pont executives could not take comfort in the great popularity of their new paint products or in their high quality, for to do so meant bankruptcy.

Government bureaucracies do not have such a clear gauge of their success or failure. They do not go broke, they do not count profits, and they can claim great credit when their actions are popular without asking if their actions are effective or efficient. This does not mean that the effectiveness of government bureaucracies cannot be measured. But often it just simply isn't measured.

Recently many political scientists have proposed that measures of government effectiveness be required. Of course, they do not suggest that government agencies should operate on the basis of profit and loss. They do suggest that government agencies should measure their results objectively so that their performance can be evaluated. Such measures are not hard to devise if an organization's goals are clearly identified.

Imagine that we are going to reorganize a welfare agency. First, we would need to set its goals. One goal might be to provide jobs for the maximum number of welfare workers. While some people suspect that this is often the goal of public agencies, it would not be acceptable as an official goal. Suppose that we set the goal as getting the maximum amount of welfare money into the hands of poor people. Then we might want to close the welfare agency and send all its administrative funds to poor people. That is precisely what proposals such as guaranteed income or a negative income tax intend to accomplish.

However, we might choose as our goal to minimize the time people spend on welfare by returning a maximum number to economic self-sufficiency as soon as possible. Then we would evaluate the agency by keeping track of the proportion of persons leaving the welfare rolls and the average length of time people were on welfare. With these measures one program could be compared with another. Then we could see if a cheaper program worked as well as or better than a more expensive one, whether some welfare workers were more effective than others, and whether different programs were needed in different places. If decentralization theory is correct, then we would expect a program to work better when local welfare offices were given maximum authority and responsibility to achieve the stated goal.

■ Conclusion

This chapter's fundamental theme is that organizations are human inventions intended to serve human needs. The rational, or formal, organization based on bureaucratic principles was a major social invention necessitated by the great increase in the scale and complexity of human activities in modern times. Perhaps the primary lesson we have learned from our brief experience with formal organizations is that there is no such thing as a perfect organization. Instead, organizational forms and principles that serve extremely well under some conditions can be inadequate or even harmful under others.

Effective organizations are therefore the momentary results of constant reassessment and redesign. When the effectiveness of organizations is not tested, they rapidly tend to become unresponsive and inefficient, taking on the negative features associated with the term *bureaucracy*. In the final analysis, we get the kinds of organizations we deserve. We create them; we run them. If they make our lives unpleasant, we can change them. The fundamental truth about organizations is this: Organizations never do anything; only people do things. While much of what people do is the result of their positions in formal organizations, the fact remains that organizations never make decisions, pursue goals, assess means, or adopt new policies. Only people, acting in the name of organizations, do such things.

By the same token, societies don't change. Society didn't invent the steam engine; James Watt did. Societies don't have babies; women do. And societies become urban only as people move to town. Thus, it is time to shift the focus of this introduction to sociology away from large social structures and back once more to human behavior. To conclude this book, we shall examine how people cause and resist social change.

■ Review Glossary

formal organization Synonymous with rational organization, a group created to pursue definite goals wherein tactics and procedures are designed and evaluated in terms of effectiveness in achieving goals, members are selected and trained to fulfill their roles, and overall operations are based on written records and rules. (p. 584)

divisional system As initially used in armies, the organization of troops into small, identical units, each containing all military elements (infantry, artillery, and cavalry). (p. 587)

geographical divisions Divisions resulting from breaking an organization into smaller units on the basis of geography and making each division relatively independent. (p. 588)

functional divisions Divisions resulting from breaking an organization into smaller units on the basis of specialized activities or functions, such as when a corporation has separate divisions for manufacturing, purchasing, and marketing. (p. 588–589)

vertical integration The inclusion within an organization of the divisions that control every step in the production and distribution of some product or service. (p. 589)

spoils system System in which the winners take over government jobs after each election. (p. 592)

bureaucracy A formal organization that, according to Weber, is based on (1) functional specialization, (2) clear, hierarchical lines of authority, (3) expert training of managers, (4) decision making based on rational rules aimed at effective pursuit of goals, (5) appointment and promotion of managers on their merit, and (6) conducting activities by written communications and records. (p. 593)

management Coordination of the work of others. (p. 593)

rational system approach Emphasis on the official and intended characteristics of organizations. (p. 594)

natural system approach Emphasis on the informal and unintended characteristics of organizations. (p. 595)

goal displacement What occurs when the official goals of an organization are ignored or changed. (p. 596)

goal conflict Situation in which one goal of an organization limits the ability of that organization to achieve other goals; for example, the desire to avoid losses due to strikes will conflict with an organization's goal to minimize labor costs. (p. 596)

span of control The number of subordinates one manager can adequately supervise, often estimated as seven. (p. 600)

diversified organization An organization that is not very specialized but instead pursues a wide range of goals. (p. 600)

autonomous divisions Parts of an organization, each of which includes a full set of functional divisions. (p. 600)

decentralization Dispersing of authority from a few central administrators to persons directly engaged in activities. (p. 601)

Blau's administrative theory Theory stating that the larger the organization, the greater the proportion of total resources that must be devoted to management functions. (p. 601)

management by objectives Situation in which managers and subordinates agree on goals that subordinates will try to achieve; subordinates then have maximum freedom in how they will try to reach their objectives. (p. 602)

■

Suggested Readings

Chandler, Alfred D., Jr. 1962. *Strategy and Structure: Chapters in the History of the American Industrial Revolution.* Cambridge, Mass.: M.I.T. Press.

Drucker, Peter F. 1974. *Management.* New York: Harper & Row.

Fligstein, Neil. 1985. "The Spread of the Multidivisional Form Among Large Firms, 1919–1979." *American Sociological Review* 50: 377–391.

Perrow, Charles. 1979. *Complex Organizations*, 2nd ed. Glenview, Ill.: Scott, Foresman.

Peters, Thomas J., and Robert H. Waterman, Jr. 1982. *In Search of Excellence: Lessons from America's Best-Run Companies.* New York: Harper & Row.

Collective Behavior and Social Movements

By William Sims Bainbridge

21

ALVIN "SHIPWRECK" KELLY sat high atop the flag-pole on the Steel Pier at Atlantic City for 49 days and 1 hour back in 1930. Who would want to do anything so crazy? Several people, apparently. Soon after Shipwreck invented this stunt, "Hold 'em" Joe Powers spent 16 days at an altitude of 647 feet on the flagpole of the Morrison Hotel in Chicago. Elsewhere other daredevils sat on flagpoles, and the news media began calling this phenomenon a *craze* or *fad*.

Since the early days of Shipwreck and Hold 'em Joe, this craze has reappeared several times in the United States. In 1976 Frank Powers set a new record by perching for 400 days on a flag-pole in San Jose, California, coming down on the nation's bicentennial. Several news stories at that time stressed that a person has to be "a little bit nuts" to do something like this.

In New York in 1970, during a march staged to protest the Vietnam War, one group of demonstrators carried a Viet Cong flag and chanted communist slogans. As they passed a building site, a group of construction workers became angry about what they regarded as anti-American behavior. The workers rushed into the street, seized the flag, destroyed it, and beat up some of the demonstrators. The press called their behavior a *riot*. Many people believe that rioting is crazy behavior—that rioters have temporarily lost their sanity, swept away by "mob psychology."

On July 20, 1969, Edwin "Buzz" Aldrin saluted the U.S. flag as it flew from the "highest" flag-pole ever—on the moon. To some people this seemed like a glorious thing to do. To others it seemed as crazy as sitting on a flagpole or tearing up a Viet Cong flag.

Chapter Preview

This chapter is not about flags or flagpoles or about crazy behavior, although it is about behavior that is sometimes called crazy by people who do not understand the reasons behind it. The kind of behavior this chapter is about often is misunderstood because it is *novel*—people are acting in unusual ways, outside of conventional channels. However, this chapter is not about just any kind of unusual behavior. It is not, in other words, a chapter on deviance. Rather, the unconventional behavior discussed here is limited to *actions related to social change*.

Author's note   Although the topics covered in this chapter are of great importance to sociology and are definitely related, the field has lacked a clear conceptual scheme that integrates them. This has posed great difficulties for textbook authors. As I grappled with the problem of how to fit together such diverse topics as the spread of Hula Hoops, riots, economic panics, and the rise of new political movements, I discovered that my friend William Sims Bainbridge had developed a very effective conceptual framework. However, he had not published it, having used it only in his courses. If I had adopted his ideas, I could not cite any published work, and thus I urged him to publish his new ideas quickly so that I could draw on them in good conscience. As we talked, it became obvious that the best solution was simply to have Bill write this chapter. So he did. Since he and I have often written together, our styles are much the same. I lightly rewrote the chapter to integrate it with the rest of the book.   **Rodney Stark**

608

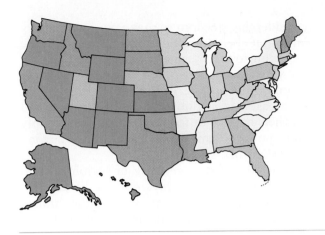

Circulation of *Survive* per 100,000 Population

Missouri	7.83	Oklahoma	20.40
New York	7.92	Louisiana	21.92
Mississippi	8.85	Texas	21.92
Rhode Island	9.29	Idaho	22.14
Maryland	9.32	Washington	22.17
Kentucky	10.38	North Dakota	22.36
Arkansas	10.41	New Hampshire	22.69
South Carolina	11.24	Maine	23.20
North Carolina	12.41	California	22.43
Wisconsin	12.98	South Dakota	24.17

Iowa	13.18	Montana	25.54
West Virginia	13.33	Wyoming	29.79
Michigan	13.55	Oregon	31.86
Indiana	13.61	Hawaii	35.54
Massachusetts	13.87	New Mexico	36.61
Vermont	13.89	Arizona	37.38
Minnesota	14.30	Colorado	37.85
Alabama	14.51	Kansas	43.15
New Jersey	14.72	Nevada	59.50
Virginia	14.96	Alaska	84.72

Pennsylvania	15.10
Illinois	15.80
Ohio	16.14
Connecticut	16.25
Georgia	16.64
Tennessee	17.25
Delaware	17.34
Nebraska	17.64
Utah	19.16
Florida	20.23

Circulation of *Survive* per 100,000 Population

Yukon	0.00	Nova Scotia	8.97
Pr. Edward Island	0.82	N.W. Territories	11.11
Quebec	2.39	British Columbia	15.52
Newfoundland	3.70	Alberta	19.58

New Brunswick	6.37
Manitoba	7.60
Saskatchewan	7.75
Ontario	8.66

Figure 21-1 ■ **The survivalist social movement.** Recently some people in the United States and Canada have become convinced that a great catastrophe soon will destroy civilization—caused by World War III, an acute change in climate, or various other disasters. Many of these people have become convinced that they, their families, and close friends can be among the small numbers of survivors *if* they prepare now. So they have identified themselves as survivalists. For some, being a survivalist means moving to a remote area and building a fortified fallout shelter. For others it involves stockpiling supplies and arms. Still others practice guerrilla military tactics. Whatever their outlook and activities, many survivalists seek to maintain contacts with others elsewhere and to share ideas. One way they do so is by subscribing to *Survive* magazine. These maps use the circulation of *Survive* per 100,000 population to locate the survivalist social movement. In both Canada and the United States, survivalism is strongest in the western areas—perhaps because that's where retreat to the mountain wilderness is possible.

Actions may be related to social change in four ways:

1. The action itself may be a social change. It may be an activity that is new in a society, such as sitting on flagpoles or going to the moon.

2. The action may be undertaken to cause social change, such as staging a peace march.

3. The action may be aimed at preventing social change, such as attacking those who mock patriotism.

4. The action may be caused by social change, such as when rapid economic changes prompt people to act in new ways.

However, we shall not concern ourselves with the individual actions of isolated individuals, even if these are related to social change. Instead, we shall only examine actions involving a number of people who influence one another. When these people form an organization and therefore attempt to coordinate their actions according to a plan, we may refer to them as a *social movement*. Often, however, group activities related to social change lack organization and planning. Such actions are called *collective behavior*. In both instances, people are acting together, but differences in the amount of organization and planning involved frequently prove critical, as we shall see. We shall also see that collective behavior sometimes develops into social movements—hence the need to consider these two patterns of activity together.

This chapter's theme is *how individuals can get together to cause, prevent, or otherwise respond to social change and why their efforts so often fail.* To pursue this theme, we must focus on the behavior of people in particular circumstances. By doing so, we can assess two of the most vital tasks of sociology—perhaps the two primary reasons for doing sociology.

The first of these tasks is to *understand the interplay between the individual and society*—or, in other words, between us and our history. Some sociologists argue that we are almost entirely the creations of our society and that our history determines our destiny. Other sociologists disagree. They believe that we have

considerable freedom to make our own history and that people create and change people according to their desires, capacities, and actions. As you read this chapter, you may want to examine the actions of the people involved in each case and ask how much impact they had on their history or to what extent they simply were puppets dancing to social forces beyond their control.

The second primary task of sociology is to *make social life less mysterious*—to uncover the reasons behind events so that the strange and alarming become understandable and ordinary. At first glance, the behavior of the people described in the introduction to this chapter may have seemed crazy to you. But social behavior is seldom really crazy. When we look carefully, we usually find that there is rhyme and reason to what groups of people do. If we fail to recognize why they are acting as they are and dismiss them as nuts or fools, then we are the ones who don't understand what is going on. Remember, too, that behavior can be reasonable without being "good" or even acceptable. Indeed, we often seek the reasons behind behavior in order to put a stop to it.

With these points in mind, we shall examine the flag-related activities described earlier and clarify some essential concepts.

A Framework for Analysis

Crazes or fads, such as flagpole sitting, are instances of what sociologists call **collective behavior.** For a behavior to be classified as collective, each of the following elements must be present:

1. The act must be unusual.

2. The action must be taken by a group of people, not by lone individuals.

3. The people involved must influence one another in some way.

4. This influence must occur with little or no planning, and there must be little or no organization of the group.

■ Alvin "Shipwreck" Kelly poses for an aerial photographer while sitting on a flagpole. The rapid spread of flagpole sitting during the 1920s can be classified as a craze. But there was nothing crazy about this behavior—Shipwreck and the others earned huge fees for doing it.

Shipwreck Kelly was an out-of-work sailor and movie stuntman. One day in 1924 he hit upon flagpole sitting as a scheme for making money. It worked like this: When he sat on a flagpole, crowds gathered and the news media gave him publicity. Therefore, sponsors would pay him to publicize a product, a new building, a fair—anything that could profit from a publicity gimmick. Soon he was able to earn $100 a day, a huge sum at that time. In his best year, 1929, he spent a total of 145 days on top of flagpoles and earned about $29,000. He wasn't really so crazy. It was the lure of money, too, that drew Hold 'em Joe and others to copy Shipwreck's novel actions.

Let's see how flagpole sitting fits the defi-nition of collective behavior. First, the actions of flagpole sitters are unusual. That's why they attract so much public attention. If thousands of Americans celebrated every Fourth of July by sitting on their flagpoles, flagpole sitting would not be unusual. Instead of collective behavior, it would merely be behavior governed by custom and tradition. Second, Shipwreck was not the only person who sat on flagpoles; a number of people did so. Third, the flagpole sitters influenced one another. Hold 'em Joe and the others took up flagpole sitting when they saw that Shipwreck was on to a good thing. Soon they competed with one another for records of height and duration. Finally, the flagpole sitters never did get together to plan future activities, and they never formed a flagpole sitters' organization. Thus, all four characteristics of collective behavior apply to flagpole sitting.

The construction workers who rioted against demonstrators carrying a Viet Cong flag also engaged in collective behavior. The workers' action was unusual: running around beating up people and destroying flags are not normal occupational or recreational activities. In addition, the men influenced one another, but they acted on the spur of the moment, without planning or organization.

However, the demonstrators who carried the Viet Cong flag were not engaged in collective behavior. They were members of a political organization, and they had planned their actions. However, the demonstrators' behavior was related to social change; they were trying to end a war and promote radical politics. When people get together in an organized way to cause or prevent social change, we identify them and their actions as a **social movement.** Had the construction workers been members of an organization that arranged for them to attack the marchers in order to prevent the changes that the marchers wanted, then the workers, too, would have represented a social movement.

Social movements consist of *organized groups dedicated to causing or preventing social change.* Social movements may be concerned with many kinds of social changes, including changes in religion, politics, economics, technology, art, morals, or ethics. But not every group devoted to causing or preventing social change constitutes a social movement. *Only an organized group acting in unconventional or unusual ways or acting outside of conventional channels to promote or prevent change constitutes a social movement.* When police are ordered to halt a riot, even though the officers and their actions may promote or prevent change, they are not a social movement because they are acting in a typical fashion and within conventional channels. Yet sometimes social movements are so successful or skillful that they transform themselves into conventional social institutions or enlist such institutions to pursue their goals.

Let's look again at Buzz Aldrin standing on the moon. How did he get there? His action was the result of a massive engineering project, directed by the U.S. government, staffed by thousands of scientists and engineers, and costing $24 billion. What could be more within conventional channels? But when we look closely, as we shall at the end of this chapter, we see that the astronauts did not reach the moon because of conventional government actions (although much social change is the result of conventional actions). They reached the moon because an intensely dedicated international social movement promoted and sustained government investments in rocket flight, first in Germany and then in the United States and the Soviet Union.

Obviously, to argue that spaceflight was the work of a social movement is not to suggest that the space program was therefore "bad" or that the money was misspent. Nor are marchers waving a Viet Cong flag conspirators simply because they are behaving as members of a social movement. How one feels about the activities that give life to social movements depends upon how one feels about their methods and goals. The question for sociologists is not whether social movements are good or bad but why and how they arise and function. You must keep that in mind throughout this chapter, for as you read on you will undoubtedly find you are for some of the movements described in the chapter and against others. That is as it should be, for the chapter reveals that social movements

can be dedicated to good or to evil—and often to both. However, good and evil are not sociological judgments; they are moral judgments that must be made independently of sociology. Sociological tools work as well on good movements as on bad ones.

In this spirit, we will devote considerable attention to the Nazi Party in this chapter. By examining the Nazis' rise to power, we can learn something about how social movements may be transformed into social institutions. For a bloody period of modern history, the Nazi Party did in fact become virtually identical with German society as a whole.

To sum up, collective behavior and social movements differ in their degree of planning and organization. They also differ in their duration. *Collective behavior tends to be brief (like a riot), episodic (something that occurs periodically, like flagpole sitting), and unorganized.* Social movements are sustained by organization and planning, and they often endure for a long period of time (like the Nazi Party or the space program).

This chapter begins with the least organized instances of collective behavior. It then examines increasingly more complex and organized activities, culminating in an extended study of two social movements. These activities share more than the fact that they are all related to social change. Indeed, the difference between them is really a matter of degree. Social movements are more organized than collective behavior is, but there is not a sharp dividing line. Social organization can gradually grow until collective behavior evolves into a social movement.

Furthermore, all our examples illustrate an important fact sometimes overlooked even by social scientists: Collective behavior and social movements are always connected to other parts of the society in which they arise. Social change can only take place in relation to a particular set of historical and social conditions. Even the least organized cases of collective behavior are greatly influenced by the traditional customs and institutions of the society around them. Social movements often try to change or even take over the government. And some of the most radical collective behavior and social movements arise inside the most powerful and respected institutions. Let's see how actions related to social change evolve.

From Thievery to Bureaucracy: A Case Study

Our particular interest in collective behavior and social movements is to see how they work as social enterprises: What are their internal structures and dynamics? How do they gain and hold members? How do they interact with their social environments? But before we examine particular kinds of change-related human actions, we need to understand that they have a common root. For this purpose, we will consider a hypothetical example.

Imagine a town in a country ravaged by famine. Some citizens have food; others do not. At night, starving individuals sneak into their neighbors' houses to steal a crust of bread or a scrap of meat. They have not conspired together to plan these raids, and some are not even aware that many other people are also nocturnal thieves. Each person is doing the same thing for the same reason, but each is doing it alone. This is called **parallel behavior.** Although it takes place in a social context, it is not socially organized.

Now suppose that a number of hungry people collect in the town square and mill about in front of the food warehouse. After a few have gathered, word spreads: "There's a hungry crowd in the town square!" Others come to see what all the fuss is about. Folks urge each other, "Come to the square!" They argue excitedly about the famine for a while, then they start demanding that somebody give them bread. Finally, they break down the doors of the warehouse and take everything that is inside. An unplanned gathering of hungry people has turned into a riot for food. People facing a common problem or opportunity tend to communicate informally and influence each other's actions so that they end up doing similar things in a somewhat unified way. Interaction among people reveals to

them their common concerns and turns parallel behavior into collective behavior.

Now that the famine has become a public issue and starving people have shared a social experience (breaking into the warehouse), they start discussing their mutual problem at length in order to find a solution. First in little groups and then in mass meetings, they plan and organize. After several meetings, they set up an organization called "Food for All," dedicated to making the town government solve the crisis. The organization is now a social movement: Many people are working together toward a specific goal through coordinated action. Continued, focused interaction has transformed collective behavior into a social movement.

In response to the growing strength of the movement, the town council appoints the leaders of Food for All to head a new government agency, the Department of Food. New laws empower the Secretary of Food to distribute bread to the needy and to set up a grain reserve to be ready for the next famine. Social agitation in this crisis has led to the establishment of a social institution in which bureaucrats occupy set positions in a hierarchy, perform standard roles, and work together according to established procedures.

Social institutions derive their identity from their recognition by other social institutions. The Department of Food meets this criterion because it is integrated into the established government. Through legitimate, formal procedures, a social movement has become a social institution.

In everyday life, parallel behavior sometimes becomes collective behavior, which becomes a social movement, which leads to the establishment of a social institution. This is a success story. However, individuals often remain caught in unproductive parallel behavior and never succeed in getting together. A particular collective behavior may arise again and again without ever producing an effective movement. And movements themselves frequently disappear after they have had a slight impact on society. Failure can break the evolutionary sequence at any point. In this chapter, we shall look at several different kinds of collective behavior and social movements, keeping in mind the question: How do people get together to do something new?

Collective Behavior

We shall first examine three types of collective behavior: crazes, panics, and riots.

Although these forms of collective behavior are not formally organized, as social movements and institutions are, they do show a degree of order. People act together, even though they do not follow a plan. The task of sociology is to uncover the orderly aspects of collective behavior and to explain them. We shall begin with crazes, because they are the simplest type and also because they provide a good introduction to panics and riots.

Crazes

Webster defines a **craze** as a "transient infatuation," meaning a quick and fleeting love affair with a fashion or style. *Mania* and *fad* have a similar meaning. Crazes are not really crazy. There is nothing insane about enjoying novelty, and nothing loony about becoming bored with an activity once it is no longer novel. Crazes provide antidotes to the high degree of order that modern institutions impose on people. However, crazes themselves are in many cases direct products of those very institutions.

Crazes have been big business for decades. Corporations and churches, periodicals and political parties have consciously hunted for attractive new products, images, and ideas to sell to the general public. Usually a craze fails to get off the ground. Sometimes one grips public fancy for a few months and then fades away. Occasionally a novelty starts as a craze but then establishes itself as a beloved and permanent part of the culture. A good example is the Frisbee Flying Saucer, a favorite toy of college students and the terror of campus airspace.

■ **The Frisbee**   Frisbee is the traditional name for the game of skimming paper plates through the air. A former air force pilot came up with the idea of a plastic, aerodynamic plate that could boomerang and hover. He gave the idea to the Wham-O Company of San Gabriel, California. It sold like any other fad at first, but the demand for it continued and it now seems destined to become a permanent part of our recreational culture. Today there are organized Frisbee competitions.

The Wham-O Company had its first great success with the Hula Hoop, which burst upon the scene in 1957 and peaked in sales in the spring of 1958. By the end of the first year, 20 million hoops had been sold, many of them imitations put out by competitors. Not all Wham-O products became crazes, but it takes only one or two to make a company successful.

■ **Tulipomania**   When we think of Holland, romantic images of windmills, wooden shoes, and tulips come to mind. In actuality, the Netherlands, which has been one of the most advanced countries of Europe for hundreds of years, is not the quaint land of our imagination. There is, however, a valid reason for associating tulips with that country. In the early 1600s, the Netherlands experienced great economic growth and came to be a major trading and financial power. The Dutch built a colonial empire overseas, and at home great artists such as Vermeer and Rembrandt flourished. During this prosperous period, the Dutch were gripped by the craze known as *tulipomania*. This "disease" apparently addled the brains of many Dutch speculators and caused them to invest great sums in tulips. Several scholarly writers have delighted in calling this the craziest of crazes.

The tulip had entered Europe in the 1550s. Before then it had not been found west of Constantinople (now Istanbul). Soon after 1600, tulips became well known and highly desired for their beauty. Florists began not only to sell tulips but also to cultivate them and create new varieties. Price rose above those for other flowers. In a book on tulips, Joseph Jacob (1912) wrote:

In addition to the impetus which arose from the legitimate needs and rivalry of the florists, there seems to have grown up in Paris a fashion for ladies of the higher classes to wear flowers, especially tulips, in their low-cut dresses, so that competition of the wealthy beaux to obtain the rarest and most novel to present to their lady friends drove prices still higher.

Rare tulips had become status symbols, indicators that the owner was a person of high social status. In this way, tulips gained a social value. Historian Charles Mackay wrote that in Holland in the early 1630s, "it was deemed a proof of bad taste in any man of fortune to be without a collection of them." Prices shot through the ceiling.

In 1634, the rage among the Dutch to possess them was so great that the ordinary industry of the country was neglected, and the population, even to its lowest dregs, embarked in the tulip trade. As the mania increased, prices augmented, until, in the year 1635, many persons were known to invest a fortune in the purchase of forty roots [Mackay, 1852].

A single bulb of the rare Viceroy variety sold for 2,500 florins, enough money at the time to buy twenty oxen! A price like this certainly encourages the interpretation that tulipomania was insane.

The sad story is told of a sailor, home in Holland after a long voyage, who was sitting in a warehouse about to eat a herring for his breakfast. He noticed what looked like an onion sitting on a counter and picked it up to have with his fish. The sailor sat down on a pile of ropes and began munching on alternate pieces of herring and onion. Suddenly a merchant rushed up and shrieked that the sailor was eating his prize tulip worth 3,000 florins! Horrors! For his mistake, the sailor spent several months in jail.

In fact, of course, the financial side of tulipomania was nothing more than a particularly colorful example of an entirely normal economic phenomenon: speculation on rising prices in a well-organized market. So long as the price of tulips went up, it was to the advantage of investors to buy them, even if they personally detested tulips. The classic way to make a quick profit is to buy something for a low price and sell it for a high price. When many people decided to invest in tulips for this reason, the price was

driven up even faster. So long as the price continued upward, it was completely rational for each individual investor to buy more.

Soon the collective behavior of tulipomania had been partly institutionalized. Stock exchanges in several Dutch cities began trading in tulips, just as the exchanges had done in other investment arenas. Then the tulip market acted very much like the American stock market just before the great crash of 1929. As George Edmundson (1922) commented:

Perfectly inordinate sums were offered in advance for growing crops or for particular bulbs; most of the transactions being purely paper speculations, a gambling in futures. Millions of guilders were risked, and hundreds of thousands lost or won. In 1637 the crash came, and many thousands of people in Amsterdam, Haarlem, Leyden, Alkmaar, and other towns in Holland were brought to ruin.

The craze ended in a crash once people saw that tulip prices were dropping. Realizing that the longer they held on to their tulips, the more they stood to lose, investors quite rationally tried to sell out as quickly as possible. Because everyone else was also unloading tulips, prices were driven down even more quickly. Many investors lost their shirts, and tulipomania—which had been based more on greed than craziness—died out.

Panics

Financial crashes like the one that ended tulipomania are sometimes called **panics,** a word also used to describe situations in which terrified people attempt to flee danger. Crazes and panics are mirror images of each other. In a craze, a group of people rushes toward something they all desire. In a panic, people rush away from something they all fear. Panic can be inspired by a real danger, particularly one that is immediate and difficult to avoid (such as a fire in a crowded theater), but panic can also be caused by imaginary dangers and rumors of danger.

Although panics seldom spawn formal social organizations, panics do have a strong social aspect in that individuals often react to the panic of others in a way that spreads the panic further. Frequently panics contribute to social change by fueling the growth of social movements. As we shall see later in this chapter, the German Nazi Party gained much popular support during the financial panics of 1923 and 1929. Another case we shall discuss is the American panic reaction to the first Russian space satellites, a collective response that did much to promote the later Apollo missions to the moon. Therefore, panic is an important form of collective behavior.

■ **Crowd behavior**   A widespread belief is that crowd behavior is crude and almost mindless. Gustave Le Bon's little book *The Crowd* (1895) is the classic statement of this point of view. Le Bon said that crowds are guided by primitive, subconscious motives and that the crowd is stupid, impulsive, and frequently rendered mad by fantastic images. "Like a savage, it is not prepared to admit that anything can come between its desire and the realization of its desire. . . . Its acts are far more under the influence of the spinal cord than of the brain." Le Bon believed that the individual member of a crowd "is no longer himself, but has become an automaton who has ceased to be guided by his will."

Moreover, by the mere fact that he forms part of an organized crowd, a man descends several rungs in the ladder of civilization. Isolated, he may be a cultivated individual; in a crowd, he is a barbarian—that is, a creature acting by instinct. He possesses the spontaneity, the violence, the ferocity, and also the enthusiasm and heroism of primitive beings, whom he further tends to resemble by the facility with which he allows himself to be impressed by words and images—which would be entirely without action on each of the isolated individuals composing the crowd—and to be induced to commit acts contrary to his most obvious interests and his best-known habits. An individual in a crowd is a grain of sand amid other grains of sand, which the wind stirs up at will.

Although most people agree with this view of crowds, it is entirely false. Le Bon despised the common people and had no sympathy for the masses, their problems, or their attempts to solve those problems. The behavior of individuals in a crowd should be regarded as rational, and research can be conducted to determine the factors that are at work.

■ ***The War of the Worlds***   In 1897, crowds went wild with terror in London when malevolent and powerful invaders from Mars launched a devastating attack. Of course, this happened only in H. G. Wells's science fiction novel *The War of the Worlds*. (Although the book was pure fantasy, its description of people's reactions fits our definition of panic behavior.) The Martians had landed and were killing everyone with ray guns and poison gas. The transportation system could not get everyone out of London in time. People fought with each other for places on the trains. A mob looted a bicycle store.

Although motivated by extreme fear, this panic was quite reasonable behavior. People were suddenly thrown into a life-or-death competition for scarce resources, and there were a limited number of chances to escape doom. On those rare occasions when people have panicked in a burning nightclub or theater and blocked the exit in their struggle, it is clear that a better coordinated, less violent evacuation might have saved more lives. But there was no chance to organize one.

One evening in 1938, thousands of Americans believed they had heard a radio news broadcast informing them that real Martians were actually invading the country and killing everyone in sight. Legend has it that the roads were immediately choked with panicked families, and thousands ran about hysterically. "The Martian invasion panic" was widely reported in the newspapers and was regarded as a striking example of mass craziness.

What actually happened was that CBS Radio had broadcast a dramatization, produced by actor Orson Welles and his Mercury Theatre company, of *The War of the Worlds*. According to one estimate, 6 million people heard the broadcast; about 1.7 million mistakenly thought the realistic play was a news event, and about 1.2 million were frightened by it. In his social psychological book on the incident, Hadley Cantril (1941) says, "Thousands of Americans became panic-stricken. . . . Probably never before have so many people in all walks of life and in all parts of the country become so suddenly and so intensely disturbed as they did on this night."

Public expression of fear over a specific danger may often be magnified if people have other worries that they can do nothing about. The fictitious Martian invasion came at a time when people all over the world were anxious about the possibility of a real invasion. Hitler had begun his march toward war and was just about to seize a big chunk of Czechoslovakia. War fear had been constantly stimulated by all the papers. It is possible, therefore, that the Martian invasion gave people the opportunity to express their anxiety by focusing on a specific disaster. It could be called a *summary event*—a concrete representation of a vague but intense social and emotional situation.

In their issues for November 7, 1938, both *Time* and *Newsweek* made this point. *Newsweek* explained that on many people "already made danger-conscious by the recent war scare the effect of Wells-Welles realism was galvanic." *Time* was surprised that so many people had failed to understand that the program was pure fiction and concluded:

The only explanation for the badly panicked thousands—who evidently had neither given themselves the pleasure of familiarizing themselves with Wells's famous book nor had the wit to confirm or deny the catastrophe by dialing another station—is that recent concern over a possible European Armageddon has badly spooked the U.S. public.

The original H. G. Wells novel was set in England. When a Boston newspaper carried it in serialized episodes, it renamed the story "The War of the Worlds—In and Around Boston." The Mercury Theatre broadcast had the Martians land in New Jersey, just a few miles from its New York studio. When Hollywood produced a movie version in the early 1950s, the scene was shifted to California.

These moves illustrate the principle that panic is most likely when an ambiguous threat is seen as immediate—when its potential victims are suddenly endangered right where they are. If you were to hear that Martians had landed on the other side of the world or that they had just left Mars and were not expected to land on Earth for a few weeks, then you would have time for a leisurely response—time to discuss the situation at length, to gather the best possible information, and to make careful plans for concerted action. But when the Martians suddenly land in your backyard and disintegrate your neighbor, the only sensible thing to do is drop everything and run.

Of course, the Martians didn't land in anybody's backyard. Perhaps the most interesting question Cantril's study asked was why some people misunderstood the radio broadcast and thought it was news instead of a play. The format of the show did indeed imitate radio news journalism, but at the beginning and at intermission it was clearly stated that the program was fictitious. Not surprisingly, one of the factors that made listeners mistake the show for a news item was tuning in late and missing the disclaiming announcement. Another finding (based on an analysis of a poll conducted by CBS) was that better-educated listeners were less likely to believe that the dramatization was real. However, the most striking impression conveyed by Cantril's book was a false one—that real mass panic followed the broadcast. By quoting the stories of a few people who claimed to have been very frightened, Cantril implies that there was widespread panic. *There wasn't.* A few people did drive like maniacs along the roads or went in terror for help, but a few isolated incidents of fearful behavior do not make a panic.

Remember that 1.2 million people were frightened to some extent by the show. Out of such a large number, we would expect at least a thousand to be out doing loony things that night anyway! Afterwards, they could have attributed their actions to the Martian invasion. Many of them found that news reporters delighted in hearing extreme tales of fear or valor. Old Bill Dock, a New Jersey farmer, reenacted his brave defense of America from the Martians for a *Life* photographer by taking cover behind a pile of grain sacks with his shotgun. The whole affair was more a news media craze

■ According to *Life*, Bill Dock, a New Jersey farmer, was prepared to shoot it out with the Martian invaders. Here he reenacts his behavior on the night of the famous radio broadcast. Today, sociologists tend to think there was no widespread panic that night, despite press reports.

than a mass panic. Cantril, whether intentionally or not, reinforced the popular misconception that insane panic is the common response of normal people to real or imagined danger. Since the 1930s, sociologists have continued to study how people react—whether they do in fact follow the maxim: "When in danger or in doubt, run around and scream and shout!"

■ **The Barsebäck incident**   On November 13, 1973, sociologists in Sweden were presented with

a golden opportunity to use scientific methods to study a similar panic. To dramatize concerns about the dangers of atomic power, Swedish Radio broadcast a short play about a fictional accident said to have taken place at the Barsebäck nuclear power station. Quantities of deadly radioactive substances had supposedly been ejected into the air, where they were spreading out and threatening the lives of people for miles around. In fact, the real Barsebäck station had not even been completed yet. Sociologists Karl Erik Rosengren, Peter Arvidson, and Dahn Sturesson of the University of Lund were waiting to study the effects of the broadcast. "Within an hour the broadcast media reported widespread panic reactions in southern Sweden, and the next day the morning and afternoon newspapers followed suit, carrying page-wide headlines on the panic" (Rosengren, Arvidson, and Sturesson, 1975).

Using a random sample of more than a thousand adult residents drawn from area population registers, the researchers conducted telephone interviews and mailed questionnaires. They also interviewed police and other authorities. The researchers discovered that, in fact, no panic had occurred at all. Although 7 or 8 percent of the population had taken the program seriously and had been frightened by it, only 2 percent had taken action of any kind. These actions, far from constituting mass panic, had been reasoned responses to danger. Some folks contacted family members; others closed their windows to keep radiation out; a few made plans to evacuate the area.

Whereas Cantril had found that education and a few other variables were linked to whether persons had misunderstood the Martian invasion broadcast, the Swedish researchers found no variables (in personality or social status) that seemed to relate to the mistake of believing the Barsebäck disaster. In fact, only two things mattered. First, the vast majority of people who happened to know that the reactor was not yet finished were not fooled. Second, very few of the listeners who had tuned in at the beginning of the show and heard that they were about to hear a play were fooled. Only those people who tuned in late and who did not know the reactor was not yet operative were likely to mistake the broadcast for an authentic news report. And who is to suggest that theirs was a foolish mistake or a reflection of public craziness? Once the show was underway, every effort was made to simulate an authentic live report of a disaster.

How, then, did a panic get reported when none had occurred? For one thing, the police and news reporters received a number of telephone calls from worried citizens. These calls, which came from a tiny minority of the population, were nearly all rational attempts to find out what was really happening. But they were misinterpreted as indicative of widespread terror. A news reporter at the Malmö radio station thought that there might be a panic in progress, and phone calls to two police departments seemed to support his idea. With no other information and an approaching deadline for a regularly scheduled news broadcast, he apparently decided to gamble and announce a panic in order to scoop other reporters.

Panic was the main theme of his message, panic in a whole country, perhaps two. The telephone exchanges of the police stations, fire stations and mass media in two counties were reported to be jammed. People queueing up before the civil shelters. Large crowds in the communities around Barsebäck taking to the roads. People in Malmö collecting their valuables and heading southward in their cars [Rosengren et al., 1975].

Although this story was almost completely fabricated, it was widely broadcast by other reporters. Newspeople sometimes invent something exciting to report. Soon opponents of nuclear power had climbed on the bandwagon and were recounting the fable of the great panic that had never happened. The phenomenon was nothing but a media craze. It sprang not from disorganized mobs but from two standard institutions of Swedish society—the police and the press. Real panics do occur—when a financial market crashes, when an army is routed, or when a theater catches fire. But crazy panics in which people act in unreasonable ways are in fact very rare.

Riots

The term **riot** is often used very broadly. Here we will use it in a restricted sense as referring to a hostile outburst of collective behavior in which a crowd of people threatens or attacks other persons or property. As we have seen, mistakes in reporting can happen, and sometimes what seem to be riots are not really so. In some cases, police may attack a crowd of peaceful demonstrators and it may be reported that the crowd rioted (Stark, 1972). In general, true riots or hostile outbursts are political actions in which a group of people (called a mob by their opponents) seeks changes in their social and economic positions.

Sometimes terms like prepolitical or primitive "rebels" are used to describe rioters. Both of these terms imply that the issue behind the outburst is a political one (as indeed it is) but that the rioters have not yet built a sufficiently coherent movement to work effectively through conventional political channels. Often these conventional channels are closed to the persons who resort to riot. If the political establishment refuses to deal with their grievances, then riot may be the most effective political action open to the group. It has been frequently suggested that the riots by American blacks in the 1960s were the only possible response by ghetto residents to their dismal situations. White resistance to reform and a stalling of the Civil Rights Movement prevented ghetto residents from obtaining effective action through conventional political channels (Howard, 1974).

■ **Blues and Greens**   Once upon a time (from A.D. 527 to 565, to be exact), the Emperor Justinian ruled over the Byzantine Empire. From his capital at Constantinople (now Istanbul), he sent his generals out to conquer Italy and North Africa until much of the old, broken Roman Empire was in his grasp. Justinian was actually a Roman himself, a Christian who wanted to rule the Roman world in the name of his God. He built great buildings and had scholars codify laws. Superficially, everything was grand.

However, beneath the surface were intense conflicts and terrible grievances. The govern-

■ The Emperor Justinian and his entourage are depicted in this mosaic. Justinian undertook a major codification of Roman law, yet his disregard for legality and his repressive practices caused riots that nearly toppled his government.

ment was exceedingly corrupt. All of Justinian's great enterprises were paid for by heavy taxation squeezed out of the common people. Government officials committed many hideous crimes without being punished. The fine laws of Justinian protected no one—his goodness was a lie and his greatness an illusion.

The Byzantine people had no legitimate mechanisms by which they could work to improve their system. Although personal politics abounded within the imperial court, there was no political structure, in the modern sense, to which the people could turn. Justinian and his wicked wife Theodora made the decisions, and all others had to do as they were told. There

was only one way to remove an emperor—to kill him.

The empire was ready to explode at any moment, like a pressure cooker with no safety valve and no way to turn off the heat. Hundreds of thousands of people were intensely unhappy and angry. However, these people were not organized in any kind of political movement that allowed concerted action toward solving their common problems. How could enough people get together to make a powerful political force since political parties were outlawed?

The answer, surprisingly enough, was at horse races. Like ancient Rome before it, Byzantium loved chariot races. For a time there had been four major teams of charioteers, named after the colors of their decorations: white, red, blue, and green. Over the years the Whites and the Reds disappeared, leaving two teams, the Blues and the Greens. Informal fan clubs sprang up, and racing enthusiasts divided themselves into rabid factions behind the Blues and the Greens. Constantinople's immense outdoor stadium, the Hippodrome, had room for many thousands of spectators. It was the scene of exciting races, at which the two factions would cheer, boo, and sometimes resort to violence when their team lost. Other cities throughout the empire also held races, and much of the urban population divided into the two fan factions.

The Blues and the Greens developed into highly partisan, aggressive associations, the nearest thing to political parties within the system. Emperors themselves supported one or the other group. Justinian supported the Blues, who in turn supported him, while the Greens were attached to the relatives of an earlier emperor, Anastasius. The favored Blues persecuted the Greens, often robbing or beating them with little fear of punishment. However, both groups were victims of Justinian's tyranny; the Blues were simply a little better off than the Greens.

In January 532, Justinian presided over the races in the Hippodrome, and the Greens used this opportunity to express their grievances to him. Throughout the first twenty-two races, they shouted their discontent, getting angrier and more disrespectful with each race. When he reprimanded them, they argued back. The Blues were finally so enraged that they chased the Greens out into the city, where they spread riot and disorder. Had a modern political system existed, these events might have taken the form of a peaceful election, with Blues and Greens as rival parties.

Right in the middle of chaos, one of those random events that frequently spark rebellion occurred. A group of seven assassins from both factions were dragged through the city by guards. Four were beheaded, a fifth hung, but the remaining two, a Blue and a Green, escaped to the sanctuary of a church. The Blues, who had been suffering almost as much as the Greens under Justinian, now turned their anger against the emperor, too. The two factions stopped fighting each other and joined forces against the government. They massacred palace guards. For five days they battled Justinian's unprepared forces, until the sly Empress Theodora was able to revive the loyalty of the Blues and again set them against the Greens. These riots are called the Nika uprising, because the rioters shouted "Nika" ("Victory") as they ran through the streets.

Like all historical events, the Nika uprising had complex motives behind it. However, some sociological principles are clearly applicable. Major riots are not random, insane outbursts. Participants are motivated by feelings of resentment, injustice, frustration, and outrage. Some social mechanisms are necessary to coordinate the behavior of the many people involved, and there is always a triggering event. In this case, the sports factions were the organizing structures, and the races that day provided the sparks that ignited the riot. The result was a five-day coalition that rivaled Justinian's government in strength. Only the collapse of that coalition allowed him to survive.

■ **The Luddites** Anyone who is opposed to technological progress, who fights to block it, or who actually breaks machinery is called a **Luddite.** The original Luddites were English textile workers who smashed machines in a series of riots from 1811 to 1816. Their legendary leader, Ned Ludd, gave the uprising its name. Some English newspapers at the time believed Luddism was a sinister conspiracy to overthrow society, and frightened members of the upper classes urged harsh action. There was in fact no conspiracy, and the rioters concentrated their attacks on the little textile factories in their own areas, often on their very places of employment. Luddism was an instance of collective behavior in which groups of workers beset by the same problems acted in an uncoordinated way to solve them, with only the most rudimentary communication about the best course of action.

The standard explanation of the Luddites' behavior is that they smashed the new machinery because it was so efficient that it threatened to take over many jobs. Earlier, thousands of workers weaving or knitting by hand were needed to make woolen cloth; now machines did it all. Earlier, workers had used huge, 40-pound shears to cut the fuzz off the cloth; now machines were taking over that job. In order to hold their jobs, these "backward" textile workers were trying to stop progress. This theory pictures the Luddites as stubborn diehards caught up in a historical process entirely beyond their control.

The major problem with this theory is that the machinery had been in use long before 1811. Although mechanization had increased in some factories, the smashed machines were only a symbol of the real grievances. England was suffering a great loss of foreign markets for its textiles in this period, mostly because of the wars against Napoleon and the war from 1812 to 1816 against the United States. Food prices soared sky high, while wages dropped into the cellar. The unemployed had no bread, and many employed workers did not have enough to eat. Hunger, misery—what some sociologists dispassionately call *strain* or *deprivation*—drove desperate people to do something. The only question was, What?

In many cases of collective behavior, two sets of factors are at work: the factors that make people want to do something (general motivation) and the factors that narrow people's choices so that they do something specific (channeled motivation). The Luddites were motivated in a general way by their own deprivations, but the specific form that their action took was determined by social and cultural factors.

They could not act through the standard political process because, since they were not property owners, they were not allowed to vote. They could not demand help through labor unions, because unions were illegal at the time and their organization had been effectively suppressed. The workers must have been reluctant to kill their employers, and the rebels did not want to destroy the factories, because they needed jobs. But the Luddites had to get across the message that they needed higher wages, and they had to give employers some reason to grant them. So they smashed the machines. The machines were a relatively safe and available target, and attacks on them were not crazy orgies of anger but logical and rational actions. In his book on the Luddites, Malcolm I. Thomis points

out how near to modern labor union practices the uprising really was by describing it as "collective bargaining by riot" (Thomis, 1970).

■ **Failure to organize** The Blues and Greens and the Luddites were ultimately unable to organize effective movements to improve their living conditions. The Byzantine and British governments effectively blocked the rebels in each case with military force. However, government prohibition is not the only barrier to the organization of social and political movements. Obviously, some groups of people—infants, the very poor, the seriously mentally retarded, and the seriously mentally ill—may lack the resources to organize at all.

A very different kind of social barrier has been discussed by Mark Granovetter, a sociologist who has analyzed networks of human relationships and social ties. In a well-known article (1973), he refers back to Herbert Gans's book *The Urban Villagers* (1962), which describes the failure of residents in Boston's West End section to organize to keep their neighborhood from being destroyed by urban renewal. The Boston city government, in which West Enders had little influence, decided that the neighborhood was a blight, and officials took the necessary steps to replace it with high-income housing. The West Enders were thrown out and dispersed to other parts of the city, where they found it hard to get cheap housing and where they missed the fellowship of their long-time neighbors. The city bulldozers came in and scraped away the West End to ground level.

Gans gives several plausible explanations for the feebleness of the efforts to stop the bulldozers, but Granovetter's explanation is particularly interesting. He stresses the kinds of social relations that had linked West Enders, who were tightly bound into small groups or cliques with weak bonds between groups. Gans characterizes the West Ender of that time as first and foremost a member of a small peer group, and he says that

peer group society dominates [the West Ender's] entire life, and structures his relationship with the community and the outside world. . . . The West End, in effect, may be viewed as a large network of these peer groups, which are connected by the fact that some people may belong to more than one group [Gans, 1962].

Granovetter likes this idea, but argues that these groups were too isolated from each other to build a movement. Members of one group would not trust the leaders of other groups, and there was not enough time before the bulldozers arrived to develop the new relations necessary to form a successful movement. Both Gans and Granovetter are convinced that the neighborhood would have had a much better chance to survive if it had already been organized as a community.

Granovetter further emphasizes the fact that social relations are the primary means by which movements are built. Less personal means are rather ineffective:

Leafletting, radio announcements, or other methods could insure that everyone was aware of some nascent organization; but studies of diffusion and mass communication have shown that people rarely act on mass-media information unless it is also transmitted through personal ties; *otherwise one has no particular reason to think that an advertised product or an organization should be taken seriously. Enthusiasm for an organization in one clique, then, would not spread to others but would have to develop independently in* each one *to insure success* [Granovetter, 1973].

Social Movements

Crazes, panics, and riots may all influence social change, but only when people are able to organize into an effective social movement can they have a good chance of achieving their goals. We have used the Blues and Greens, Luddites, and West Enders to indicate how collective behavior may evolve in the direction of a true movement and how the efforts of such groups may be thwarted, but it is time to look at a movement that really succeeded. You may have been sympathetic to the people we have just been dis-

cussing, but you will most likely deplore the mass movement now to be analyzed: Hitler's Nazi Party. Although it is essential for individuals to make judgments of good and evil, these are not scientific judgments. Sociologists approach an appalling phenomenon like Nazism with dispassionate spirit in order to conduct scientific research for determining the social factors behind the movement.

A successful mass movement: the Nazis

The Nazi Party was a political movement that began in complete obscurity after World War I. Yet from 1933 until 1945, Adolf Hitler's Nazi Party ruled Germany and terrorized the world. As the established government of a nation, it controlled a cluster of social institutions.

■ **Faulty theories** It has been long fashionable for anti-Nazi writers to explain the rise of Hitler's party as the natural result of certain aspects of "the German soul." The Germans were by nature barbarians, some have said. They had never really accepted civilization. Writers pointed to one after another piece of German culture that the Nazis had adopted and thus claimed that German philosophers and composers shared in the blame. But these cultural explanations tend to account mainly for the style of the Nazis or the specific cultural content of the movement. If Nazism had been an American movement, Nazis would have sung American marching songs, spoken English, and revered American history. It was not significant, therefore, that the Nazis sang German marching songs, spoke German, and revered German history. Some of these cultural explanations may simply be romantic literary fiction; most of them are at bottom racist, nationalist propaganda that is hardly more scientific than the Nazis' own propaganda was.

The Nazis cannot be explained in terms of some imagined German inferiority. The nation that invented the automobile and the jet plane was certainly not backward technologically. The nation that gave us Beethoven and half the philosophers of the nineteenth century was cer-

Table 21-1 ■ Sales of Hitler's book *Mein Kampf* and Nazi Party growth.

| Year | Sales of *Mein Kampf* | | Nazi Party Membership |
	Copies Sold in Each Year	Copies Sold to Date	
1925	9,473	9,473	27,000
1926	6,913	16,386	49,000
1927	5,607	21,993	72,000
1928	3,015	25,008	108,000
1929	7,664	32,672	178,000
1930	54,086	86,758	380,000
1931	50,808	137,566	800,000

Sources: Hale (1955, p. 837); Shirer (1960, pp. 169, 171); Carsten (1967, p. 143).

tainly not backward culturally. Nor can we explain the Nazis simply as the victims of some sorcery performed by Hitler. The Nazis were a social movement, and they can only be explained in terms of social factors.

Another common but feeble theory holds that movements succeed because they can transmit powerful ideologies (systems of beliefs and values) that arouse masses of people. Although ideology is not unimportant, it usually plays a passive role in the growth of a movement. As we saw in Chapter 3, attachments, not ideology, play the major role in attracting people to join movements. Perhaps the most powerful function of an ideology is to control and direct the activities of people who are already members of the group.

This seems to have been the most effective role of ideology in the Nazi movement. In countless speeches and articles, Hitler and propagandists claimed that the Jews were corrupting Germany, accused the old German political parties of having betrayed the country, and promised that the Nazis would save Germany. Specific statements were usually vague and contradictory. However, in his book *Mein Kampf (My Struggle)*, Hitler wrote at length about his ideas and plans, giving the full Nazi ideology, which he had only hinted at in his speeches. If ideology is important in recruiting new members, then we would expect sales of the book to

have led the growth of the party. In fact, the opposite was true. Table 21-1 shows sales of the book and Nazi Party membership for the years 1925 to 1931. In 1932, when Hitler received more than 13 million votes in a national election, only 90 thousand copies of *Mein Kampf* were sold, or 1 for every 149 voters. After Hitler seized power in 1933 he was able to sell 1 million copies a year.

■ **The Nazi constituency and its needs**   Two conditions are necessary for the growth of a mass movement: (1) a *natural constituency*—a segment of the population for the movement to represent that lacks effective representation and (2) a vigorous *internal society*—a cohesive network of social relationships within the movement capable of attracting and incorporating large numbers of new members. The Nazis had both. Individuals from the natural constituency were drawn in by the movement, whose internal society made sure they found membership rewarding.

In the chaos after the German defeat in World War I, literally hundreds of little movements sprang up. Some movement members seized power briefly in one city or another before being ousted by a larger movement or by the central government. These movements grew up in response to a wide range of public issues, and members proposed a great variety of solutions

■ When it was printed, this bill was worth 100,000 German marks. If Germany issued such a bill today it would be worth about $40,000 in U.S. currency. However, when this bill was printed in the 1920s, runaway inflation had made German money virtually worthless—it took trillions of marks to equal $1.

to the many serious problems facing German society. Social disorganization on a large scale often leads to increased social organization on a small scale. When a central government breaks down, smaller political units take over its functions. In the economic chaos of the early 1920s, many German towns printed emergency money, called *Notgeld*. Destruction of the national army produced many private armies, and the discrediting of old political parties produced many new ones.

Most of these new movements attracted only a few followers and soon died. But movements that addressed one of two major problems—German national weakness and economic disaster—tended to receive wide support: First, not only had the country been defeated in World War I but Germany also was still at the mercy of its enemies. When the nation was unable to pay the vast reparations demanded by its conquerors in 1923, the French moved in and took over the highly industrialized Ruhr district. German historians might well date the beginning of World War II from this French invasion of Germany, rather than from the later German invasion of Poland. Second, in 1923 and again in 1929 unemployment soared, leaving mil-

Table 21-2 ■ **The catastrophic inflation in German money, 1923.**

Date	Number of German Marks That Equaled One American Dollar
1921	75
1922	400
1923 (beginning)	7,000
January 1923	18,000
July 1, 1923	160,000
August 1, 1923	1,000,000
November 1923	4,000,000,000
After November 1923	trillions

Source: Shirer (1960, p. 95).

lions of people with neither the livelihood nor the self-respect that a job provides. Table 21-2 shows the cataclysmic inflation that rendered paper money valueless, liquidated savings and many investments, and reduced many middle-class citizens to poverty.

These two problems caused a lot of agony for the majority of Germans, making them a free-floating, natural constituency for any party that could organize them. But as a rule, parties dealt with only one of these issues, not both. With the support of the upper class and the army, the German Nationalist Party was able to capitalize on dissatisfaction over Germany's position as a nation, but it never appealed to the little people—either the workers or the members of the middle class—who suffered most from the economic dislocations. The Social Democratic Party (the Socialists) attempted to deal with the economic problems, but it was in the unhappy position of being forced to collaborate with Germany's French and British enemies. The Communists capitalized somewhat on the economic disaster, but they were unable to appeal to the large middle class; furthermore, because they were directed from Moscow, they could not express nationalist sentiments. However, the Nazi Party, with no history binding it to any one segment of the population and no ideological commitment to either one of the two issues, was able to take the broad approach necessary for a successful mass movement. The Nazis attacked both issues simultaneously and garnered membership from the widest possible natural constituency: Germans. *Nazi* is a slang word, a contraction of the first word of the official name of Hitler's party, *Nationalsozialistische Deutsche Arbeiterpartei* (the National Socialist German Workers' Party). The very name expresses the principle behind the party: Something for everyone—that is, for all Germans.

Writers often suggest that the Jews became the scapegoats for German failure because of a more or less pathological refusal by Hitler and his followers to confront the real reasons for the Germans' defeat in World War I and the economic troubles that followed. However, a sociological explanation is also possible. Each of the other political parties supported the interests of some Germans against the interests of others. The Nazi Party claimed to support the interests of *all* Germans against the interests of non-Germans such as Jews and other "foreigners."

Several of the parties described German politics in terms of a war between socioeconomic classes, and such parties fought to make

Table 21-3 ■ 1933 German occupational distributions.

Occupation	Nazi Party Members (%)	Total Gainfully Employed (%)
Manual workers	31.5	46.3
White-collar employees	21.1	12.5
Independents*	17.6	9.6
Officials	6.7	4.6
Peasants (farmers)	12.6	21.1
Others**	10.5	5.9
	100.0	100.0

Source: Gerth (1940, p. 527).
* Skilled artisans, professional persons, merchants, etc., excluding independent peasants.
** Domestic servants and nonagricultural family helpers.

their class the winner. Hitler asserted that all classes could win under Nazism. Here ideology did play an important, though passive, role. Each of the other parties was hindered by its ideology—which was simply the expression of the special interests of its constituency—from recruiting all of German society. Before Nazism, Germans faced each other as enemies fighting for a piece of the economic action. With Nazism, Germans stood shoulder to shoulder against Jews and foreign enemies. The incredible but logical consequences of this extremely effective political maneuver were the extermination camps and the war against the world.

The Nazis' greatest strength lay in the middle class. The economic disasters of the 1920s injured everyone, but none more than the millions struggling for middle-class respectability. In 1925 20 million Germans were earning lower-class incomes while attempting to live according to middle-class standards they had known (Schoenbaum, 1966). Table 21-3 shows that the Nazis drew members from all occupational groups, but particularly from white-collar

Table 21-4 ■ Age distribution in the county of Oschatz-Grimma in the German state of Saxony.

Age in Years	Percent General Population (1933)	Percent Social Democratic Party (1931)	Percent Nazi Party (1931)
18–30	31.1	19.3	61.3
31–40	22.0	27.4	22.4
41–50	17.1	26.5	8.0
51 and over	29.8	26.8	8.3
	100.0	100.0	100.0

Source: Schoenbaum (1966, p. 38).

employees and independent members of the middle class, such as shopkeepers. Sociologist Hans Gerth (1940) noted the appeal Nazism had for "persons whose career expectations are frustrated or who suffer losses in status or income" and reported:

Such "unsuccessful" persons were to be found in every stratum of German society. Princes without thrones, indebted and subsidized landlords, indebted farmers, virtually bankrupt industrialists, impoverished shopkeepers and artisans, doctors without patients, lawyers without clients, writers without readers, unemployed teachers, and unemployed manual and white-collar workers joined the movement.

■ **Youth and opportunity in the radical parties** Both the Nazis and the Communists strongly appealed to young adults. In times of high unemployment, youth suffers more than other age groups. Older people are in a better position to get jobs because of their experience and personal contacts, and they tend to hang on to whatever jobs they already have. Young people coming into the work force for the first time have a hard time finding work of any kind. Table 21-4 shows the age distribution in 1931 in one German county for members of the well-established Social Democratic Party and for members of the up-and-coming Nazi Party compared

with the distribution in the population as a whole. The Social Democrats had a small proportion of young members, while the overwhelming majority of the Nazis were young.

Political parties offer a variety of job opportunities for able and loyal followers. Such positions in the older German parties were just about filled up, while the newer Communists and Nazis had a number of jobs open for active young adults. Table 21-5 shows the age distribution in the 1930 Reichstag (German parliament), the equivalent of Congress. We see percentages in each age category for the Reichstag as a whole and for the three largest parties, the old-time Social Democrats, the Communists, and the Nazis. Notice that the young were represented in the two radical parties to a far greater degree than in the Social Democrats or all parties as a whole.

■ **The Nazi movement and its competition** The political system of the German Republic was somewhat different from the American system, but the basic structure of German politics then still exists in a number of European nations today. Americans have only two parties holding power in government, but the Germans had many parties, simply because the election laws were very different. Whereas in the United States political contests are winner-take-all, the Germans had a system of proportional representation. Each party received the same proportion

Table 21-5 ■ **Age distribution in the 1930 Reichstag and its three largest parties.**

Age in Years	Total Reichstag	Nazis	Communists	Social Democrats
under 30	4%	11%	11%	0%
30–39	25	55	58	12
40–49	30	22	29	34
50–59	31	10	1	38
60 and over	10 / 100%	2 / 100%	1 / 100%	16 / 100%
Number of Representatives	577	107	77	143

Source: Doblin and Pohly (1945, p. 43).

of seats in the Reichstag as the proportion of votes it received in the election. The American system works to the disadvantage of minor parties, but the German system favored such parties. This difference is one example of the ways societal institutions shape social movements. Election laws determine how power is divided and hence what groups have the potential to win a share. Figure 21-2 shows the percentage of representatives from the major parties in the Reichstag after nine different elections, from 1919, when Germany became a republic, until 1933, when it became a Nazi dictatorship.

A glance at Figure 21-2 shows that the major parties experienced marked changes in strength. The Nazis and the Communists rose from nowhere to become two of the strongest parties, while other groups lost strength. Germany's disastrous economic crises in 1923 and 1929 dramatically affected the voting. In the first election in 1924, the representation by Social Democrats (Socialists), the party that had been in power, dropped by nearly half; the two radical parties, the Nazis and the Communists, achieved their first great successes. The Socialists were blamed by many voters for the economic calamity of 1923, while the Nazis and Communists acted as lightning rods for voters' desperate hopes. When the economy improved again in the mid-1920s, the Nazis dropped back

and the Socialists recovered somewhat. The 1929 crash of the American stock market touched off a worldwide economic depression and led to the tremendous increase in Nazi support in 1930.

Human misery may feed the growth of a movement, but deprivation is not sufficient to explain it. Movements require organization. The Nazi Party was really an alternate society in direct competition with the German state, and the Nazi society was organized along different and more effective principles. The Nazi Party was an independent social structure made of hundreds of thousands of personal relationships. When the party set up soup kitchens to feed hungry Germans, it was not only providing a needed service that the government had failed to provide but also offering the needy the possibility of developing new human relationships. Newcomers would make friends among the party members and then become members themselves (recall the research on conversion in Chapter 3).

Like the Nazis, the German army was another state-within-a-state, for the government could not control its commanders. However, under the terms of the Versailles Peace Treaty, which had ended World War I, the army could not grow beyond 100,000 men. But there were no restrictions on the growth of the Nazis' private armies, the SA (Brownshirts) and the SS

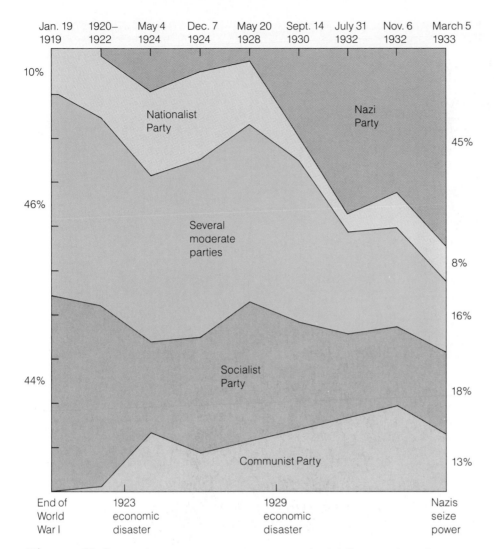

Figure 21-2 ■ **The Nazi rise to power: strength of different political parties in the German Reichstag (Parliament), 1919–1933.** The Nazi Party rose to power over the years shown in this chart, feeding on the dissatisfaction and despair of a nation constantly beset by terrible social problems. In 1923, economic disaster and the French occupation of the industrial region of Germany discredited the dominant Socialist Party, increasing the strength of the Nationalists and Communists, and gave the Nazis their first seats in the Reichstag. The economic situation improved in the mid-1920s, and the radical parties lost ground. The international economic crisis that began in 1929 and became the Great Depression gave renewed strength to the Nazis and Communists. By the end of the period, the moderate parties and Socialists had lost nearly two-thirds of their strength, and the radical movements had come to dominate German politics. In 1933, the Nazis seized absolute power, and elections were no longer held.

■ Adolf Hitler emerges from a Nazi Party meeting. Uniformed members of his private Nazi Party Army, the Brownshirts, give the Nazi salute. Since the German Army was restricted by the treaty ending World War I to only 100,000 men, the party army soon outnumbered the regulars.

(Blackshirts). By 1930 the Nazi military forces had reached 100,000 men, and the Nazi forces soon surpassed the official army in size.

Even the governmental structure of the Nazi Party was set up as an alternate state, with district leaders *(Gauleiters)* and regional leaders all giving allegiance to Hitler as their highest leader *(Führer)*. When the Nazis took over Germany by stealth and force in 1933, it was a simple matter for their state-within-a-state to become the State.

This analysis gives us a valuable perspective on social movement and leads to a conclusion that is not often stated: Society *is* movements.

Social institutions and social movements are not radically different from one another. We might say that social institutions are slow movements and that social movements are merely social institutions that happen to be evolving more rapidly. We defined *collective behavior* and *social movement*, in part, as behavior that is new, unusual, and striking. Obviously, these terms are relative, and our perspective on them depends on the particular values that we hold as individuals and as members of groups. An entire civilization can be described as a vast movement; the Nazis, on the other hand, actually believed that they were

■ Once in control of Germany, Hitler moved not only to eliminate his opponents but also to win over the whole society to support the Nazi Party. Here Nazi officers let little boys fire real machine guns during a visiting day at the Berlin barracks. Everyone, including parents, seems to be having a good time.

a civilization. All institutions and customs rise from nowhere, and most of them fall back into nonexistence. Change is the only permanent feature of human life. Hitler's Nazi Party is but one of the many movements that grew from almost nothing to become a government of a major nation and then fell into ignominy.

When the Nazis seized power, their first task was to extend their influence into every aspect of the German social structure to make it impossible for any other group to challenge Nazi rule. Under the banner of the propaganda word *Gleichschaltung* ("coordination"), the Nazis dissolved the myriad of organizations that had

made up the old society and replaced it with a few completely Nazi organizations. Labor unions, for example, were replaced by the single, Nazi-controlled German Labor Front, which was used to control the workers rather than represent them. The only potential opposition that remained was the German army. When it decided to support Hitler, effective opposition became impossible.

In his book *The Nazi Seizure of Power*, William Sheridan Allen (1965) reported on the experience of a single German town during the Nazi drive to accomplish "the atomization of the community at large." The goal was for each individual to relinquish his or her identity as a member of many interlocking social groups and become an "atom" within the huge, impersonal, Nazi institutions. Outside the context of Nazi mass meetings and organization, the citizens of the town had little opportunity to interact with one another. As one town resident put it, "There was no more social life; you couldn't even have a bowling club" (Allen, 1965). In effect, the Nazis had *created* a mass society (see Chapter 1).

Recall Mark Granovetter's analysis of the failure of Boston West Enders to organize a movement to stop the urban renewal bulldozers. German citizens were in an equally difficult situation regarding the Nazis. The atomization of social relationships had thrown individuals on their own, and only within the party apparatus or within the army could effective organizations be built. German citizens were unable to organize any kind of serious opposition to Hitler after 1933, and the Nazis had to be toppled from power by outside intervention in World War II.

A successful elite movement: spaceflight

Not all successful movements are mass movements. Sometimes a small band of dedicated people can cause great changes. Writers on social movements have sometimes made the mistake of considering only movements created by oppressed groups. In fact, middle- or upper-class individuals have initiated many of the most successful movements. As we have seen, movements often draw their strength from the misery of some natural constituency. However, this is not always true: In some cases, a movement grows up around a new opportunity rather than a new problem. Such movements gain power because they satisfy the needs or desires of upper-class, rather than lower-class, groups. The "spaceflight movement" was a response to a new opportunity for achievement in the early years of this century. Members of the middle and upper classes perceived this opportunity and supported the movement, which succeeded because it was able to exploit circumstances in three

technologically oriented nations: Germany, the Soviet Union, and the United States (Bainbridge, 1976).

■ **Origins of spaceflight** For a century before the first actual flight into space, the idea of space travel was explored and advertised in science fiction stories and popular articles on astronomy. Although astronomers have not as a rule been much in favor of spaceflight, their descriptions of astronomical discoveries for the general public have made the moon and planets seem like exciting places to visit and explore. Three authors of the late nineteenth century— Jules Verne in France, H. G. Wells in England, and Kurt Lasswitz in Germany—wrote influential novels that were read by the early rocket pioneers. Space travel became an idea that was in the air, so to speak, and at least a few people were convinced that it would be a worthwhile goal. This period can be described as one of *cultural preparation* for the later movement.

Throughout the first quarter of the twentieth century, a few far-sighted people independently developed the basic theories and essential mathematical analyses. The three most important thinkers were Konstantin Tsiolkovsky in Russia, Robert Goddard in the United States, and Hermann Oberth in German-speaking central Europe. All three worked independently, so their work can be described as parallel behavior. They were highly unusual people who shared a mystical vision and who had the mind and scientific know-how to make that vision practical. Goddard and Oberth came from upper-middle class families. All three can be described as geniuses.

The movement itself was born in Germany after Oberth published his great book *The Rocket*

■ These three photos illustrate the operations of the spaceflight movement during its purely amateur phase. Top right: A teenage Wernher von Braun and another member of the German VfR carry their homemade rockets to the launching pad sometime in 1932. Near right: A member of the American Rocket Society, working in his garage in 1932, readies a homemade rocket for launching. Far right: A homemade rocket is launched by Russian members of GIRD in 1933.

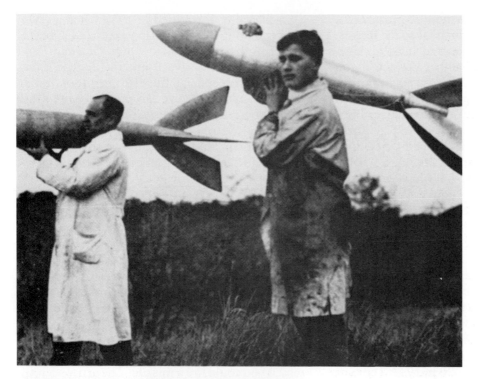

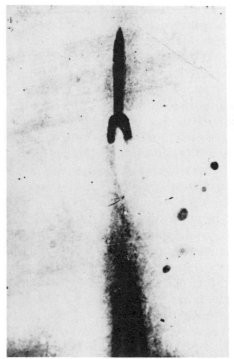

into Planetary Space, in which he presented a correct mathematical analysis of space rocketry. He had originally submitted it as his doctoral dissertation, but it had been rejected, and Oberth had to pay out of his own pocket to get this revolutionary work published. Young men at the outset of their careers flocked to him, apparently hoping that they could perform exciting, creative work in building the first spaceships. Oberth and Max Valier, one of his first converts, wrote articles for magazines and gave speeches all over the country. The two men inspired a few other young men to join together and form a German society for space travel, the *Verein für Raumschiffahrt* (VfR), in 1927.

The space activity in Germany in the 1920s fell into the category of collective behavior. It spread throughout the industrialized nations, and other space clubs like the VfR were formed: the American Interplanetary Society (AIS) in 1930, the Russian *Gruppa Izucheniya Reaktivnogo Dvizheniya* (GIRD) in 1931, and the British Interplanetary Society (BIS) in 1933. The four national space clubs constituted the real beginning of a social movement. They were formal (although amateur) organizations in which dedicated people planned and worked for a stated goal. The clubs were in close communication and attempted to cooperate despite rivalries among their countries. In the transition period from 1920 to 1940, this collective behavior gradually evolved into a social movement.

The rocket clubs tried every possible means to interest the general public, corporations, and governments in spaceflight—and failed utterly. The tiny clubs were attempting to turn their enthusiasm into an international mass movement, but there were no motives compelling enough to inspire many people to join. Spaceflight was not a solution—or even a plausible nonsolution, like Nazism—to any pressing human problem. It had no natural constituency to draw upon for support.

The VfR at its height had only about 1,000 members, and the AIS, GIRD, and BIS had hardly 100 members each. The British club spent about $1,000 on space development in the 1930s. The first liquid-fuel rocket built by the American club cost a grand total of $30.60 and included parts from a saucepan and a beverage shaker.

Max Valier was killed in 1930 when a crude rocket engine he was testing exploded. Oberth, suffering from exhaustion, left Germany and returned to his native Romania. As the Great Depression deepened, the VfR ran out of money and disbanded. However, in the midst of failure came one crucial success. The young German aristocrat Wernher von Braun, an avid young VfR member, discovered a way to get all the money he needed: He tricked the German army into buying spaceships disguised as long-range missiles.

■ **Success by exploiting political tensions**   The German army had a problem. After it lost World War I, the peace terms the Allies imposed had so weakened it that it was unable to defend Germany in case of attack. One of the terms of the Versailles Peace Treaty prohibited the manufacture of conventional heavy artillery in Germany. However, the treaty did not mention long-range rockets: This was a loophole through which you could fire a missile! The army secretly became interested in the rocket work being done by the VfR, and Wernher von Braun was able to convince the military to hire him to develop rocket engines. In 1932, the year before Hitler came to power, 20-year-old von Braun took charge of the fledgling liquid-fuel rocket program of the German army.

Over the next ten years, von Braun and a growing organization of followers outplayed the German army and the Nazi Party in a game of tricks and misrepresentation. Von Braun wanted to build spaceships; the German army wanted long-range artillery. The military, feeling at a disadvantage in the international arena, was ready to snap at any idea that might help them out of their inferior position. Von Braun sold them on the rocket as a way of getting around the restrictions imposed by the Versailles treaty—as a way of outflanking the enemy. Cultural and technological ideas of all kinds often originate as responses to such instances of conflict.

This pattern of events, which was repeated several times in the history of the spaceflight movement, can be represented by a simple interactive model involving a sequence of social interactions among three actors: the space engineer (a leader of the movement), the patron (a military officer or government official), and the opponent (the Allies). The model has four stages: (1) The patron is locked in fierce competition with his opponent. (2) The opponent gains the advantage. (3) The space engineer comes to the patron and presents the engineer's own favorite project as if it were an ideal solution to the patron's problem. (4) The patron, ignorant in the engineer's field and under great pressure, accepts the engineer's "expert" advice and invests in the project.

We can apply this same model to other kinds of movements. The intense needs of some group, either outsiders or (as in Hitler's party) movement followers, are exploited by movement leaders to give the leaders unusual power. Even the most benign leaders typically exploit their followers—at least to the extent of extracting admiration and a livelihood from them.

Without going into the details, we may note that von Braun tricked the military in two ways. First, he misled the German army into believing that long-range rockets were an efficient means of delivering conventional explosives to enemy territory, when in fact his rockets were a far more expensive way of unloading explosives than either artillery or bomber aircraft. Modern ICBMs (the successors to von Braun's rockets) are "ultimate weapons" only because they carry atomic warheads, which were not available to the Germans. Second, the liquid-fuel rockets von Braun designed were best suited for space purposes; the solid-fuel type is generally more appropriate for military uses. The V-2 was really a prototype spaceship crudely adapted to carry explosives. The V-2s were so expensive that they probably cost the Germans much more to develop than the Allies spent to clean up after them. The missiles were also costly to human life on both sides. About 5,000 persons were killed by V-2 bombardments of England and Belgium. But thousands of Germans also died, because the expenditure of something like $1 billion on the V-2 project ate deeply into appropriations for other things, including air defense.

In 1936, von Braun was able to pit the German army against the German air force (Luftwaffe) in order to get the $120 million he needed to construct his Peenemünde test station, the Cape Canaveral of Nazi Germany. In 1943, when he needed money to mass-produce the V-2 so that he could demonstrate its capabilities to the world, he personally went to Hitler and made a successful pitch, using a glowing lecture and dramatic movies of a V-2 launch. Once again, it was the same game—exploitation of the powerful in their hour of need. Hitler's air force had lost command of the air in the midst of the blitz of London, and the Allies had started blitzing German cities. Von Braun sold Hitler the V-2 as a means of continuing the bombing of London.

At the end of the war, von Braun led the scientists and engineers who were the leading members of his movement across the Atlantic. They "surrendered" to the Americans as the first step in a plan to exploit the United States in a similar fashion to produce spaceships. By the late summer of 1945, von Braun was in Boston preparing his conquest of America.

Under Stalin, the Russians had also become very interested in German rocket development by 1947. Stalin felt that he was in an inferior position, just as Hitler did. American air bases encircled the Soviet Union, and only the United States possessed atomic bombs. Stalin ordered a crash program to develop long-range rockets capable of outflanking the American aircraft. Like Hitler, he contributed to the spaceflight movement without intending to. The men who took charge of the Russian rocket programs included several who had been avid members of GIRD, the Russian amateur space club. In 1957, a team headed by Sergei Korolyov launched *Sputnik I*, the world's first artificial satellite. Korolyov, the Russian von Braun, had himself been president of GIRD back in the early 1930s! Both space engineers were leaders of branches of a social movement that had been working away—first outside and then within standard institutions—to achieve an unconventional goal.

■ **Maturity and institutionalization of the movement** Tsiolkovsky, Goddard, and Oberth were first-generation leaders of the movement; von Braun and Korolyov were second-generation leaders. The first generation developed the ideas and values of the movement. The second generation organized it and found the resources necessary to achieve practical success. Sociologist Neil Smelser (1962) has observed, "we may distinguish between two kinds of leadership—leadership in formulating the beliefs and leadership in mobilizing participants for action." Sometimes a single individual performs these two leadership functions, but it is usually worth distinguishing the *ideologue,* who invents and spreads ideas, from the *executive,* who builds and guides a social enterprise. When the executives take over a social movement, it is a sign that the movement has reached its maturity.

However, even when a social movement is well established, fresh outbursts of collective behavior in support of the movement are possible. The response of American politicians, journalists, and ordinary citizens to the first *Sputnik* was striking. A wave of self-accusation, weeping, wailing, and gnashing of teeth swept the United States. How could the Russians have been first into space? Many public figures blamed the American educational system, and for a few years there were active attempts to reform the nation's schools and colleges so that they would produce more and better engineers.

However, *Sputnik* really had nothing to do with any Russian educational superiority; the Russians had simply invested more money in rockets. The United States was actually just about to catch up with them and pass them in missile technology. The hue and cry over *Sputnik I* was a kind of panic, stimulated both by the spaceflight movement and by educators' chronic desire for more money. The *Sputnik* panic was largely an instance of movement-instigated collective behavior, or the result of previous action by an organized social movement.

With massive governmental support, von Braun was able to launch his own satellite, *Explorer I,* ninety days after getting permission. The launch rocket, a direct offspring of the V-2, had been ready for a year and a half, waiting for a go-ahead signal from Washington.

With the sponsorship of the Kennedy, Johnson, and Nixon administrations, space development progressed rapidly. *Apollo II* took Buzz Aldrin and Neil Armstrong to the surface of the moon in 1969, twelve years after the first orbit-

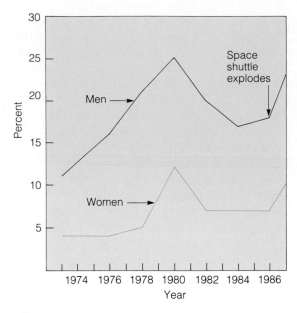

Figure 21-3 ■ **Percent who say the government is "spending too little" on the space program, 1973–1987.** At no time since the space program began have most Americans thought the government was spending too little money on it. However, the proportion wanting more spent on space more than doubled between 1973 and 1980. Concern about too little spending on space then declined through the first six years of the Reagan administration, only to rise again after the tragic explosion of the Space Shuttle on January 28, 1986. Although these patterns of support for the space program over time are similar for men and women, men are much more apt to favor the program than are women. (*Source:* prepared by the author from NORC, General Social Surveys for the pertinent years.)

ing satellite. The lunar module was launched by a huge *Saturn V* booster, designed principally by von Braun and his team of German-Americans. Now American space missions are carried out by the military and the National Aeronautics and Space Administration, a government agency organized soon after *Sputnik.* The social movement for space travel has been completely incorporated into standard social institutions.

The spaceflight movement was a success, but as such there is no longer a movement: Spaceflight is not really *moving* much any more. Despite the tragic explosion in early 1986, new space transportation systems like the Space Shuttle are prosaic compared with the first space missions, and the development of space technology has become a gradual affair. The Chinese, the Japanese, the French, and the European space agencies have independently launched earth satellites, and literally dozens of nations have participated in space projects in one way or another. Nearly $200 billion has been spent on space, not including the similar fortune invested in long-range missiles. Manned space programs are continuing, and unmanned deep-space probes have explored all the planets of the inner solar system. Space is big business, and huge government programs remain dedicated to the advancement of space technology.

Nevertheless, fluctuations in public support still influence the program. Figure 21-3 shows that in the early 1970s, few Americans thought the government was spending too little on the space program. Then, during the Carter administration, when spending on space programs did not increase during a period of very rapid inflation, the proportion of the public wanting more spending on space rose substantially, albeit only 25 percent of men and 12 percent of women ever expressed this view. Still, the active expression of support even by a minority, combined with the built-in power of NASA, proved sufficient to obtain substantial budget increases during the early years of the Reagan administration. For example, the space program was allocated $2.2 billion in the 1979 budget, while the 1983 budget provided $4.1 billion.

Studying the Spaceflight Movement

 This account of the spaceflight movement was condensed from my first book (Bainbridge, 1976), which served as my doctoral dissertation. Unlike most sociological research, it is hard to present a study in social history in a way that allows others to look over the sociologist's shoulder as the research is conducted. Although I did visit rocket installations and interview pioneer members of the spaceflight movement, most of my research was done by sitting in libraries reading books. So rather than have you sit with me in the library and read over my shoulder, perhaps I can best reveal my methods by explaining how I got interested in the subject and found it worth exploring.

As a freshman in college, I planned to major in physics because I was a dedicated spaceflight nut. I still have the junior space cadet certificate I ordered from a TV show when I was 11, and the next year I joined the American Rocket Society. However, it took me only a few months at Yale to discover that I had the wrong temperament for physics. Moreover, I found I was as interested in scientists themselves as in their discoveries. Eventually I found my way to sociology, which has allowed me to do scientific research on people, including scientists.

I chose to do my doctoral dissertation on spaceflight not only because of my interest in it but also because there had been no serious sociological research on the topic. Also, the spaceflight movement seemed to contradict a major theory of technological change.

Historians have tended to emphasize the unique character of events and to stress the importance of individual actions. Thus, in military history, emphasis is given to how one general outsmarted another. In the history of science, emphasis is given to the genius of a particular person who made a discovery. In contrast, sociologists emphasize the social environment in which a general or a scientist operated.

Surely no one could object to sociological suggestions that a famous scientist could not have made a particular discovery had he or she lived a thousand years earlier, or that not even Napoleon himself could have led the Dutch army to victory over Nazi Germany in 1939. However, some social scientists have taken the position that individuals count for nothing in the great scheme of history, and that social forces make everything happen. Thus, a dominant view of social change is called **technological determinism.**

Technological determinists such as S. C.

Gilfillan (1963) and Leslie White (1959) argue that changes in technology are the cause of all social change and that technological change is self-generating. That is, technological determinists argue that each advance in technology is the automatic response to previous advances; when technology reaches a certain stage, the next stages must occur. For example, technological determinism holds that if Thomas Edison had not invented the light bulb in 1879, within a few months someone else would have done so, because the times were right for that invention to take place. In this view, the inevitable march of new inventions drives technology forward, taking the rest of society with it.

Technological determinism leaves no room for significant exceptions—for unusually talented and dedicated people to speed up the pace of innovation or even to leap ahead of the times. (It also leaves no room for people to slow down the pace or turn the times backward.) I thought that the development of spaceflight might be a compelling counterexample for the technological determinists. If, as I suspected, a few rare individuals had in fact brought spaceflight into existence before the times were right, then we could know that at least sometimes in history individual human actions count. On the other hand, if it turned out that spaceflight was also just the expected outcome of ordinary technological advances, then technological determinism would be further supported. In effect, my study was meant to address the question, Do we make history, or does it make us?

A project such as this could not be done by an experiment or by asking a national sample of Americans whether they thought spaceflight was the result of routine science and engineering. Instead, I had to collect and analyze the history of spaceflight. To do this, I had to acquire two special skills. First, I had to learn to read the languages in which the essential documents were written. In this respect, my study began when I was 13 and read Willy Ley's popular history of the German rocket program, because that inspired me to take German in school. Later I studied Russian, only to discover that the Russian sources were completely useless—nothing but propaganda stories about rockets with very few trustworthy facts about

who designed what or why. In addition to languages, I also needed to be able to understand the science and engineering involved in rocketry. Although I had not ended up a physics major, my scientific training proved adequate.

So I began my study. To proceed, I decided to focus on about a dozen major technological advances occurring before spaceflight. Were they the expected outcome of basic trends? Would we have spaceflight today if the amateur enthusiasts of the 1930s rocket clubs had never lived? I am convinced that the historical record says no. There is no evidence of basic trends in technology leading toward space.

During the critical period, conventional scientists and engineers were not even interested in spaceflight, let alone contributing to it. Instead, spaceflight was developed by a few tiny groups of amateur enthusiasts. Later, to further their goals, they consciously deceived military leaders into financing their work by disguising spacecraft research as weapons development. How do I know this? First, because the German rocketeers wrote about what they were doing *as they did it*; they actually described their involvement in the V-2 programs at the time as a "military detour" to space. Second, the design of the rockets was inappropriate for military use. Had the military simply organized a missile program, the necessary rocket developments for space applications would not have occurred. Finally, we see the role of the spaceflight movement intervening often, in a number of countries, to deflect normal technological trends out toward space.

I intended my book only as the first sociological "space shot." As the first sociological study of this fascinating area, it was meant to be surpassed, corrected, and perhaps even refuted by others. Unfortunately, there are not many practicing sociologists, and we are thinly spread studying a large number of important topics. When I wrote a new preface for my book when it was reissued in 1983, I could not mention any subsequent work on the topic. And since I, too, have moved on to other topics, at present no one seems to be working on the many questions still to be answered about the implications of spaceflight for human societies. Perhaps one of you will relaunch the sociology of space.

■ On July 20, 1969, Astronaut Buzz Aldrin stands at attention after he and Neil Armstrong had planted the American flag on the moon. The *Apollo II* mission to the moon was not the culmination of normal scientific progress but was caused by an international social movement.

■

Conclusion

In this chapter we have taken a look at why, how, and what happens when people get together to do something new. We have seen how two interrelated concepts—collective behavior and social movements—can be applied. We have focused on whole cases to get an overview of basic principles, stressing the historical dimension. Social scientists have used various research methods to study these phenomena and to test narrow hypotheses. We selected a historical approach because it seemed most appropriate for answering our original question, which was really about social change. We have seen that the Nazi movement resulted from social changes that had brought misery and confusion to a great nation. But the Nazis themselves produced social change and laid a basis for other movements like the one dedicated to spaceflight. Thus, the Nazi Party was both the result of social change and the cause.

Collective behavior and social movements are the reactions of numbers of people to social conditions, and these people produce new social conditions to which other people then react. We, as individuals and groups, stand between past events and future ones. The course of human history presents us with circumstances to which we must respond. Our descendents will have the history we give them. To return to a question posed a few pages ago, "Do we make our history, or does it make us?" Clearly, the answer is yes!

■

Review Glossary

collective behavior Unusual action related to social change taken by a group of people who influence one another but who engage in little planning and do not form an organization. (p. 610)

social movement An organized group dedicated to causing or preventing social change and acting in unusual ways or outside of conventional channels. (p. 611)

parallel behavior Several people doing the same thing for the same reasons, but without influencing one another. (p. 613)

craze Sometimes called a fad; many people suddenly pursuing some new form of behavior, such as when millions bought Hula Hoops. (p. 614)

panics What occur when many people suddenly seek to evade something they perceive as a danger, such as when crowds flee a burning building or when investors try to sell their stock in a falling market. (p. 615)

riot A hostile, unplanned outburst in which a crowd threatens or attacks other persons or property. (p. 619)

Luddite A person who opposes technical progress (named for Ned Ludd, leader of the English textile workers who broke their machines to protest poverty). (p. 621)

technological determinism The belief that technological change is automatic and that when the time is right for the next step forward, it will occur. If Edison, for example, hadn't invented the light bulb in 1879, within a few months someone else would have invented it. (p. 637)

■

Suggested Readings

Allen, William Sheridan. 1965. *The Nazi Seizure of Power.* Chicago: Quadrangle.

Bainbridge, William Sims. 1976. *The Spaceflight Revolution.* New York: Wiley-Interscience.

Gerlach, Luther P., and Virginia H. Hine. 1970. *People, Power, Change: Movements of Social Transformation.* Indianapolis: Bobbs-Merrill.

Smelser, Neil J. *Theory of Collective Behavior.* 1962. New York: Free Press.

Zald, Mayer N., and John D. McCarthy, eds. 1979. *The Dynamics of Social Movements.* Cambridge, Mass.: Winthrop.

Becoming a Sociologist

EPILOGUE

IN CHAPTER 1, I confessed that one purpose of this book was to invite readers to become sociologists. Because I assume that you are now considering that option, it seemed useful to add a brief essay explaining how people actually do become sociologists. I have learned from my students that they often have little information about such matters as going to graduate school. For example, many students have worried about how they could afford to go on to graduate school. Clearly, these students didn't know that most graduate students receive full financial support. Nor do undergraduates usually know about how to select a graduate school.

Because it is difficult to be employed as a sociologist without a graduate degree (in fact, a doctorate is needed for many jobs), I shall devote much of this epilogue to graduate education. Then I shall describe the kinds of employment available to sociologists. First, however, something must be said about being an undergraduate major in sociology.

Majoring in Sociology

Perhaps the most important thing for a would-be sociologist to know is that graduate schools do not require applicants to have an undergraduate major in sociology. That means you have considerable latitude to select courses that interest you and to take advantage of the strengths of the curriculum offered at your school. If another social science department at your school has a stronger program than the sociology department, you could major in that department and still go on in sociology in graduate school.

You should also know that leading graduate schools in sociology place little importance on the quality of one's undergraduate college or university. You will not be handicapped if you are not now enrolled in a well-known institution. And the quality of teaching available to undergraduates is often higher at little-known schools than at famous institutions, where much of the teaching is delegated to graduate students lacking training and experience.

What you major in is not very important in becoming a sociologist; what you learn is. If my son decides he wants to be a sociologist and asks me to help him plan his undergraduate program, these are the things I would tell him (depending, of course, on what was offered at his particular school).

Take at least one course in statistics. If possible, do not take this in the math department or in the statistics department. Take it in a social science department, because then it will emphasize the statistical applications that social scientists actually use. If possible, take a second statistics course.

Take introductory economics. If micro and macro economics are separated into two courses, take micro. It is far more theoretical and more pertinent to sociology.

Take a basic course in logic. You may find a good one in the philosophy department or in the speech communications department. A course that emphasizes the rules of deductive logic may be more useful than a course devoted to modern symbolic logic.

Also, take courses that require you to write. If a good writing course is available, perhaps in the English department, take it. Later in this epilogue, I shall discuss how to learn to write, because sociologists make their living by the written word.

Take some history, especially if you can find a course or two that emphasizes social history.

Take at least one course in research methods if it is offered at your school. Research methods are not simply statistics, although it may be useful to take a statistics course first.

You will notice I have said nothing about courses in sociology. That is because your sociology department will have a set of courses it recommends or requires for a major. One of these will probably be a course in the history of social thought, and you ought to take it even if it is not required.

But whatever you do, don't specialize in one area of sociology while still an undergraduate. This is the time to sample many different parts of the field in order to discover what you really like and to gain a broad background that can serve as an adequate base for later specialization.

Finally, you may be able to gain some useful experience in doing sociology while still an undergraduate. Check around and see if some faculty members could use a volunteer assistant. Even if it only involves finding things for them in the library, you can learn from doing it, and you can include this experience in your application to graduate school.

Going to Graduate School

Most graduate schools expect students to apply by the end of December for admission in September. Details of admissions procedures can be obtained by writing departments you are considering. So by early fall you ought to have a list of schools you think you would like to attend.

Selection

How do you pick graduate schools? The first thing is to know what degree you plan to earn. If you think you want only a master's degree, which will qualify you for some kinds of research jobs (especially in government) and for teaching at some community colleges, then you have a choice of many universities. However, if you think you will aim for a doctorate, which is needed to qualify for most college and university faculty appointments and for most senior research positions, you should enroll in a school that gives a doctorate and that has a "major league" reputation.

Although the reputation of an undergraduate school has little effect on getting into a good graduate school, the reputation of a graduate school has an immense effect on a subsequent professional career. The general rule is that you will never get a job at a school with a substantially better reputation than the one from which you received your doctorate. So the better the graduate school you attend, the more opportunities you will have.

Fortunately, a number of universities have good reputations. However, the reputation of a university as a whole may not reflect the reputation of any specific department. Thus, some famous schools are not as highly ranked in sociology as some less famous places. Every few years a national study is conducted by the Council on Higher Education to rank departments in various academic fields. You may want to consult the sociology rankings in the latest of these reports (you can find it in most libraries). You can also get plenty of advice from members of your local sociology department. Moreover, you can request information on the recent placement of graduates from various departments you are considering and this will tell you how well their students are regarded.

Each year the American Sociological Association publishes a Guide to Graduate Departments, which lists all faculty and various specialties of each sociology department in the United States and Canada. This may help you determine who would be available to work with in any given department.

Be sure to apply to a number of schools, even if your grades and test scores are exceptional. That way you will have a choice. Having been accepted by several schools, you can then telephone the head of admissions at each school and seek further information to help you make your final choice. How much support do they offer? Will you have to pay tuition out of it? (Some schools require relatively high tuitions for out-of-state students; however, this tuition may be waived for graduate students.) You may also want to find out how long it takes the average graduate student to earn a degree at this school.

If you are married and your spouse plans to work while you are in graduate school, then you will want to find out the employment situations near the schools you are considering. Usually it will be easier for a spouse to find proper employment in or very near a large city than in an isolated college town. You will also want to find out about housing costs—some cities are very expensive, but that may be offset by the availability of university-owned housing.

Applying

Most departments use their own application forms and have different requirements regarding letters of recommendation and qualifying exams. You should write to each department early in the fall (or even the previous spring) to obtain these materials.

Virtually all good graduate departments require that students take the Graduate Record Examination (GRE) administered by the Educational Testing Service. Your current school will have information on when and where you can take these exams. It is best to take the GRE as early in the fall as possible so that your scores can be sent to graduate schools in time. Many students have found it helpful to prepare for this test by working through one of the practice guides available. Because undergraduate schools differ so greatly in quality and grading practices, graduate schools place great emphasis on GRE scores.

Letters of recommendation can also greatly influence graduate admissions committees. The more contact you have with several faculty members while you are an undergraduate, the more able they will be to write you an effective recommendation. That's another reason to volunteer to help some faculty with their research, especially if you are attending a very large school. It is not necessary to restrict letters of recommendation to sociology faculty—any faculty member who thinks well of you will be effective. Moreover, you can sometimes find people not in a college or university whose recommendation will be influential. Be careful, however, to ensure that nonacademics can stress your intellectual ability and motivation, not just your good character. Admissions committees tend to be a bit snobbish and do not react well to students who solicit recommendations from their minister, coach, or manager of the fast-food restaurant in which they were employed.

Succeeding in graduate school

There is a great irony about graduate education. People get into graduate schools by having been good students. They succeed in graduate school by learning to cease being students. Until graduate school, one is a consumer of knowledge— and one succeeds by learning what other people think about various matters. In graduate school, a person must become a producer of knowledge and succeeds by having his or her own thoughts about these same matters.

This is reflected in a whole new style of reading, for example. Rather than reading to understand and to be able to recall what someone has to say on a topic, one now must read to see what the underlying issues are, what remains to be said on that topic, or what is being said that is inconsistent or inadequate. One reads not just to learn but to find opportunities to contribute.

Nevertheless, the first several years of graduate school will revolve around classwork. A number of courses are required of all graduate students, and it is important to do as well as you can in each. But it is equally important to use this opportunity to get to know faculty members and discover with whom you want to work. For after the coursework is completed, graduate school turns into an apprenticeship. Finding the most suitable faculty member to work with as an apprentice will greatly shape your subsequent career.

In negotiating who will be your faculty sponsor in graduate school, let several criteria guide you. Ideally, it ought to be someone who does the kind of work you want to do. But that may be less important than finding someone who will train you well, who is interested in working with you, and who is able to place his or her students in good first jobs. Just as departments differ in reputation and ability to place students in top jobs, so do individual faculty members. Young faculty may be easier to approach and even more pleasant to work under, but they may lack the reputation to place students as effectively as senior faculty members. Sometimes, of course, a junior faculty member will be closely linked with a senior member, and thus his or her students will enjoy the sponsorship of the senior member.

In the final analysis, of course, it matters less who works with you than how well you do your work. If you begin to produce fine work, anyone will want to sponsor you, and you will be rewarded with quality job opportunities. What does it mean to produce fine work? Many things. But no matter how original and insightful your ideas, no matter how clever or creative your research, you will produce nothing until you write it down.

On Learning to Write

Perhaps the most disabling myth about intellectual activity is that writing is an art that is prompted by inspiration. Some writing can be classified as art, no doubt, but the act of writing is a trade in the same sense that plumbing or automotive repair are trades. Just as plumbers and mechanics would rarely accomplish anything if they waited for inspiration to impel them to action, so writers would rarely write if they relied on inspiration.

You learn to write by writing, just as you learn to plumb by plumbing. And just as any ordinary person can learn to plumb well, so can any ordinary person learn to write well. If you want to become a good writer, you must write. Regularly! Ideally, you should write every day.

In my teens I began to work for newspapers. Nobody taught me to write. I just began to try to do it every day. At first I was slow, and my prose was not very clear, let alone elegant. But just as one learns to make professional pipe joints as one gains experience, so one learns to write more clearly, cleanly, and easily by writing.

Never wait for inspiration; it seldom comes. Approach the job of writing as you would approach household chores, as something you do regularly and routinely. For many years I have been in the habit of getting up at the same time every morning; as soon as I have had coffee and read the paper, I settle down to write for about five hours. I never have to ask myself if I feel like writing any more than I have to ask whether I feel like brushing my teeth or not. It's just what I do at that time of day.

If you write regularly, you not only get better and better at it but you also get a great deal written. Students often fall into the habit of writing under pressure—of putting on a huge last-minute sprint to get a term paper completed. That's a bad way to write. It mixes writing with anxiety. When you write, you should be able to give your undivided attention to what you are saying, not to impending deadlines. Moreover, when you write regularly, you will find how easy it is to write a lot.

It would make me a nervous wreck had I tried to write this textbook in a series of crash sessions, trying to avert impending deadlines. The experience would have been so terrible I would have probably tried to avoid writing anything again. But that's not the way I did it. I sat down every morning and calmly knocked out 4 or 5 pages and then quit. That doesn't sound like much, but it is. In just 100 days that adds up to from 400 to 500 pages, or about half this book. Clearly, then I would have been content to average only 2 pages a day (and I write more only because I have practiced so long that I am very fast now).

So if you want to write, you should think of

it as a routine task, to be approached regularly and calmly. You will be amazed at how rapidly you improve.

When you write, don't agonize over finding the best word or the best phrasing. Get the ideas down no matter how poor your prose. After you have your ideas on paper, then worry about improving the style. When you have a draft, no matter how crude, you can work on improving the writing without getting sidetracked. You do not risk forgetting where you are going as you seek a word or wrestle with a sentence. Indeed, what you are doing now is not writing but editing.

If you are considering graduate school, no matter in what department, keep in mind that you are essentially choosing to be a writer. Great ideas do not become great sociology or great chemistry until they are written and published.

Sociological Careers

Colleges and universities are not the only places that employ people to do sociology. Much sociological research is conducted by people working for local, state, and national governments. Many other sociological researchers are employed by private firms. Thus, of the people who went to graduate school at Berkeley when I did, one ended up doing research on aging for the Social Security Administration, one plans new residential communities for a consortium of banks, one does research on drug abuse for the Justice Department, another studied parole and prison policies for New York State, two conduct market research for major advertising firms, one studies TV viewership for a rating company, and one went from research on magazine readership to being founder and publisher of a major new magazine. However, most of them ended up on college or university faculties.

College and university positions involve two very different career lines. The one most visible to students consists primarily of teaching. While virtually all college and university faculty members teach, in most schools faculty are expected to devote their major efforts to teach-

ing. In contrast, faculty at the major research-oriented universities are asked to teach only half or even a third as much as faculty in other schools. The remainder of their time is supposed to be spent on research and writing. That is, these people are hired and promoted primarily to do sociology, not to teach it, and it is to them that the rule "Publish or perish" primarily applies. In major universities, promotion and tenure are awarded almost exclusively on the basis of scholarly publications, with only modest concern given to teaching skills. Many faculty not at the major research universities also do research and publish, but less emphasis is placed on those activities (they are given less time to devote to it, for one thing) and much more importance is placed on their teaching. Most of these faculty members also did their graduate work at major universities, but they primarily chose the career of college teaching.

For people entering graduate schools today, there will be more opportunities for careers in industry and government than when I got my degree. There probably will be somewhat fewer openings in universities and colleges, since higher education was still expanding when I graduated. If you are thinking about being a sociologist, you will have each of these career lines as possibilities. Moreover, during the course of your career, you will probably have opportunities to switch from one line to another.

Before I became a sociologist, I tried some other careers. I enjoyed being a newspaper reporter. I enjoyed being an advertising writer. For several years I even enjoyed being a soldier. But there is a considerable difference between enjoying an occupation and being dedicated to it. Although newspaper writing was an interesting job, I was able to leave it without regret. But for me, sociology is different. It is not a job but a way of life. Being a sociologist is not merely what I do but what I am.

People can do a job very well and take considerable pride in it without its being essential to their self-image. But if an occupation is based on self-motivation, dedication is essential. Sociology, like any science, is fundamentally a solitary trade. Even when you are part of a research team, the most important work is not done collectively but in private. The basis of all scientific work is thought. It is very hard to force yourself to sit alone and think about things unless you enjoy thinking about them. I am sure I lack the self-discipline needed to force myself to write every morning. Fortunately, the problem never comes up. It never does when you are doing what you want to do. Dedication, then, means doing a job because you love it.

The first and most important thing I look for in graduate students is dedication. How much talent they have is of much less interest to me. The question I truly want a student to answer is, If you were so rich you didn't need a job, would you still be a sociologist? I would. If you would, too, then we need you.

References

Ackerman, Nathan W., and Marie Jahoda. 1950. *Anti-Semitism and Emotional Disorder*. New York: Harper & Row.

Adachi, Ken. 1978. *The Enemy That Never Was: A History of Japanese Canadians*. Toronto: McClelland.

Adorno, Theodore, et al. 1950. *The Authoritarian Personality*. New York: W. W. Norton.

Ages, Arnold. 1981. "Antisemitism: The Uneasy Calm." In *The Canadian Jewish Mosaic*, edited by M. Weinfeld, W. Shaffir, and I. Cotler. Toronto: John Wiley.

Ainsworth, M. D. S., et al. 1978. *Patterns of Attachment: A Psychological Study of the Strange Situation*. Hillsdale, N.J.: Erlbaum.

Alba, Richard D. 1977. "Social Assimilation Among American Catholic National-Origin Groups." *American Sociological Review* 41:1030–1046.

Alba, Richard D. 1985. "The Twilight of Ethnicity Among Americans of European Ancestry: The Case of Italians." *Ethnic and Racial Studies* 8:134–158.

Albrecht, S. L., B. A. Chadwick, and D. S. Alcorn. 1977. "Religiosity and Deviance: Application of an Attitude-Behavior Contingent Consistency Model." *Journal for the Scientific Study of Religion* 16:263–274.

Alexander, Karl L., Gary Natriello, and Aaron M. Pallas. 1985. "For Whom the School Bell Tolls: The Impact of Dropping Out on Cognitive Performance." *American Sociological Review* 50:409–420.

Allen, Leslie. 1985. *Liberty: The Statue and the American Dream*. New York: Statue of Liberty–Ellis Island Foundation.

Allen, William Sheridan. 1965. *The Nazi Seizure of Power*. Chicago: Quadrangle.

Allport, Gordon. 1958. *The Nature of Prejudice*. New York: Doubleday.

Allport, G. W. 1968. "The Historical Background of Modern Social Psychology." In *The Handbook of Social Psychology*, edited by G. Lindzey and E. Aronson, pp. 1–80. Reading, Mass.: Addison–Wesley.

Almond, Gabriel, and Sidney Verba. 1963. *Civic Culture: Political Attitudes and Democracy in Five Nations*. Princeton, N.J.: Princeton University Press.

Anderson, L. S. 1979. "The Deterrent Effect of Criminal Sanctions: Reviewing the Evidence." In *Structure, Law, and Power: Essays in the Sociology of Law*, edited by P. J. Brantingham and J. M. Kress, pp. 120–134. Beverly Hills, Calif.: Sage.

Angell, Robert Cooley. 1942. "The Social Integration of Selected American Cities." *American Journal of Sociology* 47:575–592.

Angell, Robert Cooley. 1947. "The Social Integration of Cities of More Than 100,000 Population." *American Sociological Review* 12:335–342.

Angell, Robert Cooley. 1949. "Moral Integration and Interpersonal Integration in American Cities." *American Sociological Review* 14:245–251.

Ardrey, Robert. 1961. *African Genesis*. New York: Dell.

Ardrey, Robert. 1966. *The Territorial Imperative*. New York: Dell.

Ardrey, Robert. 1970. *The Social Contract*. New York: Dell.

Arendt, Hannah. 1958. *The Origins of Totalitarianism*. New York: Meridian Books.

Asch, Solomon. 1952. "Effects of Group Pressure Upon the Modification and Distortion of Judgements." In *Readings in Social Psychology*, edited by Guy Swanson, Theodore M. Newcomb, and Eugene L. Hartley. New York: Holt, Rinehart & Winston.

Babbie, Earl R. 1973. *Survey Research Methods*. Belmont, Calif.: Wadsworth.

Babbie, Earl R. 1983. *The Practice of Social Research*, 4th ed. Belmont, Calif.: Wadsworth.

Bain, Reed. 1936. "The Self-and-Other Words of a Child." *American Journal of Sociology* 41:767–775.

Bainbridge, William Sims. 1976. *The Spaceflight Revolution*. New York: Wiley-Interscience.

Bainbridge, W. S., and Rodney Stark. 1980. "Client and Audience Cults in America." *Sociological Analysis* 41:199–214.

Bainbridge, W. S., and Rodney Stark. 1981a. "Suicide, Homicide, and Religion: Durkheim Reassessed." *Annual Review of the Social Sciences of Religion* 5:33–56.

Bainbridge, W. S., and Rodney Stark. 1981b. "Friendship, Religion, and the Occult." *Review of Religious Research* 22:313–327.

Bainbridge, W. S., and Rodney Stark. 1982. "Church and Cult in Canada." *Canadian Journal of Sociology* 7:351–366.

Ball-Rokeach, Sandra. 1973. "Violence and Values: A Test of the Subculture of Violence Thesis." *American Sociological Review* 38:736–749.

Baltzell, E. Digby. 1964. *The Protestant Establishment*. New York: Random House.

Bandura, Albert. 1974. "Behavior Theory and the Models of Man." *American Psychologist* 29:859–869.

Bardshaw, York W. 1987. "Urbanization and Underdevelopment: A Global Study of Modernization, Urban Bias, and Economic Dependency." *American Sociological Review* 52:224–239.

Barker, Eileen. 1984. *The Making of a Moonie—Brainwashing or Choice?* Oxford: Basil Blackwell.

Baron, Robert A., and Donn Byrne. 1981. *Social Psychology*. Boston: Allyn & Bacon.

Barrett, Richard K., and Martin King Whyte. 1982. "Dependency Theory and Taiwan: Analysis of a Deviant Case." *American Journal of Sociology* 87:1064–1089.

Bates, Elizabeth, et al. 1982. "Social Bases of Language Development: A Reassessment." *Advances in Child Development and Behavior* 16:7–75.

Beirne, Piers. 1987. "Adolphe Quételet and the Origins of Positive Criminology." *American Journal of Sociology* 92:1140–1169.

Bell, Daniel. 1961. *The End of Ideology*. New York: Collier Books.

Bell, Daniel. 1973. *The Coming of Post-Industrial Society*. New York: Basic Books.

Bell, Daniel. 1980. *The Winding Passage*. Cambridge: ABT.

Benbow, Camilla Persson, and Julian C. Stanley. 1980. "Sex Differences in Mathematical Ability: Fact or Artifact?" *Science*, Dec. 12.

Bendix, Reinhard, and Seymour Martin Lipset, eds. 1966. *Class, Status, and Power*, 2nd ed. New York: Free Press.

Benedict, Ruth. 1934. *Patterns of Culture*. New York: Houghton Mifflin.

Benedict, Ruth F., and Margaret Mead. 1959. *An Anthropologist at Work*. Boston: Houghton Mifflin.

Beniger, James R. 1987. "Toward an Old New Paradigm: The Half-Century Flirtation with Mass Society." *Public Opinion Quarterly* 51:S46–S66.

Benitez, J. 1973. "The Effect of Elite Recruitment and Training on Diffuse Socialization Outcomes." Doctoral dissertation, Stanford University.

Berelson, Bernard. 1978. "Prospects and Programs for Fertility Reduction: What? Where?" *Population and Development Review* 4:579–616.

Berelson, Bernard, Paul F. Lazarsfeld, and William N. McPhee. 1954. *Voting: A Study of Opinion Formation in a Presidential Campaign*. Chicago: University of Chicago Press.

Berelson, Bernard, and Gary A. Steiner. 1964. *Human Behavior: An Inventory of Scientific Findings*. New York: Harcourt, Brace and World.

Berg, E. J. 1966. "Backward-sloping Labor Supply Functions in Dual Economies—the Africa Case." In *Social Change:*

The Colonial Situation, edited by Immanuel Wallerstein. New York: John Wiley.

Berger, Peter L. 1963. *Invitation to Sociology: A Humanistic Perspective*. New York: Doubleday.

Berger, Peter L. 1967. *The Sacred Canopy*. Garden City, N.Y.: Doubleday.

Berk, R. A., K. J. Lenihan, and P. H. Rossi. 1980. "Crime and Poverty: Some Experimental Evidence from Ex-Offenders." *American Sociological Review* 45:766–786.

Berk, Richard A., and Phyllis J. Newton. 1985. "Does Arrest Really Deter Wife Battery? An Effort to Replicate the Findings of the Minneapolis Spouse Abuse Experiment." *American Sociological Review* 50:253–262.

Berkowitz, Leonard. 1978. "Is Criminal Violence Normative Behavior?" *Journal of Research in Crime and Delinquency* 15:148–161.

Bibby, Reginald W. 1979. "Religion and Modernity: The Canadian Case." *Journal for the Scientific Study of Religion* 18:1–17.

Bibby, Reginald W., and Harold R. Weaver. 1985. "Cult Consumption in Canada: A Further Critique of Stark and Bainbridge." *Sociological Analysis* 46:445–460.

Bird, Caroline. 1975. *The Case Against College*. New York: David McKay.

Birmingham, Stephen. 1973. *Real Lace: America's Irish Rich*. New York: Harper & Row.

Blalock, Hubert M., Jr. 1967. *Toward a Theory of Minority-Group Relations*. New York: Capricorn Books.

Blau, Peter M. 1964. *Exchange and Power in Social Life*. New York: John Wiley.

Blau, Peter M. 1970. "A Formal Theory of Differentiation in Organizations." *American Sociological Review* 35:201–218.

Blau, Peter M. 1972. "Size and the Structure of Organizations: A Causal Analysis." *American Sociological Review* 37:434–440.

Blau, Peter M. 1977. *Inequality and Heterogeneity: A Primitive Theory of Social Structure*. New York: Free Press.

Blau, Peter M., and Otis Dudley Duncan. 1967. *The American Occupational Structure*. New York: John Wiley.

Bloch, Marc. 1962. *Feudal Society*. Chicago: University of Chicago Press.

Blumenfeld, H. 1971. "Transportation in the Modern Metropolis." In *Internal Structure of the City*, edited by L. S. Bourne. New York: Oxford University Press.

Bonacich, Edna. 1972. "A Theory of Ethnic Antagonism: The Split Labor Market." *American Sociological Review* 37:547–559.

Bonacich, Edna. 1973. "A Theory of Middleman Minorities." *American Sociological Review* 38:583–594.

Bonacich, Edna. 1975. "Abolition, the Extension of Slavery, and the Position of Free Blacks." *American Journal of Sociology* 81:601–628.

Bonacich, Edna. 1976. "Advanced Capitalism and Black/White Race Relations in the United States: A Split Labor Market Interpretation." *American Sociological Review* 41:34–51.

Bond, Horace Mann. 1934. *The Education of the Negro in the American Social Order*. New York: Prentice-Hall.

Booth, Alan, David R. Johnson, Lynn White, and John N. Edwards. 1984. "Women, Outside Employment, and Marital Instability." *American Journal of Sociology* 90:567–583.

Boudon, Raymond. 1974. *Education, Opportunity, and Social Inequality: Changing Prospects in Western Society.* New York: John Wiley.

Boulding, Kenneth E. 1970. *A Primer on Social Dynamics.* New York: Free Press.

Bourne, L. S., ed. 1971. *Internal Structure of the City.* New York: Oxford University Press.

Bowers, William J., and Glenn L. Pierce. 1980. "Deterrence or Brutalization: What Is the Effect of Executions?" *Crime and Delinquency* 26: 453–484.

Bowles, Samuel, and Herbert Gintis. 1976. *Schooling in Capitalist America.* New York: Basic Books.

Boyd, Monica, et al. 1981. "Status Attainment in Canada: Findings of the Canadian Mobility Study." *Canadian Review of Sociology and Anthropology* 18:657–673.

Brantingham, Paul J., and Patricia L. Brantingham. 1982. "Mobility, Notoriety and Crime: A Study in Crime Patterns of Urban Nodal Points." *Journal of Environmental Systems* 11:98–99.

Braudel, Fernand. 1981. *The Structures of Everyday Life.* New York: Harper & Row.

Breault, Kevin. 1986. "Suicide in America: A Test of Durkheim's Theory of Religion and Family Integration." *American Journal of Sociology* 92:628–656.

Bretherton, I., et al. 1979. "Relationships Between Cognition, Communication, and Quality of Attachment." In *The Emergence of Symbols: Cognition and Communication in Infancy*, edited by Elizabeth Bates et al. New York: Academic Press.

Broderick, Francis L. 1974. "W. E. B. Du Bois: History of an Intellectual." In *Black Sociologists*, edited by James E. Blackwell and Morris Janowitz. Chicago: University of Chicago Press.

Brophy, I. N. 1945. "The Luxury of Anti-Negro Prejudice." *Public Opinion Quarterly* 9:456–466.

Brown, Barbara. 1984. "How the Baby Boom Lives." *American Demographics* 6:5:35–37.

Brown, Roger, and Ursula Bellugi. 1964. "Three Processes in the Child's Acquisition of Syntax." *Harvard Educational Review* 34:133–151.

Brown, Roger, and Richard J. Herrnstein. 1975. *Psychology.* Boston: Little, Brown.

Bruner, Jerome. 1977. "Early Social Interaction and Language Acquisition." In *Studies in Mother-Infant Interaction*, edited by H. R. Schaffer. New York: Academic Press.

Brym, Robert, Michael W. Gillespie, and A. R. Gillis. 1985. "Anomie, Opportunity, and the Density of Ethnic Ties: Another View of Jewish Outmarriage in Canada." *Review of Canadian Sociology and Anthropology* 22:102–112.

Bullough, Vern L. 1981. "Age at Menarche: A Misunderstanding." *Science* 213:365–366.

Burchinal, Lee G. 1963. "Personality Characteristics of Children." In *The Employed Mother in America*, edited by F. Ivan Nye and Lois Wladis Hoffman, pp. 106–121. Chicago: Rand McNally.

Burgess, Ernest W., and Charles Newcomb. 1933. *Census Data of the City of Chicago, 1930.* Chicago: University of Chicago Press.

Burgess, Robert L., and Ronald L. Akers. 1966. "A Differential Association-reinforcement Theory of Criminal Behavior." *Social Problems* 14:128–147.

Burkett, S. R., and M. White. 1974. "Hellfire and Delinquency: Another Look." *Journal for the Scientific Study of Religion* 13:455–462.

Burns, Michael. 1985. "Napoleon Elevated." *The Atlantic* 256:14–16.

Bursik, Robert J., Jr., and Jim Webb. 1982. "Community Change and Patterns of Delinquency." *American Journal of Sociology* 88:24–42.

Byrne, Donn. 1971. *The Attraction Paradigm.* New York: Academic Press.

Calhoun, J. B. 1962. "Population Density and Social Pathology." *Scientific American* 206:139–148.

Campbell, Angus. 1975. "The American Way of Mating: Marriage, Sí; Children, Maybe." *Psychology Today* 8:37–43.

Campbell, Stephen. 1974. *Flaws and Fallacies in Statistical Thinking.* Englewood Cliffs, N.J.: Prentice-Hall.

Canadian Centre for Justice Statistics. 1984. *Crime and Traffic Enforcement Statistics.* Ottawa: Statistics Canada.

Cann, Arnie, and William D. Siegfried, Jr. 1987. "Sex Stereotypes and the Leadership Role." *Sex Roles* 17:401–408.

Cantor, David, and Kenneth C. Land. 1985. "Unemployment and Crime Rates in the Post-World War II United States: A Theoretical and Empirical Analysis." *American Sociological Review* 50:317–332.

Cantril, Albert H., and Charles W. Roll. 1971. *Hopes and Fears of the American People.* New York: Universe Books.

Cantril, Hadley. 1941. *The Psychology of Social Movements.* New York: John Wiley.

Cantril, Hadley. 1966. *The Invasion from Mars.* New York: Harper & Row.

Caplow, Theodore. 1968. *Two Against One: Coalitions in Triads.* Englewood Cliffs, N.J.: Prentice-Hall.

Carmichael, Stokely, and Charles V. Hamilton. 1967. *Black Power: The Politics of Liberation in America.* New York: Random House.

Carsten, F. L. 1967. *The Rise of Fascism.* Berkeley: University of California Press.

Chagnon, Napoleon A. 1988. "Life Histories, Blood Revenge, and Warfare in a Tribal Population." *Science* 239:985–992.

Chalfant, H. Paul, Robert E. Beckley, and C. Eddie Palmer. 1981. *Religion in Contemporary Society.* Sherman Oaks, Calif.: Alfred.

Chandler, Alfred D., Jr. 1962. *Strategy and Structure; Chapters in the History of the American Revolution.* Cambridge: M.I.T. Press.

Chandler, David. 1966. *The Campaigns of Napoleon.* New York: Macmillan.

Chase-Dunn, Christopher. 1975. "The Effects of International Economic Dependence on Development and

Inequality: A Cross-National Study." *American Sociological Review* 40:720–738.

Chirot, Daniel. 1976. *Social Change in a Peripheral Society*. New York: Academic Press.

Chirot, Daniel. 1977. *Social Change in the Twentieth Century*. New York: Harcourt Brace Jovanovich.

Chirot, Daniel. 1985. "The Rise of the West." *American Sociological Review* 50:181–195.

Christiansen, K. O. 1977. "A Preliminary Study of Criminality Among Twins." In *Biosocial Bases of Criminal Behavior*, edited by S. A. Mednick and K. O. Christiansen. New York: John Wiley.

Clark, John P., and Larry L. Tifft. 1966. "Polygraph and Interview Validation of Self-Reported Deviant Behavior." *American Sociological Review* 31:516–523.

Cline, H. 1980. "Criminal Behavior Over the Life Span." In *Consistency and Change in Human Development*, edited by Orville G. Brim, Jr., and Jerome Kagan. Cambridge: Harvard University Press.

Cohen, Lawrence E., and Marcus Felson. 1979. "Social Change and Crime Rate Trends: A Routine Activity Approach." *American Sociological Review* 44:588–607.

Cohen, Lawrence E., Marcus Felson, and Kenneth C. Land. 1980. "Property Crime Rates in the United States: A Macrodynamic Analysis, 1947–1977; with Ex Ante Forecasts for the Mid-1980s." *American Journal of Sociology* 86:90–118.

Cohen, Mark. 1977. *The Food Crisis in Prehistory: Overpopulation and the Origins of Agriculture*. New Haven, Conn: Yale University Press.

Cohen, Yinon, and Andrea Tyree. 1986. "Escape from Poverty: Determinants of Intergenerational Mobility of Sons and Daughters of the Poor." *Social Science Quarterly* 67:803–813.

Cohn, Werner. 1958. "The Politics of American Jews." In *The Jew: Social Patterns of an American Group*, edited by Marshall Sklare. Glencoe, Ill.: Free Press.

Cohn, Werner. 1976. "Jewish Outmarriage and Anomie." *Canadian Review of Sociology and Anthropology* 13:90–105.

Cole, George F. 1983. *The American System of Criminal Justice*. Monterey, Calif.: Brooks/Cole.

Cole, Sonia. 1975. *Leakey's Luck: The Life of Louis Seymour Bazett Leakey, 1903–1972*. New York: Harcourt Brace Jovanovich.

Coleman, James S. 1961. *The Adolescent Society*. New York: Free Press.

Coleman, James S., et al. 1966. *Equality of Educational Opportunity*. Washington, D.C.: U.S. Government Printing Office.

Coleman, James William. 1987. "Toward an Integrated Theory of White-Collar Crime." *American Journal of Sociology* 93:406–439.

Collins, Randall. 1971. "Functional and Conflict Theories of Educational Stratification." *American Sociological Review* 36:1002–1019.

Collins, Randall. 1979. *The Credential Society: An Historical Sociology of Education*. New York: Academic Press.

Collins, Randall, and Michael Makowsky. 1978. *The Discovery of Society*. New York: Random House.

Converse, Philip E. 1964. "The Nature of Belief Systems in Mass Publics." In *Ideology and Discontent*, edited by David Apter. New York: Free Press.

Cooley, Charles H. 1909. *Social Organization*. New York: Charles Scribner's.

Cortés, J. B. 1982. "Delinquency and Crime: A Biopsychological Theory." In *The Fundamental Connection Between Nature and Nurture*, edited by Walter Gove and G. R. Carpenter. Lexington, Mass.: Lexington Books.

Cortés, J. B., and F. M. Gatti. 1972. *Delinquency and Crime: A Biopsychological Approach*. New York: Seminar Press.

Cott, Nancy F. 1977. *The Bonds of Womanhood: "Woman's Sphere" in New England, 1780–1835*. New Haven, Conn.: Yale University Press.

Cott, Nancy F. 1987. *The Grounding of Modern Feminism*. New Haven, Conn.: Yale University Press.

Counts, George Sylvester. 1922. "The Selective Character of American Secondary Education." *Supplementary Educational Monographs*, no. 19. Chicago: University of Chicago Press.

Covello, Leonard. 1967. *The Social Background of the Italo-American School Child*. Leiden, Netherlands: E. J. Brill.

Criminology. 1987. Special issue on theory. 25:783–989.

Crutchfield, Robert, Michael Geerken, and Walter R. Gove. 1983. "Crime Rates and Social Integration." *Criminology* 20:467–478.

Cullen, M. J. 1975. *The Statistical Movement in Early Victorian Britain*. New York: Barnes & Noble Books.

Curtin, Philip D. 1969. *The Atlantic Slave Trade: A Census*. Madison: University of Wisconsin Press.

Cutright, Phillips. 1983. "The Ingredients of Recent Fertility Decline in Developing Countries." *International Family Planning Perspectives* 9:101–118.

Cutright, Phillips, and Lowell Hargens. 1984. "The Threshold Hypothesis: Latin America 1950–1980." *Demography* 21:435–458.

Cutright, Phillips, and Herbert L. Smith. 1986. "Multiple Thresholds and Fertility Declines in Third World Populations: Paths to Low Fertility by the Years 2000 and 2010." In *Persistent Patterns and Emergent Structures*, edited by M. Karns. New York: Praeger.

Dahl, Robert. 1956. *A Preface to Democratic Theory*. Chicago: University of Chicago Press.

Dahrendorf, Ralf. 1959. *Class and Class Conflict in Industrial Society*. Palo Alto, Calif.: Stanford University Press.

Dahrendorf, Ralf. 1968. *Essays in the Theory of Society*. Palo Alto, Calif.: Stanford University Press.

D'Andrade, Roy G. 1966. "Sex Differences and Cultural Institutions." In *Development of Sex Differences*, edited by Eleanor E. Maccoby. Palo Alto, Calif.: Stanford University Press.

Darcy, R., and Sarah Slavin Schramm. 1977. "When Women Run Against Men." *Public Opinion Quarterly* 41:1–12.

Darley, John M., and Bibb Latanè. 1968. "Bystander Intervention in Emergencies: Diffusion of Responsibility." *Journal of Personality and Social Psychology* 8:377–383.

Darroch, A. Gordon, and Wilfred G. Marston. 1971. "The Social Class Bias of Ethnic Residential Segregation: The Canadian Case." *American Journal of Sociology* 77:491–510.

Davis, James A., and Samuel Leinhardt. 1972. "The Structure of Positive Interpersonal Relations in Small Groups." In *Sociological Theories in Progress*, edited by Joseph Berger. Boston: Houghton Mifflin.

Davis, Kingsley. 1940. "Extreme Social Isolation of a Child." *American Journal of Sociology* 45:523–535.

Davis, Kingsley. 1945. "The World Demographic Transition." *Annals of the American Academy of Political and Social Sciences* 237:1–11.

Davis, Kingsley. 1947. "Final Note of a Case of Extreme Isolation." *American Journal of Sociology* 50:432–437.

Davis, Kingsley. 1949. *Human Society.* New York: Macmillan.

Davis, Kingsley. 1951. *The Population of India and Pakistan.* Princeton, N.J.: Princeton University Press.

Davis, Kingsley. 1955. "The Origin and Growth of Urbanization in the World." *American Journal of Sociology* 60:429–437.

Davis, Kingsley. 1965. "The Population Impact of Children in the World's Agrarian Countries." *Population Review* 9:17–31.

Davis, Kingsley. 1971. "The World's Population Crisis." In *Contemporary Social Problems*, 2nd ed., edited by Robert K. Merton and Robert Nisbet. New York: Harcourt Brace Jovanovich.

Davis, Kingsley. 1976. "The World's Population Crisis." In *Contemporary Social Problems*, 3rd ed., edited by Robert K. Merton and Robert Nisbet. New York: Harcourt Brace Jovanovich.

Davis, Kingsley, and Wilbert E. Moore. 1945. "Some Principles of Stratification." *American Sociological Review* 10:242–249.

Davis, Kingsley, and Wilbert E. Moore. 1953. "Replies to Tumin." *American Sociological Review* 18:394–396.

Deck, Leland. 1971. "Short Workers of the World, Unite!" *Psychology Today* 5:102.

Delacroix, Jacques. 1977. "The Export of Raw Materials and Economic Growth: A Cross-National Study." *American Sociological Review* 42:795–808.

Delacroix, Jacques, and Charles C. Ragin. 1981. "Structural Blockage: A Cross-National Study of Economic Dependency, State Efficacy, and Underdevelopment." *American Journal of Sociology* 86:1311–1347.

DeLoache, Judy S., Deborah J. Cassidy, and C. Jan Carpenter. 1987. "The Three Bears Are All Boys: Mother's Gender Labelling of Neutral Picture Book Characters." *Sex Roles* 17:163–178.

Demerath, N. J., and Phillip E. Hammond. 1969. *Religion in Social Context.* New York: Random House.

Diaz-Alejandro, Carlos, et al. 1978. *Rich and Poor Nations in the World Economy.* New York: McGraw-Hill.

Dickeman, Mildred. 1975. "Demographic Consequence of Infanticide in Man." *Annual Review of Ecology and Systematics* 6:107–137.

Dion, Karen. 1972. "Physical Attractiveness and Evaluations of Children's Transgressions." *Journal of Personality and Social Psychology* 24:207–213.

Doblin, Ernest M., and Claire Pohly. 1945. "The Social Composition of the Nazi Leadership." *American Journal of Sociology* 51:42–49.

Dohrenwend, Bruce P. 1966. "Social Status and Psychological Disorder: An Issue of Substance and an Issue of Method." *American Sociological Review* 31:14–34.

Domhoff, G. William, ed. 1980. *Power Structure Research.* Beverly Hills, Calif.: Sage.

Dover, K. J. 1978. *Greek Homosexuality.* London: Duckworth.

Driedger, Leo, ed. 1978. *The Canadian Ethnic Mosaic: A Quest for Identity.* Toronto: McClelland and Stewart.

Driedger, Leo. 1982. "Individual Freedom vs. Community Control." *Journal for the Scientific Study of Religion* 21:226–242.

Drucker, Peter F. 1946. *Concept of the Corporation.* New York: John Day.

Drucker, Peter F. 1967. *The Effective Executive.* New York: Harper & Row.

Drucker, Peter F. 1969. *The Age of Discontinuity: Guidelines to Our Changing Society.* New York: Harper & Row.

Drucker, Peter F. 1974. *Management: Tasks—Responsibilities—Practices.* New York: Harper & Row.

Drummond, J. C., and Anne Wilbraham. 1957. *The Englishman's Food: A History of Five Centuries of English Diet,* rev. ed. London: Cape.

Du Bois, W. E. B. 1904. "The Atlanta Conferences." *Voice of the Negro* 1:85–89.

Durden-Smith, Jo, and Diane DeSimone. 1983. *Sex and the Brain.* New York: Arbor House.

Durkheim, Emile. 1897. *Suicide.* Reprint, 1966. New York: Free Press.

Eaton, C. Gray. 1976. "The Social Order of Japanese Macaques." *Scientific American,* Oct.

Edmundson, George. 1922. *History of Holland.* Cambridge, England: Cambridge University Press.

Edwards, Harry. 1982. "Race in Contemporary American Sports." *National Forum* 62:19–22.

Egeland, J. A., D. S. Gerhard, D. L. Pauls, J. N. Sussex, K. K. Kidd, C. R. Allen, A. M. Hostetter, and D. E. Houseman. 1987. "Bipolar Affective Disorders Linked to DNA Markers on Chromosome 11." *Nature* 325:783–787.

Ehrlich, Isaac. 1975. "The Deterrent Effect of Capital Punishment: A Question of Life and Death." *American Economic Review* 397–417.

Ehrman, Lee, and Peter A. Parsons. 1981. *Behavior Genetics and Evolution.* New York: McGraw-Hill.

Eibl-Eibesfeldt, Irenaus. 1970. *Ethology: The Biology of Behavior.* New York: Holt, Rinehart & Winston.

Ekstrand, Laurie E., and William A. Eckert. 1981. "The Impact of Candidate's Sex on Voter Choice." *The Western Political Quarterly* 34:78–87.

El-Badry, M. A. 1969. "Higher Female than Male Mortality in Some Countries of South Asia: A Digest." *Journal of the American Statistical Association* 64:1234–1244.

Ember, Melvin, and Carol E. Ember. 1971. "The Conditions Favoring Matrilocal versus Patrilocal Residence." *American Anthropologist* 73:571–594.

Emerson, Richard M. 1962. "Power-Dependence Relations." *American Sociological Review* 27:31–41.

Epstein, Cynthia Fuchs. 1976. "Sex Roles." In *Contemporary Social Problems*, 4th ed., edited by Robert K. Merton and Robert Nisbet. New York: Harcourt Brace Jovanovich.

Erickson, Maynard L. 1971. "The Group Context of Delinquent Behavior." *Social Problems* 19:114–129.

Erlanger, Howard S. 1971a. *The Anatomy of Violence: An Empirical Examination of Sociological Theories of Interpersonal Aggression*. Unpublished Ph.D. dissertation, University of California, Berkeley.

Erlanger, Howard S. 1971b. "Social Class and the Use of Corporal Punishment in Childrearing: A Reassessment." *American Sociological Review* 39:68–85.

Erlenmeyer-Kimling, L., and L. F. Jarvik. 1963. "Genetics and Intelligence: A Review." *Science* 142:1477–1479.

Estes, Richard J. 1984. *The Social Progress of Nations*. New York: Praeger.

Fair, Charles. 1971. *From the Jaws of Victory*. New York: Simon & Schuster.

Faris, Robert E. L. 1967. *Chicago Sociology: 1920–32*. San Francisco: Chandler.

Faris, Robert E. L., and Warren Dunham. 1939. *Mental Disorders in Urban Areas*. Chicago: University of Chicago Press.

Featherman, David L., and Robert M. Hauser. 1976. "Sexual Inequalities and Socioeconomic Achievement in the U.S., 1962–1973." *American Sociological Review* 41:462–483.

Federal Bureau of Investigation. 1982. *Uniform Crime Reports*. Washington, D.C.: U.S. Government Printing Office.

Federal Bureau of Investigation. 1985. *Uniform Crime Reports*. Washington, D.C.: U.S. Government Printing Office.

Felson, Marcus. 1987. "Routine Activities and Crime Prevention in the Developing Metropolis." *Criminology* 25:911–931.

Festinger, Leon, Stanley Schachter, and Kurt Back. 1950. *Social Pressures in Informal Groups*. New York: Harper & Row.

Finke, Roger, and Rodney Stark. 1988. "Religious Economies and Sacred Canopies: Religious Mobilization in American Cities, 1906." *American Sociological Review* 53:41–49.

Finley, M. I. 1982. *Economy and Society in Ancient Greece*. New York: Viking.

Fischer, Claude S. 1975. "Toward a Subcultural Theory of Urbanism." *American Journal of Sociology* 80:1319–1341.

Fischer, Claude S. 1976. *The Urban Experience*. New York: Harcourt Brace Jovanovich.

Fishberg, Maurice. 1911. *The Jews*. New York: Charles Scribner's.

Flanigan, William H. 1972. *Political Behavior of the American Electorate*, 2nd ed. Boston: Allyn & Bacon.

Flavell, J. H., et al. 1968. *The Development of Role-Taking and Communication Skills in Children*. New York: John Wiley.

Fleming, Joyce Dudney. 1974. "The State of the Apes." *Psychology Today* 7:31–38.

Fligstein, Neil. 1985. "The Spread of the Multidivisional Form Among Large Firms, 1919–1979." *American Sociological Review* 50:377–391.

Fogel, John K., and Stanley L. Engerman. 1974. *Time on the Cross: The Economics of American Negro Slavery*. Boston: Little, Brown.

Ford, Clellan S. 1952. "Control of Conception in Crosscultural Perspective." *World Population Problems and Birth Control. Annals of the New York Academy of Sciences* 54:763–768.

Ford, W. Scott. 1973. "Interracial Public Housing in a Border City: Another Look at the Contact Hypothesis." *American Journal of Sociology* 78:1426–1447.

Frank, Andre Gunder. 1969. *Latin America: Underdevelopment or Revolution*. New York: Monthly Review Press.

Freeman, Derek. 1983. *Margaret Mead and Samoa: The Making and Unmaking of an Anthropological Myth*. Cambridge: Harvard University Press.

Freidson, Eliot. 1973. "Professions and the Occupational Principle." In *The Professions and Their Prospects*, edited by Eliot Friedson, pp. 19–38. Beverly Hills, Calif.: Sage.

Freud, Sigmund. 1927. *The Future of an Illusion*. Garden City, N.Y.: Doubleday.

Fried, Morton H. 1967. *The Evolution of Political Society: An Essay in Political Anthropology*. New York: Random House.

Friedman, Milton. 1962. *Capitalism and Freedom*. Chicago: University of Chicago Press.

Fuguitt, G. V., and J. J. Zuiches. 1973. "Residential Preferences and Population Distribution: Results of a National Survey." Paper presented to Rural Sociological Society, College Park, Maryland.

Fuller, J. L., and W. R. Thompson. 1960. *Behavior Genetics*. New York: John Wiley.

Furstenberg, Frank F., Jr., and Graham B. Spanier. 1984. *Recycling the Family: Remarriage after Divorce*. Beverly Hills, Calif.: Sage.

Galle, O., and W. Gove. 1978. "Overcrowding, Isolation and Human Behavior: Exploring the Extremes in Population Distribution." In *Social Demography*, edited by Karl Taueber and James Sweet. New York: Academic Press.

Gallup, George H. 1972. *The Gallup Poll: Public Opinion 1935–1971*, 3 vols. New York: Random House.

Gallup, George H. 1978. *The Gallup Poll: Public Opinion 1972–1977*, 2 vols. Wilmington: Scholarly Resources.

Gallup, George H. 1985. *The Gallup Poll: Public Opinion 1972–1984*. New York: Random House.

The Gallup Poll. 1967–1984. *The Gallup Report* (formerly *The Gallup Opinion Index*), published monthly.

Galtung, J. 1971. "A Structural Theory of Imperialism." *Journal of Peace Research* 8:81–117.

Gannett, Henry. 1895. *The Building of a Nation*. New York: Henry T. Thomas.

Gans, Herbert J. 1962. *The Urban Villagers*. New York: Free Press.

Gardiner, R. Allen, and Beatrice T. Gardiner. 1969. "Teaching Sign Language to a Chimpanzee." *Science* 165:664–672.

Geerken, Michael R., and Walter R. Gove. 1977. "Deterrence Overload, and Incapacitation: An Empirical Evaluation." *Social Forces* 56:424–447.

Genovese, E. D. 1974. *Roll, Jordan Roll!* New York: Pantheon.

Gerlach, Luther P., and Virginia H. Hine. 1970. *People, Power, Change: Movements of Social Transformation.* Indianapolis: Bobbs-Merrill.

Gerth, Hans. 1940. "The Nazi Party: Its Leadership and Composition." *American Journal of Sociology* 4:517–541.

Gibbons, Don C., and Gerald F. Blake. 1976. "Evaluating the Impact of Juvenile Diversion Programs." *Crime and Delinquency* 22:411–420.

Gibbs, Jack P. 1975. *Crime, Punishment, and Deterrence.* New York: Elsevier.

Gibbs, Jack P. 1986. "Deterrence Theory and Research." In *The Law as a Behavioral Instrument,* edited by Gary B. Melton. Lincoln: University of Nebraska Press.

Giddens, Anthony. 1975. *The Class Structure of Advanced Societies.* New York: Harper & Row.

Gilfillan, S. C. 1963. *The Sociology of Invention.* Cambridge: M.I.T. Press.

Girouard, Mark. 1985. *Cities and People.* New Haven, Conn.: Yale University Press.

Glazer, Nathan. 1971. "Blacks and Ethnic Groups: The Difference, and the Political Difference It Makes." *Social Problems* 18:444–461.

Glazer, Nathan, and Daniel P. Moynihan. 1963. *Beyond the Melting Pot.* Cambridge: M.I.T. Press.

Glazer, Nathan, and Daniel P. Moynihan. 1970. *Beyond the Melting Pot,* 2nd ed. Cambridge: M.I.T. Press.

Glenn, Norval D. 1987. "The Trend in 'No Religion' Respondents to U.S. National Surveys, Late 1950s to Early 1980s." *Public Opinion Quarterly* 51:293–314.

Glock, Charles Y., and Rodney Stark. 1966. *Christian Beliefs and Anti-Semitism.* New York: Harper & Row.

Goffman, Erving. 1959. *The Presentation of Self in Everyday Life.* New York: Doubleday.

Goffman, Erving. 1961. *Asylums: Essays on the Social Situation of Mental Patients and Other Inmates.* Chicago: Aldine.

Goffman, Erving. 1963. *Behavior in Public Places.* New York: Free Press.

Goffman, Erving. 1971. *Relations in Public.* New York: Basic Books.

Goldstein, Sidney. 1971. "American Jewry, 1970: A Demographic Profile." In *American Jewish Yearbook.* New York: American Jewish Committee.

Goodall, Jane. 1971. *In the Shadow of Man.* Boston: Houghton Mifflin.

Goring, Charles. 1913. *The English Convict.* London: His Majesty's Stationery Office.

Gough, E. Kathleen. 1974. "Nayar: Central Kerala." In *Matrilineal Kinship,* edited by David Schneider and E. Kathleen Gough. Berkeley: University of California Press.

Gouldner, Alvin W. 1959. "Organizational Analysis." In *Sociology Today,* edited by Robert K. Merton, Leonard Broom, and Leonard S. Cottrell, Jr., pp. 400–410. New York: Basic Books.

Gove, Walter R., ed. 1975. *The Labeling of Deviance.* New York: John Wiley.

Gove, Walter R. 1985. "The Effect of Age and Gender on Deviant Behavior: A Biopsychosocial Perspective." In *Gender and the Life Course,* edited by Alice S. Rossi. New York: Aldine.

Gove, Walter R., Michael Hughes, and Omer R. Galle. 1979. "Overcrowding in the Home." *American Sociological Review* 44:59–80.

Granovetter, Mark S. 1973. "The Strength of Weak Ties." *American Journal of Sociology* 78:1360–1380.

Grant, Madison. 1916. *The Passing of the Great Race.* New York: Charles Scribner's.

Gray, Diana. 1973. "Turning Out: A Study of Teenage Prostitution." *Urban Life and Culture* 1:401–425.

Greeley, Andrew M. 1974. *Ethnicity in the United States.* New York: John Wiley.

Green, Dan S., and Edwin D. Driver, eds. 1978. *W. E. B. Du Bois on Sociology and the Black Community.* Chicago: University of Chicago Press.

Green, Richard. 1974. *Sexual Identity Conflict in Children and Adults.* New York: Basic Books.

Gualtieri, Francesco M. 1929. *We Italians: A Study on Italian Immigration in Canada.* Toronto: Italian World War Veterans' Association.

Guerry, A. M. 1833. *Essai sur la Statistique Morale de la France.* Paris: Royal Academy of Science.

Guest, Avery M., and Stewart Tolnay. Forthcoming. "Social Variations in School Attendance."

Guest, Avery M., and James A. Weed. 1976. "Ethnic Residential Segregation: Patterns of Change." *American Journal of Sociology* 81:1088–1111.

Guttentag, Marcia, and Paul F. Secord. 1983. *Too Many Women? The Sex Ratio Question.* Beverly Hills, Calif.: Sage.

Habermas, Jurgen. 1975. *The Legitimation Crisis.* Boston: Beacon Press.

Hacker, Andrew. 1983. *A Statistical Portrait of the American People.* New York: Viking Press.

Hadden, Jeffrey K., and Theodore E. Long, eds. 1983. *Religion and Religiosity in America.* New York: Crossroad.

Halberstam, David. 1981. *The Breaks of the Game.* New York: Ballantine.

Hale, Oron James. 1955. "Adolph Hitler, Taxpayer." *American Historical Review,* July, p. 837.

Hall, Peter. 1966. *The World Cities.* New York: McGraw-Hill.

Hallam, Elizabeth M. 1986. *Domesday Book Through Nine Centuries.* London: Her Majesty's Stationery Office.

Halliday, Fred. 1979. *Iran: Dictatorship and Development.* London: Penguin Books.

Handlin, Oscar. 1957. *Race and Nationality in American Life.* Garden City, N.Y.: Anchor Press/Doubleday.

Hardin, Garrett, ed. 1964. *Population, Evolution and Birth Control.* San Francisco: Freeman.

Hare, E. H. 1956. "Mental Conditions and Social Conditions in Bristol." *Journal of Mental Science* 102:349–357.

Harlow, Harry F., and Margaret K. Harlow. 1965. "The Affectional Systems." In *Behavior in Non-Human Primates: Modern Research Trends*, vol. 2, edited by Allan Schrier, Harry Barlow, and Fred Stollnitz, pp. 287–333. New York: Academic Press.

Harris, Louis. 1971. "Political Labels Depend on Who Applies Them." *St. Petersburg Times*, January 18.

Harris, Marvin. 1979. *Cultural Materialism: The Struggle for a Science of Culture.* New York: Random House.

Hatt, Paul K., and Cecil C. North. 1947. "Jobs and Occupations: A Popular Evaluation." *Opinion News* 9:1–13.

Hay, David A. 1985. *Essentials of Behaviour Genetics.* Melbourne: Blackwell Scientific Publications.

Hayes, K. J., and C. Hayes. 1951. "The Intellectual Development of a Home-Raised Chimpanzee." *Proceedings of the American Philosophical Society* 95:105–109.

Heaton, Tim B. 1986. "Sociodemographic Characteristics of Religious Groups in Canada." *Sociological Analysis* 47:54–65.

Hechter, Michael. 1974. *Internal Colonialism: The Celtic Fringe in British National Development.* Berkeley: University of California Press.

Hechter, Michael. 1978. "Group Formation and the Cultural Division of Labor." *American Journal of Sociology* 84:293–318.

Hechter, Michael, ed. 1983. *Microfoundations of Macrosociology.* Philadelphia: Temple University Press.

Heer, David M. 1980. "Intermarriage." In *Harvard Encyclopedia of American Ethnic Groups.* Cambridge: Belknap Press.

Heider, Fritz. 1946. "Attitudes and Cognitive Organization." *Journal of Psychology* 21:107–112.

Heilbroner, Robert L. 1961. *The Worldly Philosophers.* New York: Simon & Schuster.

Hennig, Margaret, and Anne Jardim. 1977. *The Managerial Woman.* Garden City, N.Y.: Anchor Press/Doubleday.

Hexham, Irvin, Raymond F. Currie, and Joan B. Townsend. 1985. "New Religious Movements." In *The Canadian Encyclopedia.* Edmonton: Hurtig.

Heyneman, Stephen P., and William A. Loxley. 1983. "The Effect of a Primary-School Quality on Academic Achievement Across Twenty-Nine High-and-Low-Income Countries." *American Journal of Sociology* 88:1162–1194.

Heyns, Barbara. 1978. *Summer Learning and the Effects of Schooling.* New York: Academic Press.

Higgins, P. C., and G. L. Albrecht. 1977. "Hellfire and Delinquency Revisited." *Social Forces* 55:952–958.

Hill, Charles T., Zick Rubin, and Letitia Anne Peplau. 1976. "Breakups Before Marriage: The End of 103 Affairs." *Journal of Social Issues* 32:147–168.

Hiller, Harry W. 1978. "Continentalism and the Third Force in Religion." *Canadian Journal of Sociology* 3:183–207.

Hindelang, Michael, Travis Hirschi, and Joseph G. Weis. 1981. *Measuring Delinquency.* Beverly Hills, Calif.: Sage.

Hirschi, Travis. 1961. *Causes of Delinquency.* Berkeley: University of California Press.

Hirschi, Travis, and Michael Gottfredson, eds. 1980. *Understanding Crime: Current Theory and Research.* Beverly Hills, Calif.: Sage.

Hirschi, Travis, and Michael Gottfredson. 1983. "Age and the Explanation of Crime." *American Journal of Sociology* 89:551–575.

Hirschi, Travis, and Michael Gottfredson. 1987a. "Causes of White-Collar Crime." *Criminology* 25:949–974.

Hirschi, Travis, and Michael Gottfredson, eds. 1987b. *Positive Criminology.* Beverly Hills, Calif.: Sage.

Hirschi, Travis, and Michael J. Hindelang. 1977. "Intelligence and Delinquency: A Revisionist Review." *American Sociological Review* 42:571–587.

Hirschi, Travis, and Rodney Stark. 1969. "Hellfire and Delinquency." *Social Problems* 17:202–213.

Hirschman, Charles, and Morrison G. Wong. 1984. "Socioeconomic Gains of Asian Americans, Blacks, and Hispanics: 1960–1976." *American Journal of Sociology* 90:584–607.

Hirschman, Charles, and Morrison G. Wong. 1986. "The Extraordinary Educational Attainment of Asian-Americans: A Search for Historical Evidence and Explanations." *Social Forces* 65:1–27.

Ho, Ping-Ti. 1959. *Studies on the Population of China, 1368–1953.* Cambridge: Harvard University Press.

Hobbes, Thomas. 1651. *Leviathan.* Reprint 1956. Chicago: Henry Regnery.

Hodge, Robert W., P. M. Siegal, and Peter Rossi. 1964. "Occupational Prestige in the United States, 1925–1963." *American Journal of Sociology* 70:286–302.

Hodge, Robert W., Donald J. Treiman, and Peter H. Rossi. 1966. "A Comparative Study of Occupational Prestige." In *Class, Status and Power*, 2nd ed., edited by Reinhard Bendix and Seymour Martin Lipset. New York: Free Press.

Hollander, E. P. 1985. "Leadership and Power." In *The Handbook of Social Psychology*, edited by Gardner Lindzey and Elliott Aronson. 3rd ed. New York: Random House.

Hollingshead, August B., and Frederic C. Redlich. 1958. *Social Class and Mental Illness.* New York: Wiley.

Homans, George C. 1964. "Bringing Men Back In." *American Sociological Review* 29:809–818.

Homans, George C. 1967. *The Nature of Social Science.* New York: Harcourt, Brace and World.

Homans, George C. 1974. *Social Behavior: Its Elementary Forms.* New York: Harcourt Brace Jovanovich.

Hopkins, Jack. 1983. "Judge's Order Depriving Parents of Son Is Upheld." *Seattle Post-Intelligencer.* June 7. P. 1.

Hoult, Thomas Ford. 1969. *Dictionary of Modern Sociology.* Totowa, N.J.: Littlefield, Adams.

Hout, Michael. 1982. "The Association Between Husbands' and Wives' Occupations in Two-Earner Families." *American Journal of Sociology* 88:397–409.

Howard, John R. 1974. *The Cutting Edge—Social Movements and Social Change in America.* Philadelphia: J. B. Lippincott.

Howard, Michael. 1962. *The Franco-Prussian War.* New York: Macmillan.

Howe, Irving. 1976. *World of Our Fathers.* New York: Harcourt Brace Jovanovich.

Hunt, Morton. 1974. *Sexual Behavior in the 1970s.* Chicago: Playboy Press.

Hunter, Alfred A., and Margaret A. Denton. 1984. "Do Female Candidates 'Lose Votes'?: The Experience of Female Candidates in the 1979 and 1980 Canadian General Elections." *Canadian Review of Sociology and Anthropology* 21:395–406.

Huston, A. C. 1983. "Sex-typing." In *Handbook of Child Psychology,* edited by Paul H. Mussen. 4th ed. New York: Wiley.

Illich, Ivan. 1970. *Deschooling Society.* New York: Harper & Row.

Inkeles, Alex, and Peter H. Rossi. 1956. "National Comparisons of Occupational Prestige." *American Journal of Sociology* 61:329–339.

Irwin, John. 1970. *The Felon.* Englewood Cliffs, N.J.: Prentice-Hall.

Isajiw, Wsevolod W. 1977. *Identities: The Impact of Ethnicity on Canadian Society.* Toronto: Peter Martin.

Isajiw, Wsevolod W. 1980. "Definitions of Ethnicity." In *Ethnicity and Ethnic Relations in Canada,* edited by Jay E. Goldstein and Rita M. Bienvenue. Toronto: Butterworths.

Ismael, J. S., and T. Y. Ismael. 1980. "Social Change in Islamic Society: The Political Thought of Ayatollah Khomeini." *Social Problems* 27:601–619.

Jackson, Elton F. 1962. "Status Inconsistency and Symptoms of Stress." *American Sociological Review* 27:469–480.

Jacob, Joseph. 1912. *Tulips.* New York: Stokes.

Jacobs, Jerry A., and Frank F. Furstenberg, Jr. 1986. "Changing Places: Conjugal Careers and Women's Marital Mobility." *Social Forces* 64:714–732.

Jencks, Christopher, et al. 1972. *Inequality: A Reassessment of the Effects of Family and Schooling in America.* New York: Basic Books.

Jensen, Arthur R. 1969. "How Much Can We Boost IQ and Scholastic Achievement?" *Harvard Educational Review* 39:1–123.

Jensen, Gary F. 1969. "Crime Doesn't Pay: Correlates of Shared Misunderstanding." *Social Problems* 17:189–201.

Jensen, Gary F. 1972. "Parents, Peers and Delinquency Action: A Test of the Differential Association Perspective." *American Journal of Sociology* 78:562–575.

Jensen, Gary F., Maynard L. Erickson, and Jack Gibbs. 1978. "Perceived Risk of Punishment and Self-reported Delinquency." *Social Forces* 57:57–58.

Jewkes, John, David Sawers, and Richard Stillerman. 1969. *The Sources of Invention.* New York: W. W. Norton.

Johnson, Benton. 1963. "On Church and Sect." *American Sociological Review* 28:539–549.

Johnson, Paul. 1977. *Enemies of Society.* New York: Atheneum.

Johnson, Paul. 1979. *A History of Christianity.* New York: Atheneum.

Jones, Landon Y. 1980. *Great Expectations: America and the Baby Boom Generation.* New York: Coward, McCann & Geohegan.

Juhasz, Anne McCreary. 1985. "Measuring Self-Esteem in Early Adolescents." *Adolescence* 20:877–887.

Kage, Joseph. 1981. "Able and Willing to Work: Jewish Immigration and Occupational Patterns in Canada." In *The Canadian Jewish Mosaic,* edited by M. Weinfeld, W. Shaffir, and I. Cotler. Toronto: John Wiley.

Kaiser, Robert G. 1976. *Russia: The People and the Power.* New York: Atheneum.

Kanter, Rosabeth. 1972. *Commitment and Community.* Cambridge: Harvard University Press.

Kantrowitz, Nathan. 1973. *Ethnic and Racial Segregation in the New York Metropolis.* New York: Praeger.

Kelley, Dean. 1972. *Why Conservative Churches Are Growing.* New York: Harper & Row.

Kellogg, W. N., and L. A. Kellogg. 1933. *The Ape and the Child.* New York: McGraw-Hill.

Kennedy, Robert E., Jr. 1972. "The Social Status of the Sexes and their Relative Mortality in Ireland." In *Readings in Population,* edited by William Peterson. New York: Macmillan.

Kephart, William. 1957. *Racial Factors and Urban Law Enforcement.* Philadelphia: University of Pennsylvania Press.

Kihumura, Akemi, and Harry H. L. Kitano. 1973. "Interracial Marriage. A Picture of Japanese Americans." *Journal of Social Issues* 29:69–73.

Kitano, Harry H. L. 1969. *Japanese Americans.* Englewood Cliffs, N.J.: Prentice-Hall.

Klein, Malcolm W. 1976. "Issues and Realities in Police Diversion Programs." *Crime and Delinquency* 22:421–427.

Kluckhohn, Clyde. 1962. "Values and Value-Orientations in the Theory of Action." In *Toward a General Theory of Action,* edited by Talcott Parsons and Edward Shils. New York: Harper Torchbooks.

Kluckhohn, Clyde, and Henry A. Murray. 1956. *Personality: In Nature, Society, and Culture.* New York: Knopf.

Kobbervig, Wayne, James Inverarity, and Pat Lauderdale. 1982. "Deterrence and the Death Penalty: A Comment on Phillips." *American Journal of Sociology* 88:161–164.

Kohlberg, Lawrence, and Carol Gilligan. 1971. "The Adolescent as a Philosopher: The Discovery of the Self in a Postconventional World." *Daedalus* 100:1051–1086.

Kohn, M. L. 1959. "Social Class and Parental Values." *American Journal of Sociology* 64:337–351.

Kohn, M. L., and Carmi Schooler. 1969. "Class, Occupation, and Orientation." *American Sociological Review* 34:659–678.

Kohn, Melvin L., and Carmi Schooler. 1982. "Job Conditions and Personality: A Longitudinal Assessment of Their Reciprocal Effects." *American Journal of Sociology* 87:1257–1286.

Kohn, Melvin L., and Carmi Schooler. 1983. *Work and Personality.* Norwood, N.J.: Ablex.

Kornhauser, Ruth. 1978. *Social Sources of Delinquency: An Appraisal of Analytic Models.* Chicago: University of Chicago Press.

Kornhauser, William. 1959. *The Politics of Mass Society.* New York: Free Press.

Kowalewski, David. 1980. "Religious Belief in the Brezhnev Era: Renaissance, Resistance, and Realpolitik." *Journal for the Scientific Study of Religion* 19:280–292.

Kramer, Judith. 1970. *The American Minority Community.* New York: Thomas Y. Crowell.

Kroeber, Alfred L. 1925. *Handbook of American Indians of California.* Bulletin 78: Smithsonian Institution, Bureau of American Ethnology.

Kuhn, Manford, and Thomas S. McPartland. 1954. "An Empirical Investigation of Self-Attitudes." *American Sociological Review* 19:68–76.

Lacey, W. K. 1968. *The Family in Classical Greece.* London: Thames and Hudson.

Landis, Paul H. 1965. *Making the Most of Marriage.* New York: Appleton-Century-Crofts.

Langer, Judith. 1985. "The New Mature Mothers." *American Demographics* 7:29–31; 50.

Langer, William L. 1972. "Checks on Population Growth, 1750–1850." *Scientific American* 226:92–99.

Laslett, Peter. 1965. *The World We Have Lost.* London: Keagan Paul.

Laslett, Peter. 1977. *Family Life and Illicit Love in Earlier Generations.* London: Cambridge University Press.

Lavely, William R. 1984. "The Rural Chinese Fertility Transition: A Report from Shifang Xian, Sichuan." *Population Studies* 38:365–384.

Lazarsfeld, Paul F., Bernard Berelson, and Hazel Gaudet. 1948. *The People's Choice.* New York: Columbia University Press.

Leacock, Eleanor. 1978. "Women's Status in Egalitarian Society: Implications for Social Evolution." *Current Anthropology* 19:247–275.

Le Bras, Herve, and Emmanuel Todd. 1981. *L'invention de la France.* Paris: Georges Liebert.

Lemert, Edwin M. 1951. *Social Pathology.* New York: McGraw-Hill.

Lemert, Edwin M. 1967. *Human Deviance, Social Problems, and Social Control.* Englewood Cliffs, N.J.: Prentice-Hall.

Lenski, Gerhard. 1954. "Status Crystallization: A Nonvertical Dimension of Social Status." *American Sociological Review* 19:405–413.

Lenski, Gerhard. 1956. "Social Participation and Status Crystallization." *American Sociological Review* 21:458–464.

Lenski, Gerhard. 1966. *Power and Privilege.* New York: McGraw-Hill.

Lenski, Gerhard. 1976. "History and Social Change." *American Journal of Sociology* 82:548–564.

Levine, Gene N., and Darrel M. Montero. 1973. "Socioeconomic Mobility Among Three Generations of Japanese Americans." *Journal of Social Issues* 29:40–45.

Lévi-Strauss, Claude. 1956. "The Family." In *Man, Culture and Society,* edited by Harry L. Shapiro. New York: Oxford University Press.

Lewontin, R. C. 1973. "Race and Intelligence." In *The Fallacy of IQ,* edited by C. Senna. New York: Random House.

Lieberson, Stanley. 1961. "The Impact of Residential Segregation on Ethnic Assimilation." *Social Forces* 40:52–57.

Lieberson, Stanley. 1963. *Ethnic Patterns in American Cities.* New York: Free Press.

Lieberson, Stanley. 1973. "Generational Differences Among Blacks in the North." *American Journal of Sociology* 79:550–565.

Lieberson, Stanley. 1980. *A Piece of the Pie: Blacks and White Immigrants Since 1880.* Berkeley: University of California Press.

Light, Ivan H. 1972. *Ethnic Enterprise in America: Business and Welfare Among Chinese, Japanese and Blacks.* Berkeley: University of California Press.

Lilly, J. C. 1967. *The Mind of the Dolphin: A Nonhuman Intelligence.* New York: Doubleday.

Linden, Rick, and Raymond F. Currie. 1977. "Religion and Drug Use: A Test of Social Control Theory." *Canadian Journal of Criminology and Corrections* 19:346–355.

Linden, Rick, and Cathy Fillmore. 1981. "A Comparative Study of Delinquency Involvement." *Canadian Review of Sociology and Anthropology* 18:343–359.

Linton, Ralph. 1936. *The Study of Man: An Introduction.* Reprint 1964. Englewood Cliffs, N.J.: Prentice-Hall.

Lipset, Seymour Martin. 1963. "Three Decades of the Radical Right: Coughlinites, McCarthyites, and Birchers." In *The Radical Right,* edited by Daniel Bell. Garden City, N.Y.: Doubleday.

Lipset, Seymour Martin. 1976. "Equality and Inequality." In *Contemporary Social Problems,* 4th ed., edited by Robert K. Merton and Robert Nisbet. New York: Harcourt Brace Jovanovich.

Lipset, Seymour Martin, and Reinhard Bendix. 1959. *Social Mobility in Industrial Society.* Berkeley: University of California Press.

Liska, Allen E. 1981. *Perspectives on Deviance.* Englewood Cliffs, N.J.: Prentice-Hall.

Lofland, John. 1966. *Doomsday Cult.* Englewood Cliffs, N.J.: Prentice-Hall.

Lofland, John, and Rodney Stark. 1965. "Becoming a World-Saver: A Theory of Conversion to a Deviant Perspective." *American Sociology Review* 30:862–875.

Lofland, Lyn H. 1973. *A World of Strangers.* New York: Basic Books.

Lombroso-Ferrero, Gina. 1911. *Criminal Man.* Montclair, N.J.: Patterson-Smith.

Looker, E. Dianne, and Peter C. Pineo. 1983. "Some Psychological Variables and Their Relevance to the Status Attainment of Teenagers." *American Journal of Sociology* 88:1195–1219.

Lorenz, Konrad. 1966. *On Aggression.* New York: Harcourt Brace Jovanovich.

McClean, Charles. 1978. *The Wolf Children.* New York: Hill & Wang.

McClosky, Herbert. 1964. "Consensus and Ideology in American Politics." *American Political Science Review* 58:361–382.

Maccoby, Eleanor, and Carol Jacklin. 1974. *The Psychology of Sex Differences.* Palo Alto, Calif.: Stanford University Press.

McCord, William, and Joan McCord. 1959. *Origins of Crime: A New Evaluation of the Cambridge-Somerville Youth Study.* New York: Columbia University Press.

McDougall, W. 1908. *An Introduction to Social Psychology.* Boston: Luce.

McDougall, William. 1932. *The Energies of Men: A Study of the Fundamentals of Dynamic Psychology.* London: Methuen.

McEachern, A. W. 1968. "The Juvenile Probation System." *American Behavioral Scientist* 11:1–10.

McFarland, H. Neill. 1967. *The Rush Hour of the Gods: A Study of New Religious Movements in Japan.* New York: Macmillan.

McGahey, Richard M. 1980. "Dr. Ehrlich's Magic Bullet: Econometric Theory, Econometrics, and the Death Penalty." *Crime and Delinquency* 485–502.

McGovern, Thomas. 1981. "The Economics of Extinction in Norse Greenland." In *Climate and History: Studies in Past Climates and Their Impact on Man,* edited by T. M. L. Wigley, M. J. Ingram, and G. Farmer. Cambridge, England: Cambridge University Press.

Mackay, Charles. 1852. *Extraordinary Popular Delusions and the Madness of Crowds.* New York: Farrar, Straus & Giroux.

MacKay, J. Ross. 1958. "The Interactance Hypothesis and Boundaries in Canada: A Preliminary Study." *Canadian Geographer* 2(11):1–8.

McKenzie, R. F. 1933. *The Metropolitan Community.* New York: McGraw-Hill.

MacKerras, Malcolm. 1977. "Do Women Candidates Lose Votes?" *The Australian Quarterly* 40:6–10.

McKinney, William, and Wade Clark Roof. 1982. "A Social Profile of American Religious Groups." In *Yearbook of American and Canadian Churches: 1982,* edited by Constant H. Jacquet, Jr. Nashville, Tenn.: Abingdon Press.

McLanahan, Sara. 1985. "Family Structure and the Reproduction of Poverty." *American Journal of Sociology* 90:873–883.

McNeill, William H. 1976. *Plagues and Peoples.* New York: Basic Books.

McNeill, William. 1982. *The Pursuit of Power.* Chicago: University of Chicago Press.

McWilliams, Carey. 1945. *Prejudice: Japanese-Americans.* Boston: Little, Brown.

Mallory, Walter H. 1926. *China: Land of Famine.* New York: American Geographical Society.

Malson, Lucien. 1972. *Wolf Children and the Problem of Human Nature.* New York: Monthly Review Press.

Mann, William E. 1955. *Sect, Cult and Church in Alberta.* Toronto: University of Toronto Press.

Maris, Ronald W. 1969. *Social Forces in Urban Suicide.* Homewood, Ill.: Dorsey Press.

Martin, David. 1981. "Disorientations to Mainstream Religion: The Context of Reorientations in New Religious Movements." In *The Social Impact of New Religious Movements,* edited by Bryan Wilson. New York: Rose of Sharon Press.

Marx, Gary T. 1967. *Protest and Prejudice.* New York: Harper & Row.

Marx, Karl, and Friedrich Engels. 1848. *Communist Manifesto.* Reprint 1967. New York: Pantheon.

Matras, Judah. 1973. *Populations and Societies.* Englewood Cliffs, N.J.: Prentice-Hall.

Mead, George Herbert. 1925. "The Genesis of the Self and Social Control." *International Journal of Ethics* 35:251–273.

Mead, George Herbert. 1934. *Mind, Self, and Society: From the Standpoint of a Social Behaviorist,* edited by Charles W. Morris. Chicago: University of Chicago Press.

Mead, Margaret. 1928. *Coming of Age in Samoa.* New York: William Morrow.

Mead, Margaret. 1935. *Sex and Temperament in Three Primitive Societies.* New York: Dell.

Meadows, Donella, et al. 1972. *The Limits to Growth: A Report for the Club of Rome's Projection on the Predicament of Mankind.* New York: Universe Books.

Mednick, S. A., et al. 1984. "Genetic Influences in Criminal Convictions: Evidence From an Adoption Cohort." *Science* 224:891–894.

Meeks, Wayne A. 1983. *The First Urban Christians: The Social World of the Apostle Paul.* New Haven: Yale University Press.

Megargee, Edwin I. 1966. "Undercontrolled and Overcontrolled Personality Types in Extreme Antisocial Aggression." *Psychological Monographs* 80:611–617.

Melton, J. Gordon. 1978. *Encyclopedia of American Religions.* Wilmington, N.C.: McGrath.

Meltzoff, Andrew N., and M. Keith Moore. 1977. "Facial Imitation in Infants." *Science,* Oct. 7.

Meltzoff, Andrew N., and M. Keith Moore. 1983a. "Newborn Infants Imitate Adult Facial Gestures." *Child Development* 54:702–709.

Meltzoff, Andrew N., and M. Keith Moore. 1983b. "The Origins of Imitation in Infancy: Paradigm, Phenomena, and Theories." *Advances in Infancy Research* 2:266–301.

Mendelssohn, Kurt. 1976. *The Secret of Western Domination.* New York: Praeger.

Merton, Robert K. 1938. "Social Structure and Anomie." *American Sociological Review* 3:672–682.

Messick, David M., et al. 1983. "Individual Adaptations and Structural Change as Solutions to Social Dilemmas." *Journal of Personality and Social Psychology* 44:294–309.

Meyer, John W. 1977. "The Effects of Education as an Institution." *American Journal of Sociology* 83:55–77.

Miles, Betty. 1975. *Channeling Children: Sex Stereotyping in Prime-Time TV.* Princeton, N.J.: Women on Words and Images.

Milgram, Stanley. 1967. "The Small World Problem." *Psychology Today* 1:1–6.

Miller, G. Tyler. 1982. *Living in the Environment,* 3rd ed. Belmont, Calif.: Wadsworth.

Miller, Walter B. 1962. "The Impact of a 'Total Community' Delinquency Control Project." *Social Problems* 10:168–191.

Millis, H. A. 1915. *The Japanese Problem in the United States.* New York: Macmillan.

Mills, C. Wright. 1956. *The Power Elite.* New York: Oxford University Press.

Minor, W. William, and Joseph Harry. 1982. "Deterrent and Experiential Effects in Perceptual Deterrence Research: A Replication and Extension." *Journal of Research in Crime and Delinquency* 19:190–203.

Mitterauer, Michael, and Reinhard Sieder. 1982. *The European Family: Patriarchy to Partnership from the Middle Ages to the Present.* Oxford: Basil Blackwell.

Miyamoto, Frank. 1939. "Social Solidarity among the Japanese in Seattle." *University of Washington Publications in the Social Sciences* 2:57–130.

Miyamoto, Frank S., and Sanford M. Dornbusch. 1956. "A Test of Interaction Hypothesis of Self-conception." *American Journal of Sociology* 61:399–403.

Mizruchi, Ephraim H. 1964. *Success and Opportunity: A Study of Anomie.* Glencoe, Ill.: Free Press.

Moerk, E. L. 1975. "Verbal Interactions Between Children and Their Mothers During the Preschool Years." *Developmental Psychology* 11:788–794.

Money, John, and Anke A. Ehrhardt. 1972. *Man and Woman, Boy and Girl.* Baltimore, Md.: Johns Hopkins University Press.

Montgomery, Field-Marshall Viscount. 1968. *A History of Warfare.* New York: World.

Mooney, James. 1896. *The Ghost Dance Religion and the Sioux Outbreak of 1890.* Fourth Annual Report of the Bureau of Ethnology to the Secretary of the Smithsonian Institution. Washington, D.C.: U.S. Government Printing Office.

Morgan, Elaine. 1972. *The Descent of Woman.* New York: Stein and Day.

Morioka, Kiyomi. 1975. *Religion in Changing Japanese Society.* Tokyo: University of Tokyo Press.

Morselli, Henry. 1882. *Suicide: An Essay on Comparative Moral Statistics.* New York: Appleton.

Mosca, Gaetano. 1896. *The Ruling Class.* Reprint 1939. New York: McGraw-Hill.

Mowat, Farley. 1965. *Westviking.* Boston: Little, Brown.

Murdock, George P. 1949. *Social Structure.* New York: Macmillan.

Murdock, George P. 1967a. "Ethnographic Atlas: A Summary." *Ethnology* 6:109–236.

Murdock, George P. 1967b. *Ethnographic Atlas.* Pittsburgh: University of Pittsburgh Press.

Murdock, George P., and Douglas R. White. 1969. "Standard Cross-Cultural Sample." *Ethnology* 8:329–369.

Musmanno, Michael A. 1965. *The Story of the Italians in America.* New York: Doubleday.

Myrdal, Gunnar. 1944. *An American Dilemma: The Negro Problem and Modern Democracy.* New York: Harper & Row.

Neidert, Lisa J., and Reynolds Farley. 1985. "Assimilation in the United States: An Analysis of Ethnic and Generational Differences in Achievement." *American Sociological Review* 50:840–850.

Newcomb, Theodore M. 1953. "An Approach to the Study of Communicative Acts." *Psychological Review* 60:393–404.

Niebuhr, H. Richard. 1929. *The Social Sources of Denominationalism.* New York: Henry Holt.

Nisbet, Robert. 1980. *History of the Idea of Progress.* New York: Basic Books.

Nock, David A. 1987. "Cult, Sect, and Church in Canada: A Reexamination of Stark and Bainbridge." *Canadian Review of Sociology and Anthropology* 24:514–525.

Nordhoff, Charles. 1875. *The Communistic Societies of the United States.* Reprint 1966. New York: Dover.

North, Douglass C., and Robert Paul Thomas. 1973. *The Rise of the Western World: A New Economic History.* Cambridge, England: Cambridge University Press.

Noyes, John Humphrey. 1870. *The History of American Socialisms.* Philadelphia: J. B. Lippincott.

Nozick, Robert. 1974. *Anarchy, State and Utopia.* New York: Basic Books.

Nye, F. Ivan. 1963. "The Adjustment of Adolescent Children." In *The Employed Mother in America,* edited by F. Ivan Nye and Lois Wladis Hoffman, pp. 133–141. Chicago: Rand McNally.

Ofshe, Richard. 1967. *A Theory of Behavior under Conditions of Reference Conflict.* Unpublished Ph.D. dissertation, Stanford University.

Ofshe, Richard. 1972. "Reference Conflict and Behavior." In *Sociological Theories in Progress,* vol. 2, edited by Joseph Berger, Morris Zelditch, and Bo Anderson. Boston: Houghton Mifflin.

Ogburn, William F. 1932. *Social Change.* New York: Viking Press.

O'Kelly, Charlotte G., and Larry S. Charney. 1986. *Women and Men in Society,* 2nd ed. Belmont, Calif.: Wadsworth.

Olsen, Mancur. 1965. *The Logic of Collective Action.* Cambridge: Harvard University Press.

Omenn, G. S., E. C. Caspari, and L. Ehrman. 1972. "Epilogue: Behavior Genetics and Educational Policy." In *Genetics, Environment, and Behavior: Implications for Educational Policy,* edited by L. Ehrman, G. S. Omenn, and E. Caspari, pp. 307–310. New York: Academic Press.

Ornstein, Michael D. 1981. "The Occupational Mobility of Men in Ontario." *Review of Canadian Sociology and Anthropology* 18:183–214.

Ossowski, Stanislaw. 1963. *Class Structure in the Social Consciousness.* New York: Free Press.

Paige, Jeffery M. 1974. "Kinship and Polity in Stateless Societies." *American Journal of Sociology* 80:301–320.

Park, Robert E., Ernest W. Burgess, and Roderick McKenzie. 1925. *The City.* Chicago: University of Chicago Press.

Parker, J., and H. G. Grasmick. 1979. "Linking Actual and Perceived Certainty of Punishment: An Exploratory Study of an Untested Proposition in Deterrence Theory." *Criminology* 17:366–379.

Patterson, G. R. 1980. "Children Who Steal." In *Understanding Crime: Current Theory and Research,* edited by Travis Hirschi and Michael Gottfredson. Beverly Hills, Calif.: Sage.

Patterson, Orlando. 1982. *Slavery and Social Death: A Comparative Study.* Cambridge: Harvard University Press.

Peaker, Gilbert F. 1971. *The Plowden Children Four Years Later.* London: National Foundation for Educational Research in England and Wales.

Pearlin, L. I., and M. L. Kohn. 1966. "Social Class, Occupation, and Parental Values: A Cross-national Study." *American Sociological Review* 31:466–479.

Perrow, Charles. 1979. *Complex Organizations*. 2nd ed. Glenview, Ill.: Scott, Foresman.

Peters, Thomas J., and Robert H. Waterman, Jr. 1982. *In Search of Excellence: Lessons from America's Best Run Companies*. New York: Harper & Row.

Petersen, William. 1971. *Japanese Americans: Oppression and Success*. New York: Random House.

Petersen, William. 1975. *Population*. New York: Macmillan.

Petersen, William. 1978. "Chinese Americans and Japanese Americans." In *Essays and Data on American Ethnic Groups*, edited by Thomas Sowell. Washington, D.C.: The Urban Institute.

Pfeiffer, John E. 1977. *The Emergence of Society*. New York: McGraw-Hill.

Phelps, Edmund S., ed. 1975. *Altruism, Morality, and Economic Theory*. New York: Russell Sage Foundation.

Phillips, David P. 1980. "The Deterrent Effect of Capital Punishment: New Evidence on an Old Controversy." *American Journal of Sociology* 86:139–148.

Piaget, Jean. 1926. *The Language and Thought of the Child*. New York: Harcourt.

Piaget, Jean. 1970. "Piaget's Theory." In *Carmichael's Manual of Child Psychology*, 3rd ed., edited by Paul Mussen, pp. 703–732. New York: John Wiley.

Piaget, Jean, and Barbel Inhelder. 1969. *The Psychology of the Child*. New York: Basic Books.

Piliavin, Irving, and Scott Briar. 1964. "Police Encounters with Juveniles." *American Journal of Sociology* 70:206–214.

Pineo, Peter C. 1961. "Disenchantment in the Later Years of Marriage." *Marriage and Family Living* 23:4.

Pineo, Peter C. 1976. "Social Mobility in Canada: The Current Picture." *Sociological Focus* 9:1091–1123.

Pineo, Peter C. 1977. "The Social Standing of Ethnic and Racial Groupings." *Canadian Review of Sociology and Anthropology* 14:147–157.

Pineo, Peter C. 1981. "Prestige and Mobility: The Two National Surveys." *Canadian Review of Sociology and Anthropology* 18:615–626.

Pineo, Peter C., and John Porter. 1967. "Occupational Prestige in Canada." *Canadian Review of Sociology and Anthropology* 4:24–40.

Pirenne, Henri. 1925. *Medieval Cities*. Princeton, N.J.: Princeton University Press.

Pomeroy, Sarah B. 1975. *Goddesses, Whores, Wives, Slaves: Women in Classical Antiquity*. New York: Schocken Books.

Pope, Whitney. 1976. *Durkheim's Suicide*. Chicago: University of Chicago Press.

Popper, Karl R. 1959. *The Logic of Scientific Discovery*. New York: Basic Books.

Porter, John. 1965. *The Vertical Mosaic: An Analysis of Social Class and Power in Canada*. Toronto: University of Toronto Press.

Porter, John. 1975. "Ethnic Pluralism in Canadian Perspective." In *Ethnicity: Theory and Experience*, edited by Nathan Glazer and Daniel P. Moynihan. Cambridge: Harvard University Press.

Portes, Alejandro. 1987. "The Social Origins of the Cuban Enclave Economy of Miami." *Sociological Perspectives* 30:340–372.

Portes, Alejandro. 1981. "Modes of Structural Incorporation and Present Theories of Immigration." In *Global Trends in Migration*, edited by Mary M. Kritz, Charles B. Keely, and Sylvano M. Tomasi. Staten Island, N.Y.: CMS Press.

Portes, Alejandro, and Robert L. Bach. 1985. *Latin Journey: Cuban and Mexican Immigrants in the United States*. Berkeley: University of California Press.

Portes, Alejandro, and Robert D. Manning. 1986. "The Immigrant Enclave: Theory and Empirical Examples." In *Competitive Ethnic Relations*, edited by Susan Olzak and Joane Nagel. New York: Academic Press.

Powell, Brian, and Lala Carr Steelman. 1984. "Variations in State SAT Performance: Meaningful or Misleading?" *Harvard Educational Review* 54:389–412.

Powers, Edwin, and Helen Witmer. 1951. *An Experiment in the Prevention of Delinquency: The Cambridge-Somerville Youth Study*. New York: Columbia University Press.

Preston, Samuel E. 1975. "Estimating the Proportion of American Marriages That End in Divorce." *Sociological Methods and Research* 3:435–460.

Preston, Samuel H. 1984. "Children and the Elderly in the United States." *Scientific American* 251:44–49.

Pullum, Thomas W. 1982. "The Eventual Frequencies of Kin in a Stable Population." *Demography* 19:549–565.

Quinley, Harold E., and Charles Y. Glock. 1979. *Anti-Semitism in America*. New York: Free Press.

Rapp, Rayna, and Ellen Ross. 1983. "The Twenties' Backlash: Compulsory Heterosexuality, the Consumer Family, and the Waning of Feminism," in *Class, Race and Sex: The Dynamics of Control*, edited by Amy Swerdlow and Hanna Messinger. Boston: Hall.

Reiss, Albert J., Jr. 1961. *Occupations and Social Status*. New York: Free Press.

Reiss, Ira L. 1980. *Family Systems in America*. New York: Holt, Rinehart & Winston.

Renshon, Stanley A. 1977. *Handbook of Political Socialization: Theory of Research*. New York: Free Press.

Rhodes, A. L., and A. J. Reiss, Jr. 1970. "The Religious Factor and Delinquent Behavior." *Journal of Research in Crime and Delinquency* 7:83–98.

Richardson, James T., and Mary W. Stewart. 1978. "Conversion Process Models and the Jesus Movement." In *Conversion Careers*, edited by J. Richardson. Beverly Hills, Calif.: Sage.

Richer, Stephen. 1984. "Sexual Inequality and Children's Play." *Review of Canadian Sociology and Anthropology* 21:166–180.

Riesman, David. 1961. *The Lonely Crowd*. New Haven, Conn.: Yale University Press.

Robinson, P., Jerrold G. Rusk, and Kendra B. Head. 1968. *Measure of Political Attitudes.* Ann Arbor, Mich.: Survey Research Center, Institute for Social Research.

Roncek, Dennis W., and Antoinette Lobosco. 1983. "The Effect of High Schools on Crime in Their Neighborhoods." *Social Science Quarterly* 64:598–613.

Ropp, Theodore. 1959. *War in the Modern World.* Durham, N.C.: Duke University Press.

Rosenberg, Charles E. 1975. "Introduction: History and Experience." In *The Family in History,* edited by Charles E. Rosenberg. Philadelphia: University of Pennsylvania Press.

Rosenberg, Morris. 1965. *Society and the Adolescent Self-Image.* Princeton, N.J.: Princeton University Press.

Rosenberg, Stuart E. 1970. *The Jewish Community in Canada.* Toronto: McClelland and Stewart.

Rosengren, Karl Erik, Peter Arvidson, and Dahn Sturesson. 1975. "The Barsebäck 'Panic': A Radio Programme as a Negative Summary Event." *Acta Sociologica* 18:147–162.

Rosenthal, David. 1970. *Genetic Theory and Abnormal Behavior.* New York: McGraw-Hill.

Ross, E. A. 1914. *The Old World in the New.* New York: Century Company.

Ross, Marc Howard. 1983. "Political Decision Making and Conflict: Additional Cross-Cultural Codes and Scales." *Ethnology* 22:169–192.

Rossi, Peter H., R. A. Berk, and K. J. Lenihan. 1980. *Money, Work, and Crime: Experimental Evidence.* New York: Academic Press.

Rossi, Peter H., Richard A. Berk, and Kenneth J. Lenihan. 1982. "Saying It Wrong with Figures: A Comment on Zeisel." *American Journal of Sociology* 88:390–393.

Rosten, Leo. 1968. *The Joys of Yiddish.* New York: McGraw-Hill.

Rothman, Sheila. 1978. *Woman's Proper Place.* New York: Basic Books.

Rubinow, Israel. 1970. "The Economic Condition of Jews in Russia." *Bulletin of the Bureau of Labor,* no. 72. Washington, D.C.: U.S. Government Printing Office.

Russell, J. C. 1958. "Late Ancient and Medieval Population." *Transactions of the American Philosophical Society* 48:1–152.

Sack, Benjamin G. 1965. *History of the Jews in Canada.* Montreal: Harvest House.

Sagarin, Edward. 1975. *Deviants and Deviance.* New York: Praeger.

Sanders, Jimy M., and Victor Nee. 1987. "Limits of Ethnic Solidarity in the Enclave Economy." *American Sociological Review* 52:745–773.

Sanders, Ronald. 1969. *Downtown Jews.* New York: Harper & Row.

Sann, Paul. 1967. *Fads, Follies and Delusions of the American People.* New York: Bonanza.

Sauer, William. 1975. "Morale of the Urban Aged: A Regression Analysis by Race." Unpublished Ph.D. dissertation, University of Minnesota.

Sawyer, P. H. 1982. *Kings and Vikings.* London: Methuen.

Schachter, Stanley. 1951. "Deviation, Rejection, and Communication." *Journal of Abnormal and Social Psychology* 46:190–207.

Scheff, Thomas J. 1966. *Being Mentally Ill: A Sociological Theory.* Chicago: Aldine.

Schmidt, Constance R., and Scott G. Paris. 1984. "The Development of Verbal Communicative Skills in Children." *Advances in Child Development and Behavior* 18:2–47.

Schmookler, Jacob. 1966. *Invention and Economic Growth.* Cambridge: Harvard University Press.

Schoenbaum, David. 1966. *Hitler's Social Revolution.* Garden City, N.Y.: Doubleday.

Schollaert, Paul T., and Donald Hugh Smith. 1987. "Team Racial Composition and Sports Attendance." *The Sociological Quarterly* 28:71–87.

Schuckit, Marc, et al. 1972a. "The Half-Sibling Approach in a Genetic Study of Alcoholism." *Life History Research in Psychopathology* 2:120–127.

Schuckit, Marc, et al. 1972b. "A Study of Alcoholism in Half-Siblings." *American Journal of Psychiatry* 128:1132–1136.

Schuckit, Marc, et al. 1979. *The Genetic Aspects of Psychiatric Syndrome Relating to Antisocial Problems in Youth.* Seattle, Wash.: Center for Law and Justice.

Schultz, L. G. 1960. "The Wife Assaulter." *Journal of Social Therapy* 6:103–111.

Schur, Edwin. 1971. *Labeling Deviant Behavior.* New York: Harper & Row.

Schwartz, Richard, and Jerome H. Skolnick. 1962. "A Study of Legal Stigma." *Social Problems* 10:133–138.

Selznick, Gertrude J., and Stephen Steinberg. 1969. *The Tenacity of Prejudice.* New York: Harper & Row.

Selznick, Philip. 1948. "Foundations of the Theory of Organization." *American Sociological Review* 13:25–35.

Selznick, Philip. 1949. *TVA and the Grass Roots.* Berkeley: University of California Press.

Selznick, Philip. 1957. *Leadership in Administration.* New York: Harper & Row.

Semyonov, Moshe, and Noah Lewin-Epstein. 1986. "Economic Development, Investment Dependence, and the Rise of Services in Less Developed Nations." *Social Forces* 64:582–598.

Sewell, William H. 1964. "Community of Residence and College Plans." *American Sociological Review* 29:24–38.

Sewell, William H., Robert M. Hauser, and Wendy C. Wolf. 1980. "Sex, Schooling and Occupational Status." *American Journal of Sociology* 86:551–583.

Shah, Saleem A., and Loren H. Roth. 1974. "Biological and Psychophysiological Factors in Criminology." In *Handbook of Criminology,* edited by Daniel Glaser. Chicago: Rand McNally.

Shanas, Ethel. 1973. "Family-Kin Networks and Aging in Cross-Cultural Perspective." *Journal of Marriage and the Family* 33:505–511.

Shattuck, Roger. 1980. *The Forbidden Experiment.* New York: Farrar, Straus & Giroux.

Shaw, Clifford R., and Henry D. McKay. 1929. *Delinquency Areas.* Chicago: University of Chicago Press.

Shaw, Clifford R., and Henry D. McKay. 1931. *Report on the Causes of Crime,* vol. 12, no. 13. Washington, D.C.: National Commission on Law Observance and Enforcement.

Shaw, Clifford R., and Henry D. McKay. 1942. *Juvenile Delinquency and Urban Areas*. Chicago: University of Chicago Press.

Sheldon, W. H. 1940. *The Varieties of Human Physique*. New York: Harpers.

Sherif, Muzafer, and Carolyn W. Sherif. 1953. *Groups in Harmony and Tension: An Integration of Studies on Intergroup Relations*. New York: Harper & Row.

Sherman, Lawrence W., and Richard A. Berk. 1984. "The Specific Deterrent Effects of Arrest for Domestic Assault." *American Sociological Review* 49:261–272.

Shirer, William L. 1960. *The Rise and Fall of the Third Reich*. Greenwich, Conn.: Fawcett.

Shirer, William L. 1969. *The Collapse of the Third Republic*. New York: Simon & Schuster.

Shorter, Edward. 1975. *The Making of the Modern Family*. New York: Basic Books.

Sigelman, Lee P. 1977. "Multi-Nation Surveys of Religious Beliefs." *Journal for the Scientific Study of Religion* 16:289–294.

Silberman, Charles E. 1971. *Crisis in the Classroom: The Remaking of American Education*. New York: Vintage.

Sills, David L. 1957. *The Volunteers*. Glencoe, Ill.: Free Press.

Silverman, Robert A., and James J. Teevan, Jr. 1980. *Crime in Canadian Society*, 2nd ed. Toronto: Butterworths.

Simcha-Fagan, Ora, and Joseph E. Schwartz. 1986. "Neighborhood and Delinquency: An Assessment of Contextual Effects." *Criminology* 24:667–699.

Simmel, Georg. 1905. "A Contribution to the Sociology of Religion." *American Journal of Sociology* 11:359–376.

Simmons, James W. 1970. "Interprovincial Interaction Patterns in Canada." Mimeographed. Toronto: University of Toronto, Centre for Urban and Community Studies.

Simon, Julian L. 1981. *The Ultimate Resource*. Princeton, N.J.: Princeton University Press.

Simon, Rita J., and Sharma, N. 1979. "Women and Crime: Does the American Experience Generalize?" In *Criminology of Deviant Women*, edited by F. Adler and R. J. Simon. Boston: Houghton Mifflin.

Simpson, Miles E. 1985. "Violent Crime, Income Inequality, and Regional Culture: Another Look." *Sociological Focus* 18:199–209.

Sjoberg, Gideon. 1960. *The Preindustrial City*. New York: Free Press.

Sjoberg, Gideon. 1965. "Cities in Developing and in Industrialized Societies: A Cross-cultural Analysis." In *The Study of Urbanization*, edited by P. H. Hauser and L. F. Schnore. New York: John Wiley.

Skeels, H. M. 1966. *Adult Status of Children with Contrasting Early Life Experiences*. Monographs of the Society for Research in Child Development.

Skeels, H. M., and H. A. Dye. 1939. "A Study of the Effects of Differential Stimulation in Mentally Retarded Children." *Proceedings of the American Association for Mental Deficiency* 44:114–136.

Slater, Miriam K. 1969. "My Son the Doctor: Aspects of Mobility among American Jews." *American Journal of Sociology* 34:359–373.

Smelser, Neil J. *Theory of Collective Behavior*. New York: Free Press.

Smith, Daniel S., and M. S. Hindus. 1975. "Premarital Pregnancy in America, 1640–1971: An Overview and Interpretation." *Journal of Interdisciplinary History* 4:537–570.

Smith, Hedrick. 1976. *The Russians*. New York: Quadrangle.

Smith, M. D., and R. N. Parker. 1980. "Type of Homicide and Variation in Regional Rates." *Social Forces* 59:136–149.

Snow, David, and Cynthia L. Philips. 1980. "The Lofland-Stark Conversion Model: A Critical Reassessment." *Social Problems* 27:430–447.

Sorokin, Pitirim A. 1937. *Social and Cultural Dynamics*. New York: American Books.

South, Scott J., and Steven F. Messner. 1986. "The Sex Ratio and Women's Involvement in Crime: A Cross-National Analysis." *The Sociological Quarterly* 28:171–188.

Sowell, Thomas, ed. 1978. *Essays and Data on American Ethnic Groups*. Washington, D.C.: The Urban Institute.

Sowell, Thomas. 1981. *Ethnic America: A History*. New York: Basic Books.

Sowell, Thomas. 1983. *The Economics and Politics of Race: An International Perspective*. New York: William Morrow.

Spada, A.V. 1969. *The Italians in Canada*. Ottawa: Canada Ethnica VI.

Spiro, Melford E. 1966. "Religion: Problems of Definition and Explanation." In *Anthropological Approaches to the Study of Religion*, edited by Michael Banton, pp. 85–126. New York: Praeger.

Squire, Peverill. 1988. "Why the 1936 *Literary Digest* Poll Failed." *Public Opinion Quarterly* 52:125–133.

Stack, Steven. 1983. "Religion and Suicide." *Journal for the Scientific Study of Religion* 22:239–252.

Stack, Steven. 1987a. "The Effect of Female Participation in the Labor Force on Suicide: A Time Series Analysis, 1948–1980." *Sociological Forum* 2:257–277.

Stack, Steven. 1987b. "Publicized Executions and Homicide, 1950–1980." *American Sociological Review* 52:532–540.

Stark, Rodney. 1972. *Police Riots: Collective Violence and Law Enforcement*. Belmont, Calif.: Wadsworth.

Stark, Rodney. 1981. "Must All Religions Be Supernatural?" In *The Social Impact of New Religious Movements*, edited by Bryan Wilson, pp. 159–177. New York: Rose of Sharon Press.

Stark, Rodney. 1984. "The Rise of a New World Faith." *Review of Religious Research* 26:18–27.

Stark, Rodney. 1987a. "Deviant Places: A Theory of the Ecology of Crime." *Criminology* 25:893–909.

Stark, Rodney. 1987b. "Estimating Church Membership Rates: 1971–1980." *Review of Religious Research* 29:69–77.

Stark, Rodney, and W. S. Bainbridge. 1980. "Secularizations, Revival, and Cult Formation." *The Annual Review of the Social Sciences of Religion* 4:85–119.

Stark, Rodney, and W. S. Bainbridge. 1981. "American-Born Sects: Initial Findings." *Journal for the Scientific Study of Religion* 20:130–149.

Stark, Rodney, and W. S. Bainbridge. 1985. *The Future of Religion: Secularization, Revival and Cult Formation.* Berkeley: University of California Press.

Stark, Rodney, and W. S. Bainbridge. 1987. *A Theory of Religion.* New York and Bern: Peter Lang.

Stark, Rodney, Daniel P. Doyle, and Lori Kent. 1980. "Rediscovering Moral Communities: Church Membership and Crime." In *Understanding Crime: Current Theory and Research*, edited by Travis Hirschi and Michael Gottfredson. Beverly Hills, Calif.: Sage.

Stark, Rodney, Daniel P. Doyle, and Jesse Lynn Rushing. 1983. "Beyond Durkheim: Religion and Suicide." *Journal for the Scientific Study of Religion* 22:120–131.

Stark, Rodney, and Charles Y. Glock. 1968. *American Piety.* Berkeley: University of California Press.

Stark, Rodney, Lori Kent, and Daniel P. Doyle. 1982. "Religion and Delinquency: The Ecology of a 'Lost' Relationship." *Journal of Research in Crime and Delinquency* 19:4–24.

Stark, Rodney, and Victor Reinking. *Rediscovering André Guerry and the Birth of Empirical Sociology.* Forthcoming.

Stark, Rodney, et al. 1971. *Wayward Shepherds: Prejudice and the Protestant Clergy.* New York: Harper & Row.

Stark, Rodney, et al. 1983. "Crime and Delinquency in the Roaring Twenties." *Journal of Crime and Delinquency* 20:4–23.

Steinberg, Stephen. 1974. *The Academic Melting Pot.* New York: McGraw-Hill.

Stinchcombe, Arthur L. 1968. *Constructing Social Theory.* New York: Harcourt Brace Jovanovich.

Sunahara, Ann. 1981. *The Politics of Racism: The Uprooting of Japanese Canadians During the Second World War.* Toronto: Lorimer.

Sutherland, Edwin. 1924. *Criminology.* Philadelphia: J. B. Lippincott.

Sutherland, Edwin. 1983. *White-Collar Crime: The Uncut Version.* New Haven, Conn.: Yale University Press.

Swanson, Guy E. 1968. "To Live in Concord with Society: Two Empirical Studies of Primary Relations." In *Cooley and Sociological Analysis*, edited by A. J. Reiss. Ann Arbor: University of Michigan Press.

Swanson, Guy E. 1969. *Rules of Descent: Studies in the Sociology of Parentage.* Ann Arbor: Museum of Anthropology, University of Michigan.

Taeuber, Cynthia M., and Victor Valdisera. 1986. *Women in the American Economy.* Bureau of the Census, Current Population Reports, Special Studies Series P-23, no. 146. Washington, D.C.: U.S. Government Printing Office.

Taeuber, Karl E. 1983. *Report of the Citizens' Commission on Civil Rights.* Washington, D.C.: Center for National Policy Review, Catholic University.

Taeuber, Karl E., and Alma F. Taeuber. 1964. "The Negro as an Immigrant Group: Recent Trends in Racial and Ethnic Segregation in Chicago." *American Journal of Sociology* 69:347–382.

Taeuber, Karl E., and Alma F. Taeuber. 1969. *Negroes in Cities.* New York: Atheneum.

Tanner, James M. 1970. "Physical Growth." In *Carmichael's Manual of Child Psychology*, 3rd ed., edited by Paul Mussen, pp. 77–155. New York: John Wiley.

Tarde, Jean-Gabriel. 1886. *La criminalite comparee.* Paris: Alcan.

Tardola, H. 1970. "The Needle Scene." In *The Participant Observer: Encounters with Social Reality*, edited by G. Jacobs. New York: George Braziller.

Taylor, Marylee C. 1983. "The Black-White Model of Attitude Stability: A Latent Class Examination of Opinion and Nonopinion in the American Public." *American Journal of Sociology* 89:373–401.

Taylor, Ralph B., et al. 1980. "The Defensibility of Defensible Space." In *Understanding Crime: Current Theory and Research*, edited by Travis Hirschi and Michael Gottfredson, pp. 53–71. Beverly Hills, Calif.: Sage.

Tepperman, Lorne. 1976. "A Simulation of Social Mobility in Industrial Societies." *Canadian Review of Sociology and Anthropology* 13:26–42.

Thomas, Hugh. 1979. *A History of the World.* New York: Harper & Row.

Thomis, Malcolm I. 1970. *The Luddites.* New York: Schocken.

Thompson, James D. 1967. *Organizations in Action.* New York: McGraw-Hill.

Thornberry, Terrance P. 1973. "Race, Socio-Economic Status and Sentencing in the Juvenile Justice System." *The Journal of Criminal Law, Criminology and Police Science* 64:90–98.

Tittle, C. R., et al. 1978. "The Myth of Social Class and Criminality: An Empirical Assessment of the Empirical Evidence." *American Sociological Review* 43:643–656.

Toby, Jackson. 1957. "Social Disorganization and Stake in Conformity: Complementary Factors in the Predatory Behavior of Hoodlums." *The Journal of Criminal Law, Criminology, and Police Science* 48:12–17.

Toby, Jackson. 1965. "Early Identification and Intensive Treatment of Pre-delinquents: A Negative View." *Social Work* 6:3–13.

Toch, Hans. 1969. *Violent Man: An Inquiry into the Psychology of Violence.* Chicago: Aldine.

Treiman, Donald, and Kermit Terrell. 1975. "Sex and the Process of Status Attainment: A Comparison of Working Men and Women." *American Sociological Review* 40:174–200.

Trow, Martin. 1973. "The Second Transformation of American Secondary Education." In *The School in Society: Studies in the Sociology of Education*, edited by Sam D. Sieber and David E. Wilder. New York: Free Press.

Truzzi, Marcello. 1968. "Lilliputians in Gulliver's Land: The Social Role of the Dwarf." In *Sociology and Everyday Life*, edited by M. Truzzi. Englewood Cliffs, N.J.: Prentice-Hall.

Turnbull, Colin. 1965. "The Mbuti Pygmies of the Congo." In *Peoples of Africa*, edited by James L. Gibbs. New York: Holt, Rinehart & Winston.

Turner, R. Jay, and Morton O. Wagenfeld. 1967. "Occupational Mobility and Schizophrenia: An Assessment of the Social Causation and Social Selection Hypotheses." *American Sociological Review* 32:104–113.

Ujimoto, K. Victor. 1976. "Contrasts in the Prewar and Post-war Japanese Community in British Columbia: Conflict and Change." *Canadian Review of Sociology and Anthropology* 13:81–89.

U.S. Department of Justice. 1982. *Sourcebook of Criminal Justice Statistics: 1981.* Washington, D.C.: U.S. Government Printing Office.

U'Ren, Marjorie B. 1971. "The Image of Women in Textbooks." In *Women in Sexist Society: Studies in Power and Powerlessness,* edited by Vivian Gornick and Barbara K. Moran. New York: Basic Books.

Vallee, Frank G. 1981. "The Sociology of John Porter: Ethnicity as Anachronism." *Canadian Review of Sociology and Anthropology* 18:639–648.

van den Berghe, Pierre L. 1967. *Race and Racism: A Comparative Perspective.* New York: John Wiley.

van den Berghe, Pierre L. 1973. *Age and Sex in Human Societies.* Belmont, Calif.: Wadsworth.

Veblen, Thorstein. 1899. *The Theory of the Leisure Class.* New York: Macmillan.

Vigod, Bernard L. 1984. *The Jews in Canada.* Ottawa: Canadian Historical Association.

Vogt, William. 1948. *Road to Survival.* New York: Sloane.

von Bertalanffy, Ludwig. 1967. "General System Theory." In *System, Change and Conflict,* edited by N. J. Demerath III and Richard A. Peterson. New York: Free Press.

Waldo, Gordon P., and Simon Dinitz. 1967. "Personality Attributes of the Criminal: An Analysis of Research Studies, 1950–1965." *Journal of Research in Crime and Delinquency* 4:185–202.

Wallace, Anthony F. C. 1956. "Revitalization Movements." *American Anthropologist* 58:264–281.

Wallace, Anthony F. C. 1966. *Religion: An Anthropological View.* New York: Random House.

Wallace, W. L. 1966. *Student Culture: Social Structure and Continuity in a Liberal Arts College.* Chicago: Aldine.

Wallace, Walter L. 1971. *The Logic of Science.* Chicago: Aldine-Atherton.

Wallerstein, Immanuel. 1974. *The Modern World System.* New York: Academic Press.

Wallis, Roy. 1975. *Sectarianism.* New York: John Wiley.

Wallis, Roy. 1982. *Millennialism and Charisma.* Belfast, Northern Ireland: The Queen's University.

Wallis, Roy, and Steve Bruce. 1984. "The Stark-Bainbridge Theory of Religion: A Critical Analysis and Counter Proposals." *Sociological Analysis* 45:11–28.

Walzer, Michael. 1963. *The Revolution of the Saints.* Cambridge: Harvard University Press.

Ward, David. 1971. *Cities and Immigrants.* New York: Oxford University Press.

Washington, M. H., ed. 1975. *The Black Woman and the Disappointment of Romantic Love.* Garden City, N.Y.: Anchor Books.

Webb, Eugene J., Donald T. Campbell, Richard D. Schwartz, and Lee Sechrest. 1966. *Unobtrusive Measures: Nonreactive Research in the Social Sciences.* Chicago: Rand McNally.

Weber, Max. 1946. "Politics as a Vocation." In *From Max Weber,* edited by Hans Gerth and C. Wright Mills. New York: Oxford University Press.

Weber, Max. 1904–05. *The Protestant Ethic and the Spirit of Capitalism.* Reprint, 1958. New York: Charles Scribner's.

Weed, James A. 1980. "National Estimates of Marriage Dissolution and Survivorship." *Vital and Health Statistics,* series 3, no. 19.

Weis, J. G. 1977. "Comparative Analysis of Social Control Theories of Delinquency: The Breakdown of Adequate Social Controls." In *Preventing Delinquency: A Comparative Analysis of Delinquency Prevention Theory.* Washington, D.C.: National Institute for Juvenile Justice and Delinquency Prevention.

Weitz, Shirley. 1977. *Sex Roles: Biological, Psychological and Social Foundations.* New York: Oxford University Press.

Weitzman, Lenore J., et al. 1972. "Sex Role Socialization in Picture Books for Preschool Children." *American Journal of Sociology* 77:1125–1149.

Welch, Kevin. 1983. "Community Development and Metropolitan Religious Commitment: A Test of Two Competing Models." *Journal for the Scientific Study of Religion* 22:167–180.

Wells, H. G. 1897. *The War of the Worlds.* Reprint 1964. New York: Airmont.

Westhues, Kenneth. 1976. "Religious Organization in Canada and the United States." *International Journal of Comparative Sociology* 17:245–261.

Westoff, Charles F., Robert G. Potter, Jr., Philip C. Sagi, and Elliott G. Mishler. 1961. *Family Growth in Metropolitan America.* Princeton, N.J.: Princeton University Press.

White, Burton L. 1971. *Human Infants: Experience and Psychological Development.* Englewood Cliffs, N.J.: Prentice-Hall.

White, L. A. 1949. *The Science of Culture.* New York: Farrar, Straus & Giroux.

White, Leslie A. 1959. *The Evolution of Culture.* New York: McGraw-Hill.

White, Lynn, Jr. 1963. *Medieval Technology and Social Change.* London: Oxford University Press.

White, Lynn K., and Alan Booth. 1985. "The Quality and Stability of Remarriages: the Role of Stepchildren." *American Sociological Review* 50:689–698.

Wilkinson, Karen. 1980. "The Broken Home and Delinquent Behavior." In *Understanding Crime: Current Theory and Research,* edited by Travis Hirschi and Michael Gottfredson, pp. 21–42. Beverly Hills, Calif.: Sage.

Williams, R. M., Jr. 1947. *The Reduction of Intergroup Tensions.* New York: Social Science Research Council.

Wilson, Bryan. 1959. "An Analysis of Sect Development." *American Sociological Review* 24:2–15.

Wilson, Bryan. 1961. *Sects and Society.* Berkeley: University of California Press.

Wilson, Bryan. 1970. *Religious Sects.* New York: McGraw-Hill.

Wilson, Bryan. 1973. *Magic and the Millennium.* New York: Harper & Row.

Wilson, Bryan. 1975. "The Secularization Debate." *Encounter* 45:77–83.

Wilson, Bryan. 1979. "The Return of the Sacred." *Journal for the Scientific Study of Religion* 18:268–280.

Wilson, Bryan. 1982. *Religion in Sociological Perspective.* New York: Oxford University Press.

Wilson, Edward O. 1975. *Sociobiology: The New Synthesis.* Cambridge: Harvard University Press.

Wilson, James Q., and Richard J. Herrnstein. 1985. *Crime and Human Nature.* New York: Simon & Schuster.

Winks, Robin W. 1971. *The Blacks in Canada: A History.* Montreal: McGill-Queen's University Press.

Wirth, Louis. 1928. *The Ghetto.* Chicago: University of Chicago Press.

Wirth, Louis. 1938. "Urbanism as a Way of Life." *American Journal of Sociology* 44:8–20.

Witkin, H. A., et al. 1976. "Criminality in XYY and XXY Men." *Science* 196:547–555.

Woodsworth, James S. 1909. Reissued 1972. *Strangers Within Our Gates: Or Coming Canadians.* Toronto: University of Toronto Press.

World Vision. 1979. *Mission Handbook.* Monrovia, Calif.: World Vision.

Wrigley, E. A. 1969. *Population and History.* New York: McGraw Hill.

Wuthnow, Robert. 1976. *The Consciousness Reformation.* Berkeley: University of California Press.

Wylie, Ruth C., et al. 1979. *The Self Concept.* Lincoln: University of Nebraska Press.

Yearbook of American and Canadian Churches. 1985. Nashville, Tenn.: Abingdon Press.

Yunker, James A. 1982. "The Relevance of the Identification Problem to Statistical Research on Capital Punishment." *Crime and Delinquency* 28:96–124.

Zald, Mayer N., and John D. McCarthy, eds. 1979. *The Dynamics of Social Movements.* Cambridge, Mass.: Winthrop.

Zborowski, Mark, and Elizabeth Herzog. 1962. *Life Is with People: The Culture of the Shtetl.* New York: Schocken.

Zeisel, Hans. 1982a. "Comment on the Deterrent Effect of Capital Punishment." *American Journal of Sociology* 88:167–169.

Zeisel, Hans. 1982b. "Disagreement over the Evaluation of a Controlled Experiment." *American Journal of Sociology* 88:378–389.

Zeisel, Hans. 1982c. *The Limits of Law Enforcement.* Chicago: University of Chicago Press.

Zuckerman, Michael. 1975. "Dr. Spock: The Confidence Man." In *The Family in History,* edited by Charles E. Rosenberg. Philadelphia: University of Pennsylvania Press.

Illustration Credits

Page 4, © Bibliotheque Royale Albert, Bruxelles (Cabinet des Estampes), Jean-Baptiste Madou, artist
Pages 6–7, Library of Congress
Page 10, Kent Reno/Jeroboam
Page 13, courtesy of Lynne Roberts
Page 14, © Elizabeth Crews
Page 20, © Charles Harbutt/Archive Pictures
Page 25, New York Public Library
Page 26, © Elizabeth Crews
Page 31, Culver Pictures
Page 39, Brown Brothers
Pages 44–45, The Granger Collection
Page 49, Library of Congress
Page 53, Alter Kacyzne/Raphael Abramovich Collection, Yivo Institute
Page 54, Brown Brothers
Page 55, Library of Congress
Page 56, Library of Congress
Page 60, Eaton's of Canada Archives
Page 61, Museum of the City of New York
Page 62, Library of Congress
Page 64, Bank of America
Page 69, Hilde Moray/Photo Researchers
Page 71, Library of Congress
Page 72, Mary Ellen Mark/Archive Pictures
Page 75, left, Bentley Historical Library/University of Michigan
Page 75, right, University of Chicago
Page 76, courtesy of Lynne Roberts
Page 77, © Jill A. Cannefax/EKM-Nepenthe
Page 84, UPI/Bettmann Newsphotos
Page 85, © Abigail Heyman/Archive Pictures
Page 95, © Miro Vintoniv/Stock, Boston
Pages 108–9, Robert Gardner/Film Study Center, Harvard University
Page 116, courtesy of Lynne Roberts
Page 119, Library of Congress
Page 122, from A. Meltzoff & M. K. Moore, *Science*, 1977, 198, 75–78

Page 125, © Elizabeth Crews/Stock, Boston
Page 127, Special Collections Division, University of Washington Libraries
Page 128, LeJeune/The Mansell Collection Ltd.
Page 129, © Charles Kennard/Stock, Boston
Page 133, National Archives
Page 135, News and Publication Service/Stanford University
Page 137, Ian Berry/Magnum
Page 138, Baron Hugo van Lawick, © National Geographic Society
Page 141, Wisconsin Primate Laboratory
Page 143, courtesy of Lynne Roberts
Page 149, © Thomas Hopker/Woodfin Camp
Page 151, © Yves de Braine/Black Star
Page 157, Neg. #2A 5161 American Museum of Natural History
Page 159, © Barbara Kirk/Peter Arnold
Page 163, courtesy of Lynne Roberts
Page 165, © David Burnett/Contact
Page 174, © Tony Howarth/Daily Telegraph Magazine 1980/Woodfin Camp
Page 175, Bettmann Archive/BBC Hulton Picture Library
Page 179, Philadelphia Museum of Art, purchased: Harrison Fund
Page 182, St. Duroy/Rapho
Page 183, Richard Kalvar/Magnum
Page 186, AP/Wide World Photos
Page 187, Museo Del Prado, foto MAS
Page 194, Bettmann Archive
Page 195, Robert Crutchfield
Page 198, AP/Wide World Photos
Page 213, © Sepp Seitz/Woodfin Camp
Page 214, Library of Congress
Page 220, © TIME Pix Syndication
Page 223, top, *The Denver Post*
Page 223, bottom, Carl Iwaski, *Life Magazine* © 1956 Time Inc.
Page 226, American Correctional Association

Page 228, © Alex Webb/Magnum
Page 233, Library of Congress
Page 237, Archives of Labor and Urban Affairs, University Archives, Wayne State University
Page 238, Library of Congress
Page 239, © German Information Center
Page 240, Bettmann Archive
Page 244, © Ken Heyman
Page 248, Library of Congress
Pages 260–61, © George Rodger/Magnum
Page 262, Neg. #17023 photo R. M. Anderston, American Museum of Natural History
Page 265, © Henri de Chattillion/Rapho
Page 267, Bulloz
Page 269, Art Resource
Page 271, © Jean Gaumy/Magnum
Page 273, French Cultural Services
Page 283, © Jeffry W. Myers/Stock, Boston
Pages 294–95, Bradley Smith
Page 297, © Lionel Delevingne/Picture Group
Page 301, New York Public Library
Page 302, © Jim Anderson 1978/Woodfin Camp
Pages 304–5, Library of Congress
Page 306, Library of Congress
Page 312, Special Collections Division, University of Washington Libraries, Negative #UW 526
Page 313, Brown Brothers
Page 314, Public Archives Canada/PA-37468
Page 316, California Historical Society, San Francisco/Arnold Genthe FN #23115
Page 320, Library of Congress
Page 323, Margaret Bourke-White, *Life Magazine* © Time Inc.
Page 326, © Brent Jones
Page 331, State Historical Society of Wisconsin

Page 336, © David Powers, 1988
Page 338, Seattle Museum of History and Industry
Page 339, Pierre Berton Enterprises
Page 340, National Museums of Canada, Ottawa
Page 342, Culver Pictures
Page 344, left, The Metropolitan Museum of Art
Page 344, right, Art Resource
Page 349, Culver Pictures
Page 351, Library of Congress
Page 352, Library of Congress
Page 353, top, Culver Pictures
Page 353, bottom, George Middleton Papers, Library of Congress
Page 355, Museum of American Textile History
Page 356, Special Collections Division, University of Washington Library, photographer Clifford, neg. #11
Page 357, Colorado Historical Society
Pages 358–61, Library of Congress
Page 362, top, UPI/Bettmann Newsphotos
Page 362, bottom, California Historical Society/Ticor Title Insurance, Los Angeles
Page 364, National Maritime Museum, San Francisco
Page 365, UPI/Bettmann Newsphotos
Page 366, John Phillips, *Life Magazine* © Time Inc.
Page 368, Pavlovsky/Sygma
Page 371, Freer Gallery of Art, Smithsonian Institution, Washington, D.C.
Page 377, © Abigail Heyman/Archive Pictures
Page 380, Art Resource
Page 381, Bulloz
Page 383, State Historical Society of Wisconsin
Page 384, Hirshhorn Museum and Sculpture Garden, Smithsonian Institution
Page 386, courtesy of Lynne Roberts
Page 399, © Alan Carey/The Image Works
Page 401, © Karen Stafford Rantzman
Pages 406–7, © Rene Burri/Magnum
Page 409, © Abraham Menashe from *The Face of Prayer*, an Alfred A. Knopf publication
Page 411, © Abraham Menashe from *The Face of Prayer*, an Alfred A. Knopf publication
Page 412, Paolo Koch/Photo Researchers

Page 414, © Serge Schmemann/NYT Pictures
Page 415, Townsend P. Dickinson/ Photo Researchers
Page 423, © Gerhard E. Gscheidle/ Peter Arnold
Page 424, © Jack Prelutsky/Stock, Boston
Page 429, © Abraham Menashe from *The Face of Prayer*, an Alfred A. Knopf publication
Page 434, British Crown Copyright/ RAF Photograph
Page 437, courtesy of Lynne Roberts
Page 438, © P. P./Magnum
Page 440, © Burt Glinn/Magnum
Page 445, © Carrie Boretz/Archive Pictures
Page 446, © Kas/Picture Group
Page 447, © George Bellerose/Stock, Boston
Page 449, UPI/Bettmann Newsphotos
Page 451, UPI/Bettmann Newsphotos
Page 452, Capital Press Services/ Miller Services Ltd.
Page 453, Public Archives Canada/ PA-127295
Page 459, © Paul Conklin
Page 469, Kansas State Historical Society
Page 470, Historical Photography Collection, University of Washington Libraries
Pages 472–73, Library of Congress
Page 480, © Susie Fitzhugh/Stock, Boston
Page 481, © Michael Grecco/Stock, Boston
Page 483, © Michael Heron 1980/ Woodfin Camp
Page 491, Library of Congress
Page 494, Mansell
Page 495, © Werner Bischof/Magnum
Page 496, Neg. #326744 Photo: Botlin/American Museum of Natural History
Page 498, © Marc Riboud/Magnum
Page 501, Neg. #232240 Photo: D. B. MacMillan, American Museum of Natural History
Page 505, Bulloz
Page 509, Ken Heyman
Page 510, © Philippe Billere/Rapho
Page 511, courtesy of Lynne Roberts
Page 514, © Marc and Evelyn Bernheim 1981/Woodfin Camp
Page 517, Giraudon/Art Resource
Page 518, top left, Art Resource
Page 518, bottom left, Bildarchiv Foto Marburg

Page 518, right, Mansell
Page 525, © Bruce Davidson/Magnum
Page 526, Imperial War Museum
Page 530, left, Popperfoto
Page 530, right, Bibliotheque Nationale, Paris
Page 532, Bettmann Archive
Page 535, Minnesota Historical Society
Page 537, Library of Congress
Page 541, WHO photo by J. Abcede
Page 542, © John Running/Stock, Boston
Page 553, © Elliott Erwitt/Magnum
Page 557, Bulloz
Page 558, State Historical Society of Wisconsin
Page 559, Jacob A. Riis Collection, Museum of the City of New York
Page 561, University of Chicago
Page 563, United States Department of Agriculture
Page 565, United States Department of Agriculture
Page 567, Library of Congress
Page 569, Chicago Historical Society/ Negative #ICWi-04191
Page 571, © Bill Owens/Archive Pictures
Page 577, © Gilles Peress/Magnum
Page 580, © Evelyn Hofer/Archive Pictures
Page 587, Bettmann Archive
Page 589, William England, "Niagara Suspension Bridge," 1859. Albumen print, $9\frac{1}{2} \times 11\frac{1}{2}$". Collection, The Museum of Modern Art, New York, purchase
Page 590, Chicago Historical Society
Page 591, National Gallery of Art, Washington, Alisa Mellon Bruce Fund, 1967
Page 592, © Burk Uzzle/Woodfin Camp
Page 595, March of Dimes Birth Defects Foundation
Page 597, © Richard Kalvar/Magnum
Page 599, Hagley Museum and Library
Page 604, Metropolitan Museum of Art, George A. Hearn Fund, 1956
Page 611, Brown Brothers
Page 618, © N.Y. Daily News
Page 620, Hirmer Fotoarchiv
Page 625, Mansell
Page 630, Imperial War Museum
Page 631, Popperfoto
Page 633, top, Smithsonian Institution
Page 633, bottom, Smithsonian Institution
Page 639, NASA

Name Index

Subject Index/ Glossary

A

Abstractions Ideas or mental constructions rather than material objects. All scientific concepts are abstractions. 32

Accommodation An agreement between two groups to ignore differences between them. 45–46, 50–51, 294

Achieved status A position gained on the basis of merit (in other words, by achievement). 42, 244–245

Administrative theory. *See* Blau's administrative theory

Adult socialization Processes by which adults are enabled to perform new roles. 163

African Genesis (Ardrey), 136

Age
  and deviance, 177–178, 188
  and happiness, 398
  and Nazism, 627, 628
  and voting for women, 454

Age-specific death rates The number of deaths per year of persons within a given age range divided by the total number of persons within that age range. 524–525

Age structure The proportions of persons of various age groups making up a total population. 527

Aggregate A collection of people lacking social relations; for example, pedestrians waiting for a walk light. 9, 10

Agrarian societies Societies that live by farming. Although these were the first societies able to support cities, they usually require that about 95 percent of

the population be engaged in agriculture. 263
  culture and status in, 267–268
  military in, 266–267
  population trends in, 528–531
  productivity in, 263–264
  surplus and stratification in, 265–266
  warfare in, 264–265

Agricultural development, 264, 266, 440, 441

Agricultural revolution, 541, 562–564

Allocation theories Argue that the primary function of schools is to allocate status, to place students in the stratification system, rather than to train them. 485, 486–487

Allport's theory of contact A theory holding that contact between groups will improve relations only if the groups are of equal status and do not compete with one another. 296–297

Altruism The name applied to behavior that is alleged to be contrary to self-interest and to occur entirely for the benefit of someone else. 72

American Dilemma, An (Myrdal), 298

American dilemma, the Term used by Myrdal to describe the contradiction of a society committed to democratic ideals but sustaining racial segregation. 298

American Journal of Sociology, 25

American Notes (Dickens), 355

Analysis
  cultural, 42–46
  social, 41–42

Anarchists Followers of a political

philosophy that regards the state as inevitably repressive and unjust and who, therefore, propose to destroy the state and live without laws or government. 247, 251

Animals
  and feral children, 146
  Goodall's studies of, 136–140
  language of, 140–143
  societies of, 143–144

Anomie A condition of normlessness in a group or even a whole society when people either no longer know what the norms are or have lost their belief in them. 192, 577
  and integration of societies, 192–194
  theories on, 578–581
  and urbanization, 577

Anti-Semitism Prejudice and discrimination against Jews. 50

Arithmetic increase A constant rate of growth (or decline); the same number of units are added (or subtracted) each cycle, as in 1-2-3-4-5. 531

Ascribed status A position assigned to individuals or groups without regard for merit but because of certain traits beyond their control, such as their race, their sex, or the social standing of their parents. 42, 244–245, 267–268

Asians, 290, 291

Assimilation The process by which an individual or a group reacts to a new social environment by adopting the culture prevalent in that environment. 45, 50–51, 294

Astrology, 16, 17, 18